ENCYCLOPEDIA OF
AMERICAN
IMMIGRATION

ENCYCLOPEDIA OF
AMERICAN
IMMIGRATION

Volume 1

James Ciment
Editor

 SHARPE REFERENCE

An imprint of M.E. Sharpe, INC.

SHARPE REFERENCE

Sharpe Reference is an imprint of *M.E. Sharpe*, INC.

M.E. Sharpe, INC.
80 Business Park Drive
Armonk, NY 10504

© 2001 by *M.E. Sharpe*, INC.

All rights reserved.

Library of Congress Cataloging-in-Publication Data

Encyclopedia of American Immigration / James Ciment, editor
p. cm.
Includes bibliographical references and index.
ISBN 0-7656-8028-9 (set; alk. paper)
1. United States—Emigration and immigration—Encyclopedias. 2. Immigrants—United States—Encyclopedias. I. Ciment, James.

JV6465.E53 2000
304.8′73′03—dc21

00-026560

Printed and bound in the United States of America

The paper used in this publication meets the minimum requirements of American National Standard for Information Sciences—Permanence of Paper for Printed Library Materials,
ANSI Z 39.48-1984.

BM (c)   10   9   8   7   6   5   4   3   2   1

To my
immigrant grandparents

Henry Ciment and Rebecca Tannenbaum
Israel Miller and Ida Rosenberg

CONTENTS

Editor

James Ciment

Board of Advisors

Carl Bankston III
Tulane University

Héctor R. Cordero-Guzmán
New School University

Nancy Foner
State University of New York at Purchase

Nazli Kibria
Boston University

Rubén Rumbaut
Michigan State University

Contributors

Zain A. Abdullah
Rutgers University at Newark

Rogaia Mustafa Abusharaf
University of Connecticut

Nobuko Adachi
Illinois State University

Michael B. Aguilera
State University of New York at Stony Brook

Rafael Alarcón
University of California at Los Angeles

Sandra Dalis Alvarez
Kansas State University

A. Aneesh
Rutgers University

Benjamin Bailey
Brown University

Susan González Baker
University of Texas

Carl Bankston III
Tulane University

John Herschel Barnhill

Christopher Bates
University of California at Los Angeles

Pamela Boehm
Bowling Green State University

Mehdi Bozorgmehr
City College of New York

Amelia Brown
Carnegie Endowment for International Peace

Steve Burnett
Carnegie Mellon University

Lionel Cantú
University of California at Santa Cruz

Gretchen S. Carnes
Central Michigan University

Nancy C. Carnevale
Rutgers University

James Castonguay
Sacred Heart University (Connecticut)

Adrienne Caughfield
Texas Christian University

Patricia Cedeño-Zamor
Salem State College School of Social Work (Massachusetts)

Matt Clavin
American University

Linda J. Collier
Cabrini College

Michelle Stem Cook
Johns Hopkins University

Héctor R. Cordero-Guzmán
New School University

Bruce P. Dalcher
U.S. Coast Guard Academy

Dominique Daniel
Université de Tours (France)

Arnold Dashefsky
University of Connecticut

Bénédicte Deschamps
Université de Paris

Martha Donkor
University of Toronto

Timothy Draper
Northern Illinois University

Grace Ebron
University of Kent,
Canterbury (United Kingdom)

James R. Edwards Jr.
Claremont McKenna College

Edward Eller
University of Louisiana at Monroe

Cecelia M. Espenoza
St. Mary's University (Texas)

Thomas J. Espenshade
Princeton University

Maureen Feeney
University of Michigan

Carolyn Forbes
State University of New York at
Buffalo

Brian N. Fry
Southern Nazarene University

Navid Ghani
State University of New York at
Stony Brook

Cristina Gomes
Facultad Latinoamericana
de Ciencias Sociales, Sede
Academia (Mexico)

Pamela Graham
Columbia University

Michael Lloyd Gruver
Johns Hopkins University

David Haines
George Mason University

Jennifer Harrison
North Carolina Wesleyan College

Ulf Haeussler
University of Konstanz, School
of Law (Germany)

David M. Heer
University of Southern California

Lawrence K. Hong
California State University,
Los Angeles

Christine Inglis
University of Sydney (Australia)

David Jacobson
Arizona State University

Daniel James

Ted G. Jelen
University of Nevada at
Las Vegas

William Jenkins
University of Toronto

Tomás Jiménez
Harvard University

Akel Kahera
University of Texas

Kevin Keogan
Rutgers University

Caitlin Killian
Emory University

Richard S. Kim
University of Michigan

Njoki Kinyatti
York College (City University of
New York)

Kanta Kochhar-Lindgren
Central Michigan University

I. Steven Krup, J.D.

Nathalie M. Krup

Prema Ann Kurien
University of Southern California

Nancy Haekyung Kwak
Columbia University

David Kyle
University of California at Davis

Patricia Landolt
Simon Fraser University

Terese Lawinski
City University of New York—
Graduate Center

Ellyn Lem
De Paul University

Tom Macias
University of Wisconsin

Paul Magro
University of Notre Dame

H. Nasif Mahmoud
Indiana University

Leticia Marteleto
University of Michigan

P. Rudy Mattei
Arizona State University

William C. McDonald
University of Virginia

Cecilia Menjívar
Arizona State University

Beth Merenstein
University of Connecticut

Ronald L. Mize
University of Wisconsin

Carol Moe
St. Augustine College (California)

Ewa Morawska
University of Pennsylvania

Ann Morning
Princeton University

Andrew R. Murphy
Villanova University

Njoki Nathani-Wane
University of Toronto

Immanuel Ness
Brooklyn College

K. Bruce Newbold
McMaster University

Paul David Numrich
University of Illinois at Chicago

Regina Ostine
University of Michigan

Lisa Sun-Hee Park
University of Colorado

Yoonies Park
University of California at Irvine

Vincent Parrillo
William Paterson University

Wayne J. Pitts
University of New Mexico

Luis F. B. Plascencia
University of Texas

Sara Z. Poggio
University of Maryland at Baltimore

Angela F. Pulley
University of Georgia

Enrique S. Pumar
Catholic University

John Radzilowski

S. Karthick Ramakrishnan
Princeton University

Ty Reese
University of North Dakota

Rose Ann M. Rentería
Trinity College (Virginia)

Horacio N. Roque Ramírez
University of California at Berkeley

Marc Rosenblum
University of New Orleans

Teal Rothschild
Roger Williams University

Arlene M. Sánchez-Walsh
University of Southern California

Saskia Sassen
University of Chicago

Suzanne Shanahan
Duke University

N. Mark Shelley
Grand Canyon University

Stephen Sills
Arizona State University

Audrey Singer
Carnegie Endowment for International Peace

Martin D. Smith
Nuffield College, University of Oxford (United Kingdom)

Susanna Smulowitz
City University of New York— Graduate Center

Frances G. Sternberg
University of Missouri at Kansas City

Aonghas Mac Thòmais St.-Hilaire
Johns Hopkins University

Ayumi Takenaka
Columbia University

Daniel J. Tichenor
Rutgers University

Jeanine Ton
American Immigration Lawyers Association

Faedah Totah
University of Texas

Nick Unger
Union of Needletrades, Industrial and Textile Employees

Zulema Valdez
University of California at Los Angeles

A. James Vázquez-Azpiri

Judith Warner
Texas A & M International University

Susan Wierzbicki
University of Washington

Philip Q. Yang
Texas Woman's University

Grace J. Yoo
San Francisco State University

Steven S. Zahniser

Robert F. Zeidel
University of Wisconsin-Stout

Scott Zeman
New Mexico Institute of Mining and Technology

ACKNOWLEDGMENTS

The *Encyclopedia of American Immigration* is one of the most ambitious reference projects ever published by M.E. Sharpe. To say that I received help along the way from some very talented and dedicated people would be like saying Neil Armstrong got a little lift from some folks at NASA for his trip to the moon. This project would have never come into being without them.

First, I would like to thank my good friend and colleague Andrew Gyory, whose ancestors came from Russia, Poland, and Hungary. His wit and wisdom sustained me throughout; his ability to see the forest and the trees simultaneously places him at the top of the list of editors I have worked with over the years. Wendy Muto (Russia/England)—who oversaw the production of this encyclopedia—proved herself once again to be the consummate professional. Aud Thiessen (an immigrant from Norway) did her dependably remarkable job of trafficking over 150 articles and dozens of documents, charts, and photos—making sure they ended up in the right place at the right time. Alice Thiede (England/France) and Will Thiede (England/Germany/France) did a fantastic job of taking sketchy scratch maps and notes and turning them into clear and elegant cartographic creations. Anne Burns (France/Ireland) was the exceptional researcher who dug up the captivating photos in these volumes. Fastidious and exacting, the copyeditors were Nancy Raynor, Susan Warga, Sandy Koppen, Lynne Lackenbach, and Richard Adin. The all-important fact-checkers were Gina Misiroglu, Anne Newman, and Kenneth Weuzer.

And last, I would like to thank Evelyn Fazio (Italy) for coming up with the marvelous idea of an encyclopedia devoted to immigration and then allowing me to tackle it.

Finally, my heartfelt appreciation goes out to all the writers and advisers who contributed to these volumes (their names and affiliations can be found on pp. xi–xiii). All exceeded expectations and the requirements of the assignment to produce thorough, readable, and compelling entries.

As noted above, whatever merits this *Encyclopedia of American Immigration* possesses are due to the efforts of this extraordinary team; any defects are the responsibility of the editor.

James Ciment

INTRODUCTION

Welcome to the *Encyclopedia of American Immigration.* Like virtually everyone who worked on these four volumes, I am an immigrant. I was born in Canada and came to this country as an infant. My grandparents came to Canada at the turn of the twentieth century from what are now the various countries of the former Soviet Union. All the people who helped in the production of this encyclopedia are immigrants or the children of immigrants or the descendants of immigrants: Andrew Gyory (Russia; Poland; Hungary); Aud Thiessen (Norway); Wendy Muto (Russia; England); Evelyn Fazio (Italy); and the others listed in the acknowledgments.

The vast majority of the 100-plus contributors to this encyclopedia are also immigrants or descendants of immigrants to the United States (the exceptions are the contributors who do not live in the United States). And chances are the men and women who printed these volumes are immigrants or descendants of immigrants, as are the dockworkers who loaded the trucks, the truck drivers who delivered the books, and the librarians who purchased them. Finally, of course, you—along with most of the other readers of this encyclopedia—probably came to the United States from somewhere else or are descended from people who came from somewhere else either recently or long ago. In short, the *Encyclopedia of American Immigration* is about you, me, all of us.

Although the United States is largely a nation of immigrants, we agonize over the issue of immigration to a remarkable degree. Everybody (Native Americans being the notable exception) knows that they or their ancestors came from somewhere else and all of us would agree with the fundamental truth that this country was built on the sweat, the ingenuity, and the ambition of immigrants. Yet we understand that while diversity is our greatest strength, it is also our biggest challenge as a people. Questions, disagreements, even conflicts proliferate: open frontiers or closed borders; incorporation or assimilation; bilingualism or English

only; multicultural education or culturally unifying curriculum; "melting pot" or "mosaic." It is virtually impossible to pick up a newspaper, tune into a news broadcast, or listen to a political candidate and not hear references to—or opinions about—one of these contentious issues.

We not only live in a nation of immigrants but also are living in an age of immigration. In absolute terms, the number of immigrants to this country is surpassing the totals from the peak years of the early twentieth century. (In relative terms, they remain smaller as America now has roughly three times the population it had then.) And while in many superficial ways the immigration of today is very different from the immigration of a hundred years ago, the fundamentals are much the same.

Take the origins of immigration. True, a far greater diversity exists among contemporary immigrants—geographically, racially, culturally, religiously—than there was among the immigrants of yesteryear. And yet there are basic similarities in the causes of immigration. As disruptive market forces, along with the occasional war or natural catastrophe, unsettle region after region around the globe, so they set in motion millions of people. This is as true of the Caribbean or Mexico or South Asia today as it was of Italy, Poland, or Russia at the turn of the twentieth century. Moreover, the same pull factors are at play today as they were then, even if they are a bit louder and more colorful. Whereas the United States once promoted itself through railroad and steamer handbills about endless farmlands and good-paying jobs, now the country presents itself as the land of excitement, opportunity, and the good life through consumer advertising and the products of film, television, and recording studios.

And for all the greater diversity of today's immigrants, there is much that unites them with one another and much that links them to their predecessors 100 years ago. Whether Islamic or Buddhist, farm-

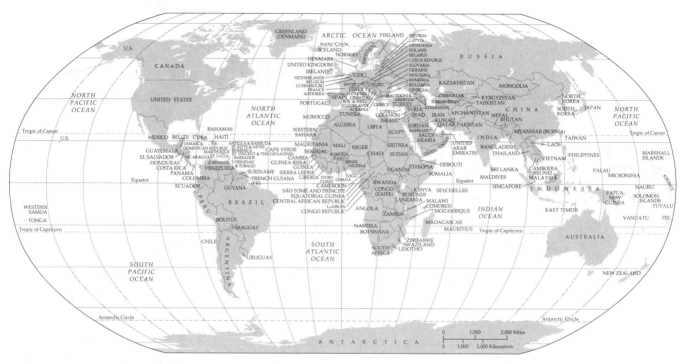

(CARTO-GRAPHICS)

worker or computer technician, parent or single, Chinese or Mexican, immigrants are the ones willing to take a chance, to open themselves up to new experiences, and to shed a bit of their cultural identity. Finally, most of the contentious issues that arise around immigration today—and are noted above—have arisen before. Like Americans today, Americans at the turn of the twentieth century wondered whether the country should welcome or bar immigrants, whether immigrants could or could not assimilate, and whether they contributed to or detracted from the economy. In short, Americans are as ambivalent about immigration today as they have always been.

Yet it would be fatuous to say there have been no changes in immigration over the past 100 years. Technology, for one, has altered things. Today's (legal) immigrants can hop on a jet and be in their native land in a few hours; they can pick up the phone or the mouse and be in instant communication with friends and relatives back home. These ongoing links make it possible to retain cultural and economic ties that resist assimilation. Of course, the countervailing forces of assimilation are, arguably, far stronger today. The immigrant parent of the early twentieth century did not have to contend with six hours of daily television, blockbuster movies, MP3 music, video games, or Internet chat rooms.

And, of course, there are notable differences in the attitudes of native-born Americans toward immigrants, immigration, and the process of assimilation. (Sociologists rightly prefer the word "incorporation" to assimilation, as it better conveys the selectivity of immigrants in adopting American culture.) While there are important pockets of resistance, native-born Americans are more willing to accept—and even celebrate—immigrants who retain elements of their native culture. In part, this has been a product of native-born Americans becoming more interested in their own roots and coming to rue the intense assimilation process in which their own ancestors were forced, or chose, to participate.

Lastly, America—as a land of immigrants—is no longer as exceptional as it once was. That is not to say that it was ever a special case. Australia, Canada, and Latin America have all been shaped by mass immigration throughout their modern history. But, today, immigration is a phenomenon that embraces all the industrialized nations of the world—with the partial exception of Japan (and, even in that ethnically homogeneous nation, things are changing). Just as the United States once pioneered the idea of the "melting pot," so now it is setting the pace for the creation of the multicultural state.

HOW TO USE THIS ENCYCLOPEDIA

The *Encyclopedia of American Immigration* is divided into four parts: Part I: Immigration History; Part II: Immigration Issues; Part III: Immigrant Groups in America; and Part IV: Immigration Documents. The titles are self-explanatory, though a few words of explication are in order here. Part I is designed to be as inclusive as possible and therefore covers the coming to America of peoples who are generally not thought of as immigrants—Native Americans and their prehistoric ancestors, and Africans who arrived involuntarily via the transatlantic slave trade.

Part II of the encyclopedia deals with contemporary immigration issues but also includes two sections that are not exactly about issues or even America for that matter. Section 12 covers immigrant destinations, examining several key American cities and regions where immigrants have settled in large numbers in recent years. To place immigration in a global context, Section 13—"International Perspectives"—deals in part with immigration to *other* major countries and regions around the world.

The third part of this encyclopedia—which focuses on immigrant groups—is organized a bit differently from other ethnic encyclopedias. To avoid repetition, countries with similar immigration patterns to the United States have been placed together. Thus, rather than individual entries on each country in Eastern Europe or West Africa, there is a single entry on the specific region. Of course, for important sources of immigrants to America—such countries as Mexico, China, and Ireland—there are separate national entries.

Finally, Part IV of the encyclopedia includes original documents connected to immigration. Covering both historical and contemporary subjects, they were chosen to provide background, context, and support for the various entries in the other three parts of the encyclopedia. They are printed in full or in significant excerpts.

As for the individual entries, each contains a bibliography at the end, as well as cross-referencing to related entries and documents. There is a glossary of terms in the fourth volume of this encyclopedia, as well as a general bibliography. Finally, there are three indexes to this encyclopedia: an all-inclusive general index, an index based on geography, and an index based on legal and judicial subjects.

James Ciment

Part I

IMMIGRATION HISTORY

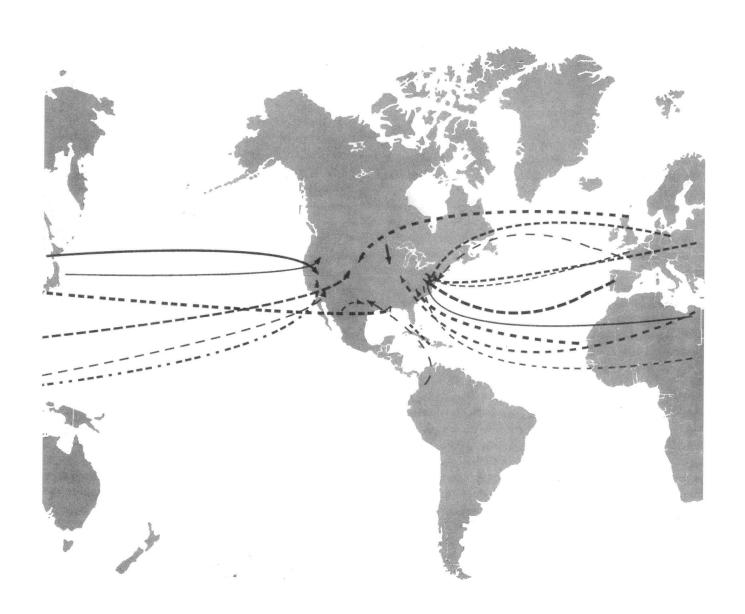

INTRODUCTION

Part I of the *Encyclopedia of American Immigration* is devoted to the history of immigration to America and the history of immigrants in America. It is divided into five sections: Prehistory to 1800; 1800 to the 1880s; the 1880s to World War I; World War I to 1965; and 1965 to the present. Within each section, the entries are listed in roughly chronological order.

The section on prehistory to 1800 covers the period from the first arrival of Native Americans in what is now the United States to about 1800 and the end of the Federalist era. The section from 1800 to the 1880s covers the early republic, the antebellum years, the Civil War and Reconstruction eras, and the Gilded Age. The section from the 1880s to World War I deals with the massive influx of immigrants that arrived on American shores in the period; in this section, entries tend to be more thematic than chronological. The section called World War I to 1965 examines the period in which immigration numbers dropped due to European wars and restrictive legislation. And, finally, the section on 1965 to the present deals with the dramatic rise in immigration from Asia, Latin America, and elsewhere that has occurred in the wake of the Immigration Reform Act of 1965.

It is no less true for being a cliché: The history of immigration and immigrants is the history of America itself. Nor is this truism merely confined to matters of genealogy—that all of us, with the exception of Native Americans, trace our immediate ancestry to other regions, continents, and islands of the world. Rather, it is because the broad contours of our national story have been shaped by immigration in the most fundamental of ways. It begins with the nation's colonial origins. It is not too far-fetched to say that the United States is a predominantly English-speaking country, with an Anglo-Saxon legal inheritance, because of early immigration patterns. Simply put, neither France, the Netherlands, or Spain—Britain's main colonial rivals for North America—had as large a population of economically redundant people as did England. Where Spain's colonies in North America were largely garrisons—and France's oriented toward trade with the Indians—Britain's were settler colonies from the beginning and, as such, attracted people from all over Western Europe.

Indeed, it is also safe to say that this multiethnic influx had a profound impact on the form of government that Americans adopted after breaking loose from Britain in the late eighteenth century, and not just in the most obvious case of freedom of religion enshrined in the First Amendment. The balance of power, the protection of minority interests, and the emphasis on local representation—the core values of the American democratic experiment—are premised on the idea of a nation of multifarious groups and interests. While this variety included economic and regional groupings unrelated to national origin per se, the fact that America was so ethnically diverse reinforced the idea—encapsulated in the *Federalist Papers*—that an interplay of interests was the best means of protecting and fostering a working democracy in a vast and diverse nation.

The dominant themes of nineteenth-century American history—the establishment of a popular democracy, early industrialization, westward expansion, and the great crisis over slavery and race—have also been fundamentally shaped by immigration and immigrants. As numerous scholars have pointed out, the American political landscape has been dominated by ethnic alliances and divisions since expansion of the franchise to nearly all white men in the early 1800s. Throughout the course of the nineteenth century, then, the Democratic Party loosely represented the interests of immigrants, while its opponents—first the Whigs and then the Republicans—were said to be bulwarks of native-born Americans. But it was more than a matter of party affiliation. The Democrats were said to stand for the workingman, the petty capitalists, the strivers—all those who had come to this country with an expectation of improving their condition of life. The Whigs and the Republicans represented the established interests, the landed farmers, the successful merchants and capitalists—all those who considered themselves true, native-born Americans.

The history of early industrialization was also inextricably linked with the history of the immigrant. Again, this is so not merely because newcomers to this country came to staff the textile factories of New England, the meatpacking plants of Chicago, or the coalfields of Pennsylvania. Numerous historians have pointed out that the most glaring particularity of America's industrialization—most notably, its failure to engender a strong tradition of working-class solidarity, socialist politics, or even a labor-based political party—was due to the divisions of a multiethnic workforce, itself, of course, a product of ongoing immigration. It has even been argued that the individualism inherent in the immigrant experience has served to undermine the possibility of socialism in America.

As far as westward expansion is concerned, the impact of immigration is more defuse and subtle. Clearly, immigrants have always been an important contingent of the frontier population, from the Scotch-Irish yeomen who settled the Piedmont and Appalachian backcountry of colonial times to the Scandinavian immigrants who broke the sod of the upper Midwest in the late nineteenth century. At the same time, the single most important political issue on the West Coast involved keeping out immigrants from a different shore. In 1882, the Chinese became the first ethnic group to be systematically and legally excluded as immigrants to America.

Immigration—or, rather, the lack of it—was also an important component in the greatest crisis this nation has ever faced: the Civil War. Between 1619, when the first contingent arrived in Jamestown, through the banning of the slave trade in 1808, some six hundred thousand Africans were imported into British North America and the United States as slaves. Natural reproduction increased that population to nearly 4 million by 1860 and the eve of the Civil War. Tensions between free and slave states existed from the beginning of the republic. Indeed, the Constitution contains a basic compromise on the subject, designed to keep the peace between the regions—that is, slaves will be counted as three-fifths of a person for purposes of representation in the federal government.

Yet despite that concession, the South could not keep pace with the North in terms of population and,

therefore, representation—and that for a simple reason. Immigrants generally shunned the South because they either disagreed with slavery or, more typically, did not want to compete economically with planters and their human chattel. As the South lagged behind the North, it increasingly felt itself under siege and reacted with increasingly extreme demands on the national government that eventually provoked a northern political backlash in the rise of the Republican Party and Abraham Lincoln.

The vast waves of immigrants from southern and eastern Europe in the late nineteenth and early twentieth centuries remains one of the key elements in the cultural history of modern America. By 1920, the U.S. Census had reported that for the first time in American history more people lived in urban areas (leniently defined as any town with over 2,500 inhabitants) than rural ones. This represented, of course, more than a mere demographic shift; it signaled a fundamental shift in America's cultural orientation. The rise of the city, to many at the time, meant the rise of an alien and un-American culture. Indeed, much of the history of the early part of this century represents a playing out of this conflict between city and country, immigrant and native-born, Democrat and Republican, Catholic and Protestant, "wet" (pro-alcohol) and "dry."

In retrospect, it is clear that the tide of history was moving against the long-held dominance of the rural, native-born, Protestant majority. Demography may not be destiny but, by as the early as the 1930s, it was the city and the immigrant who had won. Not only was Prohibition defeated and a new and triumphant political alliance built on the foundation of white ethnic voters (the New Deal coalition), but the very culture of immigrant America became transmogrified into the mass culture that has been the hallmark of the American way of life ever since: movies, popular music (with a heavy borrowing from African Americans), ethnic foods, spectator sports, and so forth.

Today, since the historic Immigration Reform Law of 1965 that ended national origin quotas, America is experiencing a wave of immigration whose size—in absolute numbers, if not in proportion to the country's overall population—rivals that of the turn of the twentieth century. As this part of the encyclopedia is devoted to immigration history, it is only fitting to raise a concern familiar to historians, that is, the difficulty of making sense out of recent and ongoing events. Still, it is safe to say that this latest wave of immigration is simultaneously different and the same as those which have preceded it. Now, the immigrants come in a variety of racial hues and from around the world, raising fears of an unassimilable mass of aliens in the midst of America. But, of course, that was said about the Irish of the mid-nineteenth century and the Italians, Jews, Poles, and the rest at the beginning of the twentieth. Undoubtedly, the American assimilation—or, to use a word favored by sociologists, "incorporation"—machine will continue doing its job of milling foreigners of various types into Americans of various types.

PREHISTORY TO 1800

$\mathcal{I}$NTRODUCTION

$\mathcal{E}$ntitled "Prehistory to 1800," Section 1 explores the history of immigration to what is now the United States from prehistoric times to 1800, and the end of the Revolutionary era in American history. While most of the entries in this section deal with traditional kinds of immigrants, two entries focus on groups not normally considered as such: Native Americans and African Americans. Their inclusion in this section and this encyclopedia is part of the effort to make this work as complete a portrayal of the arrivals of newcomers into the United States as possible.

In entry one, "Native Americans," Daniel James discusses the prevailing theory among archaeologists that Native Americans migrated to the Western Hemisphere tens of thousands of years ago during the Ice Age, when lower sea levels revealed a land-bridge between Siberia and Alaska. He also examines the two competing theories about how these Native Americans made their way southward into what is now the United States and territories beyond: that they made their way over water via the inlets and fjords of the Alaskan panhandle and British Columbia, or through gaps in the ice along the eastern slope of the Canadian Rockies.

In "Spanish Settlers," Njoki Nathani-Wane looks at the role of the Spanish, the first European explorers and settlers of what is now the United States. Wane investigates the reasons the Spanish came to the Western Hemisphere and the various explorations they conducted in the sixteenth century. She also examines how the Spanish ruthlessly conquered the native people of the region, particularly in the modern-day Southwest. Finally, she discusses the ways in which the Spanish administered the vast new region they had conquered, and the methods they used to exploit resources and people.

In his entry "Puritans and Other Religious Dissenters," Andrew R. Murphy discusses the critical role religious nonconformists played in the settlement of the British colonies, particularly those north of Virginia. Among the subjects explored are the Puritans of New England, Roger Williams and the dissenters of Rhode Island, the various religious sects of New Netherlands (and later New York), the Quakers of Pennsylvania and other mid-Atlantic colonies, and the Catholics of Maryland.

The entry on indentured servants by H. Nasif Mahmoud begins with a description of this kind of immigrant of the seventeenth through nineteenth centuries, before discussing the different ethnic groups and classes involved. The author also describes the colonial situation at that time in which indentured servants found themselves. Mahmoud also examines the laws involving indentured servitude, and how indentured servants were eventually replaced by slaves, particularly in the Southern colonies.

In "Free Immigration," Edward Eller examines the history of immigrants who paid their own way to America in colonial times, from New England through Virginia. He also adds a discussion of the various ethnic groups who came to the British colonies in the period between the early 1600s and the American Revolution, including Germans, Scots-Irish, French, Welsh, and other ethnic groups.

In his entry on the slave trade, Ty Reese begins by tracing its history from the earliest years of European conquest in the Western Hemisphere through the outlawing of the trade by the United States in the early years of the nineteenth century. In addition, Reese examines the size of the slave trade over those centuries.

In the final entry, "Immigrants and the American Revolution," Daniel J. Tichenor discusses the effect the

(CARTO-GRAPHICS)

American Revolution had on immigrants and immigration, and the role those immigrants played in the Revolution. He begins with a discussion of the impact of colonial-era immigration on the Revolution before turning to the events leading up to the war. Finally, Tichenor offers a discussion of how the founding fathers viewed immigration, and how they chose to deal with it in the Constitution.

$\mathscr{N}$ATIVE AMERICANS

$\mathscr{T}$echnically speaking, Native Americans, as their name implies, are not immigrants to the United States. They are, of course, the country's first inhabitants. And although many Native American peoples possess legends that insist their origins lie in the territories they inhabited when the first Europeans arrived, archaeologists and historians disagree.

ARRIVAL AND DISPERSION IN THE AMERICAS

According to the most widely accepted view, Native Americans were originally inhabitants of northeast Asia, who gradually migrated to North America between 12,000 and 15,000 years ago. At that time, the planet was gripped in the last of the major ice ages. With greater amounts of water trapped in the polar ice caps, sea levels dropped by as much as several hundred feet. Lowered sea levels created a number of land bridges, including one between modern-day Siberia and Alaska. Once on North American soil, these ancestors of modern-day Native Americans made their way southward and, within a couple of thousand years, inhabited all of the Americas from the sub-Arctic to the tip of South America.

This timeline is largely premised on archaeological findings made near Clovis, New Mexico, in the 1930s. There, archaeologists unearthed arrowheads some 13,000 years old that were believed to be among the earliest human relics in the hemisphere. Findings of similar arrowheads in other parts of North America have confirmed to many scientists that the date of the Clovis arrowheads represents the best starting point for figuring the beginnings of human habitation of North America.

Many Native Americans and some archaeologists dispute this, however, pointing to Clovis-type arrowheads found in Texas that have been carbon-dated to some 37,000 years ago. Mainstream scientists argue that the Texas findings are flawed, since it is highly unlikely that there would have been no technological innovation in the manufacturing of arrowheads over a 25,000-year period. Other findings, as far south as Chile, point to an earlier introduction of human beings to the Americas, though these findings are also subject to dispute and are not accepted by the vast majority of archaeologists studying the origins of Native Americans.

In addition, most theories concerning the arrival of peoples from other continents before 1492 are widely disputed by archaeologists, who say there is no conclusive proof. Among these theories are ones that hypothesize the arrival of West Africans in eastern Central America or Brazil, Irish monks to the eastern United States, and Japanese and Chinese to the northwest coast of North America. Still, the only conclusive archaeological evidence for pre-Columbian contact has come from the remains of settlements built in Newfoundland by Viking seafarers around the year A.D. 1000.

The scenario of the majority viewpoint for the southward dispersion of early Native Americans rests on the imperatives of hunting. According to this viewpoint, the first Native Americans lived mostly in small bands of hunters and gatherers, much like people throughout the world in the final millennia before the development of agriculture. The first Native Americans were blessed in finding a land full of large mammals unused to the presence of human hunters. Easily killed, such fauna as giant sloths and woolly mammoths were quickly killed off by rapidly expanding human populations, forcing the latter to move southward in search of more game, as well as the richer vegetation to be found in warmer climes.

Meanwhile, just as the origin dates for Native Americans are the subject of dispute—with archaeologists divided between majority and minority viewpoints—so the subject of how Native Americans dispersed across the Americas is argued between mainstream scientists and those who question the mainstream viewpoint. The majority of archaeologists believe that the earliest Native Americans made their way southward along the eastern slopes of the Rocky Mountains, utilizing ice-free valleys until they emerged below the glacier line in modern-day southern Canada and the northern United States. A minority of scientists, however, believe that the first Native Americans made their way to the south of the glaciers via the west coast of North America, using simple watercraft to navigate the complex waterways of what is now the Alaskan Panhandle and the coast of the Canadian province of British Columbia.

RISE OF MESO-AMERICAN CIVILIZATION

Around seven thousand years ago, various groups of Native Americans—like their counterparts in the Middle East, East Asia, South Asia, and North Africa—switched from a hunting-and-gathering economy to horticulture. In the Americas, this transformation first occurred in the valley of Central Mexico and the highlands of Peru. In the former, early Native Americans discovered how to cultivate a wild grass known as *teocentli*, an ancestor of modern corn with an edible ear about the size of an acorn. Over the next 3,000 years or so, these early farmers gradually developed teocentli into a crop with a nutritional value that significantly exceeded such Old World crops as wheat and barley. At the same time, early American farmers began the cultivation of beans and squash, which offered both essential protein for the diet as well as renewed fertility to the soil. By about 4,000 B.C., then, farmers in both Central and South America had developed a sophisticated agricultural economy capable of supporting millions of people.

By about 1,000 B.C., the first complex civilization in the Americas had arisen along the Gulf Coast of modern-day Mexico. The Olmecs—famous for their huge stone head carvings—are believed to have been the mother culture for all subsequent civilizations of Mexico and Central America, including those of the final centuries before the arrival of the first Spanish conquistadors in the early sixteenth century. Both the Mayans of the Mexican Yucatan and modern-day Guatemala as well as the Aztecs of the Valley of Mexico derived much of their artistry and many of their religious beliefs from the Olmec civilization.

The Mayans, in particular, created a remarkable civilization, with magnificent pyramids elaborately decorated with carved friezes. A literate culture—though writing was confined to an elite class of priests and royalty—the Mayans developed one of the most sophisticated calendars known to humanity before the current scientific era, one far more accurate than any other in existence at the time. Around A.D. 900, however, the Mayan civilization died out, with the cities and temples being abandoned and many of the inhabitants dispersing to other parts of Central America and Mexico. Archaeologists have posed a number of possible causes, including wars, rebellions, epidemics, or environmental collapse caused by overfarming the thin soil of the Yucatan jungle.

In the Valley of Mexico, the Aztecs were the successors to a series of great civilizations that included those based at Teotihuacán and Tula. Originally from the north of Mexico, the Aztecs were a warrior people who settled on uninhabited islands in giant but shallow Lake Texcoco, which once encompassed much of what is now the Mexico City metropolitan area. There they built their capital, Tenochtitlán, and subdued through warfare most of the peoples of the region. By 1500, the Aztec area of control stretched from the Gulf Coast to the Pacific Ocean, and encompassed most of the Valley of Mexico. Militaristic and brutal, they subjected the peoples they controlled to a ruthless system of tribute and sacrifice, earning them many enemies who would eventually side with the Spanish when the latter arrived in 1519 and conquered the Aztecs in 1521.

NATIVE AMERICANS OF NORTH AMERICA

In contrast to the cities and hierarchical civilizations of Mexico and Central America, the Native Americans of what is now the eastern United States lived in small, self-governing tribes that, in turn, were organized into clans of persons tracing their connectivity back to a common real or fictive ancestor. Most were governed by the elders of the clan and property was held collectively, with traditional rights to certain lands subject to negotiations—and, when negotiations failed, warfare—between neighboring tribes. Many of the Native American peoples of North America did not live in fixed, year-round settlements, but moved with the seasons to take advantage of good farmland, hunting, or wild-plant gathering.

There were some important exceptions to this seminomadic, clan-based society. In modern-day New

York State, the Five Nations of the Iroquois organized a broad federation in which each tribe governed its own internal affairs but worked together on defense and diplomatic issues. In the lower Mississippi River Valley, a number of Native American peoples settled in large communities of thousands, where they erected huge earthen mounds for their temples. Unlike the clan-based tribes of the Eastern Woodlands, these so-called Mississippian cultures—possibly influenced by distant civilizations in Mexico—developed more elaborate hierarchical structures of government and religion, with a class of priests and nobles ruling over them. Like the Mayans, however, the Mound Builders of the Mississippi Valley disappeared as a culture in the final centuries of the pre-Columbian era, victims—say archaeologists—of either disease or military conquest.

In all, North America—in its final precontact centuries—was home to hundreds of independent tribes, speaking more than a thousand different languages. Most of these languages fell into broad language categories that archaeologists have used to trace the movements of peoples in the millennia before the coming of Europeans. Algonquian and Iroquian languages were spoken in what is now the northeastern United States; Algonquian, Iroquoian, and Muskogean dominated in the southeast; Siouan languages were predominant on the Great Plains; Athabaskan in the Canadian sub-Arctic; Eskaleut in the Canadian and Alaskan Arctic; Uto-Aztecan, Salishan, and Sahaptian in the Great Basin and Mountain regions of the American West; and a host of distinct language families along the West Coast of the United States and Canada. But there are anomalies in this pattern. The Navajo, for example, speak an Athabaskan language, indicating that the history of this people stretches back to the sub-Arctic region of Canada, a theory that fits in well with the Navajos' own origin beliefs.

Pre-Columbian population estimates for North America and what is now the United States are difficult to make and vary greatly among different archaeologists and Native American scholars. Figures at the low end of the scale put the population at 10 million Native American people living in North America above the Rio Grande in 1492. At the top end of the scale, the figure is about 50 million. The general consensus among archaeologists is closer to the former figure, with an accepted range of 10 to 20 million Native American inhabiting what is now the United States and Canada at the time of Columbus's arrival.

Daniel James

See also: Immigrants and Westward Expansion (Part I, Sec. 2); Act Conferring United States Citizenship on Native Americans, 1924 (Part IV, Sec. 1).

BIBLIOGRAPHY

Kehoe, Alice B. *North American Indians: A Comprehensive Account.* Englewood Cliffs, NJ: Prentice Hall, 1992.

Terrell, John Upton. *American Indian Almanac.* New York: Barnes and Noble, 1991.

Wright, Ronald. *Stolen Continents: The "New World" Through Indian Eyes.* Boston: Houghton Mifflin, 1992.

EARLY SPANISH SETTLERS

Between Christopher Columbus's first voyage in 1492 through the Spanish-American War in 1898, Spain and Spanish settlers have had a presence in the Western Hemisphere. Spain's nearly three-century-long exploration and settlement of what is now the United States began with Juan Ponce de León's expedition to Florida in the early 1500s and ended with Father Junípero Serra's 20-year-long effort to establish a string of religious and military missions in California from the 1760s through the 1780s.

Spain's initial ventures in the New World were prompted by several aims: an all-sea route to China and the East Indies; a desire for gold, silver, and other precious metals; the development of plantations for the production of commercial crops (sugar, most importantly); political prestige; military power; and a determination to spread the Catholic faith to a population of non-Christian Indians.

Spain's conquests of the early 1500s—particularly in Mexico and Peru, but also in the Caribbean, much of South America, and the present-day U.S. Southwest—brought great fortune to the Crown and to a select group of merchants, largely situated in Seville, the entrepôt for much of the wealth imported from the Western Hemisphere. At first, most of this wealth came in the form of plunder, taken by conquistadors from the fabulously wealthy Aztec and Inca empires of the Valley of Mexico and the Peruvian highlands, respectively. Gradually, as Spain consolidated its hold over the Americas, the economy shifted to one of mining, ranching, and plantation agriculture.

But all this wealth brought woe in its wake. American silver and gold produced economy-ruining inflation and encouraged and paid for the military pursuit of religious orthodoxy through a series of European wars in the sixteenth and seventeenth centuries. With its economy in ruins, Spanish dominance of European politics faded as well, especially as other European powers challenged Spain's economic and political dominance in the Americas.

By the late eighteenth century, the Spanish settlers of Mexico, Central and South America—many of whom were the mixed-blood offspring of Spanish fathers and Indian mothers—were chafing under imperial rule. During the first two decades of the nineteenth century, these regions broke free of Spain to form over a dozen independent republics, including Mexico, which, when it achieved independence in 1821, controlled much of what is now the American Southwest.

Facing the loss of most of its colonial empire, Spain also chose to sell its remaining holdings in continental North America—largely the modern-day state of Florida—to the United States in 1819. The Dominican Republic—the eastern half of the island of Hispaniola—permanently broke free of Spain in the 1860s. Spain's remaining holdings in the Americas—Cuba and Puerto Rico—were lost during a brief war with the United States in 1898.

During its nearly four centuries of rule in the Americas, Spain settled hundreds of thousands of its people, including military officials and soldiers, church leaders, laborers, and planters. However, its territories in what is now the continental United States always remained peripheral to the Spanish colonial endeavor and thus attracted few settlers. Still, the impact of Spain and Spanish settlers on the contemporary United States—and particularly its southwestern quadrant—remains evident in the form of customs, culture, people and place names.

SPANISH EXPLORATION OF THE AMERICAS

Beginning with the Crusades of the eleventh century, Europeans began to develop a renewed taste for the luxuries of Asia, primarily silks and spices. For centuries, Europeans obtained these goods overland through Arab intermediaries, who charged enormous mark-ups. With the conquest of Constantinople by the Muslim Turks in 1453, Europe found itself nearly cut off from Asia.

By the 1400s, two nations, first Portugal and then Spain, began to seek an all-sea route to the East. Both were well situated for such a pursuit. Both faced the Atlantic; both had access to Arab navigation innovations (and both improved on them); and both had developed strong national monarchies—capable of envisioning and financing expensive expeditions—earlier than most other European states.

At the same time, the two countries pursued different routes. Over the course of about half a century, Portugal headed south and east, around Africa and across the Indian Ocean, reaching the subcontinent of India by the 1490s and the East Indies by the early 1500s. Spain, meanwhile, gambled on a western route, financing a voyage by Genoese navigator Christopher Columbus in 1492.

Although the unanticipated encounter with the Americas—and the unexpected expanse of the Pacific—made a western route to the Indies impractical, it did open up a new world of exploration, exploitation, and settlement for Spain. Over the course of the next 100 years, Spanish explorers would map most of the Caribbean, Central America, South America, and southern North America. (Northern North America was left largely to English and French colonists.)

In North America, Spanish exploration began with Ponce de León. A Spanish noble who was a member of Columbus's second voyage to the Americas in 1493, de León served as governor of Puerto Rico before setting out for Florida in pursuit of the legendary "fountain of youth" in 1513. Failing in this endeavor, he launched a second expedition in 1521, but was mortally wounded by Indians.

In 1527, an expedition under the command of Pánfilo de Narváez landed at what is now Tampa Bay, Florida, but was quickly overcome by disease. Over the next eight years, the few remaining survivors wandered along the Gulf Coast of the modern United States, until they encountered a party of Spanish soldiers in northern Mexico. The survivors of the de Narváez expedition spread stories of seven legendary cities of gold—El Dorado—believed to be situated in what is now the southwestern United States.

These stories inspired Hernando de Soto, a Spanish *conquistador* who had participated in Francisco Pizarro's conquest of the Incan empire of Peru and the Andes in the early 1530s. In 1539, de Soto led a ten-ship, 600-man expedition from Spain in search of El Dorado. After landing in Florida, de Soto and his men, led by native guides, made their way through the present-day Carolinas and Tennessee, becoming the first Europeans to encounter the Mississippi River. De Soto died of fever on the Mississippi in 1542. Yet another Spanish explorer—actually a Portuguese native who took on the Spanish name of Juan Rodríguez Cabrillo—became the first European to set eyes on what is now California, when he landed in modern-day San Diego in 1542.

CONQUEST AND EXPLOITATION

After exploration came conquest and exploitation. By the mid-sixteenth century, Spanish dominions stretched from central Mexico to the tip of South America, although some regions were not brought fully under administrative control for another century or so.

Spanish conquest and exploitation had a devastating impact on the native peoples of the Americas, though the effects varied from region to region. Worst hit was the Caribbean, with the native Arawak, Carib, and Taino Indians suffering near-total genocide, largely from Spanish-borne diseases, with just pockets of survivors holding on in the interiors of some of the larger islands or on mountainous smaller islands unsuited for large-scale plantation agriculture.

The much larger concentrations of Native Americans in Mexico and Peru also suffered horrendous losses from European pathogens, yet enough people survived to continue Indian life in most of the continental Americas. At the same time, the Spanish conquest had a devastating effect on native cultures, destroying their political order, redirecting their economies to European interests, and largely replacing native faith and language with Catholicism and Spanish.

Again, with few obvious sources of wealth and more dispersed populations, the territories of Spanish America that are now within the continental United States saw far less destruction of Native peoples and cultures, at least as far as the Spanish were concerned. How many Indians in the Southwest and Florida died from diseases introduced by the Spanish is unknown, though estimates place the loss at up to 50 percent. In California, the effect was even greater. The 21 missions founded by Junípero Serra in the late eighteenth century had a profound impact on the Native peoples, particularly in the coastal regions between what is now San Diego and San Francisco. Large numbers died from Spanish diseases, while most of the rest were herded into missions where they were indoctrinated with the Catholic faith and forced to work on

BALBOA SETTING UP THE CROSS ON THE SHORE OF
THE PACIFIC OCEAN, SEPTEMBER 25, 1513.

This late-nineteenth-century linecut offers a romantic depiction of the encounter between Spanish conquistadors and Native Americans. In fact, Spanish settlers—who founded colonies in Arizona, California, Florida, New Mexico, and Texas—were responsible for wide-spread destruction of Native American cultures. *(Library of Congress)*

Spanish farms and ranches. The priests were industrious in "saving" souls. For example, priests baptized 500,000 in 1597, and a million were baptized during the first eight years of colonization.

SPANISH GOVERNANCE AND SETTLEMENT

To regulate its empire, Spain created two organizations, the House of Trade to deal with commerce and the Council of the Indies to make laws. The system of colonization was called the viceroyalty. It began in

1535 when Antonio de Mendoza was sent to govern Mexico. The viceroys, responsible to the king, were the chief colonial officials. Under them were the proprietors, charged with direct administration of the colonies.

Initially, the Indians were enslaved, but later a head tax was charged on all natives, thus forcing them to work in the mines or on ranches. Gradually what developed was a controversial system known as the *encomienda,* a legal arrangement under which the Spanish landholders had "commended" to them the care of the Indians on their lands. The encomienda system was a feudal arrangement in which the Indians served the role of serfs and were required to perform labor and pay tribute to their lords, who, in exchange, were supposed to provide for the physical and spiritual needs of their Indians.

Meanwhile, at the colony-wide level, a government was established by Hernando Cortez in Mexico in the 1520s, but it proved weak and was soon taken over by a viceroy appointed by the home government. The colonial territories were divided into districts and provinces, with governors and deputy governors instituted with judicial authority. Small towns were planted on plots of land and established with laws according to royal edicts. Spanish missionaries influenced the civil government to a great extent and also established religious or ecclesiastical orders.

In what is now the United States, the first Spanish settlement was established in St. Augustine, Florida, in 1565, followed by Santa Fe, New Mexico, in 1610. (Pueblo revolt saw the Spanish driven from Santa Fe from 1680 to 1693.) The first Spanish settlement in Texas was at San Antonio in 1718, followed by the building of *presidios* at La Bahia on the central Texas coast in 1722 and San Saba in the center of the modern-day state in 1757. San Diego, the first Spanish settlement in California, was established in 1769, and a string of missions was built up the coast to San Francisco by 1776. The first Spanish settlement in modern-day Arizona was built at Tucson in 1772.

The immigration of Spanish settlers to the Western Hemisphere was substantial (see Table 1), particularly in the late sixteenth and early seventeenth centuries, with most immigrants settling in what is now Mexico, Central America, Peru, and Argentina.

Generally, on the periphery of the Spanish centers of colonization farther to the south, Spanish immigration to what is now the United States was slow to develop and sporadic even after settlements were established. For example, the Spanish-speaking population of Texas never stood much above 4,000 in the roughly 120 years the territory was under Spanish

and Mexican rule, from the 1710s to the 1830s. And although a Spanish presence in Florida dated back to the late sixteenth century, the settler population was hardly above 1,000 in any given year. California, a latecomer to the Spanish Empire, saw its population of Spanish-seeking settlers rise quickly after the first settlement was established in 1769, to about 8,000 in 1848, when the territory was ceded to the United States following the Mexican-American War. By comparison, in the first ten years of American statehood, from 1850 to 1860, the Anglo population of California stood at nearly 200,000. Only in New Mexico was there a substantial settlement of Spanish and Spanish-speaking settlers. By 1848 and the end of the Mexican-American War, there were about 35,000 of them.

Although Spanish settlement of what is now United States territory was never substantial, it had a profound impact on the future of the country, particularly in the Southwest. A resilient Spanish-Mexican-Native American culture survives there, evidenced in language, place names, architecture, customs, and food. Moreover, the cultural foundation laid by Spanish and Mexican settlers has undoubtedly made the region more comfortable and familiar to future Hispanic immigrants, thus playing a role in encouraging the vast waves of those immigrants who have settled in the region in the twentieth century.

Njoki Nathani-Wane

See also: Immigrants and Westward Expansion (Part I, Sec. 2); The Surge of Latino Immigration (Part I, Sec. 4); Central America, Mexico (Part III, Sec. 2); Treaty of Guadalupe Hidalgo, 1848 (Part IV, Sec. 1).

Table 1 Spanish Immigration to the Western Hemisphere	
1506–1561	86,681
1561–1600	157,182
1601–1625	111,312
1626–1650	88,504
1651–1700	40,201

Source: Carter Smith III and David Lindroth, *Hispanic-American Experience on File* (New York: Facts on File, 1999).

BIBLIOGRAPHY

Adams, Herbert B., ed. *History, Politics and Education: Johns Hopkins University Studies in Historical and Political Science*, vol. VII. Baltimore: The Johns Hopkins Press, 1890.

Anderson, Gary Clayton. *The Indian Southwest, 1580–1830. Ethnogenesis & Reinvention.* Norman: University of Oklahoma Press, 1999.

Armitage, David, ed. *An Expanding World, Vol. 20. Theories of Empire 1450–1800.* Aldershot: Ashgate, Variorum, 1998.

Hudson, Charles. *Knights of Spain, Warriors of the Sun.* Atlanta: University of Georgia Press, 1997.

Smith, Carter III, and David Lindroth. *Hispanic-American Experience on File.* New York: Facts on File, 1999.

Wills, W. H., and R. D. Leonard. *The Ancient Southwestern Community: Models and Methods for the Study of Prehistoric Social Organization.* Albuquerque: University of New Mexico Press, 1990.

PURITANS AND OTHER RELIGIOUS DISSENTERS

In a nation of immigrants, the New England Puritans must be accorded a place as one of the first and arguably most influential groups of Americans. Certainly this was the view of Alexis de Tocqueville, whose visit to the United States in the 1830s yielded the classic *Democracy in America* (1848). "The foundation of New England was something new in the world," wrote Tocqueville, and he accorded Puritanism a prominent place in that foundation. Yet the term "Puritanism" encompasses a variety of theological and political positions, and Puritanism played out differently in different places during the early years of the American experience. In addition, the seventeenth-century settlement of America along the eastern seaboard was shaped by immigrants of many religions.

PURITANS AND NEW ENGLAND

The term "Puritan" is a broad one, referring to a group of English Protestants who sought further reform within the Anglican Church after its Protestantization under the reigns of Henry VIII (1509–1547), Edward VI (1547–1553), and Elizabeth (1558–1603). Generally speaking, English Puritans emphasized personal piety, an educated ministry, and strict observance of the Sabbath. Puritans also sought to purify the church from within, opposing the authority of bishops and archbishops over individual congregations, a practice they viewed as an unsavory remnant of Catholicism in the ostensibly reformed English Church. This Puritan approach to church government gave rise to the term "congregationalism," which later became known as the New England Way on issues of church government. "Congregationalism" refers to a system that affirms the autonomy of individual, voluntarily gathered (as opposed to geographically defined) congregations in decisions affecting their own

collective life. At the same time, these independent congregations would remain bound together by a shared Calvinist Protestant theology strongly emphasizing salvation by faith alone and a commitment to the cooperation of civil and ecclesiastical authorities in creating a social climate conducive to godly individual and communal behavior.

The East Anglia region of England represented the stronghold of Puritanism during the early seventeenth century, and it supplied a disproportionate number of New England's settlers between 1629 and 1640, the years of the Puritan Great Migration. Although most Puritans remained in England to work for reform from within, the 1620s and 1630s saw an outpouring of immigration to New England: estimates run as high as 21,000 emigrants by 1640. A major cause of this immigration was political dissatisfaction with Charles I, who persecuted Puritans and attempted to rule as an absolute monarch. In 1629 Charles disbanded Parliament, where Puritans had gained a stronghold, and for the next eleven years, Parliament failed to meet. Poor harvests and economic difficulties in East Anglia also encouraged Puritans to leave. Religious factors were central to the professed intentions of the early settlers, however, including the aforementioned Puritan opposition to the hierarchical system of bishops and archbishops, Anglican ceremonialism and exclusive use of the Book of Common Prayer, and the perceived Catholic sympathies of William Laud, archbishop of Canterbury. (Laud, appointed by Charles I, reciprocated Puritans' distaste for him by expelling many Puritan clergy from their positions and harassing Puritan sympathizers whenever possible.) As a sign of the seriousness and specifically religious concern with which the English government came to view emigration, in 1634 Charles I's Royal Commission for the Plantations required all would-be emigrants to attest that they had taken oaths of supremacy (acknowledging the king as head of the Church of England) and allegiance to the king and to furnish

A modern drawing of Puritan settlers captures both the isolation and enterprise of these earliest European settlers of New England.
(Library of Congress)

a testimony to religious conformity from their parish priest.

PILGRIMS AT PLYMOUTH

The Pilgrims who landed at Plymouth in November 1620 were Separatists—that is, they denied that the Church of England was a true church and asserted that membership in it was hazardous to one's spiritual health. Furthermore, they denied that the civil government ought to have any role in church affairs, claiming that forced worship and governmentally imposed uniformity corrupted true religion. (In this respect, the Separatist position reverses the later view that religious liberty is desirable to protect the state from religious warfare.) Accordingly, Separatists withdrew into gathered congregations as opposed to the geographically defined, established parishes of the Anglican system. These Pilgrims, as they came to be known, had their origins in the English village of Scrooby around 1606, when a small number of fami-

lies gathered themselves into an independent congregation and met secretly in the home of William Brewster. Such an act was illegal, opposed by orthodox Anglicans and "nonseparating" Puritans (who, to recall, worked for reform from within the Anglican Church). After enduring imprisonment, the group emigrated to the Netherlands in 1609. Settling in Leiden and worshiping under the leadership of John Robinson, the Pilgrims continued to suffer economic hardship and struggled to maintain their strict religious principles in the tolerant Dutch culture. The decision to emigrate to America was made around 1618, and after a series of difficult negotiations, a portion of the Leiden congregation sailed for America on the *Mayflower* in 1620. The ensuing landing, difficult winter, and Thanksgiving celebration are all, of course, part of American lore. The Plymouth settlement—the first permanent English settlement in New England— remained small compared with the dynamic and growing Massachusetts Bay Colony that would later spring up in and around Boston: indeed, Plymouth would eventually be incorporated into the colony.

The Massachusetts Bay Company was made up largely of Puritans who voiced a yearning for a biblical community as a primary reason for coming to America. They did not call for formal separation from the Church of England as did Roger Williams or the Plymouth Pilgrims (see below) but instead for a reformed, national, congregational church structure. John Winthrop, the colony's first governor, arrived in Boston on the *Arbella* in 1630, and the rapid spread of Puritan settlements around Massachusetts Bay led in turn to the further settlement of New England: a group led by Thomas Hooker, a prominent Puritan minister in England and Massachusetts, established Hartford and a number of smaller settlements in the mid-1630s; another led by the merchant Theophilus Eaton and the Reverend John Davenport settled New Haven (incorporated into Connecticut in 1662) in 1643. In varying degrees, with diverse individual characteristics, these settlements diffused the New England Way throughout New England.

In journeying to America, Massachusetts Puritans, though remaining nominally loyal to the English church, sought to leave behind elaborate ecclesiastical hierarchies and rule by bishops and archbishops. As opposed to the more radical Separatists, who insisted on a formal break with the English church, they claimed to have separated only from the corruptions of the Church of England but not from the church itself. It seems more likely that Massachusetts Puritans looked forward to *reforming* the English church fully one day. The responsibility of Christians in a church that contained error, according to John Cotton, one of the architects of the New England Way, was not to withdraw but to work for its repair. Referring to the Church of England as "our dear mother," Massachusetts Puritans begged Anglicans to put away any hostility and to see them as "a church springing out of your own bowels." (Practice, of course, was another matter. In every practical sense the great distance between the two made any enforcement of Anglican discipline virtually hypothetical. But crucially, in their own minds, they were not Separatists, as became clear in their dealings with Roger Williams.)

Massachusetts Bay Puritans did not journey to America to seek religious liberty as a principle; rather, they sought a place in which to live godly lives, both individually and collectively. In their eyes, England was sorely lacking on this score. Many early Massachusetts leaders, while still in England during the 1620s and 1630s, suggested that England was provoking God's wrath—that due to its failure to reform its church fully, as well as the broader corruption in social life and mores, England was due for divine punishment. Thomas Hooker pointed out England's social problems, corruption, "popish" influences, poverty, and the general turning away of the nation from God, exhorting the faithful to repentance: "As sure as God is God, God is going from England . . . God begins to ship away his Noahs . . . and God makes account that New England shall be a refuge for his Noahs and his Lots, a rock and a shelter for his righteous ones to run unto."

Protestantism had fallen on hard times in the opening decades of the seventeenth century, and Puritans (as steeped in the providential view of history as any of their contemporaries) saw in these events signs of God's displeasure at the failure to purify "Romish" elements in English church liturgy and government. In May 1629, after reciting a litany of European Protestant defeats, John Winthrop told his wife that God was "turning the cup towards us also. . . . I am verily persuaded, God will bring some heavy afflictions upon this land, and that speedily." He expressed his faith, however, that "[God] will provide a shelter and a hiding place for us." The formation of a new society in America provided opportunities not present in existing states, possibilities for greater fidelity to the guidelines found in the Bible. If Puritans failed to walk in the Lord's ways, disaster would surely befall them, but if they remained faithful, Winthrop said on board the *Arbella*, "men shall say of succeeding plantations: the lord make it like New England." Massachusetts Puritans aimed to create a corporate, communal society with a singular focus on following God's law.

But the influence of Separatism was not limited to the Plymouth colony. Roger Williams, who arrived in New England in 1631 as a highly regarded young minister, declined the offer of a prestigious teaching post in the Boston church because the congregation there had not formally renounced their fellowship with the Church of England. As he later put it, "I durst not officiate to an unseparated people." In addition to preaching a Separatist doctrine of formal withdrawal from the Anglican Communion, Williams objected to the administration of loyalty oaths and called the colony's patent "a national sin," because the Massachusetts authorities had not compensated Native Americans for their land. Furthermore, he did this at a time when the Massachusetts Bay Company's enemies and rival claimants to the New England territories were mounting a concerted attack on the settlement at the royal court in England. In 1635, Archbishop Laud and the Royal Commission initiated legal proceedings to withdraw the colony's charter. Williams's unorthodox religious and political positions, not to mention the tenacity with which he held them and his poor sense of timing, led the Massachusetts General Court to banish him in 1635. He moved south and in 1636 founded the settlement of Providence, which he envisioned as a haven for the persecuted everywhere.

In 1644, Parliament granted Williams a land patent for the colony. From its inception, Rhode Island attracted an extraordinary variety of religious dissenters and refugees from Massachusetts. Puritan dissenter Anne Hutchinson, herself banished by Massachusetts several years after Williams's expulsion, settled for a time in the colony. Baptists settled in Newport and Providence during the late 1630s. By the early 1650s, both Baptists and Quakers (much to the chagrin of Massachusetts Bay's magistrates) were using Rhode Island as a base for evangelism in Boston and the surrounding towns: between 1659 and 1661, Massachusetts executed four Quakers. A Jewish community was established in Newport during the late 1650s. In 1663, Williams finally received a royal charter from King Charles II which affirmed Rhode Island's identity as a colony founded on religious liberty. By the first half of the eighteenth century, Anglicans and even some congregationalists had added further to Rhode Island's religious diversity.

NEW YORK

The Dutch presence in what would become New York dates back to Henry Hudson's explorations in 1609. With the purchase of Manhattan Island from Native Americans in the 1620s, the Dutch set their colonizing endeavor in motion, establishing a commercial presence in New Amsterdam (future city of New York) where the Dutch Reformed Church was officially established in 1629. A combination of (relative) economic prosperity and scant religious persecution in Holland limited religiously driven emigration by the Dutch: indeed, the Netherlands was itself an important refuge for victims of religious persecution across Europe. Still, the commercial attractions of the Dutch settlement and the attendant fur trade were considerable, and in its first few decades, New Netherland attracted Lutherans, Quakers, Presbyterians, and Catholics.

One group of religious refugees who deserves special mention in the context of New Netherland (future colony of New York) is American Jews. In 1654, in the wake of the Portuguese capture of Dutch holdings in Brazil and fears of a new Inquisition there, roughly two dozen Jews traveled to New Amsterdam. Peter Stuyvesant, director general of New Netherland, initially attempted to refuse them, but was overruled by the West India Company. (The history of Jews in America traces back, ultimately, to their expulsion from Spain in 1492, an event that set off a great migration in which many Jews journeyed to the Netherlands and later to the Dutch colony of Recife, in Brazil.) Jews represented only a tiny fraction of the American population during these early colonial years and were generally concentrated in such port cities as New York, Philadelphia, and Newport, where they benefited from the thriving commercial environment and ethnic heterogeneity. Well into the nineteenth century, Sephardic (Iberian), not Ashkenazi (European) Jews, predominated, evidence of the continuing importance of the Iberian expulsions.

Although Stuyvesant attempted to impose a measure of religious uniformity on the colony during the 1650s, specifically in his attempts to suppress Quakers, he was often overruled by the West India Company, which sought to continue in New Amsterdam the policy of moderation that had made Old Amsterdam such a thriving economic success. Ultimately, however, Stuyvesant's quest for orthodoxy became a nonissue, because the English captured New Netherland in 1664 and renamed it New York, in honor of James, Duke of York (later King James II of England). Himself a Roman Catholic and mindful of the commercial benefits of religious liberty, James continued a policy of religious toleration.

QUAKERS, PENNSYLVANIA, AND THE MIDDLE COLONIES

After the Restoration, which placed King Charles II on the throne in 1660, the Church of England regained its privileged position, and English religious dissenters—both Protestant and Catholic—faced a much more difficult situation. Charles II had signaled a willingness to extend liberty to religious dissenters in his Declaration of Breda, just prior to the Restoration, and issued Declarations of Indulgence (toleration) in 1662 and 1672. He was forced to withdraw both, however, because of parliamentary resistance. Restoration Parliaments were hostile to religious dissent (both Protestant and Catholic) and suspicious of royal attempts to govern by decree. Parliament formally reestablished the Anglican Church between 1661 and 1665 with a number of acts that restricted the right of independent congregations to assemble, reinstated the Book of Common Prayer, and required assent to the church's liturgy by all clergy. Restoration England, then, was not a hospitable place for Quakers and other sectarians, due to the hard line against religious dissent taken by the Anglican hierarchy and the gradually deteriorating relationship between Parliament and the king.

Against the backdrop of politically powerful, orthodox Anglicanism, William Penn converted to Quakerism in 1667. During the 1670s, Penn suffered a number of imprisonments for his faith, and he preached, wrote, and traveled across England and Europe, defending the Society of Friends from its detractors and promoting religious liberty as a fundamental principle of legitimate government. Notoriously unsuccessful in securing religious liberty in his own country, where Parliament continued its hostility to religious dissenters, Penn began to seek land in America. He received a royal charter in 1681: personal friendship with James, Duke of York, as well as debts that Charles II owed his father, helped secure Penn's case at a time when the king was increasingly occupied by conflicts with Parliament. In 1682, Penn crossed the Atlantic—already the colony's population had reached 4,000—and in the following spring the first Pennsylvania General Assembly adopted his Frame of Government for the colony.

The territory surrounding Penn's grant was not, however, uninhabited. As early as 1666, Puritans from New Haven had settled south of New York. In 1676, a group of Quakers including Penn established West Jersey, and nearly fourteen hundred Quakers arrived over the next five years. The governments of East and West Jersey were unified by the Crown in 1702. Both represented refuges for persecuted religious dissenters in Restoration England: the former primarily for Puritans, who were suppressed with special ferocity during the 1660s in England; the latter, for Quakers. George Fox, founder of the Society of Friends and the most prominent Quaker, himself visited West Jersey and encouraged colonization efforts there.

From Pennsylvania's inception, a socially and politically predominant Quaker majority coexisted with a wide variety of other religious groups. Penn appealed to persecuted religious dissenters to take up residence in his colony. Although Quakers occupied most influential positions in society, government, and the commercial sphere, many ethnic (German, Dutch, French, Swiss, Scotch, and Irish) and religious groups contributed to a vibrant colonial religious life. In 1683, for example, a group of German immigrants, many of them Mennonites, arrived in Pennsylvania and founded Germantown. Mennonites and Amish also settled in Lancaster County to the west. German Pietists, attempting to purify their communal religious life, also flocked to the colony: Dunkers during the 1720s, Moravians to Nazareth during the following decade, along with Schwenkfelders at roughly the same time.

German Lutherans from Landau had arrived as early as the first decade of the 1700s: initially dispersing to New York and New Jersey, after 1712 most settled in Pennsylvania. By 1730, Pennsylvania had become home to roughly fifteen thousand German Reformed Christians and, by the mid-1700s, to significant numbers of Lutherans and Presbyterians as well. Other groups represented within the colony's borders included Presbyterians from Scotland and Ireland, Methodists, Irish Catholics, and eventually Anglicans, whose first permanent church was built in 1695. A bit optimistically, perhaps, Penn described these various groups as "of one kind, and in one place and under one allegiance, so they live like people of one country," but the degree of religious diversity in the colony's early years is truly striking. Numerous descriptive accounts of early Pennsylvania life testify to the variety of religious experience in the colony, as well as the frequent contention brought about by such variety.

CATHOLICS AND MARYLAND

Maryland represents the only British colony expressly founded by and intended to serve as a refuge for English Catholics. George Calvert, the first Lord Baltimore, who initiated this search for an American haven, did not live long enough to see his undertaking bear fruit. His son Cecil (the second Lord Baltimore) carried on his father's endeavor and received a charter from Charles I in 1632. To attract settlers and increase the colony's chances of economic success, Calvert sought both Protestant and Catholic emigrants to Maryland from the beginning: the proprietor extended religious liberty to all Maryland's Christians, while counseling Catholics to worship discreetly and not give offense to Protestants. In 1634 the *Ark* and the *Dove*, carrying a religiously mixed company of passengers, reached Maryland, and shortly thereafter the Catholics among the group celebrated a public Mass.

Although conceived as a refuge from persecution for Catholics, Catholics comprised only a minority of the Maryland population from the beginning, and their political position was always precarious. Protestants were always in the majority, and over the course of the colony's first fifty years, Presbyterians, Quakers, and Baptists settled in Maryland. Religious and political disputes racked the colony for much of its early history. During the early 1640s, Protestants (primarily Puritans) gained control of the colony and expelled Jesuit missionaries. In the interest of preserving order, Calvert appointed William Stone, a Protestant, governor in 1648. In April 1649, the Maryland Assembly passed a toleration act covering all Christians; Protestants repudiated this act and gained control of the colony in 1655, outlawing Catholicism, barring Catholics from public office, and expelling all Catholic priests. By the end of the seventeenth century, the English monarch and Parliament had assumed control over the colony, and the Anglican Church was established in 1702. In 1715, the Calverts regained control; by then, however, they had rejoined the Anglican Church.

VIRGINIA

The first permanent English settlement in America had remarkably inauspicious beginnings: the population of Jamestown, Virginia, founded in 1607, was decimated in its early years by starvation, by Native Americans, attacks and disease, while fire ravaged its buildings and library. Although economic motives figured heavily in the thinking of the merchants who supported the Virginia Company, a royally chartered company organized to establish a colony in Virginia, religion was by no means absent, and the Anglican Church was established in Virginia as soon as the House of Burgesses was formed in 1619. As the seventeenth century progressed, Anglicanism became further entrenched as the dominant church in the colony: all clergy arriving in the colony were required to present their credentials to the governor, parish vestries had a great deal of authority in community affairs, and Sabbath observances were required by law. Still, the geography and nature of the Virginia settlements mitigated against any enforcement of religious uniformity: parishes often stretched for miles (in the western part of the state, hundreds of miles), which made it difficult if not impossible for clergy to discharge their responsibilities faithfully. Regular services, with clergy officiating, were the exception, not the rule. Religious gatherings of all sorts, writes the American religious historian Sydney Ahlstrom, "tended to be small, poorly supported, and isolated."

At the same time, although Virginia's geography and scattered settlements made enforcement of uniformity difficult and sporadic, dissenters initially found little refuge in Virginia, where legislation was relatively effective in keeping out Catholics and Baptists and where Quakers were confined to outlying coastal areas. During the eighteenth century, Presbyterians, Baptists, and Methodists gradually moved into the colony, remaining largely in the colony's western, mountainous portions.

CAROLINAS AND GEORGIA

The colony of Carolina was founded in 1663 largely for economic reasons and until 1712, present-day North and South Carolina constituted one unit of government by the Lords Proprietors—eight English gentlemen who had assisted Charles II prior to his restoration in 1660, and to whom he granted the colonial charter—and their descendants. Despite a grant of religious liberty to all who settled there, the settlement grew slowly. Trade in tobacco, slaves, and fur attracted a wide variety of immigrants, however, from as far away as France, Germany, Ireland, and the Caribbean. In the final two decades of the seventeenth century, after Louis XIV revoked the Edict of Nantes that had granted religious liberty to French Protestants (Huguenots), nearly five hundred Huguenots settled in Charlestown (later Charleston) and organized their own church. In 1704, the South Carolina colonial assembly established the Church of England. Baptists, Quakers, and Congregationalists had formed churches by the middle of the eighteenth century.

North Carolina did not receive its own governor until 1711 and was not recognized as a distinct colony until 1729, for many years being known primarily as the undeveloped wilderness that lay between (South) Carolina and Virginia. From the beginning, religious dissenters figured prominently in North Carolina, and as early as 1707, Quaker John Archdale served as deputy governor of the territory. (Archdale was earlier governor of South Carolina.) In 1701, the North Carolina Assembly established the Anglican Church, a measure quickly overturned by the proprietors. Baptists, Quakers, Presbyterians, and German Protestants (Moravians, Reformed)—many driven from Virginia by antidissenter legislation—contributed to the religious mix in the colony. Midway through the eighteenth century, a group of Moravians sought a refuge by purchasing a large area of land in the northwestern part of the state, creating their own congregation and community called Wachovia.

Georgia was founded in 1732, originally intended as a combination of bulwark against Spain and France, as a solution to the problem of overcrowded English debtor prisons, and, more idealistically, as a vehicle for educating and evangelizing slaves and their children. The colony also came to serve as a refuge for Austrian Lutherans, Moravians, and even a Jewish community in Savannah.

Colonial America provided an opportunity for adherents of a number of religious groups to escape persecution in Europe and to create communities and congregations to meet their own needs. Rhode Island

and Pennsylvania provide examples of colonies with an elaborated, theoretical foundation for their practices of religious liberty; many others, however, arrived at policies conducive to the settlement of persecuted religious dissenters primarily due to pragmatic or economic considerations. The immigration of Puritans and other religious dissenters created thriving societies in seventeenth-century America, and the impact of these different groups on the nation's religious diversity continues to this day.

Andrew R. Murphy

See also: Political, Ethnic, Religious, and Gender Persecution (Part II, Sec. 1); Great Britain (Part III, Sec. 4).

BIBLIOGRAPHY

Ahlstrom, Sydney A. *A Religious History of the American People.* New Haven: Yale University Press, 1972.

Bridenbaugh, Carl. *Vexed and Troubled Englishmen, 1590–1642.* New York: Oxford University Press, 1968.

Gaustad, Edwin Scott. *A Religious History of America.* 2d ed. San Francisco: Harper and Row, 1990.

Hooker, Thomas. *Thomas Hooker: Writings in England and Holland, 1626–1633,* ed. George H. Williams, Norman Pettit, Winfried Herget, and Sargent Bush Jr. Cambridge: Harvard University Press, 1975.

Murphy, Andrew R. *Conscience and Community: Revisiting Toleration and Religious Dissent in Early Modern England and America.* University Park: Pennsylvania State University Press, 2001.

Penn, William. "A Further Account of the Province of Pennsylvania." In *Narratives of Early Pennsylvania,* ed. Albert Cook Myers. New York: Charles Scribner's Sons, 1912.

Phillips, Kevin P. *The Cousins' Wars: Religion, Politics, and the Triumph of Anglo-America.* New York: Basic Books, 1999.

Tocqueville, Alexis de. *Democracy in America.* Trans. George Lawrence, ed. J. P. Mayer. 1848. New York: Harper and Row, 1969.

Williams, Roger. "Letters of Roger Williams." *Publications of the Narragansett Club* 6 (1874).

Winthrop, John. *Winthrop Papers.* 5 vols. Boston: Massachusetts Historical Society, 1929–47.

INDENTURED SERVANTS

Indentured servants were a distinct and diverse immigrant group that came to the English colonies in the seventeenth and eighteenth centuries under different circumstances than other immigrants. This article examines their reasons for coming; their contributions as immigrants; their difficulties as a class of laborers; their inefficiency as a continuous, stable, dependable working class; their transitions from indenture to freedom or from indenture to slavery; and, finally, the institution's extinction. The term "indentured" is derived from the act of indenting or folding in half the paper that contained the written terms of the labor contract between the servant and the master. The terms of the indenture were written twice (once on each side of the fold or indentation). The paper was cut or torn apart along the fold or indentation so that each party, the servant and the master, could have a copy. At the end of the term the master was to indicate on his copy that the terms of the indenture had been served and return it to the servant. This event signified the servant's manumission, or liberation, from the condition of servitude. He or she was then free to go or to continue to labor for wages. The period of service was usually five to seven years, with most terms being seven years. In the early period of transporting indentured servants to America, the indentured servants were almost exclusively male, but as the colonies grew, females and children were added. The servant was responsible for contributing all his labor to the master, in exchange for a modicum of food, shelter, and clothing, but no wages.

ETHNIC GROUPS AND CLASS

Initially, the majority of indentured servants were male and British. Soon, due to the labor needs associated with colonization, the British brought inden-tured servants of all ethnic groups, religions, and races to the colonies. They were English, Irish, Scots, Welsh, German, Dutch, French, African, Spanish, and Portuguese. The indentured servants came from the lower classes who were sometimes too poor to maintain themselves, or who had no money to make the voyage. The indenture was sometimes the cost of passage to America; therefore, some indentured themselves to masters for five to seven years just to get the opportunity to come to the colonies. Some of these indentured servants were in debtor's prison and were released upon a master paying the debt and then taking the prisoner as an indentured servant to the colonies. Some indentured servants were criminals who the British wanted to get rid of so they were sold to masters traveling to the colonies and were to be in servitude to the master under an indenture, as a way of fulfilling the remainder of their prison sentences. While it can be said that mainly the impecunious became indentured servants, it was not always a choice on the part of the servant. When the need for indentured servants became more and more acute the British companies that had invested in the business of supplying such servants began to go to extreme measures to trick, hoodwink, swindle, highjack, kidnap, and cajole individuals into indentured servitude. Some were even framed for a crime and then brought to the colonies to work off their penal sentences. Children were stolen from their parents. Drunks were taken from the gutters. These people, of the mostly lower classes, comprised of various ethnic groups, races, and ages, were brought to the colonies to work if they survived the voyage.

THE BRITISH ROUNDUP

The British scouted the North American coast area as early as 1497 when John Cabot of England ex-

On the eve of the American Revolution in 1775, Britain's North American colonies included a mélange of ethnic groups from America, Europe, and Africa. *(CARTO-GRAPHICS)*

plored the Atlantic coast of Canada for Henry VII. The British, however were stymied in further exploration for almost one hundred years because of the strength of the Spanish navy and their ruling of the high seas, especially in exploration of the Caribbean, Mexico, Peru, Cuba, and Florida. In 1584, Sir Walter Raleigh landed on Roanoke Island in present-day North Carolina and named the sur-

rounding area Virginia, in honor of Queen Elizabeth I of England. In 1588, the defeat of the Spanish Armada by the British led to their replacing the Spanish as the dominant imperial power in North America.

In June 1606, King James I granted a charter to a group of London entrepreneurs, who formed the Virginia Company to establish a settlement in the Chesapeake region of North America. This company is sometimes referred to as the London Company. By December, the settlers had sailed from London with orders to settle Virginia, and to find gold and a water route to Asia. Half of this group according to Captain John Smith, was composed of "gentlemen" of refined birth and upbringing, who were wholly unsuited for the daunting task of settling a colony. The remainder were artisans, craftsmen, and laborers. The laborers were indentured servants. These initial indentured servants were from England, Scotland, and Ireland. On May 13, 1607, the settlers founded Jamestown.

By December, there were only 32 survivors of the original 105 settlers. In January 1608, an additional 110 settlers arrived at Jamestown and almost one-fourth of these were indentured servants.

England was not yet the great imperial power that it would grow to be. In fact conditions for the poor were desperate, with high unemployment, rampant crime, and overpopulation in London and the other major cities. In many instances the lower classes were outright starving. The Virginia Company during this period offered potential settlers passage to America in exchange for indentured servitude in the colonies. Many were eager to take the opportunity. They did not know of the real perils of starvation, poverty, and brutal conditions that awaited them. When knowledge of these conditions filtered back to England, the Virginia Company resorted to strong-arm tactics. It was not uncommon for potential settlers to be drugged, kidnapped, seduced, or knocked senseless in seaport towns, and then transported to the colonies to be sold as labor. In one year during the reign of King Charles II, more than ten thousand persons were transported to the colonies against their will. The other group brought unwillingly into servitude were the convicts and criminals who were forced to serve out the remainder of their sentences as indentured servants. It is estimated that when the period of indentured servitude was at its zenith, half of the persons being transported aboard ship were from the British jails.

Irish Servants.

JUST ARRIVED, *in the* Ship JOHN, *Capt.* ROACH, *from* DUBLIN,
A NUMBER of HEALTHY, INDENTED
MEN and WOMEN SERVANTS:

AMONG THE FORMER ARE,
A Variety of TRADESMEN, with fome good FAR-
MERS, and ftout LABOURERS: Their Indentures will be difpofed
of, on reafonable Terms, for CASH, by
GEORGE SALMON.

Baltimore, May 24, 1792.

Although technically not slaves, indentured servants paid for their passage across the Atlantic with up to seven years or more of servitude and were often auctioned off to the highest bidder. *(National Parks Service, Statue of Liberty National Monument)*

THE COLONIAL REALITY

Many of the indentured servants did not survive the voyage. Of those that survived the voyage many did not survive their period of servitude. Often the promises and propaganda from the representatives of the London Company were that at the conclusion of the period of servitude land, tools, and clothing would be given to the newly freed indentured servant. The bestowing upon these servants of land, tools, and clothing was a rare exception and not the rule. The masters found quickly that five to seven years was just not enough for the consistent labor needed to tame the wilderness, clear land, plant crops, build houses, and cook food. Indentured servants performed duties including, but not limited to, skilled and unskilled labor, farming, domestic work, blacksmithing, hunting, trapping, and fishing; some educated servants were even teachers who were required to instruct the children of the wealthy. Soon rules and laws were developed specifically for the purpose of extending the period of servitude. Colonial laws were passed prohibiting indentured servants from marriage, fornication, having children, or trading in goods. When these laws were violated, the perpetrator was subject to public flogging and humiliation, in addition to an extension of the period of servitude.

There were many attempts at escape among the unwilling indentured servants who were convicts or who had been kidnapped or tricked into servitude. Those who had come willingly to the colonies but had based their decision on the deceit and misrepresentations made by the Virginia Company were prone to escape. Of the 15,000 people who came to Virginia from 1607 to 1622, only 2,000 survived disease, ill treatment by masters, starvation, and wars with Native Americans.

As to the willing indentured servants, many came "prepurchased" by colonial masters, but others were not prepurchased. They were indentured to the Virginia Company for the initial cost of the passage but once they survived the trip, they could not land and had to stay aboard ship, sometimes up to thirty days, until a colonist purchased the labor contract from the

Virginia Company. Many times for both willing and unwilling indentured servants, families were split apart if they had been indentured as a married couple. Further, if the spouse of one indentured servant died, the surviving spouse would be required to fulfill both terms of the indenture, one for themselves and the other for the deceased spouse. If young children were involved, the 7-year rule was ignored and the child was required to serve until the age of 21 years.

Despite the high death toll for indentured servants during the voyage and after arrival, the British Crown still supported the continuance of the system because of its profitability. It is estimated that the king made more on taxes and duties on the indentured servant than the master received in value. Further, the tobacco crop in the colonies became an extremely profitable commodity for the king due to the taxes and duties that the traders had topay for its importation into the British Isles. The tobacco crop is labor-intensive and many indentured servants were needed to plant, grow, tend, harvest, and dry the huge tobacco leaves. The system of indentured servitude both enriched the king and enabled him to get rid of the desperately poor and lower-class citizenry, and to clear the jails of unwanted convicts.

THE COURT AND THE LAWS

By law, masters were obligated to provide for the servant and the servant was, by law, obligated to obey the master. Servants who disobeyed faced harsh punishment. In 1619, a case was filed in Jamestown, against a servant by his master for neglect of his business, for wantonness with a female servant, for falsely accusing his master of drunkenness, and for falsely accusing his master of stealing from the governor. The servant's punishment for his crimes was to stand for four days with his ears nailed to the pillory, a public whipping on each of those days, and an extension of his period of servitude.

Indentured servants were on the lowest rung of the social ladder and often suffered brutal treatment. In 1642, a law was passed in Jamestown that prohibited the marriage of indentured servants. If the law was violated the male would have his period of servitude extended for one year and the female's period would be extended for two years. If a freeman married a female indentured servant, he had to give satisfaction by doubling the value of the service to the master and pay a fine of 500 pounds of tobacco. If a person hired an escaped servant the new employer had to pay the master twenty pounds of tobacco for every day that he hired the servant. When escapees were captured, their terms of service were often extended for a period that was double the time that they had been absent. If a servant escaped a second time they could be flogged and branded by burning a letter "R" into their cheek.

TRANSITION TO SLAVERY

Indentured servants grew increasingly restless, and the colonists began to pass laws giving them some protection. Every master was required to provide a competent diet, clothing, and lodging. They were not allowed to go beyond the "bounds of moderation" in punishing the servant for an offense. If the servant felt the master was not meeting these obligations, the servant could make a complaint to the colonial commissioner. Upon a finding by the commissioner that the master was not meeting his obligations, the master was warned and the servant given a remedy for his or her complaint. There appeared to be a certain unity among indentured servants that often crossed racial lines. Indentured servants yearned to be free whether they had been willing or unwilling conscripts.

The first Africans were introduced to the colony in 1619, the same year that the Virginia House of Burgesses, the first legislative assembly in America, convened in Jamestown. The legislature consisted of twenty-two burgesses representing eleven plantations. The Africans were from the Dutch ship *Man of War* that had raided a Spanish ship and taken twenty Africans from them. The Dutch put into port at Jamestown and traded the twenty Africans for food and provisions. These Africans became indentured servants, for at this point slavery in the colonies did not legally exist. These Africans served their periods of indenture, and had the opportunity to become free men. Many did so and some became wealthy enough to get indentured servants of their own.

This large labor class of indentured servants grew during the seventeenth century. The ruling class in colonial Virginia—made up of wealthy farmers, landowners, government appointees, and other freemen—began considering ways to deal with this increasingly restless population. The solution they turned to was slavery.

In the mid-1600s, colonies began enacting racially based laws that legalized slavery for blacks. By the end of the century, indentured servitude had become an almost exclusively white institution.

The indentured servant system was the initial means utilized to do the extremely hard, backbreaking work of developing colonies in the Americas. It proved far more popular in the southern colonies than in the northern colonies. During the colonial period, more than half of the nation's immigrants south of New England came as indentured servants. The institution began declining during the American Revolution and died out in the early nineteenth century.

H. Nasif Mahmoud

See also: Free Immigration, Slave Trade (Part I, Sec. 1); Memorial of James Brown, 1819 (Part IV, Sec. 3).

BIBLIOGRAPHY

Breen, Timothy. *Tobacco Culture: The Mentality of the Great Tidewater Planters on the Eve of the Revolution.* Princeton, NJ: Princeton University Press, 1985.

Kettner, James H. *The Development of American Citizenship, 1608–1870.* Chapel Hill, NC: University of North Carolina Press, 1978.

Kim, Sung Bok. *Landlord and Tenant in Colonial New York: Manorial Society, 1664–1775.* Chapel Hill, NC: University of North Carolina Press, 1978.

Morgan, Edmund. *American Slavery, American Freedom: The Ordeal of Colonial Virginia.* New York: Norton, 1975.

Rutman, Darrett, and Anita Rutman. *A Place in Time: Middlesex County, Virginia, 1650–1750.* New York: Norton, 1984.

Tate, Thad W., and David L. Ammerman, eds. *The Chesapeake in the Seventeenth Century: Essays on Anglo-American Society.* Chapel Hill, NC: University of North Carolina Press, 1979.

FREE IMMIGRATION

European immigration to North America during the 1600s was sporadic and slow. Unlike Central America and South America, North America lacked easily exploited riches and a vast Native American population of potential laborers. Discouraging immigration further were early failed attempts—like that of Sir Walter Raleigh's colony at Roanoke Island (North Carolina) in the 1580s, which disappeared after a couple of years without a trace—and the rigors of the long and often fatal transatlantic passage. Thus, the European population remained small through 1600, with no more than a handful, including several hundred Spanish soldiers, established at permanent bases in Florida and New Mexico.

The first successful English colony in mainland North America was established at Jamestown, Virginia, in 1607. And while about 5,000 persons emigrated there over the following decade, most died of disease and starvation during their first season. By the time the first English Pilgrims landed at Plymouth in 1620, only about 2,400 English settlers remained in and around Jamestown.

This slow and sporadic start persisted despite the aggressive promotional literature written by investors anxious to encourage immigration and see financial returns. Right from the first, Christopher Columbus himself, finding no treasure or spices as expected, emphasized, instead, the capital-producing potential of the country—the thick forests, the abundant game, the "cultivatable land." In his 1589 book, *The First Voyage Made to the Coasts of America*, Arthur Barlowe, an English navigator subsidized by Raleigh, described the Virginia area as if it were a new Eden, a promised land of abundance, full of produce ready for the picking, cutting, and fishing, and the natives as amiable, "gentle savages" posing no threat at all.

In *A Brief and True Report of the New Found Land of Virginia* (1588), fellow writer and promoter Thomas Harriot provided a somewhat more negative account of native relationships but still emphasized the amenable nature of the "savages," who "are not to be feared, but . . . shall have cause both to fear and love us." And early Virginia governor John Smith boldly stated that "Heaven and earth never agreed better to frame a place for man's habitation."

Still, immigration to North America was driven primarily by economic necessity and religious intolerance, not by the promotion of corporate investors and royal charters.

Both economic redundancy among many peasants pushed off the land by the ongoing enclosure movement—whereby landlords turned small peasant holdings into commercial sheep pastures—and the persecution of minority sects such as the Puritans pushed people to leave England in the 1600s. During the "Great Migration" from 1620 to 1650, Puritan dissenters and separatists, harassed by the church and state machinery in England, poured into New England. Thirty years later, by 1650, New England's population, driven both by the need to escape religious intolerance at home and the promise of economic well-being in the New World, had grown to 30,000 and overtaken that of the Virginia area's 20,000 persons.

NEW NETHERLANDS

Only the Dutch and Swedish settlements—the latter being taken over by the former in the mid-seventeenth century—which grew up along the Hudson Valley, the New Jersey peninsula and the present-day New York City metropolitan area, would significantly challenge the hegemony of English colonial settlement along the Atlantic seaboard in the 1600s. Henry Hudson's 1609 explorations had established the Dutch claim to this area later to be divided into New York, New Jersey, and Pennsylvania. Amsterdam investors in the Dutch East India and New Netherland companies aggressively pursued the fur trade in the area, but the first Dutch immigrants to attempt settlement did not arrive until 1624, when the West India Company supported the emigration of thirty French Belgian families (Walloons), who founded New Amsterdam on the southern tip of Manhattan Island.

During the 1600s, this initial seed of non-English settlement represented by the Walloons would grow into a large and diverse population stimulated by liberal land, mercantile, and political policies. The royal charter of New Netherland expressed the colony's tolerance, saying, "all the inhabitants of these countries [United Netherlands, or the various independent states that came to make up modern Netherlands], and also of other countries . . . may be admitted into this Company." This liberal policy intended to generate wealth by allowing the distribution of lands and subscriptions to all comers who had the wherewithal to bring settlers and produce wealth, although much of the best land of the Hudson Valley went to a handful of well-connected *patroons,* or landlords.

The tolerance of various ethnicities and religions, the relative liberality of land distribution, and the confusion of constantly changing proprietorship and claims among various groups of settlers served to attract a diverse population. In 1643, a French missionary reported that 400 people speaking eighteen languages had settled in New Amsterdam. Beleaguered Quakers, suffering intense persecution in the Old World and finding already established areas of the New World (especially New England) hostile, gravitated to the New Jersey area during the mid-1600s. By 1664, visitors' estimates put the population of New Amsterdam at 1,600 and the population of the whole New Netherlands area at 10,000.

Meanwhile, in 1681, William Penn obtained his proprietorship of Pennsylvania from England's King Charles II and began his "Holy Experiment" to allow all races and creeds of immigrants to be "governed by laws of your own making, and live a free, and, if you will, a sober and industrious people," opening up the floodgates of free immigration to the colony. At the end of the century, then, New Netherland—or New York, after control of the colony was ceded to Britain in 1664—had an estimated population of 80,000 persons of various faiths and ethnicities, including a small contingent of Africans, both free and slave.

VIRGINIA

From the beginning, attempts to settle the Virginia area were thwarted by bad management and natural disaster. The settlers were overstocked with "adventurers" who knew next to nothing about the practical affairs of farming, much less the necessity of work and food conservation. Plagued with mismanagement, corrupt governors, and slow supply ships, the colony was constantly on the verge of failure during its first five years, and in sore financial arrears until James I revoked the Virginia Company charter and took control directly in 1622.

Of the 140 Englishmen who started out from the Canary Islands in 1607, only 104 arrived in Chesapeake Bay on April 26, 1607. Despite specific instructions to the contrary, they settled on a low, swampy point of land. They were surrounded by 5,000 Native Americans, who looked upon the colonists as both potential allies and land usurpers. Consequently, after "seasoning"—an initial period of about six months in which many settlers died of disease, overwork, or starvation—only 46 remained. In 1608, another several hundred English settlers made their way to Virginia. But even under Captain John Smith's more practical and experienced leadership (he had them plant corn, not hunt for gold), the fledgling colony was again reduced to 50 settlers and teetered on the edge of failure. All in all, of the some 450 to 500 settlers who set out for the Jamestown area in the first two years of settlement, over 400 either died or abandoned the project.

By 1609, this time under the leadership of acting governor George Percy, the colony had again built up to 500 settlers. Yet again, because of the disorderliness of the colonists, malaria and dysentery, crop failure, starvation, Native attacks, and their resistance to hard labor and judicious rationing, they were reduced—in the words of Sir Thomas Gates, to just sixty crazed survivors "not able . . . to step into the woods to gather other firewood." Meanwhile, during this "starving time" in Jamestown, the London Company was reorganizing. In an attempt to rejuvenate the flagging colony, the company was issued a new charter by the Crown, which drew investors and potential colonists from a much broader base. In addition, new incentives of land distribution were instituted and stockholders had more control over the management and governorship of the colony.

The new London Company also organized a small fleet of nine ships, and 800 settlers left for Virginia in 1609 under the leadership of Sir Thomas Gates and Sir George Somers. Unfortunately, this tiny army of would-be settlers was blown off course and landed on the Bermuda Islands, which they immediately claimed for the Crown. It was not to be until a year later that some of them would make it to the James River. When Gates and Somers finally arrived in 1610 and saw the condition of the colonists, they decided to abandon Jamestown, taking the remaining 60 survivors with them. This would have been the end of the Jamestown project had Lord Delaware not arrived with reinforcements: three ships, 150 new settlers, and sufficient supplies, all of which persuaded the survivors to return.

From this point on, immigration to the Virginia area became steadily more successful. Gates and Sir Thomas Dale instituted rigid control and discipline over the colonists. Dale's administration (1611 and 1614–1616), in particular, helped reorganize the colony, again liberalizing land distribution, but now eliminating the communal system of farming. In addition, Dale helped bring in a new crop—tobacco—although the governor insisted that all settlers leasing land from the company grow edible crops on two of their three acres before planting tobacco. In short, Dale instituted a "no work, no food" rule. Despite Dale's tyrannical rule, settlers to the immediate Jamestown area began arriving—and staying—in greater numbers. By the end of 1616, 350 settlers arrived, this time with sixty women and children and 200 servants. In addition, the arrivals settled inland, establishing small settlements mostly to the north of the James River.

Conditions improved, and from 1619 to 1622 more than 3,000 new settlers arrived. There were setbacks, however. As tobacco plantations spread inward, Native Americans found themselves displaced. Meanwhile, a new native leader named Opechancanough had succeeded Powhatan, the Indian leader of the local Algonquins who had welcomed the first English settlers as potential allies in his struggle against neighboring tribes. Opechancanough was not as cooperative as Powhatan had been. In 1622, he led his warriors in a war that saw 350 settlers killed, homes destroyed, and livestock driven off. The war also caused hundreds of other settlers to flee the colony, leaving the population at just 1,200.

The commitment of government troops, money, and supplies improved the colonists' situation considerably. After the transfer of the colony to the control of the Crown, the native-born population of settlers began to grow proportionally relative to new immigrants. In 1635, 1,600 immigrants filtered into the colony, which had now grown to 5,000; more stayed, more were born, and fewer died of disease and as a

result of Native warfare. During the last half of the century Virginia grew tenfold so that, by 1700, more than 60,000 colonists and their descendants had settled in Virginia.

Early immigrants to the colonies were, in general, a rich mix of classes: a large percentage of lesser gentry and free English laborers mixed with servants. Some 535 of the 1,275 Virginia immigrants in 1625 were servants. In addition, a constant influx of undesirables"—Scottish and Irish war prisoners, convicts, debtors, orphans, vagrants, and impressed recruits—were mixed into this brew. As the English economy revived in the 1630s, the colonies suffered a decline in free English emigration to the colonies. However, the continued forced deportation of ex-convicts and other servants served to mitigate the decline in free immigration, and so the total influx remained relatively constant.

By the late seventeenth century, former indentured servants—those who had exchanged several years of labor for passage across the Atlantic—made up one of the largest segments of the population and provided one of the most important sources of skilled artisan labor in the colonies. However, they were an increasingly dissatisfied lot. Unable to buy farmland in the rich tidewater district, they were either forced to work for more established planters or settle their own farms on the frontier, where they increasingly came into conflict with Native Americans. In 1676, the dissatisfaction at being forced onto the frontier and having little say in the governance of the colony exploded in Bacon's Rebellion, a revolt against the planter-controlled regime at Jamestown. Several months of fighting and looting nearly destroyed the colony, until the well-timed arrival of an English warship ended the revolt.

Adding to the unsettled and transient nature of the colony was the sex imbalance. Typically, the indentured servants who flooded the immigrant ranks were males between the ages of fifteen and twenty-five. The 1624 Virginia count showed that of the 1,253 whites counted, 938 were males but only 225 were women and 45 were children. In the Chesapeake area's early years of settlement, three-quarters of the incoming colonists were male, and in 1650, New England's male population was still as high as 60 percent. Not until the eighteenth century did the ratio of men to women even out. The improving ratio of men to women, the near universal marriage of fertile women, and high birth rates with large broods and low infant mortality had a more significant impact on population growth than any other factor. Averaged out over the century, natural increase possibly accounted for as much as 30 percent of the population growth.

FREE IMMIGRATION TO THE COLONIES: 1700–1776

Historians have habitually described North America, especially the Atlantic seaboard of the seventeenth and eighteenth centuries, as "British." The designation "British" is legitimate from the perspective of military might and legal right. The thirteen colonies had, after all, developed from a series of agreements and treaties among governments that basically deeded North America to England, and English kings did claim legal control over settlers and immigrants. These royal "rights" and contracts yielded a population that up until the 1700s was overwhelmingly English. In 1625, 92 percent of the 1,275 settlers in Virginia were English immigrants. By 1700, the situation in the colonies as a whole had not changed that much. Of the approximately 100,000 immigrants who had arrived in the colonies by 1700, fully 80,000 were of English origin, 10,000 were African, and another 10,000 were from various European countries. Whether they were Protestant dissenters escaping Anglican domination, adventurers seeking wealth, the poor lured by promises of land and economic freedom, indentured servants whose years of labor were bought in England to be sold in America, or just convicts and impressed sailors dumped on the coast, almost all were of English origin.

And yet the British colonies began to lose their ethnic homogeneity after 1700. Either forced out of their homeland or emigrating by choice, Germans, Scots-Irish, Swiss, and Africans poured into the colonies. By century's end, fully half the population south of New England was non-English by birth or descent. In 1790, Pennsylvania's population was 65 percent non-English, the balance being made up mostly by Germans and, to a lesser extent, by Scots and Scots-Irish.

They came in roughly two waves: the Germans and Scots-Irish from 1710 to 1740 and then the Scots-Irish and regular Scottish in the 1760s and 1770s. They were Protestants for the most part, and drawn from the middle and lower classes. Both groups spread into the backcountry as far as the eastern slopes of the Alleghenies and the Appalachians. Many of the Scots-Irish were combative, hardy frontiersmen opening up the country to further European settlement; the Germans tended to be stable, skilled farmers who managed the land carefully.

GERMAN MIGRATION

During the 1600s the migration of Germans and German-speaking Swiss was negligible, limited mostly to small religious groups separating themselves from the persecution and corruption of the state Church, whether it happened to be Lutheran or Catholic. William Penn had visited the Rhineland in 1677 and convinced a group of dissenters to purchase a significant tract of land in Pennsylvania. When they arrived in 1683, they founded Germantown and then various smaller settlements during the next ten years. The 1700s, however, was a time of aggressive colonial promotion by England and the colonies and aggressive persecution of dissenting sects in Germany and France. Led by lawyers and Lutheran divines, artisans and professionals, thousands of the poor and indentured sought refuge from the economic devastation and religious persecution in Europe in the perceived security and freedom of America. They established a toehold on the frontier. German enclaves throughout the backcountry up along the Hudson and Shenandoah valleys and through ports in South Carolina and Georgia formed a colonial buffer zone against the Spanish to the south and southwest, the French to the North, and Native Americans all around. In all, from 1700 to 1776, over 100,000 Germans emigrated to the colonies.

By now the Crown and the colonies had realized fully the principle that "population equaled wealth," and so began an aggressive campaign of books and tracts encouraging movement to the "Edenic" colonies, promising refuge and the easy life. These publications, along with other "recruiting" activities, played a significant part in bolstering the ranks of German colonists. The English Crown sponsored a sizable number of emigrants from Germany. In addition, a small percentage had enough cash to pay their own passage. The vast majority, however, were indentured servants, or "Redemptioners" as they were called, because they were forced to labor to "redeem" their passage. Many sold their labor to "Newlanders," earlier immigrants and others who traveled up and down the Rhine pretending to be the newly rich hailing from America.

It took, however, the wars of Louis XIV—which wreaked havoc with crop production and the economy of the Palatine region in southwest Germany—

to set off the migration of Germans in earnest. The repeated devastation of war and the severe winter of 1708–09 drove 12,000 to 15,000 German Protestants to seek refuge in England. England, however, was neither willing nor able to commit the resources needed to support a large refugee migration, so most (excepting the Catholics, who were "deported" back to Germany) were shipped on to the colonies at government expense. Three thousand of these immigrants were incorporated into a failed New York attempt to produce tar and other naval supplies. When that project failed, the immigrants settled for a while in the Hudson Valley, but several years later moved south to Pennsylvania. Another large contingent settled in back-country South Carolina, only to be ruined in the Tuscarora War of 1711–1712.

When European war spilled over into the American theater in the early and mid-1700s, these foreign groups became even more desirable—but only if they could be lured to the backcountry and used as a shield between the already entrenched English colonies and the colonies of France and Spain, as well as the Native American population. German immigrants settled in New Bern, North Carolina, founded by a company of German-speaking Swiss. They spread along the Susquehanna River, south along the eastern slopes of the Appalachians, into Virginia and western Maryland, and south as far as North Carolina. In 1732, 400 Germans and German-speaking Swiss formed a colony in South Carolina, about thirty miles inland on the Savannah River. From there, they quickly spread west to the mountains. Three thousand or more German families had settled on the western edge of the North Carolina frontier by 1771. In 1750, German immigrants began showing up at the ports of Charleston and Savannah. Thus, by 1750, they were an established population in South Carolina and Georgia.

With its religious tolerance and liberal land policies, Pennsylvania became a mecca for dissenting German and Swiss Protestants, and Philadelphia their point of entry. Three thousand tried to settle in the Mohawk Valley of New York, where they were promptly evicted by the colonial landlords, so they took refuge in western Pennsylvania. Moravians—German-speaking people from what is now the Czech Republic—first went to Georgia, then on to Pennsylvania in 1738–1739, under duress and public persecution because they refused to carry arms against the Spanish. Most of the immigrants were Lutheran and German Reformed, but the pacifist Mennonites, Moravians, and Quakers came in increasing numbers to Pennsylvania too. A host of other minor sects settled in Pennsylvania as well, including Swiss Mennonites (1710), German Dunkards (Protestants who baptized

by total immersion, 1720s), and Silesian sectarians (1733–34). By 1775, more than one-third of the Pennsylvania population was of German origin. They became such a strong presence in the colonies that Benjamin Franklin complained that "unless the stream of importation could be turned from this to other colonies . . . they will soon outnumber us, that all the advantages we have, will in my opinion, be not able to preserve our language, and even our government will become precarious."

THE SCOTS-IRISH

The Scots-Irish came in larger numbers than any other non-English immigrants during the 1700s. Even though they were consistently confused with the Irish themselves, the Scots-Irish was a distinct group of colonists—originally from Scotland—who were settled in the Ulster region of northern Ireland in the seventeenth century by James I and Oliver Cromwell. The Crown and the Commonwealth intended that these transplanted Scots carve out a British stronghold in the troublesome Catholic Irish territories. Ironically, the Scottish success led to their subsequent undoing. In 1700, 100,000 Scots were settled in the Ulster lowlands and had made such a success of wool and stock production that they threatened English exports. The Crown withdrew its support, the export of woolens and other products was prohibited except to England itself, their long-time leases from the government began to expire, and English landlords began charging exorbitant rents on lands farmed by the Scots-Irish. Finally, in 1704, Presbyterians were excluded from all civil and military Crown offices, removed from their state jobs, excommunicated for marriage by their own ministers, and compelled to pay tithes—or church taxes—to Anglican parishes. In addition, crop failures in 1727–28 and 1740–41 reduced most Ulsterites to abject poverty.

However, the Crown was dealing with a Protestant group that had been defending itself for nearly 100 years in the heart of Catholic country. Under constant threat and civil strife in the Irish stronghold, they had become hardened defenders of the Presbyterian faith and combative political foes. Instead of paying the new rents and submitting to the indignities of religious and civil persecution, many thousands emigrated to America. As many as 300,000 Scots-Irish arrived in the colonies during the 1700s, distributing themselves throughout the backcountry along the Allegheny and Appalachian ranges.

When they arrived, however, they were often just

as ill-treated and frowned upon as they had been in Ireland. When thousands of them began arriving during the early 1700s, they were mistaken as Irish possessing suspicious religious beliefs and resented for the cost of poor relief. One observer noted that "these confounded Irish will eat us all up." What with the poverty-stricken condition of the new arrivals and the rising cost of provisioning them, Boston officials began meeting the shiploads of immigrants at the docks and telling them to move on. During the ten years following 1719, 500 of the "strangers" were told the same. One immigrant ship in 1729 was met by a mob that prevented them from landing.

Those who did settle in the New England area were forced to attend Puritan services and pay tithes to the local church. When they asked to be relieved of these obligations, the local magistrates refused. When they tried to build a church in Worcester, Massachusetts, the locals burned the new Presbyterian church and carried off the building supplies. Finally, the Scots-Irish immigrants succeeded in buying themselves a township and they began to scatter to more remote parts, moves that were advocated by Massachusetts officials. As with the German immigrants, it was thought that the Scots-Irish would make excellent frontier settlers, who would be able to carve out a buffer zone between the English colonies and those of France, as well as providing protection against Native Americans.

For their part, the immigrants were all too happy to comply, given the cheap and free land, the freedom of the wilderness, and their natural hardihood. They moved toward the Alleghenies up the Connecticut River's western shore into Vermont and the Kennebec River into Maine and southern New Hampshire. Always they moved farther inland, following the valleys and rivers to the south into Delaware and up the Susquehanna as far west as modern-day Pittsburgh. They invaded the western Pennsylvania backcountry, driving out the remaining Natives on the way and forming a protective shield around the pacifist Quakers and Germans. By this time, Philadelphia had become the port that received the majority of immigrants and Pennsylvania the colony where most of the new immigrants settled. Again, as with the German immigrants, they were seen as a mixed blessing, valued for the barrier they formed on the frontier but distrusted for their "strange" ways and their "audacious and disorderly manner." Unlike the Germans, however, they were so audacious that they pushed out the frontier, disregarding the colony's land ownership and payment rules, and arguing that Pennsylvania officials "had solicited for colonists and they [the Scots-Irish immigrants] had come accordingly. . . . [I]t was

against the laws of God and nature that so much land should be idle while so many Christians wanted it to labor on and to raise bread." And so they simply squatted, taking open lands southward through Virginia and into the Carolinas and north Georgia, where they mixed with Ulsterites coming in through the port of Charleston in South Carolina.

FRENCH, THE WELSH, AND OTHER ETHNIC GROUPS

Even though the German and Scots-Irish Ulsterites provided the bulk of the immigrants to the thirteen colonies, other groups had a significant impact on regional cultures. In particular, French Calvinists, or Huguenots, suffering persecution after the Edict of Nantes was revoked in 1685, yielded a wave of immigration to the colonies. (The Edict of Nantes, 1598, had protected the Protestants from the excesses of the Catholic-dominated government.) However, when the edict was revoked, Louis XIV unleashed troops that, along with the long-repressed prejudices of the majority Catholic population, sent more than 300,000 Huguenots to Canada, South America, and the English colonies. Some ten thousand to fifteen thousand made their way to the mid-Atlantic and Southern colonies, settling for the most part in Virginia and North Carolina. Among all the immigrants to the colonies, however, they may have had the most disproportionate cultural impact. They came with money and were better educated, moving easily into leadership roles and bringing industrial, agricultural, and business skills not possessed by the average indentured servant.

The Welsh, like the French Huguenots, arrived in better condition than the typical impoverished immigrants from Germany, Ulster, and even England. Defeated by the English at the battle of Culloden in 1746, their clan system and social habits right down to the way they dressed came under fire. With English soldiers taking over their businesses and large estates, thousands fled Wales singing their new drinking song, "Going to seek a fortune in North Carolina."

In addition, the ever-persecuted and impoverished Catholic Irish trickled in over the decades, until their numbers nearly matched those of the Scots by the time of the American Revolution, even though they would not begin to migrate in large numbers until the nineteenth century.

In 1654, the first shipload of Jews landed in New Amsterdam, having been driven from Brazil. They, too, would continue to show up here and there throughout the colonies. In addition, various Swiss and Greeks and others would mix into the brew, thus diluting the term "English" in the phrase "English colonies."

The rise of European immigration in the 1700s was stunning. Always under the pressure of religious persecution, government harassment, and impoverishment at home, the European population in America practically doubled every twenty to twenty-five years, from 629,000 in 1730 to 1,170,000 in 1750, and to 2,148,000 by 1770. The growth rate by this time was so fast that in 1798 Thomas Malthus looked worriedly on this phenomenon, noting that it was "a rapidity of increase probably without parallel in history" and predicting the first great population crisis would occur in the Americas.

Edward Eller

See also: Indentured Servants, Slave Trade (Part I, Sec. 1); Look Before You Leap, 1796, Letters from an American Farmer, 1782 (Part IV, Sec. 3).

BIBLIOGRAPHY

Barck, Oscar T., and Hugh T. Lefler. *Colonial America*. New York: Macmillan, 1968.

Bureau of the Census. *Historical Statistics of the United States: Colonial Times to 1957*. Washington, DC: Bureau of the Census, 1960.

Dickson, R. J. *Ulster Immigration to the United States*. London: Routledge, 1966.

Faust, Albert B. *The German Element in the United States*. New York: Arno Press, 1969.

Graham, Ian C. C. *Colonists from Scotland: Emigration to North America, 1707–1783*. Ithaca, NY: Cornell University Press, 1956.

Hansen, Marcus L. *The Atlantic Migration, 1607–1860*. Cambridge, MA: Harvard University Press, 1940.

Hofstadter, Richard. *America at 1750: A Social Portrait*. New York: Knopf, 1971.

Klees, Frederic. *The Pennsylvania Dutch*. New York: Macmillan, 1950.

Leyburn, James G. *The Scots-Irish: A Social History*. Chapel Hill: University of North Carolina Press, 1962.

Potter, J. "The Growth of Population in America, 1700–1860." In *Population in History: Essays in Historical Demography*, ed. David V. Glass and D. E. C. Eversley. Chicago: Aldine Publishing, 1972.

Wells, Robert V. *The Population of the British Colonies in America before 1776: A Survey of Census Data*. Princeton, NJ: Princeton University Press, 1975.

SLAVE TRADE

One of the most profound, and largest, pre-nineteenth-century movements of people to the Americas occurred through the auspices of the transatlantic slave trade. The growth and development of the slave trade resulted from European expansion into the Americas, beginning in 1492, and the desire of various European states and settlers to profit from America's abundant land and resources. The slave trade was a unique migration in that European merchants acquired workers from one region, Africa, and transferred them to another, the Americas, without the slaves being brought to or extensively utilized in Europe. The migration caused by the slave trade was also unique in that it was forced. While the vast majority of Europeans who migrated to the Americas did so of their own free will, the Africans taken and utilized through the slave trade did not. During a period of approximately 350 years, more than 11.5 million people were brought, against their will, thousands of miles from Africa to the Americas. In the African diaspora caused by the slave trade a great diversity of Africans came to the Americas and played an important role in their development.

THE BEGINNINGS

As the Spanish conquistadors arrived and settled into the Americas, they brought with them not only sugar cane and disease, but Africans. The status of these early Africans is unclear, but in 1518 the first shipment of African slaves arrived in the West Indies. The problem for the Spanish, and for the other Europeans who followed, was that while they found economic opportunities in the Americas, such as the cultivation of sugar and silver mining, they lacked the necessary laborers to exploit these opportunities. Spanish attempts to utilize the local indigenous peoples as a labor force produced disastrous results, yet the Africans

already there survived and proved to be efficient workers. The problems with the indigenous peoples, coupled with the utility of the Africans, led Charles V to issue the *asiento* that granted control over the importation of four thousand African slaves per year into New Spain. The individual who initially received the *asiento* quickly sold it to a group of Genoese merchants, who obtained slaves for the West Indies from Lisbon. By 1520, the Atlantic slave trade had begun to develop.

The Spaniards were able to draw upon African labor because of earlier Portuguese activity along the coast of West Africa. The Portuguese started construction on a trading outpost at Elmina in 1481 only after negotiating with the local leader, King Kwame Ansa. The creation of a permanent Portuguese presence in West Africa assured them of access to Africa's natural and human resources. As the slave trade grew in importance to the colonial development of the Americas, more European states became involved in the slave trade because of the economic opportunities it presented. In the sixteenth century, the English, Dutch, French, Swedes, Brandenburgers (Prussians), and Danes all became active in West Africa, and over the next two hundred years they built forts and outposts of their own.

THE SLAVE TRADE

As colonization of the Americas increased during the sixteenth and seventeenth centuries, African slaves became an important part of both America's and Europe's economic development. For many European merchants, and eventually American merchants, the slave trade was a source of profits; the buying and selling of slaves along the West African coast also developed a market there for a global assortment of commodities. While the idea of a triangular trade—

Negroes for Sale.

A Cargo of very fine stout Men and Women, in good order and fit for immediate service, just imported from the Windward Coast of Africa, in the Ship Two Brothers.—
Conditions are one half Cash or Produce, the other half payable the first of January next, giving Bond and Security if required.
The Sale to be opened at 10 o'Clock each Day, in Mr. Bourdeaux's Yard, at No. 48, on the Bay.
May 19, 1784.   JOHN MITCHELL.

Thirty Seasoned Negroes
To be Sold for Credit, at Private Sale.

AMONGST which is a Carpenter, none of whom are known to be dishonest.

Also, to be sold for Cash, a regular bred young Negroe Man-Cook, born in this Country, who served several Years under an exceeding good French Cook abroad, and his Wife a middle aged Washer-Woman, (both very honest) and their two Children. *Likewise,* a young Man a Carpenter.
For Terms apply to the Printer.

Between 1619 when the first shipload of slaves arrived at Jamestown and 1808 when the slave trade was finally outlawed, over 600,000 Africans were brought as slaves into colonial America and later the United States. This number represents but a fraction of the total transported to the Western Hemisphere. *(Library of Congress)*

commodities from Europe to Africa, slaves from Africa to the Americas, and sugar and other products from the Americas to Europe—simplifies the complex commercial transactions in the Atlantic world, it highlights the central role of the Atlantic slave trade in this process of economic integration and globalization.

The slave trade was an expensive, time-consuming, and risky business venture that involved a vast number of people. Participation in the slave trade required a large amount of capital, which meant that only rich merchant families, companies backed by wealthy investors, or state-created monopolies could finance this forced migration. The slave trade usually began in a European port when the merchant or corporation procured a ship, captain, and crew. The merchants then needed to purchase commodities in demand in West Africa, buy insurance, retain an American middleman, and provide supplies for the crew and slaves once on board. To be successful, the

slave trader needed to be well informed of the current political, economic, and social situation along the West African coast, particularly whether the region was at war or peace. War often closed the slave paths, while peace kept them open. Traders also needed to know what commodities were currently in demand in West Africa, where slaves were most in demand in the Americas, and the price of slaves in both regions. Their final destination in the Americas often determined where in Africa they purchased the slaves, for over time American slave owners developed affinities for slaves from specific regions with specific skills.

Most captains and crews were not professional slavers because of the great risks and labor involved in the trade. The trip was long, usually from nine to twelve months, and their stay along the West African coast introduced them to diseases that caused them to consider West Africa a "white man's grave." The captain needed to supervise his crew, which consisted of the smallest number of sailors needed to ensure a successful voyage, and oversee the purchasing of slaves. He was then responsible for safely getting his human cargo from West Africa to the Americas—the part of the slave trade known as the Middle Passage. The crew faced many of the same problems, and once the slaves were loaded, the crew's position became more precarious.

A large part of the trip, three to four months, was spent on the African coast acquiring slaves. One problem for the slave trade involved finding commodities that the Africans would accept in exchange for slaves and then determining the price of a slave. The solution that developed was the ounce trade—slaves would be valued in gold ounces—and the sorting system. In the sorting system, slavers exchanged one sorting (an assortment of commodities, usually including a variety of textiles, firearms and gunpowder, alcohol, tobacco, metal wares, and other items) for one slave. If slavers arrived with the wrong commodities, their ability to purchase slaves diminished.

Slaves could be purchased in three ways. The first option was to buy slaves at one of the numerous European castles, forts, and warehouses on the African coast. By 1750, there were numerous European posts in West Africa, designed to both facilitate the slave trade and present a façade of power. This was popular in that these slave depots usually contained a ready supply of slaves, thereby reducing the voyage time and the time spent along the West African coast. Depending upon the ship's size and the number of slaves the captain was instructed to obtain, the slaver usually needed to visit several places before the holds were filled. The problem with this system was that

Conditions aboard the ships that brought Africans to America were abysmal. It is estimated that between 15 and 20 percent died en route during the early years of the trade (1500s and 1600s) and from 5 to 10 percent in latter years (1700s and 1800s). *(Library of Congress)*

the fort or company acted as a middleman, thus driving up the slaves' price.

The second option was to deal with African merchants. Here the slave's price was usually cheaper, but it took longer to acquire a shipload of slaves. The other problem was that if the slaver was not familiar with the local customs and rituals of exchange, the proposed sale could quickly fall apart.

The third option was to find either a European or African private merchant who operated trading factories on ship or shore. These private traders, like the company depots, usually maintained a surplus of slaves, thus speeding the process.

The slaves who filled the holds of slave ships and toiled in the Americas represented a variety of African cultures and peoples. The parts of West Africa that were the main suppliers of slaves to the Americas were Senegambia, Sierra Leone, the Windward Coast, the Gold Coast, the Bight of Benin, the Bight of Biafra, west-central Africa, and southeast Africa. Early on, most slaves transported to the Americas came from the West African coastal region or from along river systems that allowed European slavers access to the

interior. By the seventeenth and eighteenth centuries, more slaves came from Africa's interior; coastal African states had developed the ability both to protect their own people from being taken as slaves and to control and profit from the slave trade. As more and more slaves came from further inland, the diversity of African peoples being carried to the Americas increased.

Most enslaved Africans came from the lower echelons of their local society and were powerless to prevent their enslavement, yet at times even the elite were enslaved. Most commonly, slaves came from among those captured in war or raids, but one also could become a slave through judicial decisions, kidnapping, or debt, or in conflict. For most slavers, where the slaves came from and how they had become enslaved did not matter; what counted was their age, sex, and health. Most slavers wanted healthy young men, because they made the best plantation workers, and their youth meant a longer period of service for their masters. Young male slaves fetched the highest prices in the American slave markets.

Once the holds were filled with slaves, the Middle Passage of this forced migration began. This lasted between five to twelve weeks, depending upon the weather and where in the Americas the slaves were to be taken. Slavers had two main concerns: disease, which could decimate both slaves and crew, and a revolt. Most slave revolts occurred when the shoreline was still in sight and a chance to escape still existed.

Conditions on the ships were usually awful and were only exacerbated by the practice of tight-packing. The slaver captains who practiced tight-packing knew that a percentage of slaves would die on the trip and believed that they needed to put as many slaves as possible into their holds to ensure that the voyage would prove profitable. However, tight-packing increased the spread of disease among the slaves. On most ships, male slaves were separated from women and children; depending upon the slaver captain, some slaves were shackled together, while others were not. Most of the holds in the slaving ships had an extra floor placed in them to double the number of slaves that could be carried. This meant that when the slaves were confined to the holds, they could not stand up and usually lacked the space to move. Many crews did not clean the ship's holds, instead bringing groups of slaves to the deck to both feed and exercise them. Those slaves who refused to eat were forced to eat through a variety of means and contraptions, while other slaves, who had given up on life, attempted to jump overboard. Some slavers actually hung nets along the sides of their ships to

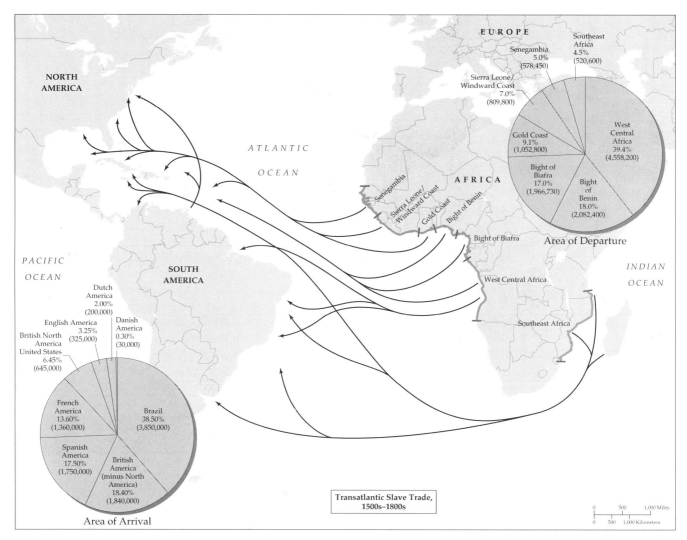

Three facts about the United States stand out on this map of the transatlantic slave trade: (1) Most African Americans trace their ancestry to West Africa; (2) many slaves came to the North American mainland from the Caribbean, rather than directly from Africa; and (3) the vast majority of slaves transported to North and South America were taken to places south of the present-day United States. *(CARTO-GRAPHICS)*

catch those slaves attempting to jump overboard. On some slave voyages, the death rate could reach 50 percent or higher.

Upon arrival in the Americas, the slaves were either kept aboard the ships or taken to a slave pen on land. The arrival of the slaves was usually advertised in handbills or newspapers to alert potential buyers of the impending auction. Before the auction potential buyers were allowed to inspect the slaves; often the period of inspection was limited to how long it took a candle to burn an inch. At many auctions, slaves were sold in lots to ensure that all slaves, both healthy and unhealthy, sold. Once sold, slaves could change hands several more times before their life of toil began.

NORTH AMERICA AND THE SLAVE TRADE

The first slaves to arrive in what would become the United States came on a Dutch ship that arrived in Jamestown, Virginia, in early 1619. The local settlers exchanged provisions for the slaves. As the colonies of North America developed and the demand for slaves increased, American merchants started to participate in the slave trade. The center of the North American slave trade was Rhode Island, which dominated the importation of slaves in the 1700s. Although the colony was not reliant upon slave labor, most of Rhode Island's economic development during this time centered on the slave trade. In the eighteenth century, Rhode Island slave ships left port over nine hundred times and carried more than a hundred thousand slaves to various slave markets in the Americas.

THE SIZE OF THE TRADE

One issue that has interested scholars of the slave trade involves the number of Africans affected by this forced diaspora. In the period of the transatlantic slave trade, more Africans than Europeans crossed the Atlantic to the Americas. While the exact number will never be known, the existing records lead scholars to estimate that more than 11.5 million Africans were carried to the Americas, with more than 5 million transported to Brazil and Spanish America, approximately 4 million to the West Indies, some 400,000 to North America, and the rest to other places. In North America, the number of slaves imported can be split into the more specific regions where they disembarked: the Carolinas (151,647), Virginia (84,247), Georgia (13,782), Maryland (12,210), New York (4,310), New England excluding Rhode Island (2,204), Rhode Island (2,153), Florida (1,599), and Pennsylvania, Delaware, and New Jersey (1,018). The nature of each region's dominant economic system determined the number of slaves being imported into it. The plantation systems of the West Indies and Central and South America absorbed the vast majority of Africans carried to the Americas as slaves, while North Amer-

ica followed far behind. Of the North American colonies, the plantations of the Carolinas imported the most slaves, followed by Virginia and then Georgia. The Carolinas, Virginia, Georgia, and Maryland all developed agricultural economies centered around the production of cash crops and staples, yet the plantation system was not the only colonial economic system that utilized slaves. By the time of the American Revolution, the dearth of laborers in the Americas, especially with the decimation of America's indigenous people through disease and warfare, created a demand for laborers within all economic sectors. Not until 1808 would the slave trade be outlawed in the United States, and slavery itself existed until 1865.

Ty Reese

See also: Indentured Servants, Free Immigration (Part I, Sec. 1); West Africa (Part III, Sec. 1).

BIBLIOGRAPHY

Berlin, Ira. *Many Thousands Gone: The First Two Centuries of Slavery in North America.* Cambridge, MA: Belknap Press, 1998.

Coughty, Jay A. *The Notorious Triangle: Rhode Island and the African Slave Trade, 1700–1807.* Philadelphia: Temple University Press, 1981.

Curtin, Philip D. *The Atlantic Slave Trade: A Census.* Madison: University of Wisconsin Press, 1969.

Eltis, David. *The Rise of African Slavery in the Americas.* New York: Cambridge University Press, 2000.

Klein, Herbert S. *The Atlantic Slave Trade.* New York: Cambridge University Press, 1999.

IMMIGRANTS AND THE AMERICAN REVOLUTION

In the decades preceding the American Revolution, most colonial leaders came to view immigration as a crucial source of fresh labor upon which the future economic development of British North America vitally depended. While nearly all colonial governments by the 1760s favored relatively open immigration policies and offered various inducements to attract new European settlers, they could not claim exclusive authority to regulate immigrant admissions and rights. Indeed, the ultimate power over immigration and naturalization in the New World rested with the English Crown, Parliament, and Board of Trade. For many years, English and colonial officials shared strong economic incentives to promote policies that spurred the recruitment of immigrant laborers.

By the late eighteenth century, however, colonial designs for enticing newcomers with attractive terms of admission, settlement, and naturalization were frustrated by imperial policies that barred colonial grants of subjectship and limited westward territorial expansion under the Proclamation of 1763 and the Quebec Act of 1774. The British government's resistance to colonial demands for more open immigration policies was one of a long train of grievances that led American revolutionaries to defy English rule in 1775. The Declaration of Independence specifically charged that King George III and the Privy Council "endeavored to prevent the population of these States" by "obstructing the laws for naturalization of foreigners, refusing to pass others to encourage their migrations hither, and raising the conditions of new appropriations of lands." Nearly all the former British colonies that became states in 1776 saw immigration as a new source of labor that was crucially needed to meet the demands of economic development. The British government's rejection of colonial efforts to better populate their territories through open immigration, revolutionary leaders alleged, was nothing short of an assault on the freedom, economic well-being, and military defense of North American colonists.

COLONIAL HERITAGE

Due to early waves of immigration, the United States was already a remarkably diverse country in terms of religion, race, and ethnicity at the time of its founding. Less than half of the new republic's white population could be described as English proper when the Revolution began. Anglo-Americans remained the dominant group in the former English colonies, but British newcomers increasingly came from Scotland, Wales, and Ireland. Moreover, one-third of the country's white inhabitants claimed German, Swedish, French, Swiss, and Dutch origins. In two of the original states, New Jersey and Pennsylvania, those of English descent were increasingly becoming a minority of the white population. Southern importation of African slaves was the principal engine of racial diversity in the early American republic, complemented by an indeterminate population of American Indians in each of the new states. Finally, the United States was more religiously diverse than any country in Europe. Despite early efforts to build a single religious orthodoxy in Massachusetts, a rich variety of sects flourished in New England by the outbreak of the Revolution. The former Middle Colonies became home to Quakers, Catholics, and other religious dissenters. In Virginia and other former southern colonies, religious revivals significantly eroded the dominance of established churches.

America's founding generation grew up in colonies with contrasting traditions of governing immigration and alien rights. Some colonies were unwaveringly hostile to outsiders during their history; some granted entry only to immigrants who adhered to dominant sectarian standards and equal membership only to those who shared their ecclesiastical goals; some vigorously recruited immigrant labor but limited the rights that newcomers enjoyed; and still others extended generous terms of immigration and membership to all white male settlers. Moreover, eth-

While foreign mercenaries fought on the British side in the Revolution, the patriot side could count on the support of many immigrant settlers, including German General Friedrich Wilhelm Ludolf Gerhard Augustin Von Steuben, shown here reviewing troops at Valley Forge. *(National Park Service: Statue of Liberty National Monument)*

nic and religious tensions surfaced from time to time before the outbreak of the American Revolution. Although Roman Catholics were few in number, authorities in every colony, including Maryland, discouraged Catholic immigration through special head taxes and other legal barriers. Ethnic animosities were most often directed in the eighteenth century against Irish and German newcomers, not surprisingly the two largest ethnic groups after English Americans. Members of Pennsylvania's English majority, for example, were especially agitated by the perceived cultural separatism of German immigrants, who were said to number roughly a third of the colony's population. Benjamin Franklin derided German settlers as unassimilable because they were reluctant to adopt English language and customs. These immigrants, he warned, would "soon be so numerous as to Germanize us instead of us Anglifying them."

CRISIS OF THE REVOLUTION

The crisis of the American Revolution provided the young nation's leaders with a special impetus to stress ethnic and religious cohesion. The Declaration of Independence took care to describe Americans as "one people" who found common cause in separating themselves from British rule. In reality, an estimated eighty to one hundred thousand American loyalists— a sizable portion of the population—fled the newly established United States for Canada and Britain after the war began. As a result, emigration out of the country far exceeded immigration into the country

during this period of upheaval. For the diverse ethnic groups that remained, however, the war largely served as a unifying crisis. Through prominent military service during the Revolution, German Americans gained new credibility and acceptance. To Revolutionary idealists, the struggle for independence produced a distinctively American national identity forged by the rigors of frontier life, the sacrifices of war, and the diverse European origins of the citizenry. Thomas Paine declared that all Europe, rather than England, was the parent country of the United States. "In this extensive quarter of the globe, we forget the narrow limits of three hundred and sixty miles (the extent of England) and carry our friendship on a larger scale," he noted. "We claim brotherhood with every European Christian, and triumph in the generosity of the sentiment." George Washington exuberantly declared a few years later that the country had a special obligation to provide asylum to persecuted Europeans of every nationality and religion. Other national founders were more pragmatic, embracing postwar immigration as a valuable means of spurring U.S. economic and territorial growth.

Although immigration slowed to a trickle during the era of the American Revolution (no more than a few thousand per year), some national leaders remained wary of future immigration. In his celebrated *Notes on the State of Virginia*, Thomas Jefferson criticized the new nation's member states for their "present desire to produce rapid population by as great importations of foreigners as possible." In 1781, Jefferson expressed a general fear that most newcomers were unable to learn republican principles, to cherish individual liberty, or to practice self-government virtuously. Immigrants, he predicted, would prove either incapable of shedding their loyalties to the "absolute monarchy" of the Old World or prone to anarchical temptations of the new one. While supporting broad rights for European immigrants already residing in the new nation, Jefferson suggested that the quality and durability of republican government in America required measured restraints on future admissions.

The French Revolution and subsequent Napoleonic warfare in Europe delayed robust immigration to the United States until well after the 1820s. Nevertheless, new state governments wasted little time in establishing their own immigration and naturalization policies soon after the nation's founding. Most of these policies were designed to entice new European settlers and to extend broad membership rights to white male newcomers.

There were important exceptions: Jewish newcomers could not vote in Maryland or hold public office in New Hampshire, and naturalized residents were made ineligible for elected office in South Carolina. Yet most states extended full citizenship rights to European immigrants after a short term of residence, some level of property ownership, and a public declaration of support for republican principles of self-government. J. Hector St. John (originally Michel-Guillaume-Jean de Crèvecoeur) a French immigrant who for a time settled and became naturalized in New York, noted the enormous opportunities for European immigrant men in the United States.

With some hyperbole, St. John blithely observed that Europe's poor enjoyed a "metamorphosis" in the new United States thanks to generous state policies. "The laws, the indulgent laws, protect [immigrants] as they arrive," he wrote, "stamping on them the symbol of adoption; they receive ample rewards for their labours; these accumulated rewards procure them lands; those lands confer on them the title of freemen, and to that title every benefit is affixed which men can possibly require."

IMMIGRATION AND THE CONSTITUTION

While state and local officials assumed the authority to regulate immigration, the architects of the U.S. Constitution reflected at some length on the relative merits of immigrant admissions and rights during their Philadelphia deliberations in 1787. The question of who should be eligible for federal elective office served as the impetus for a broad-ranging immigra-

tion debate that revealed widely divergent views among delegates. Some came to the xenophobic conclusion that immigrants could never throw off what Elbridge Gerry called "foreign attachments," making them an inherently subversive presence in the new nation. Others, like Gouverneur Morris and Pierce Butler, called for long periods of citizenship (fourteen years or more) before the foreign-born were eligible for congressional office. Ultimately, they shared Gerry's deep suspicions of immigrants. "What is the language of Reason on this subject?" asked Morris. "Admit a Frenchman into your Senate and he will study the commerce of France; an Englishman, he will feel an equal bias in favor of England." Tellingly, those favoring the exclusion of the foreign-born from public office included such decidedly pro-immigration delegates as George Mason, who welcomed the economic benefits of alien laborers but resisted extending broad political rights to "foreigners and adventurers."

Many delegates assailed this position. James Wilson, a Scottish-born delegate, spoke of "the discouragement and mortification" felt by immigrants due to "degrading discrimination" in social and political membership. An august Franklin observed that those who came to American shores were predisposed to embrace its social and political ideals. James Madison worried that excluding immigrants from public office would "give a tincture of illiberality to the Constitution." A constitution properly constructed, he insisted, would provide enduring stability that would attract "great numbers of respectable Europeans: men who love liberty and wish to partake its blessings." Madison also pointed out a more pragmatic reason to welcome European newcomers who were willing to accept republican principles: those states which most encouraged European immigration were the strongest in population, agriculture, and the arts.

The final draft of the Constitution disqualified naturalized citizens only from the presidential office. American residency of seven years was required to serve in the House of Representatives, and nine years of residency for the Senate. The Philadelphia convention also adopted with little fanfare a proposal empowering Congress to establish a uniform rule of naturalization. In contrast to British tradition, these decisions signaled a rejection of fixed gradations of membership among foreign- and native-born white men in the American political community. On the subject of immigrant admissions, the Constitution was all but silent. As such, it tacitly reinforced the authority of state and local officials to shape and implement their own immigration policies.

Ratification debates in the separate states captured widespread enthusiasm for European immigration.

But they also brought to light strong nativist resentment toward non-English newcomers among some Anti-Federalists. In the *Massachusetts Gazette*, an essayist using the name "Agrippa" challenged the power of Congress with respect to naturalization. While many states might be willing to receive foreigners as citizens, he observed, "reasons of equal weight may induce other states, differently circumstanced, to keep their blood pure." Whereas Thomas Paine and James Wilson upheld Pennsylvania as a model for the country, Agrippa cast Pennsylvania's religious and ethnic diversity in foreboding hues:

> Pennsylvania has chosen to receive all that would come here. Let any indifferent person judge whether that state in point of morals, education, energy is equal to any of the [New England] states; the small state of Rhode Island excepted. Pennsylvania in the course of a century has acquired her present extent and population at the expense of religion and good morals. The [New England] states have, by keeping separate from the foreign mixtures, acquired their present greatness in the course of a century and an half, and have preserved their religion and morals. They have also preserved that manly virtue which is equally fitted for rendering them respectable in war, and industrious in peace.

By empowering Congress to establish a uniform—and sure to be liberal—rule of naturalization, Agrippa protested, the Constitution threatened to undermine the civic virtue and martial spirit fostered by cultural homogeneity.

Agrippa's protests represented the minority view during the ratification process. Most commentary in 1787 praised the Constitution as crucial for encouraging European immigration, which most opinion leaders saw as essential to building a secure and prosperous nation. In Massachusetts, New York, Pennsylvania, Virginia, and other states, defenders of the Constitution wrote wistfully in newspapers of the territorial expansion, commercial empire, and national greatness that robust European immigration promised. "Behold America with extended arms, inviting the numerous, oppressed and distressed inhabitants of Europe," proclaimed a Massachusetts enthusiast of the Constitution. "[O]ur woods and waste lands will become at once valuable, and in great demand . . . arts and sciences will be cultivated with redoubled ardour—every kind of business will increase—and in a word, this continent will soon become, under the new government, the delight and envy of the European world."

During ratification debates at the Pennsylvania convention, speakers suggested that European immigration was consistent with "the first command given by the Deity to man, increase and multiply." In particular, it was important "to draw numbers from the other side of the Atlantic" for purposes of settling the vast North American continent. "We are representatives . . . not merely of the present age, but of future times; not merely of the territory along the seacoast, but of regions immensely extended westward."

Having asserted the desirability of European immigration for the security and prosperity of American states, various proponents of the Constitution argued that the absence of a competent national government discouraged new arrivals. One Virginia commentator observed that the peasantry, merchants, and philosophers of Europe would eschew the United States so long as it remained susceptible to "insurrections against state governments" and "the insecurity of property." Madison concurred, observing that the number of European immigrants "will depend on the degree of security provided . . . for private rights and public order." Most defenders of the Constitution seemed to endorse European immigration and its potential for spurring American development. They were not inclined to see the national government regulate immigration itself, content with having the states continue to exercise this authority. However, political leaders such as James Madison made an important connection between steady European immigration and national guarantees of citizenship rights for white newcomers. Significantly, such nativist Anti-Federalists as Agrippa drew the same conclusion.

Not all the Constitution's champions embraced white ethnic and religious diversity. Although Madison's *Federalist No. 10* emphasized the advantages that a pluralistic American society offered for taming factional threats to republican government, John Jay's *Federalist No. 2* stressed the importance of cultural homogeneity in the United States. "Providence has been pleased to give this one connected country to one united people," he averred, "a people descended from the same ancestors, speaking the same language, professing the same religion, attached to the same principles of government, very similar in their manners and customs." That Jay's longings for white ethnic and religious uniformity found their way into the *Federalist* reminds us that competing ideological streams informed how political notables of the founding era perceived membership in the political community. Pro-immigration views represented the dominant perspective during the constitutional convention and ratification process, but notions of ethnic, religious, and racial hierarchy also were unmistakably present.

It did not take long for Congress to vindicate

Agrippa's fears that it would establish generous terms of naturalization. The first Congress in 1790 enacted a uniform rule of naturalization that made citizenship very easy to acquire for European men. It provided that "free white persons" who resided in the United States for as little as two years could be naturalized by "any common law court of record in any of the States."

With the ratification of the Constitution, the young nation embraced a laissez-faire national policy toward European newcomers and left it to states and localities to regulate and recruit new settlers almost as they saw fit. The fact that most state and local governments encouraged immigration fit well with the prevailing view among national leaders that the recruitment of new European settlers was essential to the country's future development. The nation's first uniform naturalization law left little doubt that the founders favored new European immigration. Labor scarcity, abundant territory, and strong yearnings for rapid economic development were all factors that informed the framers' ultimate enthusiasm for future European immigration. Moreover, early American nationalism reflected a natural-rights philosophy and lingering revolutionary spirit that led the country's most prominent leaders to embrace tolerance, nonsectarianism, and robust European immigration. At a time when no more than between 3,000 and 6,000 immigrants arrived annually, the nation's founders could not have anticipated either the massive scale or increasing diversity of immigration in the next century. Yet their initial choices about how to govern alien admissions and rights had an impact that far outlasted the era of the American Revolution, one that decisively linked U.S. national development to immigration.

Daniel J. Tichenor

See also: Puritans and Other Religious Dissenters (Part I, Sec. 1); Immigrants and the Civil War (Part I, Sec. 2); Revolutionary War Correspondence of George Washington, 1775–1778 (Part IV, Sec. 3).

BIBLIOGRAPHY

Fuchs, Lawrence. *The American Kaleidoscope: Race, Ethnicity, and Civic Culture.* Middletown, CT: Wesleyan University Press, 1992.

Jacobson, David. *The Immigration Reader.* New York: Blackwell, 1998.

Kettner, James. *The Development of American Citizenship, 1608–1870.* Chapel Hill: University of North Carolina Press, 1978.

Kohn, Hans. *American Nationalism: An Interpretive Essay.* New York: Macmillan, 1957.

LeMay, Michael. *From Open Door to Dutch Door.* New York: Praeger, 1987.

Noriel, Gerard, ed. *Immigrants in Two Democracies: The French and American Experience.* New York: New York University Press, 1992.

Smith, Rogers. *Civic Ideals.* New Haven, CT: Yale University Press, 1998.

St. John, J. Hector (originally, de Crèvecoeur, Michel-Guillaume-Jean). *Letters from an American Farmer; Describing Certain Provincial Situations, Manners and Customs Not Generally Known.* London: Thomas Davies, 1782.

1800 TO 1880s

INTRODUCTION

Section 2 of Part I of the *Encyclopedia of American Immigration* is titled "1800 to 1880s," and covers the following periods in American history: the early Republic, the Jacksonian age, the antebellum era, the Civil War, Reconstruction, and the Gilded Age. The entries in this section include those on a specific period or event ("Early-Nineteenth-Century Immigration," "Immigrants and the Civil War," and "Immigrants and Westward Expansion"); various immigrant groups ("The Great Irish Immigration," "Germans and Other Political Refugees," and "Chinese and Chinese Exclusion Act"); and, finally, an entry on native-born reaction to immigration ("Nativism and Know-Nothings").

In "Early-Nineteenth-Century Immigration," writer Njoki Nathani-Wane examines a much overlooked period of immigration between the Revolutionary era and the great waves of Irish and German immigration in the 1840s and 1850s. Wane explores the various factors—including European wars and economic depression—that acted to curtail immigration to the United States in the first four decades of the nineteenth century. For those immigrants who did come, the author offers a picture of where they settled in America and what they did for a living once they got here.

In her entry "The Great Irish Immigration," Judith Warner discusses the mass immigration that accompanied the famine that struck Ireland in the mid-nineteenth century. The author begins with a discussion of the potato famine itself before moving on to colonial power Britain's insufficient efforts at famine relief. Next, she examines the demography and settlement patterns of the Irish immigration. In addition, the author looks at the nativist reaction against Irish immigrants and how such immigration institutions as the Catholic Church responded. Finally, she examines the economic and political adjustment of Irish immigrants to American society and their affinity for Irish nationalism.

In "Germans and Other Political Refugees," William C. McDonald discusses the wave of political immigrants who came to these shores in the middle of the nineteenth century. He examines the history of Europe in the mid-nineteenth century, exploring what led up to the revolutions of 1848 and why they sent the immigrants that they did to the United States. With a focus on the German-speaking persons that made up the bulk of this immigrant wave, McDonald looks into where they settled and what they did economically once they got here, as well as their impact on American political and cultural life.

In "Nativism and Know-Nothings," Christopher Bates looks at anti-immigrant sentiment in the United States from the beginning of the nineteenth century through the onset of the Civil War in the 1860s. He examines the nativist sentiment and politics in America in the early years of the republic, when there was relatively little immigration. Bates then goes on to examine the rise and impact of the largest anti-immigrant political organization in U.S. history, the Know-Nothings of the 1850s, and how they grew in response to the waves of Irish immigration after the famine years of the late 1840s.

For the entry "Chinese and Chinese Exclusion Act," Lawrence K. Hong examines the largest free immigration of non-European people to the United States prior to the post–World War II period. Hong discusses the few Chinese immigrants who made their way to the United States in the years before the California gold rush of the late 1840s and 1850s. He also explores the ways in which the vast bulk of gold rush and post–gold rush era Chinese got to America and what they did economically once they arrived. In addition, he discusses the rising anti-Chinese sentiment in California and the West in these years and how it led to the Chinese Exclusion Act of 1882.

In "Immigrants and the Civil War," Angela F. Pulley lays out the demographics of the foreign-born population in the United States at the time of the great conflict. She then discusses how immigrants related to the war, how they participated in it, and how they resisted participating in it. Pulley focuses on the North, where the vast majority of immigrants lived, but she also explores the role of immigrants in the Southern war effort. Finally, she adds a note about the meaning of African-American emancipation for immigrants in American society.

Adrienne Caughfield's entry, "Immigrants and Westward Expansion," offers a survey of the role of immigrants in the settling of the American frontier. The entry is divided into sections on colonial times and the nineteenth century, as well as discussions on immigrants in various frontier areas, including the trans-Appalachian West and the trans-Mississippi West. She also offers a discussion of the impact of the frontier on immigrants and how immigrants shaped the frontier experience.

EARLY-NINETEENTH-CENTURY IMMIGRATION

Compared to the great waves of Irish and German immigration in the middle of the nineteenth century and the flood of eastern and southern European immigrants at the turn of the twentieth century, immigration in the half-century from the presidency of George Washington in the 1790s to that first great wave of immigrants from Europe in the 1840s was moderate. Whereas some 4.2 million immigrants came to the United States in the 1840s and 1850s, roughly just one-fifth of that number arrived in the two decades preceding 1840. And although systematic statistics were not maintained until the passage of the 1819 Manifest of Immigrants Act, it can be presumed that the twenty-five years of near-continuous European warfare that followed the onset of the French Revolution in 1789 kept immigration to the United States at a minimum in those years.

The pattern of new arrivals in the fifty-year period from 1790 to 1840 bore a stronger resemblance to colonial times than it did to the post-1840 era, with most newcomers to the United States coming from a traditional roster of places: England, Ireland, Scotland, the various German-speaking states of Central Europe, and—until the banning of international slave trade in 1807–08—Africa. Similarly, the reasons for immigration were much the same: loss of land in the home country; skilled labor rendered redundant by the rise of factories, particularly in England; and the desire for the higher wages and cheaper lands of the United States, two economic facts of life promoted in Europe through advertising by various state governments looking for settlers.

WAR, PEACE, AND IMMIGRATION

Despite these similarities with colonial times in the causes of European immigration, there were a number of critical events in the fifty years of the early republic

period that played a role in determining the numbers of immigrants coming into the United States. First and foremost is the question of war. Like the American Revolution, but on a far vaster scale, the European revolutions and wars between 1789 and 1815—as well as the War of 1812 between Britain and America, which lasted until 1815—disrupted immigration from Europe to the United States.

On July 14, 1789, Parisian mobs attacked and occupied the Bastille, a fortress-prison symbolizing the repression of the old regime and marking the beginning of the French Revolution. Over the next four years, increasingly radical elements would come to the fore in Paris in a process that would lead to the declaration of the first French republic in September 1792 and the beheading of Louis XVI in January 1793. With pressure mounting from conservative governments throughout Europe, the new republic declared war against the Netherlands and Britain in February 1793 and against Spain in March. War had already been declared between France on one side and Austria and Prussia on the other.

Meanwhile, in the United States, political divisions arose between supporters of France and revolution and backers of Britain and conservatism. The Federalists, in power from 1789 to 1801, were conservative in outlook and, while officially maintaining neutrality in the European wars, continued to emphasize trade and political ties with Britain. Attempting to isolate Britain from its American markets, France went on the offensive in the Atlantic, leading to an undeclared naval war with the United States. In addition, the revolutionary government in Paris sent agents to the United States to try and influence the American political process to favor France. Outraged over this interference and fearful that new immigrants were joining the pro-French Democratic party of Thomas Jefferson, President John Adams, the last Federalist to serve in the White House, imposed the Alien Act of 1798, authorizing the deportation of foreigners for political reasons and increasing the residency requirement for naturalization from five to fourteen years. (The law would be allowed to lapse in 1801, after the Democrats came to power in the election of 1800.)

In Europe, revolutionary France went from victory to victory in the 1790s, culminating in a kind of military coup in Paris by the republic's leading general, Napoleon Bonaparte. Ruthless and ambitious, Napoleon soon led France into renewed warfare against Britain as well as Austria and Prussia in the first decade of the nineteenth century. In the Atlantic, London and Paris attempted to impose naval blockades against each other. In doing so, they seized American ships attempting to trade with the enemy. To keep the United States out of war, President Jefferson imposed a blockade on all American overseas trade in 1807–8. Four years later, his successor, James Madison, took the United States into war against Britain for the latter's practice of seizing immigrant English seamen serving on American ships. Wars in both Europe and the United States continued from 1812 through 1815, leading in the former to a total defeat for Napoleon and in the latter to a stalemate.

With the return of peace to both continents in 1815 came an upsurge in European immigration, to about 150,000 in the 1820s and around 600,000 in the 1830s. Still, the arrival of peace alone cannot explain the in-

creasing numbers, as other factors came into play. In England, for instance, the postwar period witnessed widespread protests among tenant farmers and urban workers, culminating for the latter in the so-called Battle of Peterloo, where armed cavalry gunned down numerous workers protesting at Saint Peter's Field, in Manchester. Both the economic conditions that precipitated these rebellions—and the political repression that followed them—contributed to the rising immigration numbers from Britain. In the German-speaking states of Central Europe, increasing economic integration—culminating in the *zollverein*, or German customs union, of 1834—was breaking down barriers between states in the interior and the great ports on the North Sea, making immigration to the United States far easier.

Yet there were other factors that continued to act as a break on immigration in the post–Napoleonic war decades. In England, Parliament passed laws that restricted the number of craft workers seeking to immigrate to America, even as it limited the number of settlers each ship crossing the Atlantic could carry. Moreover, the economic collapse that hit both the United States—and, to lesser extent, Europe—in the late 1830s and early 1840s discouraged many from coming.

This 1805 woodcut depicts immigrants from Basel, Switzerland, embarking on the first leg of their journey to the United States. *(Library of Congress)*

SETTLEMENT PATTERNS

While different immigrant groups tended to settle in different parts of the country for reasons of their own, one crucial factor applied to all immigrants. For the most part—with the major exception of the Scots-Irish—the vast majority tended to settle in the free states of the North, especially from the 1820s on. There is no great mystery behind this tendency. The existence of slave labor depressed wages, and the prohibitive costs of slaves made the economics of immigrating to the South unattractive, not to mention the fact that many immigrants were ideologically opposed to the institution.

Still, where immigrants settled in the United States depended much on their ethnic backgrounds, skills, and the amount of money they brought with them, if any. For the most part, English and lowland Scottish immigrants were the wealthiest immigrants of the period, with the highest level of skills. Many settled in urban areas—particularly Boston, New York, Philadelphia, Baltimore, and other towns and cities of the Northeast—where they became involved in retailing, wholesaling, and skilled artisan work. Those who were farmers often came with enough capital to buy lands in the more settled eastern portions of the country, although many established communities in the newly opened lands of the Upper Midwest.

Highland Scots and the Protestant Scots-Irish of modern-day Northern Ireland were generally poorer and lower-skilled. As was the case with their colonial-era predecessors, most of these immigrants made their way to the frontier, where land was far cheaper. Most of these immigrants settled along the eastern slopes of the Appalachians in the earlier part of the period in question. The effective removal of Native Americans from the southeastern states opened up these lands to immigrants as well, and thus many Scots-Irish and others made their way to western slopes of the Appalachians. Wars that removed Native tribes from the Old Northwest (today's Upper Midwest) led to migration there, particularly by English immigrants.

Finally, a word should be added about the arrival of Africans in the United States in this period. Obviously, as slaves, they had no choice in coming and no say in where they settled. But between 1800 and America's decision to join Britain in ceasing the international trade in slaves, some 15,000 Africans were imported to the United States, most coming via the Caribbean.

Njoki Nathani-Wane

See also: The Great Irish Immigration, Germans and Other Political Refugees (Part I, Sec. 2); An Act to Establish a Uniform Rule of Naturalization, 1790, Alien Act, 1798, Manifest of Immigrants Act, 1819 (Part IV, Sec. 1); Look Before You Leap, 1796, History of the English Settlement in Edwards County, Illinois, 1818, Memorial of James Brown, 1819, Tour Through the United States, 1819, Letters from Illinois, 1818, How an Emigrant May Succeed in the United States, 1818 (Part IV, Sec. 3).

BIBLIOGRAPHY

Adams, Henry. *History of the United States during the Administration of James Madison.* New York: The Library of America, 1986.

Berthoff, Rowland Tappan. *British Immigrants in Industrial America: 1790–1950.* Cambridge, MA: Harvard University Press, 1953.

Erikson, Charlotte. *The Invisible Immigrants: The Adaptation of English and Scottish Immigrants in Nineteenth-Century America.* Miami, FL: University of Miami Press, 1972.

Grabbe, Hans-Jurgen. "The Demise of the Redemptioner System in the United States." *American Studies [West Germany]* 29:3 (1984): 277–96.

———. "European Immigration to the United States in the Early National Period. 1798–1820." *Proceedings of the American Philosophical Society* 133:2 (1989): 190–214.

———. "Before the Great Tidal Waves: Patterns of Transatlantic Migration at the Beginning of the Nineteenth Century." *American Studies [Germany]* 42:3 (1997): 377–89.

Leach, Kristine. *Walking Common Ground. Nineteenth and Twentieth Century Immigrant Women in America.* San Francisco: Austin & Winfield, 1995.

Shepperson, Wilbur S. *Emigration & Disenchantment: Portraits of Englishmen Repatriated from the United States.* Norman: University of Oklahoma Press, 1957.

Young, Donald. *American Minority Peoples: A Study in Racial and Cultural Conflicts in the United States.* New York: Harper & Brothers, 1932.

THE GREAT IRISH IMMIGRATION

Ireland has experienced a long history of colonization by Great Britain, a status still maintained in Northern Ireland in the late twentieth century. To foster control of the Irish, Irish Protestants initiated between 1695 and 1746 a series of legislative acts establishing the Penal Laws. These laws had the explicit purpose of maintaining an ethnic stratification system in which Roman Catholic Irish were denied access to economic, political, and social resources. Protestants, a numerical minority, were at the apex of the power structure and formulated laws discriminating against Catholics. While the Penal Laws were lifted in the nineteenth century, their legacy was that many Irish Catholics were impoverished and still subject to social discrimination.

Discrimination in Ireland was a result of a system of racial oppression. Although twenty-first-century Irish are categorized as "white," in nineteenth-century Ireland, Catholics were referred to as "native Irish," "Celts," or "Gaels" and regarded as members of a "race" that had a lower-caste status. The Penal Laws precluded social acceptance of Irish Catholics, enabling Irish Protestants and the British to act as a dominant group. In 1800, however, Great Britain passed the Act of Union, joining the British and Irish Parliaments into one body. Protestant Irish were no longer dominant over Catholic Irish, and both groups were subject to the British. British rule fostered resentment among Irish Catholics, which intensified in the nineteenth century and resulted in eventual independence for southern Ireland and intensely hostile relations in twentieth-century Northern Ireland.

PRE-FAMINE IRISH EMIGRATION

In the first three decades of the nineteenth century, Ireland had one of the highest rates of emigration in Europe. Between 1800 and 1845, prior to the Great Famine, it is estimated that 1 million left Ireland. Although the century-long pattern of emigration fostered a stereotype of the poor Irish Catholic immigrant, the actual flow was more diverse. In the eighteenth century and from 1815 to 1830, a majority of Irish emigrants were Protestant, primarily Presbyterian dissenters and Anglicans. They were descendants of Scotch who had intermarried with Irish women; although initially the Scotch were of privileged ethnic status, their children grew up Irish. These settlers were as frustrated with the British landholding and business systems as Catholics. Emigrants included farmers, artisans, tradespeople, and professionals. Less than one-quarter were laborers; the poor could not afford passage. Prior to the famine, even Catholic Irish immigrants were not necessarily poor.

In the United States, the descendants of Scotch-Irish unions were regarded as Irish. After the development of anti-Irish nativism, however, the term "Scotch-Irish" developed in America, as earlier arrivals sought to differentiate themselves from the perceived Irish influx. The racialized differentiation between Scotch and Irish that characterized Ireland reemerged as an ethnic distinction in the American Irish diaspora population, indicating the socially constructed nature of ethnicity as well as race.

Discrimination was a primary motive for the emigration of Irish Catholics. Starting in the 1820s, prior to the onset of famine, individuals began to leave Ireland, and even after the Great Famine was over, massive emigration continued. This extensive migration was internationally regarded as due to poverty and overpopulation, in effect blaming the Irish victims. The Irish, however, eventually attributed the mass exodus to British oppression, primarily the British handling of the Great Famine. The Great Famine itself occurred because the diet of Irish Catholic tenant farmers and laborers was largely reliant on one basic crop, potatoes, which failed.

THE GREAT IRISH IMMIGRATION

Irish immigrant workers, shown here laying track for the first transcontinental railroad in 1869, were indispensable in the construction of America's transportation system. *(Library of Congress)*

THE POTATO ECONOMY IN IRELAND

Potatoes, the primary subsistence crop of the peasantry, were blighted by the fungus *Phytophthora infestans* in various Irish regions for a period of seven years. The disproportionate impact of the blight was due to peasants' and laborers' high dependence on the crop. As a result of the association of potatoes with poverty, however, they were a stigmatized food. Also, the cultivation requirements of potatoes kept families bound to the land and permitted the repeated subdivision of tenant-occupied lands. Great Britain, as overseer of Ireland, had sought to modernize and diversify Irish agriculture. Reducing dependency on the potato and changing tenant and landlord practices were viewed as the way to agricultural development.

Irish landlords had a low degree of capital investment in their tenanted estates and had allowed repeated subdivision, in the process gaining more labor to produce cash crops. Peasants resisted agricultural change because it would mean changes in their diet, use of turf as fuel, and communal village lifestyle as well. Prior to the famine, the Irish had begun a period of demographic transition, in which births greatly exceeded deaths yet fertility remained high. The resulting rapid population growth led to the type of overcrowding characteristic of the developing economies of the twenty-first century. A key difference, however, was the extreme degree of peasant reliance on a single crop. The Great Famine occurred in the potato peasant subsistence economy, but more than 75 percent of Irish agriculture involved other crops. The agricultural cornucopia of Ireland included livestock and dairy products, corn and other grain crops, which comprised a large agricultural surplus. These crops were exported to Great Britain for profit. Thus, the Great Famine was inherently a social famine rather than an all-encompassing ecological disaster.

THE GREAT FAMINE

The immediate motivation for accelerated emigration was a social famine in which Irish Catholic tenant farmers suffered starvation in the midst of plenty. It is estimated that between 1 million and 2.1 million left Ireland between 1845 and 1851. As mentioned, the social structure of British-controlled Ireland was responsible for the disaster. In the nineteenth century, Protestant landlords owned the vast majority of the land in Ireland and rented it to predominantly Catholic tenant farmers at exorbitant rates of return. Land leases were fragmented, and profit to those who worked the land was minimal. Tenant farmers raised a variety of crops for landowners and barely survived on a separate crop, potatoes. When blight struck the potato crop, food available for tenant-farming families was minimal; they did not have the right to consume the cash crops and livestock they raised to pay rent. Individuals starved in the midst of abundant grain crops, which were exported to England. Landlords maintained their profit margins and took advantage of the potato crop failure to reorganize farming.

Eviction was one harsh response of landlords to the Great Famine. It is estimated that at least five hundred thousand people were evicted. Tenant farmers resisted eviction through a series of burnings, livestock mutilations, and murders directed at landlords, their agents, and prospective new tenants. Victims of eviction, however, were only a minority of the emigrants, as many simply relinquished farming as a way of life in a massive redistribution of population to the United States, Canada, and Australia.

The Great Irish Famine of 1842–52 resulted in both high mortality and extensive emigration from Ireland. It is estimated that between 1.1 million and 1.5 million Irish died between 1845 and 1855. Approximately 25 percent of the population emigrated or perished within a period of five years. Perhaps as many as 2.1 million Irish emigrated, nearly 1.9 million to North America. The pre-famine population of 8.5 million was reduced to 4.5 million in the harshest food crisis of modern times.

INITIAL BRITISH FAMINE RELIEF

In 1845, the potato blight arrived in Ireland by ship, having spread from the United States and Europe. Initial British efforts to respond to the famine were fairly effective: The government imported inexpensive corn, or maize, from the United States and sold it through a network of food relief committees. These committees were controlled by the British treasury and organized by regional gentry; the committees were also responsible for public works. In 1845, when about 40 percent of the potato crop was lost, government intervention was effective in averting mass starvation.

Although Great Britain was the richest and most industrialized nation in the nineteenth century, the socially engineered manner in which Great Britain responded to the famine was ultimately ineffective. In 1846, 90 percent of the potato crop was destroyed, but changes in the mechanism of relief greatly reduced government capacity to respond. The European corn harvest was also poor. The successful government intervention through food relief was abandoned due to complaints from merchants who felt that their businesses had been harmed, and food relief sales were replaced with a public works program.

THE BRITISH POOR LAW

The new relief program was bureaucratically controlled by the British treasury and provided low wages for twelve hours of work per day, in order to discourage freeloaders. Despite the criteria for aid, the demand for work by men, women, and children was greater than the supply. Approximately half a million participated, many working during a cold winter without adequate clothing; some even lacked footwear. Food prices soared, and wages were below subsistence level. As a result of these changes to relief mechanisms, disease and mortality soared. It is estimated that four hundred thousand died.

Because of the British government's desire to socially reengineer Ireland's peasant society and its political and budget concerns, relief became based on free-market principles. The changes in provision of relief and transfer of the burden to Ireland were meant to rationalize Irish landholding by ridding the land of tenants. This occurred through forced immigration, forced relief, or starvation. In an act of blaming the victims, Protestant politicians suggested that poor Irish Catholics were being punished by God for being lazy and lacking motivation. A countervailing tendency in the nineteenth-century world was the emergence of international humanitarian concern, which led to debate about the British handling of the Irish crisis and fostered a long-term resentment among Irish at home and abroad. Indeed, the mismanagement of famine relief is central to understanding the formation of the Irish diaspora and long-term nationalism among Irish-Americans.

BLACK '47

The social famine experienced by the Irish poor in the year 1847 brought such intense and widespread suffering that the year became known as "Black '47." In a time of political and capitalist opportunism, the British government refused to intervene in the process of importation and exportation of food. Lack of constraints on market forces allowed continued export of cash crops, while various navigation acts in force since the seventeenth century, specifying that all imports should enter on British vessels, hampered the bringing in of food. Irish and British merchants were more interested in export profits than importing foodstuffs and did little to assist the impoverished. As a result, the British removed import duties on some goods. It was painfully clear that British government policy, no longer based on humanitarian principles, was adding to rather than reducing Irish suffering.

Ireland's Great Famine was different from many other modern famines because emigration was a safety valve for those who could afford it. Usually, modern famine has resulted in internal rather than external displacement. Over half a million received assistance from Irish landlords for their passage, while others were helped by Irish immigrants already in the United States. Ireland's emigrants headed toward the United States, Canada, Australia, and Great Britain, but because of recession in Great Britain and Australia and a booming American economy, a preference was established for emigration to the United States. Post-1846 emigrants were unskilled and extremely poor. The trans-Atlantic crossing made by immigrants was marked by crowded and unhygienic conditions, which led to the use of the term "coffin ships" to describe the vessels used. It is estimated that forty thousand died during the crossing or in American and Canadian hospitals.

In Ireland, the attempt to ameliorate suffering using the tool of the English poor laws failed. The potato famine continued, and although corn imports increased, many began to starve, as public relief wages were too low to purchase food at inflated prices. Simultaneously, a European industrial recession subjected many Irish textile mill workers to layoffs and reduced hours. The property crime rate increased as individuals turned to theft in an effort to survive, and individuals with property requested and received increased policing in the form of mounted officers and armed forces. The constabulary, assisted by the British military, began to engage in mass tenant evictions and seizure of assets of small tenant farmers unable to pay local tax. The military also guarded food shipments and policed food riots. The British government began to reconsider the anti-poor ideology of its food policy.

TEMPORARY RELIEF ACT

In 1847, the Temporary Relief Act, passed in Great Britain, replaced the public works program with soup kitchens. The Society of Friends, or Quakers, had pioneered this activity in 1846. This was a direct attempt to reduce hunger without requiring work or payment, thus reversing the victim-blaming ideology of public works efforts. Soup kitchens were, nonetheless, regarded as a temporary expedient. Soup was chosen to reduce taxpayers' ire because it was cheap and could not be readily resold. The soup provided varied greatly in quality and was often not sufficiently nutritious. The timing of the end of the public works program preceded the establishment of soup kitchens, increasing Irish hardship and mortality. By mid-1847, 3 million were receiving soup daily, and mortality began to decline. Government assistance was supplemented by private donations, many from working-class British citizens who responded to the suffering of the Irish, and by the Catholic Church. Pope Pius IX issued an encyclical asking international Catholics to pray for the Irish. Irish immigrants in America contributed funds for the suffering Irish population as well.

The 1847 food harvest was free of blight but limited, and it marked the final collapse of the potato economy. The British government announced that the famine was over, despite continuing high levels of malnutrition and disease among impoverished Irish peasants and laborers. Relief was reorganized based on the model of the British workhouse system, based on the poor laws, and each jurisdiction in Ireland was responsible for poverty in its area. The landlords and other members of the propertied class gained the motive to keep aid as limited as possible. The destitute Irish were subjected to additional stigmatization, as they went from being public works employees to soup kitchen visitors and then were designated as "paupers." Closure of the soup kitchens and reduction in private aid forced individuals with no other option to enter the workhouses. The infirm, aged, and thousands of orphaned children had to accept the dress code, work, status of pauper, and forced familial separation practiced in workhouses. Many resisted the workhouse program, in which the impoverished inmates were forced to labor for their handouts, until no other option remained.

OUTDOOR RELIEF

In 1847, to adapt to conditions in Ireland, the British poor laws were amended to provide for "outdoor relief," assistance for individuals not residing in workhouses. Outdoor relief was limited to a ration of cooked food, which was not always sufficient to meet the recipients' needs. Local Irish governments, however, were encouraged to rent additional workhouse accommodations in order to make absolute destitution the criteria for relief. To further deter relief applications, all "paupers" able to work were required to break stones for up to ten hours a day. By mid-1848, over eight hundred thousand were receiving daily outdoor relief, and more than 1 million depended on measures specified by the poor laws for survival.

In 1848, the requirement that Irish jurisdictions finance their own impoverished populations was problematic for two reasons: the extent of the famine was greater than Irish taxation could meet, either because the upper classes paid insufficient tax or regular taxpayers could not pay; and localization of tax funding placed the most impoverished districts at a disadvantage. The situation was a precursor of the institutional discrimination that occurs due to inequality of resources between districts today. The initial government response was to increase pressure to collect revenues.

The amended poor laws contained the "Gregory Clause," also referred to as the Quarter Acre Clause, which stipulated that no individual who resided on more than one-quarter acre could receive relief. Many small tenant farmers faced a choice of starvation or losing their land. Some landlords took advantage of this situation to evict tenants, occasionally through mass removals. Other landlords softened the blow by assisting emigration. From 1849 to 1854, a quarter of a million were officially removed. This is an underestimate, as it does not include both voluntary and illegal removal. After 1847, homelessness emerged as a major cause of mortality.

1848–1849: ENCUMBERED ESTATES ACTS AND RATE-IN-AID ACT

Landlords were faced with increased taxes and declining rents and were especially hard-pressed if they were already indebted. British government officials in favor of agricultural modernization viewed this as a golden opportunity to rid Ireland of absentee and/or undercapitalized landlords. To further this objective, the 1848 and 1849 Encumbered Estates Acts were passed. Landlords lost their farms if they could not meet taxation demands.

The potato blight reappeared in 1848 and one-half the crop was lost, but despite continued hunger, the British poor laws remained the only remedy. The workhouses themselves were overcrowded and were an independent cause of increased mortality.

In 1848, famine conditions inspired the failed "Young Ireland" rebellion against Great Britain. This uprising, although it was opposed by the Catholic clergy and most Catholic politicians, became a symbol for Irish nationalism. Resentment against the British increased in Ireland and among Irish immigrants in the United States.

The British were committed to having the Irish address Irish poverty, and responded with the 1849 Rate-in-Aid Act, which sought to redistribute funds from more-prosperous jurisdictions to less-prosperous ones. (This effort is similar to a contemporary method used to deal with institutional discrimination through redistribution of property taxes.) This legislation served to encourage emigration for the purpose of tax relief and further galvanized the Catholic clergy and the Irish middle class in a nationalistic response. The famine and related emigration became politicized, and famine immigrants in America began to perceive their decision to migrate as a forced choice motivated by political tyranny.

In 1850–51, the potato blight was localized, but the reorganization of Irish agricultural tenancy and emigration had been established as permanent patterns. At this point, the Irish lower class had been dramatically reduced, and continued emigration began to threaten Irish Catholic farmers, clerics, and shopkeepers with a loss of the population base needed to perpetuate their society. As a result, the social structure of Ireland was permanently transformed. The rural Irish community never fully recovered, and the youngest, healthiest, and most enterprising continued to leave, causing a major drain of human capital.

POSTFAMINE IRELAND

After the famine, the Irish continued to emigrate; those who remained in the country tended to postpone marriage, causing the birthrate to stagnate. Social distress in the Irish population was great. Destitute Irish did not immediately emigrate, however, as they lacked the means to pay for passage. Relatives and friends in an emerging migrant network provided funds, sending an estimated $260 million to Ireland. These remittances provided the means for over three-quarters of Irish immigration to the United States in the period 1848–1900. Estimates of the number of emigrants between 1851 and 1871 range from 2.1 million to 2.6 million. Between 1871 and 1921 an additional 2.5 million are estimated to have left Ireland. The exact rate of departure for the United States varied according to the viability of the American economy, which was subject to periodic recession.

SOCIAL DEMOGRAPHY OF IRISH IMMIGRATION

After the Great Famine, emigration was more likely to originate from rural counties with many small holdings of little value. Emigrants to the United States were especially likely to be from rural, impoverished areas. Irish immigration was unusual in that the sex ratio among immigrants was balanced. During the Great Famine, social constraints against emigration of women were relaxed. Positive experiences and the development of an American migrant network led to continuation of Irish women's emigration.

Catholic Irish women who were motivated by a need to escape low status were a major segment of the emigrant stream to the United States. In nineteenth-century Ireland, the favoring of sons over daughters created a system of extreme gender inequality characteristic of intensive agricultural societies. Daughters were subject to a life of childbearing and gender-segregated drudgery. Men and older boys ate before women, receiving better nutrition. Women's work was considered unimportant, and women were expected to work in the fields, cutting turf, harvesting hay, and planting, cultivating and harvesting potatoes, as well as doing the household chores.

Gender inequality in nineteenth-century Ireland was sufficiently extreme to result in higher female mortality. The intersection of gender inequality and inequality based on religion motivated many Irish women to emigrate to American cities, where social opportunity structures favored them more than in the rural areas of Ireland. A preference for urban residence among Irish women contributed to concentration of the Irish population in American cities, where Irish women immigrants found ready employment as domestic servants.

Catholics predominated among post-famine Irish immigrants, although a substantial component of the migration stream was Protestant. Prior to the famine, the Irish did not tend to emigrate as family units because of lack of means. During the Great Famine, however, many tenant farmers sold off their assets to enable emigration as a family group. After the famine, family and children's migration was once again greatly reduced. Immigration was especially frequent among 20–24-year-olds. Between 1820 and 1840, unskilled working-class Irish greatly outnumbered farmers among immigrants. After 1850, many of these unskilled workers were joined by servants.

Irish immigrants, who were part of a network in which the loyalty of relatives and friends was important, had an immediate need for a cash income to pay for the passage of additional immigrants. As a result, they were attracted to urban jobs rather than rural homesteading, which necessitated capital investment. Seeking work in urban areas was facilitated by the fact that almost all later Irish immigrants could speak English (although with an accent), which gave them an advantage. Rates of literacy in Ireland, however, were low, and emigrants were likely to be illiterate. It was not until the end of the nineteenth century that Ireland had almost universal literacy.

URBAN SETTLEMENT

Irish immigrants to the United States often settled in northeastern cities and were more likely to be laborers than those Irish emigrating to Britain and Australia. The social stratification system in rural Ireland had been a major motivator for leaving. Irish tenant farmers received a low rate of return for their labor because of the system of land tenure, in which only 12 percent owned their farms, and periodic crop failures. Their overwhelming preference for urban destinations and occupations upon arriving in the United States was due to differences in farming methods in the two nations. Irish farmers had small plots and used manual tools: spade, pitchfork, scythe, and wooden rake. American farms were extensive, often over a hundred acres, in contrast to the Irish average of fifteen acres. Horses and associated equipment, which required extensive capital investment, were necessary. Irish immigrants were not interested in large tracts of uncleared land and were not knowledgeable about farming methods requiring horses.

By 1850, the majority of Irish immigrants were settled in just three industrializing states: New York, Pennsylvania, and Massachusetts. In 1890, one-half of the Irish were still settled in these states, but additional dispersion had occurred to New Jersey, Illinois, Connecticut, and California. The urban preference of the Irish explains this pattern of population concentration, which is similar to the urban spatial concentration of post-1965 immigrants to the United States.

Irish immigrants primarily settled in northern and midwestern cities, including New York City, Jersey City, Boston, Philadelphia, and Chicago. They also settled in San Francisco. The high level of population concentration, which peaked at one Irish resident out of every five individuals in New York City and Boston, increased the ethnic visibility of the Irish and fostered nativistic reactions.

CATHOLIC INSTITUTIONS AND NATIVISM

After 1840, Irish Catholic immigrants resisted pressure to assimilate to Protestant denominations. Their loyalty to the Catholic Church was in part due to resentment of English oppression in Ireland. One impact of the Irish development of the Catholic Church as a significant non-Protestant institution in America has been to reinforce the constitutional separation of church and state and the right to religious freedom.

Irish Catholics were subject to extreme prejudice and acts of violence in establishing their churches. The hierarchical structure of the Catholic Church prompted fears that the Irish immigrants were politically controlled by the Pope. The practice of celibacy by Catholic priests and nuns led to lurid speculation about sexual relations between priests and nuns, abuse of female students by confessors, and infanticide practiced upon illegitimate offspring.

Mob attacks occurred, such as the one on August 11, 1834, when the Ursuline convent community in Charlestown, Massachusetts, was ransacked and burned after the adults and children had been driven out. Beginning in the 1820s, verbal altercations and physical assault often resulted from American Protestant and Irish Catholic encounters. In 1844, two armed riots in Philadelphia, prompted by a public school authority decision to allow use of the Catholic Bible in the schools, resulted in sixteen deaths, many injuries, and the burning of more than thirty homes and two churches. As of 1850, Protestants had demonstrated or rioted in most major American cities. The nativistic Know-Nothings, a Protestant group, played a major role in these violent conflicts.

Protestant Irish tended to enter the American public school system, but between 1820 and 1840, numerous Catholic parochial schools were built. Although some Irish Catholic children entered public schools, Anglo-Protestant pressure led to separate church-associated schools as a means of maintaining Irish Catholic identity in the face of pressure to assimilate.

A parish with a parochial school system, a hospital, and charitable organizations was the focus of Irish Catholic immigrant life.

RACIALIZATION AND ANTI-IRISH DISCRIMINATION

Nativists targeted the Irish because of their social visibility as immigrants and their status as Roman Catholics. The late-nineteenth-century stereotype of the Irish "Paddy" was the basis of populist humor, depicted as an anti-British, drunken, childlike, indolent spendthrift controlled by priests. Alternatively, Irish women were stereotyped as the "Queen of the Kitchen," hardworking but unpredictable servants who would later squander their wages on innumerable children, drunken husbands, and lazy relatives. From the 1820s on, the Paddy stereotype ascribed character traits such as wickedness, lack of intelligence, and shiftlessness. As intergroup conflict developed, however, the stereotype began to emphasize conflict and hostility, adding words such as *quarrelsome* and *reckless* to describe the Irish.

Caricatures of the Irish drew them as protosimians. The ape image had originated in England and represented the Irish as the "missing link" between gorillas and humans. The British preferred to see themselves as extremely physically differentiated from the Irish and black Africans. Animal stereotypes, which deprived individuals of their humanity, were a means of rationalizing the low wages, unsafe work environment, and inhumane living conditions of poor immigrants. The parallel usage of these stereotypes for both Irish and African Americans was to heighten conflict between the two groups. Stereotyping and caricaturization of the Irish led to the social construction of the "Irish race" as inferior.

In the nineteenth century, racialization, the identification of the Irish as a group believed to be biologically distinct from other Europeans, contributed to the development of prejudice and discrimination. The "Irish race" was believed to be biologically inferior to the "Anglo-Saxon race" and suitable only for unskilled employment. Noel Ignatiev points out that the Irish were described as an intermediate category socially positioned between "black" and "white." This created a social obstacle for Irish advancement as nonwhite was a caste status with limited opportunity.

In 1790, the U.S. Congress had decreed that only white individuals were eligible for naturalization. In 1798, the Congress passed the Alien and Sedition Act, which restricted the naturalization and voting rights of immigrants. Irish immigrants were not accepted as white, but later generations wanted to become politically active. Their desire for political representation was shaped by the politics of slavery and the African-American presence in the cities and led to a rupture in relations between the Irish and African Americans. The Irish had often mixed with African Americans at work and in neighborhoods, and a small mulatto population developed. Both the Irish and the general population came to regard this development with disapproval, and the native-born often characterized the Irish as like Negroes through the use of such terms as "White Negroes" and "Smoked Irish," which led to interracial hostility between Irish and African Americans. Because the designation of whiteness carried social privilege, the Irish gradually opted to pursue a political strategy of racialization as white, separating themselves from African Americans and abandoning the cause of the abolition of slavery.

ECONOMY AND ANTI-IRISH DISCRIMINATION

Irish workers were a major labor source for the economic development of the northeastern United States. After 1830, Irish men were often employed as miners, railroad laborers, textile workers, and other unskilled labor in the factories and on the wharves. The many single Irish women often worked in domestic service.

In an atmosphere of racialized intergroup tension and conflict between American Protestants and Irish Catholics, extensive discrimination was openly practiced. Advertisements for jobs frequently included a notice stating "No Irish need apply." In-group collusion among American Protestants created a barrier for those with Gaelic names and accents, regardless of personality traits and employment qualifications. Often, potential employers asserted that intergroup tension prohibited Protestants or Irish Catholics from working with the native-born.

IRISH LABOR CONFLICT

Irish immigrants did not respond to harsh treatment with passive resignation. In the 1830s, Irish laborers began to organize and strike for higher wages. Initially, the Irish worked alongside African Americans, but by the 1840s, competition for work had caused

intergroup hostility. From 1840 until the Civil War, attacks by Irish against African-American workers in northern cities occurred. During the Civil War, the intense competition for low-wage laboring positions and fear that freed African-American slaves would increase competition intensified hostility. The use of African Americans as strikebreakers added to the tension.

In mining, Irish workers were pitted against English Protestant mine owners and higher-paid English-origin workers. One racialized practice involved creation of a contract-slavery status whereby wages were used to pay for necessities and rent, referred to as a "bobtail check." During the Civil War, Irish miners in Pennsylvania were opposed to the military draft and maintaining the Union, which they saw as a cause of the wealthy. As noted above, another reason was a fear that freed African-American slaves would compete for their jobs.

Because Irish immigrants were viewed as non-whites in a society where social categorization as members of racial groups was important in determining social status, they sought to socially distance themselves from blacks. From 1830 to 1890, the Anglo-American elite began to respond to immigrant labor's concerns by stressing white racial unity and superiority. To gain acceptance as white, the Irish participated in the racialization of blacks, stereotyping them as wild apes or savages. Irish immigrants socially constructed their whiteness in a racist relation to African Americans, whom they discriminated against. Responding to the persuasion of the Anglo-American press and both Anglo-Protestant and Roman Catholic religious leaders, the Irish adopted techniques of racialization to raise their own social status.

AID FOR IRISH IMMIGRANT POOR

Discrimination was rationalized through racist rhetoric characterizing the Irish as an unintelligent people suited for menial work. Commentators of the time blamed Irish immigrants for urban poverty. The cost of public aid and medical assistance was decried. Some Irish did receive charity, but very little was expended on social programs for the poor of any nationality. In 1818, the racialized climate of discrimination in the United States prompted Irish separatists to petition Congress for financial assistance and an area in which to settle Irish charity cases. Congress did not accept this request on the grounds that groups of many nationalities might make such requests and fragment the nation. The immigration historian Marcus Hansen considers this an auspicious decision in the history of American policy because it precluded state support for ethnic communities. Instead, the formation of ethnic settlements has remained a voluntary process without state assistance. The Catholic Church and charitable community organizations were instrumental in assisting the impoverished. The Ancient Order of Hibernians is a well-known example of an Irish voluntary relief association.

IRISH POLITICS AND SLAVERY

In the mid-nineteenth century, the abolition of slavery was a critical issue in the United States. In Ireland, Daniel O'Connell and sixty thousand Irish signed a petition requesting that the Irish abroad support abolition. Pro-abolitionism was viewed as a way of acknowledging the equality of African Americans, an important parallel to realizing Irish freedom. Irish immigrants, however, while expressing sympathy toward the abolition of slavery, refused to recognize blacks as their equal due to job competition and the desire to attain "whiteness" to avoid discrimination.

The crisis over slavery was reaching a height as the Irish presence increased in the United States. In the 1840s, presidential and other national candidates solicited Irish votes. The Democratic Party advocated an ideology of white supremacy and had a base of support among both northern workers and southern planters. Noel Ignatiev considers that support of assimilation of the Irish into the white race was a key source of Irish Democratic votes. The Democratic Party rejected anti-Irish nativism and strengthened the use of the color line as a mechanism for maintaining slavery. The Irish gradually became advocates of slavery and the color line, advertising their "whiteness." Indeed, African-American labor was viewed as a competitive threat.

Many artisans had resented Irish immigration and resented their willingness to accept low wages, but tensions were displaced toward African Americans. The rejection of nativism by the Democratic Party was coupled with the social construction of a division between whites, inclusive of the Irish, and blacks. As a result, the Democratic Party is said to have created the white vote. Movements that expanded the white franchise often simultaneously created restrictions upon African Americans, such as the property-holding requirement for blacks established at the New York constitutional convention in 1821. Indeed, the Irish remained loyal to the Democratic Party even to the point of not supporting the Civil War. In 1863, the

New York City Draft Riot (also known as the Irish Riot) was an expression of discontent with the federal government. The Draft Riot was the most serious American street conflict of the nineteenth century, and free blacks, a few white police officers and soldiers, and an estimated four hundred whites were killed.

Throughout the nineteenth century, the Irish in America pursued separation from blacks. Irish Catholic priests and scholars rejected notions of Anglo-Saxon racial superiority in which the Irish were represented as an inferior race. Instead, in collusion with other white immigrant groups, they advocated that western Europeans constituted a superior white race. Because the Irish had developed a substantial political base in the nation's cities, Anglo-Americans gradually accepted the idea that European immigrants, particularly the Irish, were "white."

IRISH SOCIAL MOBILITY

After the Civil War, Irish Catholics achieved a measure of social mobility. In Philadelphia, which had emerged as a major industrial and transportation hub, the Irish began to obtain semiskilled and skilled work. Although many remained in Irish neighborhoods with run-down housing, some began to move to middle-class areas. As the nineteenth century ended, the emergence of many of the urban centers where the Irish had settled as major manufacturing centers facilitated Irish advancement. The movement of Irish into public jobs, facilitated by the political machines, was accompanied by the emergence of Irish entrepreneurs. In Philadelphia, Irish contractors and builders outnumbered those of other immigrant ethnicity by two to one. By the 1900s, the Irish were heavily involved in unions for longshoremen, construction workers, and miners.

By the 1870s, Irish Americans were more socially accepted than the famine immigrants had been nearly three decades earlier, and spoke and behaved according to the norms of the time. In the mid-nineteenth century, Irish Protestants and some Irish Catholics were business owners and professionals. A few Irish had attained sufficient wealth to attain elite status. By the turn of the century, however, many Irish remained poor and subject to discrimination.

THE IRISH AND AMERICAN POLITICS

The Irish response to blatant hostility was to develop cohesiveness as an ethnic community and to enter urban politics. The nineteenth-century Irish are often stereotyped as the developers of the "political machine," an ethnicized voting mechanism in which corruption guaranteed turn-out and election results. City political systems, however, lacked a secret ballot, and Anglo-Protestant politicians had set a corrupt precedent. Irish politicians merely followed a tradition of providing food, housing, loans, and jobs for their constituents. The Irish, like other immigrant groups, used local political office as a means of attaining group social mobility. The Anglo-Protestant establishment did not favor economic assistance, and immigrants turned to local politicians and organizations for assistance. Once in office, Irish politicians developed local programs for the poor. The political machine dispensed jobs in construction and other areas of city development.

New York City's Tammany Hall was originally an Anglo-Protestant political machine. In historical treatment of the time of Irish patronage, William M. "Boss" Tweed has achieved notoriety as an icon of greed and corruption. However, an examination of his life reveals that Tweed supported Irish and Jewish immigrants, working to help them out of poverty and building schools and hospitals. He rewarded his supporters with jobs and provision of social services. Although he was hated by the Anglo-Protestant leadership, Boss Tweed may not have been as politically corrupt as many other machine politicians of Anglo-Protestant and other ethnicities.

In 1880, William R. Grace, the first Catholic Irish-American mayor of New York, was elected, and after that point, the Irish won many posts and were substantially represented in appointed positions. Other urban areas with major Catholic populations, including Boston, Philadelphia, New Haven, and Chicago, were the sites of Irish political victories. Urban Irish Catholic immigrant political success was paralleled by the political achievements of Irish Protestants.

Because of the low social visibility of the Irish Protestants who immigrated to the United States in the later eighteenth century and early nineteenth century, recognition of the first Irish president has been limited. Andrew Jackson, president from 1829 to 1837, was the son of two Scotch-Irish immigrants; he was Presbyterian. Woodrow Wilson (1913–1921) was Scotch and Irish. By the twentieth century, the Irish background of politicians was not so important. When John F. Kennedy ran for president in 1960, it was his religion, more than his ethnicity, that mattered to voters. After Kennedy, a politician's Irish background mattered even less. Ronald Reagan is of Scotch Protestant and Irish Catholic descent, while Bill Clinton is of both English and Irish ancestry, but few people remarked on this. Intriguingly, none of these elected presidents took a strong stand on freeing southern or Northern Ireland, despite extensive and persisting nationalism among Irish Americans. Clinton, however, worked hard to forge a peace settlement among Protestants and Catholics in Northern Ireland.

IRISH NATIONALISM

The harsh measures taken during the Great Famine galvanized the Irish diaspora, which repeatedly took measures to remove British landlords and free Ireland. The Fenian movement of 1858–67 was a product of the immigrant Irish in New York City. Motivated by revenge, Irish exiles, especially ex–Civil War soldiers, aspired to return and reestablish their families on Irish soil.

Skibbereen, an impoverished community that had received a great deal of nineteenth-century newspaper attention, was an especial focus of Irish desire for revenge. In 1847–48, Catholic clerics and nationalists began to attack Great Britain's rule and derided the famine immigrants as exiles. In the 1850s, the famine was being represented as a plot to exterminate or exile the Irish peasantry. Many nationalists advocated both a political revolution against British rule and a social revolution to remove the Protestant landlords.

In the United States, the desire to free Ireland began to be viewed as a way to fight anti-Irish nativism. By restoring Ireland to freedom and prosperity, Ireland's famine exiles hoped to achieve positive recognition. In this manner, Irish-American nationalism promoted the notion of emigration as a form of exile due to British oppression. The Fenian movement was a product of the Great Famine and related immigration. The impoverished, socially isolated Irish immigrants involved as Fenians lived in American urban centers as a socially alienated group dissimilar from later, relatively assimilated Irish Americans. Nevertheless, the Fenian movement established a precedent for Irish-American support of Irish nationalism through fund-raising and influence on politics in Ireland.

Famine memories have informed the Irish diaspora in America and many Irish-Americans, brought up on stories of trauma and dislocation, viewed themselves as involuntary exiles. In the nineteenth century, a post-famine culture of despair expressive of sorrow at leaving Ireland and anger toward Great Britain was well-rooted. The sorrow of the Irish diaspora fuels the problems in restoring social harmony in Northern Ireland in the twenty-first century.

Judith Warner

See also: Nativism and Know-Nothings (Part I, Sec. 2); Ireland (Part III, Sec. 4); Stimulating Emigration from Ireland, 1837, Four Years of Irish History, 1845–1849, Emigration, Emigrants, and Know-Nothings, 1854, Irish Response to Nativism, 1854 (Part IV, Sec. 3).

BIBLIOGRAPHY

Bernstien, Iver. *The New York City Draft Riots: Their Significance for American Society and Politics in the Age of the Civil War.* New York: Oxford University Press, 1990.

Diner, Hasia. *Erin's Daughters in America.* Baltimore: Johns Hopkins University Press, 1983.

Dolan, Jay P. *The Immigrant Church: New York's Irish and German Catholics, 1815–1865.* Baltimore: Johns Hopkins University Press, 1975.

Handlin, Oscar. *Boston's Immigrants: A Study in Acculturation.* Cambridge, MA: Harvard University Press, 1959.

Hansen, Marcus Lee. *The Immigrant in American History.* Cambridge, MA: Harvard University Press, 1940.

Ignatiev, Noel. *How the Irish Became White.* New York: Routledge, 1996.

Knobel, Dale. *Paddy and the Republic: Ethnicity and Nationality in Antebellum America.* Middletown, CT: Wesleyan University Press, 1986.

Wittke, Carl. *The Irish in America.* Baton Rouge: Louisiana State University Press, 1956.

GERMANS AND OTHER POLITICAL REFUGEES

According to the 1990 census, almost 58 million Americans claim some degree of German origin or ancestry, making German Americans 23.3 percent of the total population. This is a great increase over 1800, when they made up less than one-tenth of the population. The present population owes its origin in great part to the influx of immigrants in quest of Germania-in-America during the nineteenth century. In contrast to pre-1800 immigrants, who by and large came to America to avoid religious oppression, the nineteenth-century Germans arrived in search of personal freedom and economic opportunity. Political upheaval, principally the failed democratic revolution of 1848, impelled scores of disillusioned activists and patriots to leave Germany. Early-nineteenth-century Germany was no country in the modern sense of the term, but a hodgepodge of kingdoms, duchies, principalities, and free cities melded together by fiat at the Congress of Vienna in 1814–15. Until 1871 and unification under the aegis of Prussia, Germany was a collection of often antagonistic territories linked by little more than language and cultural traditions.

EVENTS LEADING UP TO THE 1848 REVOLUTIONS

The defeat of Napoleon in 1815 raised hopes in the German cultural area for constitutional reform and political unity. Both were dashed, however. The emerging political entity was the German confederation, which lasted until 1866. Prince Metternich, the Austrian chancellor who helped reorganize Europe after the Napoleonic era, had intended the confederation to maintain the status quo, and thus to oppose nationalist, liberal, and republican movements wherever these might arise. He had the cooperation of self-interested rulers, for example, the German-speaking states in Saxony and Bavaria, who made a mockery of the federal parliament (Bundestag) at Frankfurt am Main. Nobles everywhere in Germany were reluctant to cede influence to any central political organ that might create a union from the disparate states. Thus, the Bundestag had very limited powers and was unable even to pass laws binding on citizens. In fact, it was not even a legislative assembly. It soon became evident to citizens of every political stripe that the German Confederation was an imposed alliance of states in the interest of political conservatism and uninterrupted dynastic rule. Regionalism, particularism, and parochialism in the German states therefore proceeded unhindered, frustrating a national union of Germany.

Frustrated, too, were German patriots, especially liberals, who had hoped for unity, and uniformity, of laws and customs. Since each state retained full sovereignty over internal affairs, justice was arbitrary and regional. Each state wrote its own legal code, levied its own taxes, and raised its own armies. Not only was there no supreme court in Germany, but there were no universal rights. No right of assembly or free speech protected individuals who protested against the regime. In this climate of political suppression, in which every impulse toward liberty was thwarted, it is not surprising that the 1830 revolution in Paris was a sensation. The revolution and reign of the "Citizen King" Louis-Philippe, the so-called July Monarchy (1830–48), inspired and frustrated Germans, who had hoped to follow the model of France. Especially auspicious to those outside France was the victory of the middle class over the aristocracy. Domestic conflicts throughout Europe between dynastic-conservative and nationalist-liberal movements sharpened from the 1830s onward, culminating in 1848, the year of revolution. Everywhere, it appeared—Poland, Greece, Belgium, Norway, Croatia, Italy, Hungary, the Balkans—citizens ever more stridently demanded constitutional reform and national unity.

Repeatedly, anticipation of reform in the German

CHARGE OF TROOPS, AT BERLIN.

This woodcut depicts German revolutionaries fending off a charge of Prussian troops in Berlin in 1848. When the uprisings that unsettled much of Europe in the mid-nineteenth century failed, many of the revolutionaries left for the United States. *(Library of Congress)*

states resulted in frustration. For example, the euphoria that greeted the accession of King Frederick William IV of Prussia in 1840 soon turned to disappointment when the hoped-for constitutional reformer and national unifier revealed himself to be but another believer in the divine right of kings. The representative assembly (Prussian United Diet) that Frederick William IV permitted in 1847 was so powerless as to be ineffective. It was soon dismissed. However, by 1848, following the murder of protesters in Berlin, Frederick William felt under sufficient pressure to humble himself by apologizing to the city and by wearing the colors of the insurgents (black, red, and gold). Demonstrations in Prussia were by no means isolated; throughout Germany and Austria there were cries for constituent assemblies and human rights. Reformers spoke of elections, constitutional states and, indeed, of the Republic of Germany.

Again the spark for reform came from outside Germany, and again France was the model for reform, if

not revolution. The February Revolution in 1848, introducing the Second Republic, established that new rulers from the middle class could effect change in a range of difficult problems, including unemployment, educational reform, and universal suffrage. Some conceived of a social, and socialist, utopia, promoting the brotherhood of man and emancipation of all the oppressed. Events in Paris inspired nascent republican reforms across the entire German cultural area: first Munich (Bavaria), then Baden, next Vienna and Berlin. Schleswig-Holstein protested against Danish political influence; meetings were held in Heidelberg and Constance; in Budapest Louis Kossuth proclaimed the freedom of Hungary from Habsburg rule. From north to south, from east to west, there were gatherings, demonstrations, and protest. Historians allude to general unrest and to the holiness of the concept of the constitution.

German efforts to achieve a new society were by no means monolithic. There existed a range of forces in the period 1830 to 1848, embracing the political spectrum from reform monarchists to Junge Deutschland (Young Germany) and Linkshegelianer (Left-wing Hegelians). All factions promoted patriotism and argued for a loosening of restrictions against student societies and political censorship. Out of a radical plan for societal change arose the Communist Manifesto of the Germans Karl Marx and Friedrich Engels, which appeared in early 1848. In that year Marx, an émigré, returned to Germany and to the profession of journalism, but was expelled in the 1849 counterrevolution.

1848 REVOLUTIONS

Spring 1848 was the high point of reform, and hope, when in Frankfurt am Main reformers met in parliament and called for elections throughout Germany, for universal male suffrage, and for a parliament to represent all Germans. Although all shades of political opinion were represented, the assembled leaders were mostly from the upper middle class. University professors were among the leaders. The group created a full, written statement of the rights of German citizens, which, in conjunction with a new constitution, served as the basis for a proposed federal state. Whereas legislative power was to rest in a bicameral congress, a hereditary emperor, with limited veto power, was to rule. But the person chosen to be the first emperor, Frederick William IV of Prussia, rebuffed the offer. His refusal to accept the title *kaiser der Deutschen* (emperor of the Germans) in 1849, with the justification that a ruler could receive the crown only from God and not from the people, dealt a blow from which the parliamentarians did not recover. The Prussian ruler's refusal to accept the crown highlighted the weaknesses of the Frankfurt reform movement, not least of which were military forces to enforce any proposed legislation from the assembly.

The final revolts in support of the Frankfurt constitution, in Baden and Saxony, were put down in 1849 by Prussian troops. Clearly, the 1848 revolution was now over in the German states. The reform movement, with its three streams of liberalism, republicanism, and nationalism, had been unable to effect lasting change at the national level. Among the opponents of a united Germany were rulers unwilling to sacrifice local dominion. In 1849 a German counterrevolution followed quickly on the heels of the revolution, dashing the hopes aroused by the Frankfurt national assembly for basic human rights throughout Germany.

With the exception of the aristocracy in Germany,

dissatisfaction swept all social strata. City artisans and apprentices, peasants, the intelligentsia, the professions—all had grievances with their querulous, fractured homeland. And all of the disaffected, agitators and silent sufferers alike, wanted remedy. One of these was emigration. America was for most a place synonymous with freedom; they called the country the "Land of Freedom" (*das Land der Freiheit*). America represented what millions of Germans sought: a stable, united nation with representative democracy, a written constitution, and a president—not an aristocracy that promoted feudalism. The extreme solution to political and social turmoil in the homeland was the "wandering out" that the German word for "emigration" and "migration" implies: *Auswanderung.* The failure of liberal revolution in Europe was thus the chief impetus to the migratory impulse across the continent after 1849. Scholars speak of America as a kind of safety valve. Comparing the numbers of immigrants in the decades 1821–30, 1831–40, and 1841–50, when expectations of political reform ran high, with the decades 1851–60 and after, the loss of hope correlates significantly with immigration. What they did dream of was a vague concept of a Germania in America.

GERMAN MIGRATION TO THE UNITED STATES

Statistically, massive immigration of Germans to America began after 1815 and the Congress of Vienna, reaching a peak in the 1850s. Each revolution in Europe produced its own German Americans, be these the refugees of the 1830s (the so-called Dreißiger) or the 1840s (the Forty-Eighters). Throughout the nineteenth century Germans made up the largest single ethnic group to enter the United States. But around 1900, in response to the new United Empire, German immigration slowed. In all, over 8 million Germans have come to America over three centuries. German immigrants were at Jamestown, and in 1683 families from Krefeld established an all-German community in Germantown, Pennsylvania. During the Revolutionary War, General Friedrich Wilhelm von Steuben was recruited to aid the Americans, while the English conscripted German soldiers, known popularly as the Hessians. A large number of those in the Hessian regiments decided to remain in America after the war to become citizens and to farm the soil. When the first U.S. Census was taken in 1790, Germans made up about one-third of the residents of Pennsylvania, with smaller but significant population concentrations in Maryland, New Jersey, and New York. Settlement patterns of German-born immigrants in the nineteenth century show a band from the upper Northeast to the Dakotas, Nebraska, and Kansas. (The middle Northwest in 1990 still had a population that was almost 10 percent German-American.)

Researchers use aquatic metaphors to characterize the emigration of German and other nineteenth-century political refugees: The émigrés were part of a flood, a wave, a tide, a deluge; they poured and flowed into the United States. The extent of immigration to America in the century was, most claim, unprecedented. In fact, the influx of immigrants between 1840 and 1860 was the largest in the history of America. Between 1840 and 1890, 4 million Germans came to the United States. Although social unrest and discontent with political systems during the liberal-national revolutions account for much German immigration, economic concerns also played a role. German-American immigration thus cannot be reduced to a single equation. During the European economic revolution of 1830–48, some émigrés who wanted to better their social and economic situation left Germany willingly. Others, particularly in domestic manufacture or the so-called cottage industries (weaving, for example), were forced out, abandoning Germany in the face of mechanized competition. Handicraftsmen, therefore, stood alongside farmers on the ships to America. Famine was also a cause for emigration, for example, in the German southwest in 1817 (Württemberg, Baden); crop failures in 1846 and 1847, the resultant agricultural crisis, and widespread famine in Germany motivated many to abandon the country. Additional factors in immigration were a labor surplus in Germany and great demographic growth in the first half of the nineteenth century, expanding the rural population by millions.

Most German-Americans before 1830 were Protestant and of southwestern origin. This changed by midcentury, when a broad spectrum of Germans, as measured by religious faith and geography, made the trip to America. (Among these were the so-called Germans of the Hebrew faith, many of whom knew German far better than Yiddish.) So singular was the German exodus to the United States that Germans made up almost half the number of arrivals in the decade 1851–60. In America they joined fellow failed revolutionaries from Italy, Ireland, Poland, and Austria-Hungary. The largest groups came after the collapse of the revolutions of the 1840s all over Europe, be they adherents of the Burschenschaften (the associations of German university students) or the Young Ireland movement. The Forty-Eighters was the name borne by the German-Americans fleeing the Continent. Deeply committed to democracy, a significant number were intellectuals who remained politically active. The historian and journalist Friedrich Kapp, attempting in 1856 to explain German immigration for the newspaper *New York Daily Times*, said: "We are all either social or political refugees. . . . Dissatisfaction with the political or social relations of Europe led us hither."

The fault line in German immigration to the United States is 1848–49. Before that date, German immigrants, who were mainly farmers, laborers, and artisans, had clustered on the East Coast, for example, Maryland and Pennsylvania. Most were Democrats, in part because Jacksonian democracy promoted Irish and German immigration. The Forty-Eighters, on the other hand, tended to be intellectuals and political activists; they supported Abraham Lincoln and the Republican Party with its antislavery stance. One who may be included in their number, although he arrived as a boy in New York City in 1846, was Thomas Nast, the renowned political cartoonist and caricaturist. So effective were his pro-Union drawings for *Harper's Weekly* and other publications that Lincoln called the artist the best recruiting sergeant in the republic.

The nineteenth-century German immigrants ventured westward into the upper Mississippi Valley, establishing important settlements in Chicago, St. Louis, Milwaukee, and Cincinnati. The Midwest, from Ohio to North Dakota, remains the home of preference for German Americans. Wisconsin, with over 50 percent, is the state with the largest population of Americans of German descent; Missouri also has significant numbers. Agriculture was by no means the chief profession of German Americans. By 1870, for example, only about one-fourth were so engaged; the others took urban professions, for instance, baker, tailor, carpenter, brewer, blacksmith, butcher, shoemaker, optician, and furniture maker, as well as jobs in manufacturing. Proportionally few German Americans were unskilled laborers. German immigrant craftsmen and tradesmen were instrumental in organizing labor organizations in the United States.

GERMAN CULTURAL AND POLITICAL ACTIVITY IN AMERICA

German Americans assimilated at a record pace, thus sparing themselves animosity and hardship in establishing communities. Although there were clusters of German population, supported by German-language newspapers and church services in the mother tongue, nineteenth-century immigrants from Germany were arguably the group most committed to the ideal of the melting pot. They actively promoted cultural pluralism in the United States, perhaps as a reaction to their experience in Germany with widely divergent political entities and markedly different spoken dialects. German Americans held, to be sure, a positive attitude toward their heritage, preserving cultural events (Oktoberfest) and gymnastics clubs (Turnverein) and transplanting a strong devotion to education (for instance, the kindergarten), as well as to the dramatic, pictorial, and plastic arts (Chicago alone had several German theaters in the nineteenth century). The singing society was a prominent custom imported from home, and some argue that the transformation of America into a mecca for music in the nineteenth century is the achievement of German Americans, who promoted music festivals, opera, and symphony orchestras. Having left a Germany that in literature (Goethe, Johann von Schiller) and philosophy (Immanuel Kant, Georg Hegel) alone had attained world prominence, immigrants could scarcely ignore, or forget, a civilization of vast richness. But in spite of devotion to the culture of their homeland, German settlers adapted rapidly to American culture, particularly to the political culture. Within several decades German Americans were so well assimilated that one of their number, Herbert Hoover, became president.

Significant numbers of Germans who took asylum in nineteenth-century America pursued a liberal agenda in this country. Hungry for social reform, survivors of political upheavals on the continent were understandably sensitive to oppression and set about to oppose any tyranny in the United States. Tenacious defenders of freedom of the press, they opposed capital punishment, imperialism, and bigotry toward Jews. They raised their voices in support of suffrage, reform of the civil service system, and equality for African Americans. For German refugees themselves, the Civil War had an unexpected benefit: It contributed materially to the process of Americanization. Approximately 200,000 German Americans took the field for the North, constituting entire regiments. Although some fought for the Confederacy (the Prussian aristocrat Heros von Borcke is a prominent example), those coming to America were mostly opposed to slavery, reflective of a passion for democracy. Strong opposition to American slavery and support for Abraham Lincoln and the Union in the Civil War were the norm for German-American political exiles. Some attribute the failure of Missouri to join the Confederacy at the beginning of the Civil War to German Ameri-

cans living in the state. A Union regiment there, the Twelfth Missouri, was made up of German immigrants.

Military experience and skills were a perhaps unexpected dividend that the German Forty-Eighters could share with America. As an educated bourgeois elite, many had training in warfare. Prominent among the German-American Civil War officers were Franz Sigel and Alexander von Schimmelpfennig. The latter, a general active at the battle of Gettysburg, had first been a member of the Prussian army as an officer, but then in 1848 opposed the actions of his own army in the Palatinate. This political refugee commanded the Eleventh Corps of the Army of the Potomac, made up primarily of German Americans. But it was Carl Schurz, himself a refugee and a Union general in the American Civil War, who became synonymous with the term *Forty-Eighter.*

Schurz (d. 1906), erstwhile university student, political publicist, and revolutionary, was forced to leave Germany for participating in the political uprisings of 1848. In Baden, Schurz was one of the rebels fighting alongside Ludwik Mieroslawski, the Polish patriot, against the Prussian army. Schurz, after rescuing a prominent dissident professor from prison, fled to Switzerland, France, and England, and then to America in 1852—the same year in which Louis Kossuth visited the United States in support of Hungarian independence. In America, Schurz, who had started out as a Wisconsin farmer, soon became a political activist. He was an early supporter of Lincoln and gave speeches opposing the Fugitive Slave Law. At the outbreak of the conflict, Schurz became a prominent general in Lincoln's army and fought in many battles, including Chancellorsville. After the war Schurz was a journalist *(Harper's Weekly, New York Evening Post),* politician, and public servant, holding cabinet posts under Presidents Ulysses S. Grant and Rutherford B. Hayes. Schurz, an early champion of American diversity, vigorously espoused the rights of Native Americans, believing in the inalienability of basic freedoms for all those living in the United States.

If searching for a single family to represent the immigrant experience of German political refugees in the nineteenth century, one need look no further than that of Carl Schurz. His wife, Margarethe Meyer Schurz, contributed significantly to American educational reform. A pupil of the renowned pedagogue Friedrich Froebel, she founded the first kindergarten in the United States during the 1850s in Wisconsin. Under the Schurz roof are thus found, *in nuce,* the contributions of a vast movement of people, the German Americans. In agriculture, politics, journalism, the military, and education, German immigrants left their mark. And their passion for freedom and learning, combined with the activism of the social reformer, indelibly shaped American culture and civilization.

William C. McDonald

See also: Political, Ethnic, Religious, and Gender Persecution (Part II, Sec. 1); Western and Southern Europe (Part III, Sec. 4); "What Does America Offer to the German Immigrant?" 1853 (Part IV, Sec. 3).

BIBLIOGRAPHY

Bailyn, Bernard. *From Protestant Peasants to Jewish Intellectuals: The Germans in the Peopling of America.* Oxford, New York, and Hamburg: Berg, 1988.

Bittinger, Lucy F. *The Germans in Colonial Times.* 1901. Reprint, New York: Russell and Russell, 1968.

Dill, Marshall, Jr. *Germany: A Modern History.* Ann Arbor: University of Michigan Press, 1961.

Helbich, Wolfgang. *Amerika ist ein freies Land. Auswanderer schreiben nach Deutschland.* Darmstadt and Neuwied: Luchterhand, 1985.

Hess, Earl J., ed. *A German in the Yankee Fatherland: The Civil War Letters of Henry A. Kircher.* Kent, OH: Kent State University Press, 1983.

Hoerder, Dirk, and Jörg Nagler, eds. *People in Transit: German Migrations in Comparative Perspective, 1820–1930.* Cambridge: Cambridge University Press, 1995.

Kamphoefner, Walter D., et al., eds. *News from the Land of Freedom: German Immigrants Write Home.* Trans. S. C. Vogel. Ithaca and London: Cornell University Press, 1991.

Krewson, Margrit W. *German-American Relations: A Selective Bibliography.* Washington, DC: Library of Congress, 1995.

Levine, Bruce C. *The Migration of Ideology and the Contested Meaning of Freedom: German-Americans in the Mid-Nineteenth Century.* Washington, DC: German Historical Institute, 1992.

———. *The Spirit of 1848: German Immigrants, Labor Conflict, and the Coming of the Civil War.* Urbana and Chicago: University of Illinois Press, 1992.

Luebke, Frederick C. *Germans in the New World: Essays in the History of Immigration.* Urbana and Chicago: University of Illinois Press, 1990.

McCormick, E. Allen, ed. *Germans in America: Aspects of German-American Relations in the Nineteenth Century.* Brooklyn, NY: Brooklyn College Press, 1983.

Moltmann, Günter, ed. *Aufbruch nach Amerika. Die Auswanderungswelle von 1816/17.* Stuttgart: J. B. Metzler, 1989.

O'Connor, Richard. *The German-Americans: An Informal History.* Boston and Toronto: Little, Brown and Co., 1968.

Rippley, Lavern. *Of German Ways.* New York: Gramercy Publishing Co., 1986.

Rothan, Emmet H. "The German Catholic Immigrant in the United States (1830–1860)." Ph.D. diss., Catholic University of America, Washington, DC, 1946.

Shinagawa, Larry H., and Michel Lang. *Atlas of American Diversity.* Walnut Creek, London, and New Delhi: AltaMira Press, 1998.

Sowell, Thomas. *Ethnic America: A History.* New York: Basic Books, 1981.

Trommler, Frank, and Joseph McVeigh, eds. *America and the Germans: An Assessment of a Three-Hundred-Year History.* Philadelphia: University of Pennsylvania Press, 1985.

Walz, John Albrecht. *German Influence in American Education and Culture.* Philadelphia: Carl Schurz Memorial Foundation, 1936.

NATIVISM AND KNOW-NOTHINGS

Nativism is anti-immigrant sentiment. Since the time of its founding, the United States has had a seemingly paradoxical attitude when it comes to immigrants. On the one hand, America has portrayed itself as a sanctuary for the victims of poverty and oppression throughout the world. Since 1892, for example, new Americans entering the country through Ellis Island in New York have been greeted with the inscription on the foundation of the Statue of Liberty, which reads:

> Give me your tired, your poor,
> your huddled masses yearning to breathe free,
> The wretched refuse of your teeming shore.
> Send these, the homeless, tempest-tossed, to me:
> I lift my lamp beside the golden door.

In part, this reflects the fact that America is a country largely created by immigration, first from western Europe and Africa (whose people were forced here), and eventually from Eastern Europe, Latin America, and Asia.

At the same time, hostility to immigration has been a theme in American politics as long as there has been American politics. Political nativism has almost always attracted votes. In the more than two centuries since the Constitution was written, the nation's political parties have consistently engaged in a complicated dance with America's immigrants, rejecting or embracing them as circumstances dictated.

1800–1820: POLITICAL NATIVISM MAKES ITS BOW

When drafting the Constitution in 1787, the framers hoped that America could be a nation without political factions. However, the new government had hardly been founded before it became clear that this was not to be the case. By the time George Washington's second term was under way in the 1790s, a pair of rival political parties began to coalesce under the leadership of two of his cabinet secretaries. The Federalists were led by the secretary of the Treasury, Alexander Hamilton. They favored a strong centralized government, dedicated to supporting economic growth through the promotion of trade. The Democratic-Republicans were led by the secretary of state, Thomas Jefferson. They felt that the Federalist philosophy favored the country's economic and social elites, and they stressed the importance of equality and of creating opportunity for every American.

New immigrants tended to be poor, and so it is not surprising that the vast majority of them flocked to the Jeffersonian banner. The immigrant vote quickly became a source of strength for the Democratic-Republicans and a source of consternation for the Federalists. In 1798, looking toward the elections of 1800, the Federalists passed the Alien Acts, the first overtly anti-immigrant U.S. legislation. Three laws made up the Alien Acts. The Naturalization Act made citizenship requirements vastly more stringent, requiring fourteen years of residence in the United States before an immigrant could be granted citizenship. The Alien Act gave the president, John Adams, a Federalist, the authority to deport any foreigner he deemed to be "dangerous" to the nation's welfare. The Alien Enemies Act allowed for the capture and detention of "enemy" foreigners in times of war. Both the Alien Act and the Alien Enemies Act went to great pains to avoid defining "dangerous" and "enemy," respectively, so as to allow the laws to be applied as broadly as possible.

The Federalists hoped to achieve two complementary goals with the Alien Acts. They wanted to limit the vote of immigrants while at the same time attracting support from nativists who might otherwise be inclined to vote for the Democratic-Republicans. While they may have been partially successful, the

Federalists failed to achieve their larger objective—namely, retaining control of the presidency and the Congress. Jefferson and the Democratic-Republicans were swept into power, and the Alien Acts were left unenforced until they expired in 1801.

1820–1860: POLITICAL NATIVISM REACHES ITS HIGH TIDE

With the rise of Jefferson and his Democratic-Republican successors James Madison and James Monroe, the nation came as close as it ever would to achieving the founders' vision of a country without political factions. The Federalists declined, in part because of their own political blunders and in part because many of their policies were adopted by the Democratic-Republicans, so much so that they were accused of "out-Federalizing the Federalists" in some quarters. In the absence of serious partisan debate, nativism largely disappeared from American politics for several decades.

In the 1830s and 1840s, however, a pair of concurrent developments resurrected the issue and thrust it to the center of American politics. First, with the ascension of Andrew Jackson, parties became increasingly important in organizing voters. Following a controversial election in 1824, in which John Quincy Adams narrowly defeated Jackson, Jackson's followers had organized themselves as the Democratic Party. Soon thereafter, Jackson's enemies coalesced into the Whig Party. In 1828, Jackson was elected president. During this period, economic depression and famine in Europe led to an explosion in immigration. In the 1820s, a mere 8,400 immigrants came to America. Between 1830 and 1850, however, nearly 5 million immigrants, largely German and Irish Catholics, arrived in the United States

The United States had historically viewed itself as a Protestant nation, and so the nativism of this period focused on the Catholicism of the new immigrants. Insinuating that Catholics were superstitious, ignorant, and under the control of their priests and the Pope, Protestants argued that Catholics were not fit to be part of a republican government. There were numerous anti-Catholic magazines and newspapers, including *Protestant, The Anti-Romanist,* and *Priestcraft Exposed*. In 1836, a book entitled *Awful Disclosures of the Hotel Dieu Nunnery of Montreal* was published. Purportedly written by a young Protestant woman named Maria Monk, it ostensibly recounted the story of Monk's imprisonment and torture in a Catholic

monastery in Montreal. This anti-Catholic tract became a best-seller before it was proven to be a hoax.

On the national level, neither the Whigs nor the Democrats were especially vocal about immigrant-related issues, in part because both parties hoped to attract the support of immigrant voters, and in part because other issues, nost notably expansion, were dominating national politics. On the local and state levels, however, there was a great deal of squabbling between pro-immigrant and nativist forces, especially over the issue of education. Many Catholic immigrants came from a tradition where religion was heavily intertwined with normal classroom study. Protestants, by contrast, preferred to maintain a certain level of separation between education and religion. Catholics developed an educational system with their own separate parochial schools, but paying the bills often proved difficult, so they wanted a portion of the funds allotted by the state governments for support of schools. Protestants objected, and the issue sparked controversy and tension in every state with a large number of Catholic immigrants.

As the education issue suggests, the Irish and German immigrants were not uncomfortable asserting themselves politically. As such, they became an increasingly more prominent force in American politics, in particular serving as the foundation for the powerful political organizations, or "machines." A congressional committee formed in 1845 reported on the practice of naturalizing large numbers of immigrants on the eve of an election as a means of padding the ballot box. New York City's Tammany Hall, a Democratic organization and the most influential and notorious political machine in the country, drew considerable support among Irish immigrants.

In response to the rise of the machines, nativism became increasingly vitriolic. Some employers tried to cripple immigrants economically by refusing to give them jobs. It was not uncommon in some areas to see signs in the windows of businesses that read "Help Wanted—No Irish Need Apply." At the same time, groups organized solely around the issue of nativism appeared on the scene. Some of these organizations were local political parties, such as the Native American Democratic Association or the American Republican Party. More common were secret nativist societies, such as the Sons of '76, the Druids, and the Sons of America. The most prominent secret society was the Order of the Star Spangled Banner, founded in 1849 by Charles B. Allen. Its members were required to take an oath of secrecy, and if asked about the activities of the group, they were instructed to answer, "I know nothing about it." Soon members of all secret nativist societies were called "Know-Nothings."

At the same time, ethnic tensions led to violence in many American cities, particularly in New York City, the nation's largest metropolis and main port of entry for immigrants. In 1849, some twenty-two persons were killed when Irish-American and nativist gangs clashed outside the Astor Place opera house. While the immediate source of the dispute was the performance of a hated English actor, there were long-simmering ethnic disputes behind the violence. Many of those killed in the rioting were members of Irish-American street gangs that had been formed to defend immigrant neighborhoods against nativist marauders and police, the latter seen as biased against the Irish. Eight years later, a smaller riot broke out in the Kleindeutschland, or Little Germany, section of Manhattan. Again, the initial spark for the violence was a drunken street brawl, but many German Americans in the community resented nativist, anti-immigrant bias and police harassment of immigrant Americans.

In the 1850s, political nativism reached the zenith of its influence in American political history. The Whig Party was in the process of disintegrating, torn apart by internal squabbles over slavery and other issues. This created a vacuum that the nativists tried to step into, and for a few years they were successful. They founded a national political organization, called the American or Know-Nothing Party, dedicated almost exclusively to anti-immigrant policies. By 1855, the party had over a million members and had elected a dozen governors and more than a hundred congressmen. In some states, the Know-Nothings' hold on power was almost absolute. In Massachusetts, for example, the Know-Nothings won every statewide office and an overwhelming majority of the seats in the state legislature in the election of 1854. At the height of their power, Know-Nothing leaders looked forward to the election of 1856 with their eye on the presidency.

The Know-Nothings' hopes were dashed, however, by the rise of the slavery issue. Slavery evoked a much deeper response from most Americans than nativism, and it was nationally relevant. When the Republican Party arose in response to the slavery question in the 1850s, it had an issue much more suited to

winning a national election than anti-immigrant rhetoric. By the time the Know-Nothings met for their presidential convention in 1856, the slavery issue had become so prominent that it was necessary for the party to address it in its platform. However, the delegates could not reach agreement what position to take, and when a pro-slavery plank was finally adopted, many delegates bolted the convention and joined the Republican Party. The party nonetheless forged ahead, nominating for president former president Millard Fillmore. Given the split, the Know-Nothings were largely irrelevant in the election. In fact, they became the butt of jokes in many parts of the country, as antinativists organized "Do-Nothing" and "Say-Nothing" clubs to ridicule the Know-Nothings. Fillmore won a credible 874,534 popular votes, about 20 percent of the total cast, but only eight electoral votes. The party disappeared soon thereafter.

Christopher Bates

See also: The Great Irish Immigration (Part I, Sec. 2); Nativist Reaction (Part I, Sec. 4) Anti-Immigrant Backlash (Part I, Sec. 5); Anti-Immigrant Politics (Part II, Sec. 6); Imminent Dangers, 1835, Emigration, Emigrants, and Know-Nothings, 1854, Irish Response to Nativism, 1854 (Part IV, Sec. 3).

BIBLIOGRAPHY

Billington, Ray Allen. *The Protestant Crusade, 1800–1860: A Study of the Origins of American Nativism.* New York: Macmillan, 1938.

Crewdson, John. *The Tarnished Door: The New Immigrants and the Transformation of America.* New York: Times Books, 1983.

Higham, John. *Strangers in the Land: Patterns of American Nativism, 1860–1925.* New Brunswick, NJ: Rutgers University Press, 1955.

Mills, Nicolaus. *Arguing Immigration: The Debate over the Changing Face of America.* New York: Touchstone Books, 1994.

Overdyke, William Darrell. *The Know-Nothing Party in the South.* Baton Rouge: Louisiana State University Press, 1950.

Roediger, David. *The Wages of Whiteness: Race and the Making of the American Working Class.* New York: Verso, 1991.

Smith, James Morton. *Freedom's Fetters: The Alien and Sedition Laws and American Civil Liberties.* Ithaca, NY: Cornell University Press, 1956.

CHINESE AND CHINESE EXCLUSION ACT

*Y*ung Wing was the first prominent Chinese immigrant to the United States. Arriving in Massachusetts in 1847, Yung studied at Monson Academy and became an American citizen while a student at Yale College. After graduating from Yale in 1854—the first Chinese to graduate from an American college—Yung commuted between China and the United States promoting American education for Chinese youths. He directed a Chinese academy in Hartford, Connecticut, in the 1870s and later served as China's associate minister to the United States.

ANCIENT CHINESE IMMIGRATION

Chinese history, however, has an account of possibly a much earlier visit to the Americas. In the *Book of Liang* (A.D. 499), there is a detailed report of a Buddhist priest named Hui Shen (or Hwui Shan) who might have arrived on the American continents in A.D. 458, more than a thousand years before Columbus. Hui Shen told the Court of Liang that he and four other monks had traveled to a land called Fusang and stayed there for forty years. Some European and American scholars believe that his descriptions of the location, culture, and habitat of Fusang were very similar to those of pre-Columbian Mexico. The king of Fusang, according to the document, was called Itchi, which brings to mind Itza, a prominent branch of the Mayas in that period. Hui Shen's report of an excursion to a "Kingdom of Women" near Fusang raises the possibility that he might have traveled to what is today the southwestern United States. Based on his descriptions of its customs, the Kingdom of Women could very well be the ancestors of the present-day matrilineal Hopi who reside in New Mexico, Arizona, and other states. In 1973, a U.S. Geological Survey team retrieved an anchor stone of probable ancient Chinese origin off the shore of Los Angeles. Two years later, additional stones of a similar nature were found

by two divers in the waters of the Palos Verdes Peninsula, south of Los Angeles. These discoveries give tantalizing support to the pre-Columbian Chinese contact hypothesis. Some archaeologists, however, have disputed the age of the rocks or argued that Fusang was someplace other than the Americas.

A small number of Chinese immigrants came to the United States in the early 1800s. Large-scale Chinese immigration began midcentury after the discovery of gold in California in 1848. By 1852, some 25,000 Chinese immigrants had arrived in the United States. For the next thirty years, an average of 9,669 passed through U.S. Customs every year. In 1880, the census counted 105,465 Chinese residing in the United States.

Initially, the United States eagerly sought Chinese as immigrants. In 1852, Governor John MacDougall of California declared the Chinese the "most desirable of our adopted citizens." They were admirably called "celestials"—from the Celestial Kingdom, a name for China—and were often invited to public functions. When California was admitted to the Union in 1850, Chinese took part in the official celebration of statehood. One newspaper proclaimed, "These celestials make excellent citizens and we are pleased to notice their daily arrival in large numbers." The Chinese government, ruled by the Qing Dynasty, officially discouraged emigration. In 1868, the United States, desiring more Chinese immigrants for the development of the West Coast, persuaded the Qing government to ratify the Burlingame Treaty, which recognized "the inherent and inalienable right of man to change his home and allegiance . . . and the mutual advantages of the free migration and emigration of their citizens." Anson Burlingame, a former congressman from Massachusetts, had served as American ambassador to China from 1861 to 1867. While in China, Burlingame won the admiration of the Qing court, and when he retired from office, the emperor of China appointed him to the post of envoy extraordinary and minister plenipotentiary. As a Chinese minister, Burlingame

In the late 1860s, up to 12,000 Chinese immigrants found work constructing the western half of the nation's first transcontinental railroad, which included this timber trestle in the Sierra Nevada mountains of California. *(National Park Service: Statue of Liberty National Monument)*

had the unusual task of negotiating the 1868 treaty with his home country, the United States.

Seeing a business opportunity, British and American ships cruised the ports of southeast China distributing flyers, maps, and booklets enticing young men to go to America. Shipowners and their agents offered convenient payment plans for the passage, which cost between $15 in the 1850s and $55 in the 1860s. Family members or employers served as guarantors for repayment of the fare. Chinese workers of the Central Pacific Railroad signed promissory notes of $75 for the passage and other expenses. The note, guaranteed by the railroad company, stipulated that the borrowers would repay the money in seven installments from their monthly wage of $35.

In spite of easy credit, the voyage was far from easy sailing because of overcrowding and poor sani-

tation on many of the ships. The historian Sucheng Chan estimated that 5 to 10 percent of the passengers did not survive the month-long journey across the Pacific. Conditions did improve in the 1860s when the Pacific Mail Steamship Company, subsidized by the U.S. Congress, built four modern vessels for carrying mail and passengers between San Francisco and Hong Kong. While transportation had improved, the destination had not: Chinese immigrants faced hard work and hostility when they came ashore.

CAUSES OF EARLY IMMIGRATION

Even before the Burlingame Treaty removed the prohibition in 1868, large numbers of Chinese had al-

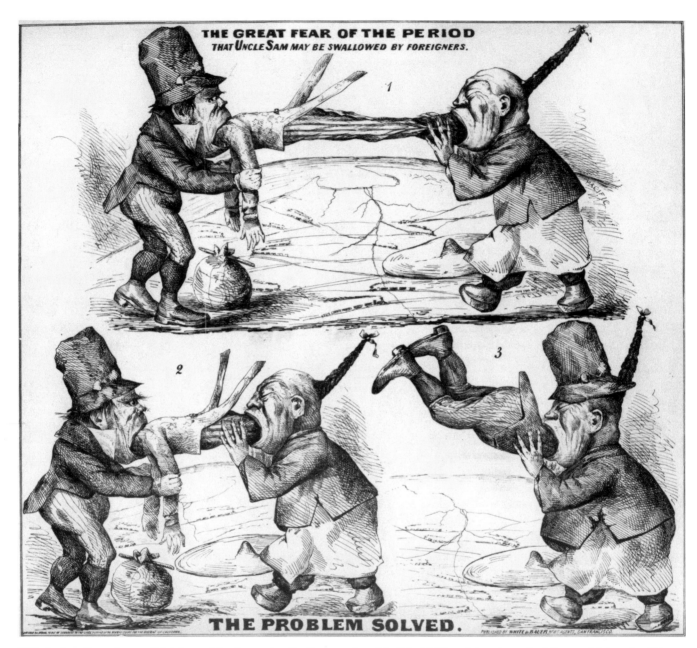

Mid-nineteenth-century nativist fear of foreigners is effectively captured in this 1869 racist cartoon depicting an Irish and a Chinese immigrant swallowing a helpless Uncle Sam. *(Library of Congress)*

ready emigrated to the United States and other parts of the world in defiance of the imperial edict of the Qing court. The vast majority of the Chinese immigrants in the United States in the 1800s and early 1900s were from Taishan (traditionally pronounced Toishan), a rural county in Guangdong Province in south China. Many others also came from the same general areas, such as the districts of Hsinhui (Sun-wui), Kaiping (Hoiping), Enping (Yanping), and the three counties collectively called San-i (Sam Yup).

After coming to America, immigrants from each

district established their own support groups, known as district associations. These groups arose by necessity because of language and cultural barriers as well as the fact that almost all the immigrants were men arriving alone. From 1860 to 1910, the average ratio of men to women for Chinese in the United States was a staggering nineteen to one. Far from their families and homes, these men relied on their district association for social and emotional support. In 1854 these groups merged into a single organization called the Six-District Association, better known as the Chinese

Six Companies. For almost a century after its inception, the Six Companies was the de facto self-government for most of the Chinese in America. It served as spokesperson for the Chinese community, fought against discrimination, offered educational and social services, settled disputes, and returned the bones of the deceased to China for proper burials.

The causes of immigration were a combination of push-pull factors. First, both the political and economic conditions in China were in disarray. The Qing Dynasty was losing control over the country due to a combination of self-indulgence, negligence, and incompetence. Foreign military intimidation, civil uprisings, and ethnic conflicts became increasingly common. In the 1800s, the Taishan area was hit especially hard by natural disasters and by ethnic strife where residents had a decade-long fight with the Hakka minority. Those situations, together with its mountainous and relatively barren landscape, did not make Taishan a wholesome place for people to stay. Proximity to the port of Hong Kong, which was ceded to the British in 1842 as a result of the Opium War, also placed the people of Taishan at the gateway to the American West. The impulse to emigrate became irresistible when inducements came from America, initially in terms of gold and, later, work on the railroad.

GOLD MINING

The first large-scale emigration of Chinese to the United States was in response to the news that large deposits of gold were discovered in California in 1848. This news quickly turned California into a mecca for migrants from within the country and for immigrants from around the world. Legend has it that James Marshall started the gold rush in California and Chum Ming started the rush of Chinese to America. Before becoming an "argonaut," as gold miners were called in those days, Chum owned a Chinese general store in San Francisco. The lure of gold led Chum to give up his business and became a prospector. Chum struck it rich quickly and told a friend in China about it. The news spread rapidly throughout south China, and it did not take long for both California and America to be called *Gum Shan* (gold mountain) among the southern Chinese.

By introducing new techniques brought from the old country to supplement panning, the Chinese soon became the most efficient placer miners in California. The Chinese were the first to use the rocker, the waterwheel, and the bucket-pulley system to dredge the river bottoms where larger nuggets were more likely

to be found. With their superior methods, they also were able to rework claims abandoned and thought to be unproductive by other miners. The success of the Chinese in prospecting was also due to their social organization. To make life in the remote mountains more bearable and also because they could not get help from white settlers, the Chinese made sure that their mining camps were self-sufficient. One of the best-known camps during the gold rush was Chinese Camp. At its prime, the camp boasted hotels, stores, a bank, a post office, joss houses (Chinese temples), a Masonic lodge, and a Catholic church. In those days, the largest hospital in the California mining territories was operated by the Chinese doctor Ah Sang, who was highly regarded by both Chinese and white patients ("Ah" is a casual way of addressing people in the dialects of south China, vaguely equivalent to "Mr.").

The importance of prospecting to the Chinese can be seen in the 1860 census. It shows that more than 70 percent of the Chinese in the United Sates were miners, almost all located in California. When placer mining began declining in California, the Chinese moved on to neighboring states and territories. By 1870, there were 4,274 Chinese in Idaho, 1,949 in Montana, 3,152 in Nevada, and 3,330 in Oregon (see table). Some went as far north as Alaska. The concentration of the Chinese in gold mining, however, also invited open hostility toward them. They were frequently chased off claims by the white miners once there were signs of gold, even though some of the claims had already been worked on and abandoned by the same people who now returned to claim them. One noted exception was the establishment of the Chinese Camp, which was made possible with the help of some friendly whites in the Washington Camp after the miners in Camp Salvado rejected the Chinese.

BUILDING THE RAILROADS

As gold mining started to wane, a new demand for Chinese labor unexpectedly emerged. In 1862, the U.S. government passed the long-awaited act to build a transcontinental railroad to link the nation coast to coast. Due to the Civil War (1861–65) and the arduous nature of the work, the Central Pacific Railroad Company, which had been commissioned to build the western segment of the railroad, was seriously behind schedule. In 1865, Charles Crocker, a partner in Central Pacific, turned to the Chinese Six Companies, over the objections of his colleagues, for help in recruiting workers.

Chinese Population by States, 1870–1890			
State	1870	1880	1890
Alabama	0	4	48
Arkansas	98	133	92
California	49,277	75,132	72,472
Colorado	7	612	1398
Connecticut	2	123	272
Delaware	0	1	37
Florida	0	18	108
Georgia	1	17	108
Idaho	4,274	3,379	2,007
Illinois	1	209	740
Indiana	0	29	92
Iowa	3	33	64
Kansas	0	19	93
Kentucky	1	10	28
Louisana	71	489	333
Maine	1	8	73
Maryland	2	5	189
Massachusetts	87	229	984
Michigan	1	27	120
Minnesota	0	24	94
Mississippi	16	51	147
Missouri	3	91	409
Montana	1,949	1,765	2,532
Nebraska	0	18	214
Nevada	3,152	5,416	2,833
New Hamsphire	0	14	58
New Jersey	5	170	608
New York	29	909	2,935
North Carolina	0	0	32
North Dakota	0	8	28
Ohio	1	109	183
Oregon	3,330	9,510	9,540
Pennsylvania	13	148	1,146
Rhode Island	0	27	69
South Carolina	1	9	34
South Dakota	0	230	195
Tennessee	0	25	51
Texas	25	136	710
Utah	445	501	806
Vermont	0	0	32
Virginia	4	6	55
Washington	234	3,180	3,260
West Virginia	0	5	15
Wisconsin	0	16	119
Wyoming	143	914	465

Source: Inter-University Consortium for Political and Social Research (ICPSR). *Historical, Economic, and Social Data: U.S., 1790–1970.* Ann Arbor: ICPSR, 1992.

At its peak, more than ten thousand Chinese were employed, constituting 90 percent of the front-line workers on the railroad. Many of the workers were directly recruited from China by the Six Companies on behalf of Central Pacific. They laid the tracks, built the bridges, chiseled the mountains, and worked through bitter winters in the Rockies and the Sierras. Four years later, in 1869, the line was completed in Utah joining the eastern segment, which had been built primarily by Irish immigrants.

Chinese also played a major role in building the Northwest Pacific and the Southern Pacific lines. They took part in constructing the Alabama and Chattanooga Railroad, the Houston and Texas Central, and numerous lines in Arizona, Nevada, and Colorado. As the railroad builder West Evans informed Congress in 1876, "I do not see how we could do the work we have done without them." Contrary to popular belief, Chinese laborers were not hired because they cost less. Central Pacific paid both Chinese and white laborers the same rate, $35 per month.

AGRICULTURE AND RECLAMATION

When work on the railroad wound down, many Chinese turned to farming. Earlier, in the mining camps, Chinese had grown vegetables that were indispensable to their diet. Some Chinese turned to full-time truck gardening as the market for vegetables and fruits expanded. In 1870, there were over three thousand Chinese farmers and farm laborers in California, compared with less than four hundred a decade earlier. By the 1880s, it was estimated that 50 to 90 percent of the farmworkers in California were Chinese.

In the South, Chinese worked on plantations. In 1880, there were 489 Chinese farm laborers in Louisiana and 133 in Arkansas. But they did not stay in the fields long, owing to poor working conditions. The advertised wage in Louisiana at that time was $22 a month. Almost all the Chinese in the South left farming within a few years and moved to cities. In Hawaii, Chinese built the first sugar mill in 1802 and worked extensively on the sugar plantations. They also introduced the cultivation of rice to the islands.

As agriculturists, Chinese were the innovators of two important crops. Ah Bing, a grower in Oregon, was credited with the breeding of the famous cherry that still bears his name. In Florida, Lue Gim Gong successfully cross-fertilized Mediterranean oranges with local varieties to create a hardy hybrid that has become the progenitor of the core of today's citrus crops in California and Florida. He also created some unusual plants, including huge perfumed grapefruits measuring twenty-one inches in circumference and a rose tree bearing flowers in seven different colors. Lue learned his horticultural skills from his birthmother in China and from his adopted mother, Fanny Amelia Burlingame, niece of Anson Burlingame. In 1911, Lue was awarded the Wilder Medal by the American Pomological Society for his contribution to the citrus industry.

Chinese were responsible for reclaiming nearly five million acres of marshland and swamps in the Sacramento–San Joaquin Delta, turning them into the richest farmland in America. They built the levees that prevented flooding as well as the irrigation systems that both drained and watered the land. It did not take long for the crops from the reclaimed land to exceed in value all the gold ever produced during the gold rush. The delta has made California the leading agricultural state in the nation. It undergirds the state's $24.6 billion agricultural economy (1998) that produces more than half of the nation's fruits, nuts, and vegetables. The land itself has risen astronomically in value. Sucheng Chan has calculated that each acre that cost the owner as little as $1 to $4 to buy in the late 1800s was worth as much as $20 to $100 soon after reclamation.

For their contributions, the Chinese laborers were paid $1 a day and worked from 6 A.M. to 6 P.M. with a break and lunch in between. Some Chinese leased the reclaimed land from their white owners to grow berries and other crops. But, very few were able to retain the farms, because when the leases expired the landowners kept the farms by not renewing the leases.

FISHING INDUSTRY

In 1854, 150 Chinese established a fishing village in Rincon Point, San Francisco. By 1892, one-fourth of the twenty-five hundred fishermen in the San Francisco Bay Area were Chinese. They founded the shrimp industry and owned all twenty-six shrimp camps in 1897. Chinese fishing fleets eventually spread northward to the border of Oregon and southward to San Diego. Along the Monterey Peninsula, Chinese harvested seaweed for food and industrial gum. In the Pacific Northwest, they worked in the salmon canneries. As many as thirty-one hundred Chinese were employed by the canneries on the Columbia River in Oregon in 1881.

In San Diego, abalone was the catch of choice. While the Chinese prized the mollusk as a culinary delicacy, whites in the nineteenth century were more interested in their shells as ornaments. The historian Pei-Chi Liu has written that Chinese in California sold $38,880 worth of abalone meat to China in 1879, whereas their shells, valued at $88,825, were exported by the Chinese to the East Coast and Europe. According to the author Stan Steiner, Chinese were responsible for popularizing the eating of shellfish—shrimp, abalone, crab, and lobster—on the West Coast.

THE LAUNDRY BUSINESS

One of the most unusual occupations for the Chinese in nineteenth- and twentieth-century America was the laundry business, because it was a totally new line of work for them, different from the kind that had attracted them to America originally. In the early 1850s, some Chinese were making a living out of washing and ironing clothes in the mining camps. The typical prospector, Yankee or Chinese, was either a bachelor or a man without the company of his family who had very little interest in washing and ironing his own clothes. Seeing a market for these chores, some Chinese became laundrymen. Reportedly, Wah Lee opened the first full-service laundry in 1851 on Washington Street, San Francisco, charging $2 for a dozen shirts.

Chinese did not engage in the laundry business in large numbers until the last part of the nineteenth century when the gold rush was over and they were barred from many jobs. The business could be started with small capital, needing only a trough, iron, and ironing board. It was estimated that only 1 to 2 percent of the Chinese in California were laundry workers in the 1860s, but by 1900, the numbers had increased to 8 percent. In the 1870s, Chinese laundries began to move eastward, opening first in St. Louis and Chicago in 1872, Baltimore in 1875, and New York in 1876. In 1900, more than 13 percent of the Chinese in San Francisco were in the laundry business. For much of the early 1900s, Chinese laundries were ubiquitous in major cities nationwide. The 1920 census shows that 30 percent of the Chinese in the United States listed their occupations as laundry work. Many Chinese also performed domestic services in the homes of whites.

ANTI-CHINESE LEGISLATION IN CALIFORNIA

In 1852, when Governor John McDougall was welcoming Chinese to America, anti-Chinese sentiments were already brewing in both the legislature and the judiciary as well as in the mining camps. In those days, Chinese and other minorities had very little legal recourse in any disputes with whites because a California law enacted in 1850 stipulated that "no black or mulatto person, or Indian shall be allowed to give evidence in favor of, or against a white man." In 1854, the California Supreme Court interpreted this to include the Chinese. The court's racist ruling declared that all Asians were American Indians because, among other things, they were "a race of people whom nature has marked as inferior, and who are incapable of progress or intellectual development beyond a certain point" (*People v. George W. Hall*). It was not until 1873 that Chinese were allowed to testify against whites in California courts.

As early as 1850, there were public cries of "California for the Americans." Enacted that year, the Foreign Miners' License Law required foreign-born miners to pay a fee of twenty dollars each month and was intended primarily to drive out Mexicans and Latin Americans. The law was soon repealed when four thousand French- and Spanish-speaking miners occupied the town of Sonora in a protest. After that incident, many non-Yankee miners gave up, leaving the Chinese to face the full force of the antiforeign hysteria. There were mob actions and local resolutions to ban "Asiatic" or "South-Sea Islanders" from mining. In 1852, another foreign miner's tax was passed. This time the specific target was the Chinese. Even though the tax was reduced to $3 per month, a companion legislation required shipmasters to pay from $5 to $10 per passenger, many of whom were immigrants from China. The foreign miner's tax, raised to $4 in the following year, was in force until 1870. When it was over, the state treasury was enriched by $5 million, most of which the Chinese paid.

Meanwhile, other state laws attempting to restrict Chinese immigration to California were enacted, but all were struck down by federal courts. In 1858, California banned Chinese immigration, and in 1860, it barred all Chinese from public schools. In the 1870s, San Francisco adopted various ordinances that had little purpose other than to harass the Chinese. For example, there was a "pole" law (1870) that outlawed the Chinese method of carrying merchandise on a pole. The "cubic air" law (1870), which required 500 cubic feet of air space for each occupant in a lodging place, was designed to reduce overcrowding in Chinatown as much as to harass both the renters and the landlords. In 1873, the first year the "cubic air" law became effective, 177 Chinese were arrested and imprisoned for its violation. County supervisors, however, were embarrassed and voided the ordinance immediately when they found the prisons had less than 100 cubic feet of air space for each prisoner. Another example is the "queue" law (1875) that authorized shaving off the queues of all Chinese held in county jails. It was a custom of Chinese to wear queues, or long, single braids of hair. In the case of *Ho Ah Kow v. Matthew Noonan*, the U.S. Circuit Court invalidated the ordinance in 1879 on the grounds that it was cruel and unusual punishment and that it violated the religion of the plaintiff. Ho had argued that, according to his religious belief, the loss of his queue would bring him misfortune.

ANTI-CHINESE RIOTS

A confluence of factors brought anti-Chinese sentiments in the urban centers to a peak in the West. In 1869, the transcontinental railroad was completed, which released more than twenty-five thousand workers to the California job market. The new railroad also brought in more job seekers from the East. The end of the gold rush further infused more people into the ranks of the unemployed.

Uninformed about labor rights and unwelcome in most of the American union movement, the Chinese unwittingly became pawns of employers in job actions. In June 1870, the owner of a shoe factory in North Adams, Massachusetts, brought in seventy-five Chinese workers from San Francisco to break a strike. This gained the Chinese the wrath of the Knights of St. Crispin, a powerful labor union representing the striking workers. Three months later, a New Jersey steam laundry plant also brought in Chinese to end a strike by its Irish employees. In Louisiana and Mississippi, with the end of slavery, the plantation owners attempted to control the wages of black workers by hiring Chinese. Such incidents fueled tension between white and Chinese workers.

In the last quarter of the nineteenth century, major anti-Chinese riots broke out in western cities and towns. While only some of the disturbances were labor related, all of them were rooted in racism and sinophobia (fear and hatred of Chinese). In March 1877, five Chinese farmers were murdered in Chico, California. Four months later, a full-fledged riot broke out in San Francisco after a seemingly well-intentioned labor meeting outside the City Hall. For three days, the rioters roamed the streets, attempting to attack Chinatown, as well as the railroads, the Pacific Mail Steamship Company, and other employers of Chinese. Even though Chinatown was saved by a determined police force, four people were killed, twenty-five laundries were completely destroyed, and many buildings were damaged. In 1880, one Chinese man was murdered in Denver, Colorado, and the entire Chinese quarter was laid waste by a white mob over an altercation between two Chinese gamblers and two drunken white men. Anti-Chinese riots broke out in Seattle, Washington, in 1885 and again in 1886. The most notorious riots occurred in Los Angeles on October 24, 1871, and in Rock Springs, Wyoming, on September 2, 1885.

The Los Angeles riot was triggered by the killing of a white man and the wounding of others who were caught in the cross fire during a shootout between two Chinese gangs over a young woman named Ya Hit. As retold by newspaper columnist Cecilia Rasmussen, a mob of five hundred Angelenos ransacked and looted Chinatown. The city marshal ordered his men to "shoot any Chinese who try to escape." When it was over, nineteen Chinese had been killed. The looters then paraded through the streets, showing off their booty. One bright spot in that dark episode was a young policeman, Emil Harris, who refused to obey the order of the marshal and took it upon himself to rescue some of the Chinese from the lynch crowd. Another righteous man was Judge R. M. Widney, who ordered the arrest of all the rioters. Later, Harris testified against the perpetrators in court, which resulted in the indictment of thirty-seven and the conviction of eight for manslaughter. Six years later, Harris became the first and only Jewish police chief in Los Angeles.

The Rock Springs incident was the worst massacre of Chinese in American history. At least twenty-eight Chinese were killed, and all Chinese-owned buildings, save one, were destroyed. Some Chinese escaped to the mountains, after which their whereabouts were never known. The rampage was triggered when Chinese coal miners refused to join white miners in their proposed strike. The white workers retaliated by setting fire to homes and businesses on the Chinese side of the town and trying to shoot every Chinese in sight. More than five hundred Chinese fled to a nearby town, where they were protected by a railroad company until federal troops arrived to restore order. Stunned by the senseless destruction of life and property and pressured by the Chinese government, the U.S. Congress indemnified the victims for a total of $147,748. The only Chinese establishment that sur-

vived was the Grand Café. According to a great-great-granddaughter of the original owner, the restaurant, renamed the New Grand Café and rebuilt on a different street many years later, was operated by her relatives, the Lui family, until the early 1990s. This would make it the oldest restaurant in the United States run by the same family. Today, many restaurants in the Rock Springs area are owned by different branches of the Lui family (also spelled Leo and Liu due to errors in immigration records common in the nineteenth century).

THE CHINESE EXCLUSION ACT OF 1882

In 1877, an anti-Chinese agitator named Denis Kearney helped organize the Workingmen's Party of California. The party's war cry was, "The Chinese must go." National politicians soon adopted this war cry, and in 1879, Congress passed a bill restricting Chinese immigration, which was vetoed by President Rutherford B. Hayes. Both the Republican and Democratic Parties, however, backed legislation limiting Chinese immigration, and in 1882, Congress passed the Chinese Exclusion Act, suspending the emigration of Chinese laborers to the United States for ten years. It was the first law ever passed banning a group of immigrants based on race or nationality. Six years later, the Scott Act banned the return of Chinese laborers to the United States and invalidated their reentry permits. Over twenty thousand Chinese were trapped outside the country, which caused enormous hardship, especially on those who had families and property in the United States. The Geary Act of 1892 extended the 1882 Chinese Exclusion Act and all immigration laws against the Chinese for another ten years. It also required the Chinese in the United States to obtain a certificate of residence. In 1904 the Exclusion Act was extended indefinitely.

Even though the 1882 Chinese Exclusion Act did not apply to merchants, students, and professionals, it exacerbated anti-American sentiments in China and drastically reduced the number of Chinese coming to the United States. For the decade after its passage (1883–92), an average of 1,308 Chinese arrived in the United States annually as compared with an average of 12,795 in the preceding ten years. Both figures included new arrivals and returnees. Between 1885 and 1888, arriving Chinese never exceeded forty per year. A combination of low immigration, low birthrate (due to scarcity of women), and aging had caused a sharp decline in the Chinese population in the United States from a high of 107,488 in 1890 to a low of 61,638 in 1920. It rose back to 77,504 in 1940 primarily due to natural increases, as the number of American-born Chinese more than doubled from 18,532 to 40,262 between 1920 and 1940. The upward trend continued after the 1882 Exclusion Act, and all its related legislation was repealed in 1943 as a result of the United States and China becoming allies in World War II. The change was small, providing a quota of 105 for Chinese immigrants. However, it did pave the way for more progressive immigration legislation in later years.

Lawrence K. Hong

See also: Restrictive Legislation, Japanese Internment (Part I, Sec. 4); Changes in the Law (Part I, Sec. 5); China, Taiwan and Hong Kong (Part III, Sec. 3); Angell Treaty, 1881, Chinese Exclusion Act, 1882, Repeal of Chinese Exclusion Acts, 1943 (Part IV, Sec. 1).

BIBLIOGRAPHY

Chan, Sucheng. *The Bittersweet Soil.* Berkeley: University of California Press, 1986.

Coolidge, Mary Roberts. *Chinese Immigration.* New York: Henry Holt, 1909.

Frost, F. "The Palos Verdes Chinese Anchor Mystery." *Archaeology* 35:1 (January/February 1982): 23–26.

Gyory, Andrew. *Closing the Gate: Race, Politics, and the Chinese Exclusion Act.* Chapel Hill: University of North Carolina Press, 1998.

Lai, Him Mark. "Chinese." In *Harvard Encyclopedia of American Ethnic Groups,* ed. S. Thernstrom. Cambridge: Harvard University Press, 1980.

———. "The United States." In *The Encyclopedia of the Chinese Overseas,* ed. L. Pan. Singapore: Chinese Heritage Centre, 1998.

Lee, Calvin. *Chinatown, U.S.A.* Garden City, NY: Doubleday, 1965.

Liu, Po-Chi. *A History of the Chinese in the United States of America, 1848–1911.* Taipei: Commission of Overseas Affairs, 1976.

McClain, Charles J. *In Search of Equality: The Chinese Struggle against Discrimination in Nineteenth-Century America.* Berkeley: University of California Press, 1994.

McCunn, Ruthanne Lum. *Chinese American Portraits: Personal Histories, 1928–1988.* San Francisco: Chronicle Books, 1988.

Mertz, H. *Gods from the Far East: How the Chinese Discovered America.* New York: Ballantine, 1972.

Pierson, L., and J. Moriarty. "Stone Anchors: Asiatic Shipwrecks off the California Coast." *Anthropological Journal of Canada* 18:3 (1980): 17–22.

Rasmussen, C. "L.A. Then and Now: A Forgotten Hero from a Night of Disgrace." *Los Angeles Times,* May 16, 1999.

Saxton, Alexander. *The Indispensable Enemy: Labor and the Anti-Chinese Movement in California.* Berkeley: University of California Press, 1995.

Steiner, Stan. *Fusang: The Chinese Who Built America.* New York: Harper and Row, 1979.

Sung, Betty Lee. *Mountain of Gold: The Story of the Chinese in America.* New York: Macmillan, 1967.

Tcheu, John Kuo Wei. *New York before Chinatown: Orientalism and the Shaping of American Culture, 1776–1882.* Baltimore: Johns Hopkins University Press, 1999.

Tung, William L. *The Chinese in America, 1820–1973.* Dobbs Ferry, NY: Oceana, 1974.

Williams, F. W. *Anson Burlingame and the First Chinese Mission to Foreign Powers.* New York: Scribner's, 1912.

Yung Wing. *My Life in China and America.* New York: H. Holt and Company, 1909.

IMMIGRANTS AND THE CIVIL WAR

Before the start of the Civil War, the United States experienced a record level of immigration, primarily from Western Europe and the British Isles. A variety of factors, including political refuge and economic opportunity, influenced the immigrants' motivations for relocation. The vast majority of these newly arrived immigrants settled in and around the port cities where they disembarked. In addition, most immigrants arriving in the middle of the nineteenth century settled in the Northern regions of the nation. Though the United States experienced a population boom in the years preceding the war, immigration statistics reveal that the total number of immigrants entering the country in the 1860s had declined, partially as a result of the Civil War, which began in 1861.

The Civil War marked the culmination of a conflict between the slave states and the free states over the extension of slavery into newly formed or acquired territories. Underlying the conflict were various emotionally and politically charged issues, including the inherent evils of slavery, the rights of states versus the rights of the federal government, congressional representation, and tariff controversies. After Abraham Lincoln's presidential inauguration in March 1861, Alabama, Florida, Georgia, Louisiana, Mississippi, South Carolina, Texas, and, later, Arkansas, North Carolina, Tennessee, and Virginia were formed into the Confederate States of America.

THE NORTH

In 1860, the population of foreign-born residents in the North far exceeded the number living in the South. The free states were home to over 90 percent of the total foreign-born population of the United States, and both newly arrived immigrants and those more established were quickly caught up in the highly charged issues of slavery and states' rights. New York,

long the nation's major Atlantic port, was the recipient of an overwhelming majority of immigrants in the mid–nineteenth century. But many other Northern cities, including Boston, Chicago, Philadelphia, and Milwaukee, were also home to substantial immigrant communities.

In both the North and the South, Europeans constituted the great majority of the immigrants who arrived in the antebellum and Civil War years. More Germans and Irish immigrated to the United States than any other group. Other newcomers also hailed primarily from western European nations, such as Britain, France, Italy, the Netherlands, Norway, Scotland, Spain, Sweden, and Wales. For a variety of reasons, many of these newly arrived immigrants, as well as a considerable number of those more solidly established, became active participants in the Civil War.

IMMIGRANT INVOLVEMENT IN THE UNION CAUSE

A significant number of nonnative inhabitants were already involved in the nation's armed forces before the war broke out. It is estimated that 50–60 percent of the enlisted men in the army during the prewar years were immigrants. Financial necessity was the primary reason many of these foreign-born settlers sought military employment before the war began. After the first shots were fired at Fort Sumter, however, motivations became more varied and complex. Conscription did not begin in the Northern states until 1863, but foreign-born inhabitants constituted just over 20 percent of the Union army (though they accounted for approximately 18 percent of the total Northern population).

For many, the decision to volunteer for service was based on a desire to prove patriotism and loy-

Italian-speaking troops of the Garibaldi Guard file past President Lincoln in the early days of the Civil War. Note the Italianate flag that reads *Deo e Popolo* **(God and People). Most immigrants lived in the North and hence fought for the Union.** *(Library of Congress)*

alty to their adopted country. Memories of anti-immigration sentiment still lingered in the minds of those—especially the Irish—who had been settled in the United States for a few decades. In some cases, immigrants felt a particularly strong incentive to volunteer as a result of the strained diplomatic ties between their home country and the United States. British settlers, for instance, were required to take special oaths of loyalty, as tensions still existed over the War of 1812 and were fueled by the perception of British support for the Confederacy. Some of these British-born foreigners took up arms against the South as a way of reasserting their renunciation of ties to Britain.

In general, a desire to prove one's "Americanness" was a motivating factor among immigrant volunteers in the Union army. That is not to say that hatred of slavery or genuine support for preserving the Union

were not also influential in their decisions. For most foreign-born volunteers, as for their native-born counterparts, attitudes and reasons were varied and often complicated. Many Northerners, both foreign- and native-born, also sought the personal and political advancement a successful career in the military might bring them. Still others, including a number who immigrated specifically to join the Union forces, simply hoped for adventure.

Many of the immigrants who joined the Union army responded to passionate solicitations in the local newspapers which urged members of ethnic communities to show their pride by enlisting. An immigrant community with its own regiment or at least its own company was a positive reflection on the ethnic politicians of the community and also removed any doubt as to the patriotism of the new Americans. Af-

Irish and German Immigrants are recruited for the Union army in front of Castle Garden, New York, which, until the opening of Ellis Island in the 1890s, was the nation's main immigrant entry point. *(Library of Congress)*

ter the start of the war, a number of distinctly German companies emerged from nearly every state in the Union, including Illinois, Indiana, New Jersey, New York, Ohio, Pennsylvania, Wisconsin, and West Virginia. Irish companies were also formed in most of these states as well as in Massachusetts, Michigan, and New Hampshire. A significant number of Irish and German soldiers also became Union officers as the war progressed, gaining notoriety for their communities as well as for themselves. The German and Irish units were most numerous, but other groups were also represented, including immigrants from France, Holland, Hungary, Italy, Poland, Scotland, and Sweden. In addition, there were over 180,000 black soldiers in the Union army and constituted about 10 percent of the total number of Union soldiers by the end of the war.

Ethnic forces, in both the Union and the Confederacy, were involved in nearly every major land battle of the Civil War, from the shots fired at Fort Sumter to Appomattox Courthouse.

Other immigrant groups also formed and fought in military units for the Northern cause. Notable among these are the French companies and the Scottish regiment of New York. New York also offered a Scandinavian company that consisted of both Norwegians and Swedes, though both these groups also formed distinct companies in Illinois, Minnesota, and Wisconsin. Represented in lesser numbers were the Dutch volunteers, who formed units in Michigan; Mexican soldiers from the New Mexico area, who formed a regiment and several militia companies; a Welsh company from New York State; and Swiss companies from Illinois, New York, and Wisconsin. Furthermore, after 1862, a number of black troops were organized from volunteers in the North and, sometimes, escaped or manumitted slaves from the Southern states. Although freed blacks often suffered racist and inhumane treatment from white officers, the Union became as dependent on their contributions to the war effort as it had on the involvement of other immigrant groups.

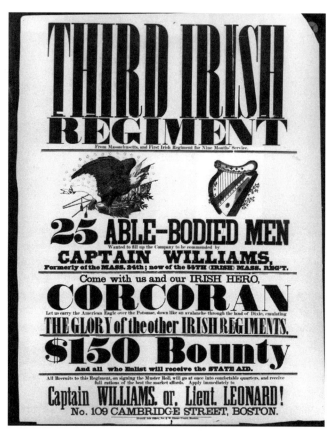

This recruiting poster, aimed at Irish immigrants, promised a little money ($150) and a lot of glory for those who enlisted for a nine-month stint. The rigors and horrors of actual warfare, however, discouraged many from re-enlisting. *(Library of Congress)*

Although the North's ethnic regiments were truly significant and distinctive, many foreign-born volunteers joined regiments that had no national affiliation whatsoever. In addition, immigrants were also involved in the Union war effort in somewhat unofficial ways. In Chicago and many other cities, immigrant women (as well as native-born women) formed sewing societies that helped keep the Union army supplied with cloth goods and garments. Support societies such as these were common among those who did not travel to the front lines. Other enterprising immigrants became involved in the war in unusual but significant ways. One such was Mme Turchin, daughter of a Russian infantry officer and wife of the colonel of the 19th Illinois Regiment, who led her husband's troops into battle when he fell seriously ill. Another fascinating participant in the Northern effort was Captain Joseph Gloskowski, a Polish immigrant who served in the signal service during the war. Gloskowski, along with a number of other Poles, was in-

strumental in transmitting communications across battle zones using a complicated system of flag signals. In addition, numerous immigrants, both men and women, were involved in diplomatic and espionage efforts during the war.

THE SOUTH

The immigrant population in the Southern states was considerably lower than in the Northern region, partially because the slave-based staple crop economy of the South afforded fewer employment opportunities for paid laborers. Certain areas did cultivate considerable immigrant settlements, however, particularly New Orleans, Mobile, and Charleston, all major ports of the Confederacy. In general, the immigrant population in the South constituted approximately 4–5 percent of the total free population. The nearly 4 million blacks enslaved in the South, while they formed the foundation of the cash crop economy, were not considered a reliable source of military potential for the Confederacy.

In every Southern state, with the exception of Texas, Irish immigrants outnumbered all those of other nationalities. Louisiana and Texas had the highest numbers of foreign-born inhabitants, with Germans dominating the numbers in Texas. British settlers, excluding the Irish, ranked third in total immigrant populations in the South. Other groups, however, were also present in the Confederacy, including French, Italian, Mexican, Polish, Scottish, Spanish, and Swedish settlers. As in the Union, many of these nonnative newcomers became involved in various facets of the war effort, whether on the battlefield or on the diplomatic front. Their reasons for participating were not unlike those of the Union's ethnic volunteers, nor were they wholly different from those motivations which spurred native-born citizens to serve.

IMMIGRANT INVOLVEMENT IN THE CONFEDERATE CAUSE

Early in the war, Southern newspapers, like those in the Northern states, were filled with advertisements encouraging men to join the Confederate forces. A number of these solicitations were specifically aimed at the formation of companies of foreign-born volunteers. There were fewer unemployed immigrants in the South, and economic inducements to join were, on the whole, less lucrative than those offered in the North. For these reasons, in the Confederacy, fewer nonnative settlers volunteered for purely financial reasons. Like their counterparts in the Union forces, many immigrants volunteered for service as a way to prove their national loyalty, in this case to the Confederate States of America. Fighting in the Confederate forces hastened the acceptance of newly arrived immigrants and bolstered the status of those long settled.

As with Northern ethnic communities, the formation of ethnic regiments and companies was extremely significant in terms of building unity among immigrants of certain nations and between those communities and their native-born neighbors. A number of military academies dotted the Southern states, and the prevailing attitude, particularly among the upper middle class, was that military service was an honor and a privilege. As a result, at the outset of the war the Confederacy possessed a clear advantage in terms of its more experienced pool of officers, both native- and foreign-born.

German companies were formed in several states in the Confederacy, including Alabama, Georgia, North Carolina, South Carolina, Tennessee, Texas, and Virginia. Irish companies, as expected, were also very prominent in the ranks of each of these Southern states as well as in Missouri. Other, less numerous immigrant groups also formed ethnic units in the Confederacy. Louisiana boasted several French companies, which often included Creoles as well. In addition, a group known as the European Brigade formed in New Orleans, largely as a civil defense mechanism, and brought together Belgian, Dutch, English, French, German, Italian, Scandinavian, Spanish, and Swiss volunteers. The motley nature of this brigade aptly reflected the cosmopolitan atmosphere of the important port city. Texas also contributed distinctive military units to the Southern cause, including several Mexican and Polish companies.

As in the Union, many foreign-born inhabitants of the Confederacy were engaged in the war effort in noncombat capacities. One interesting character was Lola Sanchez, a Cuban immigrant who settled in Florida near the St. John's River. Her entire family was involved in the Confederate cause, but they were virtually surrounded by Union troops. Sanchez engaged in a variety of espionage efforts that put her life at great risk but had a decisive hand in aiding the Confederates in Florida. Another notable foreign-born person was Captain Henry Wirz, a Swiss immigrant who acted as a special agent in the Confederacy be-

fore being appointed to oversee the Confederate prison camp at Andersonville, Georgia. Wirz was condemned to death for the criminal nature of the conditions and treatment of prisoners at the notorious prison, and though not a native-born citizen, he was the only person executed for war crimes after the Civil War.

EFFECTS OF THE WAR

The North had a greater military potential at the beginning of the war as a consequence of its larger free population. In addition, greater industrialization in the Northern states made the Union army better able to sustain and command large numbers of troops, even from a great distance. At the start of the war, many believed that the civil unrest would last only a month or so and were surprised and disillusioned when the bloody conflict continued beyond the initial months. Northern newspapers and popular opinion underestimated the tenacity of Southern forces, which, at least initially, possessed various advantages, such as greater proximity to and familiarity with crucial battle sites. The South, though rich in military talent, was ill equipped to fight a war of this magnitude. Shortages of food and supplies were chronic and the social atmosphere so volatile that the Confederacy was unable to sustain its troops effectively or to defend its territory. Almost one of every four Confederate soldiers lost his life in the Civil War, and the South itself was utterly devastated. Union forces had destroyed thousands of crops and homes resulting in over $3 billion in damage.

The end of the Civil War led to the Thirteenth Amendment, which abolished slavery in December 1865. Many freed blacks still faced economic and social injustice and, despite freedom, were bound by prejudice and oppression. Issues of race and class, in addition to labor struggles, worsened during Reconstruction. Many Southern soldiers returned to find their homes destroyed and their families scattered. Tensions between immigrants and newly freed blacks were fueled by increased competition for jobs, especially during the nationwide economic depression of the 1870s. Over the next decade, immigrant communities, like their native-born neighbors, struggled to put families back together and heal the wounds of the bloody conflict.

Angela F. Pulley

See also: Immigrants and the American Revolution (Part I, Sec. 1); Immigrants and Westward Expansion (Part I, Sec. 2); Senate Report on the Encouragement of Immigration, 1864 (Part IV, Sec. 2).

BIBLIOGRAPHY

Archdeacon, Thomas J. *Becoming American: An Ethnic History.* New York: Free Press, 1983.

Burton, William L. *Melting Pot Soldiers: The Union's Ethnic Regiments.* New York: Fordham University Press, 1998.

Lonn, Ella. *Foreigners in the Confederacy.* Chapel Hill: University of North Carolina Press, 1940.

———. *Foreigners in the Union Army and Navy.* Baton Rouge: Louisiana State University Press, 1951.

Sowell, Thomas. *Ethnic America: A History.* New York: Basic Books, 1981.

IMMIGRANTS AND WESTWARD EXPANSION

Historians, both of immigration and of the American West, have long ignored the role of immigrants in western expansion. Nevertheless, immigrants formed a substantial percentage of the population in both the trans-Appalachian and the trans-Mississippi West. By 1870, for example, 25 percent of Nebraskans and 34 percent of the residents of the Dakota Territory were of foreign birth. By 1900, 20.7 percent of those living in the west states were foreign-born, in comparison with 13.6 percent of the United States as a whole. Immigrants helped shape and adapt the West to become a vital part of the United States.

COLONIAL ERA

Expansion across the North American continent began with the arrival of the first Europeans in the late fifteenth century. Before long, several countries had laid claim to different portions of the continent. During the sixteenth century, the Spanish populated the Southwest and Florida, although not as heavily as they did the Caribbean and Latin America, and by the seventeenth century, French Jesuits, trappers, and traders inhabited Canada and the Great Lakes region. Not long afterward, French soldiers arrived to protect them. The Dutch settled New Amsterdam in 1624, later renamed New York by the English, and Swedes settled in the area that is now known as New Jersey and Delaware.

The English sent the most colonists to the continent, beginning in 1585 with the establishment of Sir Walter Raleigh's ill-fated Roanoke colonies off the coast of present-day North Carolina. Colonists first abandoned and then disappeared from Roanoke, but other settlements soon followed until the English dominated the eastern seaboard from Maine to Georgia. These early English immigrants came for several reasons, whether it be for trade and opportunity, the possibility of free land, or the right to worship without government interference.

As the European population grew, land along the coast grew scarce. Newer immigrants were forced to move inland if they wished to own farmland of their own. This process continued steadily throughout the seventeenth and eighteenth centuries. By the mid–eighteenth century, the English had expanded to the Appalachian Mountains. Were it not for the Proclamation of 1763, which declared the Appalachians the natural western border of the British colonies, anxious immigrants and more settled colonists would have quickly pushed farther.

Despite the overwhelming English majority, the British colonies were not homogeneous. Late in the colonial period, 2.64 million people lived in what would become the United States. Of these, only 60.9 percent were of English origin. The next highest percentage were not even European but African, at 20 percent. African slaves had been unwilling immigrants to the English colonies since 1619, when Dutch traders brought the first shipment to Jamestown, the first permanent English settlement in Virginia. Even after Congress outlawed their importation from abroad in 1808, slaves continued to comprise a significant portion of westward expansion. Slaves moved west along with their owners until after the Civil War. Even Native Americans owned slaves, including the Cherokees and the Creeks, who were forced to move to Oklahoma in the late 1830s.

Other immigrants were from the British Isles but were not English. Many were Scottish and Scotch-Irish. The Scotch Irish were Scots who were moved to Northern Ireland by the English to control the native Irish population. However, due in part to rent increases in County Ulster, many began to move to such areas as Pennsylvania in the 1700s. From there, immigrants took the Great Pennsylvania Road into Appalachia. It was easier to move west and begin again on new land than to face possible poverty at home.

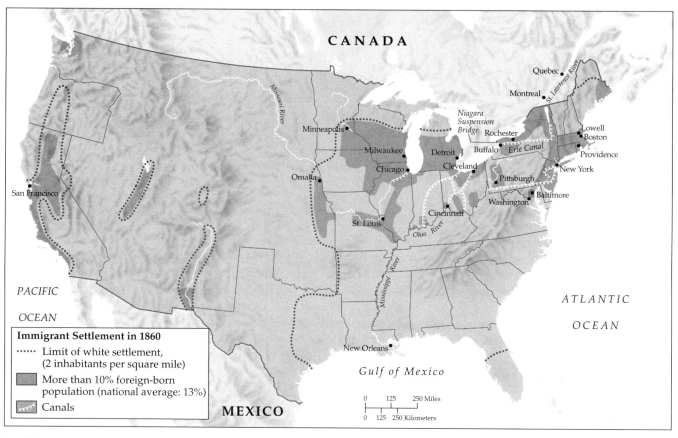

As this map of the United States in 1860 indicates, immigrants were an important part of the population that settled in the frontier regions of the Midwest and West Coast in the antebellum era. *(CARTO-GRAPHICS)*

Between 1760 and 1775, some 55,000 Protestant Irish had left Europe for North America, as did 40,000 Scots from 1770 to 1775. This equated to 2.3 percent of the Irish and 3 percent of the Scots living in Great Britain.

In the 1680s, Germans began to arrive in Pennsylvania, settling particularly in the area of Lancaster County. This influx of Pennsylvania "Dutch," as the Germans were called, continued into the eighteenth century. As a result of this and other migrations, 8.7 percent of the colonial population was German. The colonies also drew the Dutch (mainly to New York), the Irish, and French Huguenots. What was true prior to the American Revolution continued afterward. The United States remained a willing port of entry for various ethnic groups.

NINETEENTH CENTURY

Between 1750 and 1845, the population of Europe rose from 140 million to 250 million, an 80 percent increase. This was the result of better medical care and nutrition, which decreased the infant mortality rate and the

overall death rate. As the population grew, the percentage of arable land remained the same, making it difficult for rural Europeans to make a living. This problem was aggravated by inheritance practices in which the oldest children received the family's land, while younger children had no option but to fend for themselves. Many Europeans moved to the cities to try their fortune, a change that did not work for everyone.

Europe was also in the midst of a cultural flux. The Industrial Revolution contributed to the reorganization of social structure in the early nineteenth century. New factories took up even more land and displaced many farmers. Simultaneously, artisans were losing prominence as laborers of mass production took their place. Potential immigrants sensed that their traditions and beliefs were becoming outmoded, possibly even unnecessary. The pace of social and economic change was too great for some, who chose to immigrate to America to retain stability rather than lose it in countries shaken by the transition.

America held out a lure equal in power to the forces pushing immigrants out of Europe. Guidebooks on the new nation flooded the Continent, regaling

This 1852 woodcut by a Boston artist is captioned: "A company of Swedish emigrants passing our office, bound to the West"—most likely to the northern Midwest. *(Library of Congress)*

readers with stories of the golden land of opportunity that lay across the Atlantic. Adding to Europeans' temptations were letters from friends and relatives already living in the United States. These "America letters," as they were called, painted the writers' experiences in even rosier hues, in part because of the immigrants' desire to have familiar faces nearby once again.

Americans also tried to entice immigrants to move west. A number of speculating companies, or emigration companies, emerged in the 1840s. These companies took out advertisements in European newspapers in which they described the various joys of life in the United States, especially for farmers. The ads were far from altruistic. By 1866, each male immigrant was worth an average of $1,500 in direct and indirect taxes. Local governments had to bring in more people in order to increase their revenue. The end result would be beneficial to both parties.

The United States offered not only land but opportunity as well. After the American Revolution, the

nation's borders extended to the Mississippi River, which meant plenty of available land for those willing to work it. The size of the United States almost doubled in 1803 with the purchase of the Louisiana Territory from France. Texas added more land when it joined the Union in 1845 after gaining its independence from Mexico. In 1848, with the Treaty of Guadalupe Hidalgo that ended the war between the United States and Mexico, the United States had created for itself an empire that reached from the Atlantic to the Pacific. The land long inhabited by Native Americans was there for the taking, and millions of immigrants from abroad traveled west to use it.

In 1848, the discovery of gold at Sutter's Mill in northern California set off another wave of immigration westward. With and without families, tens of thousands of men the world over traveled to Sacramento and San Francisco in the hopes of striking it rich. Many remained in the area later on, becoming farmers. Others stayed in the cities to find jobs as teamsters and other common laborers. Still others capitalized on prospectors' newfound wealth, becoming merchants and traders.

The Homestead Act of 1862 made the West only more tempting. Congress designed the act to entice more settlers into the sparsely populated trans-Mississippi West. Interested parties would receive 160 acres of land for free as long as they settled their claim and produced a crop within five years. Millions of displaced Europeans flooded the region, particularly Wisconsin and Minnesota and such territories as Nebraska and the Dakotas.

As did the English in the seventeenth century, many immigrant groups traveled west in search of a new life, religious freedom, and a location where they could be left alone to rebuild communities that shared both faith and culture. Such disparate groups as Lutherans, Mennonites, Jews, and Mormons established separate settlements in the West. There they enjoyed the best of both worlds. Immigrants had vast, open territory as well as the ability to retain familiar patterns of life. By keeping traditions, language, and religion alive in the United States, immigrants created stability in what would otherwise have been insecure circumstances.

THE TRANS-APPALACHIAN WEST

Immigrant communities were a common sight in the trans-Appalachian West. Networks of families and friends relocated to establish their own enclaves of familiar culture or create ethnic neighborhoods in already settled American communities. Many remained farmers, as they had been in Europe. The soil of the Ohio and upper Mississippi River valleys was rich and fertile, perfect for growing crops. Other immigrants became merchants or laborers in one of the countless towns on the frontier. Soon they raised churches in keeping with their traditional faiths and schools in which their children could learn in their native languages.

As they had been before the American Revolution, the majority of immigrants before 1860 were of British and Irish descent. The British included individuals from England, Scotland, Wales, and even Canada. The Irish were the most numerous, but unlike their neighbors, they were not as easily assimilated into the community at large. The Irish came to the United States in large numbers beginning in the 1840s. Fleeing ever-increasing poverty and famine, they immigrated as a means for survival. Between 1847 and 1853, over 1 million Irish relocated across the Atlantic. Because they were poor and overwhelmingly Catho-

lic, they did not fit in well with the native population and were frequently subject to vicious prejudice.

Although most Irish immigrants remained in the cities of the eastern seaboard, some moved west. Few actually farmed, as they lacked the means to buy the land or the necessary supplies. Most of those who chose to go west did so along lines of transportation. These individuals worked as laborers, frequently helping to build or maintain the roads, canals, and railroads now extending into the frontier. In the 1850s, for example, the Irish were integral to the construction of the Illinois Central Railroad. The Irish continued this pattern across the Mississippi River.

Germans were the most insular of the early immigrant groups. The level of cohesion they kept was possible primarily due to their large numbers. In 1852, 100,000 Germans emigrated to the United States, and by 1860, one-third of all foreign-born Americans were German. Hoping to create a new homeland in the Midwest, particularly in Ohio, Wisconsin, Indiana, Illinois, and the trans-Mississippi state of Missouri, 47 percent of all German immigrants lived in these states alone.

German immigrants were separated from their American neighbors chiefly by language, which they fought to maintain as the language of their communities. Beyond this, however, Germans were a surprisingly heterogeneous group. Germany itself did not exist as a nation until the late nineteenth century. Anyone who spoke German was classified as German, whether he or she came from Austria, Bavaria, or Switzerland. Germans could also be Protestant, Catholic, or Jewish, and the types of Protestants were myriad. Finally, while many German immigrants remained farmers after their arrival in the United States, others were artisans forced out of work by increasing industrialization at home in the 1820s and 1830s, who plied their trades in town. Still other Germans joined the Irish in building the railroads.

Not only British, Irish, and Germans found the trans-Mississippi West a good place to settle. Many Belgians moved to Wisconsin between 1853 and 1857, establishing several of their own communities. Scandinavians moved to the region as well, primarily after the Civil War. In the North, Germans and Scandinavians settled in such cities on the Great Lakes as Milwaukee. In the late nineteenth century, Scandinavians, Poles, Czechs, and other Slavs moved to the industrial center of Chicago, hoping to find work in one of the local factories. Immigrants to the South, typically German, Irish, or French, moved primarily to New Orleans. Not including this urban element, foreign-born settlers before 1860 made up 10 to 15 percent of the frontier population.

Immigrants contributed heavily to the population and the development of the trans-Appalachian West. By the late nineteenth century, Wisconsin had the largest percentage of foreign-born residents of any state east of the Mississippi River. However, a vast territory lay beyond that river, waiting to be settled. As did native-born Americans, immigrants heard the call of the Far West and moved there in great numbers.

THE TRANS-MISSISSIPPI WEST

Immigrant settlement beyond the Mississippi continued along the same agricultural patterns as it had to the East. Germans continued to be the largest non-English-speaking immigrant group on the plains. By 1870, 25 percent of all Germans were farmers, constituting one-third of all foreign-born farmers. They located in the Upper Midwest and Texas, still holding to their homogeneous ethnic enclaves for security.

Soon the Germans were joined by other groups, particularly Scandinavians and Slavs. Most Scandinavians arrived after the Civil War, when a series of crop failures added to the pressures of life in Europe.

Between 1820 and 1860, 41,669 Scandinavians immigrated, compared with more than a million between 1860 and 1889. By 1914, about 2 million Scandinavians had emigrated to the United States. Norwegians were the most numerous. The majority moved to the Dakotas, with over half settling in North Dakota, Minnesota, and Wisconsin. Swedes and Danes lived more often in Nebraska and South Dakota.

Czechs were the most common Slavic group to head west. Primarily from Bohemia and Moravia, the first wave emigrated the late 1840s and 1850s after the European revolutions of 1848. These individuals settled in such cities as St. Louis, Chicago, or Milwaukee, as well as in Texas. In the 1860s, they settled in Illinois and the upper Mississippi River Valley, particularly Nebraska. Between 1850 and 1990, 200,000 Czechs emigrated to the United States. Other Slavs, such as Poles, who did not come to cities like Chicago, moved to Nebraska. Most arrived in the 1880s, becoming cotton farmers. Both Czechs and Poles tended to settle near Germans, as the German culture and behavior was more familiar and therefore more comfortable to them than that of native-born Americans.

Although most Irish immigrants continued to work as laborers and railroad workers, some created

As pioneers in the North Dakota Plains in the late 1800s, Norwegian immigrant Ole Myrvik and his family lived in typically primitive conditions. *(North Dakota Institute for Regional Studies and University Archives)*

farming communities in the Midwest. They were not alone. Mennonites, or Russian immigrants of German ancestry, began to arrive in the 1870s. They settled mainly in Kansas and Nebraska and grew wheat or other staples. Many Jewish immigrants also formed agricultural colonies in what they termed a "back to the soil" movement. Between 1881 and 1915, Jewish immigrants founded over forty agricultural colonies west of the Mississippi. Toward the end of the nineteenth century, Japanese immigrants began to arrive on the Pacific Coast. By the early twentieth century, Japanese comprised half of California's agricultural workers.

Immigrants also took up the herding of livestock. Many British immigrants were aristocrats hoping to make a living by owning cattle companies during the cattle boom of the late nineteenth century. West of the Rocky Mountains, Basques from the Pyrenees area of France eventually became shepherds after the Civil War.

Most Basques, however, along with countless other immigrants, first came to America in the hope of striking it rich in the gold rush of 1849. San Francisco became the hub for California's new population, beginning with the Irish, Germans, French, and British. In the 1860s, other groups, such as Italians, also arrived in the city. Many German Jews moved to San Francisco to become merchants. By 1877, 84 percent of western Jews lived in California, and 7 to 8 percent of San Franciscans were Jewish. Fifty percent of San Franciscans were foreign-born.

But not all immigrant miners were European. Lured by the promise of opportunity and prosperity, 300,000 Chinese emigrated to the United States between 1848 and 1882. Unlike Europeans, who frequently traveled in family groups, the Chinese population was overwhelmingly male, outnumbering Chinese women by a ratio of twenty to one. Fifty percent worked in mines and as laborers in western cities, primarily San Francisco. By 1873, the Chinese were the largest ethnic group of miners in California's gold region, native-born Americans included.

Immigrants took full advantage of the opportunities available at other mines throughout the West. Over twenty-five different nationalities moved to Utah to work in the mines. Cornish (England) immigrants worked chiefly in lead mining. Irishmen moved west to work in copper mines in Montana. By the turn of the century, Slavs (Croats, Slovenes, and Serbs) had moved to Montana to work in the coal mines.

The extension of railroads after the Civil War provided work and land for thousands of immigrants. In 1862, Congress passed the Pacific Railroad Act, which called for the creation of a transcontinental railroad. Approximately ten thousand Chinese went to work on the Central Pacific Railroad, heading east toward Utah. They comprised four-fifths of the labor force of railroad workers. Irish workers moved westward on the Union Pacific Railroad, continuing their pattern of labor on transportation lines. Other groups, such as Greeks, Italians, Japanese, and Mexicans, also worked on the rails. By 1909, first- and second-generation immigrants made up over 96 percent of those who built and maintained American railroads.

American railroad companies also had their own indirect link to immigrants. In 1871, the Northern Pacific Railroad created its Bureau of Immigration, which was designed to lure prospective settlers to the West. Agents then organized communities alongside the land owned by the railroads. Other railroads quickly imitated Northern Pacific's practices, supplying their own agents and recruiting settlers.

The most unusual group of immigrants transcended ethnic boundaries. After Brigham Young led his group of Latter Day Saints to Utah in the 1840s, European Mormons soon joined them. The earliest large groups of Danish arrivals in the United States were Mormons, as Mormon missionaries to Scandinavia had focused on Denmark more than Norway or Sweden. Thirty thousand Scandinavians immigrated, most of whom were Danish. Some forty thousand British Mormons did the same. By the late 1840s, 25 percent of British converts had already immigrated. They originated in a newly industrialized region of Britain, which meant they had to relearn farming when they arrived in Utah. Despite their economic differences, however, only the British integrated with American Mormons. The Scandinavians remained in separate communities, distinguished by language and culture.

ACCULTURATION AND AMERICANIZATION

People of many different ethnicities flooded the western United States in the nineteenth century. Each individual group dealt with the process of acculturation differently. Groups wishing to remain insular, for instance, took far longer accepting American ways. Americanization also depended on the willingness of native-born Americans as a whole to accept any particular immigrants. The more similar a given group's culture was to that of the majority, including language, custom, and, especially, faith, the more easily it could assimilate into the society at large. Native-born Americans felt more comfortable with immigrants with whom they shared common beliefs.

Politics also contributed to the pace of acculturation. Such ethnic groups as the Irish and Slavs generally voted Democrat, as did German Catholics and Lutherans. But other German Protestants voted Whig and later Republican. Scandinavians and British immigrants did the same. Particularly during and after the Civil War, immigrants who did not vote Republican were viewed by northern Americans with suspicion. In general, those immigrants who were more conservative politically tended to be accepted more quickly into the society at large.

Thus some ethnic groups became Americanized more quickly than others. Understandably, English immigrants acculturated faster than any other group due to their close cultural and linguistic ties to Americans. The process was slower for the Irish, who shared the same language and some of the culture but not the same faith. Of all the non-English-speaking immigrants, Scandinavians Americanized most quickly. On the other hand, Germans were in a more difficult situation. As noted above, Germans were not a homogenous group, representing various religious and cultural tendencies. All Germans were separated from the native-born by language. Beyond this, how quickly German immigrants acculturated depended on whether they were Protestant or Catholic, Republican or Democrat. German Protestants had an easier time assimilating than did their Catholic counterparts.

Jewish immigrants faced several difficulties. Early Jewish immigrants spoke German, and after 1880, they spoke Russian, Polish, Yiddish, or some other language not familiar to native Americans. They also practiced a non-Christian faith. Therefore, even after they integrated into society, they retained a sense of their distinctiveness. San Francisco became the hub of western American Judaism, publishing four Anglo-Jewish weekly newspapers devoted exclusively to a Jewish audience by the late nineteenth century.

For Chinese immigrants, acculturation was nearly impossible. Unlike European immigrants, they could not blend in physically with other Americans. They also faced the problem of combining two cultures that had little if anything in common, again unlike Europeans. Another problem was that the Chinese had saturated the California job market. In 1877, Californians upset with the prevalence of low-wage Chinese labor rioted in the streets of San Francisco. The Chinese were the first group restricted from the United States by law. In 1882, Congress passed the Chinese Exclusion Act, which banned continued immigration of Chinese laborers. They were soon replaced by Japa-

nese immigrants, who were also refused entry after 1908.

The difficulty of acculturating Chinese immigrants had more to do with the prejudices of native-born Americans than separatist tendencies on the part of the Chinese. The United States had pushed westward under the banner of Manifest Destiny, which decreed that "Providence" had given the land to white Americans to cultivate and civilize as they deemed suitable. This attitude depended in part on a belief in a racial hierarchy encompassing all humankind, later called social Darwinism. Under social Darwinism, Anglo-Saxons considered themselves the supreme race, which entitled them to dominate the continent.

Other races fell into lesser categories depending on their nation of origin. Americans considered Germans more capable of civilization than the Irish or eastern Europeans, and all Europeans were more "civilized" than Chinese or blacks. Many proponents of social Darwinism were uncertain that all immigrants could assimilate. In fact, some saw immigrants as causing the decline of civilization worldwide. As a result, many Americans became nativists, rejecting immigration as dangerous to American culture. Immigrants faced blatant discrimination, which they frequently avoided by remaining in ethnic enclaves, as did the Chinese.

Such nativist ideas also emerged in partisan politics. In the 1850s, the American, or Know-Nothing, Party established itself with distinctly anti-immigrant views. In California in the 1870s, the Workingmen's Party expressed its disgust at the flurry of Chinese entering at ports along the Pacific Coast, although Chinese immigration at its height made up only 5 percent of all immigration. In the 1890s, many midwestern and southern farmers established the People's Party, also called the Populist Party, one of whose platform planks was the limitation of immigration.

In 1890, the U.S. Census Bureau declared that the American frontier had closed, which meant that there was no longer a frontier line advancing across the continent. The population had reached 17.9 people per square mile. Americans could now consider the United States settled, said the bureau. There was no further need for western expansion. Yet this did not mean that the United States was fully developed. Much remained to be done in the American West to bring it up to the standards of "civilization" prevalent in the eastern states. Americans continued to expand their holdings in the West and establish towns and cities. Settlers and citizens worked together to shape the future of the region.

Immigrants continued to play a vital role in this effort. By 1890, 32.8 percent of the nation's population, or 20,645,542 Americans, were first- or second-generation immigrants, and most of these individuals lived in the West. In 1893, for example, Wisconsin had a higher proportion of foreign-born citizens than New York. And although the frontier had supposedly disappeared, immigrants continued to arrive in the West. Immigrants had been a part of western expansion since the beginning, with the first arrivals of Europeans on the continent. It only made sense that they would continue to aid western development after expansion had been officially completed.

Adrienne Caughfield

See also: Native Americans, Immigrants and the American Revolution (Part I, Sec. 1); Report of the Minnesota Board of Immigration, 1871 (Part IV, Sec. 2); Letters from Illinois, 1818 (Part IV, Sec. 3).

BIBLIOGRAPHY

Archdeacon, Thomas J. *Becoming American: An Ethnic History.* New York: Free Press, 1983.

Billington, Ray Allen. *Land of Savagery, Land of Promise: The European Image of the American Frontier in the Nineteenth Century.* New York: W. W. Norton, 1981.

Daniels, Roger. *Coming to America: A History of Immigration and Ethnicity in American Life.* New York: HarperCollins, 1990.

Dinnerstein, Leonard, Roger L. Nichols, and David M. Reimers. *Natives and Strangers: A Multicultural History of Americans.* New York: Oxford University Press, 1997.

Eblen, Jack E. "An Analysis of Nineteenth-Century Frontier Populations." *Demography* 2 (1965): 399–413.

Greene, Victor R. *American Immigrant Leaders, 1800–1910: Marginality and Identity.* Baltimore: Johns Hopkins University Press, 1987.

Hine, Robert V. *Community on the American Frontier: Separate but Not Alone.* Norman: University of Oklahoma Press, 1980.

Korytová-Magstadt, Stepanka. *To Reap a Bountiful Harvest: Czech Immigration beyond the Mississippi, 1850–1900.* Iowa City: Rudi Publishing, 1993.

Luebke, Frederick. "Ethnic Group Settlement on the Great Plains." *Western Historical Quarterly* 8:4 (1977): 405–30.

———, ed. *European Immigrants in the American West: Community Histories.* Albuquerque: University of New Mexico Press, 1998.

Merk, Frederick. *History of the Westward Movement.* New York: Alfred A. Knopf, 1978.

Noble, Allen G., ed. *To Build in a New Land: Ethnic Landscapes in North America.* Baltimore: Johns Hopkins University Press, 1992.

Rischin, Moses, and John Livingston, eds. *Jews of the American West.* Detroit: Wayne State University Press, 1991.

Woods, Lawrence M. *British Gentlemen in the Wild West: The Era of the Intensely English Cowboy.* New York: Free Press, 1989.

Section *3*

1880s TO 1920

Introduction

Causes of Immigration
Ewa Morawska

Immigration Stations
Robert F. Zeidel

Living Conditions
William Jenkins

Economics and Labor
Steve Burnett

Culture and Assimilation
Nancy C. Carnevale

INTRODUCTION

Entitled "1880s to 1920," Section 3 of Part I covers the history of one of the greatest waves of immigration in world history. Between 1880 and 1920, more than 20 million people immigrated to the United States. Moreover, most of these immigrants came from countries that had previously contributed few newcomers to the United States: Italy, Greece, Russia, Poland (then divided between Russia, Austria-Hungary, and Germany), and the numerous eastern and central European states that belonged to the Austro-Hungarian Empire in the pre–World War I era. The 1880s were chosen as the beginning point for this chapter because they witnessed a doubling of immigration over the previous decade, while 1920 was chosen as the endpoint because it falls roughly between World War I and passage of the restrictive quota laws of 1921 and 1924 that cut immigration to a trickle of what it had once been.

In "Causes of Immigration," Ewa Morawska primarily cites the urban-industrial transformation of southern and eastern Europe. As secondary factors that contributed to the expansion and the sustaining of the mass immigration, she examines the increasing geographic mobility of eastern, central, and southern Europeans during this period. Finally, she talks about how America had come to represent a "land of freedom" for the many oppressed peoples of the region, particularly the Jews.

In "Immigration Stations," Robert F. Zeidel looks at the various ports of entry for immigrants in the late nineteenth and early twentieth centuries, including both well-known ones—Ellis Island in New York and Angel Island in San Francisco—and the lesser known ports along the Atlantic, Gulf, and Pacific coasts.

William Jenkins' entry, "Living Conditions," opens with a discussion of immigrant neighborhoods and their institutions in America at the turn of the twentieth century. He then provides a look at daily life in the immigrant neighborhood before going on to describe housing conditions. Finally, he examines the health and sanitation conditions in the overcrowded immigrant ghettos.

In "Economics and Labor," Steve Burnett explores the economic reasons many immigrants had for coming and the ways in which they were fitted into America's new industrial order at the end of the nineteenth century. The first section of the article concerns how immigrants found jobs. Next, Burnett goes on to discuss employment patterns, whereby different immigrant groups ended up in different sectors of the economy. The author also provides a lengthy discussion of the ways in which immigrants resisted the most degrading and economically exploitative aspects of industrial work, including the formation of unions and the calling of strikes. Burnett concludes by considering the immigrant woman worker and her place in the American economy of the period.

Finally, in "Culture and Assimilation," Nancy C. Carnevale examines how immigrants during this period adapted themselves to American culture and society, as well as how these masses of newcomers reshaped American life. She begins with a survey of the most important cultural forums for immigrants—theater, music, dance, and literature. She also examines "popular folkways" as well as some of the popular cultural forms that took root in the immigrant community, including dance halls, nickelodeons, cafés, and saloons.

CAUSES OF IMMIGRATION

etween 1870 to 1914, a large new wave of European immigrants arrived on American shores, this time from the southern and eastern parts of the Continent. Whereas western and northern Europeans still constituted more than three-quarters of all arriving immigrants in 1880, twenty years later, 80 percent came from Russia, Austria-Hungary, and the southern parts of the Balkan Peninsula, Italy, Spain, and Portugal. Altogether, including returnees and multiple-entry visitors, more than 10 million southern and eastern European immigrants entered the United States during the forty years preceding the outbreak of World War I.

The causes of this mass transatlantic movement of southern and eastern Europeans were multiple, and they operated at different levels of sender and receiver society structures from large-scale socioeconomic and political forces to local communities of emigrants. Their cumulative effects accelerated the transatlantic flow over time, turning a trickle of less than 200,000 travelers in the 1870s into a multimillion flood in the 1900s that was interrupted only by the outbreak of World War I in Europe.

Two major sequences in this causal constellation can be distinguished as they evolved over the time period considered here: (1) the conditions that triggered or initiated this migratory movement, and (2) those that contributed to and sustained its growth. Each set of conditions involved multilevel factors from macrostructural economic and political forces, effects of (trans)local sociocultural norms and interactions in immigrants' communities to decisions and actions of individuals, but the specific configurations of these contributing components differed at each stage of the migratory process.

TRIGGERING CONDITIONS

Because the structure of interrelations known as the Atlantic world system provided the encompassing framework within which mass migrations of southern and eastern Europeans expanded over increasingly longer distances as the nineteenth century drew to a close, it should be considered first among the factors triggering this movement. The transatlantic system had matured from 1870 to 1914 through mutually reinforcing developments: significant improvements in long-distance transport and communication, expansion of commerce and capital flows, and, energizing all these, the acceleration of urbanization and industrialization that transformed the residential patterns and modes of production and labor both in Europe and in the Americas. Nevertheless, the duration and impetus of these developments and, therefore, their transformative effects differed significantly among regions.

The western regions of Europe, where (proto-) industrialization and urbanization had started two to three centuries earlier, were well advanced in these processes, while centrally located Germany was undergoing a forceful, centrally planned urbanization-industrialization that by 1914 had thoroughly transformed its western part. On the other side of the Atlantic, the United States developed in the same direction but much faster than did Great Britain, France, and Germany combined. (The industrial output of Germany nearly tripled between 1870 and 1910, whereas that of the United States increased sixfold.)

It was only in the last decades preceding World War I that southern and eastern Europe entered the process of accelerated urban-industrial transformation. This was a protracted, uneven, and incomplete modernization, encumbered by the ubiquitous remnants of premodern social forms and political institutions. It was constrained by the dependent character of these regions' economic advance, which lacked internal impetus and was significantly influenced by and subordinated to the far more developed Western countries. Still in 1900, the average proportion of southern and eastern European persons employed in agriculture was 70 percent (as compared with 10–15

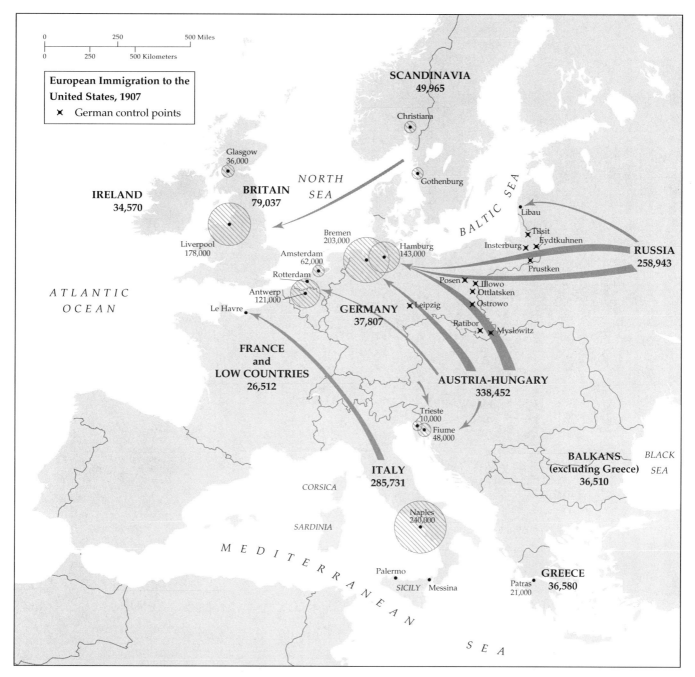

0   250   500 Miles
0   250   500 Kilometers

European Immigration to the
United States, 1907
  ✕   German control points

SCANDINAVIA
49,965

NORTH
SEA

Christiana

Glasgow
36,000

Gothenburg

BALTIC SEA

IRELAND
34,570

BRITAIN
79,037

Libau

Liverpool
178,000

Bremen
203,000

Hamburg
143,000

Insterburg ✕ ✕ Eydtkuhnen
✕ Tilsit

RUSSIA
258,943

Amsterdam
62,000

✕ Prustken

Rotterdam

Posen ✕ ✕ Illowo
✕ Ottlatsken
✕ Ostrowo

Antwerp
121,000

GERMANY
37,807

✕ Leipzig

ATLANTIC
OCEAN

Le Havre

Ratibor
✕ ✕ Mysłowitz

FRANCE
and
LOW COUNTRIES
26,512

AUSTRIA-HUNGARY
338,452

Trieste
10,000
Fiume
48,000

BALKANS
(excluding Greece)
36,510

BLACK
SEA

ITALY
285,731

CORSICA

Naples
240,000

SARDINIA

M E D I T E R R A N E A N

Palermo

SICILY Messina

Patras
21,000

GREECE
36,580

S E A

By the early twentieth century, European immigration patterns had changed dramatically from the early nineteenth century. Rather than coming from northern and western Europe, most immigrants were coming from the southern and eastern parts of the continent, although usually through northern European ports. *(CARTO-GRAPHICS)*

percent in the most advanced areas of the western part of the Continent), and per capita gross national product (GNP) in each region was only about 60 percent of that produced in the developed West. Nevertheless, profound structural relocations accompanying the belated urbanization-industrialization processes in southern and eastern Europe combined with a demographic explosion to impoverish and dislocate

large segments of the population, especially small landowners and landless peasants, as well as rural and small-town petty traders and craft workers, thus setting in motion millions of people in search of livelihoods. As modern transportation (especially rail and steamship), an integral component of the incorporation of southern and eastern Europe into the Atlantic world-system, became increasingly available in these

Irish immigrants, like these depicted in County Kerry in 1866, fled their island home because of poverty and hunger. *(Library of Congress)*

regions, those income-seeking migrants began to move in growing numbers toward more highly developed western parts of the Continent and to North America where rapidly growing economies needed large numbers of farm and industrial laborers and where even the lowest wages were 50–60 percent (western Europe) to 100–400 percent (United States) higher than in their home country.

Triggered, then, by structural relocations of masses of people in southern and eastern European economies ("push" forces), on the one hand, and by the increasing demand for manual labor in the rapidly expanding economies of the highly developed northwestern parts ("pull" forces), on the other, the increase in size and distance of migrations across and, of concern here, outside these restructuring regions was both a consequence and a constituent part of their incorporation into the Atlantic world-system. Historians estimate that the combined short- and longer-distance

seasonal and permanent migrations by southern and eastern Europeans between 1870 and 1914 affected no less than 25–30 percent of the total population in these regions.

While the push (from southern and eastern Europe) and pull (to western Europe and North America) forces at the upper structures of the Atlantic capitalist world-system created general vectors of movement or so-called compass (southeast-northwest) migrations, it was at the level of migrants' immediate surroundings that the actual decisions to travel were made and actions undertaken. In the initial phase of cross-continental and, especially, transatlantic migrations of southern and eastern Europeans, these decisions were prompted by west European and, of concern here, American employment agents who, to secure much-needed labor, combed towns and villages in these regions to recruit workers. After the contracting of labor was officially outlawed by the

U.S. government in 1885, the agents of western steamship companies took over the solicitation of potential migrants, covering European parishes, towns, and villages and visiting the marketplace. This advertising and solicitation of employment and transportation agencies performed the function, in the words of a turn-of-the-twentieth-century student of new immigrants in America, of "opening new regions [of southern and eastern Europe] which are ripe for emigration and in setting the ball rolling."

As contemporary reports indicate, the first "converts" won by these soliciting agents—the pioneer transatlantic migrants—tended to be socially peripheral members of their community. Many of them, having spent a few years in the United States, returned to their home village or town and then came back again, bringing with them a group of relatives and neighbors. For example, in a typical pattern, transatlantic migrations from Maszkienice in Galicia developed only after a seed group of the local people had formed in America. In 1888, the first pioneer, persuaded by an acquaintance from the neighboring village who had been solicited by a steamship company agent, gave up his accustomed income-seeking travels to nearby Ostrava and accompanied the acquaintance to Pennsylvania to dig coal. After one year, he brought over two of his relatives; more Maszkienicans followed—men first and then also women and children— so that by 1900, seventeen lived in the same American town.

Economic push-and-pull forces had constituted the underlying forces that triggered income-seeking migrations of southern and eastern Europeans across the Continent and to North America. But for some eastern European groups, the civic constraints that accompanied the region's economic restructuring and the concurrent development of modern nationalism and aspirations to state sovereignty among politically subordinated groups provided a reinforcing reason to emigrate.

Eastern European Jews, particularly residents of the so-called Pale of Jewish Settlement in the Russian Empire, home to nearly three-quarters of the approximately 7 million Jews in the region, were victimized by a series of expulsion decrees and restrictive legal statutes issued during the thirty-five-year period after the assassination of Czar Alexander II. The hostile policies of the czarist regime fomented popular violence (so-called pogroms) against Jewish persons and property. Although in the Polish part of the Austrian monarchy Jews had been granted civil rights and legal protection, in practice residential and occupational exclusion and harassment of Jewish citizens were common. The Hungarian political elite, concerned with

the growing nationalist consciousness and separatist aspirations among non-Hungarian, especially Slovak and Rusyn, groups in the multiethnic Hungarian monarchy, implemented hostile legal-political measures aimed at controlling and, ultimately, suppressing these developments. Considerably larger proportions of Jews (27 percent) and Slovaks (9 percent) among turn-of-the-century eastern Europeans in the United States (there are no data for Rusyns) than the proportion of these groups in home-country populations (10 percent and 2.5 percent, respectively) suggest the operation "reinforced" existing economic-political causes for their emigration.

EXPANDING AND SUSTAINING CONDITIONS

Although the U.S. share was only 30–35 percent of the southern and eastern European income-seeking travelers between 1870 and 1914, including seasonal short- and middle-distance harvest migrations, intra-regional movement from countryside to expanding cities, and long-distance migrations to farms and factories in more western parts of the Continent and across the Atlantic, the number of migrants heading for America nevertheless grew rapidly over time. Whereas in 1880 the reported foreign-born population from Russia, Austria-Hungary, Italy, Greece, Spain, and Portugal combined was smaller than 300,000, it was about 2 million in 1900 and more than 5 million in 1910.

The factors that contributed to and sustained the rapid growth of transatlantic migrations from southern and eastern Europe were not the same as those which triggered this movement. Developmental discrepancies between southern and eastern Europe and the western parts of the Continent and, still more pronounced, the United States, along with the push-and-pull economic pressures they generated within the Atlantic world-system, combined with the facilitating impact of advances in modern transportation and its soliciting agents, remained the framing conditions of southeast-to-northwest, income-seeking migrations, including those across the Atlantic. Within this macrostructural framework, however, new forces emerged over time that caused transatlantic travels to grow rapidly in volume and to continue uninterrupted until they were halted by the world war.

Most of these developments operated in immigrants' local communities. Before considering these local conditions, however, one should note an important factor in the broader political ramifications of turn-of-the-century mass immigration to the United States that made the continued expansion of U.S.-bound travels from southern and eastern Europe possible. Despite publicly expressed anxieties regarding the increasing influx from southern and eastern Europe of the so-called "New Immigrants," whom the dominant white Anglo-Saxon groups perceived as racially inferior, throughout the period considered here and with the exception of individual entrants excluded for poor health or moral conduct, the United States maintained an open-door immigration policy (excepting Chinese and Japanese)—a situation that both invited and facilitated the growing number of these new immigrants.

Even though turn-of-the-century migrations across the Atlantic had constituted just a fraction of the total volume of movement within and from southern and eastern Europe, it was only America that had a "great legend" of unmatched riches awaiting immigrants. First introduced by agents of American employers and European steamship companies, fantastic news about the "golden land" spread through European villages and towns by immigrant letters and returning migrants. Intense circulation of international mail—more than 5 million letters were sent between 1900 and 1906 alone from the United States to southern and eastern Europe—comparing immigrant laborers' earnings with those obtained at home and showing photographs of well-fed and urbanely dressed *Amerikanci* (Americans) spread "American fever" among local residents. It was further fueled by the remittances sent home from America and moneys brought by returnees. During the six years from 1900 to 1906, the total American money received in Russia and Austria-Hungary from its émigrés was a staggering $69 million. At county levels, these were huge sums of money, larger than any previously handled by local postmasters: in 1906, for example, the little village of Cetinje in Montenegro received $30,000, and in Maszkienice in 1901, the combined postal remittances and personal savings brought back by returnees averaged $850 per capita, or the equivalent of the purchase price for three to four acres of land.

The enormous amount of dollars that had come into the possession of local households as the result of American income-seeking migrations—plainly visible to all as it was turned into land, cattle, brick houses, barns, and better food and dress—fortified the belief of those who had not yet gone themselves that America was the true El Dorado. Louis Adamic, an immigrant from the small town of Blato in Slovenia, recalled experiencing "a thrill" every time someone returned from the United States urbanely dressed

and bearing opulent gifts for family and friends, as well as the ambition to go to America kindled in young men in the village by these sights. A typical recollection (from a village in Congress, Poland) describes this demonstration effect particularly well: "When, after a few years spent in America, Walenty Podlasek returned to Wierzchoslawice, such processions of people visited him every day that he was forced to hide.... [And when] with the dollars he brought with him [he] purchased a dozen or so hectares and started to build [a new house], the people went wild with envy and desire."

The demonstration effect of the successful, income-seeking Amerikanci had a strong multiplier impact on the expanding volume of transatlantic migrations. For some, the image of the United States as "that incredible land of gold" was accompanied—and reinforced—by a vision of America as "the land of freedom." As immigrant letters suggest, such fused, economic-political representation mobilized a number of eastern European peasants who understood "freedom" in terms of their own experience in a region that was still sunk waist deep in feudal remnants as a freedom from *poddanstwo*—"serfdom," in Polish, here meaning the subordination in social demeanor and cultural mores of the class of toilers to the class of *pany*, or the genteel possessors of means and status—which they contrasted with the egalitarian manners of Americans.

The representation of America as "the land of freedom" was a more common and more "energizing" contributor to the spread of American fever among Russian Jews because they were subject to harsh civic constraints at home, especially since the 1880s, and because it was reinforced by important group symbolism. The majority of Slavic, Italian, and Hungarian migrants to America intended their sojourns there to be temporary: a few years of hard labor to save enough money to secure financial independence and, they hoped, a considerably improved existence for the family at home. Indeed, large proportions of immigrants, between 35 and 60 percent, depending on the group, returned to their home country. Jews, most of whom intended their emigrations to be permanent and whose return rate was less than 7 percent, were the exception. Historians' explanations of the exodus of eastern European Jews to America at the turn of the twentieth century point out an extra factor, absent among non-Jewish migrants, that contributed to the unusually high rate of their mass emigration—namely, the symbolic joining of the collective movement to America with one of the most powerful images in the Jewish Great Tradition, that of the Exodus of the Jewish people from Egyptian slavery and their march toward the Promised Land. In Mary Antin's city of Plotsk, Poland, it became common to conclude the Passover Haggadah with "Next Year in America!" in place of the customary "Next Year in Jerusalem!"

One more factor was a constitutive component of the set of conditions responsible for the increase of transatlantic migrations across southern and eastern Europe. Regardless of travelers' provenance and their national/ethnic origins and whether their motivations were purely economic or also political or cultural, mass migrations at the turn of the century were not an individual but a collective movement. The social networks created in this process played a very significant role in channeling and expanding these ventures into the outside world and to faraway America.

Particularly important were networks of information about prospective jobs and wages; once the decision to travel was made, assistance in organizing passage, and, upon arrival, help in finding lodging and employment. According to a study by the U.S. Immigration Commission conducted in 1908–9, nearly two-thirds of the newcomers from southern and eastern Europe declared that their passage was arranged by immigrants already in this country. An even greater number were headed for destinations—primarily large industrial cities and smaller towns in the eastern and midwestern United States—where relatives or acquaintances from their hometown or village waited for them. Most new immigrants, more than 90 percent, found employment as unskilled laborers in American factories, steel mills, and coal mines (Slavs and Hungarians) and in railroad and building construction (Italians); eastern European Jews, two-thirds of whom were employed as skilled manual workers, primarily in the garment industry, were the exception. The hiring of new employees in all these workplaces relied on informal networks that the immigrants themselves provided, and the work process itself involved groups, usually of the same origin.

As social networks of information, travel, and employment assistance directed the increasing flow of immigrants to places where the original colonies of settlers had formed, home-country communities were partially reestablished in American cities. "We have here now the second Babica [a village in southern Poland]," wrote an immigrant from Detroit in his letter home thirty years after the first Babican arrived there in 1883. Podgaje, split by a long-standing feud between two groups over local pasture, transplanted this division across the Atlantic as subsequent immigrants followed their assistance networks; by 1920, a community of Podgajans from the left side of the village existed in Elizabeth, New Jersey, and from the right side, in Detroit.

This partial transplantation of home-country com-munities from southern and eastern Europe to American cities and a continuous back-and-forth flow of people created translocal communities extending across the Atlantic. These transatlantic communities were supported by complex networks of communication, travel, and employment assistance. At the same time, these communities performed an important function of sustaining the movement of people by turning transatlantic migrations into socially accepted behavior in home-country towns and villages and making migration possible through practical assistance to those who decided to go.

The outbreak of World War I in Europe in 1914 and, in its wake, the implementation of immigration restrictions by the United States that effectively ended its long-standing open-door policy, first halted completely and then cut back to a trickle the influx from southern and eastern Europe. The Great Depression on both sides of the Atlantic further diminished international travel. At the outbreak of World War II, the developmental gap between southern and eastern Europe and western parts of the Continent and North America combined still remained large. Both regions entered the postwar era economically underdeveloped, with a large rural proletariat, and were still "emigration unsaturated."

Incorporated into the Soviet bloc, eastern European countries were separated from the rest of the world by the Iron Curtain. The main form of mass migration, from the conclusion of the war through the 1960s (and in Russia throughout the next two decades), were internal population movements from the countryside to the rapidly developing cities and industries during the accelerated economic perestroikas centrally planned and administered by Communist Party authorities. After the collapse of Soviet communist regimes in the region in 1989–90 and the easing of restrictions of travel to the West, income-seeking westbound migrations resumed on a mass scale, although their American component greatly decreased. Even though they contain important elements from the turn-of-the-twentieth-century set of westbound migration causes at both macro- (the enduring, even deepened by several decades of inefficient communist management of regional economies, developmental disparity between Eastern European and Western countries) and microlevels (migrants' primary reliance on informal social support networks in their travels), the factors triggering and sustaining turn-of-the-twenty-first-century international (also U.S.-bound) travels of Eastern Europeans differ significantly from those of the last century.

In contrast, post–World War II southern Europe slaked its "migration thirst" as it became reincorpor-

This 1892 painting depicts starving Russian peasants making their way to St. Petersburg. Many immigrants moved to major cities in their homelands before coming to America. *(Library of Congress)*

ated into the Western system of exchange of capital and labor that emerged in the 1950s and 1960s. In this case, too, the role of the United States as a receiver of labor migration greatly decreased; wage-seeking migrants in southern parts of Europe were vigorously recruited by governments of western and northern European countries. As the position of southern European countries, included one after another in the economic and political structures of the European Community, progressively improved over the next thirty years, higher income-seeking compass migrations of their citizens gradually abated, and they began to attract increasing numbers of immigrants from less developed parts of the world, including Eastern Europe.

Ewa Morawska

See also: Economics I: Pull Factors, Economics II: Push Factors, Natural Disasters, Environmental Crises, and Overpopulation, Political, Ethnic, Religious, and Gender Persecution (Part II, Sec. 1).

BIBLIOGRAPHY

Adamic, Louis. "The Land of Promise." *Harper's Magazine*, October 1931.

Antin, Mary. *The Promised Land.* Boston: Houghton Mifflin, 1912; New York: Arno Press, 1980.

Balch, Emily. *Our Slavic Fellow Citizens.* New York: Charities Publication Committee, 1910; New York: Arno Press, 1969.

Berend, Ivan, and Gyorgi Ranki. *The European Periphery and Industrialization, 1780–1914.* New York: Columbia University Press, 1982.

Berger, David, ed. *The Legacy of Jewish Migration: 1881 and Its Impact.* New York: Columbia University Press, 1983.

Bodnar, John. *The Transplanted: A History of Immigrants in Urban America.* Bloomington: Indiana University Press, 1985.

Briani, Vittorio. *L'Emigrazione italiana ieri e oggi.* Detroit: Blaine Ethridge Books, 1979.

Bujak, Franciszek. *Maszkienice. Wies powiatu brzeskiego: Stosunki gospodarcze i spoleczne.* Kracow: Gebethner, 1901.

Chirot, Daniel. *Social Change in the Modern Era.* San Diego: Harcourt and Brace, 1986.

Duda-Dziewierz, Krystyna. *Wies malopolska a emigracja Amerykanska: Studium wsi babica powiatu rzeszowskiego.* Warsaw: Dom Ksiazki, 1937.

Ferenczi, Imre, and Walter Willcox. *International Migrations.* 2 vols. Geneva: International Labor Office, 1929.

Glatz, Ferenc, ed. *Hungarians and Their Neighbors in Modern Times, 1867–1950.* New York: Columbia University Press, 1995.

Gliwicowna, Maria. "Drogi emigracji." *Przeglad Socjologiczny* 4 (1936).

Gould, J. D. "European Intercontinental Emigration, 1815–1914: Patterns and Causes." *Journal of European Economic History* 8:3, (1979): 593–681.

———. "European Inter-Continental Emigration: The Role of 'Diffusion' and Feedback." *Journal of European Economic History* 9:1 (1980): 41–112.

Higham, John. *Strangers in the Land: Patterns of American Nativism, 1860–1925.* New Brunswick, NJ: Rutgers University Press, 1988.

Krajlic, Frances. "Croatian Migration to and from the United States between 1900 and 1914." Ph.D. diss., New York University, 1975.

Kraut, Alan. *Silent Travelers: Germs, Genes, and the "Immigrant Menace."* New York: Basic Books, 1994.

Kula, Witold, Nina Assorodobraj Kula, and Marcin Kula, eds. *Writing Home: Immigrants in Brazil and the United States, 1890–1891.* Transl. from Polish and Yiddish by Josephine Wtulich. New York: Columbia University Press, 1986.

Nugent, Walter. *Crossings: The Great Transatlantic Migrations, 1870–1914.* Bloomington: Indiana University Press, 1992.

Piore, Michael. *The Birds of Passage: Migrant Labor in Industrial Societies.* New York: Cambridge University Press, 1979.

Senate. *Reports of the U.S. Immigration Commission: Immigrants in Cities,* pt. 4. 61st Cong. 2d sess. S. Doc. 338. Washington, DC: Government Printing Office, 1911.

Senate. *Reports of the U.S. Immigration Commission: Immigrants in Industries,* pt. 2. 61st Cong., 2d Sess., S. Doc. 633. Washington, DC: Government Printing Office, 1911.

Witos, Wincenty. *Moje wspomnienia.* Paris: Kultura, 1964.

Wyman, Mark. *Round-Trip to America: The Immigrants Return to Europe, 1880–1930.* Ithaca: Cornell University Press, 1993.

IMMIGRATION STATIONS

The contrary experiences of the Irish woman Annie Moore and the Chinese man Lin help to convey the history of America's immigration stations. Moore, the first arrival at the newly opened Ellis Island in New York harbor, received greetings and a $10 gold piece from Immigration Commissioner John B. Weber. Lin, detained at Angel Island in San Francisco, wrote poetically on his cell wall of having been arrested and imprisoned. These disparate stories explain the dual purpose of America's immigrant portals: welcome those who were entitled to land, and screen out those whom the law excluded.

During the mass immigration period, from the 1880s to the mid-1920s, America's immigration stations processed over 25 million alien arrivals. Photographs show the diverse people, dressed in their native attire and lugging their assorted belonging, some clenching their papers in their teeth, coming ashore to begin the admission process. Inspectors checked each immigrant's health and character, thereby deciding who was fit to pass through the gates. Those deemed statutorily unfit or unwanted were denied entrance. For the vast majority who passed muster, enduring the indignities meant admission to the United States, a chance to add to America's increasingly diverse ethnic mosaic; for those denied, it meant the frustration or heartbreak of exclusion. The latter individuals did get a Board of Special Inquiry hearing and could appeal to the secretary of the treasury or (after 1903) commerce and labor, but often these procedures only postponed their deportation.

ELLIS ISLAND

Ellis Island, America largest and most famous immigration station, opened on January 1, 1892. Drawing its name from seventeenth-century owner Samuel Ellis, the island previously had served as a military fort and munitions depot. It replaced the outdated immigration station at Castle Garden, which had been in operation since 1855, and a temporary facility at the nearby Barge Office, both located at Manhattan's southern tip. Ellis Island's first structures, built wholly out of wood, burned in 1897, and the new buildings (those which survive as the National Immigration Museum) opened in 1900. During the intervening years, immigrant processing returned to the Barge Office.

From 1892 to 1924, Ellis Island welcomed about three-fourths of all U.S. immigrants. Its numerical predominance made it, along with the nearby Statue of Liberty, a universal symbol of American immigration. Representatives of literally every European group, and even some non-Europeans, passed through its doors. At its peak, the station had a staff of 700, with the capability of processing 5,000 arrivals per day. The 1900 station included the main building, a bathhouse, restaurant, laundry, and hospital, the last of which occupied an adjacent new island. When their ships docked, immigrants passed through the "great registry room," where they received their medical examinations and background checks. Those admitted then could buy tickets, at times from decidedly corrupt agents, for several railroads and coastal steamship lines, which would take them to their final destinations. Those detained remained on the island until they won an appeal or were sent back. Most stayed only from one to two weeks, and some returned on the same ship that had brought them to America.

With immigration's decline, due first to World War I and then to the implementation of restrictive quotas, Ellis Island devoted more time to detention and deportation and less to immigrant processing. The station admitted 878,000 arrivals in 1914, but only 327,000 in 1915. By 1918, the number had declined to about 29,000. The numbers increased significantly in the immediate postwar years, but the quotas quickly brought them back down. During the war, the gov-

Between its opening in 1892 and the passage of the 1924 quota act that cut immigration dramatically, the Ellis Island immigration station welcomed more than three-quarters of all newcomers to America. *(L.A. Raman/Impact Visuals)*

ernment interned German seamen and suspected alien enemies at the station; after the war, during the Red Scare, this focus changed to subversive radicals, including those deported on the *Buford*, or "Red Ark." Ellis Island thereafter continued to serve as a detention and deportation station, but its years as an immigrant entry point had ended. The station closed in 1954.

Ellis Island subsequently reopened as America's National Immigration Museum. In 1965, President Lyndon Johnson made the deteriorating station part of the Statue of Liberty National Monument, and planning began for its preservation and restoration. After several fits and starts, the museum opened amid great fanfare in September 1990.

ANGEL ISLAND

Angel Island occupies a far different place in American immigration history. If Ellis Island was a gateway,

Angel Island was a gate. During its years of operation from 1910 to 1940, an estimated 100,000 immigrants, mostly Asians, passed through the station. Chinese, numbering some 60,000, made up the largest group, and while most of these did gain entrance, their exclusion rate of one in six was much higher than that for the overwhelmingly European immigrants who passed through Ellis Island. The historian Roger Daniels has aptly described Angel Island as "a useful symbol of the invidious ways in which the American government treated Asian immigrants between 1875 and 1965."

Angel Island consists of 740 acres in San Francisco Bay. Named by the Spanish explorer Juan Manuel de Ayala in 1775, it served a variety of purposes—Russian fur trade post, Mexican cattle ranch, and U.S. army post—before its use as an immigration facility. San Francisco's quarantine station opened on its northwest side in 1892, and an immigration station began operation at the island's north-shore China Cove in 1910. Prior thereto, immigrants landed at the city's wharfs. The Angel Island station, allegedly modeled on Ellis Island, included barracks, a hospital, and various administrative and support buildings, all made of wood. A forty-minute ferry ride across the bay separated the immigrants from their coveted new home on the mainland. The station remained in operation until 1940, when a fire destroyed the administration building, and the last immigrants were moved to the mainland.

Squalid conditions and poor treatment characterized Angel Island. Complaints of filthy accommodations and a lack of proper sanitation plagued the station from the start. Acting Commissioner Luther C. Steward called it an "outrage on civilization," but nothing was ever done to alleviate this terrible state of affairs. Inadequate surroundings amplified the asperity of the immigrants' entry examinations. Inspectors grilled the arrivals, looking for any discrepancy in their story, any reason to order their exclusion. Hearings could take a week or more, and some immigrants waited for months to learn their fate. It was at these times that they inscribed the walls with their poignant poetry, venting their frustration at what they saw as abusive treatment.

Angel Island later became a state park. Starting in 1954, it first encompassed the quarantine station and in 1962 added the immigration station. Appreciation for the poems led to conversion of the old barracks into the Angel Island Museum. Clearly, Angel Island manifested the anti-Asian-American attitudes and policies, as well as the various exclusionary laws, that persisted through passage of the Immigration and Nationality Act of 1965 and beyond. The museum stands as an enduring reminder of America's historically poor treatment of Asian immigrants.

OTHER IMMIGRANT PORTS

Although New York and San Francisco were the predominant immigrant ports of entry, other stations also welcomed or rejected large numbers of new arrivals. These included Boston, Philadelphia, and Baltimore on the East Coast; New Orleans and Galveston on the Gulf of Mexico; Portland on the Pacific Coast; and Hawaii. The particular groups that landed at each place enhanced the development of local ethnic communities.

ATLANTIC STATIONS

Boston began the nineteenth-century as one of America's most Anglo-Saxon communities, but by the time that the restrictive quotas ended the period of mass immigration, it trailed only New York City as an immigrant entry point. The bustling New England port received little immigration until 1847, when the potato famine Irish began their influx. The American terminus of the British Cunard Line, Boston attracted over 20,000 Irish immigrants annually until 1854, and while the numbers declined during the Civil War years, the Irish thereafter again predominated. Others, including Italians, Jews, and substantial numbers of Canadians from the Maritime Provinces, began to join the influx in the 1880s and 1890s. The number of Boston immigrants reached an all-time high of 70,164 in 1907. These new arrivals contributed to the city's increasing ethnic diversity. For example, the North End saw the decline of its original Yankee character and culture, as the neighborhood filled first with Irish, then Jews, and, later, Italians.

Philadelphia, conversely, from the time of its colonial origins, always has been an immigrant city, but it never became a major immigrant port. Its inland location on the Delaware River and its proximity to New York City limited the number of foreigners who arrived directly from Europe. Of these, British, Germans, and Scandinavians predominated during the 1870s and 1880s, giving way in the 1890s to growing numbers of southern and eastern Europeans. The immigration station was located on Washington Avenue, in the heart of the city's wharf district, and although not all ships docked at the station, it supplied inspectors for those docking at several nearby piers. In 1909, in an effort to alleviate some of the crowding at Ellis Island, Congress appropriated funds for building several new stations, including one at Philadelphia. Construction began, but first World War I and then the restrictive quotas effectively eliminated its need. The facilities were never completed, and destruction of the inadequate Washington Avenue station in 1915 necessitated that inspections thereafter be done on board the ships.

Baltimore completed the triumvirate of smaller Atlantic Coast immigrant entry ports. Its station, initially a privately run boarding house, was located on Piers 8 and 9 at Locust Point. Because of its connection with the nation's interior via the Cumberland Road, Baltimore began to attract significant numbers of immigrants in the 1820s. Railroads and canals soon augmented its inland transportation options. These, as well as the jobs that they created, attracted English, Irish, and German settlers. Immigration, which rebounded after a decline during the Civil War, reached an average annual high of about forty thousand during the early part of the years 1910–19. The government built new processing facilities in 1913, but their use was short-lived. World War I began Baltimore's permanent decline as an immigrant port.

GULF STATIONS

Early immigrants arriving at New Orleans entered a decidedly non-American city. When President Thomas Jefferson initiated its purchase in 1802–3, he helped to buy a city with a deeply embedded Spanish, French, and African-American culture. Unlike its Atlantic and Pacific Coast counterparts, New Orleans's most significant immigration took place prior to the Civil War, about 550,000 or 10 percent of the U.S. total. Sizable numbers of German, Irish, French, and Italian immigrants then arrived in the Crescent City, and while many moved on, others stayed, adding to the existing ethnic diversity. A yellow fever outbreak in 1853–54 led the city to build an outlying quarantine station, followed by a permanent onshore processing facility in 1859. By that time, railroad lines from the Atlantic ports made redundant New Orleans's Mississippi River connection with the nation's interior. Immigration began to decline, and although the U.S. government built a new station in 1913, New Orleans did not play a major role during the mass migration period.

Galveston, Texas, located on a small island approximately thirty miles south of Houston, did make a notable contribution to early-twentieth-century immigration. The Galveston movement, directed by philanthropist Jacob H. Schiff, sought to settle large numbers of persecuted eastern European Jews throughout the American West. This highly organized effort decided to route them through the Galveston station because of its small size, railroad connections, and direct service from Germany by steamship line. Between 1907 and 1914, 10,000 eastern European Jews passed through the station.

PACIFIC STATIONS

San Francisco's Angel Island processed most Asian immigrants, but Seattle, Portland, and Los Angeles did welcome small numbers. At Portland, for example, the U.S. government employed state officials to process immigrants. After its acquisition by the United States in 1898, large numbers of Asian immigrants continued to go to Hawaii. Japanese Americans eventually became Hawaii's largest ethnic group.

Robert F. Zeidel

See also: Transit and Transportation of Recent Illegal Immigrants (Part II, Sec. 2).

BIBLIOGRAPHY

Coan, Peter Morton. *Ellis Island Interviews: In Their Own Words.* New York: Facts on File, 1977.

Daniels, Roger. "No Lamps Were Lit for Them: Angel Island and the Historiography of Asian American Immigration." *Journal of American Ethnic History* 17 (Fall 1997): 3–18.

Lia, Him Mark, Judy Yung, and Genny Lim. *Island: Poetry and History of Chinese Immigrants on Angel Island, 1910–1940.* San Francisco: Hoc Doi, 1980.

Marinbach, Bernard. *Galveston: Ellis Island of the West.* Albany: State University of New York Press, 1983.

McGinty, Brian. "Angel Island: The Door Half Closed." *American History Illustrated* (September/October 1990): 50–51, 71.

Perec, Georges, with Robert Bober. *Ellis Island.* New York: New Press, 1995.

Pitkin, Thomas M. *Keepers of the Gate: A History of Ellis Island.* New York: New York University Press, 1975.

Stolarik, M. Mark, ed. *Forgotten Doors: The Other Ports of Entry to the United States.* Philadelphia: Balch Institute Press, 1988.

Yans-McLaughlin, Virginia, and Marjorie Lightman. *Ellis Island and the Peopling of America.* New York: New Press, 1997.

ℒIVING CONDITIONS

By 1900, immigrants from all parts of Europe, Asia, Canada, and Mexico were present to varying degrees and numbers in American cities, towns, and rural areas. They were divided mainly between two groups. The "old immigrants" from northwestern Europe (Ireland, Britain, France, Holland, the German states, and Scandinavia), whose migration was focused around the 1830–80 period, were primarily Protestants (except the mostly Catholic Irish) who established themselves both as farmers and as prominent urban dwellers. The "new immigrants" from southern and central Europe (Italy, Austria-Hungary, Poland, and Russia), whose volumes increased sharply after 1880, consisted of a mix of Catholics and Jews (Table 1). Given the levels of poverty from which they escaped, the closure of the American farming frontier, and the advance of industrialization, these recent arrivals headed primarily for the largest cities such as New York, Philadelphia, Chicago, and Boston. Immigrants from other places, also quite impoverished upon entry, were more regionally concentrated than the Europeans. Mexicans were dispersed around rural Texas and the southwest; the Chinese resided in both rural California and in San Francisco, while most of the Japanese labored on Hawaiian sugar plantations. Dubbed "the Chinese of the Eastern States," French Canadians also crowded into New England's cities and mill towns. The national origin and economic status of all these immigrants, as well as their length of residence in the United States, did much to determine the conditions under which they lived by the turn of the century.

IMMIGRANT NEIGHBORHOODS AND THEIR INSTITUTIONS

As a key strategy of adaptation to urban America, immigrants usually strove to reside in close proximity to their fellow countrymen and countrywomen in the immigrant neighborhood. Chain migration transplanted networks of family and friends from European villages to American neighborhoods, thus the patterns of living that confronted new immigrants were not as dislocating as one might expect. Immigrant languages and customs survived, and social relations were reconstituted in secure and friendly "safe havens." Such clustering produced many a "Little Italy," "Little Poland," "Little Bohemia," or "Chinatown" in American cities by the turn of the twentieth century. Regarded with disdain by Progressive reformers of the time, these neighborhoods, many of which were deeply entrenched in poverty, were full of everyday meaning for their inhabitants.

The world of the neighborhood and its institutions facilitated the integration of immigrants, many of whom did not speak English, into American life throughout the nineteenth century. The durability of immigrant neighborhoods and their institutions would have been difficult without the support of a small but influential middle-class sector of self-employed entrepreneurs or "ethnic leaders." Although many immigrants who could afford it donated part of their household income to the institutions' development, the inspiration provided and loans negotiated by ethnic leaders were crucial for their establishment.

Such efforts produced a matrix of economic and cultural institutions in these neighborhoods. Savings and loan banks extended loans to immigrants for first mortgages on real estate or credit to immigrant businesspeople. Social clubs and nationalist societies abounded to maintain immigrants' awareness of their origins. The Germans had sport-centered *turnverein*, the Poles had the *Gminska Polska* to sponsor amateur theater, and the Chinese had the *huiguan* and *tong*. Ethnic newspapers, written in the vernacular, reinforced immigrant identities and strengthened their "ethnic world."

Religion was often central to immigrant identities. For many Irish, Germans, Italians, and Poles and other eastern Europeans, Catholic churches acted both as spiritual and as social epicenters, anchoring these groups to their urban neighborhoods. Although parish infrastructures already existed in most places, disagreements and jealousies based on nationality meant that many among the new Catholic immigrants frequently established their own "ethnic parishes" and other splinter congregations. Similar divisions were present in Lutheran and Jewish congregations, producing a rich diversity of immigrant houses of worship in urban and rural areas of America.

Immigrant churches were usually supplemented by educational facilities, but often little consensus existed between ethnic leaders in cities over what sort of schooling was most beneficial to the immigrants' children. Public schools not only exposed immigrant children to the values and norms of Americans but also were places where adult immigrants could learn English and new trades. Although the Catholic Church was expanding its network of parochial schools, public schools received Catholic Italians, Germans, and Irish, as well as Jews. Noted social reformer Jacob Riis wrote that on New York's Lower East Side in 1890, "when the great Jewish Holidays come around every year, the public schools . . . have practically to close up." For Catholic immigrants, however, parochial schools served as alternatives; Missouri Germans had Lutheran schools, and Jews had yeshivas. In 1900, Poles in Detroit had an extensive network of parochial schools, including a seminary that provided students with instruction given in both Polish and English.

DAILY LIFE IN THE IMMIGRANT NEIGHBORHOOD

The spatial contours of the immigrant neighborhood shaped its social life. Main streets radiating out from the city center were spines along which their immigrant businesses were located and off which the immigrants resided. News was diffused through such centers of interaction as the saloons, butchers, grocers, drugstores, coal and wood merchants, and others. Alleyways, street corners, and local pool halls were the domain of local gangs of immigrants' children who were only too ready to defend their ethnic turf. As Samuel Goldberg, from New York's Jewish East Side, wrote, "The Irish gangs . . . from the East Side water-front . . . invaded our district with rocks, glass bottles, clubs, and all sorts of homemade weapons."

Although some neighborhoods had problems with widespread intemperance, saloons were important to neighborhoods not only as outlets for conviviality but also as labor exchanges. Their atmospheres varied, however. While the dimly lit Irish saloon was primarily a man's world, German saloons and beer gardens welcomed entire families. Saloons also acted as centers of political mobilization. The boardinghouse and saloonkeepers of Buffalo's Irish First Ward, for example, directed the votes of their Irish grain-scooping clientele toward local Democratic candidates. In other places such as San Francisco's Chinatown, which covered an area of fifteen blocks by the early 1900s, smoky and crowded opium dens, although reviled by the majority whites as a moral threat, offered valuable outlets for companionship for Chinese males.

Whether they lived in the tenement or in less congested housing elsewhere in the city, privacy was not something that came easily within the immigrant household. Not only parents and their children made up immigrant households. Members of the extended family, such as other cousins and siblings of the parents, were also taken in, as were nonrelated boarders, usually of the same nationality. Outside, the streets were teeming with petty traders and merchants' horses and carts from morning until night, which, when combined with the lack of space within the home, meant that children had few options in terms of playing space. While the roofs of tenements provided an outlet for games such as marbles, many who did not do so well education-wise ended up as so-called street kids.

Although Italians and Poles dominated certain sections of American cities by the turn of the century, other immigrants were always present. Even when immigrants from various countries shared a common street, the institutional structures into which their lives were channeled often served to maintain a sense of apartness. Their capacity to interact with each other on a social or emotional level was deflected by their involvement in ethnically defined friendship and community networks and was reflected in low rates of intermarriage. Exposure to American ways of life was within the reach of some immigrants more so than others. Irish immigrant females frequently lived and worked as servants in the homes of society's well-to-do families in exclusive sections of cities, acquiring exposure to Victorian values of housekeeping and cleanliness. In contrast, Jewish mothers remained at home and, when not preparing dinner, often worked tirelessly at sewing machines while directing their off-

The Guadina family apartment on Manhattan's Lower East Side was both workplace and living space, a frequent arrangement in the crowded immigrant ghettos of late nineteenth-century America. *(National Archives)*

spring and other members of the family in the ways of sewing. These homes were dubbed "sweatshops" by social reformers, though this term could also refer to small factories as well.

The capacity to mix with immigrant groups other than their own was less of a daily reality for so-called immigrants of color. Labor camps, housing either Mexican railroad workers or Japanese laborers, were frequently segregated along ethnic lines. The work was hard; whether it was clearing or reclaiming land for agriculture, constructing the transcontinental railroad network, or harvesting cotton or sugar on plantations, desertions and physical ill-treatment were frequent as workers came and went.

Immigrant neighborhoods in cities also experienced high rates of population turnover. Because of the changing location of work opportunities or, more frequently, eviction, the immigrant's address was rarely fixed. Many immigrant families moved through a succession of rented lodgings around the same city

neighborhood. Such mobility usually culminated in homeownership, a move to another area, or, in some cases, return to the homeland.

IMMIGRANT HOUSING CONDITIONS

Tenements dominate the image of immigrant housing in late-nineteenth-century urban America. Developed since the 1860s as a way to squeeze profits from limited and expensive urban space, tenements became common features of American inner cities, and those of the "dumbbell" variety on New York's Lower East Side had a notoriety few other cities could match. In 1900, that district's Tenth Ward, 109 acres in area, contained no less than 1,179 tenement houses, with a population density of 679 people per acre. Cheaply built structures, usually four to six stories in height and scarcely ten feet distant from buildings at the

The crowded streets of Manhattan's Lower East Side were often extensions of the buildings that lined them, serving as workplace, market, and playground for the immigrants who lived there. *(Corbis)*

back of the lot, sheltered poor immigrant families in small apartments where proper access to daylight and clean air was often in short supply.

The potential for reconstructing European companionship drew new arrivals to these immigrant neighborhoods. For the arriving Italian, Pole, or Jew in the 1890s, in search of work and with little English, the appeal of such "gathering places" was obvious. With little in the way of affordable housing, the subdivision of homes and the taking in of boarders were essential for working-class immigrant families to pay the bills. Boardinghouses, clustered around the cities' inner cores and industrial districts, were occupied mostly by single male immigrants upon arrival, but these could not cope with the widespread demand for shelter. While other cities' tenements did not match New York's in terms of height, the overcrowding problem was pervasive and worsened already poor living conditions. Philadelphia's poor lived primarily in row housing of up to three stories, while Chicago's Hull House reports in 1894 showed that frame-built

immigrant housing, while usually only one or two stories high, held three tenant families on average.

Open space in the immigrant neighborhood also came under pressure from the so-called rear tenements. Rather than front the street, these alley dwellings were placed behind other buildings, occupying yard space alongside outhouses and manure dumps emanating from horses, cows, ducks, and chickens kept by other households. Robert Hunter, the author of *Tenement Conditions in Chicago* (1901), estimated the percentage of alley dwellings in that city's Little Poland to be almost one-third. Rats were in their element in such environments.

Landlords did little to alleviate the problem. In some cities, an "agent" or "lessee" system contributed to the problem of overcrowding and insufficient investment in the properties. In Buffalo's Italian District in 1900, New York State Tenement House Commission inspectors William Douglas and William Lansing found that house owners rented their premises to agents "whose whole object then is to secure as much rent as possible out of the tenant for the smallest possible amount of expense for repairs or proper sanitary provision." Inside such houses, furnishings were of a minimal nature; floorboards were unlikely to be covered, while linen, utensils, and tables were likely to be scarce and well-worn entities.

Settlement of the new immigrants from southern and eastern Europe in the central areas of cities could not have been possible without the displacement of earlier inhabitants. Few among the "old immigrants" from England, Scotland, English-speaking Canada, Germany, and, to a lesser extent, Ireland remained in the congested inner city by the turn of the century. Most of these groups had abandoned their downtown working-class neighborhoods and were dispersing toward newer residential areas near the city's edge. Upward occupational mobility propelled them to the status of middle-class homeowners. Often residing in detached frame-built houses, they now lived among and mixed socially with Americans of longer generation. So-called lace-curtain Irish Catholics began to move from central Philadelphia by the 1880s into Victorian houses on the city's west side, leaving their "shanty Irish" compatriots behind.

Although new immigrant families were not all confined to city centers, conditions were often no better than they were downtown. Chicago's "Packingtown," where a mix of Europeans, old and new, lived in the shadow of the city's slaughterhouses and meatpacking plants, was a notorious industrial district that had degenerated to slum conditions by 1900. At other times, self-building in less congested surroundings on the city's frontier was one route to immigrant home-

Table 1
Characteristics of Selected Foreign-born Groups in the United States, 1900

	Number	As a % of total foreign-born in U.S.[1]	% in 160 principal cities[2]	% change 1890–1900[3]	Principal states of settlement
Germany	2,669,164	25.5	50.2	-4.2	New York, Illinois
Ireland	1,619,469	15.5	62.0	-13.5	New York, Massachusetts
England	843,491	8.1	46.3	-7.4	New York, Pennsylvania
Italy	484,703	4.6	62.4	165.2	New York, Pennsylvania
Russia	424,372	4.1	74.9	132.2	New York, Pennsylvania
French Canada	395,427	3.8	37.7	30.7	Massachusetts, New Hampshire
Poland	383,595	3.7	62.6	160.1	New York, Pennsylvania
Norway	338,426	3.2	22.4	4.4	Minnesota, Wisconsin
Austria	276,702	2.6	53.5	124.1	New York, Pennsylvania
Hungary	145,815	1.4	53.4	133.5	Pennsylvania, New York
China	106,659	1.0	No data	-6.1	California, Hawaii
Mexico	103,445	1.0	7.1	32.8	Texas, Arizona

Source: Bureau of the Census, *Census Reports,* vol. 1: *Population,* pt. 1. Washington, DC: Government Printing Office, 1902.
[1]Numbers of foreign-born include those in Alaska and Hawaii.
[2]The percentage of foreign-born in the 160 principal cities does not include those in Alaska and Hawaii.
[3]The percentage change in the numbers of Chinese-born is an estimate.

ownership. Immigrant Polish families in Milwaukee's peripheral Fourteenth Ward lived in modest one- and two-family dwellings, built by local Polish workers "on quiet residential streets, with small front yards and an occasional tree."

Immigrants to small-town America—and particularly to company towns—experienced varied quality of housing. The predominantly male and young Slavs and Hungarians that migrated to the medium-size city of Johnstown, located in the hills of western Pennsylvania and dominated by the Cambria Iron Works, were in 1900 inhabiting dilapidated company tenements of two stories that were surrounded by furnace refuse. Further south, Mexican and Asian immigrants of recent arrival fared little better than their urbanized European counterparts. In the southwest, Mexican farmworkers either lived in employer-owned housing or had to provide their own; railroad construction workers lived in rented boxcars. While some ranches provided cottages for workers, conditions were generally deplorable. Low wages and seasonal work decreased the Mexicans' capacity to establish homes and stable communities. Where such existed, as in the barrios of El Paso, one- to three-room houses built of adobe mud bricks with dirt floors and few sanitary facilities were common. In Hawaii, Japanese laborer Yoshitaka Taro described housing on a sugar plantation thus: "We lived in the bunk house, sleeping on

blankets, spread over hay, on tiers of bunks like silkworms."

HEALTH AND SANITATION

Few urban neighborhoods in which immigrants settled provided a clean and healthy environment, and sanitation was usually substandard. Since tenement housing covered most of the lots on which they were built, immigrants' apartments received insufficient light and ventilation. Moreover, the height of the building blocked the light and air from adjacent buildings. Not only were these domestic environments dim and dark, they were crowded as well. With little in the way of central heating, the burning of coal was essential for cold winters in northern cities.

Immigrants living in poverty struggled to consume a balanced diet. Finding American food too expensive, they consumed fat-rich and protein-poor diets. Italians ate bread, potatoes, some eggs, fish, and pasta, while Slavs and east European Jews subsisted on herring, pumpernickel bread, and tea, supplemented by potatoes and cheap meats. Given the economic constraints under which they lived, underconsumption was common.

Immigrant household waste was typically disposed of in a variety of ways in the late nineteenth century. Human waste was deposited into privy vaults; garbage and coal ashes were dumped into ashpits, while cesspools received wastewater. Frequently overflowing, these sites became sources of disease. Sewers had begun to replace backyard privies and cesspools by 1900, but in such tight housing markets, tyrannical and profit-hungry landlords were loath to invest in sewer connections and other improvements. As Olivier Zunz's study of the Poles and Germans in Detroit around 1900 revealed, the delaying of services such as sewers and pavements was essential to minimizing costs during the initial phase of immigrant house building in residential areas of cities. Unfortunately, the crowding of many families into these small houses was also part of these short-run sacrifices.

With space at a premium in the kitchen and inadequate refuse collection, immigrant housewives deposited their garbage into the streets, vacant lots nearby, and their own tenement air shafts. Water closets, shared between a number of households, were located in the yards of some tenements, but high population levels and fear of sickness forced residents into the streets to use the sides of wagons or vacant lots, creating a foul stench on the streets which became unbearable in the summer. The Hull House investigation into Chicago immigrant districts in 1894 revealed that fewer than 3 percent of families lived in a building with a bath, and only 26 percent had access to a "water closet," or toilet.

Such inferior sanitation, allied to poor diets, overcrowding, and a lack of adequate exposure to clean air and daylight, created serious disease problems in many immigrant neighborhoods. Tuberculosis, an airborne disease, made all the more rampant by damp and filthy conditions, was a frequent killer. The high rates of immigrant transiency also enabled its spread from one neighborhood to another. Dr. Hermann Biggs mapped the reported cases and deaths from pulmonary tuberculosis in New York City tenement districts from 1894 to 1899 and noted that "on a single street block as many as 102 cases have been reported within four years, and as many as twenty-four cases in a single house." The contamination of water also led to the spread of typhoid fever, although deaths from this disease decreased as sewer mileage increased.

While water pollution was a known source of bacterial threat in 1900, industrial waste was given scant attention. The short journey to an industrial workplace was often paid for in terms of pollution emissions into its surrounding environment. Chicago's Stock Yards District was famous for its unique smell: "a mixture of decaying blood, hair, and organic tissue (with) fertilizer dust . . . and smoke belching from the stacks of the largest plants." Suburbanizing families of the "old immigrant" populations from northwestern Europe, in contrast, were rewarded with less congested neighborhoods, cleaner air, and the prospect of water closets and treated sewage.

William Jenkins

See also: Housing (Part II, Sec. 7); The Immigrant and the Community, 1917 (Part IV, Sec. 3).

BIBLIOGRAPHY

Barrett, James R. *Work and Community in the Jungle: Chicago's Packinghouse Workers.* Urbana, IL: University of Illinois Press, 1987.

Chen, Yong. *Chinese San Francisco, 1850–1943: A Trans-Pacific Community.* Stanford, CA: Stanford University Press, 2000.

DeForest, Robert W., and Lawrence Veiller, eds. *The Tenement House Problem.* 2 vols. New York: Macmillan, 1903.

Duis, Perry R. *The Saloon: Public Drinking in Chicago and Boston, 1880–1920.* Urbana, IL: University of Illinois Press, 1983.

Garcia, Mario T. *Desert Immigrants: The Mexicans of El Paso, 1880–1920.* New Haven, CT: Yale University Press, 1981.

Goldfield, David R., and Blaine A. Brownell, eds. *Urban America: From Downtown to No Town.* Boston: Houghton Mifflin, 1979.

Howe, Irving, and Kenneth Libo, eds. *How We Lived: A Documentary History of Immigrant Jews in America, 1880–1930.* New York: R. Marek, 1979.

Hunter, Robert. *Tenement Conditions in Chicago.* Chicago: City Homes Association, 1901.

Kraut, Alan. *The Huddled Masses: The Immigrant in American Society, 1880–1921.* Arlington Heights, IL: Harlan Davidson, 1982.

Melosi, Martin. *The Sanitary City: Urban Infrastructure in America from Colonial Times to the Present.* Baltimore: Johns Hopkins University Press, 2000.

Moriyama, Alan T. *Imingaisha: Japanese Emigration Companies and Hawaii, 1894–1908.* Honolulu: University of Hawai'i Press, 1985.

Philpott, Thomas L. *The Slum and the Ghetto: Neighborhood Deterioration and Middle-Class Reform, Chicago, 1880–1930.* New York: Oxford University Press, 1978.

Riis, Jacob. *How the Other Half Lives: Studies Among the Tenements of New York.* New York: Charles Scribner's Sons, 1890.

Simon, Roger D. "Housing and Services in an Immigrant Neighborhood: Milwaukee's Ward 14." *Journal of Urban History,* 2:4 (1975): 435–58.

Zunz, Olivier. *The Changing Face of Inequality: Urbanization, Industrial Development, and Immigrants in Detroit, 1880–1920.* Chicago: University of Chicago Press, 1982.

ECONOMICS AND LABOR

America's second Industrial Revolution arose from the ashes of the Civil War and the harsh economic downturns of the 1870s. The industries that forged this expansive period in the history of American capitalism utilized modern transportation networks, technological advances, and streamlined production processes to turn out steel and other metals, packaged food, ready-to-wear clothing, chemicals, tobacco, oil, and drug products. Most importantly, they made use of America's greatest commodity, the steady stream of new immigrants that transformed American life and culture around the turn of the century. Immigrants accounted for one-third of the increase in the labor force between 1870 and 1910, roughly the years of America's ascendance as the world's foremost industrial power. These new immigrants built modern industrial America.

Economic need defined the immigrants' experience in America. In the period from the 1870s to the 1920s, most came for financial reasons, and the economic role they filled upon arrival profoundly influenced their lives in America as well as their decisions to remain or to return to their homeland. The depression of the 1890s slowed immigration, but an industrial resurgence after 1898 created millions of new jobs in the factories of the urban North. Advances in intercontinental transportation enabled rural peasants from the economically stricken regions of central, southern, and eastern Europe to come to America to fill these new positions.

Beginning in the late 1870s, but especially at the turn of the century, immigrants streamed into the expanding urban centers of the industrial North. But unlike earlier waves, the majority of new European immigrants did not come from northern Europe. From 1890 through 1917, central Europe contributed 4,879,000 immigrants, or 27.1 percent of the total. Next came southern Europe with 4,369,000 (24.3 percent), northern Europe with 3,637,000 (20.2 percent), and eastern Europe with 3,328,000 (18.5 percent). The peak years were from 1905 to 1914, and at the apex of immigration in 1914, nearly three-quarters of the total number of immigrants came from southern, central, and eastern Europe including Greeks, Italians, Poles, Russians, Jews, Turks, and Slavs, a pan-ethnic term used to denote a number of ethnic groups from Austria-Hungary. After a series of treaties limited and then cut off Chinese immigration after 1882, and following the "Gentlemen's Agreement" which introduced Japanese exclusion in 1907, Asia contributed only 468,000 or 2.6 percent of the overall total immigrants during this period.

LOOKING FOR A JOB

The new immigrants flocked to burgeoning turn-of-the-century northern industrial and midwestern cities like New York, Pittsburgh, Milwaukee, Cleveland, Detroit, Buffalo, St. Louis, and Chicago. By 1900, almost three-quarters of Slavic, Hungarian, and Italian immigrants lived in the seven major industrial states, which produced more than half of America's manufacturing and mining output. Meanwhile, the West also absorbed hundreds of thousands of immigrants. Mexicans worked the cotton fields of Texas, laid railroad lines, and helped the sugar-beet industry to expand. And Japanese immigrants worked on the railroads and in the service industry. A number of Japanese immigrants also opened small businesses or truck farms outside of western cities. In general, immigrants went where there was work to be had. They had come all this way to find a job.

Though some immigrants around the turn of the century had prior experience working in industry and a few were even union members, the majority came from rural backgrounds and therefore lacked industrial skills. Instead, they possessed agricultural and craft skills that were not of use to modern factory em-

Factory conditions for immigrant laborers were harsh and often dangerous, as this early-twentieth-century photograph of unprotected spinning machines in a textile factory makes clear. *(National Archives)*

ployers. Only craft-oriented, skilled industrial work commanded a substantial wage in this era. The immigrants were therefore subject to the dictates of a job market that was continually deluged with other newcomers desperate for work and similarly lacking in industrial experience and sellable skills. To a large extent, immigrants had to take what industry gave.

Skilled, native-born workers who could afford both a home and transportation tended to drift toward residential neighborhoods away from the pollution of the teeming urban areas of the North. However, economic necessity forced new immigrants to live near their places of work in cheap tenements and shoddy wood-frame houses. In places like the mill towns of Pennsylvania and Chicago's "back-of-the-yards" community of immigrant meatpackers, immortalized by Upton Sinclair in *The Jungle* (1906),

choking smoke, open sewage, and pervasive industrial and human pollution rendered immigrant communities dangerous and dirty places. At the same time, overcrowding cut down on privacy, inflated housing prices, and gave greater salience to the American dream of home ownership. Russian Jewish immigrant Anzia Yezierska articulated the craving for space and cleanliness in her classic novel *Bread Givers*. When she first leaves the city for a small college town, the main character comments, "Before this, New York was all of America to me. But now I came to a town of quiet streets, shaded with green trees. No crowds, no tenements. . . . So these are the real Americans. . . . They had none of that terrible fight for bread and rent that I always saw in New York people's eyes."

In a foreign land, often lacking English-language skills and inexperienced in the ways of modern in-

This clothing workshop is an example of the sweatshops that filled the immigrant neighborhoods of most American cities at the turn of the twentieth century. *(National Archives)*

dustry, many of the new immigrants, especially those from southern or eastern Europe, turned first to a *padrone,* or labor contractor, specializing in securing employment for newly arrived immigrant men. Usually a more established member of a specific ethnic group fluent in both English and the language of his clients, the padrone helped immigrants get their feet in the door of industry by finding them their first American jobs. For a fee, the contractor would place the immigrant in a mill, on a railroad, with a construction crew, or in a logging camp. Sometimes the padrone's middleman role was even more complete, with employers dispersing wages only through him. Not surprisingly, the padrone's power over the desperate newcomers led to high levels of corruption. Some overcharged for their services or misrepresented the kind of jobs they were selling, and in some cases the padrone absconded with savings that an immigrant worker had placed in his care. But once the newly arrived immigrant had actually attained the job, he or she had other things to worry about.

IMMIGRANTS AND INDUSTRY

The employment patterns, as well as the gender ratios, of turn-of-the-century immigrants varied according to ethnicity. Immigrant groups struggled to establish niches in a particular industry. When entire ethnic communities worked together, it helped to ease both the struggles of newcomers to find work and their difficult transition to the disciplines of industry. Some employers explicitly set out to destroy this practice, fearing that ethnic enclaves cultivated a shop-floor solidarity that might lead to organized resistance. In many cases, employers purposefully mixed ethnic groups, putting Swedes, Italians, and Poles together in one crew, for example. Still, some immigrant communities successfully established substantial beachheads in various industries. For example, Cubans dominated the cigar industry in Tampa, Florida, while in Detroit, Polish women dominated the industry. In Philadelphia, cigar-making was done by Russian Jews, and in Newark by Hungarian women. Italian men comprised the vast majority of public-works employees in New York and Chicago. They dug the Bronx aqueduct, constructed New York's Grand Central Station, and built the Empire State Building. Italians also made up the majority of railroad builders east of the Mississippi by 1890. Along with Italians, Poles and Slavs found work in coal mines, heavy industry, and the building trades. Sixty-nine percent of Slovak males living in America were coal miners by 1920. Many others worked in the steel industry. By 1920, Jewish and Italian women dominated New York's garment trade. They all shared one thing in common: The work they did was difficult, dangerous, dirty, and long.

Many immigrants found wages in American industry to be a tremendous improvement over their earnings in previous jobs. Though they often earned only a percentage of what skilled workers received, immigrants still considered work in America to be quite profitable, especially for men hoping only to make enough to return with a nest egg for the future. However, though wages could be good, the conditions under which many of the new immigrants worked were deplorable at best. Moreover, irregular employment cut into the value of some wages, stretching them to cover periods without a regular paycheck.

Simply put, immigrant labor worked many of the worst jobs that industrial society had to offer, and they worked them for long hours, with little or no hope of ever advancing. Employers usually considered labor their most costly form of overhead. Beginning full-scale in the 1870s, American industrialists endeavored to increase profits by increasing efficiency and expenditure, which meant reducing wage levels as much as possible. Skilled workers, both because their skill was a valuable commodity and because many had established national craft unions, were by far the costliest employees. Logically then, reducing the need for skill and destroying the power of the national unions would undercut the bargaining power of skilled workers, reduce overhead, and increase profits.

Around the turn of the century, industrialists increasingly introduced new technology aimed at reducing the need for skill. To lower overhead, industry reversed the relationship between master and machine. Henry Ford instituted a system of production that he insisted anyone could learn in two days, and by 1914, 95 percent of the employees at one of Ford's foundries were unskilled laborers. To fill these new unskilled positions, employers turned to immigrant labor. In time, "unskilled work" came to be equated with "immigrant work." On several occasions, Mike Urban of Homestead, Pennsylvania, "asked for [a] promotion but was told that the good jobs are not for hunkies." He felt that "the clean jobs are for Americans only." In 1907, the Carnegie Steel Works near Pittsburgh employed 14,359 unskilled workers, 11,694 of whom were eastern Europeans. In the years from 1907 to 1911, the Dillingham Commission found that 57.7 percent of iron and steel manufacturing employees east of the Mississippi were foreign-born, and 64.4 percent of those had come from a rural background in Europe.

Employers also increasingly began to adapt scientific methods to the production process in order to streamline their mills. Just as the skilled work formerly done by well-paid unionized workers began to be appropriated by machines, a new breed of middle-level managers codified the thought processes inherent in skilled labor into a new science of shop-floor production. College-trained technicians armed with stopwatches broke down complex work into a simple routine of highly repetitive, thoughtless motions. The founder of "scientific management," Frederick Winslow Taylor, justified these dehumanizing transformations in work by arguing that the average iron puddler is "so stupid and so phlegmatic that he more nearly resembles in his mental make-up an ox." No wonder then that one researcher found *Ameryka dla byka, Europa dla chlopa*" ("America for the oxen, Europe for the men") to be a prevalent saying among Slavic steelworkers.

The new immigrants filled these newly deskilled and routinized jobs. In most cases, they were asked for their brawn only; their brains were not profitable to industry. However, some companies found it to be in their best interest to teach their immigrant workers about American life and customs and also to teach them English. In numerous corporate-sponsored Americanization programs, immigrants learned to be both good workers and good Americans. For example, International Harvester in Chicago provided its Polish employees with a brochure to help them learn to speak and read English:

> I hear the whistle. I must hurry.
> I hear the five minute whistle.
> It is time to go into the shop.
> I take my check from the gate board and hang it on the department board.
> I change my clothes and get ready to work.
> The starting whistle blows.
> I eat my lunch.
> It is forbidden to eat until then.

Even while employers tried to Americanize them, many immigrant workers complained of "un-American conditions" in the factories. Worst of all may have been the hours. The demand for an eight-hour day had been a linchpin of the American labor movement since the end of the Civil War, but only during the World War I era did substantial numbers of American workers achieve it. By 1919, about half of the nation's waged employees worked for eight hours. However, eight hours was slow to trickle down to the lowliest of unskilled workers, and some industries continued to cling tenaciously to traditional schedules. The steel industry, for example, refused to go to three shifts instead of two until the mid-1920s. Therefore, the Slavs, Italians, Lithuanians, and Poles that comprised steel's unskilled workforce stoked the fires and kept the furnaces roaring for twelve hours at a time (or, in many cases, for ten hours when on day turn, and fourteen when on night). Inconceivably, every other week brought the dreaded long-shift when day and night turn rotated and unskilled workers spent an entire twenty-four-hour period in the mill. In testimony before Congress, one Polish striker described this life:

> Just like horse and wagon. Put horse in wagon (i.e., hitch it to the wagon). Work all day—put in stable. Take horse out of stable. Put in wagon. Same way like mills. Work all day, come home—go sleep. Wife say, "John, children sick. You help with children." You say, "Oh go to hell"—go sleep. Wife say, "John, you go to town." You say, "No"—go to sleep. No know what the hell you do. For why this war? For why we buy Liberty Bonds?

For the mills! No, for freedom and America—for everybody. No more horse and wagon.

Echoing this sentiment, Mike Stephan, a Hungarian working at a U.S. Steel mill in McKeesport, Pennsylvania, said of the twelve-hour day, "A man is like a mule—he sleeps and eats at home and spends the rest of the time in the mill."

The consequences for immigrant families were devastating. One woman referred to her husband's biweekly shifts on the night turn as "the lonesome week." Another said of her husband's relationship to their two children: "He really doesn't know them." This sentiment echoes achingly throughout the testimony of immigrant working families in the early years of the twentieth century. Collectively, they weave a wrenching narrative of lives shattered by industrial demands for efficiency and low overhead. Long hours and poor wages could act like a cancer on personal relations as drones in the mill became drones in the home. Observed one immigrant woman, "When a man works as long as that he can't see his babies, he can't see the daylight—all he can do is just come home and lie and sleep." Work and home entwined inextricably in men's, women's, and children's lives. Moreover, the wages the immigrant men brought home for these hours often did not meet the needs of their children and families. In other words, immigrant men did not earn a family wage. For the most part, industrial work was "a single man's job."

IMMIGRANT LABOR RESISTANCE

Immigrant workers resisted such attempts at indoctrination into the world of industrial efficiency and sought to preserve some control over the daily regimentation of their lives by both individual and organized means of resistance. They observed "St. Mondays" or "Blue Mondays," which extended their weekends and gave them time to recover from its excesses. Also, immigrants worked collectively to establish their own pace of work in opposition to time standards demanded by scientific managers. Moreover, immigrant workers simply quit jobs at often alarming rates. America may not have offered the immigrants quality jobs enabling them to support their families in decency, but it did offer an abundance of opportunities for work. The bad jobs were often plentiful, and immigrants exercised their freedom by quitting excessively exploitative labor. In the early decades of the twentieth century, some industries experienced dramatic turnover ratios in the lowest-paid positions. In-

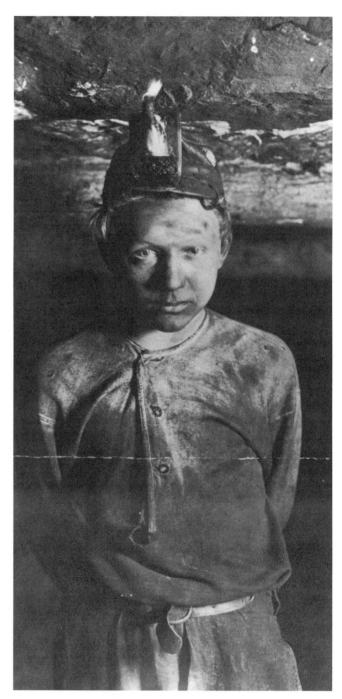

Like this young coal miner, immigrant children were often put to work to supplement meager family incomes. (National Park Service: Statue of Liberty National Monument)

credibly, one Ford plant weathered a 416 percent turnover rate in 1913. In the steel, mining, and metal industries, turnover routinely was near 100 percent for a single year. In some industries, employers actually hoped to keep turnover rates for unskilled workers high in order to counteract worker cohesion. Many also manipulated ethnic divisions for the same purpose, refusing to put workers of the same ethnic group onto the same work crews.

Immigrant workers also articulated trenchant political critiques of industrial society. Ethnic communities established fraternal and worker organizations centered on politics that often embraced socialist ideology. This was especially true of the vibrant political culture of New York's Lower East Side Jewish community. Increasing political and economic turmoil near the end of the nineteenth century, coupled with vicious outbreaks of anti-Semitic violence and bloody pogroms, induced thousands of Jewish families from Russia and Poland to leave for America. Political thought and a growing revolutionary movement began to flower in the cities and towns of the Pale just as Jewish immigration to America reached its zenith. Jewish immigrants transplanted their revolutionary fervor in New York's crowded ghettos. There they established a flourishing socialist press and a tradition of street-corner proselytizing. However, despite its tradition of resistance to the demands of industry, immigrant labor did not enjoy a warm relationship with America's institutionalized labor movement.

IMMIGRANT WORKERS AND THE UNIONS

According to its official policy, the American Federation of Labor (AFL) represented all of America's workers without regard to ethnicity, skill level, race, gender, or nationality. However, Japanese and Chinese workers had never been admitted into the house of labor, and an 1895 reversal of policy introduced the color bar banning African Americans in many of the national AFL-affiliated unions. Moreover, at the local level, the craft unions associated with the AFL never lived up to official national policy. Their constitutions featured egalitarian wording, but their actions were not so inclusive. Either by rule or by practice, the AFL represented America's skilled workers, who made up only about one-sixth of the nation's workforce but dominated its unions. Skilled workers were usually native-born or the children of immigrants from northern and western Europe. Originally, they secured these position with the help of friends and relatives, much like the padrone system used by many of the new immigrants. By the turn of the century, however, native-born workers explicitly sought to defend their hold on these relatively privileged positions from the aspiring new immigrants.

With increasing macrolevel changes in industrial production at the turn of the century, unskilled immigrant workers pushed national unions in the garment industry and coal mining toward an industrial union model later adopted in the 1930s by the Congress of Industrial Organizations (CIO). However, at about the same time, most craft unions instead opted to protect their interests against the incursions of the unskilled. Fearing that the influx of immigrants would threaten their tenuous hold on skilled positions and potentially devalue their wages, the native-born workers of the AFL heartily endorsed immigration restrictions. Moreover, Samuel Gompers, the head of the AFL, increasingly resorted to racial and ethnic slurs in criticizing the masses of immigrant, unskilled workers. Native-born workers used racially charged terms like "Hunky," "Ginny," or "Coolie" to describe poorly paid and degraded work, and the national craft unions associated with the AFL refused to organize workers in such positions. At the turn of the century, the new immigrants, African Americans, and women found themselves unwelcome or segregated within the labor movement.

"BIRDS OF PASSAGE"

Idealists have cherished the image of huddled masses fleeing persecution to the shores of America, however, most of the immigrants in the years between 1880 and the 1920s came for the explicit purpose of filling industrial positions. Indeed, many, especially Polish and Slavic immigrants from eastern and central Europe, planned only to make enough money in America to return to their European homes with savings.

Without a long-term commitment to life in America, some "birds of passage," or single men intent on working long hours to save wages for a return to their homeland, were as opposed to unionization as the skilled workers who refused to welcome them into their fold. For immigrant workers singly intent on accumulating savings and returning home, unions meant union dues (a sap on wages) and the possibility of a strike (a time without wages). In some industries, near the end of the nineteenth century, immigrant workers gained a reputation among organized coworkers as being antiunion due to their reluctance to join.

Between 1880 and 1920, only about half of Italian immigrants actually became permanent citizens. Between one-half and two-thirds of east-central European immigrants between 1908 and 1923 returned to their homeland. Though almost half of Jewish immigrants were women, and entire families of Jewish immigrants often came at once, Greeks and Slavs were especially known to come as birds of passage. This practice made them especially open to criticism from native-born workers who worried that they would undercut wage rates by working longer hours for less pay. Skilled workers, hoping to protect their claim to a family wage, came to see birds of passage as an even greater threat to their status than the scientific manager.

However, the ravages of World War I changed the plans of many European immigrants. With their homelands in economic chaos, many for the first time committed themselves to a future in America. Consequently, formerly transient immigrant communities increasingly came to be active in labor struggles in the period immediately following the war. In a wave of strikes in 1919, immigrant workers demanded some of the privileges enjoyed by the native-born skilled workers, including shorter hours, safer conditions, opportunities for advancement, and union representation. However, this time it was the native-born who refused to join. For example, in the Great Steel Strike of 1919, skilled workers in the Pittsburgh and Gary districts stayed on the job, chastising what they called a "Hunky strike." Over a quarter of a million east-central European immigrants waged a prolonged struggle against the steel industry, but they also practiced exclusion. The striking immigrant steelworkers refused to welcome African-American migrants from the rural South into the union cause, and the migrants, in turn, effectively broke the strike. Industrial unionism across boundaries of race, ethnicity, and skill would not come to most American industries until the Great Depression of the 1930s.

WOMEN AT WORK

In order to counteract the inadequate wages of the male breadwinner, economic necessity forced some immigrant families to send other family members in search of waged work. A common practice for immigrant women, especially among Chicago's meatpackers or the steel communities of western Pennsylvania, was to take in boarders from the population of unmarried immigrant workers, many of them birds of passage. In many cases, boarders represented the only paid employment immigrant women could find. Yet the boarder system had clear disadvantages. Not only did it mean incessant toil for the mother and daughters who now had to cook, clean, and launder for even more persons, it also meant a lack of privacy and overly crowded conditions for immigrant families. In some cases, boarders working different shifts took

turns in a cot set up in a kitchen or a front room. Finally, in order to supplement family incomes, many immigrant families were forced into putting their children to various forms of paid work at a very early age. When Progressive Era reformers and social activists exposed these cramped conditions and the abuses of child labor to a broader public, they mixed their compassion with condescension and were often as likely to chastise the immigrants for their low standards or "un-American" habits as to criticize the industrial conditions that led families to these ends.

Italian and Polish families were especially reluctant to allow a wife or daughter to seek waged employment outside the home. These women accommodated this cultural mandate with the need to supplement family wages by finding ways of performing paid labor from within the home by taking in boarders, laundry, neighborhood children, or industrial homework. This was especially true of Italian women in New York City, who came to dominate certain forms of garment labor done in the house rather than in the factory. Yet some immigrant women, in Buffalo, for example, found factory work. Through the teaching profession, some immigrant women actually entered white-collar employment while their male relatives continued to populate factories and construction crews.

Finally, immigrant women waged one of the crucial labor struggles of the early twentieth century. On the night of November 22, 1909, hundreds of young women garment workers, most of them Jewish and Italian, crowded into New York's Cooper Union. As women, as unskilled workers, as new immigrants, and as workers who would not continue for long in the labor force, these women constituted the absolute antithesis of the labor movement's ideal unionist. Males in the garment industry thought they could not be organized. Yet, after a round of cautious and restrained speeches, young Clara Lemlich requested to take the stage and proclaimed: "I have listened to all the speakers. I would not have further patience for talk, as I am one of those who feels and suffers from the things pictured. I move that we go on a general strike." The next day at least fifteen thousand shirtwaist makers went out, and thousands more joined the cause in the weeks to come. Called "The Uprising of the 20,000," the strike broke long-held stereotypes about the complacency of immigrants, women, and unskilled workers. The garment workers were eventually able to negotiate contracts with many employers, securing better wages and improved conditions. Unfortunately, however, the Triangle Shirtwaist Company was not one of these firms, and on March 25, 1911, a devastating fire claimed the lives of 146 immigrant garment workers trapped on the tenth floor of a supposedly fireproof building. The tragedy brought national attention to the exploitative conditions faced by many immigrants in industry and inspired a generation of political activists who fought for industrial unionism and protective legislation for women and children.

Steve Burnett

See also: Entrepreneurs, Impact on the Home Country Economy, Income and Wealth, Poverty (Part II, Sec. 7); Labor Markets for Recent Immigrants, Sweatshops and Factories, Unions and Union Organizing (Part II, Sec. 8); Contract Labor Act (Foran Act), 1885 (Part IV, Sec. 1); The Immigrant and the Community, 1917 (Part IV, Sec. 3).

BIBLIOGRAPHY

Bell, Thomas. *Out of This Furnace: A Novel of Immigrant Labor in America*. Pittsburgh: University of Pittsburgh Press, 1993.

Buhle, Paule, and Dan Georgakas, eds. *The Immigrant Left in the United States*. Binghamton: State University of New York Press, 1996.

Debouzy, Marianne. *In the Shadow of the Statue of Liberty: Immigrants, Workers, and Citizens in the American Republic, 1880–1920*. Urbana: University of Illinois Press, 1992.

Foley, Neil. *The White Scourge: Mexicans, Blacks, and Poor Whites in Texas Cotton Culture*. Berkeley: University of California Press, 1997.

Gabaccia, Donna. *From the Other Side: Women, Gender, and Immigrant Life in the U.S., 1820–1990*. Bloomington: University of Indiana Press, 1994.

Mink, Gwendolyn. *Old Labor and New Immigrants in American Political Development: Union, Party and State, 1875–1920*. Ithaca, NY: Cornell University Press, 1986.

Montgomery, David. *The Fall of the House of Labor: The Workplace, the State, and American Labor Activism, 1865–1925*. New York: Cambridge University Press, 1987.

Orleck, Annelise. *Common Sense and a Little Fire: Women and Working-Class Politics in the United States, 1900–1965*. Chapel Hill: University of North Carolina Press, 1995.

Sinclair, Upton. *The Jungle*. Urbana: University of Illinois Press, 1988.

Wyman, Mark. *Round-Trip to America: The Immigrants Return to Europe, 1880–1930*. Ithaca, NY: Cornell University Press, 1993.

Yezierska, Anzia. *Bread Givers: A Struggle Between a Father of the Old World and a Daughter of the New*. New York: Persea, 1975.

CULTURE AND ASSIMILATION

Immigrants to the United States at the turn of the century came predominantly from southern and eastern Europe. Italians, mainly from the southern part of Italy, constituted the single largest group, followed by Jewish immigrants from eastern Europe, largely from Russia. Gentiles from eastern Europe such as the Slavic groups, including Polish, Slovak, and Czech immigrants, represent another significant component of this migration stream. The Slavic immigrant groups are culturally diverse, but historians have not yet examined their cultures to any great extent. Most has been written on the Poles, the largest of the Slavic groups.

All of these immigrants brought elements of their own unique cultural heritages with them, including languages, arts, and folkways. Once in the United States, these cultural traditions came into contact with American forms and were often transformed in the process, creating entirely new identities along the way. For example, initially, the immigrants tended to identify with their own regions, each with its own variations of language, food, dress, religious feasts, and forms of entertainment. It was only in the United States that distinctions between regional groups tended to fade as immigrants slowly came to identify on a national rather than on a more local basis.

One of the more striking examples of the type of hybrid identity immigrants formed in the New World, neither wholly of the country of origin nor completely American, can be found in the language of Italian immigrants. While immigrants brought their own distinct dialects of standard Italian with them, some of which were virtually unintelligible outside of one's own region, once in America, Italians developed a unique linguistic form of their own. This idiom, which some have referred to as "Italglish," was largely Italian in terms of sound and structure. It incorporated elements of standard Italian, Neapolitan (a widely understood dialect), and Italianized English. The immigrants coined words to describe uniquely New World

objects or phenomena for which no Italian equivalent either existed or was commonly known. Examples include *baccauso* (literally, back house) for the outhouse and, subsequently, the indoor flush toilet and *uliveto* for the elevated train. The immigrants also coined their own versions of everyday English words that they would hear and use repeatedly such as *storo* for store or *bosso* for boss. This idiom was not limited to nouns but included new verb forms that were conjugated according to Italian principles of grammar.

Italglish was spoken from New York to California, wherever an immigrant colony existed, at home, on the job, and in social contexts. Even store signs and newspaper ads made use of this language. Italian contractors for the New York City garment factories advertised for *pressatore* (pressers) in the Italian-American press, for example. Some variation in words and expressions existed, depending on the location of the immigrant settlement. The phrase *andarre a Flabusse,* (to go to Flatbush), a reference to a cemetery in Queens, was an idiomatic expression for "to die" that immigrants outside of New York would not have understood. Depending on the region of origin of the colonists, the local version of Italglish also took on different pronunciations.

While Italglish served the utilitarian function of enabling the immigrants to communicate with each other in their New World context, it also allowed for creative expression in the form of wordplay. Such wordplay often contained a critique of American life based on the immigrant experience. The term *Mericane,* for example, meaning "American," contained the Italian word for dog (*cane*) and so could also mean American dog. This linguistic phenomenon was not unique to Italian immigrants. Similar fusions of immigrant languages and English occurred in Yiddish- and Polish-speaking communities as well.

Ethnic identity was maintained and transformed as immigrants, and especially their children and grandchildren, became more Americanized, at least in

Americanization of immigrants was considered essential for national security, as this World War I-era poster promoting English language instruction emphasizes. *(National Park Service: Statue of Liberty National Monument)*

terms of outward appearance and practices. Indeed, the second generation—children of immigrants—actively participated in the creation of a vibrant, new working-class American culture. While the common understanding of assimilation or Americanization is that immigrants become incorporated into a dominant, uniform American society, in recent years historians have presented a more complex portrait of assimilation. Rather than a single predominant American society to which immigrants assimilate, historians describe a variety of coexisting ethnicities, including the dominant culture, that continually evolve through their interaction with each other to create new ethnic identities. Through their experience, immigrants themselves transform the meaning of what it means to be an American. This does not preclude the possibility of fading immigrant ethnicities nor of adopting some version of an American identity.

THEATER

Although culture can be defined in various ways, it was largely through their expressive cultural practices of their arts as well as folkways that the immigrants helped shape new American identities. These included artistic as well as traditional cultural forms.

Italian immigrants were mainly drawn to comic variety theater, best represented by Eduardo Migliaccio, the premier comic performer of the Italian immigrant stage from the turn of the century until well into the 1930s. Performing under the stage name of Farfariello, or Little Butterfly, Migliaccio created comic character sketches of immigrant life, known as *macchiete coloniale,* for which he was famous in the Bowery theaters of New York City's Lower East Side. Performing in the tradition of the Italian *commedia dell'arte,* he portrayed a variety of characters, from the lowly immigrant *cafone* (peasant) to the great Caruso, with an artistry that drew the attention of uptown patrons of the arts as well as Italian immigrant laborers.

Unlike those of other vaudeville and variety performers, Migliaccio's character sketches were not just crude caricatures, but sensitive characterizations of everyday types from New York's Little Italy. He achieved this realistic effect in large part by using the immigrant idiom. Through his depictions of immigrant types, Migliaccio gave expression to Italian immigrant life as it was lived through its unique linguistic form. Indeed, much of his humor relied for its effect on confusion of language.

New York City's Italian immigrants also enjoyed other forms of theatrical entertainment, from dramas by well-known Italian performers of the day such as Antonio Maoiri to Sicilian marionette theater staged by Remo Buffano. Other cities with large Italian enclaves such as San Francisco, St. Louis, and Boston all had their own immigrant theaters, each with a somewhat different emphasis.

The Yiddish theater was a central feature of Jewish cultural life in New York City and other urban centers with large Jewish populations. In New York at the turn of century, 1,100 performances were being given annually before an estimated 2 million patrons. The Yiddish theater encompassed a greater variety of theatrical genres than its Italian counterpart. "Greenhorn" comedy based on immigrant life, as well as historical dramas, romantic musicals, and dramas dealing with events of the day and biblical themes were all represented on the Yiddish stage.

Serious Yiddish theater is exemplified by the plays of Jacob Gordin, who dominated Yiddish theater in the 1890s and early 1900s. Gordin's plays were loose adaptations of the works of Shakespeare, Goethe, Ibsen, and others, set in the immigrant context and using its language. (*The Jewish King Lear* was one of his first successes.) The well-known Jewish actor Jacob Adler was the foremost exponent of Gordin's plays. Together, they brought a unique brand of realism to the Yiddish stage, a theater steeped in the realities of immigrant life but acted in a grand style. This theater reached its peak at the turn of the century, giving way in popularity to the Yiddish variety theater, which featured one-act performances incorporating comedy and music. A number of famous American vaudevillians with broad appeal—such as Eddie Cantor and Fanny Brice, known for their Yiddish dialect humor—had their roots in the Yiddish variety theaters or music halls.

Other eastern European groups had their own forms of theatrical entertainment, though they were not as developed as the Yiddish or the Italian theater. The larger Polish communities, for example, often had dramatic societies and sometimes even professional theater groups, but they generally did not enjoy any longevity.

MUSIC AND DANCE

Immigrant Italian America's musical culture encompassed opera as well as band music. The two, in fact were related in surprising ways. Italy's tradition of local bands continued in America. Indeed, in the latter part of the nineteenth century, Italian musicians were in demand by native-born Americans to perform in military and circus bands. Many Italian settlements had community bands that performed for weddings, funerals, and religious processions. As early as 1900, there were hundreds of these amateur musical groups, composed of coronetists, clarinetists, trombonists, and other instrumentalists. Their repertoires included traditional marching music and Italian *bel canto* but operatic pieces as well, primarily by the well-known nineteenth-century Italian composer, Gioacchino Rossini.

Opera was still the music of everyday people in Italy at the turn of the century. Italian opera took the United States by storm with the arrival of the celebrated tenor, Enrico Caruso, who first came to perform in America in 1903. His arrival coincided with that of tens of thousands of Italian immigrants, who were among his most ardent fans. The immigrants quickly recognized him as one of their own—a southerner from Naples who came from a large impover-

ished family. Although the grand opera houses of American cities were not very receptive to Italian immigrant audiences, the newcomers enjoyed local productions of opera.

Italians also brought their own regional folk musical traditions with them. The primary instruments included the accordion and the mandolin, although different regions produced their own unique music. Immigrant musicians from the mountainous regions of Calabria, Campania, Basilicata, and Abruzzi, for example, might play bagpipes in addition to the more familiar *organetto,* or button accordian.

Music was not only a major component of the Yiddish variety theater, it was also a cornerstone of Jewish religious life. Exceptional cantors were often treated as celebrities. Synagogues vied with each other for the best cantors in order to draw the largest audiences, and it was not unusual for worshipers to travel some distance for the promise of an especially fine voice. A number of Jewish virtuosi string instrument musicians from Russia made their American debuts in the early 1900s. Indeed, Jewish musicianship came to be linked very closely with string instruments and the violin in particular.

Eastern European Jewish folk music, known as *klezmer,* which featured the clarinet, made its way to America in the late nineteenth century. Klezmer musicians were sought out for such festive family occasions as weddings. Popular Jewish music, such as street songs and vaudeville numbers from the era, survives in the form of broadsides that were sold individually on the streets of the Lower East Side and in collections of sheet music. Broadsides encompassed a range of subjects and styles, including bawdy songs as well as parodies and songs dealing with religious themes. Song sheets also reveal a wide variety of Yiddish popular songs including Yiddish versions of American melodies.

Music and dance were also a central part of eastern European immigrant culture. Polish music and dance traditions were long a mainstay of Polish culture. In America, Poles organized singing ensembles through their local churches—such as the Polish Singers Alliance, established in 1888 in Chicago. The local parish church, together with the "Dom Polski" (Polish house), formed the cultural centers of Polish immigrant communities that sponsored musical as well as other events. Folk and patriotic songs formed the bulk of the repertory for the singing groups.

Traditional Polish melodies, like the folk music of other immigrant groups, had their origin in various religious and other activities including family events, local holidays, and religious celebrations. Like that of other groups, Polish music varied, depending on the region and whether it was urban-based or rural. Both the rural-style and urban-style Polish bands shared a reliance on stringed instruments like the bass and the violin as opposed to the predominantly brass bands that characterized Bohemians and Germans, for example.

Polka music was the favored musical genre—and dance form—among the mass of eastern European immigrants. A favorite Czech composer and bandleader famous for his polka compositions was Frantisek Kmoch, known as the Bohemian March King. Kmoch combined polka with marches, emphasizing the traditional folk music over the military, nationalistic style. These proved very popular with the immigrants, who brought over his sheet music. Due to the heavy concentration of eastern Europeans in the Midwest, Chicago became a center for this music. It was there that Andrew Grill gained fame for his own compositions as well as for his arrangements of this Bohemian-style of traditional ethnic music. Like the Poles, Czech immigrants also had many musical institutions, including musical societies and brass bands that played the marches and dance tunes favored by the immigrants.

LITERATURE

The literature of the Italian immigrant generation is sparse, since Italian immigration was largely limited to peasants and laborers with minimal formal education. However, several notable autobiographies were produced dealing with the early years of settlement, primarily for an English-speaking audience. Pascal D'Angelo's *Son of Italy* details the author's transformation from semiliterate railroad worker to award-winning author. Pietro Di Donato's *Christ in Concrete* tells the harrowing story of a young boy growing up in New York City who finds work in the construction trade after his father's grisly death. In *The Soul of an Immigrant,* Constantine Panunzio attempts to explain the southern Italian to Americans by tracing his own difficult adjustment to the New World. Like D'Angelo's, his is a story of hard manual labor interwoven with study. Arturo Giovannitti was probably the most widely known early Italian-American writer. He achieved critical acclaim with his book of poems, *Arrows in the Gale,* based on his experiences during the famous 1912 Lawrence, Massachusetts, strike of largely immigrant textile workers.

Italian immigrant women were even less likely to be literate than men, which helps explain the absence of Italian immigrant women authors among the first

generation. An exception of sorts is *Rosa, The Life of an Italian Immigrant,* an oral narrative that details life during the immigrant generation. A maid in a Chicago settlement house, "Rosa," using her pseudonymous name, told her story to one of the social workers, Marie Hall Ets. Ets took some liberties in transcribing the tale. Rosa's own colorful English is thus lost in Ets's version. Nevertheless, her story of immigration and survival in America as a mother, wife, and worker, under often desperate conditions, provides a vivid picture of immigrant life from a female perspective.

Unlike the Italian peasantry, the more urban Jewish immigrants tended to be literate. Indeed, literacy and learning were highly esteemed, in part due to the central importance of religious scripture to Jewish life. Jewish immigrants built on this tradition to create a distinctive literary culture in America both in Yiddish and in English.

Although Yiddish first came to the United States as a dialect, the popular press helped to establish it as a literary language while providing an important forum for writers. Journalists who wrote in Yiddish, particularly Abraham Cahan, did much to legitimize the language. A measure of the stature Yiddish achieved can be found in the 1891 publication of Alexander Harkavy's *Complete English-Jewish Dictionary.* In turn, the maintenance of Yiddish was facilitated by the outpouring of Yiddish language writing. Dozens of daily, weekly, monthly, and quarterly publications appeared between the 1880s and the World War I years. Periodicals of all types, literary but also political, commercial, and entertainment were available in Yiddish. At its height in 1885, the popular Yiddish weekly, the *Yiddishe Gazetten,* had over eight thousand subscribers. Even though Americanisms, in the form of expressions such as "alle right," seeped into Yiddish over time, it remained intact as a language.

A literary genre that was born directly out of Jewish immigrant life was the sweatshop school of poetry. The name derives from the crowded, ill-ventilated shops in New York's garment district where the largely Jewish immigrant workers were "sweated." This Yiddish poetry vividly recalled the harsh conditions under which Jewish workers labored, and it contained an implicit call for social justice. The poems were either sung or recited. Morris Rosenfeld was one of the most famous of the sweatshop poets, both within the Jewish community and among a larger American audience, thanks to an 1898 English translation of his poems from the Yiddish.

Another literary movement was centered around the magazine *Yugend* (Youth) established in 1907. The newly arrived immigrants who formed *Di Yunge,* as they came to be known, marked a sharp break with the sweatshop poets and other Jewish writers in their refusal to write about the political or social issues affecting the Jewish community. Instead, poets such as Mani Leib and the novelist Joseph Opatashu embraced a more personal style, both in terms of content and language.

The immigrant generation also produced important English-language works. Among the most well known are the works of two women, Mary Antin's *The Promised Land*, first published in 1912, and Anzia Yezierska's novel *The Bread Givers*. As the title suggests, Antin's memoir offers a very positive appraisal of immigrant life in America. Yezierska's autobiographical novel relates her struggles with her Old World father. One other outstanding work of immigrant fiction is Abraham Cahan's *Rise of David Levinsky,* the story of a Jewish immigrant who gains success in America but pays a heavy price for it.

Like the Italians, Poles lacked both the education and the literate tradition of Jewish immigrants. They tended to focus instead on the practicalities of everyday existence, leaving little room for creative endeavors. Thus, the immigrant generation of Poles can point to only one author who detailed their struggle in the New World, Henry Sienkiewicz and his novel *After Bread: A Story of Polish Emigrant Life in America*. In a naturalistic style, the novel details the experiences of a Polish father and daughter from their passage to America through the course of their ultimately tragic lives.

FOLKWAYS

In addition to more commonly recognized cultural traditions, immigrants brought with them various folkways that formed an integral part of their cultures. Traditional foods, celebrations, and storytelling are some examples of immigrant folkways.

Immigrants celebrated religious holidays in particular with traditional foods. For the largely Roman Catholic Italians and Slavs, Christmas Eve, Christmas Day, and Easter were the most important holidays of the year. Polish immigrants celebrated Christmas Eve, for example, with a menu of odd-numbered dishes, often as many as eleven, including different types of *pierogi* stuffed with cheese, mushrooms or sauerkraut; various fish dishes; noodle soups with beets or mushrooms; herring with boiled potatoes; and poppy seed cake. Slovaks marked Easter Sunday with the meats and dairy products that they had given up during the fasting period of Lent. They ate cheeses like hrudka

and syrek, as well as meats such as klobasa, along with the traditional Easter bread, *Paska*.

The Italian *feste* combined traditional food with regional folk religious practices. Southern Italian religiosity found expression in devotion to local patron saints and the Virgin Mary, a tradition that carried over to America. The *feste* featured a procession through the neighborhood with a statue of the saint or the Madonna held aloft. Italian Americans honored their saints with large family meals and foods served in the local streets where the *feste* took place. Although the foods varied according to Italian region of origin, celebrants of the *festa* of Our Lady of Mount Carmel in Italian East Harlem in New York City, for example, could expect street vendors to offer such traditional foods as pasta; nougat candy; fried, sugared dough balls known in some areas as zeppole; and beans cooked in oil and red pepper.

The foodways of eastern European Jewry reflected their region of origin. These included potato-based soups, dark rye breads, fatty meat and fishes like herring, but few vegetables beyond pickled cucumbers, beets, and dried legumes. The foods and rules of food preparation necessary for religious observances were more uniform. Jewish immigrants followed the rules of *kashruth* in determining what foods to eat and how to prepare and serve them. For example, Jewish law required the avoidance of pork and prohibited meat dishes from coming into contact with milk-based dishes at any point in their preparation. Religious high holidays like Passover dictated specific symbolic foods such as the unleavened bread, *matzoh,* as well as specialty foods such as gefilte fish or pastries made from *matzoh* meal.

Storytelling was an important folkway for Italian immigrants, who brought with them a rich oral tradition that included many forms such as personal stories, local legends, folktales, jokes, anecdotes, and proverbs. Although some men and women were known for their abilities to tell intricate, traditional stories from memory, everyday immigrants had at their disposal a stock of proverbs from the old country (some of which were more suited to their new environment than others) to draw upon, along with material from their own lives. The ability to tell a good story was a valued skill.

DANCE HALLS, NICKELODEONS, CAFÉS, AND SALOONS

Italian and other immigrants patronized the new working-class American forms of entertainment which were developing at the turn of the century. Indeed, immigrants and their children helped create these new forms, including the dance halls, nickelodeons, cafés, and saloons.

By 1907, young second-generation Jewish men and women on the Lower East Side could choose from thirty-one dance halls to indulge their passion for the latest dances. The dance halls offered affordable entertainment; single girls could enter the halls for ten cents, a couple for twenty-five cents. There were even instructors on hand for those who were not seasoned dancers. The more sheltered Italian girls found their way to the dance halls only against their parents' wishes. The dark side of the dance halls was their association with prostitution; "dance instructors" sometimes turned out to be pimps or procurers.

Perhaps the most popular entertainment for the immigrants and their children was the newly emerging movies. Indeed, the tenement districts of large cities provided the first audiences for the early cinema. In 1909, New York City could count over three hundred and forty nickelodeons, movie houses that charged five cents per person, which were visited by over two hundred and fifty thousand people each day of the week except Sunday—when attendance mushroomed to five hundred thousand. The movie-going experience of the time was quite different from what modern audiences have come to expect. It was not uncommon for audiences to sing along with the music or read the captions of the silent films aloud. Socializing in the aisles was commonplace. Italian mothers were so reassured by the familiar neighborhood atmosphere of the nickelodeons that they allowed their daughters to attend them. Although the movies themselves were not made by their immigrant working-class audiences, the conventions of movie watching were dictated by and reflected the culture of this audience.

The coffeehouses and saloons were a predominantly male domain, but women frequented the movies, constituting 40 percent of the total audience. Nor was female attendance limited to young women as in the case of dance halls. Many middle-age and older women regularly patronized the nickelodeons.

Immigrant neighborhoods were dotted with coffeehouses that offered sociability and entertainment of various forms. Jewish coffeehouses were centers of intellectual and cultural life, where journalists, playwrights, and others engaged in lively debate. By 1905, the Lower East Side coffeehouses numbered more than two hundred and fifty, each catering to the specific interests, whether political or cultural, of its patrons.

While the Jewish coffeehouse occasionally featured music, the Italian equivalent, the *caffe chantant*, was a popular neighborhood café that was much more oriented toward entertainment. Italian immigrant popular music was kept alive through the *caffes*, which featured musical fare for working-class immigrants. These *caffes* existed in Little Italys all over America. They varied in terms of form (some for example, resembled saloons or restaurants more than *caffes*) and types of music offered.

The music performed in the *caffes* was regionally based. The most popular *caffe chantant* in New York's Little Italy, the Villa Vittorio Emanuele III on Mulberry Street, for example, featured Neapolitan music. It was in these local popular establishments that Eduardo Migliaccio and other figures of the Italian immigrant musical stage launched their careers.

Saloons were popular neighborhood institutions for eastern European gentiles and Italians, but not for Jewish immigrants, who shunned alcohol. In Polish communities, it was not uncommon to find two or three saloons at each intersection. The saloons have been called "poor men's clubs." In addition to providing a place for working men to enjoy their favorite drinks, they often offered amenities such as free lunches and meeting rooms for ethnic groups. In New York City, Italian men frequented drinking establishments on the docks, where they could drink wine and play cards while waiting for work. Saloons offered opportunities to barter steamship tickets or lodging. Perhaps most importantly, they provided a space for immigrants to enjoy some leisure time with co-ethnics.

Nancy C. Carnevale

See also: Immigrant Aid Societies and Organizations (Part II, Sec. 2); Segmented Assimilation (Part II, Sec. 4); Foreign and Immigrant Influence on American Popular Culture (Part II, Sec. 10); The Immigrant and the Community, 1917 (Part IV, Sec. 3).

BIBLIOGRAPHY

Conzen, Kathleen, and David A. Gerber, Ewa Morawska, George E. Pozzetta, and Rudolph J. Vecoli. "The Invention of Ethnicity: A Perspective from the U.S.A." *Journal of American Ethnic History* 12 (Fall 1992): 3–41.

D'Acernio, Pellegrino, ed. *The Italian American Heritage: A Companion to Literature and Arts.* New York: Garland Publishing, Inc., 1999.

Ewen, Elizabeth. *Immigrant Women in the Land of Dollars: Life and Culture on the Lower East Side 1890–1925.* New York: Monthly Review Press, 1985.

Gabaccia, Donna R. *We Are What We Eat: Ethnic Food and the Making of Americans.* Cambridge, MA: Harvard University Press, 1998.

Green, Victor. *A Passion for Polka: Old-Time Ethnic Music in America.* Berkeley: University of California Press, 1992.

Howe, Irving. *The World of Our Fathers.* New York: Harcourt Brace Jovanovich, 1976.

Kazal, Russell A. "Revisiting Assimilation: The Rise, Fall, and Reappraisal of a Concept in American Ethnic History." *American Historical Review* (April 1995): 437–71.

La Sorte, Michael. *LaMerica: Images of Italian Greenhorn Experience.* Philadelphia: Temple University Press, 1985.

Mathias, Elizabeth, and Richard Raspa. *Italian Folktales in America: The Verbal Art of an Immigrant Woman.* Detroit: Wayne State University Press, 1985.

Obidinski, Eugene E., and Helen Stankiewicz Zand. *Polish Folkways in America.* Lanham, MD: University Press of America, 1987.

Orsi, Robert Anthony. *The Madonna of 115th Street: Faith and Community in Italian Harlem, 1880–1950.* New Haven, CT: Yale University Press, 1985.

Peiss, Kathy. *Cheap Amusements: Working Women and Leisure in Turn-of-the-Century New York.* Philadelphia: Temple University Press, 1986.

Rischin, Moses. *The Promised City: New York's Jews, 1870–1914.* Cambridge, MA: Harvard University Press, 1962.

Slobin, Mark. *Tenement Songs: The Popular Music of the Jewish Immigrants.* Urbana: University of Illinois Press, 1982.

Stolarik, M. Mark. *Growing Up on the South Side: Three Generations of Slovaks in Bethlehem, Pennsylvania, 1880–1976.* Cranbury, NJ: Associated University Presses, 1985.

Section 4

1920 TO 1965

INTRODUCTION

Section 4 of Part I of the *Encyclopedia of American Immigration* focuses on the period between roughly 1920 and 1965. These two years mark the beginning and end of a unique period in American history, a time of relatively light immigration between two great waves of incoming people. The first demarcation year—that is, 1920—represents a compromise of sorts. Two factors were critical in the falling off of European immigration from its peak at the turn of the twentieth century: World War I and the pieces of immigration restriction legislation passed between 1917 and 1924.

The second demarcation year—1965—is more clear-cut. In that year, Congress passed and President Lyndon Johnson signed the landmark Immigration and Nationality Act, ending the strict national quotas established in 1921 and 1924. With this law, immigration from countries outside of western and northern Europe was opened up for the first time in two generations. Aside from the law, however, there were other factors that led to reduced immigration to the United States in this period—most notably, the Great Depression of the 1930s and the Second World War of the 1940s.

Nevertheless, despite these domestic and international factors, there was a steady, albeit reduced, stream of immigrants to the United States in the period between 1920 and 1965. In "Nativist Reaction," Brian N. Fry explores the political climate in the United States immediately before, during, and after World War I that led to the restrictive legislation from 1917 through 1924. Fry also discusses the anti-immigrant sentiment of the period between the 1930s and 1950s that helped keep immigration restriction legislation on the books, despite an increasingly liberal political climate open to more immigration and an expanding U.S. economy that needed new workers.

In a related entry on the Red Scare of the immediate post–World War I era, John Herschel Barnhill shows how immigrants and foreigners became associated in the popular imagination of the period with treason and anarchy. He discusses how antiforeign propaganda and popular sentiment during World War I fueled the wave of hysteria against liberals and leftists that followed. Barnhill then examines the wave of strikes and political radicalism that occurred in the United States directly after World War II, events and trends that also helped to fuel antileftist and anti-immigrant hysteria. Finally, he explores the impact that the Red Scare had on immigrants and the means by which several thousand individuals suspected of being communist-leaning foreigners were deported from the country.

In "War Refugees," Richard S. Kim discusses those immigrants who came to American shores because of the great global struggles of the early and mid–twentieth century. Among the topics discussed is the Jewish refugee crisis of the 1930s, when the United States largely turned a deaf ear to the appeals of Jews trying to flee Nazi Germany and Nazi-threatened Europe. Exploring the American response to the Holocaust, Kim discusses how few Jews and other persecuted people were allowed into the United States. He also examines U.S. policy toward displaced persons immediately after World War II. Finally, Kim looks into the way in which Cold War politics shaped U.S. policies toward refugees from such Communist countries as Hungary and Cuba and how those refugees were more openly welcomed than those people escaping brutal but noncommunist regimes, many of which were supported by the United States.

In "Japanese Internment," Nobuko Adachi discusses the U.S. government's decision to intern West Coast Japanese nationals and Japanese-American citizens in concentration camps for the duration of World War II. In this entry, Adachi examines the history of Japanese immigration to the United States from the late 1800s through the beginning of World War II. Adachi also explores the reasons leading up to the internment order as well as what life was like in the camps themselves. The author also discusses the several cases brought by Japanese internees to challenge the constitutionality of the internment order, and why and how those cases failed. Finally, Adachi looks into the movement to redress the internment policy and the ultimately successful effort to win reparations for remaining survivors of the camps and their descendants.

Timothy Draper's entry, "The Surge of Latino Immigration," explores the anomaly created by the immigration restrictions acts of the late 1910s and early 1920s, whereby peoples of the Western Hemisphere were largely exempt from the quotas. The author ex-

amines how this exemption—as well as the need for low-cost farm labor—led to a growing tide of immigration from south of the border. In addition, Draper discusses why Puerto Ricans began coming to this country in ever greater numbers after World War II and what they experienced once they got here. He also looks into the impact of the Cuban revolution on immigration from that country beginning in the late 1950s. Finally, Draper examines the small but steadily growing numbers of immigrants from Central America and the Caribbean during the period between World War I and the immigration reform act of 1965.

NATIVIST REACTION

A lesson about the domestic casualties of war and war's aftermath rests between the bookends of World War I and 1965. Even though some of the most egregious examples of American nativism occur during or around wartime, scholars routinely explain nativism in terms of economic downturns and immigration flows. Unlike recessions and migration rates, wartime encourages patriotic displays of loyalty and makes immigrant customs and activities into matters of national security.

Wartime antagonisms belong to a tradition of intolerance in which "natives" view national and ethnic populations as potential subversives because their former homeland is at war with their new home. In the course of conflict, some are branded as "fifth columnists," internal saboteurs who aid their former homeland through acts of sabotage.

Describing reactions as "nativist," however, is not a straightforward matter because nativism is associated with a variety of beliefs and behaviors. Social scientists use the term to describe hostility toward immigrants and aspiring immigrants, the dislike of "foreigners," and attempts to reduce the "rights" of immigrants. But because its meaning is constantly changing, so are its expressions, which is especially true when looking at past events from the vantage point of the present. For the sake of consistency and clarity, then, a brief definition of nativism is required.

"Nativism" is "a policy of favoring native inhabitants as opposed to immigrants," and includes a native defense of exclusive claims over and against the encroachment of aliens. The meanings of "native" and "alien" are not firmly planted but shift with perception, identifiability, and sociohistorical context. Newly arrived immigrants as well as third-generation residents can be perceived as alien and unwittingly threaten the exclusive claims of natives. For example, the tensions of World War I transformed German-*American* behaviors into *German* acts of treason.

Natives not only make distinctions between "us" and "them" but also—out of a sense of entitlement—arrogate certain rights and privileges unto themselves. Like "native" and "alien," the exclusive claims of natives fluctuate. At various points throughout American history, natives have defined education, employment, and government benefits as exclusively theirs. These definitions depend, though, on power and perceptions of legitimacy. When aliens encroach on the exclusive claims of natives, the responses of a native population will vary according to its relative power, ability to identify and monitor aliens, the perceived legitimacy of the proposed actions, and overall social and legal contexts.

THROUGH WORLD WAR I

During the French and Spanish wars of colonial times, Americans viewed Catholics as potential saboteurs, a fifth column cooperating with the armies of French Canada and Spanish Florida. Tagging Catholics as the "enemy within" was not uncommon. Anti-Catholicism was the most prevalent form of nativism up until the Civil War. Some Protestants considered the "authoritarian" and "secretive" religion of Roman Catholicism a menace to their God-given liberty, and Catholics as pawns of the pope.

Anti-Catholicism eased after the Civil War but still remained potent in the early 1900s. An anti-Catholic weekly called *The Menace* enjoyed 1.5 million subscribers in April 1915, but its subscription base shrank to around 500,000 in just over a year. Fears about immigrants—specifically, their racial makeup and purported radical tendencies—overshadowed nativist fears about disloyal Catholics as the United States readied itself for World War I.

The Great War directed the public's attention to German Americans, whose opinions and activities allegedly threatened the national interest. Americani-

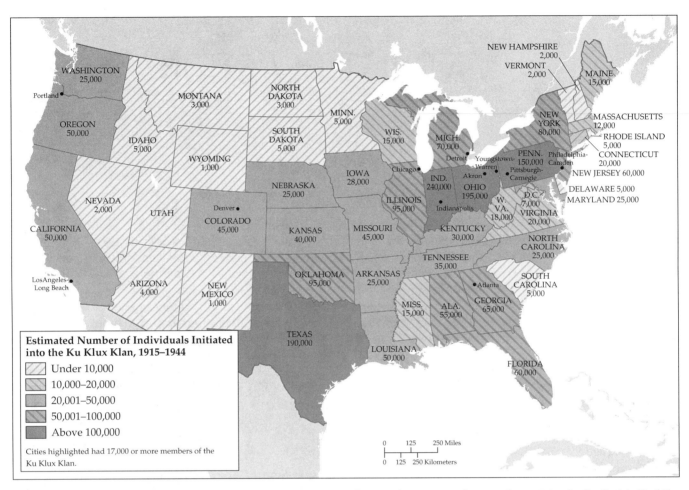

As this map makes clear, the Ku Klux Klan had more members in key northern states than southern states in the first half of the twentieth century. *(CARTO-GRAPHICS)*

zation propaganda and preparations for World War I placed Germans under the national microscope. Dissent looked like disloyalty. Americans championed the standard of "one hundred percent American," just as German Americans highlighted their heritage and insisted on American neutrality.

Accustomed to friendliness and even praise, German Americans insisted on American neutrality with little thought of reprisal. The German-American Alliance, with 2 million members and branches in forty states, solicited support from the general population and, of course, German Americans—the largest population of first-generation immigrants in the United States between 1880 and 1920. According to the 1910 census, 8.3 million people considered Germany their land of origin, and almost one-third of them (2.5 million) were born in Germany. Comprising nearly 9 percent of the American population, German Americans participated in American politics and, as did other immigrant groups, took a special interest in matters involving their ethnic homeland.

In December 1914, Representative Richard Bartholdt (R-MO) proposed an arms embargo bill prohibiting the export of war munitions. The German-American Alliance (and the Irish-based American Neutrality League) lobbied for its passage by sending telegrams, letters, and petitions to their national representatives. Mass rallies were also staged in support of the bill, further confirming American suspicions of divided loyalties. At a rally in St. Louis, the assembly sang the German national anthem before the orators criticized American and British diplomacy and adopted a resolution backing the arms embargo bill. The American press emptied their editorial quivers, criticizing German Americans for their tactics and questioning their loyalty.

In January 1915, representatives from every large German American organization met in Washington. Munitions shipments to the Allies had increased, adding to Great Britain's natural advantage over Germany in receiving American supplies. The conference of embargo supporters claimed that an embargo was

PUCK.

LOOKING BACKWARD.
They would close to the New-Comer the Bridge that Carried Them and their Fathers Over.

This early twentieth-century cartoon mocks nativist reaction to immigrants as the height of hypocrisy. The original caption reads: "Looking backward: they would close to the new-comer the bridge that carried them and their fathers over." Note how the shadows of these respectably dressed gentlemen depict their humble immigrant origins. (U.S. Department of the Interior, National Park Service)

the only true, neutral course. The press was nearly unanimous in its condemnation. Some of the New York papers tagged the conference as the work of "German agents," while others reminded German Americans that flirting with treason invited reprisals.

German diplomats and their agents had already established a propaganda machine in New York to generate newspaper articles and pamphlets absolving Germany of initial aggression. Making matters worse, German agents working out of Germany's Washington embassy perpetrated the first acts of German sabotage just a few days after the Washington conference. In the ensuing months, agents attempted to smuggle bombs aboard American ships and destroy American factories. Their efforts usually failed, but some saboteurs bombed a New Jersey assembly plant in 1917. On May 7, 1915, however, the sinking of the *Lusitania*, a casualty of Germany's submarine campaign, that cost British and American lives, converted amorphous misgivings and suspicions into a concretely defined threat.

Between 1915 and 1917, national and international events sapped President Woodrow Wilson's "too proud to fight" slogan of its persuasiveness, while American reporters applauded his denunciation of both the German government and the adherence of German and Irish Americans to their countries of origin. In short, the German-American Alliance's bold support for Germany, the virtually unanimous pro-Germany stance of the German-American press, and acts of sabotage by German agents (and some German Americans) were intolerable to a country feverishly trying to prepare for war.

German Americans tried to pacify the American public by Americanizing German names—for example, Schmidt became Smith; East Germantown, Indiana, was renamed Pershing, and sauerkraut became "liberty cabbage." But these last-minute demonstrations of loyalty did little to pacify official or public sentiment. Volunteer "spy-hunting" organizations, such as the American Protective League, continued to harass German Americans, and in 1919, fifteen states passed laws requiring all public and private schools to teach only in English. Across the country, nativists humiliated Germans by painting them yellow, gumming them with tar and feathers, destroying their property, and forcing them to kiss the flag. One unfortunate immigrant was even dragged to the outskirts of Collinsville, Illinois, and hanged for no other apparent reason than his German nationality.

On the same day Congress declared war against Germany, April 6, 1917, President Wilson announced twelve "enemy alien regulations"; by the following November he had added another eight. The regulations restricted the movement of enemy aliens, required them to carry registration cards, and laid the legal groundwork for the ensuing internments. Federal agents used the 1798 Alien Enemy Act to intern 6,300 German nationals ("enemy aliens"), of whom 2,300 were alleged civilian enemy aliens. Congress also enacted the 1917 Espionage Act and the 1918 Sedition Act to prosecute U.S. citizens of German origin who obstructed the draft or condemned the war effort.

Civilian enemy aliens residing east of the Mississippi River were interned at either Fort Oglethorpe or Fort McPherson in Georgia. Those living west of the Mississippi found their new internment camp in Fort Douglas, just outside Salt Lake City, Utah. Civilian and foreign enemy aliens encountered different receptions at Fort Douglas, but both groups endured insulting indignities and ridicule. Attempted escapes made local headlines and illuminated the less-than-inviting conditions of the camp.

The fate of the prisoners, however, changed little with the end of the war on November 11, 1918. The suspension of war regulations did not apply to internment, although internees were freed if they could demonstrate a job was waiting for them upon release. But the tight, postwar labor market slowed the rate of release, as did the Red Scare of 1919, which kept "dangerous radicals" in the camps until 1920. The American fear of foreign radicals did not subside with the war's end but actually grew during the postwar years, as communists and bolshevists replaced Germans as the new enemy within.

THE 1920s

After the war, Attorney General A. Mitchell Palmer institutionalized America's fear of foreign subversives by creating the General Intelligence Division in 1919 to weed out "radicals." In a series of "Palmer raids" conducted between 1919 and 1920, agents from the Department of Justice stormed the meeting places of Russian workers in twelve cities. Thousands were arrested, and hundreds of aliens were deported to Russia. Some were even forced to leave their families behind. A false prediction of terrorism by Palmer in 1920, however, brought the Red Scare to an end. His debacle marked a turn in nativist apprehension, from a fear of foreign radicals increasingly to a general uneasiness with "inferior races."

Between 1920 and 1927, Henry Ford's *Dearborn Independent* periodically deplored the control allegedly exerted by "International Jews." At one point, the newspaper reached a circulation of 700,000. The editorials expanded the anti-Semitic campaign beyond the reaches of Detroit when they were converted into a four-volume work entitled *The International Jew*. Ford's articles not only deceived American audiences about the alleged dangers of a Jewish takeover but fed Nazi prejudices as well.

In his book *Mein Kampf* (1925–1927), Adolf Hitler praised Ford for resisting the control of American Jews, and Baldur von Shirach, head of the Hitler youth program, told his prosecutors during the Nuremberg Trial that Ford's book had had a profound impact on German youth. The Nazis awarded Ford the Grand Cross of the German Eagle in 1938 after Thomas J. Watson, founder and president of International Business Machines (IBM), refused to accept it. But Ford took little pleasure in Nazi compliments and decorations once he saw the horrors of Germany's Final Solution. After watching a newsreel on the Majdanek concentration camp in 1945, Ford was so dismayed, some say, that he experienced a serious stroke that laid the foundations for his death in 1947.

The Ku Klux Klan also stepped up its restrictionist and racist initiatives in the early 1920s, acquiring somewhere between 2 and 3 million recruits by 1924. Although white supremacy played an influential role, the organization's ideas converged on populations that seemed especially "foreign." Klan members selected Catholics, Jews, and foreigners as their main targets, while recent Jewish immigrants from eastern Europe encountered extensive discrimination in housing, employment, and college admissions.

Two new editions of Madison Grant's *The Passing of the Great Race* were published in the early 1920s. Grant warned that the extinction of the Nordic race was inevitable unless the hordes of Alpines, Mediterraneans, and Jewish "hybrids" were turned back. Even though the book was relatively insignificant when it first appeared in 1916, eugenicists and other race-oriented thinkers received what later became an indispensable tool in reducing legal immigration—a racial typology. Much of the Immigration Act of 1924 was predicated on a cultural and racial logic, as evidenced by the new national origins quota system that limited immigration from southeastern Europe. The system lowered the annual immigration ceiling, and immigrants from northwestern Europe received over 80 percent of the visas.

THE 1930s

Irony riddled the aspirations of many immigrants in the 1930s. Those who wanted to stay were forced out, and those who wanted to enter were kept out. The deportation or repatriation of five to six hundred thousand persons of Mexican ancestry in the wake of the Great Depression symbolizes those who desired to stay but were forced out. By the end of the decade, it is estimated that more than half of those who returned to Mexico were American citizens and that a third of the Los Angeles Mexican community had emigrated to Mexico.

Those who tried to enter but were kept out—primarily Jewish refugees—encountered a president and State Department hesitant to admit them as refugees or expand the immigration quotas. The government did not act alone but took its cue from the American public. Public opinion polls conducted between 1938 and 1941 reveal a pervasive anti-Semitism that clearly influenced President Franklin D. Roosevelt's position.

Anti-Semitism was steered through the air waves by Father Charles Coughlin, a Detroit-area Catholic priest. While his Christian Front against Communism focused on "the problem of the American Jews," Coughlin reprinted the speeches of Nazi propaganda minister Joseph Goebbels in his widely read newspaper, *Social Justice*, and personally praised the "social justice" meted out by the Third Reich. With an estimated 30 million listeners by the mid-1930s, Coughlin had amassed the largest radio audience in the world. But his support for Germany against the "British-Jewish-Roosevelt conspiracy" and the banning of *Social Justice* from the mails—for violating the Espionage Act—contributed to his downfall.

WORLD WAR II THROUGH 1965 IMMIGRATION REFORM

Fearful of "another" fifth column, Congress established a set of internal and external barriers when war

erupted in Europe. From April to June 1940, Germany's string of victories in Norway, Denmark, France, and the Low Countries convinced American and British officials that such successes were due in part to the work of fifth columnists. As a result, they took unparalleled action against an essentially imaginary threat.

First, admissions from Nazi-occupied countries were drastically reduced, and in 1940, Congress enacted the Alien Registration Act, which required all resident aliens fourteen and older to be fingerprinted and to register annually. Second, Congress moved the Immigration and Naturalization Service (INS) from the Department of Labor to the Department of Justice for purposes of national security. The executive branch also authorized a network of agencies—the Federal Bureau of Investigation (FBI), Military Intelligence, the War Department, and the Office of Naval Intelligence—to compile a list of aliens to be interned in the event of a war.

The list would be used soon enough. On December 7, 1941, the Japanese attacked Pearl Harbor, killing over three thousand Americans stationed in Hawaii. That very day, the Japanese American Citizens League telegraphed their allegiance to President Roosevelt, pledging their support, as citizens of the United States, to drive out the Japanese invasion with their fellow Americans. But the Pearl Harbor attack, along with Japan's initial victories in the Pacific, became a symbol of America's vulnerability to fifth columnists and galvanized public opinion against the Japanese, precipitating a string of reactions against Japanese Americans.

A congressional commission, a quickly formed committee to investigate the Pearl Harbor attack, erroneously concluded that fifth columnists contributed to the surprise attack. The press heightened the public's fear of a fifth column with sensationalist headlines about subversive Japanese-American tactics, but the public and the press broadened the indictment by pressuring public officials to do something about German and Italian aliens. President Roosevelt, the War Department, and the FBI were already two steps ahead of them.

On December 8, 1941, the day that the United States declared war against Japan, President Roosevelt directed the FBI and other agencies to arrest all Italian and German aliens they considered a threat to national security. By February 4, 1942, the FBI had arrested 261 Italians and 1,361 Germans, and by October 5, 1943, 5,300 Japanese, 3,503 Italians, and 5,977 Germans had been taken into custody. Of those arrested, none were convicted of sabotage, although 228 Italians were interned for various lengths of time.

On February 19, 1942, President Roosevelt signed Executive Order 9066 by which he authorized the army, under the secretary of war's direction, to "prescribe military spaces" and exclude "any or all persons" as military necessity required. While Japanese and Japanese Americans are never mentioned in the order, officials singled them out for mass internment. By August 7, 1942, nearly all the West Coast Japanese (112,704 in all, almost two-thirds of whom were American citizens) were either in War Relocation Authority (WRA) camps or in Wartime Civil Control Administration Assembly centers. The camps were scattered throughout the U.S. interior and reached as far as Jerome, Arkansas.

Life in the camps was harsh, although with the exception of barbed wire and armed sentries, it bore little resemblance to the concentration camps in Germany. Still, the "evacuees" dwelled in barracks, ate in mess halls, used communal toilets and showers, dressed in identical clothing, and endured days marked by monotony, tension, and violence. By 1943, the WRA had begun to release individuals who satisfied certain requirements, and by January 1945, it had allowed most Japanese to leave the camps.

The fate of German and Italian aliens came frightfully close to that of the Japanese but in the end took a different course. From January to May 1942, various officials at the local, regional, and federal level called for the internment of all enemy aliens and their families during the war. The failure to realize this objective can be attributed to, among other things, bureaucratic infighting between the War and Justice departments, racism, the logistics of relocating and interning possibly millions of German and Italian Americans, and the recognition that such an action would inevitably interrupt the war effort.

German and Italian aliens lived throughout the United States. In 1940, over 264,000 German aliens and 599,000 Italian aliens resided in the United States. If the military interned the immediate descendants of the European alien populations (as they had with the Japanese), the number of potential internees could have approached the 11 million mark. The number of German and Italian aliens was intimidating, but their heavy concentration in jobs vital to the war industry and the inappreciable degree of racial and cultural distinctiveness (compared with the Japanese) kept dreams of a mass internment in the heads of government officials.

The Japanese, on the other hand, were relatively concentrated and small in number. By 1940, only 126,947 Japanese Americans lived in the contiguous United States, 90 percent of whom resided on the Pacific Coast, mostly in California. In addition, seven out of eight West Coast Japanese worked in three sectors somewhat peripheral to the war effort: agriculture, forestry, and fishing. When their racial distinctiveness was added to the cognitive mix, the Japanese emerged as *the* scapegoat for a plan originally devised, in the eyes of some officials, for all enemy aliens.

The military ordered all three groups to evacuate certain military areas in March 1942 (approximately twenty-five hundred to three thousand Italians were required to leave Monterey Bay alone), but in April, while officials transported Japanese Americans to internment camps, German and Italian aliens tolerated minor inconveniences such as a 9 P.M. to 6 A.M. curfew, travel restrictions, and the confiscation of their cameras, radios, and firearms. The restrictions lasted approximately nine months and affected most of the German and Italian aliens on the West Coast.

Mexican Americans in Los Angeles also bore the label of "fifth column," albeit for a shorter period of time. Between 1942 and 1943, descriptions of Mexican juvenile delinquency complemented or replaced headlines about the alleged disloyalty of Japanese Americans. The list of internal enemies expanded to include Chicano youth. Press accounts inflamed public opinion, and in June 1943, Anglo servicemen and Mexican-American youth clashed in Los Angeles for ten days in the Zoot Suit Riots. Tearing off the youths' oversized suits and assaulting them, Anglo servicemen were joined by civilians in their provocations and confrontations with the zoot-suiters.

Primarily because of the Cold War, a fear of foreign radicals outlived World War II. Congress passed the McCarran Internal Security Act in 1950, making membership in a supposedly subversive group grounds for denaturalization, as well as deportation and exclusion. But Congress slowed the restrictionist impulse in 1952 by passing the massive McCarran-Walter Act. The legislation removed race as a barrier to admission and naturalization (and lifted the ban on Asian entry and naturalization) but left the 1924 immigration preferences basically intact. Not until 1965 would the national origins system—and the face of U.S. immigration—undergo considerable change.

Brian N. Fry

See also: Nativism and Know-Nothings (Part I, Sec. 2); Anti-Immigrant Backlash (Part I, Sec. 5); Anti-Immigrant Politics (Part II, Sec. 6).

BIBLIOGRAPHY

Barkan, Elliott R. *And Still They Come: Immigrants and American Society, 1920 to the 1990s.* Wheeling, IL: Harlan Davidson, 1996.

Bennett, David H. *The Party of Fear: From Nativist Movements to the New Far Right in American History.* 2d ed. New York: Vintage Books, 1995.

Bosniak, Linda S. " 'Nativism' the Concept: Some Reflections." In *Immigrants Out! The New Nativism and the Anti-immigrant Impulse in the United States,* ed. J. F. Perea. New York: New York University Press, 1997.

Brown, Mary E. *Shapers of the Great Debate on Immigration: A Biographical Dictionary.* Westport, CT: Greenwood Press, 1999.

Conzen, Kathleen N. "Germans." In *Harvard Encyclopedia of American Ethnic Groups,* ed. Stephen Thernstrom, pp. 405–25. Cambridge: Harvard University Press, 1981.

Daniels, Roger. *Prisoners without Trial: Japanese Americans in World War II.* New York: Hill and Wang, 1993.

Ellis, Mark, and Panikos Panayi. "German Minorities in World War I: A Comparative Study of Britain and the USA." *Ethnic and Racial Studies* 17 (April 1994): 238–59.

Fernandez, Ronald. "Getting Germans to Fight Germans: The Americanizers of World War I." *Journal of Ethnic Studies* 9 (1981): 53–68.

Fox, Stephan R. *The Unknown Internment: An Oral History of the Relocation of Italian Americans during World War II.* Boston: Twayne, 1988.

Gold, Steven J., and Bruce Phillips. "Mobility and Continuity among Eastern European Jews." In *Origins and Destinies: Immigration, Race, and Ethnicity in America,* ed. Silvia Pedraza and Rubén G. Rumbaut, pp. 182–94. Belmont, CA: Wadsworth, 1996.

Grant, Madison. *The Passing of The Great Race.* 4th edition. New York: Charles Scribner's Sons, 1922.

Harrington, Mona. "Loyalties: Dual and Divided." In *Harvard Encyclopedia of American Ethnic Groups,* ed. Stephen Thernstrom, pp. 676–86. Cambridge: Harvard University Press, 1981.

Higham, John. *Strangers in the Land: Patterns of American Nativism, 1860–1925.* New Brunswick, NJ: Rutgers University Press, 1992.

Kitano, H. "Japanese." In *Harvard Encyclopedia of American Ethnic Groups,* ed. Stephen Thernstrom, pp. 561–71. Cambridge: Harvard University Press, 1981.

Myer, Dillion S. *Uprooted Americans: The Japanese Americans and the War Relocation Authority during World War II.* Tucson: University of Arizona Press, 1971.

Nagler, Joerg A. "Enemy Aliens and Internment in World War I: Alvo von Alvensleben in Fort Douglas, Utah, a Case Study." *Utah Historical Quarterly* 58 (1990): 388–405.

Nelli, Humbert. "Italians." In *Harvard Encyclopedia of American Ethnic Groups,* ed. Stephen Thernstrom, pp. 545–60. Cambridge: Harvard University Press, 1981.

Sánchez, George J. *Becoming Mexican American: Ethnicity, Culture, and Identity in Chicano Los Angeles, 1900–1945.* New York: Oxford University Press, 1993.

Simon, Rita J., and S. H Alexander. *The Ambivalent Welcome: Print Media, Public Opinion, and Immigration.* Westport, CT: Praeger, 1993.

Ueda, Reed. *Postwar Immigrant America: A Social History.* Boston: Bedford Books of St. Martin's Press, 1994.

IMMIGRANTS AND THE RED SCARE

By 1919 the Great War was over. Four million American soldiers were demobilized hurriedly and without plan. Nine million industrial workers were converting to peacetime work, again without plan. Inflation had raised prices nearly 100 percent since 1914. The year 1919 saw 3,600 strikes by 4 million workers, almost all of which failed. A Republican Congress overturned wartime economic controls and much of the labor legislation of the Progressive Era, and emphatically rejected American involvement in the League of Nations. America was becoming isolationist, leaderless, and divided.

WORLD WAR I AND ANTIFOREIGN PROPAGANDA

During World War I, absolute loyalty was mandatory. Hyperpatriotic groups such as the National Security League, the American Defense Society, and the government-sponsored American Protective League cast aspersions on German Americans and foreigners generally as being antithetical to the American way of life. These and other grass-roots vigilante committees also engaged in direct action, including violence against those who did not meet their standards of "Americanism" or even those who refused or failed to buy war bonds. Led by George Creel's Committee on Public Information, the American press was rabidly patriotic and xenophobic as well. Symptomatic of the impulse to Americanism were the outlawing of the German language and the renaming of towns with German or German-sounding names. Sauerkraut was renamed "victory cabbage." And when they returned, many servicemen joined the patriot organizations.

Wartime legislation included the Espionage Act of 1917, which outlawed false reports or statements intended to hamper the military campaign, morale, recruiting, and the general effort. The Sedition Act of 1918 prohibited the printing, writing, or publishing of disloyal, profane, scurrilous, or abusive language about the form of government, the Constitution, the armed forces, or any language promoting the cause of American enemies or resistance to the American effort. Anti-immigrant legislation of 1918 called for the deportation of aliens advocating anarchism, assassination of government officials, or violent overthrow of the American government. On warrant of the secretary of labor, any resident advocating any prohibited idea could be detained and deported without due process.

American Socialists, of whom there were hundreds of thousands when the war began, were caught in the middle, as the party had opposed American entry into World War I. The government launched a series of prosecutions against prominent Socialists under the Sedition Act, including Milwaukee mayor Victor Berger (who may have lost his race for a Senate seat because of the trial) and perennial presidential candidate Eugene V. Debs, who actually ran for the White House from jail in 1920 and received almost 1 million votes. In addition, Charles Schenck, general secretary of the party, was convicted for distributing antienlistment leaflets during the war.

POST–WORLD WAR I RADICALISM

Rabid anti-Germanism switched easily to rabid anti-communism. After the Bolshevik revolution of 1917 in Russia and the creation of the Communist International (or Comintern) in 1919, it appeared to many as if communism was triumphing in Europe and potentially threatened America. This fear was exacerbated by other events across the Atlantic, including the temporary rise to power of a communist government in Hungary and its evident popularity and strength in Germany, Poland, and Italy. At home, two

American communist parties, small but highly visible, paraded and leafleted, thereby helping to fuel the hysteria.

In January 1919 the Industrial Workers of the World (IWW), one of the foremost radical labor organizations in the United States, led a general strike in Washington State. The IWW was an anarchosyndicalist labor organization that advocated economic as opposed to political action, confronting industry bosses through strikes and direct action rather than trying to fight them at the ballot box. Yet for all the fear it conjured up among capitalists and the middle class, the IWW was hardly a threat to the existing order. At its peak before and during the war, the IWW, or Wobblies as they were popularly called, had a membership of no more than 60,000 to 100,000 people. Still, it was very effective in using its limited numbers to target its enemies.

The IWW's strongest appeal was to Western migrant farm workers, timber workers, miners, and others in the extractive industries, though it also had a signficant presence among Midwestern steel and meatpacking workers and textile laborers in the Middle Atlantic and New England states. IWW tactics included the wildcat strike and violent rhetoric, neither of which was conducive to sustained, long-term struggle or success. The IWW message was spread by freelance anarchists such as Emma Goldman, and by Alexander Berkman's publications, *Mother Earth* and *The Blast*. In 1892, Berkman had attempted to murder industrialist Henry Clay Frick during the Homestead strike, and served fourteen years of his twenty-one-year sentence. Goldman, a well-known organizer, was believed to be the mentor of Leon Czolgosz, the assassin of President William McKinley in 1901. Goldman also had a twenty-five year history of radical speech and arrests. By 1919 the IWW was defeated, dispirited, and voiceless, serving as little more than as a bogeyman for the right. In the aftermath of the Washington State strike, fifty-four alien radicals were held incommunicado while awaiting deportation. Three finally were deported.

Adding to the sense of social unrest, riots spread across the country as communists and anticommunists clashed in the streets of Boston, Cleveland, and New York City on May 1, International Labor Day. Even more threatening to those in power, some thirty-six bombs came in the mails, including one to the mayor of Seattle. To the hyperpatriots of the day, it appeared that a "red" takeover of America was imminent. To leading industrialists and their supporters in government, however, the crisis seemed to present an opportunity to crush their long-time enemies—that

is, the socialists and the IWW—and so those in power began to fan the flames of anticommunist hysteria that were beginning to sweep the nation.

The presence of numerous immigrants among the ranks of radicals—and the prominence of foreigners among the leadership of the anarchist movement—tarred all newcomers with the brush of sedition, even though the vast majority of foreigners in the United States were hard-working, law-abiding residents and citizens. Immigrants dominated the leftist socialist groups. Still, the latest wave of immigration, from 1880 to 1920, had split the American left generally and the socialists specifically. Older socialists such as Debs and Berger advocated peaceful change through participation in the American electoral process. Many of the new immigrants, however, had come from the Russian Empire, where there was virtually no democratic tradition. They were encouraged by the revolution in their homeland and believed that something similar could be achieved through direct action and even violence here. To most Americans, they seemed extremely alien; they were European radicals who often spoke and wrote in foreign languages, using incendiary words to convey their demands for change.

EARLY ANTI-IMMIGRANT ACTIONS

Politicians in Washington, seeing what they believed was a threat to the American way of life and an opportunity to score points with their constituents, took action. In Congress, Representative Lee Overman's (D-NC) Judiciary Committee heard anti-Bolshevik witnesses, whose Christian patriotism reflected the charged nationalism of the war and immediate postwar years. One of the charges leveled by the witnesses—and accepted as truth by the committee members—was that the Russian Revolution itself had been organized and led by Jews living on Manhattan's Lower East Side. (Ridiculous as this sounds, it was true that Leon Trotsky, one of the prime movers of the Bolshevik uprising, had lived in that neighborhood before the war.)

Meanwhile, in New York State, a committee headed by state senator Clayton Lusk organized a police raid—which included its own undercover agents, local police and private detectives—on the Soviet Russian consulate, then claimed that the United States housed no less than 500,000 reds. Further raids on the offices of the radical wing of the Socialist Party, the IWW, and a Socialist Party educational center produced little evidence of revolutionary planning, but the actions added to the climate of fear. Also fueling the fear were race riots, the occasional ouster of a communist or socialist school teacher, and government and press propaganda. The process fed on itself, as public panic increased public pressure for the government to solve the crisis and the actions taken by the government fueled public fears. Finally, in the fall of 1919, the federal government began to act against aliens. Leading the fight was Attorney General A. Mitchell Palmer.

PALMER RAIDS

A. Mitchell Palmer was a Quaker reform Democrat who had declined the secretaryship of war in 1913. He was Wilson's alien property custodian (APC) from 1917 to 1919, which put him in charge of property seized from enemy aliens during the war. In March 1919, Wilson appointed him attorney general. He was seen as an able, diligent, intelligent, ambitious, pro-League of Nations reformer whose time as APC had sensitized him to the perils of radicals, anti-Americanism, and sabotage. Indeed, his home was actually bombed within three months of his taking office.

Palmer moved quickly. In August 1919, he set up the General Intelligence Division (GID) of the Bureau of Investigation (later, the Federal Bureau of Investigation, or FBI) and appointed an ambitious young agent named J. Edgar Hoover to run it. The GID quickly established card files on more than 200,000 radical organizations and publications, including membership lists. It also compiled 60,000 case histories of radicals.

By October, congressional and public opinion was pressing for "Red Specials," a popular term for the deportation of foreign radicals. And while Palmer recognized that the espionage and sedition acts were void in peacetime, he decided to call a nationwide raid on the radical Union of Russian Workers (URW) as a means to stir up so much popular hysteria against aliens that a way around the peacetime exception could be found or created.

The URW was an ideal target for Palmer. Founded in 1905, it had around four thousand members and defined itself as atheist, communist, and anarchist—all fighting words to most Americans. Still, most of the organization's members were apolitical, having joined the organization for the services it offered, including a boarding house, community center, and social activities for foreigners a long way from home.

Government raids on the URW on November 7, 1919, resulted in the arrests of 250 members in eleven cities—200 in New York alone. All but 39 were released in a short time. In one case, the city of Hartford, Connecticut, held a member in jail without a hearing for five months. State and local governments, following the federal example, raided other radical organizations. In New York City, the Lusk committee, back by 700 policemen, raided 73 locations, arrested 500, and seized tons of literature. Lusk turned over 256 of the aliens to the federal immigration and justice agency, mostly members of the Union of Russian Workers who were deemed deportable. For their part, the radicals reacted with calls for revolution and revenge.

For all the noise about deportation, however, the government outside Palmer's office was often slow to act. An investigation by the House of Representatives into the administration of Ellis Island revealed that only sixty of six hundred detainees had been deported between February 17 and November 19. The commissioner of immigration, Frederic C. Howe, resigned in 1919 rather than deport *en masse*, but his replacement, Byron Uhl, showed no reluctance.

When a November 25 raid on the Russian People's House found bomb-making materials, the press and government exaggerated the extent of the find. Many patriotic and social organizations—such as the Elks, Rotarians, Kiwanians, Legionnaires—petitioned Congress to act. Congress responded by introducing bills to shift deportation power to the attorney general, revoke the citizenship of radicals, and establish a penal colony on Guam for American radicals. The Labor Department announced that membership in the Union of Russian workers was a deportable offense. The first deportees would sail on an army transport, the *Buford*, before Christmas.

On December 21, 249 deportees (including 3 women) and accompanied by 250 soldiers, set sail on the *Buford* for Hanzo, Finland, thence by train to Russia. The deportees included 199 members of the URW, 43 previously detained anarchists, and 7 public charges, criminals, and misfits. Twelve left behind families, whose attempt to break through the ferry gates to join them was reported as a red attempt to free the radicals. Mostly the deportees were radicals without criminal records, but a few, such as Berkman and Goldman, supported the public perception that all were criminals and murderers. The deportations generated some opposition from the respectable press; the radical and liberal papers were outraged, but the press mostly enthusiastically supported the deportation.

Hyme Kaplan was one of many labor leaders rounded up during the Palmer raids in January 1920. He is shown here in his jail cell on Deer Island, Boston. *(UPI/Corbis-Bettman)*

FURTHER ANTICOMMUNIST RAIDS

In January 1920 Palmer targeted the Communist and Communist Labor parties. Labor secretary William Wilson was ill, and his antideportation deputy, Louis Post, was otherwise occupied. By default, Labor's immigration affairs became the preserve of solicitor general John W. Abercrombie, a Justice Department employee. Commissioner of Immigration Anthony J. Caminetti was antiradical. On December 27, 1919, Abercrombie signed more than three thousand warrants; four days later, he ended the administrative rule that reading of the warrant and notification of right to counsel occur at the beginning of each deportation hearing. He just required reading and notification sometime during the proceeding. On January 2, the raids netted four thousand victims in 33 cities in 23 states.

Raids, often without warrants, targeted both offices and residences. Police tactics were rough, and usually everyone in a given place was arrested. Detainees were often held incommunicado and deprived of right to counsel. American citizens were given to the states for action; aliens were held for deportation. Of the 800 seized in New England, 400 were sent in chains to the Deer Island detention center in Boston Harbor. Poor heat and sanitation contributed to three deaths there. The raids in New York City featured police brutality; Philadelphia used the "third degree" on suspects, subjecting them to browbeating and intimidation; Pittsburgh and New Jersey used warrantless arrests.

Raids also occurred in Chicago and Detroit, but the Midwest and West was mostly quiet after the massacre of IWW members by the right on Armistice Day, November 11, 1919, in Centralia, Washington. (In that city, mob violence ended a smoldering conflict between local mill owners and the IWW, as vigilantes captured hundreds of IWW members and the government put eleven on trial, convicting nine.) These raids generated some opposition from government quarters, organized labor, and the radical/socialist/liberal press, but the overwhelming majority of Americans applauded the actions. The raids were largely successful and had a devastating effect on radical organizations across the country, leaving many of them all but defunct.

DEPORTATIONS

As 1920 moved on, the states continued to enact antisyndicalism laws, restrictions on free speech, and bans on the red flag. But the Communist expansion in Europe stopped, and attempts to stifle socialists led to Democrat and Republican recognition that they could be similarly outlawed. Even Palmer had lost some of his ardor for antiradical action.

Meanwhile, Department of Labor antideportation deputy Louis Post investigated the manner in which the raids had been carried out. His investigation revealed major civil liberties violations. In many cases, there was very little evidence to justify deportation; most detainees were not communists, even if they were members of organizations affiliated with communists. In the end, Post voided 1,293 warrants and, by April 1920, nearly half of the detainees had been released. Congress, angry at Post's actions, called him to testify. At his hearing, Post showed that the raids had produced little evidence and few weapons. Congress, which had contemplated ousting Post, backed off.

But Congress had not given up the effort entirely. On May 5, 1920, Secretary of Labor William Wilson ruled in a key case that mere membership in or affiliation with a proscribed organization was insufficient cause for deportation. Congress reacted by authorizing the deportation of all aliens convicted under the espionage and sedition acts, not just the Alien Act.

On June 23, in *Colyer et al. v. Skeffington*, Judge George W. Anderson ruled that even membership in the Communist Party was not in itself a deporta-ble offense. He chastised the federal authorities for their use of warrantless arrests and general rights violations, and he released seventeen Communists. This ruling shocked the liberal Labor Department, but the government acted on the judge's order nevertheless. As time passed and police abuses gained wider public awareness, even the conservative press came to recognize that preservation of constitutional safeguards mattered more than the elimination of the communist threat. The Red Scare was over, for now.

The Red Scare was a large effort for a small result. Between November 1919 and January 1920, approximately five thousand arrest warrants were issued, and three thousand used. In the end, Post cancelled 2,202 of them. When all was over, the United States deported 591 aliens from the Palmer raids. These people, although scattered throughout the United States, did not try to fight their deportations and were deported in small groups to their native lands.

Still, Palmer continued to keep up the pressure. Citing the threat of a major uprising for May Day (May 1), 1920, he got local authorities to mobilize their police and bomb squads, as well as putting up guards in public places and in front of the homes of prominent officials. In Chicago, 360 suspected radicals were arrested in advance of May Day. But Palmer was proved wrong, as the day came and went without incident. Ironically, the greatest act of violence committed by suspected anarchists—the Wall Street bombing of September 16, 1920, an attack that killed thirty-three and injured more than two hundred—failed to revive the antiradical hysteria.

In the end, the Red Scare was the product of many factors, including xenophobia and excessive patriotism, as the war and immediate postwar years were marked by political, social, and economic dislocations. Government leadership that might have forestalled the excessive reaction of police and justice officials was absent. And, with the Russian Revolution fresh in people's minds, the fear of communism was great. New immigrants made easy scapegoats with their foreign languages, customs, and—in some cases—politics. They paid the price for this in arbitrary arrest and deportation. Later in the 1920s, they would pay an even higher price in draconian anti-immigration legislation.

John Herschel Barnhill

See also: Nativist Reaction (Part I, Sec. 4); Collapse of Communism, Anti-Immigrant Backlash (Part I,

Sec. 5); Anti-Immigrant Politics (Part II, Sec. 6); Act Banning Naturalization of Anarchists, 1903 (Part IV, Sec. 1).

BIBLIOGRAPHY

Bennett, David. *The Party of Fear: From Nativist Movements to the New Right in American History.* Chapel Hill: University of North Carolina Press, 1988.

Claghorn, Kate Holladay. *The Immigrant's Day in Court.* New York: Harper and Brothers, 1923.

Hoyt, Edwin P. *The Palmer Raids, 1919–1920: An Attempt to Suppress Dissent.* New York: Seabury Press, 1969.

Labor Research Association. *The Palmer Raids.* New York: International Publishers, 1948.

Murray, Robert. *Red Scare: A Study in National Hysteria, 1919–1920.* New York: McGraw-Hill, 1964.

Preston, William, Jr. *Aliens and Dissenters: Federal Suppression of Radicals.* 2d ed. Urbana: University of Illinois Press, 1995.

Shulman, Alix. *To the Barricades: The Anarchist Life of Emma Goldman.* New York: Thomas Y. Crowell, 1971.

Ulam, Adam. *The Bolsheviks.* Cambridge, MA: Harvard University Press, 1998.

RESTRICTIVE LEGISLATION

In the 1920s, Congress passed the most comprehensive, restrictive immigration laws in American history. The legislation, referred to as the national origins quota system, greatly reduced the flow of incoming immigrants and largely guided American immigration policy until 1965, when Congress replaced it with a more equitable system. Policymakers reinforced the restrictionist impulse with naturalization laws and judicial decisions that made it difficult, if not impossible, for some of the foreign-born to naturalize. This potent union of immigration and immigrant laws, combined with a mixture of historical and international forces, decreased the size of annual admissions and critically shaped the destinies of immigrants and refugees.

A RESTRICTIONIST REHEARSAL

Between the late 1800s and World War I, Congress limited immigration, but not until the 1920s did a comprehensive system emerge. Congress began using national origins to restrict immigration with the 1882 Chinese Exclusion Act. The law prohibited Chinese laborers from entering the country and declared all foreign-born Chinese "aliens ineligible for citizenship." Some states used the category to bar aliens from various occupations and owning property. The law reinforced the Naturalization Act of 1870, which had extended naturalization rights only to persons of African nativity and descent (previously only "free whites" had been eligible), thereby excluding other racial groups.

Lawmakers used a combination of immigration and immigrant policies to prevent not only Chinese entries but also Asian admissions in general. The Immigration Act of 1907 doubled the head tax from two to four dollars and authorized the president to deny admission to immigrants he considered detrimental to

U.S. labor conditions. This provision was primarily aimed at Japanese laborers, but a diplomatic arrangement between the United States and Japan—the Gentlemen's Agreement of 1907–08—augmented the legislation. In exchange for incorporating Japanese Americans into the San Francisco public school system, Japan agreed to prevent the immigration of Japanese laborers to the United States.

After 1910, policymakers and judges typically used a mixture of legal precedents, scientific guidelines, and popular race sensibilities to declare most Asians ineligible for citizenship. But the net of racial inferiority began to expand. In 1911, the U.S. Immigration Commission (1907–10) released its forty-two-volume report, in which it argued that the unassimilable, "degenerate" racial stock hailing from southern and eastern Europe was provoking a host of social problems. In 1913, the head of the commission, Senator William P. Dillingham (R-VT), proposed an immigration bill based on national origins, but President Woodrow Wilson killed the bill by withholding his signature. Not until 1917—the year of America's entrance into World War I—was Congress able to override Wilson's veto and pass its first piece of restrictive legislation in ten years.

WORLD WAR I AND THE 1920s

The Immigration Act of 1917 created an Asian "barred zone" and excluded illiterate aliens, but World War I proved to be an even more restrictive force. The international disruption fueled by the First World War precipitated a slowdown in arrivals and an increase in departures. Almost 4.5 million immigrants entered the United States between 1911 and 1915, but between 1916 and 1920, the number of entries dropped to around 1.3 million. Between 1911 and 1915, thirty-two people left the country for every one hundred that

THE AMERICANESE WALL, AS CONGRESSMAN
BURNETT WOULD BUILD IT.
UNCLE SAM: You're welcome in—if you can climb it!

The 1917 literacy act blocked the immigration of all foreigners who could not read and write in English or their native language. *(Library of Congress)*

arrived, but between 1916 and 1920, fifty-five people departed for every hundred that entered. While the war in Europe modified migration flows, Americanization advocates turned the American conception of loyalty into a magnifying lens—tiny departures from undying allegiance started to look like subversion.

During the early stages of World War I, the German-American Alliance and German-American press lobbied for American neutrality, holding rallies in support of an arms embargo. Americans interpreted their efforts as a threat to national security primarily for two reasons. First, the United States was in the throes of an Americanization campaign, and second, a war with Germany seemed likely. Had German Americans supported their homeland in a different setting (e.g., during peacetime or in a war of little consequence to the United States), their ensuing arrest and internment would probably not have occurred. Their actions would have been considered an exercise

in free speech, ethnic pride, or an unwillingness to assimilate, but not a threat to the national interest.

But the social meanings assigned to German-American activities typically converged on matters of national security as the United States feverishly prepared for war. In December 1917, President Wilson restricted the movement and rights of "enemy aliens" with a set of twelve "enemy alien regulations." These regulations helped federal authorities to intern 6,300 "enemy aliens" (including 2,300 civilians) during the war. Supplementing the 1798 Alien Enemy Act, Congress passed the 1917 Espionage Act and the 1918 Sedition Act to prosecute citizens who obstructed the draft or criticized the war effort. Attorney General A. Mitchell Palmer used the 1917 deportation law to jail 6,000 suspects and to deport 600 aliens.

After the war, immigrant education and language assumed center stage in the Americanization crusade. Idaho and Utah required their non-English-speaking aliens to take Americanization classes, and fifteen states passed laws in 1919 requiring all private and public schools to instruct only in English. Several states ruled that only citizens could serve as public schoolteachers. These and similar efforts began to fade by the end of 1920, but the growing number of immigrant arrivals kept the issue of immigration restriction alive in Congress.

The flow of immigration dropped substantially during the war, but lawmakers worried that prewar levels would accompany the hard-won peace. In late 1920, monthly arrivals suggested that the postwar movement would soon equal the prewar influx. In addition to the numbers, committees told Congress that millions of Germans and Polish Jews wanted to enter the United States, and Albert Johnson, chair of the House Committee on Immigration, circulated a memo from a State Department official stating that America faced a flood of "unassimilable" and "abnormally twisted" Jews.

Congress knew that the literacy requirement it had inserted into the 1917 Immigration Act could not prevent mass immigration. The literacy rate in Europe was rising, and a loophole in the literacy test permitted thousands of illiterate immigrants from southern and eastern Europe to enter the country. Congress needed a new formula to restrict immigration, and within a year, the House and Senate hammered out their first quantitative immigration law—the 1921 First Quota Act.

In November 1920, the House overwhelmingly passed a plan to suspend immigration (with some exceptions) for one year. Even though the plan was temporary, the Senate Committee on Immigration allowed cotton growers, beet producers, and such

THE ONLY WAY TO HANDLE IT.

In 1921, the United States passed the first immigrant quota law, which limited immigrants coming from a given country to just 3 percent of their number already in America in 1910. A 1924 law cut the quota to 2 percent and set the base year in 1890. *(Library of Congress)*

organizations as the National Association of Manufacturers to challenge the proposal in a series of relaxed hearings. The Senate committee did not share the House of Representatives's sense of urgency, but the majority of senators and the public wanted less immigration. The Senate had to suggest something.

Senator Dillingham proposed that the number of immigrants accepted annually from a country be limited to 5 percent of the foreign-born population of that nationality living in the United States in 1910. The plan did not interfere with the ban on Asian entry or restrict the movement of eligible immigrants from Canada and Latin America. The bill quickly passed the Senate. The House accepted the quota system but convinced the Senate to reduce the annual quota from 5 percent to 3 percent. President Wilson killed the bill by ignoring it, but it was reintroduced the following May, and the newly elected Warren G. Harding signed it into law.

Representative Johnson and the other members of the House Committee on Immigration wasted little time in designing a permanent policy to replace the stopgap measure. Between 1921 and 1923, Johnson ac-

tively corresponded with Madison Grant, author of *The Passing of the Great Race* (1916), and enlisted the expertise of Harry H. Laughlin, a prominent eugenicist, whom the committee promptly appointed as its eugenics expert. By late 1922, the committee had drafted a bill to lower the annual ceiling (particularly the inflow from southern and eastern Europe) by reducing the quotas and moving the census base year from 1910 to 1890. But the bill encountered a strong economy and a tight labor market. Without the support of industry, Republican leaders in both houses deferred the issue until 1924.

After much tinkering and posturing, Congress passed the Immigration Act of 1924, which did not assume its full form until 1929. Primarily designed to limit immigration from southeastern Europe, the system lowered the quota from 3 percent to 2 percent and used 1890 as the base year for determining annual quotas for eligible nationalities. The House Committee on Immigration intended to discriminate against immigrants from southeastern Europe but realized they could not openly defend the bill on grounds of Nordic superiority or shift to an older census base without revealing their biases for immigrants from northwestern Europe.

This Second Quota Act fortified the ban on "aliens ineligible for citizenship" and instituted the "national origins quota system." In 1929, Congress set the annual ceiling at approximately 150,000. Immigrants from northern and western Europe procured 83 percent of the visas, southern and eastern Europe secured 15 percent, and the rest of the world received 2 percent.

Some politicians justified the legislation by advancing the idea of Nordic superiority and decrying the perils of "mongrelization." The new immigrants some argued, mongrelized the old. In a popular 1921 article, Vice President Calvin Coolidge contended that Nordics deteriorate when they breed with other races. When signing the National Origins Act of 1924, he captured the sentiment by stating, "America must be kept American." Such opinions were widely held and discussed in the early 1920s and, contrary to being the ravings of a few extreme xenophobes and racists, enjoyed the backing of prominent legislators and scientists.

The research and lobbying efforts of eugenicists may have contributed to the passage of the Immigration Act of 1924. During World War I, Harvard professor Robert M. Yerkes supervised the administration of intelligence tests for 1 million army recruits. Although his research design was conceptually unsound and methodologically flawed, Yerkes and his assistant, E. G. Boring, had little problem accounting for the low mental age of Nordics—the intelligent native stock was being swamped by the southern and eastern Europeans. This conclusion was followed by an even more "scientific" finding—European immigrants could be ranked by their country of origin. In their estimation, southern and eastern Europeans were less intelligent than northern and western Europeans.

C. C. Brigham transformed their results into a social prescription with his 1923 *Study of American Intelligence*. Relying on Grant's typology of three races, Brigham concluded that the only way to arrest the deterioration of "American intelligence" (i.e., Nordic intelligence) was to regulate reproduction and restrict immigration. Brigham recanted in 1930, recognizing that the tests measured one's fluency in English and culture, not intelligence. Still, the influence of his political advice and "hard" army data on the national origins system is difficult to determine.

The movement to restrict immigration had been gaining ground since the 1890s, and only one reference to intelligence testing results appears in the records of the congressional floor debates surrounding the 1924 act. Brigham's research and that of his predecessors probably had little to do with the Immigration Act of 1924 but most likely exacerbated interethnic tensions and indirectly contributed to America's growing concern with social cohesion and national unity. The racial underpinnings of the 1924 act, however, appear in the official record. Members of the House Committee on Immigration listened to prominent biology professors warn them of the alleged dangers of "racial mixing" and went to great lengths to hide their biases for northwestern Europeans.

THE GREAT DEPRESSION AND WORLD WAR II

Congress devoted little attention to immigration in the 1930s. Congress tweaked the national origins laws and lengthened the list of deportable offenses but basically left the system alone. After the market crashed in 1929, some legislators requested more reductions in immigration, and others suggested that the quota laws be extended to the Americas, but the majority of lawmakers considered the existing policies sufficient. The quota system, coupled with the Great Depression (and the string of actions it precipitated), provoked a net out-migration of 138,400 in the early 1930s: The government admitted 159,400 persons between July 1931 and June 1936, but 297,800 persons left.

At the request of President Herbert Hoover, the State Department instructed officials to enforce strictly the immigration caveat that immigrants "likely to become a public charge" be denied admission. Federal, state, and local authorities pressured Mexicans and Mexican Americans to participate in repatriation programs to Mexico, but they often resorted to deceit and illegal tactics to accelerate the process. The Mexican government often cooperated with officials because they wanted more laborers. Between five and six hundred thousand persons of Mexican ancestry (many of them American citizens) left the United States and returned to Mexico during the 1930s. Later in the decade, President Franklin D. Roosevelt and Congress refused to receive extra Jews beyond those allowed under the quota laws (and other refugees) fleeing Nazism.

Congress guarded the quotas in the 1930s but in 1940 started to focus on internal security. It passed the Nationality Act to unify and tighten the myriad of naturalization, citizenship, and expatriation laws sitting on the books; moved the Immigration and Naturalization Service (INS) from the Department of Labor to the Department of Justice for national security purposes; and passed the Alien Registration Act. The last measure required all resident aliens fourteen and older to register annually with the government. By the end of the year, the list contained 5 million names. On December 8, 1941, the president instructed the Federal Bureau of Investigation (FBI) and other government agencies to use the national registration list—and their own shortlists—to arrest and intern German and Italian nationals, Japanese nationals, and Japanese Americans. Officials arrested thousands of German and Italian aliens but (for a variety of legal, logistical, and social reasons) interned only the Japanese en masse.

While the Japanese lived in internment camps, immigrants were busy naturalizing. Over 1.5 million aliens became citizens between 1941 and 1945, including some Asians. As a sign of goodwill, the United States lifted the ban on Chinese immigration and naturalization in 1943 to thank its Chinese allies and, in a similar 1946 gesture, allowed Filipinos and East Indians to naturalize. The United States not only revised the naturalization process but also restored the former World War I guest-worker program with Mexico. Between 1942 and 1947, an estimated two hundred thousand contract laborers called *braceros*, or farmhands, came to the United States temporarily as "foreign laborers" instead of as immigrants. Congress regularly renewed the program, keeping it alive until December 1964.

The final batch of legislation passed by Congress in the 1940s addressed a different kind of migration—the forced and fleeing kind. In mid-1945, almost 2 million displaced persons (DPs) were living in European camps. To facilitate the migration of DPs, President Harry Truman issued an executive order in December to increase the speed of refugee admissions. Congress concentrated on military personnel. It passed the 1945 War Brides Act to allow soldiers who had married non-citizens during the war to reunite with their wives and children. Over 119,000 people (mostly brides) took advantage of the special visas between 1946 and 1950.

Over 41,000 DPs arrived between Truman's directive and the 1948 Displaced Persons Act, which permitted over two hundred thousand refugees to settle permanently in the United States over a two-year interval. Technicalities in the law, however, discriminated against Jewish applicants and favored immigrants from the Baltic states. The act also "mortgaged" the visas—Congress charged the refugee visas against future annual quotas. Countries with small annual quotas consumed *decades* of quotas when they sent thousands of DPs to the United States. Congress removed the provisions that tended to disadvantage Jewish refugees in 1950 and later relinquished the mortgage system (and allowed another 214,000 aliens to become permanent residents) when it enacted the 1953 Refugee Relief Act. After 1948, all refugees had to pass stringent security screenings before securing their visas. This precaution was designed to prevent the migration of spies and saboteurs, but the provision also symbolized a recurring national anxiety— the fear of being destroyed from within.

THE COLD WAR

Primarily because of the Cold War, a fear of foreign radicals did not subside with the end of World War II. Senator Patrick McCarran (D-NV) worried that Truman's program would, in the rush to accommodate DPs, allow communist spies and saboteurs—posing as refugees—to enter the country. McCarran, who shared Senator Joseph McCarthy's (R-WI) fear of communist subversion, offered Congress a new internal security law, one that protected it against communist infiltration. The bill denied admission to members of communist parties and authorized the attorney general to deport aliens without a hearing. In short, the proposed legislation made membership in a supposedly subversive group grounds for denaturalization, deportation, and exclusion.

President Truman vetoed the bill, calling it unnecessary and reactionary. The plan, he said, complicated foreign relations and interfered with established procedures for identifying subversives. But the House and Senate overrode his veto and passed the McCarran Internal Security Act on September 22, 1950. Later that same year, McCarran proposed another plan to discard obsolete immigration laws, reinforce useful ones, and tackle new issues. After weathering a couple of congressional storms, the bill finally arrived on Truman's desk in mid-1952, full of amendments and controversy. Truman vetoed the legislation, arguing that the quota system conflicted with the country's democratic and religious principles. McCarran challenged his colleagues to reverse the president's "un-American" action, and two days later, Congress complied by overriding the veto.

The McCarran-Walter Immigration and Nationality Act of 1952 brought previous immigration and naturalization laws under one legislative roof. Although the act preserved the basic national origins formula and fortified the federal government's deportation powers, it removed race as a barrier to naturalization, thereby eliminating the infamous category "aliens ineligible for citizenship." But the act continued to emphasize what wartime actions had already made clear—that the rights of naturalized citizens were not equal to those of native-born citizens. Membership in a supposedly subversive group was grounds for denaturalization, as well as deportation and exclusion.

From the early to mid-1950s, the federal government addressed another phenomenon connected to wartime—its guest-worker program. At the request of U.S. employers, the United States and Mexico revived the bracero program in 1942 to supply American companies with cheap labor replacements during the wartime labor shortage. Although Congress extended the program several times until its cessation in 1964, an increasing number of border apprehensions in the early 1950s prompted Eisenhower to appoint a new INS commissioner to curb illegal border crossings. In 1954, the INS officially launched Operation Wetback to tighten the border and apprehend Mexicans who overstayed their visas. Between 1950 and 1955, the U.S. government expelled almost 4 million Mexicans.

Congress abolished the national origins system, as well as the last trace of Asian barriers, with the noncontroversial passage of the 1965 Immigration and Nationality Amendments to the 1952 McCarran-Walter Act. Although not fully implemented until 1968, the amendments aligned the country's immigration policy with its new commitment to ending racial discrimination. The changes, however, placed a numerical cap on immigration from the Western Hemisphere for the very first time. The architecture of the law, combined with a number of push-and-pull factors, precipitated a variety of legal and illegal migration pathways. The amendments unintentionally exacerbated illegal immigration from such Western Hemisphere countries as Mexico by imposing a numerical cap in the absence of a guest-worker program, but they paved the way for millions of immigrants, particularly those hailing from Latin America and Asia, to enter legally.

Brian N. Fry

See also: Chinese and Chinese Exclusion Act (Part I, Sec. 2); Changes in the Law (Part I, Sec. 5); Immigration Act, 1917, Quota Act of 1921, Quota Act of 1924, Immigration and Nationality Act, 1965 (Part IV, Sec. 1).

BIBLIOGRAPHY

Barkan, Elliott R. *And Still They Come: Immigrants and American Society, 1920 to the 1990s.* Wheeling, IL: Harlan Davidson, 1996.

Brown, Mary E. *Shapers of the Great Debate on Immigration: A Biographical Dictionary.* Westport, CT: Greenwood Press, 1999.

Daniels, Roger *Prisoners without Trial: Japanese Americans in World War II.* New York: Hill and Wang, 1993.

Degler, Carl N. *In Search of Human Nature: The Decline and Revival of Darwinism in American Social Thought.* New York: Oxford University Press, 1991.

Ellis, Mark, and Panikos Panayi. "German Minorities in World War I: A Comparative Study of Britain and the USA." *Ethnic and Racial Studies* 17 (1994): 238–59.

Fox, Stephan. *The Unknown Internment: An Oral History of the Relocation of Italian Americans during World War II.* Boston: Twayne, 1988.

Gould, Stephen J. *The Mismeasure of Man.* New York: W. W. Norton, 1981.

Higham, John. *Strangers in the Land: Patterns of American Nativism, 1860–1925.* New Brunswick, NJ: Rutgers University Press, 1992.

Immigration and Naturalization Service. *1994 Statistical Yearbook of the Immigration and Naturalization Service.* Washington, DC: Government Printing Office, 1996.

Portes, Alejandro, and Ruben G. Rumbaut. *Immigrant America: A Portrait.* Berkeley: University of California Press, 1996.

Reimers, David M. *Unwelcome Strangers: American Identity and the Turn against Immigration.* New York: Columbia University Press, 1998.

Romo, Ricardo. "Mexican Americans: Their Civic and Political Incorporation." In *Origins and Destinies: Immigration, Race, and Ethnicity in America,* ed. S. Pedraza and Ruben G. Rumbaut, pp. 84–97. Belmont, CA: Wadsworth, 1996.

Rumbaut, Ruben G. "Origins and Destinies: Immigration to the United States since World War II." *Sociological Forum* 9 (1994): 583–621.

Sánchez, George J. *Becoming Mexican American: Ethnicity, Culture, and Identity in Chicano Los Angeles, 1900–1945.* New York: Oxford University Press, 1993.

Ueda, Reed. "Naturalization and Citizenship." In *Harvard Encyclopedia of American Ethnic Groups,* ed. Stephen Thernstrom, pp. 734–48. Cambridge: Harvard University Press, 1981.

———. *Postwar Immigrant America: A Social History.* Boston: Bedford Books, 1994.

WAR REFUGEES

The period between the end of World War I in 1918 and the passage of the Immigration and Nationality Act in 1965 reveals the tremendous challenges and conflicts faced by the United States in formulating policies regarding war refugees that would balance humanitarian concerns with practical national interests. In light of such inherent tensions, U.S. refugee legislation during this period was administered primarily on an *ad hoc* basis in response to specific political crises around the globe. This piecemeal response to war refugees was determined largely by the restrictive quota limits set in the Immigration Act of 1924.

WORLD WAR I AND RESTRICTIVE LEGISLATION

The end of World War I ushered in a period of conservatism, nativism, xenophobia, and isolationism within the United States. During the war, an Americanization movement that demanded near-total social and political conformity created a deep sense of distrust and antipathy toward foreigners on American soil. The 1917 Russian Revolution heightened these anxieties, culminating in the infamous 1919 Red Scare. By the start of the 1920s, many Americans perceived immigrants, particularly those from southern and eastern Europe, to be inextricably linked to political subversion and radicalism. Given the intense antiforeigner sentiments that gripped the nation, large numbers of Americans began to demand restrictions on immigration after the war. In response, Congress passed the 1924 Immigration Act, which severely cut immigration to the United States. The new law established a stringent national origins quota system that institutionalized preferences for "desirable" immigrants from northern and western Europe while re-stricting those from southern and eastern Europe, Asia, and Latin America.

The start of the Great Depression in 1929 increased demands for further limits on immigration to the United States. In response, President Herbert Hoover implemented the strict enforcement of a "likely to become a charge" (LPC) provision contained in immigration law. The LPC clause denied visas to any prospective immigrant who was unlikely to find employment in the United States or unable to provide evidence of a financial sponsor if unemployed. The enforcement of the LPC provision, along with the restrictive quota system, virtually halted immigration to the United States. More than 4.1 million immigrants entered the United States in the 1920s. During the 1930s, immigration dropped drastically, to roughly five hundred thousand. As restrictionist legislation was taking effect in the United States, events in Europe created an international refugee crisis.

1933–1938: JEWISH REFUGEE CRISIS

In 1933, Adolf Hitler's ascendancy to power in Germany precipitated the mass exodus of Jewish refugees from Germany. Though there is considerable scholarly debate concerning the U.S. response to the Jewish refugee crisis, most scholars agree that it was conspicuously inadequate. Nearly all scholars maintain that the social and political climate of the 1930s was decisively hostile to the entrance of large numbers of Jewish refugees from Europe. In his seminal work, *Paper Walls: America and the Refugee Crisis, 1938–1941*, historian David S. Wyman asserts that economic depression, nativist anxieties, and anti-Semitism were the primary factors for the unresponsiveness of the United States to Hitler's systemic persecution of German Jews. Though generally sympathetic to the plight of Germany's Jews, President Franklin D. Roosevelt was unwilling to take the political risks associated with aiding foreign Jews. Upon assuming the presidency in 1933, Roosevelt continued Hoover's policy of enforcing the LPC clause.

In the late 1930s, however, the Jewish refugee crisis became more acute as Nazi violence against Europe's Jews increased dramatically. In March 1938, Hitler's troops annexed neighboring Austria, in what is commonly known as the *Anschluss*. The Nazis employed a campaign of widespread violence and terror against Austrian Jews in the wake of annexation, causing the large-scale emigration of Jews from Austria. Similar pogroms against Germany's Jews occurred later in the year. On November 9, 1938, a wave of violence and destruction against Jews swept Germany. Often referred to as the "Night of the Broken Glass" or *Kristallnacht*, angry mobs destroyed and looted Jewish residences, businesses, and synagogues. Tens of thousands of Jews were also assaulted, beaten, and arrested without charges. In the aftermath of the *Kristallnacht*, large numbers of German Jews sought refuge outside Germany.

The systematic violence and persecution against

Perhaps the most notable refugee to flee Nazi Germany in the 1930s was physicist Albert Einstein, whose theories helped America develop the atomic bomb. *(Library of Congress)*

Austrian and German Jews in the *Anschluss* and *Kristallnacht* prompted the United States to act with greater urgency. Eleven days after the *Anschluss*, President Franklin Roosevelt announced that the German and Austrian quotas would be fully opened, marking the first time the White House openly addressed the Jewish refugee crisis. In April, Roosevelt took further action by declaring that the annual quotas for Germany and Austria would be combined, setting the total quota limit at 27,370. In the days following the November *Kristallnacht*, Roosevelt announced that the twelve to fifteen thousand German Jewish refugees who had already entered the United States under visitors' visas would not be required to return to Germany after the expiration of their visas.

In response to the March *Anschluss*, President Roosevelt also summoned a thirty-two-nation conference in Evian, France, to discuss possible solutions to the Jewish refugee crisis in Europe. Meeting in July 1938, the Evian Conference accomplished very little, because no nation was willing to make a commitment to accept large numbers of Jewish refugees. The conference, however, managed to establish a new international refugee organization, the Intergovernmental Committee on Refugees (IGCR), which sought to negotiate with Nazi Germany for the peaceful and orderly resettlement of Jewish refugees. During its eight-year tenure, the actions of the IGCR were ineffective due to constant shortage of funds and general apathy from the international community.

Though Roosevelt took special emergency measures to aid the victims of Nazi persecution in Austria and Germany, the White House refused to commit to any attempts to work outside the quota system. Always keenly sensitive to public attitudes and political pressure, Roosevelt consistently avoided advocating the unpopular position of altering U.S. immigration laws. Nevertheless, Roosevelt's actions in 1938 marked the first easing of immigration quotas since the implementation of the "likely to be a public charge" policy in 1930, which had effectively kept immigration levels well below the quota limits.

Though the mood of the United States was emphatically hostile to any changes in the nation's immigration laws, advocates of a more liberal refugee policy proposed a series of bills between 1933 and 1939 to assist the victims of Nazi persecution. The most notable attempt came in the aftermath of the *Kristallnacht*. A group of private voluntary groups introduced the Wagner–Rogers bill in early 1939, which proposed the annual admission of 20,000 German refugee children under the age of fourteen, beyond the quota limits, for a two-year period. Named for its sponsors, Senator Robert F. Wagner (D-NY) (who was born in Germany) and Representative Edith Rogers (R-MA), the Wagner–Rogers bill garnered support from a wide range of political, labor, and religious figures and organizations. Nevertheless, the children's bill encountered a formidable wall of opposition from restrictionist forces in Congress and the public at large. Moreover, President Roosevelt failed to provide critical support for the bill by remaining conspicuously silent when approached for his endorsement. Ultimately, the bill died in Congress in mid-1939.

Despite the failure of the Wagner–Rogers bill, scholars agree unequivocally that the period between March 1938 and September 1939 marked the most liberal phase in U.S. immigration policy than at any other time between 1931 and 1946. During this eighteen-month period, nearly twenty thousand German refugees, most of whom were Jewish, entered the United States each month as quota immigrants. In all, approximately eighty-five thousand refugees were admitted to the United States from March 1938 to September 1939.

WORLD WAR II AND THE HOLOCAUST

The beginning of World War II, marked by Germany's invasion of Poland in September 1939, quickly reversed the loosening of immigration policy administered during the previous eighteen months. As the White House devoted its full attention to the war, President Roosevelt turned over the primary responsibilities related to refugee policy to Assistant Secretary Breckinridge Long in the State Department. Under Long's direction, the State Department instituted a series of policies over the next several years that drastically cut the number of refugees who could enter the United States. Motivated by intense fears of a "fifth-column," or traitorous, threat from Nazi agents infiltrating through the refugee flows into the United States, Long imposed a set of rigid requirements for the issuance of immigration visas. All prospective immigrants had to pass through a number of extremely stringent security reviews, making it virtually impossible for anyone to enter. Moreover, State Department officials considered Jews in particular to be threats to the nation's security. These anti-Semitic perceptions were rooted in the antiradicalism and nativism displayed during the 1919 Red Scare, when Jews were branded as subversive radicals. By June 1940, the quotas for refugees coming from Germany and Austria were half-filled. The number of refugees entering the

United States continued to drop during the war. By 1942, only 4,883 German and Austrian refugees entered the United States, a sharp decline from the quota limit of 27,370 who had arrived in 1939. By 1944, the number of refugees issued immigration visas had plummeted to 2,300, or roughly 5 percent of the quota limit.

The sudden reversal of U.S. refugee policy during World War II had catastrophic consequences for Europe's Jews. Until 1941, the Nazis had emphasized a policy of forcing Jews to emigrate, initially through social and economic pressures and later through the widespread use of violence and terror. In 1942, however, the emigration policy shifted to the mass genocide of the Holocaust, in which 6 million Jews perished in Nazi concentration camps. Scholars such as David Wyman assert that Hitler turned to the "Final Solution" of genocide after the continued failure of the forced emigration policy, due in large part to the international community's refusal to provide sanctuary to Jewish refugees. With the implementation of the Final Solution, the Nazis permanently closed the doors to any further emigration. In *The Politics of Rescue: The Roosevelt Administration and the Holocaust, 1938–1945*, historian Henry L. Feingold argues that the period between September 1939 and January 1942 represented the most opportune time to save thousands of Europe's Jews from mass extermination. In his critical assessment of the Roosevelt administration's response to the Holocaust, Feingold notes that 62,000 to 75,000 additional refugees could have entered the United States through the quota system between 1939 and 1942. He further states that those figures do not take into account the scores of lives that could have been saved during the Holocaust years between 1942 and 1944 if more lenient precedents in refugee policy had been set earlier. The Roosevelt administration, in fact, would not seek an active rescue policy until late in the war in 1944.

As news of the Holocaust began filtering into the United States, American Jews initiated a mass campaign to aid their brethren in Europe. During the previous years, their response to Nazi persecution of Europe's Jews had been limited, due in part to bitter factional disputes among various Jewish organizations. In 1943, however, many of the quarreling factions united their efforts to raise public awareness of the Holocaust and to pressure United States government officials to act. This mobilization campaign generated sufficient public agitation to impel the governments of the United States and Great Britain to convene a conference in Bermuda to discuss rescue strategies for Jews in Europe. Held in April 1943, the Bermuda Conference, which excluded any Jewish organizational representation, failed to produce any plans or strategies. Concerted efforts at international cooperation to aid Jewish victims of the Holocaust were constantly impeded, not only by the unresponsiveness of the United States but also by Britain's persistent refusal to ease restrictions on Jewish immigration into Palestine.

Greatly disappointed and angered by the blatant failure of the Bermuda Conference, American Jews stepped up their efforts to alter United States refugee policy. By 1944, Jewish organizations in the United States had garnered significant non-Jewish support to pressure the White House to take more substantive action. On January 22, 1944, President Roosevelt issued Executive Order 9417, which established a new independent agency named the War Refugee Board (WRB). Given cabinet status, the three-member board of the WRB consisted of the secretaries of state, war, and the treasury. The WRB's primary objective was to develop and to coordinate rescue plans for European Jews under Nazi control. Through its various activities, the WRB saved thousands of Jewish lives. In one of its more well-known missions, the WRB, working in conjunction with Swedish diplomat Raoul Wallenberg, prevented at least twenty thousand Jews in Hungary from being deported to Germany, where they would have met certain death. Other notable WRB projects included attempts to create temporary havens in the United States for Jewish refugees. However, the WRB managed to establish only one haven. In the summer of 1944, a refugee camp at Fort Ontario in Oswego, New York, provided temporary asylum for approximately a thousand Jews from Italy. In *Token Refuge: The Story of the Jewish Refugee Shelter at Oswego, 1944–1946*, Sharon R. Lowenstein documents thoroughly the volatile political and public debates sparked by the efforts to create havens in the United States such as the one in Oswego. In spite of such conflicts, the WRB's actions marked a significant departure from the inaction exhibited throughout much of the war. Even so, most scholars agree that U.S. rescue efforts not only came much too late but were also egregiously inadequate.

Though over one hundred twenty thousand refugees, most of whom were Jewish, entered the United States between 1933 and 1944, the U.S. government during this period never established a clearly defined policy regarding the admission of refugees. The restrictive quota system in U.S. immigration law presented a formidable institutional barrier to the formulation of a refugee policy capable of dealing with the immensity of the Jewish refugee crisis. The immediate years following the end of World War II further revealed the inadequacies of U.S. immigration laws to deal with the postwar refugee situation.

POST–WORLD WAR II REFUGEE POLICIES

The postwar refugee situation posed problems of staggering proportions for the Allied occupying forces in Europe. By the end of the war there were approximately eight million displaced persons in Europe, with nearly one million permanently residing in refugee camps. The vast number of displaced persons included survivors of the Holocaust as well as other uprooted persons who were unable or unwilling to return to their homes. In response to the massive refugee crisis in Europe, President Harry S. Truman issued a presidential directive in 1945 that admitted over forty-one thousand displaced persons under the quota system for the next two-and-a-half years.

The immensity of the refugee crisis, however, indicated the pressing need for further action. In 1948, Congress passed the Displaced Persons (DP) Act. The new law provided for the admission of over a hundred thousand persons over a four-year period. The DP Act established a preference system that operated within the quota system and created the ability for a country to "mortgage" its quotas against future annual quotas.

The DP Act was largely the outcome of vigorous lobbying by segments of the American Jewish community, who initiated a mass campaign under the name of the Citizens' Committee on Displaced Persons (CCDP). Enlisting a broad constituent of influential non-Jewish supporters, the CCDP sought to admit Jewish displaced persons to the United States through special legislation. Though intended to aid the survivors of the Holocaust, the 1948 DP Act contained loopholes that rendered nearly all Jewish survivors of Nazi concentration camps ineligible to enter the United States. In *America and the Survivors of the Holocaust*, Leonard Dinnerstein notes that the general antipathy in the United States to the plight of Jewish victims of Nazi persecution persisted after the war, as manifested in the failure of the DP Act to address the needs of Jewish displaced persons. The CCDP mobilized immediately after the passage of the 1948 DP Act to eliminate the anti-Semitic provisions of the bill. Their lobbying campaign culminated in the passage of an amended Displaced Persons Act in 1950, which liberalized Jewish refugee admissions to the United States. Dinnerstein, however, points out that the amended act brought only small increases in Jewish immigration to the United States. By 1950, many Jewish survivors had already immigrated to the newly created Jewish state of Israel, established in 1948.

Though the 1948 Displaced Persons Act (DPA) and its 1950 amendment did not alter the basic provisions of U.S. immigration law, the DP Act was the first substantial piece of refugee legislation in U.S. history. In his survey text of U.S. immigration policies, *From Open Door to Dutch Door: An Analysis of U.S. Immigration Policy Since 1820*, Michael C. LeMay argues that the DP Act represented a significant shift in U.S. immigration policy, representing the first time in the twentieth century that the U.S. Congress enacted legislation that eased earlier restrictive and exclusionary policies. This shift in immigration policy that gradually eroded the quota system would become more evident in the 1950s and 1960s.

COLD WAR REFUGEES

As Cold War tensions between the United States and the Soviet Union intensified in the years after World War II, immigration and refugee admissions served as a potent weapon in the battle against communism. U.S. policymakers increasingly advocated more liberal admissions legislation to advance an anticommunist foreign policy, even to the extent of working beyond the national-origins quota limits. In 1953, Congress passed the Refugee Relief Act (RRA), which authorized over two hundred thousand nonquota visas for individuals escaping from communist nations.

In the following years, the White House continued to take additional special "emergency" measures to aid refugees from communist nations. In 1956, President Dwight D. Eisenhower authorized the admission of 38,000 Hungarian "freedom fighters," who had fled Hungary after a failed anticommunist revolt. Using an obscure executive prerogative that bypassed the need for congressional approval, Eisenhower admitted a large number of Hungarian refugees under a special mass parole program. In the following years, Presidents Eisenhower and John F. Kennedy invoked the same executive privilege to grant parole status to nearly two hundred and fifty thousand Cubans, who entered the United States between 1959 and 1962 in the aftermath of Fidel Castro's communist revolution. Other mass parole refugees admitted to the United States during the same period included smaller numbers of Chinese from Hong Kong and Dutch Indonesia.

The development of U.S. refugee policy in the late 1950s and early 1960s continued to reflect Cold War foreign policy concerns. Under the 1957 Refugee-Escapee Act, refugees were defined as victims escaping communist or communist-dominated nations. This definition stood until the passage of the Refugee Act of 1980. The Refugee-Escapee Act also abolished the mortgaged quota practice, further chipping away at the quota system. In 1960, Congress enacted a more comprehensive refugee policy. The Refugee Fair Share Law provided for the general admission of refugees over a set period of time rather than admitting refugees from a particular country or in response to specific political crises. In 1965, the Fair Share Law was discontinued with the passage of the Immigration and Nationality Act. The monumental 1965 immigration act abandoned the national-origins quota system and for the first time included provisions for refugee admissions in basic immigration law.

Richard S. Kim

See also: Wars and Civil Unrest (Part II, Sec. 1); President Truman's Directive on European Refugees, 1945 (Part IV, Sec. 1).

BIBLIOGRAPHY

Bauer, Yehuda. *American Jewry and the Holocaust: The American Jewish Joint Distribution Committee, 1939–1945*. Detroit: Wayne State University Press, 1981.

Berman, Aaron. *Nazism, the Jews, and American Zionism*. Detroit: Wayne State University Press, 1990.

Breitman, Richard, and Alan M. Kraut. *American Refugee Policy and European Jewry, 1933–1945*. Bloomington: Indiana University Press, 1987.

Dinnerstein, Leonard. *America and the Survivors of the Holocaust*. New York: Columbia University Press, 1982.

Feingold, Henry L. *The Politics of Rescue: The Roosevelt Administration and the Holocaust, 1938–1945*. New Brunswick, NJ: Rutgers University Press, 1970.

Friedman, Saul S. *No Haven for the Oppressed: United States Policy toward Jewish Refugees, 1938–1945*. Detroit: Wayne State University Press, 1973.

LeMay, Michael C. *From Open Door to Dutch Door: An Analysis of U.S. Immigration Policy Since 1820*. New York: Praeger, 1987.

Loescher, Gil, and John A. Scanlan. *Calculated Kindness: Refugees and America's Half-Open Door, 1945 to the Present*. New York: The Free Press, 1986.

Lowenstein, Sharon R. *Token Refuge: The Story of the Jewish Refugee Shelter at Oswego, 1944–1946*. Bloomington: Indiana University Press, 1986.

Stewart, Barbara McDonald. *United States Government Policy on Refugees from Nazism, 1933–1940*. New York: Garland Publishing, 1982.

Wyman, David S. *The Abandonment of the Jews: America and the Holocaust, 1941–1945*. New York: Pantheon Books, 1984.

———. *Paper Walls: America and the Refugee Crisis, 1938–1941*. Amherst: University of Massachusetts Press, 1968.

Zucker, Norman L., and Naomi Flink Zucker. *The Guarded Gate: The Reality of American Refugee Policy*. New York: Harcourt Brace Jovanovich, 1987.

JAPANESE INTERNMENT

During World War II, when the United States was at war with Japan, over 120,000 Americans of Japanese descent were removed from their homes and sent to one of ten detention camps in the country. About seventy-seven thousand of them—almost two-thirds—were American citizens. None had committed any act of sabotage or disloyalty to the United States. Any person with even one-eighth Japanese blood was subject to internment. The justification given for this imprisonment was that these were people who still might hold allegiance to their country of origin, now an enemy of the United States. However, most German Americans and Italian Americans—or anyone with ancestry from any other enemy nation—were never subjected to internment.

HISTORICAL BACKGROUND

Before 1900, most Japanese immigrants had settled in Hawaii. There were only several thousand people of Japanese ancestry on the mainland of the United States, and these were mostly elites. After the United States annexed Hawaii in 1898, massive numbers of Japanese farmworkers began migrating to the West Coast. In 1899, for instance, two thousand Japanese moved to the mainland, and in the following year, that number swelled to some twelve thousand. Over 70 percent of these Japanese settled in California, where the majority of people were European Americans. These "white" people had a long history of feeling threatened by Asian immigration, ever since the 1850s, when large numbers of Chinese began to arrive. Thus, they were also very uncomfortable with this influx of new Japanese settlers. As a result, in 1907, with the so-called Gentlemen's Agreement between President Theodore Roosevelt and the Japanese

government, Japanese immigration to the United States was effectively stopped.

Through a loophole in the law, however, wives of Japanese immigrants already in the country were excluded from these restrictions. Thus, many Japanese men in the United States rushed to bring their wives over (or to quickly marry and do so). Many single men not financially able to return to Japan asked their parents or relatives back in Japan to help find partners for them. These "picture brides"—whom their new husbands knew only through photographs—attended wedding ceremonies in Japan and crossed the ocean by themselves under visas sent to them by their grooms in the United States.

Seeing the vast numbers of picture brides arriving in the West Coast angered many Californians, who felt tricked by this legal technicality and who were appalled by these "immoral" and loveless marriages practiced by the Japanese. As a result, the Immigration Exclusion Act passed in 1924 officially ended all kinds of Japanese (and most European) immigration to the United States. Not until 1965 would Japanese immigration become legal. In the meantime, numerous state, local, and federal statutes greatly restricted the civil rights of people of Japanese ancestry. For example, California's Alien Land Act of 1913 prohibited Japanese immigrants from owning farmland, even though a majority of them were farmers. Often these laws were also applied to native-born Japanese Americans, who were American citizens by birth.

Japanese people faced similar kinds of discrimination in Canada. Around the turn of the twentieth century, upward of four thousand Japanese arrived annually in British Columbia, a majority of them engaged in the fishing industry. The Canadian equivalent of the Gentlemen's Agreement (the Lemieux Agreement) also greatly restricted Japanese immigration (to about four hundred people a year).

CANADA

WASH.
14,565

MONTANA

NORTH
DAKOTA   MINN.

OREGON
4,071

IDAHO
Minidoka

SOUTH
DAKOTA   WIS.

Tule Lake

WYOMING

NEBRASKA   IOWA

NEVADA
UTAH
Topaz

COLORADO
Granada
(Amache)

KANSAS   MO.

ILL.

CALIFORNIA
93,717

Manzanar

ARIZONA
Poston
Gila River

NEW
MEXICO

OKLA.   ARK.
Rohwer.
Jerome

PACIFIC
OCEAN

TEXAS   LA.

**Japanese-American Relocation
Camps during World War II**

•   Relocation camp

   States with more than 1,000
   Japanese-American residents, 1940

Gulf of Mexico

0   125   250 Miles

0 125 250 Kilometers

**During World War II, more than 120,000 Japanese Americans—
almost two-thirds of whom were United States citizens—were
incarcerated in a series of camps in the West and Arkansas. The
action only involved Japanese Americans living west of the
Rocky Mountains but, ironically, did not include Hawaii, which
was the only heavily inhabited American territory actually attacked by Japan.** (*CARTO-GRAPHICS*)

DETENTION CAMPS

Soon after the Japanese attack on Pearl Harbor in Hawaii on December 7, 1941, both the United States and
Canadian governments passed a series of executive
orders and laws restricting the freedom of people of
Japanese ancestry. One key measure was President
Franklin D. Roosevelt's Executive Order No. 9066 of
February 19, 1942. These acts stipulated that "all Japanese persons, both alien and non-alien, will be evacuated from the [Japanese residential areas] by 12:00
o'clock noon, Tuesday, April 7 in 1942. . . . No Japanese person will be permitted to enter or leave [their
residential areas] after 8:00 a.m., Thursday, April 2,
1942 without obtaining special permission." People of
Japanese ancestry were commanded to dispose immediately of their real and personal property, livestock, homes, and businesses. Of course, most of these
were liquidated at a tremendous financial loss. By August 1942, over 120,000 people of Japanese descent
were sent to detention camps in Arizona, Arkansas,
California, Colorado, Idaho, Utah, and Wyoming.
Most were allowed to take only two suitcases. Some
30,000 of those interned—one out of four—were

school-aged children. (However, because over a third
of the Hawaiian population was Japanese, it was not
possible to intern them all, so no people of Japanese
ancestry in Hawaii went to the camps.)

Life in the camps was not only a physical and economic struggle but also a battle against racial discrimination. At the same time, there was a crisis of ethnic
identity for these Japanese Americans. This was especially true for the nisei (the second generation of
Japanese Americans who were born in the United
States), who usually thought of themselves as real
Americans and identified themselves as holding
American cultural and social values. Their sense of
betrayal was profound. At the same time, the issei
(first-generation Japanese immigrants) held little allegiance to the Japan of their distant past but were
also not yet fully assimilated into mainstream American culture. These differing cultural and genera-
tional values often made life in the camps tense and
tenacious.

Physically, these internment camps were like prisons, being surrounded by barbed wire fences with
armed guards. Physical conditions, especially at first,
were stark. Each camp housed about ten thousand
people, and conditions were often crowded. But the
residents gradually organized themselves, and by the
end of the war, something of a community had grown
in each camp. There were newspapers, amateur theaters, schools, and sports teams. Many people had
jobs, working as cooks, janitors, or health care workers. As time passed, some Japanese were given a
chance to be released temporarily from the camps if
they would engage in agricultural work in the local
areas.

In 1943, President Roosevelt, acting on the sugges-
tion of Lieutenant General John L. DeWitt, head of the
Western Defense Command, suggested to the War Department that Japanese Americans might join the
army in a unit of all Japanese Americans as one means
to prove the loyalty of the Japanese-American community. This unit became known as the 442nd Regimental Combat Team. As a result, by 1943, young
Japanese-American men had become eligible to be
drafted, even though they had been denied most
other rights and responsibilities enjoyed by American
citizens. The War Relocation Authority even asked all
internees over the age of eighteen if they were loyal
to the United States and would defend the country
against Japan if called on. The issei, who previously
had been denied American citizenship because of
their race, were uncomfortable with the idea of facing
their parents, old friends, and relatives back in Japan
at gunpoint. At the same time, if they refused to declare their loyalty to America, they could become

During World War II, these government-built barracks in Salinas, California, were an assembly center for Japanese Americans destined for internment camps. *(National Archives)*

stateless. Some second-generation nisei, too, were very suspicious of a government that had taken away their rights as American citizens. As a result, about 12,000 internees became "disloyal." However, about 1,500 Japanese-American volunteers from the mainland and some 2,700 from Hawaii served in the armed forces at the time the unit was formed. Over 18,000 men ultimately served in the 442nd. In extremely tough European combat, approximately 9,000 of them were wounded, and over 600 were killed. The 442nd went on to become one of the most decorated units in U.S. military history. By the end of World War II, more than 33,000 Japanese-American men and women had served in the American armed forces.

The West Coast exclusion orders were removed in December 1944, and the last camp was closed in March 1946. Japanese Americans were free to go any-

where in the country, and many returned to the West Coast. Yet no provisions were made to compensate them for any losses they incurred during the war or as a result of internment, except for the $25 they were given when they left the camps.

There were also some Latin Americans who were sent to the American internment camps. For example, over 10 percent of the Japanese-Peruvian population (about seventeen hundred people) were deported at gunpoint to America between 1942 and 1945. In 1945, when the war ended, these Japanese Peruvians became stateless when they could not obtain either American or Peruvian passports. Some returned to Japan, a few to Peru, and many remained in the United States as refugees and later became naturalized citizens.

All Japanese Americans living west of the Rocky Mountains were given just a few days to dispose of their property and report to assembly centers after President Franklin Roosevelt signed Executive Order 9066 in February 1942. *(National Archives)*

COURT CASES

There are three important Supreme Court cases that directly addressed issues of internment. Minoru Yasui, an American-born lawyer, challenged the legality of the curfews imposed on Japanese Americans. In 1942, he deliberately violated curfew in his hometown of Portland, Oregon. He was arrested, and his American citizenship was taken away under suspicion of disloyalty. In *Yasui v. United States* (1942), the Supreme Court ruled that the curfew was constitutional.

Also in 1942, Gordon Hirabayashi turned himself in to police in Seattle for failing to report for relocation. Being an American citizen, a Quaker, a leader of a Boy Scout troop, and a student at the University of Washington, he did not feel he could allow himself to be evacuated without practicing civil disobedience. He was sentenced to six months in prison, and in 1943, the Supreme Court upheld his conviction in *Hirabayashi v. United States*.

The case of Fred Korematsu was a little different from these other two. Korematsu escaped from a camp, as he wished to be with his non-Japanese fi-

ancée. He had plastic surgery and changed his name to a Spanish Hawaiian–sounding name. He was arrested and ordered to go to a detention camp. Once again, the Supreme Court upheld the constitutionality of the evacuation order in *Korematsu v. United States* (1944). However, throughout World War II, the Court always evaded directly taking up the issue of the constitutionality of the actual internment camps themselves.

REDRESS MOVEMENT

After World War II, Japanese Americans fought to rectify the injustices done to them. They demanded an apology from the federal government and compensation for the people who were interned. Some Americans, including several World War II veterans groups, felt that such action would be inappropriate. After years of lobbying, however, Japanese Americans won their case. In 1988, Congress passed the Civil Liberties Act, which authorized each internee or survivor to receive $20,000 and an apology from the United States. Some sixty thousand Japanese Americans received this compensation.

Japanese Latin Americans who were also interned with Japanese Americans were denied the apology and compensation in 1988 because they were not technically American citizens or residents at the time of their internment. In 1998, these Japanese Latin Americans were finally recognized and received an official apology from the U.S. government. Nonetheless, their compensation was only $5,000 each, one-fourth of the amount given Japanese Americans. This difference in treatment between Japanese Americans and Japanese Latin Americans is one reason why some tension remains today in Japanese-American society.

Nobuko Adachi

See also: Japan (Part III, Sec. 3); President Roosevelt's Executive Order 9066 (Japanese Internment), 1942, *Hirabayashi v. United States*, 1943 (Part IV, Sec. 1); Reparations for Japanese-American Internees, 1988 (Part IV, Sec. 2).

BIBLIOGRAPHY

Emmerson, John K. *The Japanese Thread*. New York: Holt, Rinehart, and Winston, 1978.

Hatamiya, Leslie T. *Righting a Wrong: Japanese Americans and the Passage of the Civil Liberties Act of 1988*. Stanford: Stanford University Press, 1993.

Herman, Masako. *The Japanese in America, 1843–1973*. Dobbs Ferry, NY: Oceana, 1974.

Irons, Peter. *Justice Delayed*. Middletown, CT: Wesleyan University Press, 1989.

Spickard, Paul R. *Japanese Americans: The Formation and Transformations of an Ethnic Group*. New York: Twayne Publishers, 1996.

THE SURGE OF LATINO IMMIGRATION

While citizens of the United States during the late nineteenth and early twentieth centuries increasingly conceived of immigration in terms of regulation, restriction, and, in some cases, exclusion, policymakers, nonetheless, left wide open the door to neighboring peoples, especially those from Mexico and the Caribbean. From the onset of the First World War to the Immigration and Nationality Act of 1965, the United States of America witnessed a rising tide of immigration from Latin America. For example, in the decade prior to the First World War, immigration to the United States from the Western Hemisphere, excluding Canada, represented little more than 2 percent of the total number of immigrants, but in the next decade, that figure swelled to nearly 7 percent. By the period 1951–60, Latinos comprised nearly a quarter of all immigrants coming to the United States.

This vast movement of people reflected both similarities to other migratory experiences, such as chain immigration, reverse immigration, and ethnic clustering, and profound differences, as in issues of proximity to homelands, significant native-born populations already in the United States, and the geopolitical realities of the Western Hemisphere. Specific historical developments both in Latin America and the United States also influenced the mass movement of people. Revolutionary conditions in Mexico, Nicaragua, Guatemala, the Dominican Republic, Cuba, and elsewhere facilitated the movement of Latinos, particularly in the context of the Cold War. Issues of development, including natural disasters, foreign capitalist hegemony, and accelerating population growth, also functioned as factors pushing migratory people north to the United States. Moveover, developments within the United States served to attract Latinos. A strong, vibrant Mexican-American presence in the Southwest provided comfort for newcomers. Rapidly expanding labor demands in agriculture, light industry, and construction offered new job opportunities. Improvements in transportation and communication made it easier for Latinos, particularly Puerto Ricans, to relocate and stay in contact with family and friends left behind. Finally, national policy, particularly efforts at supplying labor markets and utilizing refugees as propaganda tools in the Cold War, offered significant opportunities for Latino immigration to the United States.

IMMIGRATION POLICY AND LATINOS

Immigration policy in the United States has traditionally treated Latinos differently from people of Asia and Europe largely because of the special patterns of Western Hemisphere geopolitics. While immigration restrictionists finally succeeded in their efforts with the literacy legislation of 1917, the Quota Act of 1921, and the Quota Act of 1924, immigrants from the Western Hemisphere were not limited, as were those from Europe, or excluded, as were Asians. Several factors contributed to the exclusion of Western Hemisphere people from the quota systems, notably capitalists' needs for cheap sources of labor and policymakers' desires for warm relations with neighboring states. The 1942 treaty between Mexico and the United States creating the Bracero Program, whereby contract laborers crossed the border to work in industry and agriculture, represented a major initiative embracing both labor and diplomatic objectives of the United States.

By the Cold War, policies dealing with political refugees expanded immigration opportunities, and by 1960, under the World Refugee Year Law, thousands of Cubans fleeing the revolution in their homeland flocked to the United States. By 1965, however, previous preferential policies toward Latinos ended with the Hart-Cellar Act, which placed a ceiling of 290,000

Mexicans make their way through customs in El Paso, Texas, in 1938. Unlike immigrants from Europe and Asia, immigrants from the Western Hemisphere were not subject to national quotas. *(Library of Congress)*

on annual immigration, with only 120,000 visas available to people from the Western Hemisphere.

THE CHALLENGES OF LATINO IMMIGRATION

While traveling to the United States in increasing numbers and benefiting, at times, from preferential federal policies, Latinos coming to the United States between the First World War and 1965 nevertheless encountered significant challenges. While "Americans," Latinos were perceived as quite different by most residents of the United States, many of whom judged historical Spanish and Portuguese traditions

and institutions as somehow "inferior" to Anglo ones. In addition, cultural construction of race and identity often served to categorize Latinos among nonwhite groups who found themselves marginalized economically and politically.

In the West, Mexicans faced both de facto and de jure discrimination in states such as Texas and California, the latter of which witnessed the brutally notorious Zoot Suit Riots of 1943, where Anglo sailors and youths attacked young Chicanos in Los Angeles. In the 1960s and 1970s, Cuban immigrants, many of whom brought greater skills and capital as political refugees, found themselves lumped by the native-born with poorer and less-educated Puerto Ricans in eastern cities. Caribbean peoples from Cuba, Puerto Rico, the Dominican Republic, Haiti, and elsewhere

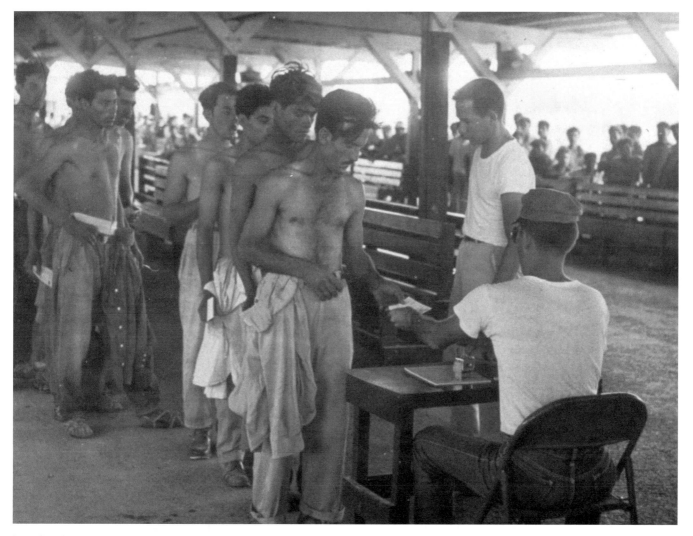

Introduced during the labor shortages of World War I, the Bracero Program offered tens of thousands of Mexicans temporary farm work in the 1920s. The program was ended during the Great Depression. *(INS)*

have also had to negotiate racial boundaries in the United States that include ingrained prejudices by both native-born whites and African Americans. Finally, lingering nativism and pejorative labeling as in the term "wetback" have created obstacles to full participation in public life in the United States by Latinos, particularly for undocumented visitors. Both in the 1930s and 1950s, for example, the federal government operated repatriation campaigns meant to soothe public concerns over the increasing numbers of Latinos in the United States.

The rising tide of Latino immigration between the First World War and 1965 represented a shift in immigration trends from people of the developed to the developing world. In terms of the Western Hemisphere, the numbers of people immigrating from specific regions reflected various factors, including geography, history, economics, and geopolitics. On a

decade-by-decade basis, the proportion of Latinos in terms of all immigrants to the United States progressively increased (save for the depression years) from roughly 2.1 percent in the decade before the First World War to around 39.2 percent in the decade of the Hart-Cellar Act.

The vast majority of that immigrant population came from Mexico. Of the nearly 3 million documented immigrants to the United States from Latin America between the First World War and 1965, nearly one-half came from Mexico, reflecting both the efficacy of geographic proximity and labor markets in facilitating immigration. Immigrants from the republics of South and Central America constituted roughly 15 and 7 percent, respectively, of Latino immigration to the United States in the period. The remaining three-tenths of non-Canadian immigrants to the United States from the Western Hemisphere came from the Caribbean, including people of both Latin (e.g., Dominican Republic) and non-Latin (e.g., British West Indies) heritage. While not necessarily analogous, proportionality of representation among immigrant groups has generally intersected with the visibility and impact of specific Latino immigrant groups; thus, one may expect Mexican immigrants, for example, to have played a larger role in United States immigrant history than, say, Bolivians. Analysis of immigration by specific nationality group, therefore, must reflect both numbers of immigrants to the United States and impact of specific immigration streams on national historical experience.

MEXICANS

While Mexican immigration to the United States had been steadily increasing before the First World War, largely because of expanded agricultural labor needs coupled with the exclusion of Chinese, the outbreak of the revolution in 1911 greatly facilitated movement over the border for the next decade. Census records indicate that Mexican immigration to the United States more than quadrupled from the decade of 1901–10 to that of 1911–20 and then doubled again during the 1920s. Between 1900 and 1930, the Mexican population in the United States grew from 100,000 to nearly 1.5 million, with the population of Mexicans in the Los Angeles barrio second only to that of Mexico City. Similar population increases appeared throughout the Southwest, particularly in already established barrios in southern Texas, and for the first time, visible Mexican enclaves appeared in the Midwest, particularly in the Plains states. While many new arrivals found support in established barrios, they also faced increasing Americanizing pressures, particularly during the First World War. For example, the 1915 Home Teacher Act in California sought to combine instruction in English, Americanism, and domestic skills to foster assimilation; however, the social pressures of such schemes often turned immigrants inward to their own community, thus helping to reinforce Mexican culture.

During the 1920s, the Obregón and Calles administrations sought to stabilize Mexico through the institutionalization of the revolutionary government, but the debate over agrarian reform and rural unrest, coming at a time when the neighbor to the north witnessed incredible economic growth, contributed to even greater numbers of Mexicans immigrating to the United States. While much of the Mexican immigrant population remained agricultural workers, during the 1920s new opportunities opened up in mining, transportation, construction, processing plants, and manufacturing. And, while much of this growth occurred in the West, the traditional locale for the great bulk of Mexican immigrants, greatly expanded opportunities presented themselves in the industrial center of the country. Industries such as steel, meatpacking, and automobiles offered new, better-paying opportunities for Mexicans willing to relocate to cities such as Detroit and Chicago.

Despite their increasing numbers and expanded economic opportunities, Mexican immigrants and Mexican Americans began encountering strong prejudices, especially in the Southwest. By 1929, concern over continuing discrimination led to the creation of the League of United Latin American Citizens (LULAC) in Corpus Christi, Texas, an organization dedicated to forging a new politics aimed against inequality. Ironically, however, the new organization allowed only United States citizens to join and adopted English as its official language, thereby revealing cultural boundaries between Mexican Americans and recently arrived immigrants from Mexico.

The need for Chicano solidarity became more readily apparent during the 1930s as the Great Depression witnessed shrinking labor markets, social disruption, and increased anti-Mexican sentiments among United States citizens and policymakers. During the depression decade, 1931–40, immigration from Mexico to the United States dropped to just over 22,000, a dramatic decrease from the nearly 460,000 immigrants of the previous decade. Much of this decline, obviously, may be attributed to the dearth of economic opportunities north of the Rio Grande as well as the lack of financial wherewithal to finance laborer movement back and forth across the border. Those Mexican immigrants already in the United States during the Great Depression faced a new set of challenges such as wage cuts and layoffs, restrictions on mobility, and repatriation efforts by private employers, state governments, and the federal government. From 1928 to 1933, for example, California farmers sliced laborer wages more than half. Rocky Mountain states such as Colorado sought to bar new migrants. In Michigan, Henry Ford personally financed the repatriation of 3,000 of his own employees to Mexico. Finally, the federal government manipulated relief policy to force Mexicans to return home, often taking their U.S.-born children with them.

Mexican immigrants and Mexican Americans, however, did not passively accept official discrimination and restricted opportunity. Increasingly, these people created organizations to express self-interests and organized politically to ensure representation of those interests at the public policy level. A great stride forward occurred in 1932, when Maverick County, Texas, voters elected Griff Jones, the first Mexican-American county commissioner in the United States, setting the stage for increased political activism in the years to come. Since economic need dominated much of the public consciousness during the 1930s, it is not surprising that Chicanos exerted great efforts in labor organization. Unions such as the Confederación de Uniones de Obreros Mexicanos and La Union de Trabajadores del Valle Imperial provided opportunities for Mexican Americans and Mexican immigrants to organize collectively. The Confederación de Uniones de Campesinos y Obreros Mexicanos, the largest such organization, embraced over four dozen locals. In 1933, over 12,000 agricultural workers in the San Joaquin Valley fought against wage reductions. The years to come witnessed Chicano job actions in fruit orchards, cotton fields, food processing plants, canneries, and other operations from northern California down to southern Texas. A particularly noteworthy job action occurred in 1939, in Los Angeles, when Eastside Brewery refused to hire Mexican workers even though most of their consumers were of Mexican heritage. In response, Josefina Fierro de Bright organized a successful boycott of the brewery, employing such celebrities as Dolores Del Río and Anthony Quinn in the effort.

Despite the economic turnaround brought by the Second World War, people of Mexican heritage in the United States continued to confront formal and informal barriers, which required that earlier organizational efforts continue throughout the 1940s. Some of these efforts were ably aided by the Mexican government, such as the 1942 treaty specifying more favorable working conditions of contract laborers, or *braceros*, including both government- and employer-provided transportation, living, and repatriation expenses and exemption of such brazenly anti-Mexican areas as Texas from participation in the program. Economic activism also continued. In 1946, workers in the El Paso local of the International Union of Mine, Mill, and Smelter Workers, a member union of the Congress of Industrial Organizations, challenged the powerful Guggenheim interest over ethnic job segmentation, forcing the World War II–era Office of Price Administration to broker a significant wage increase.

The notorious Zoot Suit Riots of June 1943 in Los Angeles also showed the vulnerability of Chicanos to ethnocentric forces. Although roughly 350,000 Mexican Americans participated in the war effort, garnering various decorations and honors, and Chicanos at home participated in such wartime organizations as

the Coordinating Council for Latin American Youth and the American-Mexican Victory Youth Club, virulent anti-Mexican sentiments appeared along with the increased visibility of Chicanos in urban areas and in factories. Wartime Los Angeles witnessed such pressures, especially after the mysterious death of José Díaz at Sleepy Lagoon resulted in the mass arrests of young men of Mexican derivation and the conviction of seventeen during a controversial trial. Governmental ethnocentrism and press sensationalism at the time fanned the flames of anti-Mexican xenophobia, leading to rioting in early to mid-June by Anglo sailors and soldiers who rampaged through the barrio, pulling Chicanos, especially those dressed in the flamboyant Zoot Suit style of the time, into the streets and beating them savagely while civilian and military police watched without intervening. Such behavior portrayed the marginality of Chicanos in the United States and the need for organizations such as the Sleepy Lagoon Defense Committee and the American G.I. Forum to fight for equal rights before the law.

The need to confront personal and institutional discrimination made Mexican Americans key players in the burgeoning Civil Rights movement of the postwar period. Throughout the United States but particularly in Texas and the Southwest, Mexicans and Mexican Americans encountered various forms of discrimination, including segregated schools, residential property restrictions, and ethnic labor segmentation. As early as 1939, Chicanos confronted such prejudices through the court system. Mexican-American organizations brought suits against segregated theaters, public swimming pools, housing, and prisons throughout the 1940s and 1950s in California and Texas. In May 1954, the Supreme Court ruled in the Hernández case that the defendant had been denied his civil rights because of the exclusion of Mexican Americans from the jury. Like African Americans, Mexican Americans concentrated many of their efforts on discrimination in public education, realizing that equal access to learning facilities had been a traditional helping hand to previous immigrants. In 1948, such efforts paid off when a federal court ruled in *Delgado v. Bastrop Independent School District* that it was unconstitutional to segregate Mexican-American students in separate schools or classrooms.

The postwar years witnessed additional gains by Mexican Americans on various fronts. These achievements were attributable to diverse factors, including the growing numbers of immigrants, expanding labor demands in the West, the ascendancy of the civil rights agenda, and the increased importance of friendly relations with the developing world in the

Cold War. Raymond L. Telles' election as mayor of El Paso in 1957 represented a major milestone in Mexican-American politics, impressing on southwestern politicians the growing importance of the Chicano vote. Telles' victory also reflected the significance of border crossing as part of the Mexican immigration experience, especially in light of the support his campaign received from both local businesspersons dependent on Telles' constituency and Ciudad Juárez mayor René Mascarenas. Apart from the legal and political arenas, Mexican Americans worked to undermine prejudice by confronting negative cultural portrayals. In 1950, the *Asociación Nacional México Americana* focused on anti-Mexican stereotypes rife in the media, including a boycott of the sponsor of Judy Canova's radio show.

As important as such strides appeared, the postwar period also witnessed significant challenges still confronting Mexican immigrants and their descendants who sought equal opportunity and rights before the law in the United States. The Bracero Program continued until 1964, bringing nearly 5 million Mexican laborers to the United States, but growers became increasingly restive in the postwar period over having to pay up to fifty cents an hour. To lower labor costs, these farm operators and other capitalists tapped into the increasing pool of undocumented immigrants from Mexico, thus accelerating the rate of illegal immigration. Ironically, the Bracero Program stimulated undocumented immigration, because many working-class Mexicans knew of employment opportunities to the north but could not enlist in the government program. Concerns over undocumented aliens led the Immigration and Naturalization Service (INS) to conduct a series of raids known as Operation Wetback on agricultural operations in the West. Between 1954 and 1958, INS reported that its raids had led to the deportation of nearly 3.8 million people to Mexico, although only a few over 63,000 had been provided formal hearings.

Demographic changes occasioned by economic realities also profoundly affected Mexican immigrants and Mexican Americans. While agricultural labor continued to engage many Chicanos, an increasing number relocated to the cities, where overcrowding and scarcity of good-paying jobs appeared the norm. More and more Chicanas entered the wage labor force during this period, supplementing family income and empowering themselves economically but also occasioning a paradigmatic shift in traditionally paternalistic family structures. Finally, while income figures for Chicanos improved over the years, the lack of income parity with Anglo workers remained stark. For example, in 1959, income levels for workers of Mexican heritage in the Southwest remained less than two-thirds of that of Anglo workers.

Clearly, the important efforts made by Mexican Americans before and immediately after the war had not brought equality of opportunity by the 1960s. Continuing high levels of immigration, however, both highlighted the need for addressing persistent discrimination and further empowered organizational efforts in the United States by augmenting the number of Chicanos. While LULAC and other established groups pressed for institutional change through the courts, younger Mexican Americans sought quicker change through political activism. Emboldened by Henry González's unsuccessful 1958 gubernatorial bid in Texas, Mexican Americans brought a new agenda to politics in the 1960s, creating the Political Association of Spanish-Speaking Organizations, which, in 1963, combined with the Teamsters Union to win control of the city council in Crystal City, Texas. Two years later, in California, a strike by grape pickers led by Cesar Chavez received national press coverage, especially after catching the eye of Robert F. Kennedy. Chavez's efforts contributed to a growing Chicano movement, which would link to broader civil rights and empowerment movements. At the same time, the Hart-Cellar Act reconstituted American immigration policy, contributing significantly to new controversies over illegal immigration from Mexico. The two phenomena would represent intimately linked interests in the next chapter of Mexican immigration to the United States.

PUERTO RICANS

While not sharing a border with the United States as Mexico does, Puerto Rico does enjoy a rather intimate relationship with the North American republic because of the political ties between the island and the mainland. Taken from Spain during the 1898 war, Puerto Rico as a U.S. possession held an ambiguous position until 1917, when the Jones Act unilaterally declared the island's inhabitants to be citizens of the United States. The move was designed to preempt nationalist sentiments from crystallizing at a time when various peoples throughout the globe sought self-autonomy. In terms of immigration policy, United States citizenship meant that Puerto Ricans coming to the mainland were not technically alien immigrants but migrating Americans without the legal restraints placed on noncitizens. Nevertheless, differences in language, tradition, culture, and ethnicity meant that Puerto Ricans traveling to the mainland from 1917 to 1965 were much more like foreign immigrants than native-born citizens, at least in material reality and popular perceptions.

Historically, Puerto Rico has been a generally harmonious multiracial society. While virtually all of the original Taino inhabitants were killed by the Spanish or died out from newly introduced European diseases, some Indian culture remains evident among the island's people, although African heritage brought by slaves appears much more evident. Because of interracial marriage and childbirthing patterns, Puerto Ricans settling on the mainland have often found themselves consigned to similar status as African Americans, especially as many Puerto Ricans, unlike the early Mexican immigrants, moved heavily into urban areas. While Puerto Rican nationalists struggling for independence from Spain migrated to the United States in the late nineteenth century, the great bulk of Puerto Rican migration did not occur until after the Second World War. One estimate for the prewar period places the total number of Puerto Ricans on the mainland at only 53,000 by 1930, and of course, the years of the Great Depression and Second World War precluded significant immigration streams because of economic and security reasons.

By the 1950s and 1960s, however, several key developments had brought the mainland and island together, contributing to greater political continuity, expanded cultural contact, and increased migration. First, the United States government sought to improve political relations with the island, especially after the failed assassination attempt on President Truman by Puerto Rican nationalists. The Puerto Rican Federal Relations Act allowed Puerto Ricans to write their own constitution, which was inaugurated in July 1952, granting the island commonwealth status. An economic development program entitled Operation Bootstrap invested heavily in Puerto Rico after the Second World War, resulting in 300 new factories, but rising expectations due to such development, combined with rapid population growth, only served to facilitate out-migration to the mainland. Finally, improved transportation infrastructure made the movement from Puerto Rico to the mainland much cheaper and faster, thus increasing the pool of potential migrants as well as reinforcing the urban nature of migration, given that the airlines serviced major hubs such as New York City.

While pre–World War II Puerto Rican migrants worked as contract agricultural workers in rural areas and established vibrant communities in the Midwest and California, the largest Puerto Rican community on the mainland centered in New York City. Puerto Ricans began migrating to New York City in significant numbers around the First World War, and by the 1930s, East Harlem had become the focal point of Puerto Rican culture on the mainland. Following the Second World War, Puerto Ricans began spreading throughout the metropolis, especially into the South Bronx and parts of Manhattan. For the most part, these migrants were young and brought little capital and few skills with them, so they tended to take unskilled, low-paying jobs often left behind by former European immigrants. Because of material deprivation, they tended to settle in urban areas suffering from municipal neglect and economic stagnation.

Despite vibrant and nurturing communities established in New York City and elsewhere, much of the post–World War II Puerto Rican migration constituted an internal movement from the island to the mainland and back again partly because of the lack of opportunity in the States but also because of ties back home. To help ease the migrating experience, Puerto Ricans on the mainland created or adapted institutions to their own liking as have other ethnic groups. In religion, Puerto Ricans advocated a policy of pluralism in the Catholic Church meant to incorporate some of the more communitarian aspects of Puerto Rican faith. On the secular side, Aspira, a Puerto Rican education promotion organization (meaning "aspire" in English), begun in New York City in 1961, sought to develop among Puerto Rican youth on the mainland the ideals of cultural pride and self-confidence. Finally, the easy accessibility of the island to mainland Puerto Ricans proved indispensable in maintaining family ties and preserving traditional culture.

CUBANS

Like the Puerto Ricans, Cuban immigrants and their descendants came from a Caribbean island where the importation of African slaves meant to replace the lost labor power of indigenous peoples profoundly altered the ethnic matrix of the society. Also like the Puerto Rican experience, many of the early Cuban immigrants were self-exiled nationalists seeking refuge from Spanish colonialists. In addition, its historical experience bound up Cuba's history closely with that of the United States, particularly when considering the legacy of the Platt Amendment, U.S. military intervention and occupation, and disproportionately high levels of foreign capital investment. Despite the close contact between Cuba and the United States, immigrants from Cuba had little impact on the United

States before 1959, even though nearly half a million Caribbean peoples had emigrated to the United States since 1920. What differentiated the Cuban immigration experience from that of Puerto Rico and made it especially significant was, of course, the revolution of 1959 and its aftermath.

While increasing numbers of Cubans immigrated to the United States throughout the 1950s as the Batista dictatorship became more oppressive and then began to crumble, the great bulk of Cuban immigration did not come until 1960. After the revolution's victory, Fidel Castro made clear his plans to socialize the state and slowly embraced support from domestic and foreign communists. Alarmed by the radicalization of society, over 150,000 Cuban bourgeoisie, Batististas, and anticommunists fled the island for the mainland between 1959 and 1962. Unlike fellow immigrants from the Caribbean, Cubans found themselves generally welcomed by Americans who conceived of the flight from Cuba as an ideological aspect of the Cold War rather than a class cleavage wrought by revolution. Because many of the early Cuban immigrants had been accommodationists with the Batista regime or foreign capitalists, they brought skills and capital with them, thereby easing the transition to the United States. In addition, anticipating a United States invasion to topple the revolution, which, of course, was attempted in the Bay of Pigs fiasco, many immigrants settled in south Florida, especially Miami, whose vibrant Cuban community became known as Little Havana. The suspension of direct air flights between the United States and Cuba during the missile crisis of 1962 effectively closed immigration for the rest of the period.

CENTRAL AND SOUTH AMERICANS

Immigration to the United States from the republics of Central and South America has traditionally lagged far behind that from Mexico and the Caribbean. In the period 1911–20, immigrants from these regions accounted for only about 27 percent of the total from the Western Hemisphere excluding Canada; during the decade before enactment of Hart-Cellar, that percentage actually fell to 25 percent, with most of the decline occurring on the South American side. Various factors account for the small proportion of immigration to the United States from Central and South America from the First World War to 1965. As client states of the United States throughout the period, Central American republics found their economies locked into monoculture conditions, thereby provid-

ing little access by the middle class and poor to the extra capital needed to immigrate. Distances and lack of efficacious transportation facilities also account for lack of immigration, especially in the case of South America. During the war years, transition to certain types of manufacturing provided increased opportunities for laborers in Argentina, Brazil, Chile, and Peru, thus eliminating one major motive for immigration.

While often lumped together in the popular mind as "Spanish Americans," immigrants from Central and South America during the period in question represented a wide diversity of cultural traditions. Ethnic differences abounded with Spanish, Portuguese, Amer-Indian, African, Chinese, Japanese, and other types of heritage dependent on the area of outmigration. Again, different degrees of rurality or urbanity existed depending on whether the immigrant came from regions dominated by plantations or haciendas or from major metropolitan regions such as Santiago or Buenos Aires. For Central America, most immigrants clustered in urban centers, with roughly one-third finding professional or managerial work, although many remained in the semi- or unskilled labor sector, and many women worked as domestics. For South Americans, Colombia, Argentina, Brazil, and Ecuador produced the greatest number of immigrants. South American immigrants were more likely than Central Americans to evince balanced sex ratios and higher degrees of professional employment. Like Central Americans, however, immigrants from South America gravitated to the larger metropolitan areas, especially in the industrial Northeast, along the Gulf of Mexico coast, and in the Pacific Rim states.

CARIBBEAN PEOPLES

The Caribbean supplied significant numbers of immigrants to the United States from the First World War to 1965. But not all island peoples of the Caribbean belong in the category "Latino"; for example, in the West Indies, British culture and institutions have been more influential than Latin ones. Nonetheless, Spanish influences have been felt in parts of the Caribbean, and in the North American popular mind at least, immigrants from the Caribbean have often been lumped together as part of "Latin America." Sharing a Spanish heritage with neighboring Cuba and Puerto Rico, the Dominican Republic did not send large numbers of immigrants to the United States during much of the period, principally because of the restrictive policies of the dictator Rafael Trujillo (1930–61). With the fall of Trujillo, Dominicans began immigrating in larger numbers (less than 1,000 in 1960 as compared with almost 11,000 in 1965), generally settling in eastern metropolitan areas, south Florida, and Puerto Rico. Other islands sending substantial numbers of immigrants to the United States included Haiti, which abuts the Dominican Republic but has more of a Franco-African heritage than Spanish, and those of the West Indies, which have more of an Afro-British influence, although Chinese, Hindus, Germans, and others have lived on the islands. For Haitians, the United States occupation of their homeland (1915–34) and the repressive regime of François Duvalier stimulated significant immigration streams with many out-migrants settling in New York, particularly in Harlem, where many participated in the self-empowerment movement of Marcus Garvey in the 1920s. West Indian immigration peaked after World War II but encountered the Immigration and Nationality Act of 1952, which barred entry by British colonials; therefore, larger numbers came from the independent nations of Jamaica and the Bahamas. West Indians in the United States often brought higher levels of skills and education and proved to be institution builders, creating among other organizations the West Indian Reform Association.

From World War I to the 1965 Immigration and Nationality Act, immigration by Latinos to the United States represented less a series of streams than a major surge. The large majority coming from Mexico and Puerto Rico, Latino immigrants represented a broad cross section of national, geographic, racial, ethnic, class, and cultural types. Because many were poor, non-English-speaking, and nonwhite, Latino immigrants encountered various cultural and institutional prejudices as they settled in the United States. While

many, especially those from Mexico, Puerto Rico, the West Indies, and Ecuador, practiced reverse migration, large and vibrant Latino communities developed throughout the United States but particularly in California, the Southwest, south Florida, and the industrial Northeast. As their numbers increased and the national consciousness turned increasingly to issues of social and economic justice, Latino immigrants contributed increasingly to the fight for civil rights for all and greater respect and fairness for their own peoples.

Timothy Draper

See also: Early Spanish Settlers (Part I, Sec. 1); Mexico, Puerto Rico (Part III, Sec. 2); Treaty of Guadalupe Hidalgo, 1848, Puerto Rico Citizenship Act, 1917, "Bracero Program" Act, 1949 (Part IV, Sec. 1).

BIBLIOGRAPHY

Beezley, William H., and Colin M. MacLachlan. *El Gran Pueblo: A History of Greater Mexico, 1911–Present.* Englewood Cliffs, NJ: Prentice Hall, 1994.

Cardoso, Lawrence. *Mexican Emigration to the United States.* Tucson: University of Arizona Press, 1980.

Dinnerstein, Leonard, Roger L. Nichols, and David M. Reimers. *Natives and Strangers: A Multicultural History of Americans.* New York: Oxford University Press, 1997.

Parrillo, Vincent N. *Strangers to These Shores: Race and Ethnic Relations in the United States.* New York: Wiley, 1985.

Reimers, David M. *Still the Golden Door: The Third World Comes to America.* 2d ed. New York: Columbia University Press, 1992.

Romo, Ricardo. *East Los Angeles: History of a Barrio.* Austin: University of Texas Press, 1983.

Takaki, Ronald. *A Different Mirror: A History of Multicultural America.* Boston: Little, Brown and Co., 1993.

1965 TO THE PRESENT

INTRODUCTION

The entries in Section 5 of Part I of the *Encyclopedia of American Immigration* explore recent immigration history. The starting point for this section is 1965, the year President Lyndon Johnson signed the landmark Immigration and Nationality Act, ending national quotas for immigrants. While its effects took more than a decade to occur, the act created the legal conditions for the greatest wave of immigration to the United States since the turn of the twentieth century. In addition, the law inaugurated a period in which the vast majority of immigrants no longer came from Europe but from Asia, the Caribbean, Latin America, and elsewhere. And, as was the case in the early twentieth century, this sudden wave of immigrants from unfamiliar cultures created a backlash among many native-born Americans, who sought to put limits on immigration.

In "Changes in the Law," James R. Edwards Jr. examines the landmark 1965 act. He begins with a discussion of both popular opinion and government policy in the years preceding passage of the act, including the Cold War and the liberalization of American public sentiment on immigration. He then examines the act itself, discussing in detail how its different provisions led to the mass wave of immigration that followed.

The entry titled "Southeast Asian Refugee Crisis" by David Haines explores the greatest wave of war refugees ever to reach American shores. The author begins with a brief introduction to the Vietnam War, which was the ultimate cause of the exodus, and then discusses the various stages of the crisis, beginning with the immediate exodus of Southeast Asians following the communist victories in Cambodia, Laos, and Vietnam in 1974 and 1975. He then examines the "boat people" phenomenon of the late 1970s and early 1980s, when thousands more fled poverty and renewed warfare in Vietnam and the genocide of the Khmer Rouge regime in Kampuchea (now Cambodia). Haines also looks at the various resettlement programs initiated by the U.S. government to settle Southeast Asia refugees in communities around the United States and how those refugees adjusted to their new lives.

In her essay "Increase in Immigrants from the Developing World," Dominique Daniel examines the post-1965 phenomenon in which millions of persons from the developing world have immigrated to the United States. She begins with discussion of the many ethnicities coming to the United States and then examines the causes of their immigration. Next, she looks into the various groups and discusses such developments as the Asian "brain drain," the importance of family reunification, the different uses of family-based visas, illegal immigration, and the new Latin American refugees fleeing political persecution and war in their homeland. Finally, she explores what happens to these immigrants once they get to the United States—where they settle, what they do for a living, and ways in which they have had an impact on American society.

In the entry "Collapse of Communism," Maureen Feeney explores the impact that the fall of communist regimes around the world has had on immigration to the United States. She begins with a discussion of that collapse and then looks at how immigration law coped with it. The entry "Immigrant-Minority Relations" by Suzanne Shanahan begins with a discussion of the pattern of those relations since 1965; she then provides a discussion of the perspective on group dynamics among immigrants and minorities.

In his essay on the major immigration legislation of the post-1965 era—"Immigration Legislation of the 1980s and 1990s"—Thomas J. Espenshade first examines the 1986 Immigration Reform and Control Act, which sought to limit illegal immigration by stepping up border patrols and imposing sanctions against employers who hired illegal immigrants, even as it offered amnesty to millions of illegal immigrants already living in the United States. Espenshade then goes on to look at the 1996 welfare and immigration reform acts, including the Personal Responsibility and Work Opportunity Reconciliation Act—which set strict limits on the social service benefits that immigrants could receive—and the Illegal Immigration Reform and Immigrant Responsibility Act, which also beefed up border patrols, employer sanctions, and restrictions on family sponsorship.

Finally, in "Anti-Immigrant Backlash," Brian N. Fry looks at anti-immigrant politics that have developed in the wake of rising immigration numbers in the 1980s and 1990s. He begins with a look at the early years of the movement before discussing the Official English movement, which seeks not only to make English the official language of the United States but also looks to end bilingualism in education and government. Finally, he examines how the anti-immigrant politics led to the legislation of the 1980s and 1990s which sought to halt illegal immigration and limit the social services that are available to all immigrants.

CHANGES IN THE LAW

The Immigration and Nationality Act Amendments of 1965 built on the 1952 Immigration and Nationality Act, which structure U.S. immigration law today. However, the 1965 immigration law fundamentally rewrote American immigration policy. Rather than basing admission of immigrants on one's national origin, which had been the law for more than forty years, the 1965 law laid the groundwork for a new immigrant flow and for much greater numbers.

The most notable change in the 1965 law was the repeal of the national origins quota system. This change abolished the preference given western and northern Europeans. Another change involved putting greater emphasis on "family reunification," which refers to the ability of immigrants to bring other family members to join them in the United States. These include a spouse, children, and brothers and sisters. A third major change in the law made "refugee" a category of immigration.

LEADING UP TO REFORM

In the 1880s and 1890s, immigration levels surged, and the newcomers came increasingly from southern and eastern Europe. Americans became concerned about these changes and responded with calls for new laws. These laws erected barriers to mass immigration. The Immigration Act of 1917 included a literacy test and placed further restrictions on Asians.

In the 1920s, the United States adopted an immigration system that was designed to preserve the racial and ethnic makeup of the population. The 1921 Immigration Act limited immigration directly. Immigrants gained admission on the basis of their national origin—the country from which their ancestors came—as it was represented in the U.S. population in the 1910 census, according to which each country received a quota. The U.S. ethnic composition in 1920 stemmed predominantly from British, Irish, and German origin. The 1924 Immigration Act first temporarily lowered quotas from the 1921 act based on the 1890 census, then established a permanent quota based on national origin as counted in the 1920 census.

One reason for this policy was to ease assimilation, or adaptation to American life. Americans equated nationality and ethnicity with one's value system. It was believed that immigrants from countries sharing a similar culture would share American democratic values. Thus, the future life of the nation would experience less political disruption.

Besides this overriding rationale for the national origins quotas, other reasons existed for restricting immigration. Many Americans believed that the United States had matured as a nation and that large numbers of immigrants were no longer "needed" to settle the frontier. Also, the Red Scare caused Americans concern over the presence of many eastern Europeans, who had recently arrived from 1881 until 1920. It hurt immigration enthusiasts' case mightily when many recent Russian immigrants supported the Bolshevik movement in Russia and joined the Communist Party in the United States.

Many restrictionists were motivated by racial theories in vogue at the time. Prominent social scientists advanced ideas of the superiority of the white race and cited the threat to whites' supposed inherent superiority posed by the mixing of races. Finally, economic recession in 1921 ensured that Americans, whose job security suffered with the economic upheaval, did not want a lot of foreigners who would work for lower wages threatening their already precarious economic situation. Thus, restrictive immigration laws were adopted in the early 1920s.

Coupled with a low worldwide quota of about 165,000 annually under the 1924 law, the national origins quota caused immigration to plummet. (Immigration in the middle part of the twentieth century also remained low in part because of strong "public charge" enforcement, or excluding those likely to rely on public charity for support rather than self-sufficiency. Other factors were the economic and political turmoil of the Great Depression and World War II.)

During the subsequent years of low immigration in the mid–twentieth century, the United States underwent major social changes. The civil rights movement won significant gains for African Americans, and many whites came to support the struggle for social justice and equality. These notions were soon applied to foreigners. World events also transformed American attitudes toward immigration. The United States emerged from World War II in a position to help other nations recover, and these nations, in turn, looked to America for assistance. In the postwar period, the Marshall Plan and General Douglas MacArthur's superintendence over the rebuilding of Japan—including its democratization and economic restructuring—gave America much contact with people around the globe, especially in Eastern Hemisphere countries from which immigration to the United States had remained low. And U.S. troops were stationed abroad, some taking "war brides" of other nationalities.

As the only nation that initially had nuclear weapons, the United States held much clout among its peers. As communism spread through Eastern Europe, China, and elsewhere, large numbers of people began fleeing their homelands. The United States responded to these refugee crises, albeit in piecemeal fashion. But the public value of helping individuals escape communism and the foreign policy interest in aiding displaced persons worked toward America's taking a lead role in providing assistance to refugees throughout the 1950s.

The Cold War climate produced the Immigration and Nationality Act of 1952. Also known as the McCarran-Walter Act, after its sponsors Senator Patrick McCarran (D-NV) and Representative Francis E. Walter (D-PA), the law continued the national origins quota system and authorized strict national security measures that made it easier to exclude communist subversives. The bill also established a four-category preference system. Half the visas of each nation's quota went to immigrants with more education and exceptional abilities. The other half of the visas were divided among three preference categories for various family members of U.S. citizens and permanent resident aliens. Additionally, the law exempted the husbands, wives, and children of U.S. citizens from their home nation's quota. The McCarran-Walter Act also relaxed the long-standing policies that had excluded Asians. Now, immigrants from Asian nations could become naturalized U.S. citizens. The law also extended a 100-visa quota to each Asian country.

Beginning with President Harry Truman, the national origins quota system came under increasing criticism from the White House. In 1958, Senator John F. Kennedy (D-MA) published a book called *A Nation of Immigrants*. After his election to the presidency in 1960, Kennedy sought to change the immigration system so that each nationality could have a chance at immigration.

After Kennedy's assassination in 1963, Lyndon B. Johnson pressed the issue. Following his own election as president in 1964, Johnson pursued a range of liberal social issues collectively known as the Great Society programs. These included not only immigration reform but also civil rights, antipoverty measures, and Medicare, which provided government-run health insurance for the elderly. Reforming the immigration system fit into the civil rights views making headway in the early 1960s. Policymakers in Washington predominately shared liberal views and a strong belief in the capacity of government to right wrongs and deliver services efficiently. Their faith in government activism led to enactment of the 1965 Immigration and Nationality Act Amendments.

IMMIGRATION REFORM IN 1965

The nation's reaction to Kennedy's untimely death—the late president had expressed interest in immigration reform—and the subsequent election of Lyndon Johnson, who vowed to fulfill Kennedy's legislative agenda, set the stage for the passage of immigration reform legislation in 1965. After years of low immigration, the public, though uninterested in immigration reform, did not mobilize in opposition to legislative efforts in 1965. And other factors also helped the reform effort to succeed.

First, President Johnson enjoyed large Democratic majorities in both the House and the Senate, with Republicans outnumbered two to one in both houses. Reform-minded legislators advanced to hold key congressional committee leadership posts and to serve on key committees, including those in charge of immigration, which gave Johnson allies where he needed them. Also, Johnson placed immigration reform fairly high on his legislative agenda. His administration proposed changes, and the president called for reform in his State of the Union address in January 1965.

Coordinated activity by a variety of pressure groups, such as ethnic organizations, some labor un-

At a ceremony on Liberty Island in New York harbor, President Lyndon Johnson signs the landmark Immigration and Nationality Act of 1965. The act ended national quotas for immigrants. *(Hias)*

ions, mainline religious groups, and an ad hoc group of influential people, factored into the legislation's enactment. On the other hand, few opponents of the legislation massed sustained lobbying efforts. The Johnson administration compromised early on the fundamental sticking points that opponents had long voiced. The administration accepted a quota of 170,000 for the Eastern Hemisphere. The later addition of a Western Hemisphere quota was viewed as essentially placing a yearly overall immigration quota of about three hundred thousand worldwide—the average annual immigration level at the time.

Whether to impose a Western Hemisphere quota presented the major issue of contention during the legislative debate on immigration legislation in 1965. Once that question had been settled, the bill passed

each house of Congress by wide margins: 318–95 in the House of Representatives, 76–18 in the Senate.

REPEALING THE NATIONAL ORIGINS QUOTA SYSTEM AND CHANGING THE FOCUS

The 1965 Immigration Act was designed to end discrimination based on race and nationality in the immigration system, much as civil rights laws passed at the time were intended to accomplish domestically. The immigration reform bill that became law in 1965 replaced the national origins quota system with a new immigration system. To be phased in over three years, the new system represented the most significant change in U.S. immigration policy since 1921. The law was named the Hart-Celler Act after its primary sponsors, Senator Philip Hart (D-MI) and Representative Emanuel Celler (D-NY).

The Eastern Hemisphere would have an annual quota of 20,000 visas per country. The entire hemisphere would be limited to an overall quota of 170,000 immigrants each year. A seven-category preference system would govern the allocation of immigrant visas within the Eastern Hemisphere.

The preference system expanded and modified the four-category preference system established in the 1952 Immigration and Nationality Act. The new system shifted the emphasis from individuals with needed job skills to the admission of family members, a significant and pronounced change. The 1952 law had allocated 50 percent of each country's quota for immigrants having special skills or education regarded as important to America's economy. Furthermore, skilled immigrants under the 1952 system received the first preference, or the greatest priority. But under the 1965 system, just 20 percent of immigrants would gain admission on the basis of job skills (the sixth preference) and educational attainment (the third preference), 10 percent in each category.

In addition, the new system exempted even more classes of family members from the preference quotas. These nonquota immigrants had formerly included the husbands, wives, and unmarried children under age twenty-one of U.S. citizens. Now, however, the parents of U.S. citizens would also gain entry as nonquota immigrants, when they had formerly received only 30 percent of visas. Also, ministers and certain others could formerly immigrate apart from the preference system. But under the 1965 scheme, ministers and other special groups would be subject to the Western Hemisphere's overall quota, although they remained free from the Eastern Hemisphere quota system.

Other family relations received broader opportunity for U.S. immigration under the new system. Spouses and unmarried children of permanent lawful resident aliens would now gain admission as second-, rather than third-, preference immigrants. The same proportion of the quota, 20 percent, was allocated to this category as under the 1952 system. The former fourth preference allowed up to 25 percent of unused visas of a country's quota to go to the brothers, sisters, and adult children of U.S. citizens. But the 1965 preference system gave these relatives higher priority and a larger quota. Unmarried adult sons and daughters of U.S. citizens received the first preference of visas,

up to 20 percent. Married adult sons and daughters of U.S. citizens received 10 percent of visas as the new fourth preference. The fifth preference, the largest category, which allocated 24 percent of visas plus any unused from the first four categories, went to the brothers and sisters of U.S. citizens.

Immigrants from the Western Hemisphere would gain admission on a first-come, first-served basis. That is, the preference system that applied to the Eastern Hemisphere did not apply in the Western Hemisphere. No per-country quotas would be in force for Western Hemisphere nations. But the hemisphere would be restricted to an annual quota of 120,000 visas; immigrants of Western Hemisphere national origin had not been subject to the overall cap on immigration under the 1952 McCarran-Walter Act. Of course, immediate relatives were exempt from the quota, as were those from the Eastern Hemisphere.

The 1965 law took special notice of refugees and displaced persons and provided for refugee admission under the new preference system. The seventh preference of the Hart-Cellar Act was set aside for refugees, who would receive up to 6 percent of a country's visas. The law defined "refugee" as it had been defined under a 1957 refugee law, plus one addition. Refugees were individuals fleeing persecution from communism or tensions in the Middle East, for example, as before, but now also those uprooted by natural catastrophe, as determined by the U.S. president. Refugees would gain admission for two years as "conditional entrants." After that time, refugees could change their status to that of permanent resident alien. The new law repealed the ability of certain groups to be admitted not subject to quotas.

OTHER CHANGES

Additional changes in the 1965 law raised the bar for protecting U.S. workers from job displacement by immigrants, a safeguard that labor unions had sought and secured. Foreigners wishing to immigrate in one of the employment categories would now have to obtain U.S. Labor Department certification in order to receive a visa. The Labor Department would confirm that not enough U.S. workers were available in the prospective immigrant's field and that the person's employment would not harm workers' wages and working conditions. Prior certification put the burden on the would-be immigrant, whereas formerly, foreign workers could be excluded if the secretary of labor ruled that admission of foreign labor in a particular occupation would cause undue competition for Americans. This change further oriented the new system away from employment-oriented immigration and toward family reunification.

Finally, the 1965 Hart-Celler Act abolished the Asia-Pacific triangle. The McCarran-Walter Act had created the triangle as a way of extending minimal per-country visa quotas to the nations of South and East Asia. The national origins quota system had charged visas against these nations' quotas for Western Hemisphere immigrants of Asian ancestry, instead of against the quota of their country of birth. This policy, of course, served to limit immigration from Asia-Pacific nations to even fewer immigrants than the small (a maximum of 100) number of visas allotted them.

To determine which hemispheric set of rules applied to an immigrant, the 1965 act applied a "birth rule." Those born in an independent Western Hemisphere nation would be subject to Western Hemisphere rules, even if they had moved to and naturalized in an Eastern Hemisphere country. Those persons born in the Eastern Hemisphere would be considered Eastern Hemisphere immigrants, even those who now lived in a country in the Western Hemisphere. Under the birth rule, the 20,000 per-country quota of the Eastern Hemisphere also applied to one's country of birth.

Interestingly, the 1965 law did not expressly increase the annual number of immigrants to be admitted into the United States. None of the proponents of the Hart-Celler bill advocated mass immigration or a greater volume of immigrant admissions. Indeed, supporters denied that their legislation would lead to mass immigration. Some, such as Senator Edward M. Kennedy (D-MA), openly derided the bill's opponents when some of them argued that the Hart-Celler Act would open the doors of America to mass immigration. Officials of the Johnson administration predicted that the number of immigrants in nonquota categories would range between 30,000 and 40,000 each year.

However, family members exempt from the per-country quotas almost immediately outpaced the estimates, reaching about ninety thousand on average each year—far greater than projections—after a decade. Nonquota immigrants passed 200,000 annually in the 1980s. Also, the source countries of the immigrant flow changed dramatically because of the 1965 immigration system—something else proponents of the bill denied would happen. In the 1950s, 53 percent of immigrants came from Europe, whereas just 6 percent came from the continent of Asia. By the 1990s, Europeans made up only 15 percent of immigrants, while Asians composed 29 percent of immigrants.

Thus, the shift of the 1965 act away from national origins and skills preference and toward Third World countries and family reunification preference led to a marked rise in immigration levels and in the makeup of the immigrant flow.

The 1965 immigration law fundamentally changed America's immigration system. Going far beyond removing racial and ethnic discrimination from the system, the law put the breaks on immigration from former source nations because the new system gave those first in line the opportunity to continue a long-term familial chain, while those with a desirable education and skills no longer enjoyed an ample opportunity to start a chain of their own. It led to a marked increase of immigration from Third World countries and in the number of immigrants, due to the expansion of nonquota entries through marital and blood ties. It discriminated against individuals with occupational abilities and educational attainment and favored those with some family connection in the United States but lacking skills or education. For all the good intentions of the Hart-Celler Act's authors, the law's unintended consequences went far astray from what the American public would have supported as a change in public policy, judging by public opinion polls of the time. And the 1965 law strayed from the equality and nondiscrimination its authors advocated in congressional debate.

James R. Edwards Jr.

See also: Restrictive Legislation (Part I, Sec. 4); Immigration Legislation of the 1980s and 1990s (Part I, Sec. 5); Legislation I: Immigration (Part II, Sec. 5); Immigration and Nationality Act (McCarran-Walter Act), 1952, Immigration and Nationality Act, 1965 (Part IV, Sec. 1).

BIBLIOGRAPHY

Beck, Roy. *The Case against Immigration: The Moral, Economic, Social, and Environmental Reasons for Reducing U.S. Immigration Back to Traditional Levels.* New York: W. W. Norton, 1996.

Congressional Quarterly. "Immigration Reform." In *Congress and the Nation, 1965–1968.* Vol. 2. Washington, DC: Congressional Quarterly Service, 1969.

Gimpel, James G., and James R. Edwards Jr. *The Congressional Politics of Immigration Reform.* Boston: Allyn and Bacon, 1999.

Heer, David. *Immigration in America's Future: Social Science Findings and the Policy Debate.* Boulder, CO: Westview Press, 1996.

Hutchinson, E. P. *Legislative History of American Immigration Policy, 1798–1965.* Philadelphia: University of Pennsylvania Press, 1981.

Reimers, David M. *Still the Golden Door: The Third World Comes to America.* 2d ed. New York: Columbia University Press, 1992.

SOUTHEAST ASIAN REFUGEE CRISIS

In the spring of 1975, the American-supported governments in Cambodia, Laos, and Vietnam collapsed. Thus began what became the largest refugee program ever undertaken by the United States. Between 2 and 3 million people left those countries, and about half of those—more than 1.25 million by 1990 and 1.4 million by 1998—were ultimately resettled in the United States. These people, with their children and grandchildren, now constitute a major new set of Asian-origin groups in America. Their experience has also had profound effects on the way refugee crises have been managed in more recent years.

The story of the Southeast Asian refugee crisis is a complicated one. Its historical origins lie with French colonialism and the creation of a five-part French Indochina: Cambodia, Laos, and a Vietnam split into three distinct administrative segments—north, center, and south. Although many in the U.S. government had considerable sympathy for the Vietnamese Communists during World War II, in the aftermath of that war, the United States became a supporter of French attempts to regain control of the country and, with the 1954 Geneva Accords, became the major actor supporting the creation and maintenance of a separate Republic of Vietnam in roughly the southern half of the country. American influence was initially far less in Laos and Cambodia, but increased with the war effort in Vietnam. In Cambodia, that involvement escalated with a 1970 coup that replaced the neutralist monarch Norodom Sihanouk with a new government more sympathetic to American interests. The Southeast Asian refugee crisis—in reality a series of crises—is the aftermath of the collapse of that American influence.

INITIAL EXODUS

The initial Southeast Asian refugee crisis came directly with the fall of American-supported govern-

ments in 1975 and the need to evacuate those people who were so closely allied with these governments that they would be at risk under the new regimes. Events permitted the evacuation of sizable numbers only for Vietnam. The fall of Phnom Penh in Cambodia in mid-April was abrupt, and only a few people managed to escape—either on their own or through the small American evacuation known as Operation Eagle Pull. In Laos, there was in May also a small-scale evacuation of about twenty-five hundred Hmong, a highland group that had been recruited into the CIA's so-called secret war in Laos. Over time, however, refugees did escape from those two countries westward into Thailand. Some, especially ethnic Lao, merged into the general Thai population. Most, however, ended up in refugee camps, whose total population approached seventy thousand by the end of 1975.

In Vietnam, however, there was enough time to permit a larger evacuation. In March 1975, communist forces scored a major victory in taking the provincial capital of Banmethuot in the central highlands. The South Vietnamese government initially made a decision to withdraw forces southward, then reversed itself, but by then North Vietnamese troops were streaming south in what quickly became a rout. Refugees flooded toward the south with North Vietnamese forces not far behind them. South Vietnamese forces put up serious resistance at Xuan Loc as communist forces neared Saigon, but it was rapidly apparent that the South Vietnamese government would fall. Evacuation of those particularly closely tied to the United States began with flights out of some of the cities north of Saigon as they were being overtaken and from Tan Son Nhut Airport in Saigon itself. This evacuation continued up until the moment that the last U.S. helicopters left from the roof of the U.S. embassy in Saigon on April 29.

In addition to those evacuated by the United States, there were also those who escaped by their

Crewmen aboard the USS *Durham* rescue Vietnamese refugees during the collapse of the American-supported Saigon regime in April 1975. *(National Archives)*

own means, either through commercial flights or because, as the government finally fell, they had access to boats. As this flotilla left, it moved out into the open sea, where refugees were picked up by U.S. craft. Both those evacuated and those picked up from the sea were generally sent first to transit camps in the Pacific (particularly Guam and Subic Bay in the Philippines) and from there were processed through camps set up in the continental United States: Eglin Air Force Base, Florida; Camp Pendleton, California; Fort Indiantown Gap, Pennsylvania; and Fort Chaffee, Arkansas. By the end of 1975, the processing of these 130,000 largely Vietnamese refugees was complete and the camps were closed.

During this initial refugee crisis, the U.S. government itself managed the evacuation and transport of Vietnamese refugees to the United States, including the logistics of the processing camps both overseas and in the United States. As with earlier refugee groups, the government relied on voluntary agencies (the so-called VOLAGS) to do the actual resettlement of the refugees into local American communities once

they were released from the camps. Since the Vietnamese (and the few Cambodians and Laotians in this early flow) lacked any significant preexisting ethnic communities in the United States, this system of sponsorship of refugees made practical sense. It also enabled refugees to be spread out very broadly across the country, thus avoiding the kind of dense concentration that had occurred for Cuban refugees in Miami.

Although there was some hostility toward the resettlement of the refugees, and public opinion polls showed a very mixed response, the process nevertheless had broad political support: The refugees were closely allied to the United States, had strong backing from people in the departments of Defense and State, were symbolically useful as people who had "voted with their feet" against the evils of communism, and also fit well into conventional notions of successful Asian immigrants, who worked and studied hard to succeed in America. Although there was much hardship in these refugees' lives, the general expectations were positive. Surveys during the late 1970s on their economic status, for example, suggested a population

These refugees were among the more than 100,000 who made their way to the United States after the end of the Vietnam War in 1975. *(Hias)*

that was indeed working hard and making significant economic strides.

BOAT PEOPLE

By 1978, America had successfully completed its largest-ever refugee resettlement program, and the data suggested relatively positive prospects for the refugees. However, in 1978 and 1979, a number of events gave rise to a second refugee crisis, which was different in many respects from the first and which also served to highlight the continuing plight of those who remained in temporary asylum in Southeast Asia. This second crisis had partially to do with factors pressuring people to flee. In Vietnam, border tensions with China—and finally a border war with China in early 1979—made Vietnamese authorities anxious to disfranchise the large Chinese communities that existed in both the northern and southern parts of the country. In Cambodia, the ravages of the Khmer

Rouge were pushing even those who had supported it toward exile, and the Vietnamese invasion of Cambodia in early 1979 then pushed even the Khmer Rouge into flight. In Laos, the intransigence of the new government pressured ethnic Lao to move into Thailand, and the hardships faced by the Hmong continued to push them west into Thailand.

Also important to this second crisis were events that made escape possible where it had not been before. Thus, in Vietnam, the government itself became involved in refugee escapes, most notoriously with what became known as the "big boat" trade. During the second half of 1978, rusty ocean freighters like the *Southern Cross* and *Hai Hong* (found going south from Vietnam) and the *Huey Fong* (going northeast from Vietnam to Hong Kong) were discovered packed with Vietnamese refugees. The magnitude of escape was manifestly clear, and reports from passengers indicated the collusion of Vietnamese authorities in it. In Cambodia, the Vietnamese invasion pushed the Khmer Rouge west toward the Cambodian border and in the process opened up a route through the

Like this family in Tulsa, Oklahoma, thousands of Vietnamese refugees were settled in all parts of the United States. The vast majority, however, now live in California. *(Hias)*

western part of the country into Thailand for those who wished to escape Cambodia altogether. Thus, in addition to what had been a small but steady stream of people fleeing their countries, there were new large flows of land refugees across the Thai border and boat refugees leaving from various parts of Vietnam.

Unlike in the situation during 1975, there was no immediate acceptance of these refugees for final resettlement by the United States. Instead, there was an effort to expand the temporary refuge that had existed in Southeast Asia since 1975. That expanded asylum system was intended to stabilize the situation and permit a more orderly consideration of what the refugees' futures would be—couched in terms of the standard UN options of repatriation, settlement in

place, and resettlement in so-called third countries such as the United States. Existing camps expanded and new camps were quickly developed. In Thailand, camps were largely for refugees fleeing by land—Laotian refugees toward the north and Cambodian refugees toward the south—although there were also some Vietnamese who crossed by land or by boats that hugged the coast toward Thailand rather than sailing directly across the South China Sea. Most of the Vietnamese escaping by boat headed across the open sea and landed in Malaysia, Indonesia, Hong Kong, and the Philippines. Although the population of land refugees had been significant even in 1975, it now increased sharply. Much more dramatic, however, was the increase in the number of "boat peo-

A plaque attached to this sculpture, the work of Vietnamese refugee artist Luu Nguyen Dhat, located at Camp Pendleton, a U.S. Marine Corps base in California, informs the reader that the giant hand was created to thank the "United States of America for accepting, housing, and relocating more than 40,000 Vietnamese and Cambodian refugees and immigrants . . . during the spring and summer of 1975." *(Hias)*

ple"—from approximately 62,000 at the end of 1978 to 292,000 by the middle of 1979.

Since the host countries in Southeast Asia were not interested in having the refugees settle permanently in their countries, and since few were willing at that time to consider repatriating the refugees, the problem was to find a way to resettle enough refugees to keep countries like Thailand, Malaysia, and Indonesia willing to maintain temporary camps. To that end, the UN convened a conference in Geneva in late June 1979, at which time the total camp population was estimated at three hundred and fifty thousand. The result was a set of commitments to resettle refugees from a wide variety of nations. A related 1979 effort by the UN

was a program that would permit the emigration of refugees by more normal immigration channels. This Orderly Departure Program (ODP), developed with the concurrence of the Vietnamese government, aimed to provide an alternative to the extraordinary dangers of sea escapes and the administrative problems posed by the temporary camps.

Through the 1980s this process of maintaining asylum but reducing camp size and regularizing the flow continued. In terms of resettlement, for example, the numbers quickly dwarfed the 130,000 that had seemed so large in 1975. Yet at the end of the decade, despite extensive resettlement, problems remained. The Vietnamese government suspended processing under the ODP in 1986, and there was another increase in boat escapes. The Vietnamese camp population in Southeast Asia had been gradually declining to 100,000 at the end of the 1980s. The need to empty the camps and to keep them from refilling brought about another Geneva agreement, the Comprehensive Plan of Action (CPA), which was approved in mid-1989 and in operation by the end of the year. The CPA included provisions for processing refugees to resettlement countries but also addressed the inevitable repatriation of those in the camps who did not qualify, under international laws and standards, as refugees.

The closing down of the Southeast Asian refugee program through the CPA was neither immediate nor easy. Initial efforts to increase resettlement went well, but things were more difficult when it came time to repatriate those who were not granted refugee status. Critics were vocal in their opposition to what they considered a violation of the central principle of non-repression embodied in the United Nations Convention and Protocol on the Status of Refugees: People are not to be forcibly returned to the country from which they have fled. Concern over repatriation led to attempts to track those returned to their home country, provide economic assistance to them, and enable them to apply to leave again but as legal emigrants through the Resettlement Opportunities for Returned Vietnamese (RORV) program. By the time of the formal ending of the CPA in June 1996, the resolution of the Vietnamese and Laotian refugee situations was largely complete, although a camp population lingered in Hong Kong through the end of the decade. Riots in 1999 among the few remaining refugees there again brought attention to the problems of forced repatriation.

In Cambodia, which was not part of the CPA, the Paris peace agreement of October 1991 among the contending Cambodian forces led rapidly to a massive voluntary repatriation effort aimed at returning refugees from the border in time for the 1993 elections scheduled as part of the peace agreement. Over three hundred and sixty thousand Cambodians returned with assistance from the United Nations High Commissioner for Refugees (UNHCR), permitting the closing of most of the refugee camps in Thailand. In Laos, which was incidentally mentioned in the CPA, repatriation was also generally voluntary, although the negotiations among Laos, Thailand, and the UNHCR were difficult and Hmong willingness to return was conditional on questions of security in Laos and internal conflicts within the Hmong community in the camps and in the United States. But by the end of 1993, most refugees had returned on their own or through UNHCR assistance.

U.S. RESETTLEMENT PROGRAM

Refugee resettlement programs in the United States operate on the premise that, since refugees usually lack the preparation for a new life that most other international migrants have, they are likely to need some transitional assistance before they can fully support themselves in their new country. Such assistance includes housing, medical attention, language training, employment orientation and training, and often general cultural orientation as well. It also often entails some cash and further medical assistance until refugees can get on their feet.

In the United States, the responsibility for assistance to refugees involves a combination of public and private organizations. The major precedents that were available to the United States at the time of the initial influx of Southeast Asian refugees in 1975 included a short-term program for Hungarian refugees in 1956, the far larger and longer-lasting program for Cuban refugees that began formally under the Kennedy administration, and what was growing to be a large resettlement program for Soviet Jews. These programs varied in their constituencies: The Cuban program, for example, involved a very strong influence of the Cuban community in Miami, and the Soviet program benefited from the impressive social-service expertise of Jewish community agencies. What characterized all of these programs was that they were focused on a particular population through a particular combination of public and private resources.

The initial Southeast Asian program (IRAP—the Indochinese Refugee Assistance Program) was, like these earlier refugee programs, designed specifically for this population. It had its own enabling legislation

that required at least annual revisions in admission and funding authorities. However, the growth of the number of refugees in the late 1970s and a long-delayed need to bring U.S. refugee law into conformity with the international conventions on refugees led to the passage of comprehensive refugee legislation: the Refugee Act of 1980. That act regularized procedures for determining how many refugees would be allowed in each year, formalized the role of the voluntary agencies in providing initial assistance (largely under the direction of the U.S. Department of State), and reorganized cash, medical, and other subsequent assistance to refugees under federal and state government (largely under the direction of the U.S. Department of Health and Human Services and its newly created Office of Refugee Resettlement).

The legislation continued and formalized a system in which refugee cash and medical assistance would be provided through the same kinds of mechanisms used to assist other Americans, although with more complete federal reimbursement of state and local costs. Thus refugee assistance was linked into precisely the welfare system upon which the incoming Reagan administration would launch a strong attack. Refugee assistance therefore became more visible and contentious. It also became subject to radically shifting funding levels. The period of availability of *special* cash and medical assistance for refugees, for example, was reduced over the course of a decade from thirty-six months (established by the Refugee Act of 1980) to eighteen months in 1982, twelve months in 1988, and eight months in 1991. During the same period, the federal government's reimbursement period for state costs for *regular* cash and medical assistance provided to refugees dropped from thirty-six months (established by the same act) to thirty-one months in 1986, twenty-four months in 1988, four months in early 1990, and zero months in late 1990. Early ideas about how best to help refugees make the transition to a new life—which often included well-documented arguments that retraining and education up front would have a net positive effect—thus went quickly by the board.

In other ways, the history of the program was more positive. Those concerned with it, for example, quickly realized the importance of refugee involvement in the resettlement process. Much support thus went to the development of ethnic organizations ("mutual assistance associations" in program terms) and to the inclusion of ethnic staff in both private and governmental program offices. With the wide variation among Southeast Asian refugees in terms of nationality, ethnicity, class, and education, this was not always a smooth process, but the net result was probably a more balanced program than would have otherwise existed. In addition, despite frequent comments about compassion fatigue, many Americans have remained committed to the program for moral or religious reasons. Even when refugees and those who assist them go in different directions, there usually remains at least some sense of having had the opportunity to serve and to broaden one's horizons.

EXPERIENCE OF THE REFUGEES

The experience of exodus is one of difficult decisions, often terrifying events, and usually sharp personal losses. The decision to leave can in itself be harrowing. For the early 1975 refugees, the press of events often required a rapid decision that often meant leaving relatives behind as well as making an irrevocable break with one's home country. One study from 1975, for example, indicated that over half of the refugees made the decision to leave in less than ten hours and one in four decided in less than an hour. Later on, in Vietnam in particular, escape was still possible but difficult, dangerous, costly, and unpredictable. Thus relatives might well be left behind because of cost or age, and last-minute changes in arrangements could separate a planned travel group.

The journey itself was often deadly. Refugees who tried overland passage had to cross mountains and rivers that were dangerous in their own right, were often dense with land mines, and sometimes treated as free-fire zones for police and military on both sides of the border. Those whose passage was by sea often died as unseaworthy ships sank or rations of food and water were depleted. There are no firm counts on how many people lost their lives in the journey, but there are enough accounts to indicate the proportion was significant. Even those who survived faced problems along the way. At sea, pirate attacks were frequent and ranged in severity from robbery to murder. Women were often victims of assaults and sometimes kidnapped—later either killed or sold into servitude. The memories for the survivors are ineradicable.

Those who survived the journey met with frequent hostility in neighboring countries. They were sometimes pushed back to sea or back across borders. At best, they were relegated to refugee camps where they frequently languished for long periods of time. The situation in the camps varied greatly. Some were relatively well run and insulated from the politics of the local country and the recruiting efforts of warring factions in the source country. As long as the hope of return remained alive, camps near the border had considerable appeal. Other camps, however, were subject to very limited international oversight, permitted limited freedom of movement, and were, in effect, recruiting grounds for ongoing wars. In most, security was far from adequate, with women and children at significant risk. Even with good security, life was difficult: The uncertainty about the future was severe, the opportunities for work and education limited. For those who were ultimately approved for resettlement in the United States or other countries, there was often additional time in camps waiting for transit and a lengthy period of time in yet another camp where they waited for the resolution of medical problems and were exposed to language and orientation programs.

Once refugees reached their final destination, life remained difficult. Even with some prior language training and cultural orientation, most refugees remained largely unprepared for their new lives. Although some spoke good English, many did not. Their education had often been limited and interrupted, and their job skills often lacked clear equivalents in the United States. By and large, they were not able to bring out much capital, and there was not an existing ethnic community structure—so the options of self-employment in small business were limited. For many, then, life in the United States meant living in relatively poor neighborhoods where they faced hostility from other minorities. Parents, intent on the education of their children, found a dangerous influence from the streets and an often disturbing influence even from the educational system. For many, long work hours for multiple members of the household helped provide an adequate household income, but at the cost of much time together and much oversight of children. Even basic religious practices could pose problems. Buddhists, for example, faced the difficulties of earning merit in a society where temples are few and far between, yet contributions to the temple are essential to earn that merit. Christians found few existing churches that reflected their own experience and thus faced the arduous task of creating new churches or parish programs.

Over the twenty-five years since Southeast Asian refugees began coming to the United States, no single pattern of adjustment has emerged. Many have done well economically; even more have had their children go on to successful lives in the United States. Others have been less able to adapt and remain more isolated from the general society. The attempts to impose "model minority" stereotypes on the refugees have found some basis in the social-science data, but so also have more negative stereotypes about refugees who have failed to adapt and whose children drop out of school, marry young, and sometimes drift into crime. Those refugees with limited formal education, fractured households, and sharply different cultural backgrounds have tended to fare the worst.

ENDURING LEGACY

For the United States, the Southeast Asian refugee crisis has been the largest, longest-lasting, and probably most influential attempt at a coordinated program of refugee asylum, assistance, and resettlement. From 1975 until the mid-1990s, refugees from Southeast Asia were the major portion of all refugees accepted into the United States; they continued as a smaller segment thereafter. By the turn of the century, the United States had received some 1.4 million Southeast Asian refugees. The majority came from camps of temporary asylum in Southeast Asia, but over five hundred thousand came through the ODP, including eighty thousand under the Amerasian program and one hundred and sixty-five thousand under a special program for former reeducation camp detainees. The data can be confusing, since the general notions of who is a "refugee," the exact U.S. legal status given to specific individuals, and the UN's reporting of "refugees" are often different. In particular, many counted as "refugees" by the UNHCR actually arrive in the United States as immigrants, since they came through the ODP from Vietnam.

Whatever count is used, the numbers resettled are large and represent both a general humanitarian commitment and a recognition of responsibility for the American involvement in the Vietnam War. That recognition is seen not only in the regular refugee program but in special legislation to acknowledge Amerasians, those who were in reeducation camps in Vietnam, and those (especially the Hmong) who fought most closely with Americans. In the process of meeting that obligation, the United States established a traditional partnership with voluntary agencies and received considerable individual support from Americans—including those new Americans. It also invoked its own unwieldy bureaucracy and penchant for political tinkering. Attempts to better structure and unify refugee assistance through the Refugee Act of 1980, for example, were undercut by special legislation for individual refugee groups—whether it was the gray status of "entrant" for the influx of Cubans and Haitians in late 1980 or the special designations of refugees from both Southeast Asia and the Soviet Union that have been passed. The program also developed during a period when ideas about public cash and medical assistance were shifting, when a much larger influx of other immigrants had fueled a nativist resurgence, and when the collapse of the Soviet Union had undermined the ideological value of refugees as effective voices about the problems of communist systems. The results were often detrimental for refugees and the refugee program. Refugees sometimes came to be viewed not as survivors in search of refuge, but as a welfare-dependent population causing a burdensome "impact" on local communities.

The United States was the major resettlement country and the major source of financial support for asylum and assistance to Southeast Asian refugees. Yet the effort was broadly international. Ships of many nationalities rescued refugees from the South China Sea, contributed to maintaining asylum in the countries of Southeast Asia, and accepted refugees for resettlement—often at higher rates compared to their total populations than did the United States itself. The experience with Southeast Asian refugees involved significant costs for all these countries and also came to be seen in the broader light of a more general anti-immigrant sentiment. As the international community has faced increased concern about the porousness of borders, refugees from countries with which they have been less involved, and the sheer potential volume of world refugee flows, there has been a decided tendency to keep refugee situations contained in their region of origin, whether by political or economic pressure, the creation of so-called safe zones, or even the type of military intervention that occurred in Kosovo. There has been less interest in the kind of resettlement-oriented program that occurred in response to the Southeast Asian refugee crisis.

For the refugees themselves, their children, and now often their grandchildren, the legacy is mixed. Many have done very well in the United States; many more have done reasonably well. Yet they are usually far from reconciled with the countries that they left. With the reestablishment of U.S. diplomatic relations with Vietnam, a generally more stable and secure Cambodia, and a Laos more linked into the international arena, they now have additional opportunities to reconnect with their home countries. Those home countries generally desire the refugees' involvement and benefit greatly from the money they send back. Yet the refugees remain opposed to these governments. Even in 1999, a California Vietnamese shop owner's display of a picture of Ho Chi Minh and what to refugees in the United States is the North Vietnamese flag caused large demonstrations by the Vietnamese refugee community. The political events that propelled their exodus are not easily forgotten. They, like the Cubans who more recently rallied around Elián González, continue to oppose communist governments, while their host society—satisfied with the collapse of its major communist rival—often acts as if these ideological concerns no longer matter.

David Haines

See also: Wars and Civil Unrest (Part II, Sec. 1); Southeast Asia (Part III, Sec. 3); Refugee Act of 1980, Amerasian Children Act, 1997 (Part IV, Sec. 1).

BIBLIOGRAPHY

Ebihara, May M., Carol A. Mortland, and Judy L. Ledgerwood, eds. *Cambodian Culture Since 1975: Homeland and Exile.* Ithaca, NY: Cornell University Press, 1994.

Fadiman, Ann. *The Spirit Catches You and You Fall Down.* New York: Noonday Press, 1997.

Freeman, James A. *Hearts of Sorrow: Vietnamese-American Lives.* Stanford: Stanford University Press, 1989.

Grant, Bruce. *The Boat People: An "Age" Investigation.* New York: Penguin, 1979.

Haines, David W., ed. *Refugees as Immigrants: Cambodians, Laotians, and Vietnamese in America.* Totowa, NJ: Rowman & Littlefield, 1989.

———, ed. *Refugees in America in the 1990s: A Reference Handbook.* Westport, CT: Greenwood Press, 1996.

Kelly, Gail Paradise. *From Vietnam to America: A Chronicle of the Vietnamese Immigration to the United States.* Boulder, CO: Westview, 1977.

Knudsen, John. "When Trust Is on Trial: Negotiating Refugee Narratives." In *Mistrusting Refugees,* ed. E. Valentine Daniel and John Knudsen, pp. 13–35. Berkeley: University of California Press, 1995.

Liu, William T., Maryanne Lamanna, and Alice Murata. *Transition to Nowhere: Vietnamese Refugees in America.* Nashville, TN: Charter House, 1979.

Loescher, Gil. *Beyond Charity: International Cooperation and the Global Refugee Crisis.* New York: Oxford University Press, 1993.

Long, Lynellyn D. *Ban Vinai: The Refugee Camp.* New York: Columbia University Press, 1993.

Robinson, W. Courtland. *Terms of Refuge: The Indochinese Exodus and the International Response.* New York: Zed Books, 1998.

Rumbaut, Rubén. "The Structure of Refuge: Southeast Asian Refugees in the United States, 1975–1985." *International Journal of Comparative Public Policy* 1 (1989): 97–129.

Smith-Hefner, Nancy J. *Khmer American: Identity and Moral Education in a Diasporic Community.* Berkeley: University of California Press, 1999.

Tollefson, James W. *Alien Winds: The Reeducation of America's Indochinese Refugees.* New York: Praeger Publishers, 1989.

Zucker, Norman L., and Naomi Flink Zucker. *Desperate Crossings: Seeking Refuge in America.* Armonk, NY: M. E. Sharpe, 1996.

$\mathcal{I}$NCREASE IN IMMIGRANTS FROM THE DEVELOPING WORLD

$\mathcal{I}$n 1965, the lawmakers who abolished the national-origins quota system and devised a new immigration policy did not foresee that their reform would trigger a fresh influx of immigrants that was to take historic proportions and become the most heterogeneous ever. Rather, their chief purpose was to put an end to the discriminatory regime of the national-origins quotas, which gave great advantage to northern and western Europeans at the expense of immigrants from other countries. But the decision to reopen the doors of the United States, the nation that John F. Kennedy had called a "nation of immigrants," coincided with a drive for emigration in various regions of Asia and Latin America. It was that convergence that gave rise to a new wave of immigration, remarkable both for its numbers and composition, which scholars have identified as the "fourth wave" in U.S. history.

OVERVIEW

As early as 1965, but more markedly after the Immigration Act went into effect in 1968, the volume of immigration rose sharply and steadily. In the 1960s, the Immigration and Naturalization Service (INS) recorded that 3.3 million immigrants entered the United States; in the following decade the total increased to nearly 4.5 million, and soared to 7.3 million in the 1980s. Since 1970 the number of immigrants living in the United States has almost tripled: From 9.6 million, it jumped to 14.1 million in 1980, 19.8 million in 1990, and 26.3 million in 1998. Through the 1990s, the INS registered an impressive average of eight hundred thousand to nine hundred thousand legal entries annually.

The ethnic distribution of immigration also shifted. Whereas Europe had long dominated the yearly admissions, third-world countries rapidly be-

came the major sources: Between 1965 and 1970, the volume of immigrants from Asia increased by 369 percent, while the number of Europeans dropped 58 percent. Asia represented only 7.7 percent of all visas issued from 1955 to 1964, but by the early 1980s, nearly half (43.3 percent) of all immigrants came from Asian points of origin, the leading ones being China, the Philippines, India, and Vietnam. Entries from these countries soared spectacularly: The Korean total skyrocketed from 34,500 in the 1960s to 337,000 in the 1980s; the Indian total increased from 27,000 to almost 251,000. Chinese immigrants came from the Republic of China but also Hong Kong and Taiwan—nearly 110,000 in the 1960s, and an impressive 444,000 in the 1980s. Simultaneously, immigration from the Middle East, especially Iran, also began to grow.

By 1980, Europeans amounted to less than 15 percent of the newcomers. Meanwhile, the North American share (including the Caribbean and Central American countries, Mexico, and Canada), which, at nearly 36 percent from 1955 to 1964, had been well above the Asian total, remained at similar levels. In fact, in the last three decades, the absolute number of immigrants from the Americas has increased steadily, but in the years following the reform, that relative growth was dwarfed by the spectacular Asian surge.

During the 1970s, Mexicans represented an increasingly important proportion of total legal immigration. The trend climaxed in 1974, when they amounted to 18 percent of the total. When the preference and quota systems were applied to the Western Hemisphere after 1976, Mexico and its neighbors had to submit to the 20,000 per country annual limit as did the Eastern Hemisphere nations. This reduced the annual inflow from Mexico by almost half in the following two years, although many Mexicans could enter the United States outside the ceilings, as immediate relatives of U.S. citizens. After 1978, the absolute number of legal Mexican immigrants again reached

Table 1
Immigrants Admitted by Region and Selected Country of Birth: Fiscal Years 1951–90

	1951–60	1961–70	1971–80	1981–90
Europe	1,325,727	1,123,492	800,368	761,550
China	9,657	34,734	124,360	346,747
Hong Kong	15,541	75,007	113,467	98,215
India	1,973	27,189	164,134	250,786
Japan	46,250	39,988	49,775	47,085
Korea	6,231	34,536	267,638	337,000
Philippines	19,307	98,376	354,987	548,764
Vietnam	335	4,340	172,820	280,782
Mexico	299,811	453,937	640,294	1,655,843
Cuba	78,948	208,536	264,863	144,578
Domican Republic	9,897	93,292	148,135	252,035
Haiti	4,442	34,499	56,335	138,379
Jamaica	8,869	74,906	137,577	208,148
El Salvador	5,895	11,992	34,436	213,539
Other Central Am.	38,856	86,338	100,204	254,549
South America	91,628	257,940	295,741	461,847
Total	2,515,479	3,321,677	4,493,414	7,338,062

Source: 1997 Statistical Yearbook of the INS (October 1999), table 2, pp. 25–26.

record highs thanks to this nonquota channel of entry and new visa regulations.

The period 1985–94 stands out as a decade of exceptional Hispanic immigration: Mexican immigration alone then made up nearly 30 percent of the total, compared to 14.8 percent in the previous decade, while the Asian share receded to 32.2 percent. This shift is due to the 1986 Immigration Reform and Control Act, which set up an amnesty program that enabled more than 3 million undocumented aliens to legalize their status over the following years. In the 1980s, over 1.6 million Mexican citizens emigrated legally to the United States (compared to 640,000 the preceding decade); in the three years between 1991 and 1993, nearly 1.3 million became permanent residents.

In addition, immigration from other Central American countries, which had started in the 1970s, picked up as political oppression and government violence worsened. Tens of thousands of Salvadorans, Guatemalans, and Nicaraguans sought refuge in the United States. Whereas only 34,500 Salvadorans had been admitted in the 1970s, over 213,000 entered in the following decade. During the same period, the total for other Central American nations more than doubled, reaching 255,000 in the 1980s. Simultaneously, immigration from the Caribbean countries, mostly the Dominican Republic and Cuba, and to a

lesser extent Jamaica, increased significantly. The total of entries for citizens of the Dominican Republic went up from approximately 148,000 in the 1970s to 254,000 in the 1980s; that of Jamaican legal entrants nearly doubled, reaching more than 208,000 in the 1971–80 period.

Since 1995, the overall distribution of immigration has returned to its previous pattern: The North American (Mexico and Canada), Caribbean, Central American, and Asian shares were respectively 18.1, 13.1, 4.9, and 34.6 percent in 1995–97. All in all the single country that has provided the largest contingents of newcomers was and remains Mexico. Together with the Caribbean Basin countries, Mexico supplies an inordinately large percentage of immigrants: nearly one-third in the last decades. In the 1990s, the other top countries of immigration—but far behind Mexico—remained the Philippines, China, Vietnam, and India. Together, these five countries were the birthplace of nearly 40 percent of all legal immigrants in 1997. The Philippines and mainland China reached a record high in 1993, with respectively over sixty-three thousand and sixty-six thousand legal admissions, before decreasing slightly. Yet, it is safe to assume that virtually all nationalities are represented among post-1965 immigrants to the United States: The "fourth wave" stands out for its remarkable national diversity.

Table 2
Immigrants Admitted by Region and Period: Fiscal Years 1955–97 (in percent)

	1955–64	1965–74	1975–84	1985–94	1995–97
Europe	50.2	29.8	13.4	11.0	16.2
Asia	7.7	22.4	43.3	32.2	34.6
Africa	0.7	1.5	2.4	2.6	5.9
Oceania	0.4	0.7	0.8	0.5	0.6
North America	35.9	39.6	33.6	48.0	36.1
Caribbean	7.0	18.0	15.1	11.0	13.1
Central America	2.4	2.5	3.7	6.6	4.9
Other North Am.	26.4	19.0	14.8	30.5	18.1
South America	5.1	6.0	6.6	5.7	6.6

Source: 1997 Statistical Yearbook of the INS (October 1999), table B, p. 20.

CAUSES OF THIRD-WORLD IMMIGRATION TO THE UNITED STATES

Considering how unexpected the consequences of the 1965 reform were, politicians and scholars alike have pondered the reasons for the remarkable flow of immigrants from third-world, or developing, countries. The liberalization of immigration policy on the United States's part cannot in itself offer a satisfactory explanation, since it does not account for the fact that only some national groups have responded positively. But the most common answer to the questions on the origins of immigration is of course the poverty and unemployment plaguing developing countries. This simplistic interpretation ignores both the fact that many of the post-1965 immigrants to the United States were highly educated and highly skilled, as well as the large body of research demonstrating that the very poor and underprivileged rarely migrate. Neither does it explain why equally poor countries have different emigration patterns. For the same reason, the attraction of the American Dream is not a sufficient justification.

In fact, international population moves are the result of an interplay of structural and individual factors in combination with national governments' emigration and immigration policies. The countries that have sent the largest contingents to the United States from 1965 onward share certain characteristics, all of which have exerted a role in this complex interplay of forces. First, most of them have been plagued by some form of political instability, if not civil strife and war. Above all, most have experienced dramatic economic transformation since the 1950s: They are char-

acterized by rapid industrialization and gross national products that have placed them at intermediate levels of development. In fact, they are in what scholars call the situation of "peripheral" nations—that is to say, in weaker positions relative to the powerful developed countries ("core" nations) and especially to the United States, whose sphere of influence extends over them. In this perspective, most emigrants from the peripheral areas do not flee dire poverty but rather the upheavals and contradictions inherent in their economic development as they open up to the penetration of international capital.

Most of the sending nations have undergone agrarian reforms that have deeply affected their rural population, cutting their traditional ties to the land without providing meaningful alternatives for local employment. The resulting uprooting, severe unemployment and underemployment, as well as the end of the isolation of the peasantry and its often brutal contact with modern society, are factors that are strongly conducive to emigration. In addition, the policies of economic development pursued by these countries' governments have frequently led to imbalances, as heavy industries were favored at the expense of other important sectors such as agriculture and small businesses. In any case, aggregate economic growth is often accompanied by regional and social inequalities.

A corollary has been rapid and massive urbanization owing to the influx from rural areas. Neither economic development itself nor the governments' urban planning, housing, or sanitary policies have been able to keep pace with this exodus from the countryside, which has resulted in severe urban problems: unemployment, overcrowding, and air pollution. Such problems are all the more serious as the national

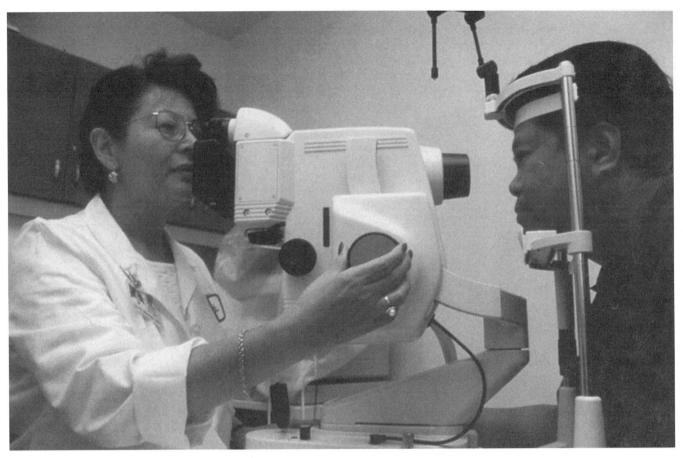

The diversity of immigration from the developing world is captured in this photo of a Mexican-American medical technician giving an eye test to a Filipino immigrant. *(David Bacon/Impact Visuals)*

populations in general keep growing dramatically, despite more or less drastic family planning and population-control measures. Even South Korea, which was rather successful in slowing down the annual rate of population increase after the implementation of family planning in 1962, saw its population continue to grow significantly in absolute numbers, from 25 million in 1960 to 38 million in 1980.

These countries are also dependent on foreign trade, investment, and aid. The strategy for economic development that they have chosen requires amounts of capital and technology that they cannot supply themselves. Their export-oriented economies are highly sensitive to international trends and are subordinated to foreign loans and markets. This is true of the United States's longstanding trading partners, such as Mexico and Caribbean countries, but also of more recent partners. Thus, in Hong Kong, Taiwan, and India, the United States's political and economic influence progressively grew to the point of taking Britain's place. In the 1950s, India and Pakistan became the largest recipients of American economic and

technical assistance. Of course, external dependence on the United States, combined with internal strife, not only affects the peripheral countries' labor markets but also deeply influences their cultures.

Indeed, one of the most important factors of out-migration may be the cultural impact of the economic and social upheavals experienced by peripheral nations under the United States's influence. The dilemma that Alejandro Portes and Robert L. Bach, two prominent specialists of immigration issues, noted in the Mexicans' case can be applied to all the major sending countries: "the profound clash between the absorption of an increasingly modern culture, with its strong attachment to the cult of advanced consumption, and material conditions that deny most Mexicans the means of participating even minimally in it." Indeed, United States's goods and mass media advertising have penetrated all of the Asian and Latin American countries in its sphere of influence, not to mention the rest of the globe. Ironically, economic development has raised the expectations of third-world countries' residents, while thwarting their desire to

The ending of national quotas in 1965 is partially responsible for the massive influx of immigrants from the developing world, including this child from Ethiopia. *(Hias)*

consume, owing to underemployment and vastly unequal incomes. The comforts and attraction of modern consumerism have become both more desirable and unreachable for large segments of these populations.

But in most cases the United States's broad influence is due to older economic, political, and cultural contacts. Revealingly, the countries that send the largest numbers of immigrants have long histories of contacts with the United States. As for the Caribbean and Central American countries (especially Cuba, Mexico, and the U.S. Commonwealth of Puerto Rico), they were the targets of some form of American expansionism, and this remolded their internal economic and social structures to such a point that their inhabitants were already attuned to the American way. Similarly, the Philippines was a colony of the United States from 1898 to 1946. In Korea and Vietnam also, the American influence has historical roots: It was exerted first through Presbyterian missionaries and then by the U.S. Army's establishments since World War

II. Consequently American mass culture diffused early and in a lasting way through direct contact between American troops and natives. In a different way, China, Taiwan, and Hong Kong also experienced political and military interventions on the part of the United States, which led to the exodus of intellectuals, students, government officials, and business leaders for political reasons after the communist takeover. Thus, the complex interaction between core and peripheral countries and the growing dependence of the latter on the former, based on historical links, help explain why specific countries in the third world responded to the 1965 immigration reform.

UNEQUAL IMMIGRATION POTENTIALS

In 1965, the Hart-Celler Act opened new opportunities for immigration to people around the world, but these opportunities varied according to the potential for immigration held by the various countries.

The act created a new admissions system—at first applied to the Eastern Hemisphere only and extended to the whole world in 1976—consisting of seven preference categories: Four of them were reserved to family members, and two were offered to immigrants with useful skills or in desirable occupations, while the remaining one was that of refugees. Since the use of family reunification provisions depends on the presence of relatives who are permanent residents or citizens of the United States, the nations' responses to the 1965 reform differed according to at least two major criteria. The first was the existence of a long history of immigration flows to the United States and of a sizable population there—which was the case for the Mexicans, as well as for the Chinese and Japanese. The second involved the experience of past discriminatory immigration policies such as the ban on naturalization imposed on Asians until 1952 and, of course, the national-origins quota system. For this reason, there were in 1965 two types of Asian Americans: on the one hand, longtime residents, mostly of Japanese, Chinese, and Filipino origins, who had entered the United States before the implementation of racial restrictions and constituted aging, isolated communities; on the other hand, more recent entrants, usually wives of American citizens (generally soldiers stationed in Korea and the Philippines). In both cases, the ethnic communities in the United States provided the bases for family reunification after the adoption of the new admissions system in 1965. However, the Japanese stood somewhat apart: Their country en-

Politics has played a role in the large number of immigrants coming to the United States from Latin America. Refugee Benito Yanez comes ashore in Key West, Florida, after escaping from Cuba in April 1980. *(Hias)*

joyed political stability and economic development, which reduced incentives to emigrate.

By contrast, Latin American immigration had not been submitted to the national quotas system before 1965, and movements to and from Latin American countries had been free. In the case of Mexico, there was a longstanding tradition of cyclical migrations to the United States, which facilitated implantation there and created a potential for family reunification.

Other nationalities, however, had few members settled in the United States at the time of the reform and therefore had an insignificant potential for family reunification: Such was the case of Indians, but also of many other Asian populations that were nevertheless to send a sizable number in the next decades. Indeed, the most spectacular consequence of the new legislation was the massive arrival of foreigners

having no family links in the United States. These came mostly from Asian countries: Now enjoying larger pools of resident visas, Asians applied in large numbers in the professional and other occupational categories (third and sixth preferences), their total for these categories increased twelvefold between 1965 and 1970.

THE ASIAN "BRAIN DRAIN"

Such increase is due to the coincidence of strong demand on the Americans' part and of significant supply on the other side of the Pacific in sectors such as medicine, civil engineering, and scientific research. In the 1965–75 period, for example, 75,000 foreign physicians came to work in the United States on permanent or temporary visas; by then, the foreign-born made up one-third of the total for this occupation. Equally impressive is the number of nurses, especially from the Philippines and Korea, who were admitted during the same period. All in all, the largest influx came from the Philippines, China, Korea, and India.

This phenomenon, which is frequently referred to as a "brain drain," can first and foremost be accounted for by the political, social, and economic conditions of the sending countries after 1965. At the time the new law was adopted in the United States, these developing countries shared a determination to improve the educational level of their populations and produce the skilled workers, the professionals, and generally the elite needed to lead and carry out the economic transformations they were planning and encouraging. Expansion of higher education was a priority in many Asian countries. New schools and universities turned out growing numbers of physicians, nurses, engineers, and technicians. But no matter how rapid and successful the economic development was, the national labor market could not absorb them entirely.

As a result, the young graduates experienced unemployment or underemployment. Even if there were jobs available for them, most of these jobs could not satisfy their ambitions, sharpened by years of hard study and large expenses necessary to obtain their diplomas. Such frustration encouraged them to look for better working conditions and wages abroad. For the many who had followed part or all of their university studies in the United States, their home country could not stand the comparison with the American superpower. In addition, young and ambitious workers complained about the red tape curbing freedom of enterprise at home and rampant nepotism, both in civil service and business, which made promotion difficult and unfair.

This made the attraction of the American Dream all the more powerful. At the same time, a combination of factors caused the United States's demand for specialized occupations, in the medical and engineering sectors especially, to grow significantly in the 1960s and early 1970s. Thus, demand for medical personnel soared as a result of shifting patterns of medical service delivery: The general practitioner gave way to big hospitals that centralized medical services and hired more and more specialists. Meanwhile, health care services were increasingly utilized because of the creation of Medicare and Medicaid in the public sector and a large expansion in health insurance plans in the private sector. As American medical schools

failed to respond positively, the import of foreign medical graduates was needed.

The demand for trained specialists combined with the United States's historical influence in several Asian countries. In the Philippines and South Korea, the education systems were modeled after those in the United States. No wonder, then, that so many Filipino and Korean physicians and nurses left for America: The diploma and training as well as hospital equipment and work methods were quite compatible on both sides of the Pacific. Moreover, the English language has remained a language of preference in the Philippines, while in Korea it is widely used in business and the civil service and is considered an essential instrument for upward mobility.

As for India, many workers there experienced similar, if not higher, frustrations and resentment. When the American government adopted the 1965 immigration reform, India had the highest rate of enrollment in higher education of any developing nation, but many of its graduates could not be absorbed by the economy, which was unable to keep pace with the demand for better wages and jobs. Many Indian nationals had pursued training in British and American institutions and were tempted to expatriate themselves when they realized that their skills could not be put to good use in their own country. Thus, Indian immigrants were the group that proportionately made the greatest use of the occupational visa categories—(45 percent in 1969), with significant numbers of physicians and engineers—particularly because in 1965 they were not in a position to use the family reunification provisions, since their population in the United States was simply too small. The immigrant group with the second-highest rate of occupational entrants was the Filipinos (42.3 percent).

Not surprisingly, these Asian populations were—and still are—extremely attentive to legislative and economic developments in the United States. The 1965 reform made headline news, and the local media kept reporting on the evolution of American immigration legislation. Universities took the American context into account. In the 1970s, for instance, Filipino medical schools adapted their curricula and tailored their training according to U.S. labor needs and regulations, thus becoming "export businesses." Similarly, the demand for specialized workers on the Americans' part was such that special schools were established in Korea for the sole purpose of teaching the skills that would qualify would-be emigrants to the United States. To respond to the situation created by American demand and Filipino and Korean supply, recruiting agencies were set up on both sides of the

Pacific to act as intermediaries and offer assistance to emigrants.

In the second half of the 1970s, however, the flow of skilled workers and professionals began to slow down. This decline is generally attributed to the recession that struck the U.S. economy and lasted through the next decade, as well as to changes in immigration law. In 1976, the number of foreign-trained physicians and surgeons entering the United States was limited as a result of the intense lobbying by the American Medical Association, which feared the competition. In addition, the entry tests and requirements were made stricter. After that date, the number of entries of highly educated and skilled immigrants diminished in absolute and, above all, relative terms, with family reunification becoming the predominant channel of entrance to the United States.

It was only after 1992, under the new provisions of the Immigration Act of 1990, that the number of visas allotted to "independent" (nonfamily) immigrants tripled the previous level. At the same time, the return of economic prosperity and the advent of the "new economy" have increased the demand for skilled workers in high technology sectors, which the native labor force cannot satisfy, and have opened new opportunities that foreign graduates have been eager to take. The Asian establishments of higher education still turn out large numbers of such graduates. Thus, a high percentage of American high-tech firms set up between 1995 and 1998 were created by natives from India, where the Indian Institute of Technology constitutes a sort of reserve of American entrepreneurs. Still, family reunification was and remains the priority of the American immigration policy, and over the past decades the large majority of newcomers have entered with family reunification visas.

THE IMPORTANCE OF FAMILY REUNIFICATION

According to the provisions of the 1965 act, nearly three-fourths of the annual total of permanent resident visas were reserved to family reunification. Aliens rushed to take advantage of the new family admission system, which not only offered many more visas than any other means of entry but also had less stringent visa requirements. Because most early beneficiaries of the 1965 reform had left relatives behind, the family preferences created an unprecedented potential for reunification and therefore had the effect of multiplying admissions from the Asian and Latin

American countries that had already become the chief purveyors of newcomers to the United States. In fact, Congress had elaborated an admission system that tended to heighten the numerical dominance of immigration from certain third-world nations and to prevent the opening of the system to other, "new" countries.

Furthermore, the family categories defined by post-1965 legislation were particularly well adapted to Asian and Latin American family ties, which further encouraged immigration. In practice, family reunification has represented an increasingly important proportion of total entries—even after 1990 and the adoption of amendments that expanded the number of independent immigrant visas. For each of the leading sending countries, the share of family-based admissions has tended to grow over time—evidence of the development of chain migration through networks of communication and assistance.

The first Asians who used the new family system were the Chinese and the Japanese, and to a lesser extent the Filipinos and the Koreans. After 1965, the developing Chinese-American family networks jumped on the new opportunities that were being offered to them. In 1969, almost 64 percent of the Chinese newcomers entered in a family category, compared to only 21 percent in an occupational category. By 1985, the respective figures were 81 and 16 percent.

The Koreans' pattern is relatively similar, with the family visas progressively monopolizing the country's annual quota (nearly 90 percent in 1985). Yet, the Korean case presents a specific pattern of family immigration due to the high number of adopted children and of women marrying American citizens (mostly servicemen) both before and after 1965. Between 1966 and 1972, Korean wives of U.S. citizens made up as much as 30 percent of the total Korean immigration, whereas the Filipino equivalent was 17 percent and that of the Chinese only 7 percent. Another difference is that the Korean women were married to native-born American citizens rather than naturalized ones, like other Asian groups.

In the same manner as for the Chinese Americans, the Filipinos' existing community in the United States facilitated further immigration for relatives after 1965. Yet, because the number of Filipino Americans was much smaller, nearly as many newcomers entered thanks to their skills in the first few years. In the late 1970s and 1980s, family reunification became dominant as well. By contrast, as stated above, Indians at first overwhelmingly used the professional categories; but they later developed a similar preference for family immigration.

In this respect, Latin American and Asian patterns differ markedly: Very few Hispanic immigrants after 1965 were professionals, and when the preference system was extended to the Western Hemisphere after 1976, nearly all visa applicants used the family categories. In the 1980s, this was the case of approximately 90 percent of Mexican legal immigrants.

THE DIFFERENT USES OF FAMILY-BASED VISAS

In case the recipient of a permanent resident visa did not come to the United States with his or her spouse and children as "dependents" (included in the same preferential visa category as his or her own), he or she can petition for them later, either through the preference system subject to numerical limitations or, if he or she obtains American citizenship, outside the annual ceilings of 20,000 per country. The latter solution was one of the most popular among the foreign-born after 1965: Because there are no numerical limits to the admission of such immediate relatives (spouses, children, and parents of U.S. citizens), the yearly total of arrivals for most sending countries greatly exceeded the 20,000 allotment. The Mexican inflow especially, as suggested above, has disproportionately high numbers of immigrants in this category. Chain migrations were established, as beneficiaries of the immediate-relative status in turn sponsored their own relatives. Over time, the annual total for this category has increased considerably: From 160,000 in 1980, it reached 220,000 in 1986, and after a few years of apparent stabilization, increased to 255,000 in 1993.

After 1965, permanent residents could also sponsor spouses and children without being naturalized, thanks to the second preference. Since it allowed a speedy reunification of families, such a procedure was very popular among newcomers, particularly Filipinos, Mexicans, and Dominicans, so much so that waiting lists developed dramatically. In 1990, by waiving the per-country limit for three-fourths of the second preference visas, Congress only temporarily managed to reduce waiting periods.

The U.S. legislation specifies that the right to benefit from family reunification is not limited to members of the nuclear household (a husband and wife and their children) but extends to parents, adult children, and brothers and sisters. Fathers and mothers have made up an important share of nonquota immigration for some Asian groups: 40 percent of nonquota Filipinos in the late 1970s and, ten years later, over 50 percent of the Chinese and Indian yearly admissions outside the quotas. As a consequence, the number of older immigrants has increased significantly—although most newcomers are still young adults in their late twenties—another feature reflecting the family orientation of post-1965 immigration.

As for brothers and sisters, they could enter through the fifth preferential category under the 1965 Immigration Act and through the fourth one since 1990. This category became the most widely used in the 1980s for all sending countries—for China and South Korea at first, and later for the Philippines and India—at times totaling over 50 percent of annual entries from these countries. Mexicans, too, make a great use of the brother and sister category, but its share has never been as important as for Asians owing to the primacy of the second preference: Since it is the only one available to noncitizens, the latter category has always been utilized by Mexican immigrants, a fact that reflects this group's low propensity to naturalize (at least until the 1990s).

In any case, the overall popularity of this channel of entry among post-1965 immigrants is in part due to cultural factors: In their countries of origin, links within the extended family, particularly between brothers and sisters, are strong and lasting. For some nations, the number of applications rose so rapidly that serious backlogs developed so that the average waiting period for a fifth-preference applicant rose to nine years in 1990 and even reached fourteen years in the Philippines. Legal restrictions brought about by the 1990 Immigration Act have further lengthened waiting lists. In short, family ties informed migration networks which, thanks to a favorable admission system, triggered chain migrations that further enhanced the pattern of third-world immigration that had emerged after 1965.

ILLEGAL IMMIGRATION

Another unforeseen effect of the 1965 reform was to boost illegal immigration. Indeed, the extension of numerical ceilings to Western Hemisphere countries and of the preference system after 1976 left would-be immigrants who did not meet the legal criteria with a single solution: illegal entry. There are basically two ways of sneaking into the United States: crossing a national border undetected or entering with a temporary visa and overstaying it. Until the 1980s, probably 90 percent of illegal entrants were Mexicans who crept across the southern border (although critics claimed that this figure reflected the emphasis placed on repression at the United States–Mexico border). To a large extent, this was the continuation of the migratory traditions inaugurated a century before and strengthened by the bracero program, which had allowed American employers to import farm workers from Mexico on a temporary basis. When the program ended in 1964, many former braceros kept coming to the United States—this time without papers. Although it is difficult to accurately calculate the number of undocumented Mexicans in the country, studies conclude that that number kept rising in the 1970s and 1980s as incentives to leave their home country and the attraction of the United States persisted. Social networks of communication and solidarity also contributed to the increase, since illegals followed in the footsteps of numerous predecessors, sometimes with the assistance of smugglers.

The 1986 Immigration Reform and Control Act, which was the result of lawmakers' awareness of the phenomenon, established sanctions against employers who hired undocumented workers and allowed for the one-time amnesty of some 3.1 million illegal aliens. But it did little to quash the influx of illegal immigrants: A 1996 INS study found that there were about 5 million of them in the United States and the number was increasing by about two hundred and seventy-five thousand each year.

Today Mexico is still by far the largest supplier of undocumented immigrants: The same INS study estimated their total at 2.7 million—that is to say, 54 percent of the total illegal alien population. Of course, there may be seasonal fluctuations, as many Mexicans come to perform seasonal work and then go home. Yet, studies show that large numbers of recent arrivals also find jobs in industries and urban services. There are many low-skill jobs for these immigrants in such sectors as plant nurseries, construction firms, foundries and shipyards, hotels and motels, and restaurants.

The national origin of the illegal population has diversified too. Numerous Dominicans and other Caribbean nationals, as well as South Americans, slip in or overstay their visas. These are mostly from El Salvador, Guatemala, Haiti, Honduras, and the Bahamas but also Canada. In fact, over 80 percent of illegals are from countries in the Western Hemisphere. The only Asian country in the top fifteen sending countries is the Philippines. But because of geographical distance, Asians are more likely to be visa overstayers than to have entered without INS inspection.

THE NEW REFUGEES

In the 1960s, the ethnic composition of the refugee flows changed too. Until then, Europe had been the chief source of refugees to the United States, but by 1960, the European political and economic scene had become more stable and the refugee issue receded in importance. Even after the first wave of Cuban expatriates between 1959 and 1962, Americans did not foresee that the destabilization and collapse of third-world regimes supported by the U.S. government would send hundreds of thousands of people fleeing. These newcomers would add their own ethnic colors to the rich tapestry of the growing immigrant populations under the 1965 Immigration Act. However, that act did not provide adequate provisions to deal with large refugee flows—which, at the time, had not seemed to be a priority.

So when Cuban leader Fidel Castro announced that his people would be allowed to leave the island freely in 1965, President Lyndon Johnson had to utilize the parole power to allow the next wave of Cuban refugees to enter the United States as exceptions, outside the ceilings. From 1965 to 1972, around three hundred thousand Cubans were thus taken in. Contrary to their predecessors, who came from the elite and middle class, this second wave represented a broader spectrum of Cuban society. Both settled in the Miami and Dade County region in Florida, and despite their initial adjustment problems, they were soon praised for their individual and collective economic achievements, especially the revitalization of urban neighborhoods. Americans were impressed by their rapid rise in Miami's construction, trade, and finance industries. Of course, not all Cubans were successful, and at the end of the 1970s, their population was divided between a sizable middle class and a disproportionate number of poor people. In 1980, however, the Mariel boatlift—Cuban Americans procuring ships to ferry their relatives and friends from the Cuban harbor of Mariel to Florida—brought a third wave of refugees (some one hundred and twenty-five thousand within a few months), who were not as welcomed by Americans because of a changed economic context in the United States and rumors that Castro was getting rid of the island's undesirable citizens. It is true that the newcomers were more apt to be of lower levels of education and skills and of working-class origin. All the same, the federal government cleared the large majority and placed them in local communities.

Very different was the fate of the Haitians who began to flee their island in 1972 hoping to escape from the violence and political unrest under the Duvalier dictatorship. They either entered the United States by air and overstayed their visas or they arrived in rickety boats on the Florida beaches. By 1980, it was estimated that there were sixty thousand Haitians in the United States, mostly concentrated in New York City. Because the American government supported the Duvalier regime, it refused to grant them refugee status, so they had to claim asylum, a more difficult procedure that can be won only by proving a well-founded fear of persecution. Not only was this done on a case-by-case basis, but the Haitians had to confront the government's claim that they were fleeing poverty rather than political oppression. Under the pressure of church and civil-rights groups, Haitians were finally granted the right to become permanent residents. But in 1982, President Ronald Reagan ordered the interception of boats suspected of carrying Haitians bound for the United States, and those who slipped through saw their asylum claim rejected, a policy that had at best limited success but condemned many Haitians to illegality. These newcomers stand out in many ways: They are overwhelmingly black, uneducated, and unskilled, penniless at the time of their arrival, speaking no English but creole (a blend of French, Spanish, and English as well as African dialects). The Haitian population is one of the poorest of the Western Hemisphere, but unlike the Cubans, they haven't benefited from any governmental assistance program. Yet, because the island's economy has not improved—although the political situation has stabilized—they keep coming and the U.S. government still tries to intercept them.

A sizable inflow from the Dominican Republic also developed in the 1970s, in the wake of U.S. intervention to stem a leftist military uprising. As the United States reasserted its hegemony, thousands of Dominicans emigrated, in such numbers that they soon represented the seventh-largest immigrant contingent to the United States. They are also one of the most concentrated groups, as their preferred destination was and remains New York City. In addition, deteriorating conditions in Central America in the 1980s also pushed out tens of thousands of Nicaraguans, Guatemalans, and Salvadorans who then found their way northward into the United States. By 1988, the INS was receiving some two thousand asylum requests per week. The Salvadorans were by far the most numerous, with up to eighty thousand legal admissions in 1990, followed by Guatemalans. Since then, political disturbances have become less frequent and the number of new refugees from Central America has declined. Still, the problem of the illegal status of many of these aliens remains: Although they are illegal, they have not been deported.

Of course, the refugee flows from these Caribbean and Central American countries cannot equal the massive influx of Southeast Asians in the 1970s and 1980s. But all in all, political refugees and those seeking asylum represent a significant addition to the post-1965 third-world inflow that deeply affected the United States.

PATTERNS OF SETTLEMENT

The new immigrants are all the more visible because they concentrate in the major cities of a few states: One in three legal immigrants in 1997 intended to live in New York City, Los Angeles, Miami, Chicago, or Washington, D.C., which have been the preferred cities of destination for the past decades. San Francisco and Houston also have large immigrant populations. In fact, the cities that are the major ports of entry possess host communities and are the fastest growing areas of the U.S. economy, providing more opportunities for newcomers. For this reason, post-1965 Mexican immigration, which was originally to rural areas, has become mostly urban.

Moreover, the five leading states of intended residence since 1965 have been California (25 percent of all 1997 legal immigrants reported that they intended to settle there), New York (15.5 percent), Florida (10.3 percent), Texas (7.3 percent), and New Jersey (5.3 percent).

New York City and Miami tend to attract immigrants from the Caribbean (Puerto Ricans and Domin-

Table 3
Immigrants Admitted by Selected State and Metropolitan Area of Intended Residence: Fiscal Year 1998 (in percent)

California:	25.8
New York:	14.6
Texas:	6.7
New Jersey:	5.3
Illinois:	5.0
New York City:	12.4
Los Angeles:	9.0
Chicago:	4.6
Miami:	4.4
Washington:	3.6
San Francisco:	2.2

Source: INS Annual Report (May 1999), p. 9.

icans to the former, Cubans to the latter), while Los Angeles is primarily the home of Mexicans but has also become the preferred destination of Guatemalans and Asians (Filipinos, Koreans, Indians, Vietnamese, and Chinese). Washington, D.C., also has a very diversified ethnic population, with large numbers of Asians (Chinese, Vietnamese, Indians, and Filipinos) and Hispanics (especially Salvadorans). As a consequence, older ethnic enclaves such as the Chinatowns have been revitalized and new ones have appeared. Thus, the post-1965 Korean influx in Los Angeles led to the official recognition of a Koreatown in 1980 (a Korean enclave that developed along Olympic Boulevard). In New York City, the older Puerto Rican neighborhoods were challenged by Dominican arrivals.

Despite the immigrants' visible preference for and concentration in certain areas, a process of diffusion has also taken place. Indeed, the different immigrant groups vary significantly in their destinations, so that a certain distribution occurs across the nation. Moreover, some groups show signs of dispersion. Thus, from the beginning, Indian newcomers manifested great geographic mobility and are today the most dispersed group. Their knowledge of English and their professional backgrounds have enabled them to seek jobs wherever they are. On the other hand, Southeast Asian refugees are equally dispersed, but for different reasons: Their geographic settlement was organized by the federal government, which tried to avoid creating cumbersome concentrations by distributing them in every state and including small cities and rural communities. After their initial placement, many drifted to existing Asian communities—especially in California (Los Angeles, Orange County, and San Diego) and Texas—but they can still be found throughout the United States.

Over time, some immigrant groups have fanned out. Mexican immigrants, who long concentrated in the South and West, began to move northward to urban centers of the Midwest—Chicago, Detroit, Cleveland, and Milwaukee—following job opportunities and are now widely dispersed across the country. In a comparable way, the Koreans, who originally favored Pacific Rim states, also settled in growing numbers in New York and Illinois. To a lesser extent, Filipinos did the same. Puerto Ricans, once extremely concentrated in New York City, now tend to disperse more and move to California, Texas, and Florida: Consequently, the share of New York City went down from two-thirds of the Puerto Rican population in 1960 to one-third in 1990. Even the Dominicans, as strongly concentrated as the Puerto Ricans until the

1970s, began to spread northward to New England and southward to Washington, D.C., and even Florida. All in all, immigrants are found in every American state, and those states with the fastest growing immigrant population are not the ones with a long-standing tradition of immigration.

ECONOMIC AND SOCIAL PROFILES

Post-1965 immigration is more heterogeneous than the preceding waves, and it covers the whole social and economic spectrum. But experts disagree on the general evolution of such immigration: Some contend that the quality of recent arrivals is deteriorating, whether it be at the educational or occupational level, while others point at evidence of stability or even improvement of economic attainment among newcomers.

What is certain is that the foreign-born population of the United States shows large variation in educational and occupational achievement depending on national origins. Some groups are above the American average, such as those from India, Taiwan, Iran, Hong Kong, the Philippines, Japan, Korea, and China. Mexico, on the contrary, provides the immigrants with the lowest levels of schooling and high-skill jobs; but El Salvador and Guatemala, as well as the Dominican Republic and Haiti, are not far behind.

According to recent Census Bureau data, the average education and occupation level of the foreign-born Asian-American population is much higher than that of foreign-born Hispanics. In 1997, nearly 36 percent of employed Asian residents in the United States held managerial and professional specialty occupations, whereas only 11.4 percent of foreign-born Latin Americans did (the corresponding figure for American citizens was 30 percent). Mexican Americans, especially, have a larger share of low-skilled workers than most immigrant groups: Nearly three-fourths are laborers, farmers, and service workers (in the food, apparel, textile, and furniture industries, for example). Incomes reveal the same discrepancy: The Asian Americans' median household income in 1997 was almost $43,000—compared to $36,000 for all households headed by natives—and the Latin Americans' corresponding income was only $24,000.

The factors accounting for such differences are numerous, but their exact influence is far from clear. It should come as no surprise that the highly selective Asian immigration should display such high average levels of schooling. Countries closer to the U.S. borders with a tradition of low-wage labor migrations, primarily in Central America, tend to send immigrants with lower socioeconomic profiles. In these countries, population displacements due to agrarian reforms or the turmoil of war or revolution are another factor of migration by the poorer elements. The case of nations that have sent large numbers of refugees, like Cuba or Vietnam, well illustrates the connection between upheavals and emigration of the more disadvantaged: As time went by and the political situation got worse, the flow of emigrants originated from increasingly lower strata of the home society. Average schooling and occupation level are further reduced by the contribution of undocumented residents, who tend to be of modest origins, some of whom manage to legalize their status in the United States. The demographic and socioeconomic profile of the illegals who benefited from the 1986 amnesty confirms that their average achievements are lower.

In addition to noting individual background factors such as the parents' schooling, studies also point to the importance of broader cultural and social factors to account for persisting inequalities in socioeconomic profiles among immigrants. Discrimination experienced in the receiving society undoubtedly plays a part, as suggested by the different socioeconomic achievements of Cubans on the one hand and Haitians and Puerto Ricans on the other. Haitians in the United States are among the poorest elements of the foreign-born population, while Puerto Ricans fare the worst in terms of occupation and earnings attainment.

Finally, it should be remembered that the family categories helped spur the immigration of individuals with a lower level of education and lower skills: Among those who enter in these categories, a majority report that they are service workers or have no occupation. For this reason, immigration from many Asian countries in effect consists of two streams: a brain drain and a flow that finds its origin in the lower classes. This bifurcation is particularly striking in the case of Chinese immigrants, who very early concentrated at both ends of the socioeconomic ladder: By the early 1980s, 32.5 percent of all Chinese living in the United States were professionals, managers, or executives, and 18.5 percent were in service work. The gap was less significant for the Filipinos (respectively, 27 and 20 percent of foreign-born Filipino Americans in 1980) as well as for the Koreans, but tended to increase as the share of family immigration grew. Indians, by contrast, long maintained an amazingly high proportion of professionals but a smaller proportion of service workers than the general population of the United States. As late as 1989,

48.5 percent reported a professional occupation. In the next decade, however, India experienced a trend comparable to that of other Asian nations, with the share of service workers rising among the recent immigrants.

THE NEW IMMIGRANT ENTREPRENEURS

Another striking feature of the new immigration is the propensity for entrepreneurship displayed by some groups. Although this is by no means a new trend, the number of small businesses run by newcomers has increased in a dramatic way since 1965, visibly transforming the cities' landscape and economy. Yet, the size and characteristics of such businesses vary significantly.

In Los Angeles, but also Chicago and New York, Korean immigrants have set up hundreds of grocery stores, restaurants, and other establishments such as liquor stores and dry cleaners. Some of the Korean entrepreneurs had been professionals in their home country, but could not satisfy American state licensing requirements and chose self-employment as an alternative. Others had limited employment prospects because they lacked skills, possessed little money, and spoke little or no English.

Many of the new Chinese immigrants were in that category; they concentrated in the nation's Chinatowns, especially in San Francisco and New York, where they labored in restaurants or toiled in the sewing shops of the booming garment industry. Smaller numbers, particularly from Taiwan and Hong Kong, succeeded in acquiring or managing small businesses themselves. This has become a very important phenomenon: Together the Koreans and the Chinese own nearly one-fifth of all businesses of Los Angeles County.

In the 1980s, Indian immigrants turned to entrepreneurship too, but generally on a different scale: They began to acquire franchise and import-export businesses, which required more capital than the Koreans' greengroceries, for example, but this was made possible because they were from the elite classes or had family financial backing.

Of all Hispanics, Cubans have by far been the most inclined toward and successful at entrepreneurship. In Miami, they have developed a complex, interdependent ethnic community that rivals the Korean achievement in Los Angeles.

POVERTY

The successful integration of Asian professionals and less educated but hard-working entrepreneurs should not blind us to the hardship and poverty that many disadvantaged newcomers suffer. The Asian immigrants' above-average statistics in terms of education, occupation, and incomes conceal significant inequalities between and within ethnic groups. As noted earlier, the Chinese-American population, for example, is divided between a successful elite and large numbers of modest or poor households, generally recent arrivals. Of those immigrants who entered between 1975 and 1980, 22.8 percent were below the poverty line in 1980, compared to 7 percent for white American households.

Adjustment problems were often severe, as illustrated by the fate of the boat people from Vietnam, Laos, and Cambodia in the 1980s: In addition to suffering the extreme disruption of getting to the United States, these refugees were less proficient in English, less educated, less experienced at holding formal jobs in urban occupations, and, in general, less familiar with Western culture. As previously mentioned, Haitians experienced similar difficulties and stand out as being among the poorest immigrant populations in the United States.

Among Hispanics, only the Cubans generally escape poverty. Mexican immigrants have a much higher poverty level than the U.S. norms, a problem most often attributed to low educational achievements. In 1996, the poverty rate for the total foreign-born population was 21 percent, that of Asians was only 14.7, and of the Mexicans nearly 34 percent. Although substantial economic and social progress was made in the 1980s, this progress was not shared by all. A study released by the California senate in 1999 found that Hispanic workers in that state—whether first, second, or third generation—lagged far behind all other groups in educational attainment and wages. Both the Puerto Rican and Mexican-American population today seem to polarize between affluent, booming communities and pockets of poverty and joblessness, especially in the first generation.

From a general point of view, recent immigrants seem to be doing worse than their predecessors and to have more difficulty trying to get out of poverty. Over one-quarter of all immigrants who arrived in the 1980s remained poor in 1997, twice the rate for natives. Some denounce the danger of the "foreignization" of poverty, which they think is because the new economy is not creating many jobs for unskilled people. But this point of view is criticized by immigrant advocates, who stress the post-1965 immigrants' contribution through enterprise and hard work, and recall that aggregate numbers do not reflect the specific achievements between and within groups. The danger today is that the most disadvantaged newcomers remain trapped at the bottom of the economic ladder, with the American Dream remaining out of reach.

IMPACT ON THE POPULATION OF THE UNITED STATES

The impact of the new wave of immigration on the proportion of native and foreign-born Americans has been remarkable: While the U.S. population had 4.7 percent foreign-born citizens in 1970, the figure reached 7.9 percent in 1990 and 9.8 percent at the end of the decade—a proportion that is nevertheless considerably less than the 14.7 percent attained in 1910.

Yet, the long-term effect of the changes in the composition of the immigrant stock becomes more evident when the continent of origin and year of immigration are taken into account. In 1960, fully 75 percent of the foreign-born were of European origin, with Asians representing only 5 percent and those of Mexican or Caribbean origin 8 percent. In the 1990 census, the foreign-born population of European origin made up only 22 percent and the Asian share had increased to 25.3 percent, while the Mexican and Caribbean foreign-born totaled nearly 32 percent. Nearly half the 32 million Hispanics living in the United States today were born outside its borders.

Because of the declining natural rate of increase in the American population, the net effect of immigration on overall population growth is becoming more pronounced and is dramatically altering the ethnic and racial balance. The linguistic, religious, and cultural diversity of the new immigrants is unparalleled. In California, the most linguistically diverse state, over two hundred languages and innumerable dialects are spoken. No wonder such dramatic changes have become the focus of attention in academic and political circles, in the media and the public at large, and have raised numerous questions about their economic, social, political, and cultural impact in the country. Some rejoice over the economic and cultural contributions that the newcomers bring to their adopted country, while others express concern over their impact. Critics doubt whether the new immigrants and their offspring—especially Hispanics, whose home countries are so close to the United States that they can easily maintain ties—will merge into American society as the Europeans of the last great migration did. In any case, inasmuch as Congress has so far shown no serious inclination to close the doors of the country, either partly or fully—despite demands from certain segments of the population—this wave of immigration is likely to continue.

Dominique Daniel

See also: Economics I: Pull Factors, Economics II: Push Factors, Natural Disasters, Environmental Crises, and Overpopulation, Political, Ethnic, Religious, and Gender Persecution, Wars and Civil Unrest (Part II, Sec. 1); Immigration and Nationality Act, 1965 (Part IV, Sec. 1); Report by U.S. Commission on Immigration Reform, 1994 (Part IV, Sec. 2).

BIBLIOGRAPHY

Center for Immigration Studies (CIS). *Importing Poverty.* Washington, DC: Center for Immigration Studies, September 1999.

Commission on Immigration Reform. U.S. *Immigration Policy: Restoring Credibility.* Washington, DC: Government Printing Office, September 1994.

Glazer, Nathan, ed. *Clamor at the Gates: The New American Immigration.* San Francisco: Institute for Contemporary Studies, 1985.

Hamamoto, Darrell Y., and Rodolfo D. Torres. *New American Destinies: A Reader in Contemporary Asian and Latino Immigration.* New York: Routledge, 1997.

Hing, Bill Ong. *Making and Remaking Asian America Through Immigration Policy, 1850–1990.* Stanford: Stanford University Press, 1993.

Hossain, Mokerrom. "South Asians in Southern California: A Sociological Study of Immigrants from India, Pakistan and Bangladesh." *South Asia Bulletin* 2:1 (Spring 1982): 74–83.

Houstoun, Marion L., et al. "Female Predominance in Immigration to the United States Since 1930: A First Look." *International Migration Review* 18:4 (Winter 1989): 908–59.

Immigration and Naturalization Service. *1997 INS Statistical Yearbook.* Washington, DC: Government Printing Office, 1998.

Ishi, T. K. "The Political Economy of International Migration: Indian Physicians in the United States." *South Asia Bulletin* 2:1 (Spring 1982): 39–58.

Jasso, Guillermina, and Mark R. Rosenzweig. *The New Chosen People: Immigrants in the United States.* New York: Russell Sage Foundation, 1990.

Kessner, Thomas, and Betty Boyd Caroli. *Today's Immigrants, Their Stories: A New Look at the Newest Immigrants.* New York: Oxford University Press, 1981.

Kim, Illsoo. *Urban Immigrants: The Korean Community in New York.* Princeton, N.J.: Princeton University Press, 1981.

———. "Korea and East India: Premigration Factors and U.S. Immigration Policy." In *Pacific Bridges: The New Immigration from Asia and the Pacific Islands,* ed. James Fawcett and Benjamin Carino, pp. 327–45. Staten Island, NY: Center for Migration Studies, 1987.

Light, Ivan. "Immigrant Entrepreneurs in America: Koreans in Los Angeles." In *Immigration Reader: America in a Multidisciplinary Perspective,* ed. David Jacobson, pp. 265–82. Malden, MA: Blackwell, 1998.

Minocha, Urmil. "South Asian Immigrants: Trends and Impacts on the Sending and Receiving Societies." In *Pacific Bridges: The New Immigration from Asia and the Pacific Islands,* ed. James Fawcett and Benjamin Carino, pp. 347–73. Staten Island, NY: Center for Migration Studies, 1987.

Muller, Thomas, and Thomas J. Espenshade. *The Fourth Wave: California's Newest Immigrants.* Washington, DC: The Urban Institute Press, 1985.

O'Hare, William P., and Judy C. Felt. *Asian Americans: America's Fastest Growing Minority Group.* Washington, DC: 1991.

Pido, Antonio J. A. *The Pilipinos in America: Macro/Micro Dimensions of Immigration and Integration.* New York: Center for Migration Studies, 1992.

Portes, Alejandro. "From South of the Border. Hispanic Minorities in the United States." In *Immigration Reader: America in a Multidisciplinary Perspective,* ed. David Jacobson, pp. 113–43. Malden, MA: Blackwell, 1998.

Portes, Alejandro, and Robert L. Bach. *Latin Journey: Cuban and Mexican Immigrants in the United States.* Berkeley: University of California Press, 1985.

Portes, Alejandro, and Rubén G. Rumbaut. *Immigrant America: A Portrait.* Berkeley: University of California Press, 1996.

Reimers, David M. *Still the Golden Door: The Third World Comes to America.* New York: Columbia University Press, 1985.

Rivera-Batiz, Francisco, and Carlos Santiago. *Puerto Ricans in the United States: A Changing Reality.* Washington, DC: The National Puerto Rican Coalition, 1994.

Rockett, Ian R., and S. L. Putnam. "Physician-Nurse Migration to the United States: Regional and Health Status Origins in Relation to Legislation and Policy." *International Migration Review* 27:3 (September 1989): 389–401.

Ueda, Reed. "The Changing Face of Post-1965 Immigration." In *Immigration Reader: America in a Multidisciplinary Perspective,* ed. David Jacobson, pp. 72–91. Malden, MA: Blackwell, 1998.

COLLAPSE OF COMMUNISM

Throughout the 1980s, U.S. immigration policy toward refugees continued to be dominated by anticommunist ideology, and refugee admissions still heavily favored applicants from communist nations. In 1980, the U.S. Congress passed the Refugee Act with the express hope of removing these ideological preferences. Little, however, changed in practice. By 1985, the largest numbers of refugees coming to the United States continued to come from communist nations, including Vietnam (23,799), Cambodia (11,380), Eastern European nations (9,169), Laos (4,035), Afghanistan (2,234), and the Soviet Union (635). Toward the end of the 1980s, applications for asylum from residents of communist nations were still much more likely to be granted than those from other parts of the world.

FALL OF COMMUNIST REGIMES

In the mid- to late 1980s, however, a series of dramatic changes within the Soviet Union led to the eventual end of the Cold War that for decades had dominated international relations and U.S. refugee policy. In 1985, soon after he was named secretary general of the Communist Party of the Soviet Union, Mikhail Gorbachev introduced a program of economic, political, and social reforms to the region. Buoyed by these changes and several coup attempts against the Soviet leadership, the individual republics gradually declared their independence from the Soviet Union. By September 1991, Soviet leaders had recognized the independence of all fourteen republics. The effects of these changes were not limited to the Soviet Union alone; other countries led by communist rulers were forced either to concede power or to adapt to the changing geopolitical climate. The Communist Party in East Germany lost power, the Berlin Wall was toppled, and East and West Germany were reunited. For Cuba and Vietnam, the end of economic assistance

from the Soviet Union foreshadowed particularly severe economic difficulties. In 1991 alone, the Cuban economy lost over $8 billion in annual Soviet subsidies. The Cuban leadership maintained power, and the nation continued to suffer not only the loss of Soviet funds but also the continuation of the U.S. embargo. Beginning in the late 1980s, the Vietnamese Communist Party introduced a series of economic and social reforms designed to mitigate the impact of the collapse of the Soviet Union.

At the same time, the end of the Cold War indicated potentially profound changes in worldwide immigration patterns. As early as 1985, the Soviet government began to ease its restrictions on travel and emigration, and approved a small number of exit visas for Russians. Within the United States, many predicted a dramatic increase in the number of emigrants from the former Soviet Union who would seek to enter the country. Others predicted that the end of the Cold War polarity would require immediate changes in U.S. immigration policy, which was left without a clear direction, since the U.S. approach toward refugees had lost its overarching rationale.

U.S. IMMIGRATION POLICY, LATE 1980s–1990s

These early predictions turned out to be either untrue or premature. Emigration escalated between the republics of the former Soviet Union, and Western Europe granted refugee status to many of the applicants from Afghanistan, Romania, the former Yugoslavia, and the republics of the former Soviet Union, but the United States was not met with a large number of requests for entrance from those same countries. Furthermore, U.S. immigration policy changed very gradually during the first decade after Gorbachev introduced his reforms. Under first the Rea-

The destruction of the Berlin Wall in 1989 signaled the collapse of East European communism and set in motion new waves of immigrants, most to Western Europe, but some also to the United States. *(Birgit Pohl/Impact Visuals)*

gan and then the Bush administrations, officials argued that people from the Soviet Union would not be given automatic latitude in their refugee applications. Indeed, at the end of 1988, the State Department announced that the U.S. government would no longer presume a well-founded fear of persecution on the part of émigrés from the former Soviet Union. That year, U.S. immigration officials denied refugee status to approximately one hundred and seventy-five Soviet Jews. In September 1989, the Bush administration announced that the United States would not admit more than 50,000 emigrants from the Soviet Union as refugees. At the same time, however, Congress passed legislation that created special short-term programs for specific groups of people who could claim past experiences with persecution under communist rule.

One of the first of these special programs facilitated the immigration of those who faced particular forms of religious persecution under communism. The liberalization of Soviet regulations regarding emigration had eased restrictions on Russian Jews

who wished to leave the country. Whereas less than 1,000 Soviet Jews had been allowed to leave in 1986, over 8,000 were granted exit visas in 1987, and over 71,000 were permitted to leave in 1989. In 1989, Congress adopted the Lautenberg amendment, drafted by Senator Frank Lautenberg (D-NJ), a provision that extended protection to residents of the Soviet Union and certain Southeast Asian nations who claimed persecution for their Jewish, Evangelical, Ukrainian Catholic, or Ukrainian Orthodox beliefs. Beneficiaries of the Lautenberg amendment did not need to demonstrate a well-founded fear of persecution, but instead needed to show a "credible basis" for fears that they would be persecuted for their adherence to a faith that has been persecuted in the past. In the first few years of the program, officials in the Bush administration moved the adjudication of refugees from Vienna and Rome to the American embassy in Moscow, prompting some critics to argue that by expecting applicants to make their claims within the former Soviet Union, those who truly feared persecution faced potential sanctions by

Soviet authorities. Since its adoption, the Lautenberg provision has been extended year by year, allowing officials to monitor conditions within the Soviet Union. By 1999, an estimated two hundred and seventy-five thousand Jews and one hundred thousand evangelical Christians had arrived in the United States. This number represents nearly 40 percent of all refugees admitted to the United States since 1989.

In the late 1980s, Congress also created an immigration program for Vietnamese who had been detained in government reeducation camps after the reunification of North and South Vietnam in 1975. In early 1979, the United Nations High Commissioner for Refugees (UNHCR), Vietnam, and the United States agreed to established in-country processing of applications under the Orderly Departure Program (ODP). The ODP favored former employees of the U.S. government, Amerasians, members of minority ethnic groups, and their close family members. Eventually, after many years of negotiation, U.S. and Vietnamese officials agreed to expand the provisions of the ODP and to facilitate the emigration of former reeducation center detainees who had been detained for more than five years or who had family members in the United States. In October 1989, U.S. officials interviewed the first group of former detainees in Ho Chi Minh City. Eventually, the program was expanded to cover those with three or more years of reeducation. Since its inception, nearly two hundred thousand former detainees and their family members have entered the United States.

SHIFTS IN U.S. IMMIGRATION POLICY

By the mid-1990s, however, the end of the Cold War began to have a greater impact on U.S. immigration policies. First, during a surge of nativist sentiment in the United States, American officials began to make changes in its overall policies toward asylum seekers. The Illegal Immigration Reform and Immigrant Responsibility Act, signed by President Clinton on September 30, 1996, created more restrictive legal standards for screening asylum seekers and gave border officials greater autonomy to reject an applicant's claims for asylum. Second, U.S. officials began to shift the emphasis away from refugee status and instead required those who wished to enter the United States from communist or formerly communist nations to apply for immigrant status, the requirements of which are often more burdensome. Applicants from former

communist countries may have difficulty persuading U.S. officials that they have the financial support for their stay in the United States. Many of those who left Vietnam by boat after 1989 were classified by the UNHCR as economic migrants rather than political refugees, were denied entrance to the United States, and were detained indefinitely in camps in Hong Kong and Southeast Asia. In the late 1990s, a large percentage of Russians who applied to enter the United States as students were denied entry. The U.S. Department of State expressed their concerns that with the economic difficulties in Russia, the applicants would not be inclined to return once their studies were completed.

The implications of this shift from a refugee-based to an immigrant-based policy has been perhaps most evident in the recent changes in U.S. policies toward Cuban immigrants. With the end of the Soviet Union as a threat to the United States, the U.S. government had less reason to want to rely on Cuban immigrants as an ideological weapon against communism. At the same time, however, official antagonism toward Cuban leader Fidel Castro did not lessen and the United States continued to impose its economic embargo on the country. During the first few years after the collapse of the Soviet bloc, U.S. refugee policy toward Cuba continued to be dominated by Cold War concerns. As in the preceding decades, the majority of Cubans who sought refugee status in the United States during the late 1980s and early 1990s were granted political asylum and allowed to apply for permanent residency. Gradually, however, the United States has modified this open-door policy. In August 1994, President Bill Clinton announced that Cubans rescued at sea would no longer be allowed to enter the United States automatically as political refugees. Instead, with few exceptions, Cubans would be offered "safe haven" at the U.S. naval base in Guantánamo Bay. By 1995, U.S. officials agreed to allow for the entrance of the Cubans being held in Guantánamo at that time. By 1997, approximately thirty-one thousand Cubans were brought to the United States from Guantánamo.

At the same time, however, U.S. officials made it clear that policies toward Cuban immigration had changed. The United States announced that any Cubans intercepted at sea in the future would have to return to Cuba for in-country processing if they wanted to apply for refugee status. These individuals would be granted only brief shipboard screenings prior to their return to Cuba. In talks, the U.S. and Cuban governments agreed to encourage immigration through legal channels as an alternative to escape by boat. The Cuban government would discourage boat departures, and the United States would increase the number of visas for Cubans wishing to emigrate legally to the United States to a minimum of 20,000 per year. Through the in-country program, Cubans who could prove their status as political prisoners, human-rights activists, forced-labor conscripts during the period 1965–68, or persons persecuted for their perceived or actual political or religious beliefs would be considered for entry to the United States.

In the mid-1990s, U.S. officials, with the cooperation of the UNHCR, also began to expand consideration of repatriation as a viable alternative to refugee status. After the end of the Cold War, the UNHCR changed some of its basic premises, began to step across national borders and work with displaced persons within their countries of origin, and began to return those displaced to their countries of origin after the original conflict had eased. The United States had established a program for refugees from the former Yugoslavia as early as 1992. Over the years, however, U.S. officials considered housing Kosovar Albanian refugees in the camps at Guantánamo Bay until they could be repatriated. In April 1999, after much public outcry, the United States announced that it would admit up to twenty thousand Kosovar Albanians to the United States as refugees, particularly Kosovars who have family ties in the country or who are in vulnerable circumstances. By 2000, approximately one hundred and seven thousand refugees from the former Yugoslavia had been admitted to the United States. Those eligible include Bosnians with family members in the United States and those who were particularly vulnerable to violence and torture based on ethnic or religious identity.

However, the Vietnamese emigrants who continued to languish in camps were not granted the same entrance. In the mid-1990s, the UNHCR began the process of returning those emigrants in Hong Kong to Vietnam. By early 1999, some one hundred and ten thousand non-refugee boat people returned to Vietnam. In an effort to speed up this repatriation process, the State Department announced that it would offer U.S. resettlement interviews to Vietnamese of special interest to the United States after they returned to Vietnam. As of 1999, the State Department estimated that only a small number of cases remain to be processed through this particular program.

Most recently, the numbers of applicants who are able to enter the United States as refugees through the special programs for applicants from communist nations have begun to decline. By the end of 1999, admissions under the Lautenberg amendment had dropped from a high of nearly twenty-five thousand in a single month to an average of less than two thousand per month. By the end of 1999, the UNHCR concluded its reintegration and monitoring assistance for returnees to Vietnam, and the UNHCR's presence in Vietnam was downsized considerably. Renewed diplomatic relations with Vietnam allowed the United States to close the Orderly Departure Program in Bangkok and to transfer remaining cases to the Refugee Resettlement Section at the newly opened U.S. Consulate General in Ho Chi Minh City. Most other Vietnamese applicants are considered for immigrant rather than refugee status. In 1998, U.S. officials conducted approximately twenty-five thousand immigrant visa interviews within Vietnam.

The end of the Cold War has also altered the direction of movement between communist and non-communist nations, as the opening of borders has allowed emigrants in the United States to return to their countries of origin, often for the first time after decades of exile. Emigrants from the former Soviet Union and parts of Eastern Europe have returned to visit family and friends, or to work in business or government enterprises during the transitional period. The government of Vietnam has simultaneously encouraged overseas Vietnamese to return with their economic capital while it expressed concerns about the potential political or cultural changes that the overseas community may introduce into the country. Still, Cuban Americans do not share this opportunity to return to Cuba. The economic embargo continued to create living conditions that encouraged the desire for emigration, while the Clinton administration's policies restricted the sending of monetary remittances to Cuba and kept the door to Cuban emigration closed.

As the twentieth century came to an end, many argued that the United States needed to reassess its current approach toward refugee, asylum, and immigrant applicants, and to adopt policies that reflect the changes introduced by the end of the Cold War.

Maureen Feeney

See also: Immigrants and the Red Scare (Part I, Sec. 4); Eastern Europe, Former Soviet Union (Part III, Sec. 4); *Whom We Shall Welcome,* 1953 (Part IV, Sec. 1).

BIBLIOGRAPHY

Department of State. "Fact Sheet: Newly Independent States and the Baltics Admissions Program." Washington, DC: Bureau of Population, Refugees and Migration. January 18, 2000.

Gibney, Mark. "The Repatriation of Soviet Emigres." In *Immigration and Ethnicity*, ed. M. D'Innocenzo and J. Sirefman. Westport, CT: Greenwood Press, 1992.

Goldman, Minton. "United States Policy and Soviet Jewish Emigration from Nixon to Bush." In *Jews and Jewish Life in Russia and the Soviet Union*, ed. Yaacov Ro'i. Portland, OR: Frank Cass, 1995.

Nackerud, Larry, et al. "The End of the Cuban Contradiction in U.S. Refugee Policy." *International Migration Review* 33:1 (Spring, 1999): 176–92.

Nguyen, D. T., and J. S. Bandara. "Emigration Pressure and Structural Change: Vietnam." UNDP Technical Support Services Report, Bangkok, 1996.

IMMIGRATION LEGISLATION OF THE 1980s AND 1990s

In 1996, an estimated 5 million unauthorized (otherwise known as "undocumented" or "illegal") immigrants lived in the United States. These are foreign-born individuals who have settled in this country but have no lawful right to be here. Depending on one's point of view, 5 million is either a small number or a large one. It represents less than 2 percent of the total U.S. population and just one out of every six U.S. residents born abroad. On the other hand, it is the largest estimate ever reliably recorded. Slightly more than half of all unauthorized migrants came to the United States without proper documents (many across the United States–Mexican border), while the remainder arrived lawfully (usually on a temporary visa—business, tourist, or student) and then either overstayed the length of their visa or did something else (for example, took a job) to violate its terms.

More than half (roughly 54 percent) of all unauthorized immigrants were born in Mexico, but other countries that contributed large numbers include El Salvador, Guatemala, Canada, Haiti, the Philippines, and Honduras. An estimated two of every five undocumented migrants live in California, but other large magnet states include Texas, New York, Florida, Illinois, and New Jersey. Many undocumented immigrants are poorly educated young adult males who come to this country looking for work. This fact has led to calls for immigration reform not only because unauthorized immigrants are breaking the law but also, it is feared, because they are harming the labor-market chances of the least-skilled, native-born workers and imposing heavy burdens on American taxpayers.

The United States did not have illegal immigrants until 1875, when Congress passed this country's first immigrant exclusion law, directed against convicts and prostitutes. Laws passed from the 1880s to the 1920s that established the first quantitative restrictions on Asians and newer immigrant groups from Europe, together with the outbreak of the Mexican Revolution, served to intensify undocumented immigration. During the 1940s, the number of unauthorized immigrants apprehended at the border rose to 1.4 million (versus fewer than 150,000 during the 1930s).

Passage of the Immigration and Nationality Act in 1952 imposed stiff penalties on persons found guilty of "harboring" illegal aliens, although in an apparent concession to Texas agricultural interests, employers of illegal aliens were not considered to be harboring them. This law did little, however, to slow the flow of undocumented Mexican migrants into the American Southwest. But in 1954 the U.S. Border Patrol launched Operation Wetback, which resulted in more than 1 million undocumented Mexican immigrants (including some U.S. citizens) being deported. For a time, this action had a chilling effect on unauthorized immigration and served to reduce the number of illegal alien apprehensions by 95 percent in five years.

But soon the illegal immigrant flow resumed and then gained momentum during the latter part of the 1960s after Congress terminated the Bracero Program. This guest-worker program, begun in 1942, permitted temporary agricultural workers from Mexico, Barbados, and other countries to pick crops in western states. After the program ended, job-seeking immigrants who had been accustomed to working in the United States legally kept coming, but now in unauthorized status. Throughout this and subsequent periods, the number of illegal alien apprehensions rose dramatically, reaching a total of 8.3 million for the 1970s. The increase continued into the 1980s and peaked at an all-time high of almost 1.8 million in 1986.

THE 1986 IMMIGRATION REFORM AND CONTROL ACT

The Immigration Reform and Control Act (IRCA) was a frontal attack by Congress on the perceived problem of illegal immigration and on the belief that the

Federal laws and budgets in the 1980s and 1990s called for increased spending for border patrols, like this one that captured a number of undocumented immigrants along the Arizona-Mexico border. *(Jeffry D. Scott/Impact Visuals)*

United States had lost control of its borders. Passed in October 1986 and signed by President Ronald Reagan one month later, IRCA's primary objectives were to slow if not entirely eliminate the flow of undocumented migrants into the country and to reduce the number of unauthorized immigrants already living here. These objectives were to be accomplished by three means: new "employer sanctions" measures to penalize employers for hiring illegal aliens, a legalization program to grant amnesty to selected undocumented immigrants, and stepped-up enforcement along the United States–Mexican border to protect against future illegal immigration.

For the first time ever in the United States, IRCA made it illegal "knowingly" to hire an unauthorized immigrant. After November 1986, all employers (including families who hired domestic workers) were subject to the new law, regardless of how many workers they employed. The intent of employer sanctions was to reduce job opportunities in the United States and thereby cut into incentives for illegal immigra-

tion. The act required every employer to verify a prospective employee's right to work by examining either a passport, a certificate of naturalization or U.S. citizenship, a resident alien card, or combinations of other documents. All workers, including persons born in the United States, were subject to the new requirements. Employers had to maintain records indicating which documents they had inspected for each new worker hired after November 6, 1986. Importantly, however, employers were not given the responsibility for verifying the authenticity of the papers they were shown, nor were they required to keep copies of the documents on file. Failure to comply could mean civil fines for initial infractions and possibly imprisonment for a "pattern and practice" of hiring undocumented workers.

The Immigration Reform and Control Act's legalization program had two parts. Beginning May 5, 1987, and continuing for a window of twelve months, undocumented aliens who could prove they had resided continuously in the United States in illegal

The 1986 Immigration Reform and Control Act, which beefed up border patrols, led to the apprehension of many more immigrants—like these men outside Douglas, Arizona—trying to make their way into the country illegally over the Mexican border. *(Jack Kurtz/ Impact Visuals)*

status since January 1, 1982, and who were not excludable as immigrants could apply for amnesty. Illegal aliens who met these conditions were then eligible for temporary resident status for a period of eighteen months, after which they could become permanent resident aliens provided they had a minimal understanding of English and knowledge of U.S. history. A second component of the legalization program extended to undocumented farmworkers who were granted temporary resident status provided they could show that they had worked in perishable-crop agriculture for at least ninety days in the twelve-month period prior to May 1, 1986. These farmworkers later became eligible to adjust their status to permanent residents. Partly to gain the support of organized growers, IRCA contained provisions to replenish the supply of agricultural workers lost to non-agricultural employment following legalization of their residency status.

Finally, the Immigration and Naturalization Service (INS) received a budgetary supplement for enforcement activities, which included a 50 percent in-

crease in the number of Border Patrol personnel (from 3,200 authorized positions in 1986 to 4,800 in 1987). Even though IRCA expanded the enforcement duties of the INS, one activity was sharply curtailed: INS officials were no longer permitted to search for undocumented immigrants in open fields without a search warrant or the consent of the owner.

Studies conducted soon after IRCA's passage indicated that the new law had at least an initial impact in reducing the flow of undocumented immigrants into the country. But that effect quickly disappeared in the face of rising numbers of border apprehensions. The lasting impact of IRCA seems to be the legalization program, through which nearly 3 million formerly undocumented migrants gained legal permanent resident status.

Annual figures on the number of INS apprehensions of illegal immigrants, which had risen to nearly 1.8 million in 1986, fell sharply to 1.2 million by 1987 and then continued a slow decline to 950,000 by 1989. But just as the U.S. economy resumed strength, the numbers began to rise again, topping 1.5 million in

To increase their mobility along the Brownsville, Texas, sector of the Mexican-American border, border patrolmen are issued mountain bikes. *(Jack Kurtz/Impact Visuals)*

both 1996 and 1997. Estimates of the *net* flow of undocumented immigrants into the United States (the annual number arriving minus the number leaving) support this picture too. Researchers at the Census Bureau estimate that the size of the U.S. undocumented alien population grew somewhere between 100,000 and 300,000 per year during the 1980–83 period. Figures for the 1986–88 period suggest the net flow was roughly 250,000 annually. Currently, the Census Bureau uses 200,000 per year in its population projections. Robert Warren, a senior scholar at the INS, believes the bureau's numbers may be too conservative. He puts the annual addition of undocumented immigrants in the United States at 275,000 for the early 1990s.

The best initial estimates of the size of the resident undocumented immigrant population set the figure at 2.1 million persons. Making an allowance for those whom the Census Bureau failed to count boosts the estimate to a range between 2.5 and 3.5 million. By 1986, between 3 and 5 million illegal aliens were estimated to be living in the United States. But these

numbers dropped dramatically following IRCA's legalization of roughly 2.8 unauthorized immigrants. By 1989, the estimated range spanned 1.8 million to 3 million. But IRCA's legalization program was a one-time occurrence, and the size of the resident undocumented population has been climbing ever since. Estimates for October 1992 put the size at 3.4 million, and for October 1996, at 5 million.

THE 1996 WELFARE AND IMMIGRATION REFORM ACTS

Two significant federal legislative developments occurred in 1996, and both have implications for future patterns of legal and undocumented U.S. immigration. The first of these, the Personal Responsibility and Work Opportunity Reconciliation Act of 1996 (also known as the Welfare Reform Act, or WRA) became law in August. The WRA, born of voter frustration over the high cost of government and what Kitty Calavita, professor of criminology, law, and society at the University of California at Irvine, has called the "new politics of immigration," reformed the entitlement policy for poor families and set new limits on noncitizen eligibility for welfare benefits and other social services.

Specifically, the Welfare Reform Act eliminated the Aid to Families with Dependent Children entitlement program, begun in 1935, and replaced it with an array of state-implemented programs designed to provide short-term cash assistance to needy families. The law also cut funding for other federal programs, including food stamps, Supplemental Security Income, child care, and child support. In all, the WRA aimed to reduce federal spending by $54 billion over the six years following its enactment. Prior to 1996, U.S. citizens, legal immigrants, and refugees had been eligible for public assistance on more or less the same basis. The WRA created a four-tier eligibility system that gave priority first to U.S. citizens, then to refugees, next to legal immigrants on whom new restrictions were placed, and lastly to undocumented immigrants who continued to be ineligible for almost all social programs. Finally, some programs now distinguish between legal immigrants who were in the United States in August 1996 and those who came later.

The Illegal Immigration Reform and Immigrant Responsibility Act (IIRIRA) of 1996 (also known as the Immigration Reform Act) became law at the end of September. Although parts of it were directed toward legal immigrants, its main purpose was to reduce the flow of undocumented immigrants and the number of unauthorized persons already in the country. Under the IIRIRA, individuals in the United States who wish to sponsor family members for legal immigration are now required to have family incomes at least 25 percent above federal poverty thresholds, whereas prior to IIRIRA there had been no income requirements. Efforts to combat illegal immigration were strengthened by increasing the number of Border Patrol officers, employing more technologically sophisticated equipment, constructing additional border fences, and fining immigrants for illegal entry. Finally, several incremental policy changes were directed toward unauthorized immigrants living within the United States, including expanding staffs to detect employment eligibility violations and visa overstayers, developing documents more resistant to counterfeiting, and expanding the pilot program to record the fingerprints of all undocumented immigrants arrested in the United States.

The consequences of the WRA and the IIRIRA for U.S. immigration are likely to be just the opposite of those which were intended. Because it is now more costly to be a poor noncitizen living in the United States, legal immigrants who came prior to 1996 have a large incentive to naturalize, and new prospective immigrants have a reduced incentive to come initially, especially if they and their potential sponsors are poor. One should therefore expect levels of legal immigration to be smaller than they would otherwise have been and the resulting legal flows to have higher average levels of income and skill. At the same time, incentives for illegal immigration have been expanded. Some potential migrants who find that legal entry to the United States is blocked by IIRIRA's requirement that financial sponsors must meet higher income tests will seek ways to enter the United States illegally. In addition, if IIRIRA succeeds in increasing the cost of illegal entry (either through fines or quicker arrests in the U.S. interior), undocumented migrants may react by returning to the United States more quickly and by attempting to stay longer on subsequent trips to recoup the costs of a prior arrest.

In the face of five challenges confronting the INS, there seems little hope of a policy change that would be acceptable to the public and also effective in terms of reducing undocumented U.S. immigration. These challenges include continued domestic economic growth, an ongoing rapid expansion in service occupations, labor shortages in the United States due to a declining size of youth cohorts, labor supply pressures in the Caribbean and in Central America, and an inability by the INS to police every aspect of illegal immigration and the necessity of relying on voluntary compliance.

Undocumented immigration appears to be increasing in both volume and complexity. Both sea and land borders (including the border with Canada) are under greater pressure, the points of destination in the United States are multiplying, and more and more countries are represented in the illegal immigrant flow. If the goal of Congress is to deter undocumented migration, then overcoming employers' objections to greater worksite verification may be the biggest challenge of all. Otherwise, we may have to conclude that unauthorized immigration at current or even higher levels is a price that most Americans are willing to pay to maintain a free and open society.

Thomas J. Espenshade

See also: Restrictive Legislation (Part I, Sec. 4); Changes in the Law (Part I, Sec. 5); Welfare and Public Benefits (Part II, Sec. 9); Immigration Act of 1990, Illegal Immigration Reform and Immigrant Responsibility Act,

1996, Personal Responsibility and Work Opportunity Reconciliation Act, 1996 (Part IV, Sec. 1).

BIBLIOGRAPHY

Espenshade, T. J. "A Short History of U.S. Policy toward Illegal Immigration." *Population Today* 18:2 (February 1990): 6–9.

———. "Unauthorized Immigration to the United States." *Annual Review of Sociology* 21 (1995): 195–216.

Espenshade, T. J., J. L. Baraka, and G. A. Huber. "Implications of the 1996 Welfare and Immigration Reform Acts for U.S. Immigration." *Population and Development Review* 23:4 (December 1997): 769–801.

Espenshade, T. J., F. D. Bean, T. A. Goodis, and M. J. White. "Immigration Policy in the United States: Future Prospects for the Immigration Reform and Control Act of 1986." In *Population Policy: Contemporary Issues*, ed. Godfrey Roberts, pp. 59–84. New York: Praeger Publishers, 1990.

Fix, M., and J. S. Passel. *Immigration and Immigrants: Setting the Record Straight*. Washington, DC: Urban Institute, 1994.

Immigration and Naturalization Service. *Statistical Yearbook of the Immigration and Naturalization Service, 1997*. Washington, DC: Government Printing Office, 1999.

Warren, Robert. "Estimates of the Undocumented Immigrant Population Residing in the United States: October 1996." Washington, DC: Office of Policy and Planning, Immigration and Naturalization Service, Department of Justice, August 1997.

IMMIGRANT-MINORITY RELATIONS

American national history has been punctuated by surges in immigration, recurrent episodes of ethnic collective conflict, exclusionary movements, and racial violence. The mid-nineteenth-century Know-Nothing movement, the anti-Chinese mobilization of the 1880s, turn-of-the-century nativism, anti-Mexican riots of the 1940s, mid-twentieth-century revitalization of the Ku Klux Klan, attacks on Jewish refugees, Korean-black violence of the 1980s and 1990s, and recent English-only movements are but a few examples of the countless movements targeting immigrants. Indeed, the notion that immigration should spark conflict appears almost natural or inevitable to contemporary observers. And yet the mechanisms by which immigration alters social relations and the conditions under which immigration prompts episodes of collective violence remains largely unexamined in the social scientific literature and thus also largely undertheorized. This review begins to address this gap with a brief discussion of current trends and research on immigrant-minority relations since 1965. Like much of the social scientific literature on immigrant-minority relations, the focus is on collective conflict.

This review highlights two points. First, immigration is critical to understanding patterns of race relations in contemporary America. Historical accounts of American race relations have emphasized the role of long-standing Western conceptions of race, the institution of slavery, or Reconstruction policies. Recent work, however, suggests that immigration and immigration policy are essential for understanding the conflictual nature of twentieth-century urban race relations. This literature views immigration and ethnic relations as interrelated political and economic processes and builds directly upon recent empirical and theoretical insights in the scholarship on racial boundaries, immigration, and collective action. According to this research, patterns of immigration explain where and when racial and ethnic collective violence will be prevalent. Thus this work also calls for a closer relationship between our explanations of immigration and social relations and our interpretations of race relations more broadly.

Second, the relationship between immigration and collective violence is not a straightforward one. Previous research has demonstrated a strong relationship between increases in immigration and rising rates of racial collective action and violence. The period between 1880 and 1930 was one of unprecedented immigration, with more than 28 million new immigrants coming to the United States. It was also a period of well-documented hostility toward these newcomers. Not surprisingly, scholars posited a causal relationship between immigration and group conflict. Yet further investigation of this claim reveals an important paradox. At approximately the same time as these new immigrants were entering the United States, urban collective conflict disproportionately targeted persons of color, not immigrants. In fact, between 1869 and 1924, two-thirds of all collective conflict targeted African Americans. In another study of seventy-six large urban centers in the post-1965 era, simple surges in immigration were found not to be associated with higher rates of racial and ethnic collective violence. Indeed, across the twentieth century, the ethnic diversity of the immigration flow and the skill level of the immigrants are much more reliable predictors of violence than is the simple rate of immigration. Not all immigration, then, poses the same likelihood of conflict. And finally, in related findings, researchers note that while there appear to be discrete moments of inclusion and exclusion in U.S. immigration policy, there are several peaks in the rates of racial and ethnic conflict even within such periods. Again, more people does not automatically mean more problems. Furthermore, merely stemming the flow of immigrants has not abated conflict occasioned by immigration. Thus, understanding the precise conditions under which immigration precipitates racial collective violence has clear implications both for immigration and

A Korean American demands that city authorities help rebuild Koreatown in Los Angeles after many businesses there were destroyed during the riots of May 1992. *(Ted Soqui/Impact Visuals)*

race policy. Perhaps alleviating social unrest is not as simple as implementing new immigration restrictions.

Three sections follow. First is a detailed profile of contemporary immigrant-minority relations since 1965. Second, dominant theoretical perspectives of immigrant-minority relations are critically discussed. And finally, these perspectives are compared in light of contemporary empirical trends in immigrant minority relations.

PATTERNS OF IMMIGRANT-MINORITY RELATIONS SINCE 1965

Anti-immigrant sentiment and collective action have been persistent features of American political life since the early nineteenth century. For centuries, immigrants have been scapegoats for a range of society's ills. In the nineteenth century, for example, immi-

grants were blamed for poor sanitation, lack of health standards, and moral decline. In the contemporary era, immigrants are disparaged for their contributions to environmental degradation and for their cultural incompatibility. Indeed, deep-rooted nativism combined with a generalized fear and mistrust of immigrants has been identified as the key factor in recent federal immigration restrictionism and anti-immigrant legislation at the state level (e.g., English-only initiatives).

Over time, however, the most consistent charge leveled against immigrants is that they take jobs, reduce wages, and destabilize the economy. A 1995 national poll cited by Rita J. Simon and James P. Lynch in "A Comparative Assessment of Public Opinion Toward Immigrants and Immigrant Policy" revealed that 52 percent of the U.S. population felt that immigrants posed a significant "burden," while a 1997 nationwide poll noted that 63 percent of the U.S. population thought immigrants took jobs away from

A furniture store focusing on Spanish-speaking customers (the sign reads: beds, bunk beds) is looted during the 1992 Los Angeles riots. *(Ted Soqui/Impact Visuals)*

Americans and created social friction. Surveys of some minority populations find even higher rates of concern over immigration. A 1992 study of Latinos found that nearly 75 percent agreed immigration levels were too high, though only 17 percent of the foreign-born Mexican population agreed. And while studies suggest that African Americans are less restrictionist than whites in their attitudes toward immigration overall, they do consistently express higher rates of trepidation where jobs and the economy are concerned. Both reflecting and reinforcing these popular worries, most social scientists have made the interplay of immigration, the economy, and collective violence their central focus.

Contemporary immigrant minority relations are shaped by historical patterns of group relations, but the "new" immigration of the post-1965 era appears to be fostering new patterns of social relations. A 1993 national poll cited by Simon and Lynch noted that while almost 59 percent of all Americans see immigration as an important ingredient in the historical development of the United States, a slightly higher number—60 percent—feel that immigration today is highly problematic. Opinions about immigration and collective mobilization against immigration are shifting. What is most striking, however, is that rates of collective violence against immigrants are not actually increasing. Recent patterns of racial and ethnic violence have yet to actually reflect the increasing disquiet about immigration expressed in survey data.

Recent research reveals a particular profile of the relationship between immigration and racial and ethnic collective action. Documenting the nature of this immigrant-minority conflict is essential if discussion about immigration and immigration policy is to move beyond perception and speculation. Furthermore, detailing these changing patterns of immigration and conflict is critical to the development of social theories to predict where and when conflict is likely to occur. An understanding of these patterns is also essential for the development of social policies to abate group tensions. Toward this end, Figure 1 arrays the immigration flow against the level of racial and ethnic col-

Figure 1
Immigration Flows and Racial or Ethnic Collective Conflict in Large American Cities, 1965–1999

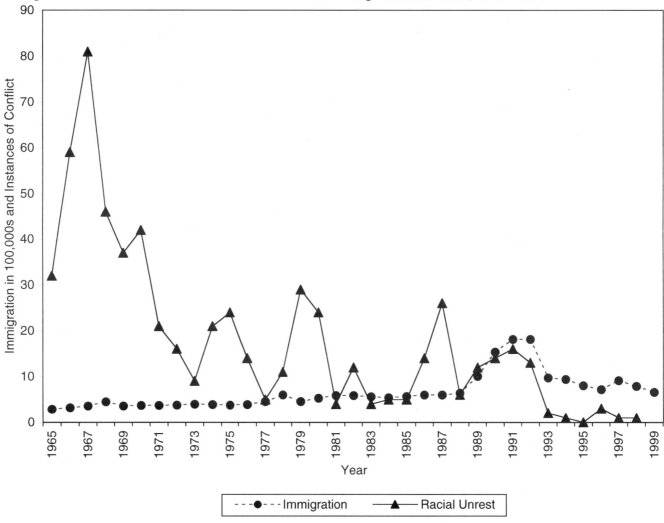

Source: Bureau of the Census. *Historical Statistics of the United States Part 1.* Washington, DC: Bureau of the Census, 1976; Immigration and Naturalization Service. *Immigration Statistical Yearbook.* Washington, DC: Immigration and Naturalization Service, 1975–2000.

lective conflict from 1965 to 1999 in seventy-six large American cities.

For this figure, instances of collective conflict were collected from the daily reports in the *New York Times*. Collective conflict is defined as the public expression of racially or ethnically based grievances against a given ethnic or racial target. Collective action takes a wide variety of forms: rallies, demonstrations, marches, attacks, and riots. It is important to recognize that this definition does not capture the full universe of street actions that involve different race groups, as in the case of interpersonal disputes, murder, or crimes such as muggings, rapes, and other violence where victims and perpetrators are from different race and ethnic group. Further, it does not

include the incredible array of nonviolent social protests that were particularly intense during the civil rights movement of the 1960s. And, of course, given the focus on large cities, events in smaller urban areas as well as rural areas are not part of the sample.

The figure demonstrates both the irregular flow of immigrants to the United States and the consistency of racial or ethnic conflict over this entire period. While mobilization is consistent throughout this period, there is a gradual decline over the observed thirty-five-year period. There are clear sharp peaks in activity observed in the 1960s. But while there is an occasional spike in activity, violence is slowly declining overall. What is most striking is that in contrast to earlier waves of immigration, which corresponded nicely to increases in racial and ethnic collective conflict, in the more recent era the figure tracks a gradual increase in immigration associated with a slow decline in conflict. The dramatic increase in immigration associated with the 1990 Immigration Act is tailed by a modest increase in conflict in the early 1990s, but this increase was short-lived. Thus, while public perceptions stress the relationship between immigration and racial tensions, more immigration clearly does not necessarily signal more violence.

Table 1 provides a more in-depth descriptive overview of racial and ethnic collective action occurring in the same seventy-six cities between 1965 and 1999. Of particular interest are the groups involved in conflict, the regional distribution of this conflict, and the scale of the conflict. Over this period there were 606 instances of collective conflict countrywide. Three critical aspects of collective violence are revealed in this table.

This table first identifies the groups most likely to participate in racial and ethnic collective mobilization. Between 1965 and 1999 the victims of conflict were overwhelmingly of African-American descent, with 471, or 78 percent of all events, involving African Americans. This figure is fairly consistent with figures for the entire twentieth century. As with earlier periods, most racial violence in the United States in this period was between native whites and native blacks. Immigrants were not the dominant perpetrators or victims of contemporary violence. In contrast to African Americans, Asians were least likely to be involved in conflict; less than 1 percent of all events involved persons of Asian descent. This figure stands in sharp contrast to the turn-of-the-century period, when conflict targeting Asians (Chinese and Japanese in particular) accounted for almost one-quarter of all racial and ethnic violence. This finding is significant

given that Asian immigrants benefited most from the 1965 Immigration Act, and that a key beneficiary of the abolition of national origin quotas was the Asian population. In the period after 1965, there is considerable immigration from Asia, and yet much less opposition to such immigration than a century earlier. However, researchers suspect that Asians are not free from nativist conflict and are likely victims of hate crimes and individual attacks. But they are not the common victims of organized collective conflict. The proportion of events involving Jews is about 10 percent, with some fifty-nine events. The number of events involving Latinos account for little of the total collective action, at only about 7 percent, but this figure was on the rise across this period. Finally, evidence reveals that the number of events involving one or more minorities (Asians, blacks, Latinos, or Jews) increased distinctly after 1965. A figure not noted in Table 1 is that between 1965 and 1999, 9.3 percent of all collective conflicts involved multiple minority populations. That is, evidence has begun to suggest that both interminority racial conflicts and cross-racial political and social coalitions are on the rise.

Second, like immigrants themselves, conflict over this period was geographically clustered. The Northeast and in particular New York, where more than 40 percent of first- and second-generation immigrants currently reside, was the most common site of collective action. Almost 60 percent of events occurred in major cities of the Northeast, most in Boston, Philadelphia, New York, and Washington, D.C. But both the Midwest and South had a fair amount of collective conflict as well, with 22 percent and 13 percent, respectively. The large proportion of violence in the Midwest differs from earlier historical periods, when conflict was comparatively rare. Chicago was the dominant site of this violence. Urbanization and black

Table 1
Patterns of Racial and Ethnic Collective Conflict, 1965–1999

Participants		Region		Scale of Conflict	
Blacks	471	Northeast	361	More than 50 Participants	353
Asians	6	South	74	Material/Physical Damage	587
Latinos	43	West	34	Organization Present	127
Jews	59	Midwest	137		
Other Minority	26				
		Total	606		

Source: Bureau of the Census. *Historical Statistics of the United States Part 1.* Washington, DC: Bureau of the Census, 1976; Immigration and Naturalization Service. *Immigration Statistical Yearbook.* Washington, DC: Immigration and Naturalization Service, 1975–2000.

migration are two possible factors for this change. Comparatively little collective conflict was located in the West despite the fact that California is one of the top six states in terms of new immigrants. This is further surprising for two reasons, one historical and one contemporary. First, during earlier waves of migration, the West was a hotbed of collective conflict, particularly anti-Asian conflict. Second, since the high-profile riots of the 1960s and 1990s in Los Angeles, it is commonly assumed that this region is particularly prone to racial tension and violence. Indeed, studies have shown that more than 40 percent of all property damage during the 1992 Los Angeles riots was suffered by Korean store owners. And yet, only 6 percent of all collective conflict occurred in this region. Again, as in earlier historical periods, the Northeast remains a key region for mobilization.

Finally, this table outlines various characteristics of racial and ethnic conflict across this period: the size of events, the level of violence (property damage, physical injury, or death), and the degree of social organization (whether social movement organizations—the National Association for the Advancement of Colored People [NAACP], for example—were present and active participants in the event). Some 60 percent of all events were large-scale and involved more than fifty people. Many of these large-scale conflicts were not well organized, as in only 21 percent of all events were racial, ethnic, or civil rights organizations present. Perhaps most striking is the fact that 97 percent of all such conflicts in the 1965–99 era involved some degree of violence. This profile reveals that while conflict was on the decline overall during this period, if conflict did occur, it was more likely to be large-scale and violent.

Two other features of contemporary immigrant minority relations also bear noting. First, while *collective* violence between immigrant and minority groups may be on the decline, instances of *individual* tensions and hate crimes may well be increasing. And second, instances of interminority conflict are increasing. That is, contemporary immigration politics aren't purely about aliens versus natives. Taken together, these indicators provide what is ultimately a far less conflictual picture of immigrant minority relations than is often depicted in the popular media and bandied about in policy debates. Though violence is present, mounting concerns over immigration flows since the early 1990s have not been met with any sharp increase in anti-immigrant collective action or immigrant-minority collective clashes.

PERSPECTIVES ON GROUP DYNAMICS

Social scientists have for decades tried to make sense of empirical patterns of immigrant minority relations. They offer several related perspectives to understand how immigration affects social relations and in particular why immigration is likely to prompt conflict. These perspectives are circumstantialist; that is, each sees identity-group dynamics as a function of group interest. Racial, ethnic, religious, and linguistic identities (among others) become a source of cohesion and a platform for mobilization. These identities enable groups to pursue their collective interests in competition with other groups. The employment of group difference as a source of solidarity serves, in turn, to further accentuate group difference and the boundaries between groups.

The first two perspectives on immigration and identity mobilization are the *cultural division of labor theory* and the *split labor market theory*. Both see economic hardship as the trigger to collective action. But while the first sees group segregation as key, the second sees integration across groups as pivotal. According to a cultural division of labor perspective, racial and ethnic solidarity is greatest when groups are segregated into subordinate economic positions. Such segregated groups may occupy a low-wage niche in a rigidly structured labor market or may be geographically segregated in an economically underdeveloped area. Group distinctions thrive because economic hardship and identity overlap. From a split labor market perspective, racial and ethnic tensions are most likely when groups receive different wages in the same labor market for the same work. Integration is central here. Wage differentials are maintained by employers to minimize cost and prevent cross-group unionization. When employers can maintain and manipulate a cheap labor supply, intergroup conflict is likely. Immigration has classically provided such a pool of cheap, exploitable labor.

The two other perspectives, *competition theory* and *middleman minority theory*, see economic opportunity as the more likely catalyst of violence. The central contention of competition theory is that racial and ethnic identities become a basis of collective action when different groups come into contact to compete for limited roles, resources, and opportunities. Thus, like split labor market theory, the interaction of distinct racial and ethnic communities is vital. When distinct identity groups compete for jobs, housing, political power, or social status, the likelihood of conflict increases. Competition theories of race relations build upon sociologist Fredrik Barth's insight that displacement and exclusion are generated by competition. They assume that initial overlap of habitats intensifies competition among groups, which in turn encourages attempts by the historically more powerful or advantaged groups to exclude the competitors. When the less powerful resist these attempts, racial conflict and violence ensue.

The middleman minority theory, also known as the ethnic enclave perspective, tends to focus on the behaviors of particular immigrant groups and how certain groups are able to carve out a niche for themselves within the broader economy, usually via entrepreneurial enterprise. Middleman minority perspectives were first developed to understand the contentious socioeconomic role played by immigrant groups such as Jews in Europe, Chinese in Southeast Asia, and Indians in Africa. According to this perspective, when social systems are rigidly stratified between elites and masses, a third, immigrant group often emerges to trade and mediate between the two. As a consequence, this third group often incurs hostility from above and below. Korean shop owners, who frequently find themselves isolated from white business owners and distrusted by African-American customers and employees, are cited as a contemporary example. Enclave entrepreneurs may follow a similar route but tend to develop dense networks of small businesses to serve and employ their fellow immigrants. In areas where immigrant populations are less dense, entrepreneurial immigrants might act as middlemen minorities serving low-income areas. In either case, these communities are a potential source of conflict. In the case of ethnic enclaves, their economic success may threaten dominant groups within the economy, and when acting as middlemen minorities, immigrants may frustrate economically disadvantaged (often minority) populations. Social isolation—either within the enclave or because of stigmatized middleman status—promotes further social cohesion among these groups or increases the likelihood of their own mobilization.

Like the popular debate on immigration, emphasis in each of these perspectives tends to highlight labor market dynamics and the effect of immigration on the economy more generally. Immigration creates economic rivalries, and such rivalries are inherently volatile. However, political and cultural interests can be equally contentious. Cultural politics may well overlap with more narrowly defined economic interests. The structure and organization of labor markets is at once both political and socioeconomic.

Indeed, recent research suggests, social boundaries and the tensions they potentially engender are predominantly a product of social policies. From this perspective, racial and ethnic social mobilization constitutes a reaction to state (and elite) articulation and manipulation of boundaries. Historical analysis of race relations in the United States reveals how intergroup tensions were resolved by state actions that used racial loyalties as instruments for subduing potentially divisive forces.

As a set, these perspectives offer rather different predictions regarding the effects of immigration. From the perspective of either the cultural division of labor approach or the split labor market theory, the economic disadvantages and relative deprivation experienced by immigrant groups is likely to create solidarity among these groups. This solidarity, in turn, has consequences for social relations as formerly disadvantaged populations fight for greater opportunity. In both theories, immigrants and their experience determine the context of social relations. In contrast, in both a competition perspective and a middleman/enclave theory, it is the very opportunities immigrants experience relative to majority and minority populations that create tension. These perspectives suggest that the relative success of immigrants can be very volatile. Here one might speculate that native minority populations, feeling squeezed in labor market competition, would initiate collective action against immigrants. All four perspectives would be likely to predict a higher rate of immigrant-minority collective conflict than there is current evidence for.

CONSEQUENCES OF IMMIGRATION

Urban race relations are defined by the nature of immigrant minority relations, and yet there is little evidence that explicit, organized collective action and violence typify this relationship. Perhaps the popular and largely taken for granted belief in the pernicious effects of immigration is misplaced. Indeed, recent research demonstrates that in the narrow arena of collective action, immigration may not promote violence against immigrants. Together with other evidence questioning the effects of immigration on the economy and wage rates of both majority and minority populations, this new evidence should prompt some serious reflection. Certainly there is no evidence that immigrant minority relations are amiable, but perhaps our classic models for understanding these dynamics need rethinking, particularly if they center on economic competition at the group level.

In the effort to understand the contemporary impact of immigration flows on immigrant minority relations, social scientists may be looking in the wrong place, both empirically and theoretically. And perhaps this disjuncture between conflict and perception may provide a starting point for new thought. It seems sure that individuals will continue to cling to negative perceptions of immigration and stereotypes of immigrants. Maybe immigrant-minority relations are best reflected in this individual-level tension. While collective discontent and action characterized turn-of-the-century responses to increased immigration, contemporary reactions may well be more individualized. We may see not large-scale social clashes, but rather more frequent day-to-day friction between individual members of minority and immigrant groups.

Suzanne Shanahan

See also: Anti-Immigrant Backlash (Part I, Sec. 5); Anti-Immigrant Politics, Public Opinion and Immigration (Part II, Sec. 6).

BIBLIOGRAPHY

Alba, Richard D., and Victor Nee. "Rethinking Assimilation Theory for a New Era of Immigration." *International Migration Review* 31 (1997): 826–974.

Barth, Fredrik, ed. *Ethnic Groups and Boundaries: The Social Organization of Cultural Difference.* Boston: Little, Brown, 1969.

Bonacich, Edna. "Advance Capitalism and Black/White Race Relations in the United States: A Split Labor Market Interpretation." *American Sociological Review* 38 (1976): 583–94.

Cummings, Scott, and Thomas Lambert. "Immigration Restrictions and the American Worker: An Examination of Competing Interpretations." *Population Research and Policy Review* 17 (1998): 497–520.

Diamond, Jeff. "African American Attitudes Towards United States Immigration Policy." *International Migration Review* 32 (1998): 451–70.

Dinnerstein, Leonard, Roger L. Nichols, and David M. Reimers. *Natives and Strangers: A Multicultural History of Americans.* New York: Oxford University Press, 1997.

Freidreis, John, and Raymond Tatalovich. "Who Supports English Only Laws? Evidence from the 1992 National Election Survey." *Social Science Quarterly* 78 (1977): 354–68.

Gans, Herbert J. "Toward a Reconciliation of 'Assimilation' and 'Pluralism': The Interplay of Acculturation and Ethnic Retention." *International Migration Review* 32 (1997): 893–922.

Garza, Rodolfo O., de la, and Louis De Spiro. "Interests, Not Passions." *International Migration Review* 32 (1998): 401–22.

Jacobson, Matthew Frye. *Whiteness of a Different Color: European Immigrants and the Alchemy of Race.* Cambridge, MA: Harvard University Press, 1998.

Marx, Anthony W. *Making Race and Nation.* New York: Cambridge University Press, 1998.

Min, Pyong Gap. *Caught in the Middle: Korean Communities in New York and Los Angeles.* Berkeley: University of California Press, 1996.

Model, Suzanne. "The Economic Progress of Europeans and East Asian Americans." *Annual Review of Sociology* 14 (1993): 363–80.

Olzak, Susan. *The Dynamics of Ethnic Competition and Conflict.* Stanford, CA: Stanford University Press, 1992.

Shanahan, Suzanne, and Susan Olzak. "The Effects of Immigrant Diversity and Ethnic Competition on Collective Conflict in Urban America." *Journal of American Ethnic History* 18 (1999): 40–64.

Simcox, David. "Major Predictors of Immigration Restrictionism: Operationalizing 'Nativism.'" *Population and Environment* 19 (1997): 129–43.

Simon, Rita J., and James P. Lynch. "A Comparative Assessment of Public Opinion Toward Immigrants and Immigration Policy." *International Migration Review* 33 (1999): 455–67.

Waldinger, Roger. *Still the Promised City? African-Americans and New Immigrants in Postindustrial New York.* Cambridge, MA: Harvard University Press, 1996.

Wilson, William Julius. *The Declining Significance of Race: Blacks and Changing American Institutions.* Chicago: University of Chicago Press, 1978.

ANTI-IMMIGRANT BACKLASH

The term "anti-immigrant" denotes hostility toward immigrants and aspiring immigrants, the dislike of foreigners, and efforts to reduce the rights of immigrants. It not only describes efforts to reduce immigration levels but also evaluates them as inappropriate or misplaced. Thus, to minimize partiality, individuals and organizations proposing lower immigration levels are called "restrictionists," whereas those seeking to maintain or increase immigration levels are termed "expansionists." Under any set of labels, however, the differences between the two sides intensified after 1965, as restrictionists aggressively tried to reduce the flow of the "new immigration."

RESTRICTIONIST ROOTS

Congress replaced the national origins quotas in 1965 with a system of preferences for family unification and employment. For the first time in American history, Congress applied numerical limitations to admissions from the Western Hemisphere and, in the visa queue, placed applicants with special job skills behind the unmarried, adult children of U.S. citizens and permanent resident aliens. The family reunification provisions increased legal immigration by permitting immediate family members to enter outside of numerical quotas, while the hemispheric ceilings and termination of the bracero program, which allowed Mexican contract laborers to work in specific U.S. industries, diverted aspiring immigrants (particularly Mexicans) toward illegal modes of entry. The increases in legal and illegal immigration took legislators and the American public by surprise.

Americans generally disliked the unexpected turn toward expansion. Between 1946 and 1993, pollsters repeatedly asked Americans if immigration should be increased, decreased, or kept at its present level. Results varied, but at no time did a majority of citizens favor an increase in immigration. The percentage of those favoring a decrease in immigration doubled from 33 percent in 1965 to 66 percent in 1982 but eased to 61 percent by 1993. Increases in legal and illegal immigration, negative perceptions of the impact of immigrants, and a growing isolationism probably pushed the percentages up. In addition, a growing group of restrictionist organizations contributed to America's dim view of immigration.

John Tanton, a Michigan ophthalmologist, led the drive to restrict immigration. As president of Zero Population Growth (ZPG) between 1975 and 1977, Tanton urged ZPG members to consider immigration restriction a prerequisite for curbing U.S. population growth. When they refused to support immigration reductions, Tanton secured some seed money and committed leaders to form the Federation for American Immigration Reform (FAIR) in 1979. The federation garnered public support through direct mail campaigns and secured small successes on Capitol Hill with its lobbying efforts.

Other organizations quickly followed in the footsteps of FAIR and Negative Population Growth (another anti-immigration organization which had been around since 1972). In 1983, Tanton asked the FAIR board and staff to broaden their agenda to include cultural division and bilingualism. They declined the offer but helped the Center for Immigration Studies (CIS), a think tank with restrictionist leanings, get off the ground in 1986. In that same year, the Environment Fund changed its name to the Population-Environment Balance to illuminate better the connections between immigration, overpopulation, and environmental degradation. The Carrying Capacity Network also entered the restrictionist camp when it committed itself to a similar set of objectives in 1989.

The American Immigration Control Foundation (AICF) waded into the immigration debate in 1983 by offering the public a wide range of criticisms, including a medley of cultural arguments against immigra-

While most nativist-inclined Americans express their anti-immigrant feelings at the ballot box, some ranchers along the Arizona-Mexico border take a more direct—and violent—approach to illegal immigration. *(Jack Kurtz, Impact Visuals)*

tion. But Tanton wanted to devote more time and money to the bilingualism issue in particular. In 1979, he established U.S. Inc. to serve as an organizational umbrella for projects pertaining to overpopulation, immigration, and the environment. Its first project, U.S. English, not only launched the Official English movement but also brought the internal workings of the restrictionist movement into full view.

OFFICIAL ENGLISH MOVEMENT

In 1983, Tanton and the late senator Samuel Ichiye Hayakawa (R-CA) launched U.S. English to place official bilingualism on the political table. Although an antibilingual ordinance had already been approved in Dade County, Florida, in 1980 and other official language laws had been passed in several states before 1980, the organized and well-financed U.S. English immeasurably contributed to what became known as the English Only or Official English movement. Between 1981 and 1990, ten southern and midwestern states established English as their official language, and by 1997, twenty-two states had designated English as their official language.

Expansionists questioned the motives of U.S. English and other related groups because of their association with restrictionist organizations. The same foundation that supports U.S. English—the Laurel Foundation—also subsidizes the work of U.S. Inc., Population-Environment Balance, and FAIR. The connection attracted little mention until the late 1980s and early 1990s, when the *Los Angeles Times* revealed that FAIR had received $1.1 million over a ten-year period from the Pioneer Fund, an intelligence organization that funds research on eugenics and the comparative intelligence quotients of different races. Tanton denied any knowledge of the group's eugenics agenda, but a 1986 memorandum to participants of an upcoming Witan meeting (a forum where prominent restrictionists met to discuss matters of culture, language, immigration, and population; the name is short for Witenagemot, a group of advisers to medieval kings of England) confirmed expansionist suspicions of impropriety.

The memo became public in 1988 when the newspaper *Arizona Republic* published portions of it shortly before Arizona voters approved the Official English initiative. Tanton contemplated the demographic future of California in his memo, speculating that an apartheid-like situation could emerge by 2030, with blacks and Hispanics at the low end of the socioeconomic ladder and non-Hispanic whites and Asians near the high end. He questioned the assumption that diversity implies strength, reflected on relations between blacks and Hispanics, and mused that the political power of whites might eventually be weakened by the higher fertility rates of immigrants. Tanton later explained that the memo was written for "a group of people who were already initiated into immigration, population, and language issues," but he nonetheless decided to resign from U.S. English before the excerpts were published, "in hopes that the crest of the controversy would pass by election day."

LEGISLATION

The controversies over Tanton's memo and the federation's funding apparently had little impact on the resolve of restrictionist organizations. They capitalized on multiple opportunities to criticize immigration and even created a few opportunities of their own. One such opportunity arose before the controversies when 125,000 Cubans arrived in the United States in 1980 and 1981. Precipitated by a three-way dispute between the United States, Cuba, and Peru—and Castro's declaration that people could leave as long as they went straight to the States—thousands of Cuban émigrés violated U.S. law by chartering boats in Miami and traveling ninety miles to Cuba's Mariel Harbor to pick up the exiles. The press and the media—in such films as Brian De Palma's *Scarface*—highlighted the criminal element among this population of immigrants.

Like the Mariel incident, the results of the 1986 Immigration Reform and Control Act (IRCA) pointed up a sizable gap between immigration policy and the realities of immigration. Although IRCA was restrictionist in intent, the status of nearly 3 million formerly undocumented immigrants was legalized, and the law did little to stop the flow of illegal aliens. Accusations that settled immigrants were "unassimilable," stealing jobs from U.S. citizens, and weakening the economy through their use of social services helped to lock in the legislation.

In early 1991, a number of actions taken in the Midwest resembled those taken by the public and the U.S. government during the First and Second World Wars. Arab Americans were the target of numerous hate crimes during the Persian Gulf War, including physical assaults, two bombings of Arab-American–owned grocery stores in Cincinnati, and a bomb threat to a Detroit-area high school where students of Arab descent constituted almost half the student body. In addition, Federal Bureau of Investigation (FBI) agents questioned hundreds of Arab Americans in the Detroit area and throughout the country about their political views and knowledge of potential terrorists.

On November 8, 1994, voters in California passed Proposition 187 by a margin of 59 percent to 41 percent; this initiative was designed to exclude all illegal aliens from tax-supported benefits, such as public education and welfare. Exit polls revealed that only 31 percent of Latino voters supported the measure but that the majority of whites (64 percent), Asians (57 percent), and blacks (56 percent) voted in its favor. Although some sections of the proposition were immediately challenged in court, a dozen other states were not dissuaded from considering similar measures. The Save Our State initiative developed in a context of rapidly increasing nonwhite immigration to the state and a prolonged recession, but few of the proposition's provisions actually addressed assimilation or employment. Instead, the measure essentially tried to prevent undocumented immigrants from using institutions that help consolidate settlement (such as public education and social services).

The publication of Peter Brimelow's *Alien Nation* in 1995 spread the seeds of Proposition 187 across the country. Recommended for serious consideration by some reviewers, the book secured newspaper headlines and television appearances for the author. One of Brimelow's suggestions—that United States–born children of unauthorized residents be denied automatic citizenship—was even adopted as part of the 1996 Republican platform. (Because of the Fourteenth Amendment's guarantee of citizenship to any person born or naturalized in the United States, such a measure would have necessitated a constitutional amendment.) Although it had been introduced to Congress prior to the Republican convention, the plank was apparently too controversial for presidential politics, as the recommendation was later repudiated by Bob Dole, the Republican candidate for president.

Controversy did not end with the proposal, however, as Congress enacted immigration law in 1996. It enacted antiterrorism and welfare reform legislation in April and August, respectively. The laws included provisions concerned specifically with noncitizens, but in September, Congress enacted the expansive Illegal Immigration Reform and Immigrant Responsibility Act. This law largely dealt with illegal immigration but also addressed—among other issues—asylum adjudication, crime, and judicial review of immigration appeals. Many of the provisions were considered fair, although expansionists considered portions of the bill unduly harsh, especially those pertaining to deportation.

Brian N. Fry

See also: Nativism and Know-Nothings, Chinese and Chinese Exclusion Act (Part I, Sec. 2); Anti-Immigrant Politics, Public Opinion and Immigration (Part II, Sec. 6); Immigration Reform and Control Act, 1986, Immigration Act of 1990, Illegal Immigration Reform and Immigrant Responsibility Act, 1996, Personal Responsibility and Work Opportunity Reconciliation Act, 1996, California Proposition 187, 1994, California Proposition 227, 1998 (Part IV, Sec. 1).

BIBLIOGRAPHY

Brimelow, Peter. *Alien Nation: Common Sense about America's Immigration Disaster*. New York: Random House, 1996.

Brown, Mary E. *Shapers of the Great Debate on Immigration: A Biographical Dictionary*. Westport, CT: Greenwood Press, 1999.

Cook, Christopher. "U.S. Arabs Assess Damage on Themselves: Many Feel Wounded, Torn by Their Loyalties." *Detroit Free Press*, January 25, 1991, p. 12A.

Crawford, James. *Hold Your Tongue: Bilingualism and the Politics of "English Only."* Reading, MA: Addison-Wesley, 1992.

Daniels, Roger. *Coming to America: A History of Immigration and Ethnicity in American Life*. New York: Harper Collins, 1990.

Delgado, Richard. "Citizenship." In *Immigrants Out! The New Nativism and the Anti-Immigrant Impulse in the United States*, ed. Juan F. Perea, 318–23. New York: New York University Press, 1997.

Edmonds, Patricia. "Hate Crimes Grow: Arab Americans Say the Rate Has Jumped since War Began." *Detroit Free Press*, February 7, 1991, 3A.

Edmonds, Patricia. "FBI Is Accused of 'Hunting' Arab Americans." *Detroit Free Press*, January 24, 1991, p. 8A.

Espenshade, T. J., and Katherine Hempstead. "Contemporary American Attitudes toward U.S. Immigration." *International Migration Review* 30 (1996): 535–70.

Federation for American Immigration Reform. "A Skirmish in a Wider War: An Oral History of John H. Tanton, Founder of FAIR, the Federation for American Immigration Reform." In *Tenth Anniversary Oral History Project of the Federation for American Immigration Reform*. Washington, DC: Federation for American Immigration Reform, 1989.

Gimpel, James G., and James R. Edwards Jr. *The Congressional Politics of Immigration Reform*. Boston: Allyn and Bacon, 1999.

Hondagneu-Sotelo, Pierrette. *Gendered Transitions: Mexican Experiences of Immigration*. Berkeley: University of California Press, 1994.

———. "Women and Children First: New Directions in Anti-immigrant Politics." *Socialist Review* 25 (1995): 169–90.

Martin, Philip. "Proposition 187 in California." *International Migration Review* 29 (1995): 255–63.

Pedraza, Silvia. "Origins and Destinies: Immigration, Race, and Ethnicity in American History." In *Origins and Destinies: Immigration, Race, and Ethnicity in America*, ed. Silvia Pedraza and Rubén G. Rumbaut, pp. 1–20. Belmont, CA: Wadsworth, 1996.

Reimers, David M. *Unwelcome Strangers: American Identity and the Turn against Immigration*. New York: Columbia University Press, 1998.

Romo, Ricardo. "Mexican Americans: Their Civic and Political Incorporation." In *Origins and Destinies: Immigration, Race, and Ethnicity in America*, ed. Silvia Pedraza and Rubén G. Rumbaut, pp. 84–97. Belmont, CA: Wadsworth, 1996.

Rumbaut, Rubén G. "Origins and Destinies: Immigration to the United States since World War II." *Sociological Forum* 9 (1994): 583–621.

Simon, Rita J., and J. P. Lynch. "A Comparative Assessment of Public Opinion toward Immigrants and Immigration Policies." *International Migration Review* 33 (1999): 455–67.

Stefancic, Jean. "Funding the Nativist Agenda." In *Immigrants Out! The New Nativism and the Anti-immigrant Impulse in the United States*, ed. Juan F. Perea, 119–35. New York: New York University Press, 1997.

Tatalovich, Raymond. "Official English as Nativist Backlash." In *Immigrants Out! The New Nativism and the Anti-immigrant Impulse in the United States*, ed. Juan F. Perea, pp. 78–102. New York: New York University Press, 1997.

Ueda, Reed. *Postwar Immigrant America: A Social History*. Boston: Bedford Books of St. Martin's Press, 1994.

IMMIGRATION ISSUES

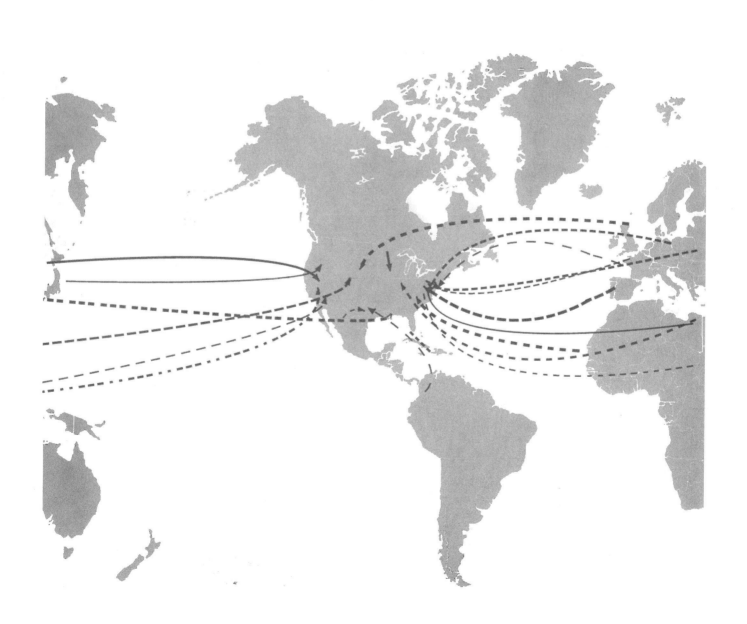

INTRODUCTION

Part II of the *Encyclopedia of American Immigration* is devoted to issues of contemporary immigration and the contemporary immigrant experience. While many of the entries include historical surveys of the subject they are covering, they largely focus on the present, defined here as the 35-plus years since the passage of the landmark Immigration and Nationality Act of 1965. That law ended over four decades of quotas and opened up America to immigrants from around the world in numbers equivalent—in absolute terms—to the great peak of immigration at the turn of the twentieth century.

This second part of the encyclopedia is divided into thirteen sections. Section 1 deals with causes, the push-and-pull factors that lead people to come to the United States. The second section explores the processes by which immigrants come to America. It includes issues of legal and illegal means of entry, the government agencies responsible for immigration and naturalization (as well as the nongovernmental organizations that help immigrants), and entries on the theories of immigration. There is also an entry on American emigration abroad.

Section 3 focuses on immigrant demographics—who they are and where they live, among other things. In Section 4, the entries explore the subject of immigrant incorporation and acculturation. These new and more subtle terms have replaced the old catchall word "assimilation" and are meant to capture the complex way in which newcomers to American shores create new identities based on the old and new.

Section 5 examines the legal issues surrounding immigration, including laws dealing with the immigration process itself as well as laws that impact on immigrants once they are in America. In addition, this section addresses civil rights and crime and the ways these phenomena affect immigrants. In Section 6, the entries explore immigrants, immigration, and politics. They provide a look at both sides of the question—how immigrants become involved in American (and their home country) politics and how politics affects immigrants and immigration.

The next two sections are concerned with the economy. Section 7 is devoted to immigrant economics, including business, wealth and poverty issues, income, investment, taxation, and consumption. In Section 8, the entries focus on labor issues. They are divided into those devoted to the role of immigrants in various sectors of the labor force, including factory work, agriculture, the professions, and services. In addition, entries cover immigrants and labor markets, unemployment, and unions.

The entries in Section 9 deal with health, education, and welfare issues. Section 10 concerns immigrant culture and society, as well as the role of immigrants in American culture and society. Topics range from the so-called fine arts—such as literature, the performing arts, and the visual arts—to the popular arts, media and pastimes like newspapers and magazines, television, film, radio, spectator sports, and food and dress. In addition, the entries in this section examine the issue of language and the acquisition of English. Finally, there is an entry on the hobby of genealogy.

Section 11 covers a relatively new field of immigrant studies—religion. The entries in this section examine how the various religions practiced by immigrants affect their experiences in America and how the arrival of new immigrants impacts the existing religions here in the United States. Section 12 covers destinations. The ten entries here examine seven key urban destinations for immigrants. In addition, individual entries concern immigrants and suburbia, immigrants in rural America, and immigrants in the border region of the American Southwest, an area often referred to as Mex-America.

Finally, Section 13 offers an international perspective, to help put the American immigrant experience in a larger context. This section is divided into two subsections. The first focuses on questions of immigration and the global economy, immigration and international law, and immigration and world politics. The entries in the second subsection provide a portrait of immigration to and the immigrant experience in other key destination countries and regions around the globe, including Australia, Canada, Israel, Latin America, and Western Europe. There is also an entry on Japan, a major industrial nation noted for its resistance to immigration.

America is undergoing a dramatic demographic change. By about 2005, it is expected that California—the most populous state and a bellwether for national trends—will become the first state in the country with a majority nonwhite population. That is to say, people of African, Hispanic, Asian, and Pacific Island backgrounds will outnumber those with European ancestry. If current trends continue, it is possible that America will experience the same demographic milestone around the midway point of the twenty-first century. The percentage of foreign-born persons living in the United States is creeping up to the all-time high that was reached in the years immediately preceding World War I.

The implications for American politics, culture, society, and economics are immense. Ever since the Alien Act of 1798, immigrants have played a major role—both as object and subject—in American politics, a role that involves the newcomer both as a political issue and a potential voting bloc. The immigrant as object of American politics has followed a familiar pattern throughout history: periods of expanded immigration—usually involving new groups who are viewed as unassimilable—lead to political reactions by nativists and, sometimes, restrictive legislation. This was the case in the late nineteenth century with Chinese immigration and with the turn-of-the-twentieth century flood of immigrants from southern and eastern Europe. In more recent years, the same pattern emerged, even if the legislation that resulted was not quite as restrictive as in earlier eras. That is to say, the massive growth of immigrants from Asia and the Americas produced a political backlash that was felt in the 1986 Immigration Reform and Control Act and the 1996 Illegal Immigration Reform and Immigrant Responsibility Act—the latter including restrictions on immigrant access to social services. In addition, there were numerous state referenda designed to limit social services to immigrants and to end the use of bilingual instruction in public schools.

As subjects, immigrants have been a critical part in America's political order, with ethnic voting blocs playing an important part in elections since at least the mid-nineteenth century. In the twentieth century, Franklin Delano Roosevelt and the Democratic Party were able to build a successful coalition of white ethnic voters in the 1930s that held together through the 1960s and, arguably, beyond. The impact of the vast wave of post-1965 reform law immigrants from Asia and the Americas has taken several decades to make its force felt in electoral politics. During the 1980s, Republicans often used illegal immigration as a wedge issue, blaming everything from unemployment to crime to the growth of welfare rolls on the new immigrants. By the late 1990s—and particularly in the wake of the Democratic sweep of California state government—Republicans began to recognize that immigrants were a key constituency of voters, rather than merely a way to galvanize white, middle-class voters. The nomination of Texas governor George W. Bush as the Republicans' presidential candidate—with his reputation for having solid support in the Latino community—indicates that the party has finally realized that it cannot win the presidency or even dominate national politics unless it can reach out to the immigrant community.

The role that immigrants and immigration have played in the nation's economic development has been, if anything, even more profound than their place in the nation's politics. In the final analysis, of course, immigrants built this country, with their role in economic development as critical as the resources of the land on which America was founded. Nevertheless, a debate has emerged in recent decades—echoing a longstanding one that goes back at least to the mid-nineteenth century—over whether immigrants, particularly illegal immigrants, provide a net gain to or drain on the economy. On one side, arguments have been made that immigrants take more in social services than they contribute in taxes or that they generate a downward effect on wages. Yet most of the empirical evidence gathered by governmental and reputable nongovernmental sources—studies noted in the entries for Section 7, "Economics," and Section 8, "Labor"—points in the opposite direction: Immigrants contribute more to than they take from government coffers, and they usually occupy low-paid positions scorned by native-born Americans.

The massive wave of immigration from around the world in recent decades is also having a most fundamental impact on American society and culture, one felt in small ways as well as large. Even as salsa has replaced ketchup as the country's best-selling table condiment, so the influx of Hispanics (and Asians) has deeply complicated America's ongoing struggle over race and national identity. The rise of Hispanic chic—as well as advertisers' attempt to reach out to this burgeoning community—in recent years is a measure of immigration's growing demographic weight. Indeed, it is estimated that by the census of 2010, America's Hispanic population will outstrip African Americans as the nation's largest minority. While Asians lag behind, there can be little doubt that as their numbers grow, so too will their cultural and social impact.

CAUSES

INTRODUCTION

Section 1 of Part II of the *Encyclopedia of American Immigration* is devoted to entries dealing with the causes of immigration. Of the seven entries in this section, two "America's Image in the Global Imagination" and "Economics I: Pull Factors"—focus on the so-called pull of the United States. Four of the remaining entries "Economics II: Push Factors," "Natural Disasters, Environmental Crises, and Overpopulation," "Political, Ethnic, Religious, and Gender Persecution," and "Wars and Civil Unrest" are concerned with the "push factors" behind immigration. And one entry deals with the phenomenon of chain migration, whereby related groups of people immigrate to the United States.

David Jacobson and Carolyn Forbes's entry "America's Image in the Global Imagination" begins with a history of how America has been seen by the rest of the world and how that vision has led people to come to the United States. After covering the early colonial era, the authors explore the way the American Revolution changed perceptions of the country. Next, Jacobson and Forbes examine how America came to be viewed as it rose to world power status. The final subsection of the entry focuses on how America is perceived in the current era of globalization.

In "Chain Migration," Steven S. Zahniser focuses on how that term came to be used by researchers in discussing how a single initial immigrant can set off a chain of immigrants from his or her family or community. He also uses the 1999–2000 case of the family of Elián Gonzalez to illustrate the process in action. Zahniser then proceeds to discuss how chain migration plays into the immigration decision and how it eventually affects immigrant employment in the United States. The author also examines how "daughter" communities—that is, re-creations of home-country communities in the United States—occur and how chain migration affects mental health among immigrants. Finally, he examines the legalities of chain migration.

In "Economics I: Pull Factors" and "Economics II:

Push Factors," P. Rudy Mattei and Saskia Sassen, respectively, examine how the forces of globalization are leading to mass immigration from around the world to the United States. In "Natural Disasters, Environmental Crises, and Overpopulation," Martha Donkor begins with an examination of how natural disasters, environmental crises, and overpopulation interconnect in the immigrant's native country. She then goes on to explore what communities and classes of people are more affected by these kinds of disasters and crises. She poses the question of classification—are people who are affected by natural disaster migrants or refugees? She then goes on to look at U.S. policy on such migrants and how such migrants fit into the overall immigration profile.

In "Political, Ethnic, Religious, and Gender Persecution," John Herschel Barnhill begins by considering the persecution as a cause of immigration in the period leading up to World War II. He then moves to a discussion of the Jewish refugee crisis of World War II. He goes on to examine the way in which America dealt with post–World War II refugees. Next, he offers a lengthy discussion of the post-1965 reform act era and its effect on people fleeing persecution in their homelands, focusing on several key groups: Cubans, Haitians, Latin Americans, and Southeast Asians. Finally, Barnhill closes with a look at a more recent source of persecution-related immigration: women and girls seeking refuge from the practice of female genital mutilation.

Finally, in "Wars and Civil Unrest," Frances G. Sternberg first discusses war-related immigration in the eighteenth and nineteenth centuries. She then examines the subject in both the pre– and post–World War II eras of the twentieth century, before turning to the post-1965 immigration reform era. Finally, she offers an accounting of war-related immigration to the United States by country, including refugees from the Korean War, the Soviet invasion of Hungary in 1956, the Cuban revolution, wars in Southeast Asia, conflict in Central America, and the war in the Balkans.

AMERICA'S IMAGE IN THE GLOBAL IMAGINATION

America, as a self-contained national entity, was first conceived by immigrants. But the understanding that early immigrants had of America, as well as the images and possibilities they foresaw, grew out of a long process of historical invention that began in the fifteenth century, not from the "discovery of America" by Christopher Columbus in 1492 but by the meanings attached to the slowly dawning realization that what Columbus had come across was, to Europeans, a huge, unexpected, and unknown landmass in the middle of the ocean somewhere between Spain and the east coast of Asia. The problem with discovering America as a separate and unique continent, as a "new world," was that it would place its discoverer in a heretical position to the Catholic Church's view of the geographic limits of the known world.

WHEN "AMERICA" WAS FIRST IMAGINED

As it happened, the discovery that this landmass was something separate and distinct from what had been known about the world took fifteen years of exploration and mapping before it was fully realized. The act of classifying this land as a continent and the naming of it "America" set off a profound revolution of thought in Europe, a revolution that enabled Europeans to turn their attention from the next world to this one. America very quickly became the screen on which these dreams and fantasies were projected. Intriguingly, Columbus was convinced until the day he died that what he had set foot on was Asia. Columbus's intransigence, despite all evidence to the contrary, marks a decisive feature of America's image in the world: it is almost always imagined to be something it is not. Because America's image is so laden with mythology and idealism, it seldom lives up to

these standards. Thus hope often gives way to disillusionment.

The global imagination that gave rise to the idea of America was decidedly Christian and European. The images that emerged from the European theological and philosophical attempt to come to terms with the discovery of this large, unexpected land continue to animate contemporary images of America. Notions of America as the land of opportunity, a paradise of untold wealth, the land of freedom, an Eden, a new world, as young and vibrant and open—all were born out of the theological, ideological, and philosophical ideas convulsing Europe at the time of Columbus's voyage and the century that followed.

A NEW NATION IMAGINED: PURITAN ROOTS

America had to be imagined before it could be seen. The Puritans were among the first to imagine America, not as a colony, not as an expansion of a European or British enterprise, but as the wilderness, the landscape in which humankind would be reborn. In America, men and women would, as God's stewards, begin anew. In America, the Protestant Reformation, which began in the early 1500s, would be completed in an apocalyptic climax. In America, politics would become the handmaiden of a godly mission, in which civic activities were a collective calling. The land had been "spied" by God, a "promised land" for a "chosen people" with a revolutionary political and civic vision. The synthesis of land, people, and civic politics would contribute greatly to the emerging idea of the modern nation-state and channel the course of history not only of America but of the world as well.

The roots of America as an idea lie in the Protestant Reformation itself, by way of its initial success, then failure, in England, and in the "discovery" of the

The immense draw of American movies and culture is evidenced in a Shanghai, China, department store by this poster of Arnold Schwarzenegger, himself an immigrant to the United States from Austria. *(Dan Habib/Impact Visuals)*

"New World" as the place where redemption would be found far from the now corrupt England. As the scholar of Puritanism Avihu Zakai wrote, the "Protestant Reformation was situated at the end of time and history, as an eschatological event preceding that moment when the whole mystery of providential history was to be resolved." Under Protestantism, England, Holland, and other Protestant countries became the Holy Land, the New Israel, driving forward history and time. They each viewed themselves (often in tandem with other Protestant peoples) as having this providential role. The land and history, as well as the people, became intertwined. For the Puritans, England was this "new Jerusalem."

But only for a period of time. For the Protestant "purists," the English failed the Reformation. In its first two hundred years in England, Protestantism was often on the defensive and in control only through bloody suppression. Mary Tudor beat back Protestant gains from Henry VIII to Edward VI, having some notable Protestants executed, while others fled into exile. With her ascension to the throne in

1558, Elizabeth sought a middle road politically—a path of compromise that was to become the hallmark of English politics—between Catholicism and the "purist" Protestants (who would receive the name "Puritans" only in the 1560s). The Elizabethan settlement was a difficult—indeed, impossible—compromise for the Puritans, as it represented for them a reversal of history, a step back from the rush onward to the apocalypse, and a betrayal of England's sacred and providential role. The very symbols and ritual that the Church of England inherited from Catholicism was an affront to the purists' desire to rid the church of "papist" corruption, dogma, and ritual. The elaborate stained glass windows, statues, and crucifixes symbolized the mediative and hierarchical role of the Catholic Church, in contrast to the austere Calvinist churches, where nothing came before man and his God. In the wake of the Elizabethan compromise, Puritans began to organize, to agitate, and to reignite the Reformation. In this context, England was desacralized, stripped of her providential role; more than that, England had strayed into the path of Satan.

Arguably the most recognizable brand name in the world, a Coca-Cola sign is akin to an American flag for many of the world's people.
(Alexandra Pais/Impact Visuals)

In the early 1600s, Anglican settlements in Virginia, when imbued with religious purpose, were viewed as the expansion of elect England in her glorious, providential role in salvation. Many Puritans, on the other hand, were now (by the early seventeenth century) so deeply alienated from the Anglican Church, or the Church of England, as to view it as the Antichrist. They saw America as God's Promised Land and refuge for his newly chosen people, the place where the Reformation would be realized.

This marked the conception, if not the birth, of the "first new nation." It is a remarkable development on a number of levels. The Puritans sought the sacred joining of a people and a land. For the Puritans, this idea was palpably captured in the notion of "covenant," which bound together God, land, and people, and the people with each other. We also see in this experiment the genesis of the nation-state; if the Reformation broke up western Europe into multiple, sovereign territorial states, Puritan New England was going to be a model, a "City upon the Hill," for an emerging international order. Though not the first expression of an emerging conception of a territorially constituted people with a historical, even apocalyptic, view of history—the Dutch republic may claim that status in terms of modern history—the Puritans established a form of nationhood that set the foundation for an independent United States. Perhaps more important, they were laying the seedbed of a nation-state that would serve as a model for much of the world.

The continuity between the Reformation and the Protestant settlement of America was a theme that remained in America well after the first generation of Puritans passed on (or, for that matter, after Puritanism itself disappeared from the American landscape by the mid-nineteenth century). "The Reformation was preceded by the discovery of America," Thomas Paine wrote in 1775, "as if the Almighty graciously meant to open a sanctuary to the persecuted in future years." The settlement of America and, later, the Revolution were viewed as a sequence of events in God's design. "I always consider the settlement of America with reverence and wonder," wrote the future president John Adams in 1765, "[and] as the opening of a grand scene and design in Providence for the illumination of the ignorant, and the emancipation of the slavish part of mankind all over the earth." Jonathan Edwards pronounced that "our nation" is "the principal nation of the Reformation." America, the new Israel, was chosen to do God's work, to push forward the course of history. This struggle would ultimately be directed for causes such as abolitionism and the spreading of democracy.

America, in this image, becomes a home from the storm, a home built by God. It anticipates the global idea, expressed later in the Statue of Liberty, of America as an *asylum* for the persecuted and destitute. This dynamic was also married to the larger Christian story of salvation, from the alienation from Eden to reconciliation with God, from the escape from Egypt to the pilgrimage to the Promised Land. We are journeying to the Promised Land, metaphorically, in the sense of some Edenic future. But that Edenic future is also located, in some sense, physically; we are journeying to America where the future will be realized. The journey would not be an easy one; it was an escape from corruption and sin, a testing of one's soul, like the wanderings of the Jews in Sinai. But in America the journey would begin again, to create a godly society.

And so the myth of immigration became part of the very sinews of America's conception of its collective self. To be rooted was contrasted with the "transient," wearying quality of travel. The poet Thomas Tillam, as he viewed the new Canaan (in his poem *Uppon the first sight of New-England June 29, 1638*), contrasted New England with the arduous voyage to reach it:

Hayle holy-land wherein our holy lord
Hath planted his most true and holy word
Hayle happye people who have dispossest
Your selves of friends, and meanes, to find some rest
For your poore wearied soules, opprest of late
For Jesus-sake, with Envye, spright and hate
To yow that blessed promise truly's given.

The issue of "belonging" that occupied the Puritans connects to later debates on immigration and citizenship. In the process of a community defining itself, questions of inclusion and exclusion became central. The covenant was by definition an attempt to assemble the godly and to exclude the degenerate. Thus one covenant, of the community of Dedham, Massachusetts, stated "that we shall by all means labor to keep off from us all such as are contrary minded, and receive only such unto us as may probably be of one heart with us." So even if the Puritans contributed to America's self-conception as a nation of immigrants through their own migration or as the source of national myths such as America as an asylum, they also illustrated that a "nation of immigrants" does not imply that it was a nation without boundaries. On the contrary, through the process of weaving together territorial, communal, and political identities into a singular, unitary, and bounded entity, the patrolling of social boundaries became more, not less, of a concern.

DECLARATION OF INDEPENDENCE AND AMERICA'S PLACE IN THE WORLD

The Declaration of Independence, in its words and for what it symbolized, was of inestimable importance for the emerging world order. Commentators have often noted the remarkable role of its framers, who, in a sense, designed a nation. In the Declaration of Independence, moreover, one can read a manifesto for the New World, a declaration that the promise of a new world order had emerged. The principles of sovereignty and national self-determination are, at least in theory, realized. Particularly striking in this regard are these words from the first two paragraphs of the Declaration:

When in the Course of human Events, it becomes necessary for one people to dissolve the Political Bands which have connected them with another, and to assume among the Powers of the Earth, the separate and equal station to which the Laws of Nature and of Nature's God entitle them, a decent respect to the Opinions of Mankind requires that they should declare the causes which impel then to Separation.

We hold these Truths to be self-evident, that all Men are created equal, that they are endowed by their Creator with certain unalienable Rights, that among these are Life, Liberty and the Pursuit of Happiness. That to secure these Rights, Governments are instituted among Men, deriving their just Powers from the Consent of the Governed. That whenever any Form of Government becomes destructive of these Ends, it is the Right of the People to alter or to abolish it, and to institute new Government.

The document refers to an event bounded in time and space, yet the language is couched in universal terms. The principles of equality and self-determination are affirmed not only internally but also as principles that apply to all nations. The principles are universal, but they are interwoven with a sense of unique *nationhood*. Boundaries are drawn through dissolving "the political bonds which have connected them with another." America's specificity is as a carrier of universal principles. There is recognition, however, that such principles transcend the United States and are not exclusively rooted in America; a "decent respect to the opinions of mankind" is called for. A sense of creating the self, of determining the self, infuses the document. The people determine their government.

The process of defining a nation would, in this revolutionary phase, culminate in the Constitution drafted in 1787. A nation defines itself—identity is not primordial—in terms of universal criteria. Political and national revolution coincided. The political identity *was* the American identity. In accentuating political beliefs, in defining the United States politically, the framers wove the moral dimension of the nation into its very definition. National identity is also rooted territorially. The Reformation's premises of changing *this* world, of self-determination, equality, and sovereignty, are finally realized in a near pristine form. The United States was a model of a new social order and the redeemer nation of the world. And yet this moral, redeemer quality is in tension with the very act of separation, anticipating an isolationist thread in American life. Republicanism could prosper only if freed of all ties with European despotism. "The attempt to realize a better social order," wrote the historian Felix Gilbert, "presupposed a critical view of the values of the Old World and aroused a fear of ties which might spread the diseases of Europe to America."

The establishment of the United States had a fundamental influence on the world at large. The Declaration was the first time a colony claimed rights to nationhood and sovereignty. The implication of this act threatened European dominance. The Americans had demonstrated that a republic could be established outside Europe. Moreover, the new state established the norm that individuals have rights prior to that of government. Such republicanism underlay the emerging world order. Finally, the Constitution provided a model for self-government that would be widely imitated.

"MAKING THE WORLD SAFE FOR DEMOCRACY," OR AN IMPERIALIST AND HEGEMONIC POWER?

In defining itself in essentially moral terms and in terms of universal values (such as equality and national self-determination), the United States was imbued with a dynamic quality that expressed itself periodically with a missionary-like zeal. The idea of chosenness and of America's moral mission had a specifically religious grounding: that the American people would bring on the Kingdom of God on Earth. By the twentieth century, more secular themes are drawn upon by Americans. Nevertheless, the same metaphors, the same imagery, rooted in Protestantism, are used: American chosenness is expressed by its self-declared mission to bring democracy and capitalism to the world, to be a light unto other nations in its democratic practice, and to, by force if necessary, rid the world of totalitarianism.

What is striking is that America's image in the global imagination comes to mirror, often in a refracted and even uncomplimentary manner, the way in which the United States has conceived of itself. Thus America's desire to make the world safe for democracy causes it be viewed as the savior, the promise, the light beckoning in the darkness. Or, conversely, its missionary zeal and self-righteousness come to be viewed as imperiousness or even the imperialistic empire building of a hegemonic power. Furthermore, the United States's informing other countries of their poor human rights record, for example, brings countercharges of hypocrisy—given its own poor record, at least historically, in the treatment of minorities and the stain of slavery. Thus the peculiar combination exists of nineteenth-century American beliefs in its "manifest destiny" to bring light to the world with the reverse image of the crushing force of imperialist power, from the vantage point of Native Americans or Mexico or, in the twentieth century, in Latin America or Southeast Asia.

Expansion and the extension of liberty were viewed as intertwined, and this belief was at its height as the country expanded westward in the nineteenth century. The United States, it was believed, was in a central position in human history and at the cutting edge of civilization. Manifest Destiny captured the interplay of chosenness, Divine Providence, liberty, millennial promise, and territorial expansion of God's kingdom, together with notions of advancing freedom and democracy. Doubts were expressed that expansion was inimical to liberty. Isolationism was just below the surface. Dissent became particularly vocal during the Mexican-American War of 1846–48.

But interventionism took on renewed vigor in 1898, in the war with Spain to free Cuba. President William McKinley ordered the occupation of Cuba, Puerto Rico, Guam, and the Philippines. How did colonization coexist with the belief in self-determination? Arguments were made that the Philippines, for example, was being freed of despotic Spanish rule. The "savage" populations in acquired territories were deemed incapable of self-government and thus became "wards" of the United States. Against promises of liberty, voices of opposition were ineffectual. Few voices favored imperialism as such, and after 1900 colonization efforts ceased. A recurrent theme, often with racist overtones, was that of the United States as "tutor." American chosenness, its calling, merged into notions of Anglo-Saxon superiority. The "backward" peoples of the world had to be brought up to American standards and values; people had to be enlightened and weaned away from despotism.

United States involvement in World War I and European politics jaded Americans into a conservative isolationism. President Woodrow Wilson promised to defeat imperialism, militarism, and autocracy. Wilson's Fourteen Points, a peace program formulated in 1918, expressed the promise of liberal interventionism. Principles of equality and self-determination were to be reexported to Europe. In 1776, the United States had shed itself of the supposed corruption of Europe. In 1918, the United States would now free Europe of its despotic past. The enormous price paid by the United States in that war, along with the lopsided settlement imposed on Germany, produced an aversion to participating in world politics. The United States, it was argued, must have a detached relationship with the world and let others follow their own path, without America's judgment. In the world, America's role as savior was replaced by disappointment. Only in the face of the Nazi and Japanese threat would the isolationism be overcome and interventionism be reasserted. Liberal interventionism merges with conservative interventionism in World War II. Once more, America's light in the world glows as savior of democracy and humanity.

However, the contradiction or paradox in the idea of American expansion in one form or another with the principles of the Declaration of Independence remains. And the opposition that American political and cultural presence engenders in the rest of the world (and the uncomfortable sense that American self-conceptions are refracted in unpleasant ways) has caused swings toward isolationism in American his-

tory. Thus the entry into Vietnam in the early 1960s under a liberal president, John F. Kennedy, on the premise that democracy was being protected from communism, generated the nadir in America's image in the world. This imperialistic imagery generated tremendous self-doubt within the country, which after Vietnam led to a period of near isolationism and a deep questioning of any attempts to make military forays in the world. This self-doubt is waning, if not disappearing, most recently with the extension of American peacekeeping troops on a humanitarian mission in the former Yugoslavia, an American involvement that engenders both the promise of democratic savior and imperialist intruder, depending on the parties concerned.

AMERICA'S IMAGE IN THE AGE OF GLOBALIZATION

Rarely has a country stood for more things to more people than America. And rarely has a country been made to stand for such wildly divergent things as America, for its images in the global imagination have rocked back and forth from paradise to wilderness, from honest and open to hypocritical, from redeemer to Satan. It is as if America sits on a pendulum, rocking back and forth between negative and positive images.

Over the last century, wildly divergent images of America on the global stage have emerged: as the savior of freedom, democracy, and the West in World Wars I and II, and as a cynical and hypocritical imperialist in Latin America and Vietnam; as representing all that was good and decent and free about humankind and as a morally depraved and satanic empire. We have witnessed revolutions that invoke the Declaration of Independence as their inspiration and revolutions that were driven by anti-American rhetoric.

There is little doubt that America's salient presence in the world's mind has acted as a catalyst for immigration. America beckons, through television, foreign aid programs, and the letters and telephone calls of family members who have already migrated. Immigration may be driven by the promises of political freedom for many refugees; for others it is the economic draw of the *golden medinah*, the golden country, as Jewish immigrants from Eastern Europe would refer to it. But even economically driven migration has a cultural root: the golden medinah was a bundle of economic promise and political freedom, the ability to begin again—or so it was perceived. It was a country said to be moving forward, animated by the idea of progress and not fettered by the past. There is and has been a curious interplay of America having a mission in the world and its magnetic attraction to outsiders. Indeed, there is a certain dialectic here: in seeking to advance a universal mission, the country considers itself the "universal nation" and thus a "nation of immigrants."

What is now raised as a question *outside* the United States, however, is to what extent the world, so preoccupied by America and so taken by American consumer culture, is itself being "Americanized." American culture is, as it were, emigrating to the rest of the world. The symbols of economic and cultural globalization—Coca-Cola, McDonald's, Nike, Hollywood, media and television programming—tend to be identified with the United States. One could argue that the United States is the epicenter of globalization, even, or especially, in the cultural sense of individual values and consumerism. Globalization, like America itself, generates a certain ambivalence: The consumer possibilities, the economic growth, and the cultural possibilities are welcomed. On the other hand, the apparent effects of homogenization and of the flattening of local cultures that appears in the wake of globalization, as well as the economic dislocations, foster a definite trepidation. No wonder, in this context, that McDonald's is attacked (quite literally) in France for, among other reasons, threatening the local culinary culture with its processed and standardized food.

David Jacobson and Carolyn Forbes

See also: Economics I: Pull Factors (Part II, Sec. 1); Look Before You Leap, 1796, Memorial of James Brown, 1819, Tour Through the United States, 1819, "What Does America Offer to the German Immigrant?" 1853, Letters from an American Farmer, 1782, Letters from Illinois, 1818 (Part IV, Sec. 3).

BIBLIOGRAPHY

Arilli, Yehoshua. *Individualism and Nationalism in American Ideology.* Cambridge: Harvard University Press, 1964.

Evans, J. Martin. *America: The View from Europe.* Stanford: Stanford Alumni Association, 1976.

Gilbert, Felix. *To the Farewell Address: Ideas of Early American Foreign Policy.* Princeton, NJ: Princeton University Press, 1961.

Hunt, Michael H. *Ideology and U.S. Foreign Policy.* New Haven: Yale University Press, 1987.

Jacobson, David. *Place and Belonging in America.* Baltimore: Johns Hopkins University Press, forthcoming.

Lipson, Leslie. "European Responses to the American Revolution." *Annals of the American Academy of Political and Social Sciences* (November 1976).

May, Ernest. *American Imperialism.* New York: Atheneum, 1968.

Thomas, George M. "U.S. Discourse and Strategies in the New World Order." In *Old Nations, New World,* ed. David Jacobson. Boulder, CO: Westview, 1994.

Tucker, Robert S. "Isolation and Intervention." *National Interest* (Fall 1985): 16–25.

Tuveson, Ernest Lee. *Redeemer Nation: The Idea of America's Millennial Role.* Chicago: University of Chicago Press, 1968.

Wattenberg, Ben. *The First Universal Nation.* New York: Free Press, 1992.

Zakai, Avihu. *Exile and Kingdom: History and Apocalypse in the Puritan Migration to America.* Cambridge: Cambridge University Press, 1992.

CHAIN MIGRATION

Chain migration occurs when one migrant facilitates the subsequent migration of another. Usually, this term refers to the later migration and immigration of immediate relatives, such as parents, children, and siblings. However, it also may be applied to more distant relatives, close friends, and even acquaintances. Thus, chain migration is very similar in meaning to the term "network migration," in that both concepts focus on how migration is aided by specific social relationships that are fostered in part by previous migration.

ORIGIN OF CONCEPT

The first person to offer a formal definition of chain migration is believed to be Reuel Anson Lochore. In his book, *From Europe to New Zealand: An Account of Our Continental European Settlers,* Lochore defines a "migration chain" as "an established route along which migrants continue to move over a period of many years from a European peasant community to a modified peasant community in the new land." Although this definition differs somewhat from the contemporary meaning of the term, Lochore touches upon many aspects of chain migration that have been studied by other researchers. These include the cumulative nature of chain migration, how chain migration sometimes leads to the formation of settlements that greatly resemble the migrants' communities of origin, and how the presence of relatives in a prospective destination helps to frame the migration decision.

Participants in chain migration often receive substantial help from previous links in the chain. As they evaluate whether to migrate, they typically weigh information provided by earlier migrants, including an assessment of the opportunities available in the contemplated destination. They also may receive useful tips about how to negotiate the migration process, such as how to deal with government officials in the origin and destination countries and how to avoid various hazards during the migratory journey. To finance the costs of migration, chain migrants may receive financial assistance from earlier migrants, in the form of loans or direct payments. Upon arrival, the new migrant may stay with family or friends and learn from them about job prospects in the surrounding area. Not surprisingly, these varied relationships have attracted the attention of researchers in numerous disciplines—including anthropology, economics, history, political science, psychology, and sociology—as well as policymakers, social-service providers, and others concerned with immigration and migration.

THE EXAMPLE OF THE GONZÁLEZ FAMILY

The unprecedented media attention given to Elián González in late 1999 and 2000—the five-year-old Cuban boy whose fateful journey to the United States triggered an international custody dispute between relatives in Cuba and the United States—resulted in the publication of numerous details about his family's migration history. This information revealed that the difficult course charted by Elián was part of a larger pattern of chain migration undertaken by his extended family over the course of several decades.

In many instances of chain migration, it is possible to identify a pioneer who constitutes the first link in the chain. In Elián's case, this pioneer was his great aunt, Caridad González, who boarded a flight from Cuba to the United States in 1966. Caridad's voyage was itself linked to that of another migrant, her ex-husband Pedro Hernández, who had fled Cuba in 1961. She had hoped that they would be able to re-

One method of coming to America is chain migration, in which one member of a family comes first, paving the way for others. That was the case with this Lebanese-American family, shown at their deli in Brooklyn. *(Hazel Hankin/Impact Visuals)*

sume their relationship once they were together in Florida, but this did not occur.

Caridad was further motivated by the plight of her brother Delfín, who was imprisoned by the Cuban government in 1962 on charges of being a counterrevolutionary. "When Delfín was arrested," she said, "I knew I had to leave because someone had to be [in the United States] to pay for passage of political prisoners." Thus, Caridad's migration was aimed explicitly at securing Delfín's migration as well. In 1979, Delfín was allowed to leave Cuba for the United States, where he has become a successful retailer of lumber and lobster-fishing supplies.

Just as Caridad had struggled to obtain Delfín's migration, she also facilitated the migration of several other siblings. In 1983, she sponsored the legal immigration of her sister Georgina, along with Georgina's husband and their three children. Roughly one year later, Caridad's brothers Manuel and Lázaro took their families—eleven persons in all—to Costa Rica with the intention of entering the United States. Al-

though U.S. officials would not permit Caridad to sponsor all eleven relatives at the same time, the two brothers eventually were able to bring their entire families to the United States. Lázaro González is the great uncle in Miami who vied with Elián's Cuban father, Juan Miguel González, for custody of the child.

Additional members of the extended family sought to leave Cuba over a period of several years, apparently with the assistance of contacts in the United States. In 1998, Caridad's sister Aide, who still lived in Cuba, lost her husband to cancer. Shortly thereafter, Aide's son and the husband of Aide's daughter made arrangements to be smuggled into the United States. Their wives and children followed in 1999. In November 1999, Caridad's niece, Elisabet Broton González, her boyfriend Lázaro Munero, and Elisabet's son Elián made a similar attempt aboard a 16-foot aluminum boat constructed by Munero and his father Rafael. During the short voyage from Cuba to the United States, the boat was swamped by heavy rain and broke apart, claiming the lives of Elisabet,

This Filipino-American family—seen at home watching TV—came to the United States one by one, a classic example of chain migration. *(Maria Dumlao/Impact Visuals)*

the two Muneros, and eight others, leaving Elián as one of three survivors.

CHAIN MIGRATION AND THE MIGRATION DECISION

For someone who is thinking about becoming a migrant, the presence of a relative or friend in a prospective destination greatly influences the migration decision. As was mentioned above, these contacts often provide important assistance that lowers the financial costs of migration and its inherent risks. Thus, it is widely believed that the opportunity of chain migration makes it more likely that an individual will migrate. For example, several econometric studies of Mexican migration to the United States, including the pioneering study by J. Edward Taylor of two rural villages in Mexico, have indicated that an individual

has a higher probability of migrating if he or she has a relative who lives in the United States.

Less is known about the decision-making process that leads to chain migration. As Lochore suggests, having the option of following in the footsteps of another migrant may help to frame the migration decision. However, there is some evidence that this narrowing of alternatives reduces the quality of the decision-making process. In a survey of Chinese immigrants (mostly from Hong Kong) in Edmonton, Alberta, Yihua Lou Lin-Yuan analyzes the decision-making process that leads to migration. She characterizes this process as one of bounded rationality, meaning that the decision maker has a limited ability to perceive and utilize information. Lin-Yuan concludes that the immigrants in her study generally considered only a few countries (including Canada) as potential destinations, that they used only a few sources of information to investigate these alternatives, and that this information search was biased in favor of factors that the decision maker deemed to be important. Moreover, this process tended to justify the individual's original inclinations, rather than involve a thorough consideration of the available alternatives.

CHAIN MIGRATION AND EMPLOYMENT

Chain migrants frequently rely on familial contacts to secure employment in the United States. Using data collected by the Mexican Migration Project from thirty-one communities in central and western Mexico, Steven S. Zahniser calculates that 23 percent of migrant heads of households obtained their most recent U.S. job with the help of family or friends. This statistic may understate the importance of family contacts in job seeking, since many of these individuals already were experienced U.S. migrants. Some chain migrants secure U.S. employment before arriving in the United States. Zahniser describes the case of one Mexican migrant in his early twenties who moved to the Los Angeles area in order to work as an automobile mechanic in his uncle's repair shop. His father, a former migrant, contacted his brother and made advance arrangements for his son.

Some of these initial positions are sufficiently attractive that the migrant will continue to work in them for an extended period of time. Others provide more transitional employment that leads ultimately to a better job somewhere else. Douglas S. Massey, Rafael Alarcón, Jorge Durand, and Humberto González provide the example of a restaurant in the San Francisco area that served as a springboard for numerous migrants from the same community in the Mexican State of Michoacán.

Job networking in conjunction with chain migration can be highly beneficial to the migrant, as it shortens the job search, may result in a higher wage than would have been obtained otherwise, and may provide the basis for further economic advancement. However, it does not guarantee a job at a living wage and tolerable working conditions. This is particularly the case for undocumented migrants, who are ineligible to work legally in the formal U.S. labor market. Zahniser, for instance, tells the story of one Mexican migrant who was referred by a relative to a restaurant where the owner was verbally abusive toward her employees. One day, the owner became so incensed with her migrant employee that she dumped a casserole on his head.

DAUGHTER COMMUNITIES AND CHAIN MIGRATION

The repeated settlement of chain migrants from a specific community or region of origin in a common destination has led to the formation of numerous "daughter communities" across the United States. One can find examples of these communities in both urban and rural areas throughout the history of U.S. immigration, and most ethnic groups and nationalities that have participated in U.S. immigration have had at least one such community in the United States at some time.

Many daughter communities are precisely connected to specific communities of origin. Rubén G. Rumbaut (citing Ronald R. Stockton) offers a contemporary example in the Arab community of the Detroit metropolitan area:

> Most Chaleans are from the village of Tel Kaif in northern Iraq and live in Southfield; Lebanese Shiites are from Tibnin or Bent Jbail near the Israeli border and prefer Dearborn; most Palestinians are from within ten miles of Jerusalem—Christians from Ramallah, Muslims from El Bireh or Beit Hanina—and live in Livonia; Egyptian Coptic Christians are in Troy, and Lebanese Maronite Catholics on the east side.

Accompanying these precise connections often are profound cultural similarities between the community of origin and the daughter community along the lines of religion, language, ethnicity, and economic activities.

Over time, the primary destination of new immigrants from a particular community of origin may shift from one daughter community to another, as a result of changing economic conditions in the original daughter community and new opportunities in other prospective destinations. Massey, Alarcón, Durand, and González examine the migration patterns of Altamira, a small rural municipality in the Mexican state of Jalisco. Initially, migrants from this community went to the San Francisco Bay Area, until the Great Depression ended this chain of migration. In the early 1940s, California's Imperial Valley became the principal destination, as the U.S. government recruited Mexicans to work in U.S. agriculture through the Bracero Program (1942–64). Starting in the late 1940s, immigrants from Altamira shifted their focus from the Imperial Valley to the San Joaquin Valley and the Los Angeles metropolitan area, as they sought employment in both agricultural and nonagricultural occupations.

Daughter communities usually feature many amenities of the home country. Residents and business owners are fluent in the immigrant's native language, and religious services are likely to be given in that language as well. In addition, newspapers, magazines, and videos published in that language may be widely available. Restaurants that specialize in the home country's cuisine operate in the community, and local grocery stores and convenience markets carry goods found in the home country. The late newspaper columnist Mike Royko, who was the son of Slavic immigrants, grew up in just such a community in his native Chicago, a city that historically has featured a wide variety of ethnic neighborhoods. Maxine Sellers offers the following recollection by Royko: "You could always tell [where] you were . . . by the odors of the food stores and the open kitchen window, the sound of the foreign or familiar language, and by whether a stranger hit you in the head with a rock."

CHAIN MIGRATION AND MENTAL WELL-BEING

Life in the destination country presents many challenges to the immigrant, including coping with language barriers, negotiating cultural differences, and making ends meet under sometimes-difficult circumstances. Removed from the social supports available in the home country, some immigrants experience tremendous emotional stress and suffer from depression and other mental illnesses. Fortunately, the social conditions that usually accompany chain migration may alleviate these pressures. Soon after arriving in the destination country, participants in chain migration are likely to have the company of relatives, friends, and other persons from their country of origin, if not their community of origin. These contacts may provide important social support to the immigrant, enabling him or her to cope more successfully with the stresses of daily life.

A number of quantitative studies support this hypothesis. Using survey data collected from 1,825 Mexican immigrant women in San Diego County, California, William A. Vega, Bohdan Kolody, Ramon Valle, and Judy Weir report that family support and family income are the best predictors of low depression scores in a multiple regression analysis. Similarly, in a study of Korean immigrants in Toronto, Ontario, Samuel Noh and William R. Avison find that persons with social support from other Korean immigrants are less likely to be depressed.

Does it matter whether this support comes from coethnics—that is, other members of the immigrant's ethnic group? Noh and Avison indicate that coethnic support does make a difference, as social support from family members, friends, and coworkers who are not of Korean origin has no significant impact on depression levels. Wen H. Kuo and Yung-Mei Tsai obtained similar results in a study of Chinese, Japanese, Filipino, and Korean immigrants in Seattle, Washington. They found that the proportion of coethnics in their closest circle of friends and relatives has a significant effect on the depression levels of the Chinese immigrants in their sample. In contrast, Sandra A. Black, Kyriakos S. Markides, and Todd Q. Miller concluded that simply having a confidant lowers the depression level of elderly immigrant women, following a study of Mexican Americans in five states in the U.S. Southwest. However, Black et al. do not distinguish between coethnic and non-coethnic confidants.

It is important to note that these studies contain a possible shortcoming, in that the dependent variable (the level of depression) and the explanatory variable (social support) may be from within. The analytical technique employed in these studies (multiple regression analysis) normally requires that the explanatory variable come from outside; otherwise, the regression may completely misstate the true relationship between the explanatory and the dependent variables. This problem is especially likely when some unmeasured characteristic of the immigrant explains both the level of depression and the existence of social support. For instance, an individual with a particular mental illness may be both more likely to feel depressed and less likely to have the support of friends and family.

Of all the researchers mentioned above, Kuo and Tsai seem to be most aware of this possibility. Their analysis incorporates an additional attribute of the immigrant: the hardiness of that individual's personality. Kuo and Tsai craft an index of hardiness that measures the immigrant's confidence about the future, whether the immigrant values planning for the future, and whether the immigrant feels capable of implementing his or her future plans. The authors find that immigrants with a hardy personality have lower levels of depression and are more likely to have social support, presumably through active networking. However, Kuo and Tsai's index of hardiness may actually measure the immigrant's state of mental health, in which case it would not be surprising to find a negative relationship between hardiness and depression.

Table 1
Family-Sponsored Immigration to the United States, Fiscal Years 1995–97

Category of admission	FY1997 Number	%	FY1996 Number	%	FY1995 Number	%
Total immigrants	798,378	100.0	915,900	100.0	720,461	100.0
Family-sponsored immigrants	535,771	67.1	596,264	65.1	460,376	63.9
Family-sponsored preferences	213,331	26.7	294,174	32.1	238,122	33.1
Unmarried sons/daughters of U.S. citizens	22,536	2.8	20,909	2.3	15,182	2.1
Spouses and children of alien residents	113,681	14.2	182,834	20.0	144,535	20.1
Married sons/daughters of U.S. citizens	21,943	2.7	25,452	2.8	20,876	2.9
Siblings of U.S. citizens	55,171	6.9	64,979	7.1	57,529	8.0
Immediate relatives of U.S. citizens	322,440	40.4	302,090	33.0	222,254	30.8
Spouses	170,263	21.3	169,760	18.5	123,238	17.1
Parents	74,114	9.3	66,699	7.3	48,382	6.7
Children	76,631	9.6	63,971	7.0	48,740	6.8
Children born abroad to alien residents	1,432	0.2	1,660	0.2	1,894	0.3
Employment-based preferences	90,607	11.3	117,499	12.8	85,336	11.8
Diversity programs	49,374	6.2	58,790	6.4	47,245	6.6
Refugee and asylee adjustments	112,158	14.0	128,565	14.0	114,664	15.9
Other immigrants	10,468	1.3	14,782	1.6	12,840	1.8

Source: U.S. Immigration and Naturalization Service (1999).

CHAIN MIGRATION AND LEGAL IMMIGRATION

The United States and many other countries have instituted legal mechanisms by which immigrants may apply for the immigration of their family members. These provisions for family reunification make it possible for chain migration to occur within the context of publicly sanctioned immigration. In fact, some people use the term "chain migration" to refer specifically to immigration resulting from these legal processes.

Under the Immigration Act of 1990, U.S. citizens and noncitizens with the immigration status of legal permanent resident may seek the lawful immigration of certain relatives. (Similar provisions have existed since the mid-1960s, as specified by earlier statutes.) Both native-born and naturalized U.S. citizens are eligible to apply for the immigration of immediate relatives. Spouses, parents, and children are considered by the act to be immediate relatives, along with cer-

tain children born abroad to alien residents. The law places no annual limit on this type of immigration. In Fiscal Year (FY) 1997 (October 1, 1996, to September 30, 1997), 322,440 immigrants were admitted as immediate relatives of U.S. citizens (see Table 1).

The act also specifies four additional categories of family-sponsored immigration, called family-sponsored preferences. These preferences cover the following groups of potential immigrants:

(1) unmarried sons and daughters of U.S. citizens and their children;

(2) spouses, children, and unmarried sons and daughters of legal permanent residents;

(3) married sons and daughters of U.S. citizens and their spouses and children; and

(4) brothers and sisters of U.S. citizens and their spouses and children, provided that the sponsoring U.S. citizen is age 21 or over.

The maximum number of immigrants who may be admitted under these preferences ranges from 226,000 to 480,000 per fiscal year; the number of immigrants admitted as immediate relatives of U.S. citizens during the previous fiscal year may affect this numerical limit. A total of 213,331 immigrants were admitted under family-sponsored preferences in FY 1997.

Family-sponsored admissions (including both immediate relatives of U.S. citizens and the family-sponsored preferences) constituted 65 percent of legal immigration to the United States during fiscal years 1995–97. Not all of these immigrants are chain migrants, as persons sponsored by U.S.-born spouses make up a sizable portion of these admissions. Nevertheless, it is clear that U.S. immigration law establishes a process by which granting permanent residency to one immigrant leads to chain migration in the form of additional legal immigrants admitted through the family-reunification provisions.

During the 1980s, some participants in political discussions about U.S. immigration policy expressed concerns that the legal provisions for family reunification were causing an explosive growth in immigration. The Reverend Theodore M. Hesburgh, chairman of the U.S. Select Commission on Immigration and Refugee Policy, offered a hypothetical example of family reunification's potential impact (as cited by John M. Goering):

> Assume one foreign-born married couple, both naturalized, each with two siblings who are also married and each new nuclear family having three children. The foreign-born married couple may petition for the admission of their siblings. Each has a spouse and three children who come with their parents. Each spouse is a potential source for more immigration, and so it goes. It is possible that no less than 84 persons would become eligible for visas in a relatively short period of time.

At the time of Hesburgh's comments, however, there was little empirical evidence of the actual size of this multiplicative effect, which is commonly referred to as the "immigration multiplier."

In 1986, the journal *Demography* published an influential article by Guillermina Jasso and Mark R. Rosenzweig in which the authors attempted to estimate the immigration multiplier using data describing the 1971 cohort of legal immigrants. In this paper, Jasso and Rosenzweig originally defined the multiplier as the number of additional persons who ultimately become immigrants due to the admission of one new immigrant. Their estimates suggested that the actual multiplier was substantially smaller than the potential multiplier, but that the multiplier was not a trivial

concern, either. For immigrants admitted under the work-related preferences, Jasso and Rosenzweig calculated a multiplier as high as 1.2. This meant that for each new immigrant who was admitted in 1971 under a work-related preference, as many as 1.2 additional immigrants would come during the next ten years through the application of the citizenship-based provisions for family reunification.

Demographers who reviewed Jasso and Rosenzweig's work identified several limitations, which are summarized by Goering in his introduction to a 1989 issue of *International Migration Review* that focuses on chain migration and the immigration multiplier. Among these criticisms was the observation that Jasso and Rosenzweig did not consider the admission of the spouses and children of permanent resident aliens. Partially in response to this criticism, the two researchers made a second attempt to estimate the immigration multiplier, which appeared in the same issue of *International Migration Review*.

The two researchers improved their methodology by providing new definitions of the immigrant sponsorship rate and the immigration multiplier. They defined the immigrant sponsorship rate as the number of additional immigrants sponsored directly by an immigrant. Then, they redefined the immigration multiplier to equal the number of immigrants sponsored directly or indirectly by one original immigrant. Jasso and Rosenzweig considered an original immigrant to be any immigrant sponsored by a native-born U.S. citizen, an employer, or the U.S. government, including both the principal immigrant sponsored for admission and his or her accompanying family members. This identification of original immigrants enabled Jasso and Rosenzweig to distinguish among the first "generation" of new immigrants sponsored directly by the original immigrants, the second "generation" of immigrants sponsored directly by the first "generation" and indirectly sponsored by the original immigrants, and so on.

These efforts yielded higher estimates of the immigration multiplier. For instance, given the admission of one original immigrant in 1971 under a work-related preference, as many as 1.4 additional immigrants might result over the next three "generations" of immigrant applications. Nevertheless, Jasso and Rosenzweig's general finding remained the same: the actual immigration multiplier was nontrivial in size but substantially smaller than the potential multiplier.

Steven S. Zahniser

See also: Settlement Patterns (Part II, Sec. 3); Family (Part II, Sec. 4).

BIBLIOGRAPHY

Black, Sandra A., Kyriakos S. Markides, and Todd Q. Miller. "Correlates of Depressive Symptomatology Among Older Community-Dwelling Mexican Americans: The Hispanic EPESE." *Journal of Gerontology: Social Sciences* 53B:4 (1998): S198–S208.

Fineman, Mark. "Cubans' Risky New Voyage Out." *Los Angeles Times*, January 4, 2000, www.latimes.com/news/nation/updates/lat_cubans000104.htm, downloaded March 30, 2000.

———, and Mike Clary. " 'A Family Divided.' " *Los Angeles Times*, February 19, 2000, A1, A8, and A9.

Goering, John M. "The 'Explosiveness' of Chain Migration: Research and Policy Issues." *International Migration Review* 23:4 (1989): 797–812.

Immigration and Naturalization Service. *Statistical Yearbook of the Immigration and Naturalization Service, 1997*. Washington, DC: U.S. Government Printing Office, 1999.

Jasso, Guillermina, and Mark R. Rosenzweig. "Family Reunification and the Immigration Multiplier: U.S. Immigration Law, Origin-Country Conditions, and the Reproduction of Immigrants." *Demography* 23:3 (1986): 291–311.

———. "Sponsors, Sponsorship Rates and the Immigration Multiplier." *International Migration Review* 23:4 (1989): 856–88.

Kuo, Wen H., and Yung-Mei Tsai. "Social Networking, Hardiness and Immigrant's Mental Health." *Journal of Health and Social Behavior* 27:2 (1986): 133–49.

Lin-Yuan, Yihua Lou. "Migration Decision-Making: A Theoretical and Empirical Study." Ph.D. diss., University of Alberta, 1993.

Lochore, Reuel Anson. *From Europe to New Zealand: An Account of our Continental European Settlers*. Wellington, New Zealand: A. H. and A. W. Reed, 1951.

Massey, Douglas S., Rafael Alarcón, Jorge Durand, and Humberto González. *Return to Aztlán: The Social Process of International Migration from Western Mexico*. Berkeley: University of California Press, 1987.

Noh, Samuel, and William R. Avison. "Asian Immigrants and the Stress Process: A Study of Koreans in Canada." *Journal of Health and Social Behavior* 37 (June 1996): 192–206.

Rumbaut, Rubén G. "Origins and Destinies: Immigration, Race, and Ethnicity in Contemporary America." In *Origins and Destinies: Immigration, Race, and Ethnicity in America*, ed. Silvia Pedraza and Rubén G. Rumbaut, pp. 21–42. Belmont, CA: Wadworth, 1996.

Select Commission on Immigration and Refugee Policy. *U.S. Immigration Policy and the National Interest. The Final Report and Recommendations of the Select Commission on Immigration and Refugee Policy to the Congress and the President of the United States*. Washington, DC: U.S. Government Printing Office, 1981.

Sellers, Maxine Schwartz. *To Seek America: A History of Ethnic Life in the United States*. Englewood, NJ: Jerome S. Ozer, 1977.

Stockton, Ronald R. "Recognize the Benefits from Our Arab Neighbors." *Detroit News*, April 3, 1994, 12A.

Taylor, J. Edward. "Migration Networks and Risk in Household Labor Decisions: A Study of Migration from Two Mexican Villages." Ph.D. diss., University of California, Berkeley, 1984.

Vega, William A., Bohdan Kolody, Ramon Valle, and Judy Weir. "Social Networks, Social Support, and Their Relationship to Depression among Immigrant Mexican Women." *Human Organization* 50:2 (1991): 154–62.

Zahniser, Steven S. *Mexican Migration to the United States: The Role of Migration Networks and Human Capital Accumulation*. New York: Garland, 1999.

ECONOMICS I: PULL FACTORS

Central to the immigration issue is the question of push-pull factors. While the notion of push-pull factors has been largely conceptualized and attributed to economic phenomena, there is an equally compelling argument that such factors should also be seen from an interdisciplinary perspective—sociological, anthropological, philosophical—and must further engage analyses that involve moral dimensions.

To be sure, immigration is largely fueled by economic considerations, but push-pull factors, particularly as those encompass education, skills, entrepreneurialism, and opportunities, elicit questions that tend to be obliterated, if not strategically stymied, from discussions on immigration. Those questions, according to Chilton Williamson Jr. in his thought-provoking book, *The Immigration Mystique: America's False Conscience*, must submit themselves to both moral and philosophical considerations. To position the push-pull factors of immigration in a framework that gives potency to both the centrality of economics and the plethora of factors that influence such decisions, it seems important that one should go beyond the notion of entry of people into spatial areas that are manifestly different from that of their native domicile.

It is imperative that one look at both the precipitating factors that encourage spatial mobility and the anticipatory factors in the host country that impel individuals hoping to improve their lives in myriad ways to move from one place to another. The very notion of immigration is questioned when one seriously considers such a configuration. Consequently, Williamson concludes that the "immigration problem is by definition a migration problem as well, produced by human dislocations, . . . [which] poses a grave moral conundrum to those concerned." Despite the fact that many persons have recognized the moral ingredient in the consideration of immigration, the prevailing analysis is basically grounded in the economic explanation.

EARLY EXPLANATIONS

Some of the earliest explanations of the push-pull phenomenon in immigration are to be found in some of the seminal works on international immigration under the aegis of neoclassical economics. Foremost among such explanations are the works of Sir W. Arthur Lewis, Gustav Ravis, John Fei, and Michael Todaro, who argue that immigration is largely based on the pull factor of a certain geographic entity manifesting a need for labor and another geographic entity having a surplus of such labor with low wages causing a push of such labor supply to the area of need.

But central to this macroeconomic theory of migration is the notion of choice on the part of individuals engaged in such movements. George Borjas, Larry Sjaastad, and Todaro have a different take on the pull factors, particularly as such factors relate to education, skills, entrepreneurialism, and opportunities. Their contention is that the individuals who engage in immigration are cognizant of the fact that while the pull factors have the real probability of increasing their chances of improving their economic base, a cost factor is involved in such transactions. Apart from the costs associated with physical relocation, there is an inherent engagement in taking risks largely predicted on both their willingness and readiness to be resocialized with respect to professional and personal issues. The push factors, ostensibly dictated by limited, if not absent, opportunities, propel them to those new situations that will, over a period of time, realize significant economic gain.

Central to the realization of such goals and objectives is the notion of entrepreneurialism—the distinct element of risk taking. This neoclassical approach to American immigration is particularly useful in looking at early immigration, primarily pre-1970s, when an individual immigrant could have come to the United States of America on a student or visitor visa

Among the factors attracting immigrants to America is the opportunity for a good education. Central American immigrant Nelson Gabino is seen here on his high school graduation day in Virginia. *(Nelson Regional Migrant Education Program)*

and elected to set up permanent residence in the country while simultaneously creating a base for the remaining members of the family to join him or her in the host country. This modus operandi was very popular in the pre-1970s, when immigrant parents were eligible for residence status as children were born out of such relationships and thereby qualified such immigrants for residence status.

"NEW ECONOMICS" THEORY

A challenge to basic tenets of the neoclassical theory of immigration, according to the sociologist Douglas Massey, is to be found in what is euphemistically referred to as the "new economic of labor migration." Scholars Oded Stark and Edward Taylor add a very interesting twist to the neoclassical theory of immigration by contending that the locus of decision making regarding immigration resides not in the individual but in a family unit that views immigration in terms of economic advancement for the family, inter alia. The focus of this rational choice approach is that emphasis is on the family and the anticipated accrued benefits are more directed to the net increase of economic advantages for the family of origin rather than the individual involved in such migratory experiences. In essence, this activity is centrally focused on entrepreneurial activity, even though in the manifestation of such activity the individual(s) of choice may be the beneficiary of educational skill advancement and poised to exploit the opportunities that are available in the host country. Again, the push factor quite likely is not large-scale migration of a family but the intent of the family to increase their economic well-being by strategically positioning a member of the family to occupy legitimately a position in the locus of the pull factor so as to be able to leverage the resources that would significantly enhance the family's

A Cambodian immigrant earns her certification in cosmetology from a school in Syracuse. Better educational and career opportunities are America's main appeal to immigrants. *(Mel Rosenthal)*

economic base "back home." It is not uncommon for many families in developing countries to support several families in developed countries who act as contact points for entrepreneurial activities back in the developing countries. This behavior was particularly manifest among citizens of Hong Kong who prior to the reannexation of Hong Kong to mainland China supported several members of the family overseas during the tense period of transition. The same example is replicated among citizens of African, South Asian, Latin American, and Caribbean countries who live in these countries but who subsidize the expenses of relatives in a developed country and are instrumental in facilitating business transactions in the de-

veloped country on behalf of the family in the country of origin.

Despite the great degree of currency that the neoclassical theory and the new economics of migration lend to an understanding of the push-pull factors in immigration, Michael Piore has challenged the basic premises in such discussions, arguing that the seeming push factors in the immigrant's home country are not contributory factors to the immigration process. His argument is that pull factors in the basic economic structure of the host country are the primary contribution to such activities. He attributes several cardinal contributory factors that serve as pull factors in attracting immigrants to a host society. Central to this analysis is what Piore refers to as "structural infla-tion." His contention is that most immigrants at the initial phases of their migratory experiences "begin as target earners seeking to earn money for a specific goal that will improve their well-being or status at home . . . [and since the immigrant] sees himself as a member of his home community, within which for-eign labor and hard currency remittances carry con-siderable honor and prestige . . . the disjunctures in living standards between developed and devel-oping societies mean that even low wages abroad ap-pear to be generous by the standards of the home community."

EDUCATIONAL FACTORS

This phenomenon is important to immigrants who are engaged in pursuing educational goals and who find that such employment opportunities are availa-ble without conformity to established legal employ-ment standards. Additionally, many immigrants can temporarily suspend judgments about the social status attached to such jobs primarily because the pull factors were not associated with achieving higher levels of social status immediately, and be-cause immigrants do not identify with the host coun-try. Hollywood popularized this notion in the motion picture *Coming to America* when Eddie Murphy played the role of a prince earmarked for succession to a tribal leadership position in an African country and accepted the lowest position at a fast-food res-taurant in the United States so that he could woo the proprietor's daughter into being his bride. The same situation is true for many international students, who will opt for work-study details on the campus of the institution at which they are pursuing their academic goals.

ETHNIC ENCLAVES

A second issue that may be attributed to the pull fac-tor of the host country is what is referred to as the secondary labor market demands of ethnic enclaves. The very nature of the main characteristics of the sec-ondary labor market lends itself to pull factors. Such markets are notorious for doling out marginal wages, tremendous insecurity in maintaining jobs, unsatisfac-tory work conditions, and so on. However, there is a silver lining for immigrants, and as the sociologists Alejandro Portes and Robert Bach clearly unearthed

in their study of the Cuban ethnic enclave, the situa-tion really is a manifestation of pull factors. What they found was that "the enclave provides immigrants with significant economic returns to education and ex-perience, as well as the very real prospect of upward socioeconomic mobility."

This phenomenon is repeated in several ethnic en-claves throughout the United States and serves in many cases as an informal route through which many recently arriving immigrants may secure employment whether that is predicated on legal or illegal arrange-ments. But this situation is not circumscribed only by economic factors; there are implications socially, po-litically, and culturally. The very manner in which the ethnic enclaves are metamorphosed positions them to generate pull factors and wield a significant amount of influence in the wider communities to which they are identified. Portes and Alex Stepick, as well as Ken-neth Wilson and W. Allen Martin, attribute the for-mation of such enclaves to both selectivity and the socioeconomic status of the central personalities as-sociated with this phenomenon. The upshot of this peculiar social and economic phenomenon is that it has a two-pronged effect on the pull factors of at least the ethnic group that is predominantly represented in that enclave. First, the enclave provides a sense of se-curity to newly arriving immigrants primarily with respect to both employment opportunities and the group solidarity that is a significant contributory fac-tor to the upward social mobility of the recently ar-rived immigrant.

Second, it offers extensive networking among var-ious strata of the enclave and positions the newly ar-riving immigrants with both a road map with which they may negotiate the various facets of the society as well as the opportunities to exploit the resources of the host society and thereby anticipate significantly greater success than those without such support sys-tems. In essence, the pull factors, from a segmented theory approach, are the legacy of the manifest dis-dain and avoidance that U.S. citizens place on em-ployment opportunities that are deemed to be at the lowest rung of the economic (and social) ladder, thereby paving the way for occupational opportuni-ties for the constant flow of immigrants.

SEGMENTED THEORY

The segmented theory approach to the burgeoning pull factors in immigration places tremendous em-phasis on the aggressive actions of targeted groups to generate pull factors that entice immigrants to the host society. The world systems theory approach pushes the analysis to a higher level and contends that the pull factors are really manifestations of the political machination of the notion of globalization. Indeed, several immigration scholars have shown how this system has really built in the push-pull factors. According to Massey, this notion of economic globalization not only orchestrates a situation whereby the net effect is to create a populace that sees migration as a relief to the severe economic hardships experienced by economic globalization but also "creates ideological and cultural links between core capitalist countries and their peripheries . . . [which] are reinforced by mass communications and advertising campaigns directed from the core countries . . . [along] with the emergence of transportation and communication infrastructure to channel international migration to particular core countries."

The push factors here are not limited to merely low-wage-earning citizens in the developing or periphery countries; they are also directed to the middle class and citizens who are in search of academic credentials that would ostensibly catapult them into lucrative positions both in the receiving countries as well as in the periphery countries had they chosen to return. In a real sense, much of this is reminiscent of the colonial and postcolonial period in which citizens of the periphery countries felt compelled to migrate to core countries in order that they may secure an educational preparation that would be easily understood by the core country and simultaneously held in high esteem in the periphery countries. This push for economic globalization perhaps creates as many push as pull factors, because the need for both skilled and unskilled workers exists at both the core and periphery geographic entities.

SOCIAL CAPITAL THEORY

To a great extent, the social capital theory of migration may be seen as a natural extension of the push-pull factors generated by the notions of economic globalization. There is a plethora of scholars who have coined several concepts under the umbrella of the social capital theory and migration. Central to this theory is the notion that both a formal network and an informal network are built up in the sending and receiving countries that facilitate migration and thereby reduce the risks that are associated with the process of migration. This phenomenon is manifested not only among individuals and families but also extends to formalized organizations that are specifically dedicated to providing services to persons who make a decision to migrate as well as the linkages that maintain the connection with such persons and their relatives remaining in the periphery countries.

Perhaps the most important factor that determines the pull factor in immigration in the United States is the response of the American legislative arm to legal immigration. The United States has had, and continues to have, a rather checkered history regarding the pull factors in immigration. From the era of unrestricted immigration (1607–1882) to the era of restricted immigration (1882–1965) to the modern period of some restrictions (1965–present), there have always been provisions within immigration legislation that propelled pull factors in U.S. immigration. Despite the legal changes with respect to who was given special privileges in American immigration over the years, the one common and reoccurring factor was that immigration was seen largely in economic terms. Immigrants from several geographic entities outside the United States anticipated a better economic standing in the United States, whereas labor entities were resistant to the influx of immigrants.

LEGISLATIVE HISTORY

A closer scrutiny of the immigration legislation since 1965 indicates that the people who wrote the legislation were very cognizant of "pulling" in immigrants who were poised to operate functionally within the U.S. economy. Perhaps one of the best examples of the legislative actions regarding immigration over the years is California. Kevin F. McCarthy and Georges Vernez, in work prepared for the secretary of defense and several private foundations including the Ford and Andrew W. Mellon Foundations, contend that "California's attraction [pull factors] to immigrants is nothing new. . . . Indeed, if the United States can be described as a nation of immigrants, this statement is even more descriptive of California."

In tracing the pull factors that attracted immigrants to California, one finds several elements that single out California's immigrant population as somewhat different from that of the rest of the nation, as well as show how the various theoretical pieces above were manifested in the case of California. Two important legislative actions led to the differential American immigration patterns in the United States.

Prior to 1910, the immigration patterns in the United States were almost identically replicated in California. By the 1970s, however, differential immigration patterns had emerged in California vis-à-vis the rest of the United States; differential situations that were attributable to pull factors manifested largely in legislative actions. Two legislative actions are particularly pertinent to an understanding of such patterns in California. First, the Bracero Program originated before World War II out of an agreement between the U.S. government and Mexico and provided for agricultural workers to have seasonal employment contracts in the United States. While this provision extended to the entire country, the bulk of the workers being pulled to the United States were disproportionately located in California. Some explanation may lie in the proximity of Mexico to California as well as the physical conditions that gave rise to a major engagement in agriculture.

Second, the immigration laws of 1917 and the 1920s were changed, and such changes had the net effect of providing fertile pull factors that favored large-scale immigration. The Bracero Program provided legal permission for thousands of laborers to enter the United States and work in the agricultural sector. However, in the early 1960s, Mexican workers were no longer eligible to engage in this contractual arrangement with the United States. The net effect was that the labor needs were now met by the same population, except that invariably the relationship was illegal. An important caveat in considering this situation is that many of the seasonal, agricultural workers from Mexico who came under the Bracero Program were afforded the privilege of obtaining legal status in the United States. This situation caused two important changes in the immigrant population of Mexican descent in California, and "as a result of this growth, California solidified its position as the most desired destination of Mexican immigrants," say McCarthy and Vernez. Consequently, what developed was an ethnic enclave that provided not only a pull factor for Mexican immigrants arriving in the United States either legally or illegally but also the economic opportunities for entrepreneurialism and the development of skills among newly arriving immigrants that enabled them to experience an easier adjustment in the host country.

The second phenomenon that has implications for pull factors in immigration was the realignment of the immigration laws that assign quotas to individual countries and the enactment of the 1965 Immigration and Nationality Act. According to McCarthy and Vernez, this reformulated immigration law had the net effect of increasing especially the number of Asian immigrants being pulled to California through provisions made for family reunification. As a manifestation of both the segmented labor theory of immigration and the social capital theory discussed

above, the Asian population in California was significantly increased through the legislation that gave preferences to this segment of the California population. The upshot of this phenomenon was that the "preferences given to family reunification also, and somewhat ironically, helped to make the new Asian immigrants the most skilled in the nation's history . . . [and as] these new Asian immigrants subsequently became citizens, they were able to bring in certain immediate family members who were exempt from the overall national ceiling, which created a 'snowball' effect that eventually allowed large numbers of their relatives to enter the country legally."

The push-pull factors that affect American immigration are still largely conceptualized and researched from the position of economic considerations. Such considerations tend to obfuscate the complexity of the push-pull phenomenon in American immigration. For example, what is euphemistically referred to as the "brain drain" issue goes well beyond economic considerations. Carmen Garcia Gaudilla, in an article on this issue, contends that "the failure of students and trainees to return home from abroad is a complex subject . . . it is independent of the wishes of those who do not return and of those in charge of the institutions concerned in home countries." There also needs to be more research to address the issue of push-pull factors in light of the realization that although "contemporary mass migration of the Third World period has made American society more diverse than before . . . lower-class immigrants in general and poor Latino and Caribbean immigrants in particular often settle in low-income minority neighborhoods . . . and assimilate to an adversarial culture."

P. Rudy Mattei

See also: Causes of Immigration (Part I, Sec. 3); Economics II: Push Factors (Part II, Sec. 1); Report on the Shortage of Technology Workers, 1997 (Part IV, Sec. 2).

BIBLIOGRAPHY

Borjas, George J. "Economic Theory and International Migration." *International Migration Review* 23 (1989): 457–85.

———. *Friends or Strangers: The Impact of Immigration on the U.S. Economy.* New York: Basic Books, 1990.

Bourdieu, Pierre. "The Forms of Capital." In *Handbook of Theory and Research for the Sociology of Education,* ed. John G. Richardson, pp. 241–58. Westport, CT: Greenwood, 1986.

Choldin, Harvey M. "Kinship Networks in the Migration Process." *International Migration Review* 7 (1973): 163–76.

Donato, Katherine M. "Understanding U.S. Immigration: Why Some Countries Send Women and Other Countries Send Men." In *Seeking Common Ground: Women Immigrants to the United States,* ed. Donna Gabaccia, pp. 159–84. Westport, CT: Greenwood, 1991.

Garcia Guadillo, Carmen. "The Brain Drain." *UNESCO Courier* 49 (1996): 24.

Goss, Jon D., and Bruce Lindquist. "Conceptualizing International Labor Migration: A Structuration Perspective." *International Migration Review* 29 (1995): 317–51.

Hagan, Jacqueline M., and Susan Gonzalez-Baker. "Implementing the U.S. Legalization Program: The Influence of Immigrant Communities and Local Agencies on Immigration Policy Reform." *International Migration Review* 27 (1993): 513–36.

Harker, Richard, Cheleen Mahar, and Chris Wilkes. *An Introduction to the Work of Pierre Bourdieu: The Practice of Theory.* London: Macmillan, 1990.

Jasso, Guillermina, and Mark R. Rozenzweig. *The New Chosen People: Immigrants in the United States.* New York: Russell Sage Foundation, 1990.

Levy, Mildred B., and Walter J. Wadycki. "The Influence of Family and Friends on Geographic Labor Mobility: An Intercensal Comparison." *Review of Economics and Statistics* 55 (1973): 198–203.

Lewis, W. Arthur. "Economic Development with Unlimited Supplies of Labor." *Manchester School of Economic and Social Studies* 22 (1954): 139–91.

Loury, Glenn C. "A Dynamic Theory of Racial Income Differences." In *Women, Minorities, and Employment Discrimination,* ed. Phyllis A. Wallace and Annette M. LaMond, pp. 153–86. Lexington, MA: Heath, 1977.

Massey, Douglas S. "Why Does Immigration Occur: A Theoretical Synthesis." In *The Handbook of International Migration: The American Experience,* ed. Charles Hirschman, Philip Kasinitz, and Josh DeWind. New York: Russell Sage Foundation, 1999.

Massey, Douglas S., Luin P. Goldring, and Jorge Durand. "Continuities in Transnational Migration: An Analysis of Nineteen Mexican Communities. *American Journal of Sociology* 99 (1994): 1492–1533.

———. "International Migration and Economic Development in Comparative Perspective." *Population and Development Review* 14 (1988): 383–414.

Massey, Douglas S., Rafael Alarcón, Jorge Durand, and Humberto González. *Return to Aztlán: The Social Process of International Migration from Western Mexico.* Berkeley: University of California Press, 1987.

McCarthy, Kevin F., and Georges Vernez. (1997). *Immigration in a Changing Economy: California's Experience.* Santa Monica, CA: Rand, 1977.

McDonald, John S., and Leatrice D. McDonald. "Chain Migration, Ethnic Neighborhood Formation, and Social Networks." In *An Urban World,* ed. Charles Tilly, pp. 226–36. Boston: Little, Brown, 1974.

Min, Pyong Gap. "A Comparison of Post-1965 and Turn-of-the-Century Immigrants in Intergenerational Mobility and Cultural Transmission." *Journal of Ethnic History* 18:3 (1999): 65–95.

Morawska, Ewa T. "The Sociology and Historiography of Immigration." In *Immigration Reconsidered: History, Sociology, and Politics,* ed. Virginia Yans-McLaughlin, pp. 187–240. New York: Oxford University Press, 1990.

Piore, Michael. *Birds of Passage: Migrant Labor in Industrial Societies.* New York: Cambridge University Press, 1979.

Portes, Alejandro, and Alex Stepick. *City on the Edge: The Transformation of Miami.* Berkeley: University of California Press, 1993.

Portes, Alejandro, and Robert L. Bach. *Latin Journey: Cuban and Mexican Immigrants in the United States.* Berkeley: University of California Press, 1985.

Portes, Alejandro, and Robert Manning. "The Immigrant Enclave: Theory and Empirical Examples." In *Competitive Ethnic Relations,* ed. Susan Olzak and Joane Nagel, pp. 47–68. Orlando, FL: Academic Press, 1986.

Portes, Alejandro, and Rubén G. Rumbaut. *Immigrant America: A Portrait.* Berkeley: University of California Press, 1990.

Ravis, Gustav, and John C. M. Fei. "A Theory of Economic Development." *American Economic Review* 51 (1961): 533–65.

Sassen, Saskia. *The Mobility of Labor and Capital: A Study in International Investment and Labor Flows.* New York: Cambridge University Press, 1988.

Schmeidl, Susanne. "Exploring the Causes of Forced Migration: A Pooled Time-Analysis, 1971–1990." *Social Science Quarterly* 78 (1997): 284–308.

Singer, Paul. "Dyamica de la Poblacion y desarrollo." In *El Papel del Crecimiento Demografico en el desarrolo Economico,* pp. 21–66. Mexico, D.F.: Editorial Siglo XXI, 1971.

———. *Economia Politica de la Urbanizacion.* Mexico, D.F.: Editorial Siglo XXI, 1975.

Sjaastad, Larry A. "The Costs and Returns of Human Migration." *Journal of Political Economy* 70 (1962): 880–93.

Stark, Oded. "Relative Deprivation and Migration: Theory, Evidence, and Policy Implications." In *Determinants of Emigration from Mexico, Central America, and the Caribbean,* ed. Sergio Diaz-Briquets and Sidney Winetraub, pp. 121–44. Boulder, CO: Westview, 1991.

Stark, Oded, and David E. Bloom. "The New Economics of Labor Migration." *American Economic Review* 75 (1985): 173–78.

Stern, Claudio. "Some Methodological Notes on the Study of Human Migration." In *International Migration Today.* Vol. 2, *Emerging Issues,* ed. Charles W. Stall, pp. 28–33. Perth: University of Western Australia for the United Nations Economic, Social, and Cultural Organization, 1988.

Taylor, J. Edward. "Differentiated Migration, Networks, Information, and Risk." In *Migration, Theory, Human Capital, and Development,* ed. Oded Stark, pp. 147–71. Greenwich, CT: JAI Press, 1986.

———. "Undocumented Mexico-U.S. Migration and Returns to Households in Rural Mexico." *American Journal of Agricultural Economics* 69 (1987): 626–38.

Tilly, Charles, and Charles H. Brown. "On Uprooting, Kinship, and Auspices of Migration." *International Journal of Comparative Sociology* 8 (1967): 139–64.

Todaro, Michael P. *Economic Development in the Third World.* New York: Longman, 1989.

———. *International Migration in Developing Countries.* Geneva: International Labor Office, 1976.

———. "A Model of Labor Migration and Urban Unemployment in Less Developed Countries." *American Economic Review* 59 (1969): 138–48.

Todaro, Michael P., and L. Maruszko. "Illegal Immigration and U.S. Immigration Reform: A Conceptual Framework." *Population and Development Review* 13 (1987): 101–14.

Williamson, Chilton, Jr. *The Immigration Mystique: America's False Conscience.* New York: Basic Books, 1996.

Wilson, Kenneth, and W. Allen Martin. "Ethnic Enclaves: A Comparison of the Cuban and Black Economics of Miami." *American Journal of Sociology* 88:1 (1982): 135–60.

ℰCONOMICS II: PUSH FACTORS

Individuals may experience their migration as the outcome of their personal decisions, but the option to migrate is itself socially produced. This fact is easily lost in much immigration analysis because immigration flows tend to share many characteristics—immigrants are mostly poor people from less developed countries, with low or medium levels of education, and are willing to take undesirable jobs. This has led to the notion that it is poverty and unemployment generally that push migrants to migrate. Yet many countries with great poverty and high unemployment lack any significant emigration history, and in others emigration is a recent event no matter how long-standing the poverty. It takes a number of other conditions to activate poverty into a push factor, and even then, it is likely to be only a small minority of poor and middle-class people who will actually try to emigrate. Emigration is not an undifferentiated escape from poverty and unemployment to prosperity.

Each country is unique and each migration flow is produced by specific conditions in time and place. But if we are to understand the possible effects of larger conditions on the formation and reproduction of migration flows, we need to abstract from these particularities so as to examine more general tendencies. For instance, one set of conditions that we now understand is significant is the fact of former colonial bonds. Thus in Europe, a majority of Algerian emigrants are in France and a majority of emigrants from the Indian subcontinent are in the United Kingdom. More controversial, economic dominance and the formation of transnational spaces for economic activity associated with the presence of U.S. firms overseas are beginning to be recognized as factors explaining some of the migration patterns into the United States. Similarly, U.S. direct or indirect overseas military activity—from Vietnam to El Salvador—is clearly a factor conditioning some of the flows of Indo-Chinese and Central Americans into the United States.

Today, the sharp growth in the organized export of workers, both legal and illegal, adds yet another dynamic to the older, long-standing ones. Organized exports can create whole new ways of linking emigration and immigration countries, beyond old colonial or new global economic linkages.

Confining the analysis to economic factors that may activate a general condition of poverty and unemployment into a migration push factor, we can see several patterns. Most migrations have been initiated through direct recruitment by firms, governments, or labor contractors. Once an immigrant community exists, the operation of the immigrant network tends to replace outside recruitment, and chain migration tends to set in. Second, recruitment by firms and governments typically takes place among countries that have already established linkages—colonial, neocolonial, military, and, increasingly, due to economic globalization. Third, economic globalization has further strengthened interdependence among a growing number of countries. It may also have contributed to create new push factors in countries with already high levels of government debt by sharpening this debt and its negative impact on overall economic conditions through the imposition of structural adjustment programs. Fourth, there has been a significant increase in the organized export of workers in the decade of the 1990s. Of particular importance here is the sharp increase in the illegal international trade in people for work and for the sex industry.

The focus in this essay is on three major aspects of these issues. They are (1) the geoeconomics of international migrations, which explain the considerable degree of patterning evident in these flows and provide the crucial context within which to understand the dynamic whereby an overall condition of poverty, unemployment, or underemployment can become activated into a migration push factor; (2) the contemporary formation of mechanisms binding emigration and immigration countries, particularly the impact of various forms of economic internationalization; and

A better chance for their children leads many immigrants to the United States. Here a young boy works at an automobile repair shop in Lucknow, India. *(Leah Vinluan/Impact Visuals)*

(3) the organized export, both legal and illegal, of workers.

THE GEOECONOMICS OF MIGRATION

It is important to note that some form of organized recruitment by employers or governments on behalf of employers often lies at the origin of immigration flows, both in the 1800s and today. But who recruits whom in terms of countries tends to be shaped by prior politico-economic bonds, for example, colonialism or current foreign investment and other cross-border operations by firms in the context of economic globalization. Eventually most migration flows gain a certain autonomy from the organized recruitment mechanisms.

The large mass migrations of the 1800s emerged as part of the formation of a transatlantic economic system binding several nation-states through economic transactions and wars, particularly war-induced flows of people. This transatlantic economy was at the core of U.S. development. There were mas-sive flows of capital, goods, and workers, and there were specific structures that produced this system. Before this period, labor movements across the Atlantic had been largely forced, notably slavery, and mostly from colonized African and Asian territories.

To take another example, the migrations to England in the 1950s originated in what had once been British territories. And the migrations into Western Europe of the 1960s and 1970s occurred in a context of direct recruitment and of European regional dominance over the Mediterranean and over some of the Eastern European countries. In brief, receiving countries have typically been participants in the processes leading to the formation of international migration.

The renewal of mass immigration into the United States in the 1960s, after five decades of little or no immigration, took place in a context of expanded U.S. economic and military activity in Asia and the Caribbean basin. The United States is at the heart of an international system of investment and production that binds these various regions. In the 1960s and 1970s, the United States played a crucial role in the development of a world economic system. It passed legislation and promoted international agreements aimed at opening its own and other countries' economies to flows of capital, goods, services and information.

This central military, political, and economic role contributed both to the creation of conditions that mobilized people into migrations, whether local or international, and to the formation of links with the United States that subsequently were to serve as often unintended bridges for international migration. This bridging effect was most probably strengthened by the Cold War context and the active ideological selling of the advantages of open democratic societies. One, albeit controversial interpretation, is that these patterns show us that measures commonly thought to deter emigration—foreign investment and the promotion of export-oriented growth in developing countries—seem to have had precisely the opposite effect, at least in the short and middle run. Among the leading senders of immigrants to the United States in the 1970s and 1980s have been several of the newly industrialized countries of South and Southeast Asia whose extremely high growth rates are generally recognized to be a result initially of foreign direct investment in export manufacturing. A parallel analysis has now been produced about the "development" effect of the North American Free Trade Agreement (NAFTA) on Mexican emigration to the United States: ongoing and new emigration and eventual stabilization in thirty years.

The specific forms of internationalization of capital we see since the postwar period have contributed to mobilize people into migration streams and to build bridges between countries of origin and the United States. The implantation of Western development strategies, from the replacement of smallholder agriculture with export-oriented commercial agriculture to the Westernization of educational systems, has contributed to mobilize people into migration streams—regional, national, and transnational.

At the same time, the administrative commercial and development networks of the former European empires and the newer forms these networks assumed under the Pax Americana (international direct foreign investment, export processing zones, wars for democracy) have created bridges not only for the flow of capital, information and high-level personnel from the center to the periphery, but also for the flow of migrants. In a 1991 article, S. Hall described the postwar influx of people from the Commonwealth into Britain and notes that England and Englishness were so present in his native Jamaica as to make people feel that London was the capital to which they were all headed sooner or later. This way of narrating the migration events of the postwar era captures the ongoing weight of colonialism and postcolonial forms of empire on major processes of globalization today, and specifically those binding emigration and immigration countries. The major immigration countries are not innocent bystanders; the specific genesis and contents of their responsibility will vary from case to case and period to period.

On a more conceptual level, one could generalize these tendencies and posit that immigration flows take place within systems and that these systems can be specified in a variety of ways. The type of economic specification contained in this article represents but one of several possibilities. In other cases, the system within which immigration takes place is to be specified in political or ethnic terms. One could ask, for example, if there are systemic linkages underlying the current Central European migrations to Germany and Austria. Thus, before World War II both Berlin and Vienna were major receivers of large migrations from a vast Eastern region. Furthermore, these practices produced and reproduced migration systems as such. Finally, the aggressive campaign during the Cold War years showing the West as a place where economic well-being was the norm and well-paying jobs were easy to get had an effect in inducing people to migrate westward; a more accurate portrayal of conditions in the West might have deterred potential migrants beyond those that would have come at all costs. These historical and current conditions contain elements for specifying the systems within which the current Eastern European migrations to Germany and Austria take place.

The fact that there is a geoeconomics of migration is suggested by major immigration patterns. If immigration were simply a matter of policy and the will to enforce controls, then many of the current unauthorized flows should not exist. In the case of the United States, the major reform passed in 1965, known as the Immigration and Nationality Act, had an immense impact because it happened at a time when the United States had a far-flung network of production sites and military operations in several Third World countries. There was not only a pent-up demand for emigration but also a broad network of linkages between those countries and the United States. That the new law as such was not enough to bring about the new immigration to the United States is also suggested by the fact that, being based on family reunion, the new law was expected to induce largely the immigration of relatives of those already in the country, that is, mostly Europeans. Instead, the vast majority of immigrants came from the Caribbean basin and several Asian countries. Policy alone cannot engender migrations.

Sixty percent of the foreign residents in the United

Kingdom are from Asian or African countries that were former dominions or colonies; European immigration is rather low, and almost three-fourths of these come from Ireland—also once a colonized territory. While the United Kingdom has few immigrants from such countries as Turkey or Yugoslavia, which provide the largest share to Germany, it has almost all immigrants from the Indian subcontinent and from the English Caribbean residing in Europe.

Continuing along these lines, in the first ten years after World War II, the vast majority of "immigrants" to Germany were the 8 million displaced ethnic Germans that resettled there. Another major group were the 3 million who came from East Germany before the Berlin Wall was erected in 1961. Almost all ethnic Germans went to Germany, and those who did not go to Germany went overseas. But also 86 percent of Greek immigrants in Europe reside in Germany, as do almost 80 percent of Turkish immigrants in Europe and 76 percent of Yugoslavs. More recently, Germany has expanded its labor recruitment or sourcing area to include Portugal, Algeria, Morocco, and Tunisia, even though the vast majority of immigrants from these countries reside in France. In brief, what we see in the case of Germany is, first, a large migration rooted in a long history of domination over the Eastern region, then an immigration originating in less developed countries following a by now classical dynamic of labor-import/labor-export countries.

The Netherlands and Belgium both received significant numbers of people from their former colonial empires. They also received foreign workers from labor-exporting countries, such as Italy, Morocco, and Turkey. Switzerland similarly receives workers from the traditional labor-exporting countries of Italy, Spain, Portugal, Yugoslavia, and Turkey. All three countries originally organized the recruitment of these workers, until eventually a somewhat autonomous set of flows was in place. Sweden receives almost 95 percent of Finnish immigrants. Also in Sweden, as in the other countries, there is a large expansion of the recruitment area to include workers from the traditional labor-exporting countries on the Mediterranean.

As a given labor migration flow ages, it tends to become more diversified in terms of destination. It suggests that a certain autonomy from older colonial and neocolonial bonds sets in. Immigrants from Italy are now distributed among several countries. Among Italian immigrants in Europe, one-third reside in Germany, 27 percent in France, 24 percent in Switzerland, and 15 percent in Belgium. The fact that it is still a limited diversity of destinations could be seen as signaling the presence of migration systems. On the other hand, younger labor migrations reveal very high levels of geographic concentration. The largest single immigrant group in any of Europe's labor-receiving countries today are the Turks, with 1.5 million in Germany.

CONDITIONS THAT OPERATE AS ECONOMIC PUSH FACTORS

We can group the variety of economic conditions that contribute to migration links between sending and receiving countries into three major categories: (1) linkages brought about by economic internationalization, (2) linkages specifically developed to recruit workers, and (3) the organized export of workers. This section discusses the first two and the next section the third.

ECONOMIC LINKAGES

Linkages created by economic internationalization range from the establishment of offshore production and the implantation of export-oriented agriculture through foreign investment to the weight of multinationals in the consumer markets of sending countries.

For instance, the development of commercial agriculture and of export-oriented standardized manufacturing have dislocated traditional economies and eliminated survival opportunities for small producers, who are forced to become wage laborers. This in turn contributes to mobilize these displaced smallholders and crafts-based producers into migrations for labor, which may initially be internal but eventually can become international. There are multiple examples of this dynamic. Sarah Mahler found that Salvadorean immigrants in the United States often had had prior experience as migrant workers to the coffee plantations. Maria Patricia Fernández-Kelly found that some of the internal migrants to the northern industrialization zone of Mexico eventually became migrants to the United States. Frank Bonilla and Ricardo Campos found a similar impact from the U.S.-sponsored "Operation Bootstraps" in Puerto Rico in promoting emigration to the United States.

Another type of economic linkage resulted from the large-scale development of manufacturing operations in low-wage countries by firms from the highly developed countries. The aim here was and continues to be to lower the costs of production of goods meant for and reexported to markets in their home countries. This creates a number of objective and subjective linkages between the highly developed countries and these low-wage countries. There are two migration-inducing conditions at work here. One is that the better-situated workers may gain special access to the contacts for migration, and the second is that the most disadvantaged workers are often "used up" after a few years and then need to find new ways of surviving and helping their families, which may in turn lead to outmigration. These workers are, partly, in an extended labor market that connects the two countries involved.

The growing use of offshore production to lower costs also helps create conditions in the highly developed countries that may lead to recruitment/demand for low-wage immigrant workers, given the growing pressure among firms and countries to lower costs to remain competitive. The internationalization of manufacturing production and of agriculture has contributed to weaken unions and has generally led to the search for low-wage workers inside the developed countries.

The case of Japan is of interest here because it allows us to capture the intersection of economic internationalization and immigration in its inception and to do so in a country with a radically different history, culture, and, to a lesser extent, economic organization from those of other advanced economies. Japan's lack of an immigration history in the recent period—it had one in the 1800s—provides us with a clearer picture of these dynamics. Though it developed much later than in most other advanced economies, Japan now has a growing unauthorized immigrant workforce in low-wage, unskilled jobs in a context where Japanese youth are rejecting such jobs.

In the case of Japan, one cannot help but ask why has this happened now rather than during the period of extremely rapid economic growth in the 1950s and 1960s, when Japan experienced very sharp labor shortages. In the 1980s Japan became a major presence in a regional Asian economic system where it is the leading investor, foreign aid donor, and exporter of consumer goods (including cultural products). In the 1980s Japanese firms began to set up large numbers of manufacturing operations, with a heavy concentration in Asian countries. This has created legal and illegal networks between those countries and Japan, and these countries emerged as some of the leading senders of immigrants to Japan. In its period of high growth, Japan lacked the types of networks and linkages with potential immigrant-sending countries that could have facilitated the formation of international migration flows. As Japan internationalized its economy and became a key investor in South and Southeast Asia, it created—wittingly or not—a transnational space for the circulation of its goods, capital,

and culture, which in turn created conditions for the circulation of people. We may be seeing the early stages in the formation of an international labor market, a market that both labor contractors and unauthorized immigrants can "step into." Once Asian immigrants had become part of the low-wage workforce in many economic sectors and given ongoing shortages, the Japanese government initiated recruitment of people of Japanese descent in Brazil and Peru, adjusting its immigration law to do so. These emergent immigrant communities have now entered the stage of chain migration.

Another type of linkage is shaped by the growing Westernization of advanced education systems, which facilitates the movement of highly educated workers into the developed Western countries. This is a process that has been happening for many decades and is usually referred to as the "brain drain." Today it assumes specific forms, given the growing interdependence among countries and the formation of global markets and global firms. We are seeing the formation of an increasingly complex and flexible transnational labor market for high-level professionals in advanced corporate services that links a growing number of highly developed and developing countries. This is also taking place in the high-tech sector, where there is explicit recruitment of computer and software experts, especially from India, by firms in highly developed countries. More generally, we can capture these and other such dynamics in the strong trend for immigration to be bimodal in terms of educational levels: with a concentration of low-wage, poorly educated workers and a concentration of very highly educated workers.

RECRUITMENT AND ETHNIC NETWORKS

The second type of linkage includes a variety of mechanisms for the organized or informal recruitment of workers. This can operate through governments in the framework of a government-supported initiative by employers, directly by employers, through the illegal smuggling of workers, or through kinship and family networks. Some of these can also function as more generalized migration channels. Ethnic linkages established between communities of origin and destination, typically via the formation of transnational households or broader kinship structures, emerge as crucial once a flow has been formed, and they serve to ensure its reproduction over time. These recruitment and ethnic linkages tend to operate within the broader transnational spaces constituted via neocolonial processes and/or economic internationalization.

A key issue facilitating the operation of ethnic networks and recruitment operations is the existence of an effective demand for immigrant workers in the receiving countries. Labor demand—more specifically, the effective labor market absorption of workers coming from different cultures with mostly lower levels of development—becomes increasingly important in the context of advanced service economies. Immigrants have a long history of getting hired in low-wage jobs requiring little education and often situated in the least advanced sectors.

Much analysis of postindustrial society and advanced economies generally posits a massive growth in the need for highly educated workers and little need for the types of jobs that a majority of immigrants have tended to hold over the last two or three decades. This suggests sharply reduced employment opportunities for workers with low educational levels generally and for immigrants in particular. Yet detailed empirical studies of major cities in highly developed countries show ongoing demand for immigrant workers and a significant supply of old and new jobs requiring little education and paying low wages. One current controversial issue is whether this job supply is merely or largely a residual partly inflated by the large supply of low-wage workers, or is mostly part of the reconfiguration of the job supply and employment relations that are in fact a feature of advanced service economies, that is to say, a systemic development that is an integral part of such economies. There are no precise measures, and a focus on the jobs by themselves will hardly illuminate the issue. We know generally what they are: low-wage, requiring little education, undesirable, with no advancement opportunities, and few if any fringe benefits. There are clearly some aspects of the growth dynamics in advanced service economies that are creating at least part of this job supply. This job supply is a crucial cog in the sets of linkages used and developed by coethnics and by recruiters.

One condition in the reproduction of these linkages is that over the last few decades, and in some cases over the entire twentieth century, certain countries have become marked as labor-export countries. In many ways, the labor-exporting country is put in a subordinate position, and keeps being represented in the media and in political discourse as a labor-exporting country. This was also the case in the nineteenth century, when some labor-sending areas existed in conditions of economic subordination and often also quasi-political subordination. The former Polish territories partitioned off to Germany were such a region, generating significant migration of ethnic Poles to western Germany and beyond. It is also the case of the Irish in England, and of Italy, which

kept reproducing itself as a labor supplier for the rest of Europe.

It does seem (and the history of economic development supports this) that once an area becomes a significant emigration region, it does not easily catch up in terms of development with those areas that emerge as labor-importing areas. Precisely because the latter have high growth, or at least relatively high growth, a type of cumulative causation effect sets in that amounts to an accumulation of advantage. Whether immigration contributes to this process of cumulative causation is a complex issue, though much scholarship shows that immigration countries have gained multiple benefits from access to immigrant labor, particularly in periods of high economic growth. Further, whether emigration contributes to the negative cumulative causation evident in sending countries is also a complex matter. The evidence shows that individual households and localities may have benefited, but not national economies. History suggests that the accumulation of advantage evident in receiving countries has tended to elude labor-sending areas because they either cannot catch up with or are structurally excluded from the actual spatialization of growth, precisely because it is characterized by uneven development. Italy and Ireland for two centuries were labor exporters, and this did not turn out to be a macroeconomic advantage. Their current economic dynamism and labor immigration have little to do with their prior history as emigration countries; rather, they result from a set of specific economic processes in each of these countries that took hold and rapidly expanded the economy.

In brief, analytically we could argue that as today's labor-receiving countries grew richer and more developed, they kept expanding their zone of recruitment/influence, covering an expanding set of countries and including a variety of emigration-immigration dynamics, some rooted in past imperial conditions, others in the newer development asymmetries that underlie much migration today. There is a dynamic of inequality within which labor migrations are embedded, and this dynamic keeps on marking regions as labor-sending and labor-receiving, though a given country may switch categories as is the case with Ireland and Italy today.

SUSTAINING MIGRATION: WOMEN AND SETTLEMENT

The reproduction of migration flows is strongly influenced by the fact of settlement. And the extent of settlement, we now know, is in turn deeply influenced by the difficulty of circulation between country of origin and country of destination. Recent literature has given us enormous insights into the dynamics of settlement and circulation, and though it covers only part of the picture, it helps us understand some of the strategic elements. Let me briefly address these.

In understanding settlement, it is essential to introduce the fact of the differential outcomes that result from gendering. There is, to some extent, a joining of two different dynamics in the condition of immigrant women. On one hand, they are constituted as an invisible and disempowered class of workers in the factories and the services of the receiving economy. On the other hand, access to wages and salaries (even if low), the growing feminization of the job supply in highly developed economies, and the growing feminization of business opportunities brought about by informalization do alter the gender hierarchies in which women find themselves.

The incorporation of women in the migration process strengthens the likelihood of permanent settlement and contributes to greater immigrant participation both in their communities and vis-à-vis the state. This, in turn, furthers settlement. For instance, Pierrette Hondagneu-Sotelo found that immigrant women come to assume more active public and social roles, which further reinforces their status in the household and the settlement process. Women gain greater personal autonomy and independence, while men lose ground. Women gain more control over budgeting and other domestic decisions, and greater leverage in requesting help from men in domestic chores. Also, their access to public services and other public resources gives them a chance to become incorporated in the mainstream society—they are often the ones in the household who mediate in this process. It is likely that some women benefit more than others from these circumstances; there are likely to be differences in terms of the impact of class, education, and income on these gendered outcomes. Sherri Grasmuck and Patricia Pessar found that Dominican women wanted to settle in New York precisely because of these gains, while men wanted to return. They found women spending large shares of earnings on expensive durable consumer goods such as appliances and home furnishings, which served to root the family more securely in the United States and deplete the funds needed for organizing a successful return. Men preferred to spend as little as possible, instead saving for the return. Mary Garcia Castro had similar results in her study on Colombian women in New York City.

Besides the relatively greater empowerment of women in the household associated with waged employment, there is a second important outcome: their greater participation in the public sphere and their

possible emergence as public actors. There are two arenas where immigrant women are active: institutions for public and private assistance, and the immigrant/ethnic community. Women are more active in community building and community activism, and they are positioned differently than men regarding the broader economy and the state. They are the ones that are likely to have to handle the legal vulnerability of their families in the process of seeking public and social services for their families.

THE ORGANIZED EXPORT OF WORKERS

The decade of the 1990s has seen a sharp growth in the export of workers, both legal and illegal. This growth in exports is not simply the other, passive side of the active recruitment of immigrants described above. This organized export has its own specific features. These are operations for profit making and for enhancing government revenue through the export of workers. In terms of economic conditioning, a crucial matter for research and explanation is what the systemic links are, if any, between the growth of organized exports of workers for private profit or for government revenue enhancement, on one hand, and major economic conditions in developing countries today, on the other. Among these conditions are growth in unemployment, the closure of a large number of typically small and medium-sized enterprises oriented to national rather than export markets, and large, often increasing government debt. While these economies are frequently grouped under the label "developing," they are in some cases struggling or stagnant and even shrinking. (For the sake of brevity, we use the word *developing* as shorthand for this variety of situations.) The evidence for these conditions is incomplete and partial, yet there is a growing consensus among experts that they are expanding and, further, that women are often a majority, including in situations that used to be mostly male.

The various types of exports of workers have strengthened at a time when major dynamics linked to economic globalization have had significant impacts on developing economies. The latter have had to implement a bundle of new policies and accommodate new conditions associated with globalization: structural adjustment programs, the opening up of these economies to foreign firms, the elimination of multiple state subsidies, and the nearly inevitable financial crises and the prevailing types of programmatic solutions put forth by the International Monetary Fund (IMF). It is now clear that in most of the countries involved, these conditions have created enormous costs for certain sectors of the economy and of the population, and have not fundamentally reduced government debt.

Among these costs are, prominently, the growth in unemployment, the closure of a large number of firms in often fairly traditional sectors oriented to the local or national market, the promotion of export-oriented cash crops that have increasingly replaced survival agriculture and food production for local or national markets, and, finally, the ongoing and mostly heavy burden of government debt in most of these economies.

Are there systemic links between these two sets of developments—the growth of organized exports of workers from these developing economies and the rise in unemployment and debt in those same economies? One way of articulating this in substantive terms is to posit that (1) shrinking opportunities for employment in many of these countries, (2) shrinking opportunities for more traditional forms of profit making as they increasingly accept foreign firms in a widening range of economic sectors and are pressured to develop export industries, and (3) the fall in revenues for the governments in many of these countries, partly linked to these conditions and to the burden of debt servicing, have all contributed to raise the importance of alternative ways of making a living, making a profit, and securing government revenue.

Prostitution and labor migration are ways of making a living; the legal and illegal trafficking in workers, including workers for the sex industry, is growing in importance as a way of making a profit; and the remittances sent by emigrants, as well as revenues from the organized export of workers, are increasingly important sources of foreign currency for some of these governments. Women are by far the majority group in the illegal trafficking for the sex industry and in the organized government export of workers.

The organized export of workers, whether legal or illegal, is partly facilitated by the organizational and technical infrastructure of the global economy: the formation of global markets, the intensifying of transnational and translocal networks, and the development of communication technologies that easily escape conventional surveillance practices. The strengthening and, in some of these cases, the formation of new global networks is embedded or made possible by the existence of a global economic system and its associated development of various institutional supports for cross-border money flows and markets. Once there is an institutional infrastructure

for globalization, processes that have basically operated at the national level can scale up to the global level even when this is not necessary for their operation. This would contrast with processes that are by their very features global, such as the network of financial centers underlying the formation of a global capital market.

Debt and debt servicing problems have become a systemic feature of the developing world since the 1980s and are contributing to the expanded efforts to export workers, both legally and illegally. There is considerable research showing the detrimental effects of such debt on government programs for women and children, notably education and health care—clearly investments necessary to ensure a better future. Further, the increased unemployment typically associated with the austerity and adjustment programs implemented by international agencies to address government debt have also been found to have adverse effects on broad sectors of the population. Subsistence food production, informal work, emigration, and prostitution have all grown as survival options. Heavy government debt and high unemployment have brought with them the need to search for alternative sources for government revenue; and the shrinking of regular economic opportunities has brought with it a widened use of illegal profit making by enterprises and organizations.

Generally, most countries that became deeply indebted in the 1980s have not been able to solve this problem. And in the 1990s, we have seen a whole new set of countries become deeply indebted. Over these two decades, many innovations were launched, most importantly by the IMF and the World Bank through their structural adjustment programs and structural adjustment loans, respectively. The latter were tied to economic policy reform rather than the funding of a particular project. The purpose of such programs is to make states more "competitive," which typically means sharp cuts in various social programs.

A growing number of countries have been paying a significant share of their total revenues to service their debt. Thirty-three of the forty-one highly indebted poor countries (HIPCs) paid $3 in debt service payments to the North for every $1 in development assistance. Many of these countries pay over 50 percent of their government revenues toward debt service or 20 to 25 percent of their export earnings; the ratios of debt service to Gross National Product (GNP) in many of the HIPC countries exceed sustainable limits. Today these ratios are far more extreme than what were considered unmanageable levels in the Latin American debt crisis of the 1980s. Debt-to-GNP ratios are especially high in Africa, where they stand at 123 percent, compared with 42 percent in Latin America and 28 percent in Asia. The IMF asks HIPCs to pay 20 to 25 percent of their export earnings toward debt service. In contrast, in 1953 the Allies canceled 80 percent of Germany's war debt and only insisted on 3 to 5 percent of export earnings debt service. These more general terms have also been evident in recent history, when Central Europe emerged from under communism. This debt burden inevitably has large repercussions on state spending composition and, through this, on the population.

There is a research literature on the devastating impact of government debt, focused on the implementation of a first generation of structural adjustment programs in several developing countries in the 1980s and on a second generation of such programs, one more directly linked to the implementation of the global economy, in the 1990s. This literature has documented the disproportionate burden these programs put on the lower middle classes and the working poor, and most especially women. These conditions push households and individuals into accepting or seeking legal or illegal traffickers to take them to any job, anywhere.

Yet even under these extreme conditions, where the traffickers often function as recruiters who may initiate the procedure, it is only a minority of people who are emigrating. The participation of traffickers to some extent alters the type of patterning associated with government and firm recruitment (discussed above), which tends to be embedded in older sets of linkages connecting the countries involved.

Remittances sent by immigrants represent a major source of foreign exchange reserves for governments in many developing countries. While the flows of remittances may be minor compared to the massive daily capital flows in various financial markets, they are often very significant for developing or struggling economies. In 1998 global remittances sent by immigrants to their home countries reached over U.S. $70 billion. To understand the significance of this figure, it should be related to the GDP and foreign currency reserves in the specific countries involved, rather than compared to the global flow of capital. For instance, in the Philippines, a key sender of migrants generally and of women for the entertainment industry in several countries, remittances represented the third largest source of foreign exchange over the last several years. In Bangladesh, another country with significant numbers of its workers in the Middle East, Japan, and several European countries, remittances represent about a third of foreign exchange.

The illegal export of migrants is above all a profitable business for the traffickers, though it can also add to the flow of legal remittances. According to a recent United Nations' report, criminal organizations in the 1990s generated an estimated U.S. $3.5 billion per year in profits from trafficking male and female migrants for work. Once this was mostly the trade of petty criminals; today it is an increasingly organized operation that functions on a global scale. The entry of organized crime is a recent development in the case of migrant trafficking. There are also reports that organized crime groups are creating intercontinental strategic alliances through networks of coethnics throughout several countries; this facilitates transport, local contact and distribution, and provision of false documents.

While most men and many women are indeed trafficked for work, women are at great risk of getting diverted to the sex trade. Some women know that they are being trafficked for prostitution, but for many the conditions of their recruitment and the extent of abuse and bondage become evident only after they arrive in the receiving country. The conditions of confinement are often extreme, akin to slavery, and so are the conditions of abuse, including rape, other forms of sexual violence, and physical punishments. They are severely underpaid, and wages are often withheld.

The next two sections focus with some more detail on two aspects of the organized export of workers, government exports and the illegal trafficking in women for the sex industry.

GOVERNMENT-ORGANIZED EXPORTS

Exporting workers is a means for governments of coping with unemployment and foreign debt. There are two ways in which governments have secured benefits through these strategies. One of these is highly formalized, and the other is simply a by-product of the migration process itself. Among the strongest examples of the formalized mode are South Korea and the Philippines. In the 1970s, South Korea developed extensive programs to promote the export of workers as an integral part of its growing overseas construction industry, initially to the Middle Eastern members of the Organization of the Petroleum Exporting Countries (OPEC) and then worldwide. As South Korea entered its own economic boom, exporting workers became a less necessary and attractive option. In contrast, the Philippine government did expand and diversify the concept of exporting its citizens as a way of dealing with unemployment and securing needed foreign exchange reserves through their remittances.

The case of the Philippines illuminates a whole series of issues about government exports of workers. The Philippine government has played an important role in the emigration of Filipinas to the United States, the Middle East, and Japan through the Philippines Overseas Employment Administration (POEA). Established in 1982, it organized and oversaw the export of nurses and maids to high-demand areas in the world. High foreign debt and high unemployment combined to make this an attractive policy. Filipino overseas workers sent home almost U.S. $1 billion per year during the 1990s. On the other side, the various labor-importing countries welcomed this policy for their own specific reasons. OPEC countries of the Middle East saw the demand for domestic workers grow sharply after the 1973 oil boom. Confronted with a sharp shortage of nurses, a profession that demanded years of training yet garnered rather low wages and little prestige or recognition, the United States passed the Immigration Nursing Relief Act of 1989, which allowed for the import of nurses. About 80 percent of the nurses brought in under the new act were from the Philippines. And Japan passed legislation that permitted the entry of "entertainment workers" into its booming economy in the 1980s, marked by rising expendable incomes and strong labor shortages.

The Philippine government also passed regulations that permitted mail-order bride agencies to recruit young Filipinas to marry foreign men as a matter of contractual agreement. The rapid increase in this trade was centrally due to the organized effort by the government. Among the major clients were the United States and Japan. Japan's agricultural communities were a key destination for these brides, given enormous shortages of people and especially young women in the Japanese countryside when the economy was booming and demand for labor in the large metropolitan areas was extremely high. Municipal governments made it a policy to accept Filipino brides.

The largest number of Filipinas going through these government-promoted channels work overseas as maids, particularly in other Asian countries. The second largest group, and the fastest growing, is entertainers, largely to Japan.

The rapid increase in the numbers of migrants going as entertainers is largely due to the more than five hundred "entertainment brokers" in the Philippines operating outside the state umbrella—even though the government may still benefit from the remittances of these workers. These brokers provide women for the sex industry in Japan, basically working through organized gangs rather than going through the government-controlled program for the entry of entertainers. These women are recruited for singing and entertaining, but frequently, perhaps mostly, they are forced into prostitution as well. They are recruited

and brought in both through formal legal channels and illegally. Either way, they have little power to resist. Even as they are paid below-minimum wages, they produce significant profits for the brokers and employers involved. There has been an enormous increase in so-called entertainment businesses in Japan.

The Philippine government approved most mail-order bride organizations until 1989. Under the government of President Corazon Aquino, the stories of abuse by foreign husbands led to the banning of the mail-order bride business, but it is almost impossible to eliminate these organizations, and they continue to operate in violation of the law.

The Philippines, while perhaps the one with the most developed program, is not the only country to have explored these strategies. Thailand started a campaign in 1998, after the 1997–98 financial crisis, to promote migration for work and recruitment by firms overseas of Thai workers. The government sought to export workers to the Middle East, the United States, Great Britain, Germany, Australia, and Greece. Sri Lanka's government has tried to export another two hundred thousand workers in addition to the 1 million it already has overseas; Sri Lankan women remitted U.S. $880 million in 1998, mostly from their earnings as maids in the Middle East and Far East. In the 1970s, Bangladesh had already organized extensive labor export programs to the OPEC countries of the Middle East. This has continued, and along with individual migration both to these countries and to various other countries, notably the United States and Great Britain, it is a significant source of foreign exchange. Its workers remitted U.S. $1.4 billion in each of the last few years.

TRAFFICKING IN WOMEN

International trafficking in women for the sex industry has grown sharply over the last decade. The available evidence suggests that it is highly profitable for those running the trade. The United Nations estimates that 4 million people were trafficked in 1998, producing a profit of U.S. $7 billion to criminal groups. These funds include remittances from prostitutes' earnings and payments to organizers and facilitators in these countries.

It is estimated that in recent years several million women and girls are trafficked within and out of Asia and the former Soviet Union, two major trafficking areas. Growth in both these areas can be linked to women being pushed into poverty or sold to brokers due to the poverty of their households or parents. High unemployment in the former Soviet republics has been one factor promoting growth of criminal gangs as well as growth of trafficking in women. For instance, Ukrainian and Russian women, highly prized in the sex market, earn the criminal gangs involved about $500 to $1,000 per woman delivered. These women can be expected to service on average fifteen clients a day, and each can be expected to make about U.S. $215,000 per month for the gang.

Such networks also facilitate the organized circulation of trafficked women among third countries—not only from sending to receiving countries. Traffickers may move women from Burma, Laos, Vietnam, and China to Thailand, while Thai women may have been moved to Japan and the United States. There are various reports on the particular cross-border movements in trafficking. Malay brokers sell Malay women into prostitution in Australia. East European women from Albania and Kosovo have been trafficked by gangs into prostitution in London. European teens from Paris and other cities have been sold to Arab and African customers. In the United States, the police broke up an international Asian ring that imported women from China, Thailand, Korea, Malaysia, and Vietnam. The women were charged between U.S. $30,000 and $40,000 to be smuggled in, to be paid through their work in the sex trade or needle trade.

As tourism has grown sharply over the last decade and become a major development strategy for cities, regions, and whole countries, the entertainment sector has undergone parallel growth and is seen now as a key development strategy. In many places, the sex trade is part of the entertainment industry and has similarly grown. At some point it becomes clear that the sex trade itself can become a development strategy in areas with high unemployment, poverty, and governments desperate for revenue and foreign exchange reserves. When local manufacturing and agriculture can no longer function as sources of employment, profits, and government revenue, what was once a marginal source of revenue now becomes a far more important one. The increased importance of these sectors in development generates growing tie-ins. For instance, when the IMF and the World Bank see tourism as a solution to some of the development impasses in many poor countries and provide loans for its development, they may well be contributing to the development of a broader institutional setting for the expansion of the entertainment industry and, indirectly, of the sex trade. This tie-in with development strategies signals that trafficking in women may well see a sharp expansion.

The entry of organized crime in the sex trade, the formation of cross-border ethnic networks, and the growing transnationalization in so many aspects of tourism suggest that we are likely to see further development of a global sex industry. This could mean greater attempts to enter into more and more "markets" and a general expansion of the industry. Given a growing number of women with few if any employment options, the prospects are grim.

Women in the sex industry become—in certain kinds of economies—a crucial link supporting the expansion of the entertainment industry and, through that, tourism; this development strategy in turn becomes a source of government revenue. These tie-ins are structural, not a function of conspiracies. Their weight in an economy will be raised by the absence or limitations of other sources for securing a livelihood, profits, and revenues for, respectively, workers, enterprises, and governments.

Saskia Sassen

See also: Causes of Immigration (Part I, Sec. 2); Economics I: Pull Factors (Part II, Sec. 1).

BIBLIOGRAPHY

Basch, Linda, Nina Glick Schiller, and Cristina Szanton-Blanc. *Nations Unbound: Transnationalized Projects and the Deterritorialized Nation-State.* New York: Gordon and Bohning, 1994.

Bonilla, Frank, and Ricardo Campos. "Bootstraps and Enterprise Zones: The Underside of Late Capitalism in Puerto Rico and the United States." *Review* (Fernand Braudel Center) 4 (spring 1982): 556–90.

Bonilla, Frank, Edwin Melendez, Rebecca Morales, and Maria de los Angeles Torres, eds. *Borderless Borders.* Philadelphia: Temple University Press, 1998.

Boyd, Monica. "Family and Personal Networks in International Migration: Recent Developments and New Agendas." *International Migration Review* 23 (1989): 638–70.

Bose, Christine E., and Edna Acosta-Belén, eds. *Women in the Latin American Development Process.* Philadelphia: Temple University Press, 1995.

Briggs, Vernon M., Jr. *Mass Immigration and the National Interest.* Armonk, NY: M. E. Sharpe, 1992.

Bustamante, Jorge A., and Geronimo Martínez. "Undocumented Immigration from Mexico: Beyond Borders but Within Systems." *Journal of International Affairs* 33 (fall/winter 1979): 265–84.

Castles, Stephen, and Mark J. Miller. *The Age of Migration: International Population Movements in the Modern World.* 2d ed. New York: Macmillan, 1998.

Castro, Mary Garcia. "Work Versus Life: Colombian Women in New York." In *Women and Change in Latin America*, ed. June Nash and Helen Safa, pp. 231–55. South Hadley, MA: Bergin and Garvey, 1986.

Chin, Christine. "Walls of Silence and Late 20th Century Representations of Foreign Female Domestic Workers: The Case of Filipina and Indonesian Houseservants in Malaysia." *International Migration Review* 31:1 (1997): 353–85.

Cohen, Robin, ed. *The Sociology of Migration.* International Library of Studies on Migration. Cheltenham, UK: Elgar, 1996.

Cornelius, Wayne A., Philip L. Martin, and James F. Hollifield, eds. *Controlling Immigration: A Global Perspective.* Stanford: Stanford University Press, 1994.

David, Natacha. "Migrants Made the Scapegoats of the Crisis." *ICFTU Online,* International Confederation of Free Trade Unions, www.hartford-hwp.com/archives/50/012.html, 1999.

Fernández-Kelly, María Patricia. *For We Are Sold, I and My People: Women and Industry in Mexico's Frontier.* Albany: State University of New York Press, 1982.

Grasmuck, Sherri, and Patricia Pessar. *Between Two Islands: Dominican International Migration.* Berkeley: University of California Press, 1991.

Hall, S. "The Local and the Global: Globalization and Ethnicity." In *Culture, Globalization and the World-System: Contemporary Conditions for the Representation of Identity,* ed. Anthony D. Hall. Current Debates in Art History 3. Department of Art and Art History, State University of New York at Binghamton, 1991.

Heyzer, Noeleen. *The Trade in Domestic Workers.* London: Zed, 1994.

Hondagneu-Sotelo, Pierrette. *Gendered Transitions.* Berkeley: University of California Press, 1994.

Isbister, John. *The Immigration Debate: Remaking America.* Bloomfield, CT: Kumarian Books, 1996.

Jacobson, David, ed. *The Immigration Reader: America in a Multidisciplinary Perspective.* Oxford: Blackwell, 1998.

Mahler, Sarah. *American Dreaming: Immigrant Life on the Margins.* Princeton, NJ: Princeton University Press, 1995.

Martin, Philip L. *Trade and Migration: NAFTA and Agriculture.* Washington, DC: Institute for International Economics, 1993.

Massey, Douglas S., Joaquin Arango, Graeme Hugo, Ali Kouaouci, Adela Pellegrino, and J. Edward Taylor. "Theories of International Migration: A Review and Appraisal." *Population and Development Review* 19:3 (1993): 431–66.

Massey, Douglas S., and L. Goldring. "Continuities in Transnational Migration: An Analysis of Nineteen Mexican Communities." *American Journal of Sociology* 99 (May 1994): 1492–533.

Morokvasic, Mirjana. Special Issue on Women Immigrants. *International Migration Review* 18:4 (1984).

OIM (Organization for International Migration). *Trafficking in Migrants* 22 (autumn 2000 quarterly bulletin). Geneva: OIM.

Papademetriou, Demetrios G., and Philip L. Martin, eds. *The Unsettled Relationship: Labor Migration and Economic Development.* Contributions in Labor Studies, vol. 33. Westport, CT: Greenwood Press, 1991.

Parnreiter, Christoff, ed. Schwerpunkt: Migration (special issue on migration), *Journal für Entwicklungspolitik* 11:3 (1995).

Portes, Alejandro, and John Walton. *Labor, Class, and the International System.* New York: Academic Press, 1996.

Portes, Alejandro, and Ruben G. Rumbaut. *Immigrant America: A Portrait.* Berkeley: University of California Press, 1996.

Safa, Helen. *The Myth of the Male Breadwinner: Women and Industrialization in the Caribbean.* Boulder, CO: Westview Press, 1995.

Sassen, Saskia. *The Mobility of Labor and Capital.* Cambridge: Cambridge University Press, 1988.

———. "Immigration and Local Labor Markets." In *The Economic Sociology of Immigration,* ed. A. Portes. New York: Russell Sage Foundation, 1995.

———. *Guests and Aliens.* New York: New Press, 1999.

———. *The Global City: New York, London, Tokyo.* New updated ed. Princeton, NJ: Princeton University Press, 2000.

Skeldon, R. 1997. "Hong Kong: Colonial City to Global City to Provincial City?" *Cities* 14:6 (1997): 323–32.

Smith, Robert C. "Transnational Migration, Assimilation and Political Community." In *The City and the World,* ed. Margaret Crahan and Alberto Vourvoulias-Bush. New York: Council on Foreign Relations, 1997.

Ward, Kathryn. *Women Workers and Global Restructuring.* Ithaca, NY: Cornell University Press, 1991.

NATURAL DISASTERS, ENVIRONMENTAL CRISES, AND OVERPOPULATION

Throughout history, humanity has been on the move. In prehistoric times, when populations were not settled, people moved in search of food or shelter or away from dangerous predators. As humans settled in organized communities, movement to sources of food diminished in importance, while wars and overpopulation became important factors in population movements. The same is true of modern times, although the causes of migration have become more complex. People migrate in response to adverse economic, political, and environmental conditions to areas where conditions are more favorable. Scholars have explained the phenomenon by push and pull factors. Push factors refer to conditions in people's original habitat that compel them to migrate, and pull factors refer to attractions in other areas that make those areas preferred destinations.

Within the push-pull framework, two explanatory models have emerged that define two groups of migrants. The neoclassical economics equilibrium framework is based on an economic determinism. It links migration with social and economic factors by positing that people migrate to areas where there are relatively abundant resources. This model suggests that migration is voluntary and is the natural result of national or regional resource imbalances. The structuralist model emphasizes the underlying factors that cause regional developmental disparities that result in population movement. While these two frameworks explain human migration from opposite angles, they both agree on one principle. Unfavorable conditions, whatever their cause, compel people to migrate to areas where conditions are favorable. The two models are important in defining voluntary migrants and involuntary migrants, otherwise known as refugees.

Among the factors that have caused large-scale immigration into the United States are natural disasters, environmental crises, and overpopulation. However, their impact on immigration to the United States is indirect, and it is difficult to determine exact numbers of people that have migrated as a result of these phenomena.

INTERCONNECTIONS BETWEEN NATURAL DISASTERS, ENVIRONMENTAL CRISES, AND OVERPOPULATION

The environment is the basis of life. We need forests and pastures, lakes, rivers, and the seas to sustain plant and animal life. We also need clean air to breathe, safe water to drink, and clean surroundings to prevent diseases. When the ecosystem—the resource base that makes up our environment—is disturbed, then there is an environmental crisis. The ecosystem can be disturbed through natural disasters and human action. The line between natural disasters and environmental crises is a fine one. Such natural disasters as floods, droughts, earthquakes, landslides, and hurricanes pose serious problems that countries around the globe have to deal with. They cause great environmental havoc and untold human suffering. While natural disasters occur without human agency, human tampering with the environment can intensify their impact and exacerbate their consequences. For example, when riverbeds and mountain slopes are overcultivated and overgrazed, they become vulnerable to floods, erosion, or landslides.

These phenomena destroy human life and habitats, ruin agricultural lands, and pollute water sources. On December 15, 1999, for instance, heavy rains caused serious flooding in Venezuela which killed over 30,000 people in four days and left more than 140,000 homeless. A tropical storm hit India in November 1999 and left thousands of people without

Overpopulation in many underdeveloped countries such as Nepal leads to environmental degradation and drives many people to immigrate to more industrialized nations like the United States. *(Alexander Contos/Impact Visuals)*

water, adequate sanitation, and shelter. Two major earthquakes struck Turkey in August and September 1999, killing more than 20,000 people and displacing thousands more. In 1998, Hurricane Mitch claimed over 6,000 lives in Central America. In Bangladesh, more than 1 million people perished from cyclonic storms and tidal surges between 1960 and 1991, while many more were displaced. In 1968, the rains failed in the Sahel, the region immediately south of the Sahara Desert in Africa. For several years, the drought continued, and animals began to die. Hope for rain and a return to normal pastoral life waned and bands of people began trekking southward, leaving behind a parched land. The nomadic nature of the population makes it difficult to know how many people died, but thousands of individuals from Chad, Burkina Faso, Mali, and Niger migrated to Ghana and the Ivory

Coast. Essam El-Hinnawi, an environmental scientist attached to the United Nations Environmental Program (UNEP), noted that the drought had not yet ended in Africa and estimated that in 1984 more than 150 million people in twenty-four African countries were "on the brink of starvation" due to the drought. When people are hungry, they look elsewhere for food. People who survive natural hazards are usually forced to leave their original habitats temporarily or permanently.

Other environmental hazards are caused by direct human action. In a study sponsored by UNEP, Essam El-Hinnawi and Mansur H. Hashmi identified military activity and development projects as two of the artificial causes of environmental degradation. El-Hinnawi and Hashmi noted that during the Vietnam War in the 1960s, the United States used chemical herbicides that completely destroyed 1,500 square kilometers of mangrove forest and damaged a further 15,000 square kilometers. The effect of this "scorched-earth policy" was rapid erosion and irreversible desertification. In 1998 and 1999, Russia and Chechnya engaged in war in which Grozny, the Chechen capital, and surrounding areas were shelled to flush out so-called rebel armies. The bombings have left the countryside desolate, making the land less useful for agricultural purposes. In December 1999, a British Broadcasting Corporation (BBC) world service report indicated that the North Atlantic Treaty Organization (NATO) bombardment of Bosnia in 1997 destroyed bridges and dams that two years later caused serious flooding in Mostar.

Similarly, the creation of lakes as sources of hydroelectric power and other development projects cause serious environmental problems. Again, El-Hinnawi and Hashmi have noted that the creation of the Volta Dam in Ghana caused 78,000 people to be evacuated. The Kariba Dam on River Zambezi displaced 57,000; Aswan High Dam, 100,000; Keban Dam (Turkey), 30,000; and Ubolratana Dam (Thailand), 30,000. In other places, vast tracts of land cleared for roads, power plants, or plantations cause original inhabitants to lose their habitats. Resettlement creates problems for host communities. Displaced persons further swell the populations of host regions, and rapidly increasing populations overutilize and degrade land. Overcultivation and overgrazing, for example, lead to soil erosion, deforestation, flooding, or desertification. When the environment is degraded, it cannot adequately support human populations, and the result is migration.

There is a clear link between natural disasters, environmental crises, and overpopulation. Large populations put pressure on the environment that intensifies the action of natural disasters. Overpopulation has serious social and economic consequences on land. It leads to reduced acreage per head, while intense cultivation leads to land degradation. And when agricultural land is degraded, crop yield may be reduced, although some studies have found evidence to the contrary. In a World Bank–sponsored study undertaken by Stefano Pagiola, Africa and Asia have the largest tracts of severely degraded agricultural lands that would be impossible to use. Thus, while degradation of agricultural land will not necessarily reduce crop yield, it can reduce the total cultivable area and force "excess" population to new land.

It should be noted that overpopulation is relational. While numbers are important in thinking about "overpopulation," the term does not necessarily mean "excess people" in a given geographic area or more births over deaths, although these are important indices of population growth. Overpopulation can also be considered to be the availability and management of resources in relation to the number of people in an area. Thus, a country is said to be overpopulated when its resources are not sufficient to support its population adequately. Population growth that is accompanied by technological advances reduces the adverse effects of environmental degradation and natural disasters. Hence, when addressing the effects of natural disasters, environmental crises, and overpopulation on migration, it is important to distinguish between the ways these phenomena are experienced by developed and developing countries.

WHO SUFFERS FROM NATURAL DISASTERS, ENVIRONMENTAL CRISES, AND OVERPOPULATION?

Several studies have emphasized that developing nations alter their environment in ways that make them more vulnerable to natural disasters. In other words, it is mostly Third World countries that do not have the technology to manage their natural resources which suffer the most from the ravages of natural disasters, overpopulation, and environmental degradation. And within Third World countries, it is the poor and powerless who are most susceptible to natural and environmental hazards. According to El-Hinnawi, an earthquake in Guatemala in 1976 that registered 7.5 on the Richter scale killed 22,000 people and left over a million homeless. Most of the affected were rural or slum dwellers. A quake that registered 6.2 in Managua, Nicaragua, killed 5,000 and sent

While natural disasters like the great Turkish earthquake of 1999, pictured above, do not usually lead to emigration, they can further undermine developing economies and create long-term conditions for later emigration. *(Fred Phillips/Impact Visuals)*

thousands more looking for shelter, while a San Fernando, California, quake that registered 6.6 on the Richter scale killed only 65 people with minimal displacement.

People who are displaced are mostly the poor living on "unclaimed" land in cities or in the countryside. That is, they live on land that governments do not want or cannot develop because of their vulnerability to disasters. In other instances, it is the poor whose land is claimed by governments to embark on "development" projects. Studies have noted that millions of the world's poorest people live in disaster-prone areas. Bangladesh's poor, for example, live on a river delta that is subject to cyclones and floods. Even in cities, the poor usually live in slums or shantytowns. Slums or shantytowns are constructed with materials that cannot withstand strong winds or floods. Therefore, when disaster strikes, the poor are the most affected. While many of them die through such occurrences, many more are displaced. Natural disasters thus have a multiplier effect on population explosion, environmental degradation, and migration; they force original inhabitants to move to new areas where they swell the population, thus putting extra burden on available resources, which further degrades the environment and causes further migration.

The differences in outcome can be attributed to the level of technological development in countries. The degree of advancement determines a country's preparedness to deal with hazards. The United States, for example, gives warning of approaching hurricanes for people to take shelter before winds and rains make landfall. When such events as earthquakes or flooding occur, the United States has the resources to evacuate and resettle victims because municipal, state, and federal government assistance is readily available. In less developed countries, however, warning systems may be nonexistent or inadequate, and governments wait for international relief assistance when disasters occur. For example, during the December 1999 flooding in Venezuela, international relief assistance was sought to prevent further human suffering. The catastrophe made headlines worldwide, and foreign donors, among them the Red Cross and the United States, flew in thousands of tons of food and medicine. Late in the same month, strong winds and rain across Western Europe caused major disasters, but none of the affected, particularly France and Germany, sought international relief assistance. Because international effort is usually geared toward the health and nutritional needs of victims, the impact of natural disasters on the environment is left unattended to. After crises have died down, victims are left to decide their fate. Some return to their old habitat to begin life anew, while others do not return. Those who are permanently displaced become migrants either in their own countries or in foreign ones.

ENVIRONMENTAL MIGRANTS OR ENVIRONMENTAL REFUGEES?

While scholars generally agree that the combined effects of natural disasters, environmental degradation, and overpopulation cause population displacement, they disagree over how to designate people displaced by these phenomena. Some see such individuals as "economic refugees" or "distress refugees" because it is essentially the destruction of the economic base that forces them to leave. However, others argue that those who flee natural disasters and other environmental crises should be called "environmental refugees." A special edition of *Refuge*, a Canadian journal devoted to refugee issues, called such people "ecological refugees." Whether ecological or environmental, people who flee natural disasters occupy an ambiguous position in international migration. To be designated a refugee, an individual or a group's situation must have political significance.

"Refugee," as originally defined by the United Nations Convention of 1951, referred specifically to displaced persons in Europe after World War II. In its expanded version in the 1967 United Nations Protocol Relating to the Status of Refugees, the time and space limitations were removed, and a refugee came to mean any person fleeing his or her country out of fear of persecution. Over the years, the definition has been expanded so that many more people can become refugees either in their own countries or in foreign lands. Only one international body—the United Nations High Commissioner for Refugees (UNHCR)—deals with refugee issues. Its preferred method of resettlement is local integration, but when local conditions can further jeopardize the safety of refugees, the UNHCR seeks safe third country resettlement. Settlement in most cases is seen as a temporary measure, for the policy is to send refugees back to their familiar environment once peace has been restored.

From the UN definition, persons fleeing disastrous natural and environmental phenomena or overpopulation cannot be called refugees since persecution implies human agency. Yet, certain contexts exist within which the term "refugee" may adequately describe the condition of individuals displaced by natural disasters, environmental degradation, and overpopulation. Putting aside the legalities and technicalities in the UN definition, there is a basic underlying cause for people to become refugees. Fear is central to the notion of refugee. For the political refugee, it is fear of persecution due to political opinion, race, religion, and so forth; for the environmental refugee, it is fear of recurrence of disaster. The difference between them is that persecution may cease with the restoration of peace. In other words, persecution can be controlled. The same is not necessarily true of environmental refugees. Natural disasters cannot be controlled, although their impact can be lessened with appropriate technology. Population explosion, on the other hand, can be controlled, but it requires massive resources that most Third World countries lack. Hence, a complex combination of factors makes the case for environmental refugees acute.

In spite of this similarity, individuals fleeing natural phenomena are technically not refugees and cannot seek protection in foreign countries under international law in the same way as can those who flee political situations. They may be resettled and given diverse forms of assistance by international donors, but they are simply seen as people displaced by disaster and not as refugees. In a sense, this characterization is appropriate because it reflects changes in the environment that adversely affect people's economic lives and not an orchestrated attempt by one group of persons to endanger the lives of others. Although this characterization does not diminish the dangers associated with natural hazards, it does point out the economic determinism inherent in migration associated with hazards. Explosive political situations such as occurred in Rwanda in 1994 or the ongoing war between Russia and Chechnya adversely affect the economies of the countries involved and can cause migration, but such movement is indirectly economically deterministic.

U.S. POLICY ON REFUGEES

Major legislation governing the admission of immigrants into the United States is the Immigration and Nationality Act (INA) passed in 1952. The INA originally spelled out the conditions and rules regarding entry and settlement in the United States, but it did not have a policy for refugees. Congress made ad hoc regulations to govern refugee admission, the first of which was the Displaced Persons Act of 1948. In 1953, Congress passed the Refugee Relief Act, and in 1978, the Fair Share Refugee Act. The first permanent refugee legislation was enacted in 1965 by amendment to the INA. Refugees were classified as a category of immigrants—conditional entrants—under a limited preference system. Refugees were defined as persons fleeing communist or communist-dominated countries or the Middle East, and the annual intake was limited to no more than 17,000. Like the UN Convention of 1951, the U.S. definition of "refugee" was restrictive and had to be revised in a new law, the Refugee Act of 1980, to remove the limitations.

According to an Immigration and Naturalization Service (INS) release, the change was to bring U.S. law into compliance with obligations under international law. But the United States went further and expanded the definition of refugee to include individuals who had been persecuted in the past as well as those who had a well-founded fear for future persecution. In the 1996 Illegal Immigration Reform and Immigrant Re-

sponsibility Act (IIRIRA), it again expanded the definition to include those fleeing forcible birth control methods. Clearly, the U.S. definition of refugee does not incorporate people fleeing natural disasters or overpopulation. A refugee is still defined in political terms. Thus, although the United States may continue to give assistance to people in distress, it does not offer them a haven on its soil. Such persons must enter the United States as immigrants. And as immigrants, they have to be admitted in one of two categories. They may enter either as businesspeople or as a family class. As businesspeople, immigrants are required to have capital to invest or skills that are in demand. To enter in the family class, they have to show proof of relationship with a family member who is legally resident in the United States.

ENVIRONMENTAL REFUGEES/ MIGRANTS AND U.S. MIGRATION

Throughout its history, the United States has been a land of immigrants. People have come from all over the world to settle in the country. Many have come as immigrants, others in chains, and still others as refugees. There are thousands of illegal aliens in the United States, and more people are still desirous of making their home in the country. Some individuals have been lured by America's affluence and democratic political institutions, others by pure adventure. Since 1970, the foreign-born population in the United States has increased rapidly due to large-scale influx from Asia and Latin America. In 1970, the number of foreign-born in the population was 9.6 million, representing only 4.7 percent; it increased to 14 million (6.2 percent) in 1980, climbing further to 19.8 million (7.9 percent) in 1990. In 1997, it was estimated that immigrants numbered 25.8 million, comprising 9.7 percent of the U.S. population. In addition, illegal immigrants numbered about 5 million by October 1996.

The majority of illegal aliens came from the Caribbean and Latin America, which suggests that proximity plays a role in this kind of population movement. People from these places can and do travel on rafts or in boats to enter the United States. While dangerous, that means of travel offers an avenue for entry that is not available to people from Asia or Africa in similar situations. Illegal entry from Mexico is the highest because in some cases migrants fall through the cracks undetected. Refugees also constitute a substantial percentage of the foreign-born population in the United States. In the fiscal year ending 1997,

122,741 refugee applications were filed, and 77,600 were approved. The leading countries—Bosnia-Herzegovina, nations in the former Soviet Union, Vietnam, Somalia, and Iraq—supplied 91 percent of all refugees who received official approvals in 1997.

For many people, the American frontier is still open, signified by the power of the dollar to open vistas for advancement, not in the acquisition of western land as originally measured. The American dollar has become an international currency. It is the measure of international wealth and is accepted in almost all countries in the world. Its international military activities, booming economy, star athletes and artists, and in the past fifteen years, dominance of computer technology no doubt make the United States the most influential country in the world. For others, the United States offers a safe haven from the ravages of war. Americans' belief in democracy and individual freedom has made the country a protector of the world's afflicted. Thus, a complex series of factors explains the desire of millions to make the United States their home.

That desire, however, may be elusive for environmental refugees and immigrants. As already indicated, the individuals who are most vulnerable to natural crises are the poor of society. They may not have the financial resources or the skills to resettle in a high-tech society such as the United States. Referring to those fleeing the drought in the Sahel, El-Hinnawi noted that these migrants trekked on foot for hundreds of miles with their livestock to reach their destinations. In West Africa, a large influx of people from the Sahel crowded the streets of such capital cities as Accra and Abidjan asking for alms. These were poor people who lived precarious lives. They slept at roadsides and in railway stations, vulnerable to the weather and the insensitivity of fellow human beings. Thus, unless they are geographically proximate, most people fleeing environmental and natural disasters as well as overpopulation will find it difficult, if not impossible, to make the journey to the United States. And the majority of those who succeed may enter as illegal aliens because they do not have the personal resources or meet the legal requirements to qualify as immigrants or refugees.

An examination of census reports and immigration statistics reveals that countries that have faced the worst disasters have not necessarily sent large numbers of immigrants or refugees. For instance, Bangladesh, which suffered eleven major cyclonic storms and tidal surges between 1960 and 1991, counted only 21,000 nationals in the United States within the same period, while Vietnam sent 543,262 people. The large number of Vietnamese immigrants can be explained

by the politics between the United States and Vietnam. Such disaster areas of high population density as India and China have not sent the largest numbers of either immigrants or refugees, although two of the highest numbers of foreign-born persons represented in the 1990 census were from these countries. The exceptions here are countries in Latin America and the Caribbean, as illustrated by immigrants from Haiti to the United States.

Much of Haiti's countryside is a wasteland, the result of poor agricultural practices that have denuded the land of its properties. Constant removal of trees and other plant cover has led to bouts of erosion, flooding, and poor crop yield. The erosion of their traditional way of life has disillusioned rural dwellers whose livelihood depends on the land. They have sought refuge in the capital city, Port-au-Prince, where there is a population explosion. It was estimated in 1983 that the population density in Port-au-Prince slums reached as high as 65,000 persons per square mile. People who could not cope with the increasingly deteriorating slum conditions migrated to other Caribbean countries or the United States.

Haitian immigrants have resorted to diverse means of entering the United States; many arrive at American ports as boat people, having no visas. And U.S. immigration gatekeepers have also devised means to check these illegal entrants. The United States has established a port at Guantánamo Bay, Cuba, to process refugee admissions from Haiti and other Caribbean countries. Illegal aliens who are intercepted in U.S. waters are sent to the center for screening. Those who are "screened in" are issued visas, and those "screened out" are sent back to Haiti. In 1996, only six people were "screened in" from Haiti. In 1998, Congress passed the Haitian Refugee Immigration Fairness Act (HRIFA) to deal with Haitian immigration. While the act enables more people from Haiti to enter the United States, the process "screens out" people who are considered to be economic immigrants. Thus, it is not certain how many of the admitted will be those fleeing disasters.

Natural disasters, environmental crises, and overpopulation are closely linked, and together, their impact causes migration. Yet, poverty and legalistic distinctions between immigrants and refugees can hamper the direction of people fleeing disasters. Because they have not been defined as refugees, victims of natural and environmental disasters as well as overpopulation do not enjoy the protection and support that the United States offers to those fleeing explosive political situations. Thus, if they have to enter the United States, they must do so as immigrants. Because many of these individuals are poor, they do not have the wherewithal to enter as immigrants. Those who are geographically close to the United States may succeed in entering as illegal aliens. Even then, it is difficult to determine the proportion of the illegal alien population who have suffered from natural disasters. Nor can we determine from immigration statistics or population censuses the percentage of the foreign-born population who have faced natural disasters and overpopulation. Until the U.S. immigration authorities designate a category to admit such individuals, knowledge of their numbers in the United States will continue to be speculative.

Martha Donkor

See also: The Great Irish Immigration (Part I, Sec. 2); Central America (Part III, Sec. 2).

BIBLIOGRAPHY

Department of Justice, Immigration and Naturalization Service. *Statistics Branch Annual Report: Refugees, Fiscal Year 1997.* Washington, DC: U.S. Government Printing Office, 1997.

El-Hinnawi, Essam. *Environmental Refugees.* Dublin: United Nations Environmental Program, 1985.

El-Hinnawi, Essam, and Mansur H. Hashmi. *Global Environmental Issues.* Dublin: Tycooly International Publishing, 1982.

"Environmental Refugees." Special issue of *Refuge* 12:1 (June 1992).

Kavanagh, Barbara, and Steve Lonergan. *Environmental Degradation, Population Displacement, and Global Security: An Overview of the Issues.* A background report prepared for the Royal Society of Canada under the auspices of the Canadian Global Change Program's Research Panel on Environment and Security, December 1992.

Pagiola, Stefano. *The Global Environmental Benefits of Land Degradation Control on Agricultural Land.* Washington, DC: World Bank, 1999.

POLITICAL, ETHNIC, RELIGIOUS, AND GENDER PERSECUTION

Throughout its history, the United States has had a mixed attitude toward immigrants generally and specifically toward those coming to this country to flee religious, ethnic, political, and other forms of persecution. On the one hand, this country has probably allowed more such refugees to enter than any other. Both official policy and unofficial public opinion has expressed a willingness to offer asylum to those facing repression at home. In the post–World War II era, the United States has been a signatory to various international treaties dealing with the humane treatment of refugees.

At the same time, however, the country has often moved to close its doors to refugees of various kinds. Most notorious, it turned a deaf ear to the pleas of German and European Jews seeking asylum from Nazi Germany in the 1930s and 1940s. In the post–World War II era, the United States has also displayed a biased selectivity to the refugees it would permit into the country. Several Latin American cases provide examples. While the United States heartily welcomed political refugees from communist regimes in Cuba and Nicaragua, it was averse to opening the gates to persons seeking refuge from repressive—and United States–supported—right-wing military regimes in El Salvador and Guatemala.

Finally, throughout history, Americans have often displayed a hostility to refugees based on the very same prejudices that caused these persons to flee their home country. Again, the Jews of the 1930s provide the most telling example of this. Many historians say the U.S. aversion to accepting large numbers of Jews fleeing the Nazis immediately before and during World War II was due to the prevalence of anti-Semitic prejudice among both State Department staff and the American populace at large.

COLONIAL AND EARLY REPUBLIC ERAS

The mixed attitude toward refugees was evident in the very first centuries of this country's settlement. The Puritans were, of course, America's first refugees, forced to flee an increasingly hostile England in the early seventeenth century for their unorthodox religious beliefs that challenged the governing alliance between the Anglican Church and the Crown. But the Puritans themselves proved less than open to other refugees. They were notoriously hostile to Quaker refugees from Britain, forcing out many who tried to settle in Massachusetts.

Nor were the Puritans of New England alone in their hostility to refugees, as the case of the French Canadian refugees of the mid-eighteenth century makes evident. Known as Acadians, these were French-speaking Catholics who were forced out of Canada during a series of British-French imperial wars that first left what would later become the Maritime Provinces of that country and then all of Canada under British rule. When the Acadians tried to settle in the mid-Atlantic colonies, they met with hostility from the existing population, who remained suspicious of all Catholics. Eventually, the Acadians were forced to make their way to the frontier or, as in the case of thousands, to find yet another refuge in French-influence Louisiana.

NINETEENTH CENTURY

Still, with the Declaration of Independence and the establishment of an independent United States in the late eighteenth century, the Republic became known as a haven for the political refugees of Eu-

Political persecution sent thousands of Salvadoran refugees to the United States in the 1980s. Here, one Salvadoran refugee reads a letter from the mother of another, telling him that he will be killed if he returns to El Salvador. *(Jeffry Scott, Impact Visuals)*

rope. The French Revolution sent thousands of refugees to America in the 1790s. First came the aristocrats fleeing the initial revolution, although the vast majority of these found refuge in neighboring conservative European states. But then, as the French Revolution turned against its own, new waves of refugees—including both moderate Girondists and radical Jacobins—came to American shores.

Another group of French refugees came to this country as the result of an entirely different revolution triggered by the incendiary events in France. Following the great slave uprising in Saint-Domingue (modern-day Haiti) in 1791, some ten thousand to twenty thousand planters and other white refugees fled to the United States. Largely settling in South Carolina and other slave states, they were welcomed warmly, receiving some $15,000 in congressional relief moneys. The French Revolution even indirectly sparked a flow of refugees from France's archenemy Britain, in the form of pro-Revolution British radicals.

The failure of the wave of revolutions that spread through Europe in 1848 sent large contingents of political refugees to the United States as well, particularly from the German-speaking states of central Europe. Many of these refugees brought with them radical ideologies, programs for political and economic change, and an affinity for labor unions. Joseph Wedemeyer, an emigrant from Westphalia in 1851, for instance, was a disciple of Karl Marx. As an advocate of immigrant involvement in labor unions and political organizing, he helped found the German Workers League in the United States in 1853. Indeed, these so-called forty-eighters and their successors played a major role in the development of unions and in the socialist politics of late-nineteenth-century America. In Milwaukee, for instance, they dominated urban politics, electing socialist mayors and members of Congress well into the twentieth century.

There were also German-speaking religious refugees in the nineteenth century, such as the Russo-

German Mennonites. Originally invited to settle in the Volga River and Black Sea regions of the Russian Empire by Catherine the Great in the eighteenth century, they saw their status and privileges eroded by the revival of Russian nationalism after the mid-nineteenth century. In the 1870s and 1880s, thousands of them fled to the United States, where they settled on the plains of Kansas, Nebraska, and the Dakotas.

JEWISH IMMIGRANTS

While Germans and German-speaking peoples represented the bulk of religious and particularly political refugees during the mid-nineteenth century, Jews made up the vast majority of refugees to America in the late nineteenth and early twentieth centuries, even though most Jewish immigrants came for purely economic reasons.

The beginning of this great influx of Jewish refugees can be dated to 1881, with the assassination of

Political unrest in Chile, illustrated in this confrontation between a Mapuche Indian and police, led thousands to flee that troubled land for the United States in the 1970s and 1980s. *(Carlos Villalon, Impact Visuals)*

Czar Alexander II by a Jewish terrorist. The murder led to anti-Jewish riots, and the Russian government responded by even more strictly enforcing existing laws that forced all Jews to live within the Pale, a proscribed territory on the borders of Germany and the Austro-Hungarian Empire. An 1882 law further restricted Jewish worship and banned Jews from agriculture, industry, the professions, public office, and many schools. Pogroms—anti-Jewish riots and massacres, often organized by the government—occurred periodically throughout the Pale from the 1880s through the first decade of the twentieth century. One pogrom in the town of Kishini, for example, left forty-seven Jews dead and more than four hundred injured. The result was a massive outflow of refugees. From just 5,000 in 1880, Jewish immigration to America rose to 81,000 in 1892 and peaked at 258,000 in 1907.

Some of the Jews who fled Russia were political refugees as well. Both persecuted as Jews and oppressed like other Russians by an authoritarian political establishment, many Jews played critical roles in the various radical political movements in turn-of-the-century Russia. And, of course, they brought and practiced their socialist and anarchist politics in their adopted country, becoming organizers and members of the trade union movement and the Socialist Party. When the Russian Revolution sparked anti-Red hysteria in this country in 1919 and 1920, many of the more political Jewish refugees found themselves persecuted here in America, and some were even deported back to their homeland.

Other political and religious refugees of the era included Finns, whose country was occupied by Russia, and Protestant Czechs fleeing the Catholic-dominated Austro-Hungarian Empire. Poles—whose country was also occupied by Russia—fled in large numbers to this country, though while some were escaping the repression of their culture and nationalism, most came for purely economic reasons. From farther afield came Christian Armenians, fleeing the repression and even genocide instituted by the Muslim Ottoman Empire.

WORLD WAR II ERA

In the 1930s and 1940s, tens of millions of Europeans were uprooted (and millions killed) by fascist regimes, most notably in Germany but also in Austria, France, Spain, Italy, and the states of central Europe. Germany annexed Austria (1938) and Czechoslovakia (1939) and conquered Poland, Norway, Denmark, the Netherlands, Belgium, and most of France from late 1939 to mid-1940. Jews and others in German-controlled

War, political turmoil, and ethnic and religious persecution have disrupted numerous Latin American countries since 1965, sending hundreds of thousands of immigrants and refugees to the United States. *(CARTO-GRAPHICS)*

territory were subject to government-sponsored assaults that included beatings; burning; the looting of stores, homes, and hospitals; and the roundup of tens of thousands at a time for the concentration camps.

Until 1939, Adolf Hitler allowed most Jews who wanted to leave a way out; the problem was that no other country was willing to take them. American excuses were high unemployment (10 million), the burden to relief rolls, and the threat that immigrants might be subversive, but the reason was mostly anti-Semitism. When Democratic senator Robert F. Wagner of New York and Republican representative Edith Rogers of Massachusetts proposed expanding the quotas to allow in 20,000 German refugees between the ages of six and fourteen, the American Legion and Daughters of the American Revolution, among others, opposed the measure. A Ladies of the Grand Army of the Republic spokeswoman feared that Congress might allow the quota to be filled with German-

Jewish children. Still, despite American fascism and anti-Semitism, there were organizations such as the National Refugee Service, the Hebrew Immigrant Aid Society, and other, less-formal groups that helped the immigrants to find jobs, homes, and community.

Of the millions displaced, only a handful escaped to the United States, for that escape required financial means and political connections. Given the correlation between education, economic status, and professional affiliations, not surprisingly the most successful escapees from the oppression were the intellectuals. Composers who fled the rising fascist and Nazi threat in Europe included Italian Arturo Toscanini (1867–1957), the Hungarian Béla Bartók (1881–1945), Darius Milhaud (1892–1974) of France, and the Russian Igor Stravinsky (1882–1971). Political thinkers include Hannah Arendt (1906–75), who wrote about totalitarianism, and Herbert Marcuse (1898–1979), whose impact as an antiestablishment critic would help to define the 1960s as a decade of youth rebellion.

There were scientists of all disciplines, writers and critics, artists, philosophers, and historians among the refugees as well. From Austria and Germany came a group that included such luminaries as the playwright Bertolt Brecht (1898–1956), the novelist Thomas Mann (1875–1955), and the theologian Paul Tillich (1886–1965). In all, the European refugee group included twelve existing or future Nobel Prize winners. Although some American academics and intellectuals initially expressed displeasure at the increased competition for academic jobs during the Great Depression, many of the Europeans made their way to American universities. Unlike most refugees, this was a professional and intellectual elite that dispersed through the country and had an impact far beyond its numbers.

While most fled for similar political reasons, different groups held various attitudes about the nature of their refugee status. French and Spanish intellectuals, for example, tended more than the others to regard their experience as simple exile, a temporary condition until they could return home. Other nationalities adjusted to permanent residence, considering themselves regardless of domicile as members of a world community. But, as with all groups, not everyone adjusted; some, such as Bartók, could never overcome their homesickness; others had family they'd left behind. Some returned. And of those who remained, not all achieved the success they had in Europe and needed to work as more traditional immigrants at menial jobs.

Most important of all, given the subsequent history of World War II, were the refugee physicists. Approximately one hundred in number, most were Jewish and came from Germany and Austria, fleeing persecution and the loss of jobs in universities there. Most eminent among them was Albert Einstein, whose theories eventually led to the development of the atomic bomb. But there were many others, including four other Nobel Prize winners—Peter Debye, Enrico Fermi, James Franck, and Victor F. Hess. Four more of these refugees—Hans A. Bethe, Felix Bloch, Emilio G. Segrè, and Otto Stern—would go on to win the Nobel Prize in subsequent years. Ironically, it was the loss of such physicists that doomed Nazi Germany's own atomic weapons program, helping to allow the Allies to develop it first and win the war.

POST–WORLD WAR II ERA

In 1945, the Daughters of the American Revolution (DAR), the American Legion, the Veterans of Foreign Wars (VFW), and other patriotic groups sought a five- to ten-year ban on immigration. Instead, Congress authorized the immigration of 205,000 displaced persons (DPs) over three years. Thus began, despite the restrictions of the McCarran-Walter Act of 1952, fifty years of legislation to help one troubled group after another. The postwar era was a more tolerant age toward minorities generally and refugees specifically. Religious passion waned; education and income levels rose; the war demonstrated the basic loyalty of Japanese, German, and Italian Americans; the Cold War gave Americans a new enemy to unite against; and immigrants were more acculturated. And there were not as many. Their proportion decreased from one-seventh of the population in 1920 to only one-twentieth in 1970.

After World War II, the first priority was to bring the soldiers home. Then, the War Brides and Fiancées acts of 1946, which relaxed tight quotas, brought 150,000 women, 25,000 children, and a few hundred men in the first five postwar years. Among the war brides were 5,000 Chinese and 800 Japanese wives under legislation of 1947 that reversed the anti-Asian laws of the previous seventy years. Once the pressure to demobilize eased, so did restriction on most types of immigrants—economic and political. Resumed immigration from Germany and England brought skilled artisans, small business people, and clerical/ white collar workers. And it brought refugees.

Late in the war and after, Europe was flooded with DPs, especially concentration camp survivors and forced laborers who had experienced uprooting, dislocation, and hardship. Many others had fled the advance of the Russian army as it defeated Germany and imposed communist regimes in Eastern Europe. Still others left to avoid revived anti-Semitism in Poland and Romania or Communist takeovers of Czechoslovakia, Yugoslavia, and Poland. The U.S. response was halting. Initially, quotas were low. A presidential order of December 22, 1945, giving preference to DPs, brought only 40,000 immigrants from war-torn Europe, including both former Nazis and anticommunists. The Displaced Persons Act of 1948 gave preference to persons of German origin from the Baltic states under the Soviet sphere of influence. An amendment of 1950 included Jews, but by then most European Jewish DPs had gone to Israel. The act allowed entry to 400,000 DPs, including Baltic German speakers and certain Greek, Polish, and Italian refugees. Also included were Europeans stranded in the Far East and orphans. The Refugee Relief Act of 1953 brought in 200,000 Europeans and a few hundred Asians. Priority went, as it would for decades, to refugees from communism. The quota system remained in effect, with refugees being counted against future years' quotas for the applicable national category.

In 1956, the Russian suppression of the Hungarian uprising produced 200,000 Hungarian refugees. American policy restricted Hungary to 5,000 visas under the Refugee Relief Act, so President Dwight D. Eisenhower asked for authority to let 30,000 more in on parole—that is, as visitors until conditions allowed them to return. These refugees and parolees came first to Camp Kilmer, New Jersey, then dispersed throughout the country. In 1956 and 1957 refugees also came from Yugoslavia, China, and Dutch Indonesia.

IMMIGRATION AND NATIONALITY ACT OF 1965

A series of international crises in the 1950s and 1960s—along with the increasing liberalism of the American political scene—created a growing consensus for change in the immigration laws. In 1963, thousands of Cubans fled Castro. The 1.5 million Chinese who had flooded Hong Kong in the previous ten years could not enter the United States, even with emergency parole, because of the small numbers they received under the national origins legislation that dated from the 1920s. President John F. Kennedy wanted to de-emphasize national origins and establish a policy that brought in people with skills needed in the United States as well as family members of those already in the United States. He also desired equity in quotas for African and Asian nations. Under then current law, Africa got 1 percent of all immigrant slots and Asia 2. In contrast, England, Ireland, and Germany received more than 70 percent of each year's limited quota.

Still, change was politically risky. A 1965 Harris poll showed sentiment running two to one in support of leaving the quota system as it was, and the people's most preferred immigrants were those from Canada, England/Scotland, Scandinavia, and Germany. Neither Congress nor the public liked the idea of masses of Asian, Latin American, and black immigrants. Still, the new immigration law of 1965 included most of Kennedy's ideas, if not in the form he wanted.

National origins restrictions would be phased out after three years, ending eighty years of laws designed to keep specific groups of foreigners out. Annual totals were 120,000 for the Western Hemisphere and 170,000 for the rest of the world. Three-fourths of each quota was set aside for family members, but the preference for needed skills was still there. And 6 percent of each quota was for refugees. Presumably, the largest number of family members would still come from Western Europe. In fact, just the opposite would prove true, as Latin Americans and Asians came to take advantage of this aspect of the law.

CUBA

Even as Lyndon B. Johnson signed the legislation in 1965, Fidel Castro was allowing any Cuban who wished to join his or her family to depart. Refugees from Cuban communism were coming to the United States at a rate of 4,000 per month. These immigrants quickly surpassed the refugee quota and had to be paroled. This group made up the second wave of Cuban immigration. The first wave had consisted of true political refugees who were mostly upper-class or skilled persons who came immediately after the revolution in 1959. The second wave was predominantly middle-class. Those in the first wave, typical of political refugees, expected only a short stay. While in the United States, they were politically active against Castro, going so far as to work with the Central Intelligence Agency in launching the failed Bay of Pigs invasion of Cuba in 1961.

Two decades after the Bay of Pigs, the Cuban-American National Foundation established Radio Marti as well as the Coalition for a Free Cuba, which contributed to sympathetic legislators. These "temporary" refugees also helped finance the anticommunist Union for the Total Independence of Angola

(UNITA, its Portuguese acronym) movement in Angola and the Contras in Nicaragua. Just as the Hungarian refugees of 1956 had volunteered for the anti-Castro forces, so the Cuban exiles fought against the Sandinistas and supported the Contras.

Three-fourths of Cubans settled in Miami despite government policy to disperse them. Once dispersed, they migrated back to Miami, even the Mariel refugees. Between 1960 and 1970, the Dade County ethnic Cuban population increased from 29,500 to 224,000, with 85 percent being foreign born.

Then came the rush of the Marielitos in 1980, the third wave. It began in April, after sentries in Havana fired on a busload of seekers of asylum heading for the Peruvian embassy. Castro then withdrew the embassy guards, and a mass of potential emigrants swamped the grounds. The Cuban government decreed that any Cuban (except those seeking refuge in the Peruvian embassy) was free to leave. Ten thousand would-be emigrants surrounded the embassy seeking exit documents. Peru refused to take all of them, and the United States was hesitant because it already had 30,000 who had qualified for immigration through proper processes. Costa Rica offered to take them in, and Castro said everyone could leave as long as they went by way of Mariel Harbor. Miami Cubans chartered boats by the score. In April and May, in boatload after boatload, these third-wave Cubans flooded Miami.

HAITI

All Cubans, because they came from a communist country, were by government definition political refugees and automatically entitled to stay. Not every group of refugees received this generous offer. In 1972, sixty-five Haitians landed on a Florida beachfront after nineteen days in a rickety sailboat. Some claimed to be escaped political prisoners. They were received cordially enough, although the expectation was that they would be deported. In 1978, when Haitians landed at Key Biscayne, some locals wanted them quarantined for tuberculosis and venereal disease. The Haitians were black and poor and fleeing the right-wing regime of Jean-Claude Duvalier. In the 1970s, the United States rejected 99 percent of Haitian applications for asylum.

Slowly, as more and more boat people were sent back, the middle-class émigré Haitian community became upset at the blatant differences in treatment of black refugees and white Cubans and Russians fleeing comparable tyranny. When President Jimmy Carter opened the gates to the Marielitos, it created even more political controversy. Carter had already obligated the United States to take in 230,000 refugees, mostly Indochinese. His administration had doubts about the cost—both financial and political—of taking on 115,000 Cubans and 16,000 Haitians. The cheap solution was to parole "Cuban/Haitian entrants" in a status somewhere between refugee and illegal alien. Costs would be about one-third what they would have been if these people had been defined as refugees under the Refugee Act, because it reduced funds that had to be spent on assimilation. Local governments would have to pay the bills. Especially hard hit was Miami, which received half the load.

The Immigration Reform and Control Act of 1986 granted asylum to pre-1982 illegal aliens and tried to end the Reagan era practice of intercepting them at sea and turning them back, but Bill Clinton continued the practice before opening the American base at Guantánamo Bay, Cuba, to Haitian refugees. In 1994, Bill Clinton sent American troops into Haiti to restore democracy and slow the exodus. In late 1998, Clinton and Congress authorized legal status for most of the Haitian illegal aliens in the country.

SOUTHEAST ASIA: VIETNAMESE

For nearly ten years—from 1965 to 1975—the United States had supported the noncommunist governments of South Vietnam, Cambodia, and Laos against communist insurgents. In 1974–75, however, these various governments finally fell, sending forth a wave of refugees. Ultimately, more than 2 million people were displaced in the war's aftermath, with better than 1 million ending up in the United States.

As Saigon fell in April 1975, 40,000 Vietnamese evacuated, with a plane landing in Guam every eighteen minutes. And almost one hundred thousand refugees escaped to the South China Sea by boat, where they were picked up by the U.S. Navy and taken to Guam and the Philippines. The United States accepted 130,000 refugees, for whom President Gerald Ford authorized parole status. Beyond that, he had no overall plan. Rejected by the Philippines and California, these refugees ended up at Camp Pendleton, California; Fort Chafee, Arkansas; and Eglin Air Force Base, Florida. Later, a fourth refugee camp opened at Indiantown Gap, Pennsylvania.

American public opinion was opposed to resettling the Vietnamese in the United States by a margin of 54 to 33 percent. There was also some congressional opposition owing to the influx of Cubans (600,000

over the previous decade), high unemployment, inflation, and a housing shortage. Nevertheless, Congress made available $450 million to relocate Southeast Asian immigrants. By the end of one year, all had left the camps and dispersed throughout the United States, although about 40 percent settled in Southern California and another 10 percent settled in Texas.

First-wave Vietnamese by the 1980s were in a situation comparable with that of first-wave Cubans of the 1960s. From the higher socioeconomic classes and less able to return, they were more likely to become naturalized and take jobs beneath their prior station in order to rebuild their lives, with former generals driving taxis and society leaders becoming maids.

Then came a second wave. In the late 1970s, as the new Vietnamese government consolidated and fought border conflicts with China and Cambodia, another group of Vietnamese refugees went to the South China Sea in small boats. By American definition, these were political refugees and eligible for entry into the United States. Rejected in many ports, they drifted helplessly, their numbers swelled by refugee Cambodians and Laotians. President Carter authorized parole for the boat people, and 23,000 more refugees from Cambodia, Laos, Vietnam, and refugee camps in Thailand entered the United States. Carter also signed a law allowing them to be permanent resident aliens and thus eligible for citizenship.

Democratic congressman Joshua Eilberg of Pennsylvania, however, wanted a moratorium on this executive usurpation of congressional power to define immigration policy. He also wanted parole for 5,000 Soviet émigrés stuck in a processing center in Rome. Senator Edward Kennedy, a Democrat from Massachusetts who headed the Senate immigration subcommittee, refused to support Eilberg unless Eilberg supported the bringing in of Southeast Asian refugees. By late 1978, an estimated 175,000 refugees were in camps, mostly in Thailand and Malaysia. Those governments began pushing refugees back into the water, where they fell victim to pirates or the sea. Malaysia stopped turning away boats after several horrible and widely publicized incidents of mass drowning. The pressure was on the United States, and 81,000 came under parole in 1978. The number the next year was over twice that, ten times the total allowed by law for all refugees.

Unlike the first wave, which had consisted of mostly educated and English-speaking Vietnamese, the boat people were to a great extent peasants without English, marketable skills, or education. The Vietnamese, whether first, second, or third wave, met with dislike from an American people tired of being host to poverty-stricken aliens. There was violence, especially in Texas and Louisiana fishing villages. By 1978–79, there was conflict, and in the summer of 1979, an American was killed. A Vietnamese was arrested, indicted, and acquitted. Between 1984 and 1985, there was a 60 percent increase in anti-Asian incidents. With federal, state, local, and church aid, acculturated Vietnamese revitalized declining neighborhoods into "Little Saigons" and began producing valedictorians and Rhodes Scholars.

At the same time, however, less-advantaged Southeast Asians struggled. Uprooted, emotionally drained, without skills or means to acculturate, struggling to survive and traumatized by a flight that could have included rape or other physical damage that produce emotional disorders, these people took low-paying jobs or faced long-term welfare. Women whose husbands were dead or missing headed one-fourth of Cambodian families in the late 1980s. The refugee population as of 1992 included 100,000 Hmong and other Laotian mountain people, 125,000 ethnic Lao, 650,000 Vietnamese, and 150,000 Cambodians.

The Hmong, Mien, lowland Lao, and Cambodians were often poor, farmers or villagers with limited education or exposure to Western culture and technology. Immigrants from Cambodia, Laos, and Vietnam prior to 1978 had an average of about ten years of education, whereas those who came between 1978 and 1983 had an average of six years; the Hmong averaged only 1.6. Lao and Cambodians had about five, Chinese Vietnamese had 6.7, and Vietnamese had around 9.8. American averages from the 1980 census: white, 12.5; Japanese American, 12.9; Chinese American, 13.4; and Korean American, 13 years.

LATIN AMERICA

Civil wars in Nicaragua, Guatemala, and El Salvador in the 1980s produced political persecution and violence. The United States was reluctant to recognize asylum seekers from these countries. The 1986 Immigration Reform and Control Act amnestied pre-1982 illegal aliens, but not until 1997 did they get federal permission that legalized their status in this country. These people generally settled in the Latino communities of Miami, Chicago, San Antonio, Houston, San Francisco, and Washington, D.C., where they started on the lower rungs of the economic ladder, taking jobs vacated by Cubans moving up economically.

Although the Refugee Act of 1980 attempted to broaden the definition of refugee to eliminate the Cold War practice of allowing asylum only to refugees from communist countries, the Reagan administration used the old definition of the term. It liberally granted refugee status for those fleeing communist regimes in Southeast Asia or Eastern Europe. Policy remained highly restrictive, however, toward refugees from right-wing regimes such as Guatemala and El Salvador. Chileans and Haitians seeking refuge were turned back because they were defined as economic, not political, refugees. By interpreting flight from leftist repression as political and flight from rightist repression as economic, Reagan legally denied refugee status to Haitians and Salvadorans. At best, these people were asylum-seekers, lacking certain rights granted to refugees. Refugees have legal status, the right to work in the open economy, and eligibility for welfare. Asylum-seekers have none of these rights; they are guests at the discretion of the government, and those who overstay their welcome become illegal aliens.

Americans who objected to the denial of protection for those in flight from right-wing regimes began hiding the illegal aliens, granting them sanctuary. The Reagan administration fought the Sanctuary movement to the extent of prosecuting cases in Arizona and Texas in 1984, winning convictions against those who sought to harbor asylum-seekers from Latin America. As late as 1987, the refugee total of 91,474 broke out as 43 percent from Vietnam, Cambodia and Laos; 29 percent from Cuba; and 8 percent from Poland, the Soviet Union, and Romania. Afghanistan represented 2 percent, and noncommunist Haiti 5 percent. Immigration reform in 1990 granted "safe haven" to Salvadoran refugees. By the late 1990s, however, Mexico had taken the lead as the country producing the most refugees seeking asylum in the United States.

OTHER NATIONS

Communism in the Soviet Union produced religious refugees. As in the days of the czars, so under the Communists—Jews and Pentecostals endured harassment. For more than twenty years, American administrations had urged the Soviet Union to let the people migrate. In 1987, Mikhail Gorbachev relaxed restrictions on the exit of Jews and Armenians (who were being hounded by Azerbaijanis). Emigrants rose from a handful in the early 1980s to 43,500 in 1989. Perhaps as many as 80 percent were Soviet Jews who wanted to flee ethnic nationalism, new anti-Semitism, and the prospect of scapegoating for the economic and political collapse expected from glasnost and perestroika.

Table 1
Asylum Claimants by Nationality, 1992–1998

Rank	Nationality	Cases Filed	Rank	Nationality	Cases Filed
	1992			1995 (continued)	
1	Guatemala	43,915	6	Honduras	2,926
2	El Salvador	8,781	7	Haiti	2,396
3	Haiti	5,374	8	Pakistan	2,318
4	former Soviet Union	4,517	9	former Soviet Union	2,211
5	Philippines	4,022	10	Bangladesh	1,778
6	China	3,464		1996	
7	Pakistan	3,348	1	El Salvador	63,174
8	India	3,224	2	Guatemala	8,857
9	Cuba	2,376	3	Mexico	7,820
10	Romania	2,097	4	India	3,942
	1993		5	Haiti	3,792
1	Guatemala	34,045	6	China	1,976
2	El Salvador	14,554	7	former Soviet Union	1,555
3	China	14,433	8	Nicaragua	1,444
4	Haiti	10,858	9	Somalia	1,140
5	Mexico	6,390	10	Mauritania	1,203
6	India	5,857		1997	
7	Pakistan	4,511	1	Mexico	13,663
8	Philippines	3,932	2	El Salvador	4,706
9	Bangladesh	3,764	3	Haiti	4,310
10	Russia	3,234	4	India	3,776
	1994		5	Guatemala	2,386
1	Guatemala	34,176	6	China	2,377
2	El Salvador	18,458	7	Iraq	2,328
3	China	10,839	8	Somalia	1,861
4	Haiti	9,403	9	former Soviet Union	1,734
5	Mexico	9,266	10	Mauritania	1,355
6	Nicaragua	4,445		1998	
7	India	4,415	1	Mexico	4,460
8	Honduras	4,318	2	El Salvador	3,553
9	Bangladesh	3,670	3	China	3,058
10	Pakistan	3,262	4	Haiti	2,676
	1995		5	Guatemala	2,526
1	El Salvador	75,138	6	Somalia	2,268
2	Guatemala	22,006	7	former Soviet Union	1,816
3	Mexico	9,148	8	India	1,764
4	China	4,822	9	Mauritania	765
5	India	3,135	10	former Yugoslavia	587

Source: L. F. B. Plascencia. "Mexican Asylum Applications—a Matter of Policy." Unpublished paper, 1999.

The United States was unable to take in all who wanted to flee. By 1990, Soviet emigrants had shifted their destination of preference to Israel. Senator Frank Lautenberg (D-NJ) authored an amendment of 1989 that gave refugee status to all Russian Jews, Armeni-ans, and Pentecostals, bringing in 300,000 over six years.

Other countries where political and other kinds of upheavals have sent refugees scrambling to America in recent years include Iran, Afghanistan, Palestine, Lebanon, Ethiopia, and Somalia. Most are poor and poorly educated, although the Iranian revolution of 1979 sent many professionals and entrepreneurs. Usually well-educated and English-speaking, they often settled in the posher neighborhoods of southern California.

FEMALE GENITAL MUTILATION

In recent years, a new category of refugee status has developed both in international law and U.S. practice: women—largely African—seeking escape from the practice of female genital mutilation (FGM). There are 135 million women in the world who have undergone FGM to one extent or another, from partial clitorectomy to total removal of external organs. Each day, 6,000 more undergo the procedure in Africa, the Middle East, Asia, Western Europe, and the United States, where it is illegal but occurs within applicable ethnic communities. In 1996, the United States granted asylum to Fauziya Kasinga of Togo. After sixteen months in detention and after having a Philadelphia immigration judge rule against her, she won protection on an appeal based on a fear that if returned she would suffer FGM. This ruling meant that the United States applied the 1951 United Nations Convention Relating to the Status of Refugees to this category.

The first attempt to avoid deportation by invoking the International Convention against Torture occurred in 1999. Torture in this case was defined as FGM and rape by relatives according to Nigerian custom. The United States signed the treaty in 1994 but did not authorize its antideportation protections until 1998. This approach grants sanctuary, not refugee status, which means that deportation becomes possible once the destination country changes its practices by law.

Refugees come from many places and from many circumstances, and their American experience varies widely. Postwar DPs had language barriers, and no money or skills, and they had survived the trauma of war or the concentration camp. Still, they had advantages as well—a welcoming environment, private and public (federal, state, and local) assistance organizations, Americans' willingness to accept those who shared their anticommunism, and an economy that was generally strong.

Throughout the Cold War period, those fleeing communism have been particularly welcome. And there is a notable pattern among these kinds of immigrants. Early arrivals tend to be the political elite; later refugees are poorer, and their persecution is mixed with economic hardship. Political refugees, especially Eastern Europeans, show up as prominent and well-paid professionals. First- and second-wave Cubans in South Florida and Vietnamese in Los Angeles and Orange counties, California, tend toward self-employment or business. Third-wave refugees with little education or work skills risk ending up on welfare.

Refugees generally have more threatening departure experiences, experience more undesirable change, and have less control over their circumstance than do other kinds of immigrants. They suffer more stress and mental illness. These conditions are compounded for those from the lower classes or who lack English, work skills, or education. Women have a harder time, as do older people.

The golden age of the open door is long gone, and anti-immigrant agitation is on the rise. Restrictionists fear that the numbers are too large for the United States to absorb. In 1960, the United Nations World Refugee Year, the United States passed the Fair Share Law, which adjusted quotas to help Europeans. Additional legislation passed in 1965, 1976, 1978, 1980, 1986, and 1990 produced steadily increasing numbers of immigrants. And asylum law changed virtually every year in the 1990s, as the Immigration and Naturalization Service attempted to streamline the process, break the backlog, and give petitioners speedy and fair treatment.

John Herschel Barnhill

See also: Germans and Other Political Refugees (Part I, Sec. 2); Causes of Immigration (Part I, Sec. 3); War Refugees (Part I, Sec. 4); Gay and Lesbian Immigration (Part II, Sec. 4); Judaism (Part II, Sec. 11); West Africa (Part III, Sec. 1); Cuba, Haiti and French-Speaking Caribbean (Part II, Sec. 2); Iran (Part II, Sec. 3); Refugee Act of 1980, Amerasian Children Act, 1997, President Truman's Directive on European Refugees, 1945, *Whom We Shall Welcome*, 1953, President Carter's Announcement on the *Marielitos*, 1980, President Bush and Courts on Return of Haitian Refugees, 1992 (Part IV, Sec. 1).

BIBLIOGRAPHY

Bennett, David. *The Party of Fear: From Nativist Movements to the New Right in American History.* Chapel Hill: University of North Carolina Press, 1988.

Bodnar, John. *The Transplanted.* Bloomington: Indiana University Press, 1985.

Countryman, Edward. *Americans, a Collision of Histories.* New York: Hill and Wang, 1996.

Dinnerstein, Leonard, and David M. Reimers. *Ethnic Americans*. 4th ed. New York: Columbia University Press, 1999.

Fleming, Donald, and Bernard Bailyn, eds. *The Intellectual Migration: Europe and America, 1930–1960*. Cambridge: Harvard University Press, Belknap Press, 1969.

Handlin, Oscar. *The Uprooted*. 2d ed. Boston: Little, Brown and Company, 1973.

Lacey, Dan. *The Essential Immigrant*. New York: Hippocrene Books, 1990.

Millman, Joel. *The Other Americans*. New York: Viking, 1997.

Olson, James Stuart. *The Ethnic Dimension in American History*. New York: St. Martin's Press, 1979.

Portes, Alejandro, and Rubén G. Rumbaut. *Immigrant America*. Berkeley: University of California Press, 1990.

Reimers, David M. *Still the Golden Door: The Third World Comes to America*. 2d ed. New York: Columbia University Press, 1992.

Takaki, Ronald. *A Different Mirror*. Boston: Little, Brown and Company, 1993.

Walker, Alice, and Pratibha Parmar. *Warrior Marks*. New York: Harcourt, Brace and Company, 1993.

Walker-Moffat, Wendy. *The Other Side of the Asian American Success Story*. San Francisco: Jossey-Bass Publishers, 1995.

WEB SITES

Amnesty International — www.amnesty.org
Raising Daughters Aware — www.fgm.org
American Bar Association — www.abanet.org
Feminist Majority Foundation Online — www.feminist.org

WARS AND CIVIL UNREST

Wars, revolutions, and other types of civil unrest have always exerted a profound demographic effect, resulting in the dislocation and displacement of large numbers of people. Forced to leave their homes or places of origin and to seek shelter elsewhere, usually abroad, such immigrants suffer great upheaval in their personal lives.

EIGHTEENTH- AND NINETEENTH-CENTURY REFUGEES

During the eighteenth and nineteenth centuries, upheavals were a by-product of the emergence and consolidation of European nation-states. As national governments assumed powers formerly reserved to the church or to local institutions such as the village, the municipality, or assemblies of notables—namely, defining the rights and obligations of their people, providing for their welfare, and validating their citizenship—they also became powerful enough to oppress nonconformist minorities. In the wake of these changes and as a consequence of the failure of the liberal revolutions of 1848 in France, Germany, Italy, and other European lands, ever-increasing numbers of people fled their homes. Indeed, such exiles or *émigrés*, as they were called, quickly became common fixtures in the literature of the period (for example, George Eliot's Daniel Deronda in her novel of the same name; Louisa May Alcott's Professor Baehr in *Little Women;* and Honoré de Balzac's Count Wenceslaus Steinbock in *Cousin Bette*). They also received widespread newspaper coverage (for example, the plight of Russian Jews fleeing czarist pogroms and expulsions in the 1880s and after).

TWENTIETH-CENTURY REFUGEES

In the twentieth century, war and civil unrest have functioned as critical and constant conditions in the politics and culture of developed as well as developing nations. Between 1900 and 1921, the collapse of the Ottoman, Romanov, Hapsburg, and Wilhelmian empires in the wake of the Balkan wars, World War I, the Russian Revolution and Russian civil wars, the Russo-Polish conflict, and the Armenian tragedy caused entire populations to be stranded in the Transcaucasian region and the slums of Constantinople or driven back and forth across the Russian-Polish borders. Japanese incursions into China during the 1920s and the proliferation of fascist and totalitarian dictatorships in Europe during the 1930s exacerbated the refugee crisis, as did the massive displacements sparked by World War II, the Cold War, and conflicts in the Middle East, Korea, Southeast Asia, Central America, Afghanistan, sub-Saharan Africa, and the Balkans.

The "refugees" (as they came to be called after World War I) of the twentieth century differ from the exiles and *émigrés* of the nineteenth century in three critical ways. First, there were exponentially more of them. Dozens of nationalities were dislocated and set adrift in the 1900s: millions of Chinese, Koreans, and Southeast Asians; hundreds of thousands in the Middle East and Africa; thousands in Central America; as well as vast populations in Western and Eastern Europe. Second, their expatriation often had no end in sight, and their aberrant status was passed on to a second generation. Third, increasingly, they had nowhere to go—many were and still are "stateless" (from the German *staatenlos*, coined to designate

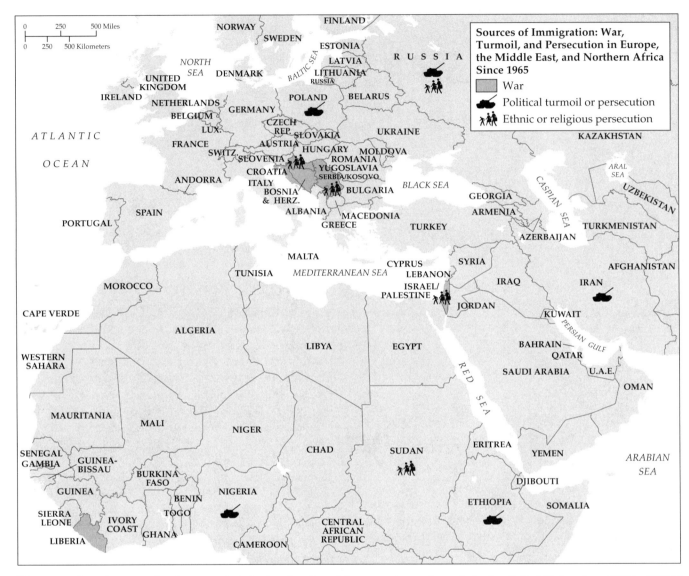

War, turmoil, and persecution have sparked the immigration of huge numbers of people to the United States since 1965. *(CARTO-GRAPHICS)*

those who fled to Germany after its unification in 1870).

Thus, these masses have come to exist outside the framework of national community. As such, they are often denied the advantages, privileges, and provisions of citizenship. This anomalous status operates on two levels. On the one hand, their nations of origin may have revoked their citizenship (such as the Jews who fled Nazi Germany) and threatened their physical safety (such as the Hmong in Southeast Asia, Hutus in Rwanda, and Albanians in Kosovo). On the other hand, their nations of refuge may not consider them eligible for citizenship and may place them in internment camps (such as Europeans in displaced-persons camps after World War II, Palestinians in Jor-

dan and Lebanon, Albanians in Macedonia, Cambodians in Thailand, and Cubans in Florida).

How such immigrants ultimately fare in their host cultures is subject to a number of variables: the extent to which their home culture enables them to respond to their host culture, the level and quality of acceptance exhibited by the host culture, and the capacity or desire of individual refugees to integrate into the host culture. Even so, given the unusual circumstances of their settlement in the host countries, it is possible to conclude that the prevalence of refugees in the twentieth century has contributed to the emergence of a new and persistent type of collective alienation.

This alienation is exacerbated by the stark contrasts that often exist between the refugees' new circumstances and the lives that they left behind, and by the traumatic circumstances of their separation from those lives. Nor, like more voluntary immigrants, can they comfort themselves with the knowledge that their home culture remains viable and that they can continue to maintain some sort of connection with it. More often than not, in this century, either their home culture has been utterly destroyed or devastated (such as the East European Jewish culture during the Holocaust or Hmong culture in Laos and Vietnam) or their continued communication with it would pose a grave threat to the safety of family and friends left behind (such as East Europeans who fled Soviet domination or mainland Chinese who fled Maoist domination of the People's Republic of China). In this context, even happy memories become burdensome and suffused with pain or a deep ambivalence. They cannot serve as a solid foundation from which to carry on the struggle between resistance and reconciliation that characterizes—for refugees and, indeed, for all immigrants—the process of accommodation to the host culture. Rather, memories provide a disturbing counterpoint, hindering assimilation and successful negotiation of tolerable social arrangements in the host culture.

REFUGEES AND IMMIGRANTS: BEFORE WORLD WAR II

A nation of immigrants, the United States has long been a beacon for those escaping the ravages of war, civil unrest, and persecution, and successive waves of such refugees have been a feature of the political and social landscape for centuries. Of course, they were not always received with unequivocal hospitality. In the early 1900s, in the face of increasing dislocation and displacement abroad, demands for curbs on immigration increased. These demands had both economic and racist overtones, motivated as they were by labor unions and significant anti-Asian sentiment. In 1921 and 1924, they culminated in immigration laws that severely reduced the total number of immigrants admitted and set national quotas that were designed to prevent any major change in the racial and ethnic makeup of the population. The laws permitted more than five times as many immigrants from northern and western Europe to enter the United States than immigrants from southern and eastern Europe, and they excluded people from Africa and Asia altogether.

REFUGEES AND IMMIGRANTS: FROM WORLD WAR II TO THE PRESENT

After World War II, the new prosperity along with a concern for the many thousands made homeless by the war led to a series of new laws. These laws implemented special programs that allowed certain groups of immigrants to enter the country outside the framework of the existing quota system or when quota backlogs became too large.

President Harry S. Truman's Presidential Directive (1945) admitted 42,000 European refugees, the War Brides Act (1946) admitted the wives and children of American servicemen, and the Displaced Persons acts of 1948 and 1950 admitted over 400,000 homeless Europeans. For its part, the Refugee Relief Act (1953), passed at the beginning of the Cold War, made special provision for "escapees" from the Soviet Union and its satellites, such as East Germany, Hungary, Latvia, Poland, and Yugoslavia. In the late 1950s, further remedial action was taken to admit refugees from China, from Hungary after the failed 1956 uprising, and from Cuba in the aftermath of Fidel Castro's overthrow of the Batista regime in 1959. In the 1970s, the Immigration and Naturalization Service administered a special program to handle the influx of refugees seeking to enter the United States from Southeast Asia.

In 1965, President Lyndon B. Johnson signed into law the Immigration and Nationality Act that not only replaced the national-origins system with one quota for the Western Hemisphere and one quota for the Eastern Hemisphere but also established a preference system for the issuing of visas that gave priority to family members of U.S. citizens or permanent residents, to immigrants with skills in demand in the United States, and to so-called conditional entrants, that is, refugees. These priorities continued to obtain even in 1978, when the separate quotas for the two hemispheres were replaced with a single annual quota of 290,000 immigrants worldwide, with a maximum of 20,000 from any one country. However, the percentages in the amendments of 1965 were too low to accommodate the flow of refugees from Southeast Asia in the late 1970s, Haiti in the early 1970s, and Cuba in 1980.

As a consequence, Congress passed the Refugee Act of 1980. This law made asylum benefits available to refugees worldwide, bringing the United States into line with international treaties and obligations. Prior to the act, asylum was available only to people fleeing the political enemies of the United States (for exam-

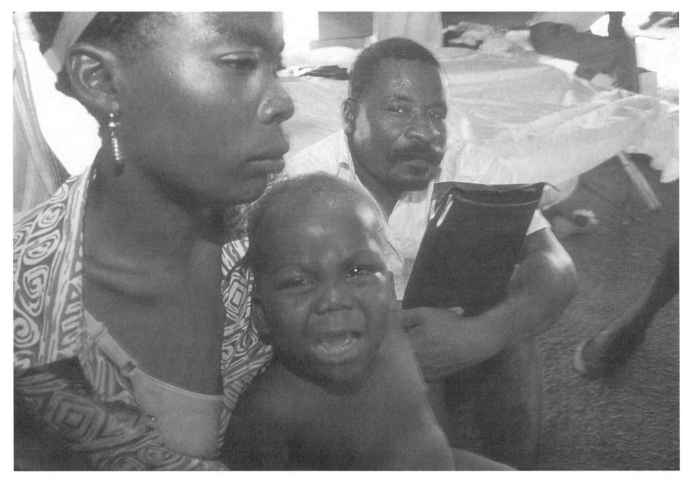

The unhappiness caused when war and civil unrest send refugees streaming from a country is captured in the faces of these Haitians being held at the U.S. military base at Guantanamo Bay, Cuba. *(Jim Tynan/Impact Visuals)*

ple, immigrants from communist countries). Furthermore, in accordance with the United Nations, the act defined a refugee as:

> Any person who . . . owing to a well-founded fear of being persecuted for reasons of race, religion, nationality, membership of a particular social group or political opinion, is outside the country of his nationality and is unable or, owing to such fear, is unwilling to avail himself of the protection of that country; or who, not having a nationality and being outside the country of his former habitual residence . . . is unable or, owing to such fear, is unwilling to return to it.

Thus, it removed such individuals from the immigrant preference system, admitting 50,000 new refugees that year, and provided for the setting of new quotas on a year-to-year basis. By the middle of the 1990s, this allocation had risen to about 110,000. In 1990, new laws fixed the quota ceilings for immigration at 700,000 annually for 1992 to 1994 and 675,000

annually beginning in 1995. They placed no limits on the number of immediate relatives of American citizens, and they did not include refugees. Rather, they granted special consideration to political refuges fleeing countries with repressive governments.

Currently, the United States accepts a certain number of refugees each year. This number is determined by the president in consultation with Congress. For example, in 1997, 78,000 refugees were permitted to enter the United States, with the total number of "refugee slots" allotted as follows: 7,000 from Africa, 10,000 from East Asia, 48,000 from Eastern Europe and the Soviet Union, 4,000 from Latin America and the Caribbean, 4,000 from the Near East (southwestern Asia) and the Middle East, and 5,000 set aside as a so-called unallocated reserve (that is, refugees fleeing unforeseen trouble). Further, the Department of State determines from which countries within these regions the United States will accept refugees. Thus, in 1997, the only nationalities designated from Africa were Somalis, Sudanese, Burundians, and Liberians.

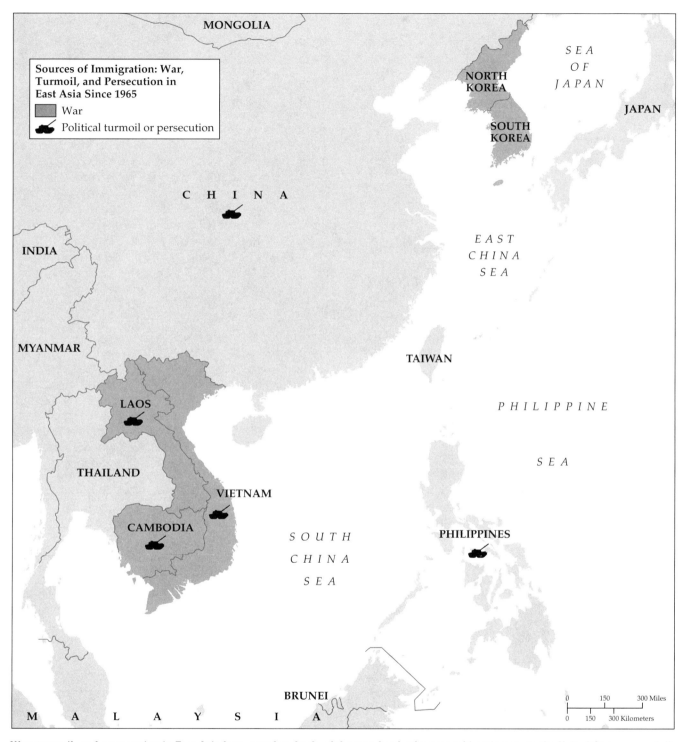

Sources of Immigration: War, Turmoil, and Persecution in East Asia Since 1965

- War
- Political turmoil or persecution

War, turmoil, and persecution in East Asia have sent hundreds of thousands of refugees and immigrants to the United States, especially since the end of Indochina wars in the mid-1970s. *(CARTO-GRAPHICS)*

Even so, the United States has continued to take in thousands of additional refugees every year since 1980.

All of these laws produced major changes in the pattern of immigration to the United States. Prior to 1965, most immigrants came from Europe and only about 5 percent came from Asia. After 1965, the number of immigrants from Asia, Latin America, and the West Indies soared dramatically, comprising at least 80 percent of the total immigrants.

KOREAN AND SOUTHEAST ASIAN REFUGEES

Clearly, the postwar years have provided no lack of immigrants fleeing the consequences of war and civil unrest. In the mid-twentieth century, Korean immigration to the United States was triggered by the Korean War (1950–53) and the civil unrest that followed it. In 1945, at the end of World War II, the United States and the Soviet Union occupied Korea. In 1948, they divided it into two separate countries, democratic South Korea and communist North Korea. The tensions inherent in this division quickly deteriorated into a conflict between the two countries and their respective allies. Between 1945 and 1965, almost 20,000 Korean immigrants had fled to the United States—among them, several thousand Korean orphans and war brides. Immigration from Korea increased more rapidly after the Immigration and Nationality Act of 1965: from 20,000 annually between 1972 and 1975 to 30,000 annually between 1975 and 1990. It reached a peak in 1987 (35,849 immigrants) and declined sharply after the 1992 Los Angeles riots, when many Korean-American stores were looted and burned.

In the 1970s and 1980s, chaotic conditions in Southeast Asia in the wake of the Vietnam War; the poor harvests of 1978 and 1979; the collapse of Cambodia and the devastation wrought by the Khmer Rouge, the border wars between China, Cambodia, and Vietnam; and the Vietnamese government's confiscation of the property of ethnic Chinese residents resulted in the dislocation of a vast population. Over 1.4 million Southeast Asians, including Vietnamese, ethnic Chinese, Laotians, and Hmong, were granted entry as refugees in the United States between 1975 and 1998.

CUBAN AND CENTRAL AMERICAN REFUGEES

Although nearly thirty thousand Cubans fled to the United States in the late 1950s, during the turbulent last years of Fulgencio Batista's dictatorship, this number increased even more sharply after Fidel Castro came to power in 1959. More than two hundred thousand people immigrated to the United States between 1959 and 1962. Another three hundred thousand fled on the "freedom flights" from Havana to Miami between 1965 and 1973. Yet another one hundred and twenty-five thousand came on the Mariel "boat lift"—a patchwork fleet of fishing boats and private pleasure craft sent by Cuban-American exiles to the port of Mariel. In addition to these mass immigrations, thousands of other Cubans have attempted to reach the United States on their own in small boats and rafts, even though many of them would lose their lives in the Straits of Florida.

Poverty, social injustice, along with political corruption, repression, and instability have persisted in many Central American republics through the second half of the twentieth century despite efforts at modernization. In a number of these republics, during the late 1970s and into the 1980s, this situation erupted into violence. Between 1960 and 1996, Guatemala was torn apart by fighting between left-wing groups and a repressive military regime—a conflict based mainly in the rural areas occupied by Indians. In Nicaragua, in 1978 and 1979, the Sandinista guerrillas overthrew the Somoza dynasty—a situation that eventually involved the United States in a major effort to support the counterrevolutionary (*contra*) forces against the leftist Sandinista government. El Salvador's people and economy were ravaged by civil war throughout the 1980s. As a consequence of these conflicts, thousands of people were killed and nearly 1 million were displaced. Of these, thousands of Nicaraguans and Guatemalan Indians, and an estimated five hundred thousand Salvadorans emigrated to the United States (about 40 percent of the latter illegally).

HUNGARIAN AND BALKAN REFUGEES

In 1956, popular discontent with the policies of the Hungarian communist regime (notably the collectivization of farms, the inclusion of communist propaganda in school curricula, and the imprisonment of Roman Catholic Hungarian leaders) led to widespread street demonstrations and eventually erupted into a revolution that, for a time, managed to drive the Communists from power. In order to reinstall them, the Soviet Union invaded Hungary. As a result, 38,000 anti-Soviet "Fifty-Sixers" and "Freedom Fighters," as they came to be called, fled Hungary for the United States. Since then, and through the 1960s, 1970s, and 1980s, more than six thousand Hungarian refugees have immigrated to the United States annually, most of them escapees from the repressive regime installed by the Soviets in 1956.

The Balkans, a region beset by long-standing ethnic, religious, and nationalistic tensions, erupted in a series of bitter and bloody conflicts during the 1990s. In 1989, Serbia tried to impose its control over the other Yugoslav republics—Slovenia, Croatia, Macedonia, and Bosnia and Herzegovina. Between June and November 1991—unable to effect a compromise with Serbia—Slovenia, Croatia, and Macedonia declared their independence. Bosnia and Herzegovina followed suit in 1992. Very soon, armed warfare broke out in Croatia (mid-1991) and in Bosnia and Herzegovina (April 1992), ostensibly as a result of internal civil discord (Muslim and Christian Croats or Muslim and Christian Bosnians), but actually abetted by Serbia, who backed the nationalist Serb campaigns in each republic. A third war erupted in 1998, following a period of increasing unrest among the Albanian population of the Serbian-controlled city of Kosovo that culminated in the killing of Serbian police officers by the Kosovo Liberation Army. All of these conflicts included atrocities and horrors that resulted in the widespread destruction of property and infrastructure, economic devastation, great loss of life (most of them Bosnian Muslims and ethnic Albanians), and massive dislocation (between 2 million and 3 million people), much of it due to Serbian "ethnic cleansing." Since 1992, more than one hundred thousand of these refugees (Bosnian, Croatian, and Albanian nationals) have been granted asylum in the United States, Canada, and Australia.

Frances G. Sternberg

See also: War Refugees (Part I, Sec. 4); Southeast Asian Refugee Crisis (Part I, Sec. 5); Central America (Part III, Sec. 2); Korea, Southeast Asia (Part III, Sec. 3); Refugee Act of 1980, Amerasian Children Act, 1997, District Court on Admissions of Haitians, 1993 (Part IV, Sec. 1).

BIBLIOGRAPHY

Arendt, Hannah. *The Origins of Totalitarianism.* San Diego: Harcourt, Brace, Jovanovich, 1968.

Ashabrenner, Brent. *Still a Nation of Immigrants.* New York: Cobblehill Books/Dutton, 1993.

Boswell, Richard A., and Carrasco, G. P. *Immigration and Nationality Law.* Durham, NC: Carolina Academic Press, 1992.

Cose, Ellis. *A Nation of Strangers: Prejudice, Politics, and the Populating of America.* New York: Morrow, 1992.

Dinnerstein, Leonard. *America and the Survivors of the Holocaust.* New York: Columbia University Press, 1982.

Goldstein, Beth L. "In Search of Survival: The Education and Integration of Hmong Refugee Girls." *The Journal of Ethnic Studies* 16: 2 (Summer 1988): 1–28.

Immigration and Naturalization Service. *An Immigrant Nation: United States Regulation of Immigration, 1798–1991.* June 18, 1991. Washington, DC: Immigration and Naturalization Service.

Marrus, Michael R. *The Unwanted: European Refugees in the Twentieth Century.* New York: Oxford University Press, 1985.

Sassen, Saskia. *Globalization and Its Discontents.* New York: New Press, 1998.

———. "Immigration Policy in a Global Economy." *The Unesco Courier,* November 1998.

Section 2

PROCESSES

Introduction

Adoption
Linda J. Collier

American Emigration Abroad
Arnold Dashefsky

Coast Guard and Coastlines
Bruce P. Dalcher

Connections to Homeland
Ewa Morawska

Human Smuggling and the Business of Illegal Immigration
David Kyle

Immigrant Aid Societies and Organizations
Héctor R. Cordero-Guzmán

The Immigration and Naturalization Service
A. Aneesh

Legal and Illegal Immigration: A Statistical Overview
Judith Warner

Marriage Market
Linda J. Collier

Sponsorship
Linda J. Collier

Transit and Transportation of Recent Illegal Immigrants
Linda J. Collier

Transnationalism: Immigration from a Global Perspective
Terese Lawinski

INTRODUCTION

Section 2 of Part II of the *Encyclopedia of American Immigration* deals with the various means by which people from around the world immigrate and settle in the United States. (It also includes one entry—"American Emigration Abroad"—that deals with the process in reverse.)

In her entry "Adoption," Linda J. Collier looks into the process by which foreign babies and children are adopted by American parents. She examines who can be adopted, who can do the adopting, how potential adoptees are located, the necessary documentation, and the issue of race and religion in the adoption process. She also offers case studies of countries that are home to many potential adoptees, including Russia and China.

Arnold Dashefsky's entry "American Emigration Abroad" deals with the little-known phenomenon whereby Americans emigrate to other countries. Dashefsky explores the extent of this phenomenon, as well as the motivation for and dynamics of emigration.

The entry "Coast Guard and Coastlines," by Bruce P. Dalcher, studies the U.S. Coast Guard's authority in protecting the nation's coasts against illegal immigration. He examines the question of how U.S. law determines the difference between migrants and refugees found at sea. He looks at the Coast Guard's recent history in this arena of immigration enforcement, as well as the Coast Guard's goals and future trends. In her essay "Connections to Homeland," Ewa Morawska examines the various personal and institutional connections that tie immigrants in the United States to their native countries.

In his entry "Human Smuggling and the Business of Illegal Immigration," David Kyle examines the multimillion-dollar industry of bringing immigrants into the United States illegally. The author begins with an examination of how the industry has changed in recent years, using immigrants from Mexico and Ecuador as examples. He then goes on to explore the question of exploitation of illegal immigrants from China before looking at the global migration industry.

Héctor R. Cordero-Guzmán's entry on immigrant aid societies and immigrant organizations begins with a history of these organizations from the early republic through the 1980s. He then examines the different types of immigrant organizations today, as well as their functions and roles. Finally, the author provides a discussion of the challenges these organizations face.

A. Aneesh's entry on the Immigration and Naturalization Service (INS) looks into that agency's enforcement of immigration law. She begins with an analysis of the INS's enforcement within the United States as well as its role in border management. She then provides a detailed history of the agency and its predecessors, beginning with its formation in the 1890s and continuing through the present day.

In her entry entitled "Legal and Illegal Immigration: A Statistical Overview," Judith Warner offers a detailed portrait of who is coming to this country both legally and illegally. She begins with a discussion of class, then moves on to discuss specific groups, including Asians, Latin Americans, and Europeans. She also looks into the numbers of refugees and asylum seekers, as well as the geographic destinations within the United States of different kinds of newcomers.

In Linda J. Collier's entry "Marriage Market," the subject is spousal entry into the United States. Beginning with a quick examination of the various ways spouses can be brought in, she goes on to study the international matchmaking business that links prospective American spouses (usually men) with foreign-born ones, including the various frauds and abuses perpetrated in this business.

The entry "Sponsorship," also by Linda J. Collier, examines the process whereby American citizens or permanent residents sponsor new immigrants to the United States. She looks at where sponsored immigrants come from and what the sponsors must do to meet the requirements of the law. She then goes into a case-by-case study of the different forms of sponsorship, including those of family, spouse, and employer.

In "Transit and Transportation of Recent Illegal Immigrants," Linda J. Collier studies the modes by which immigrants get to this country, beginning with an examination of the law as it relates to immigrant transport. She then provides an analysis of the various modes of transportation, including ship, motor vehicle, and rail transport.

In the entry "Transnationalism: A Theoretical and Contextual Overview," Terese Lawinski explores the process whereby immigrants to the United States maintain their identities and their lives in two worlds—that of the United States, their adopted country, and that of their homeland. She begins with a study of the theory and then explores its economic implications.

$\mathscr{A}$DOPTION

Although federal immigration law dictates the numbers and kinds of persons who can be admitted to the United States, the adoption of foreign-born children is regulated by the country in which the children are born and reside or the state in which the adoption originates. If the adoption occurs on American shores, then it is governed by the mandates of state law, and the procedures for accomplishing an adoption can usually be found in state statutes, legal codes, court opinions, and agency regulations. Federal statutes provide guidance in such areas as the adoption of Native American children, adoption subsidies, and determining the rights of unwed or putative fathers. Every state considers adoptions confidential and holds them in court proceedings closed to the public.

Only U.S. citizens may petition for the immediate immigration of foreign adopted children. The immigration laws do not provide for the entry of newly adopted children of legal permanent residents (green card holders) and long-term nonimmigrant visa holders. A statutory two-year waiting period frustrates attempts by legal permanent residents to secure immediate entry into the United States for children adopted abroad.

While similarities exist among the many state laws, there are decisive differences to discern before navigating the adoption route. International adoptions require adherence to stringent regulations—the rules, documents required, and length of time expended vary from country to country and depend upon many factors. Any adoption inquiry must begin with securing permission from the Immigration and Naturalization Service (INS) to bring the child into the United States and have him or her recognized as a relative of the citizen making the request. U.S. citizens are permitted to adopt children from any country as long as form I-600 or form I-600A is filed before the completion of the adoption. Form I-600 is for an orphan already known to the petitioner. Form I-600A is for an unknown orphan who will be identified by the petitioner. Approval from the INS is usually granted within several months after the filing of the petition.

WHO CAN BE ADOPTED

After all necessary authorities are satisfied that a foreign-born child is an orphan as described in Section 101(b)(1)(F) of the Immigration and Nationality Act, that child may be adopted by anyone suitable who is prepared to provide a proper home environment. A child may be adopted in all states, and all states permit the adoption of foreign-born children.

The Interstate Compact on Placement of Children, in force in every state, governs the adoption of an out-of-state child. Although the out-of-state adoption may occur in the state of the adoptive parent or placing agency, certain requirements must first be met. These requirements seek to safeguard the adoption process by ensuring that such an adoption is not contrary to the child's interests.

Due to serious concerns about "black-market babies," practically every state prohibits agencies and persons from accepting any fees for finding babies or placing a child for adoption. No person may accept or receive payment, either monetarily or with anything of value, for placing a child for adoption. Some states impose criminal penalties against anyone who violates this law.

WHO CAN ADOPT

A parent can usually adopt his or her stepchildren without the spouse (the biological parent) joining in the adoption, as long as the spouse consents to the adoption. Some states give special preferences to relatives who wish to adopt. In most states, adoption by

Since the end of the Cold War, adoption of babies from communist and former communist countries has risen dramatically. These adoptees are from China. *(Mel Rosenthal)*

preferred relatives or stepparents involves a simplified process in which waiting periods, home studies, and, in some states, even the adoption hearing may be waived.

Any single adult or a husband and wife together can adopt as long as either the husband or the wife is a U.S. citizen. According to immigration law, a married U.S. citizen of any age may adopt, or an unmarried citizen may adopt who is at least twenty-four years of age at the time of the filing of the I-600 form, but twenty-five years of age at the time of the filing of the orphan petition. The spouse may be an alien or a citizen, but the alien spouse must have lawful immigration status if resident in the United States.

If the couple is legally separated or the other spouse is unavailable or unreasonably refuses to consent to the adoption, most states allow a person to adopt without his or her spouse. A few states have special requirements for prospective adoptive parents. For example, there must be a certain age difference between the child and the adoptive parents, or the

adopting parent must live in the state for a certain period of time before being able to adopt. In some cases, the prospective adoptive parents and adoptee must live together for a period before the adoption.

LOCATING A CHILD

Prospective parents who are unsure of from which country they would like to adopt or the child whom they wish to select typically employ a facilitator or an agency to assist them in the adoption process. There are two separate functions that must be accomplished: One is the home study; the other is locating a child.

The home study must be completed by an agency within the state of residence, but the child search can be done by a facilitator or agency located anywhere. Once the home study has been completed, one copy must be submitted to INS and one to the agency locating the child.

NECESSARY DOCUMENTATION

The list of documents required for an international adoption varies by country and region, but the documentation required by the INS is more or less constant. To recognize a foreign-born child as a relative of the parent all the following are necessary:

1. Birth certificate (both spouses)

2. Marriage certificate

3. Divorce decree (if there were previous marriages for either spouse)

4. 1040 federal tax form

5. Form FD-258 fingerprint cards

6. Form I-864 affidavit of support

7. Form I-600

8. Letter of proof of employment (both spouses)

9. Net worth statement (from accountant or bank statement)

10. Police clearance letter (both spouses)

11. Approved home study

12. Medical examination report (both spouses)

13. Affidavit of health insurance

All required documents must be original or certified by a court of law to be true and correct copies of the originals. Marshaling the documents in advance saves time and money for many couples hoping to expedite the adoption process.

The home study is a very important item in the documentation process and often takes as long as four to six months to complete. An investigation and home study to determine the appropriateness of particular adopting parents are required in every state before an adoption can occur. State adoption laws specify that a child welfare or social service agency will investigate and conduct the study, but some states leave it up to the court to decide whom to appoint as an investigator. If a relative or stepparent is adopting, states exempt those family members from the investigation and home study.

The outcome of the investigation is crucial to the adoption process. Consequently, most states do not allow the adoption to take place until the investigation is completed and the court has received the resulting report. If the investigators conclude that the adopting parents are unsuitable, the adopting parents

can contest the report. In some states, this process is a separate procedure, but in other states, it is part of the same adoption hearing. When the INS processes all the aforementioned documents and approves the I-600 or the I-600A form, the petitioner receives a form I-171H. This form permits the petitioner to proceed with the adoption.

RACE AND RELIGION IN THE ADOPTION PROCESS

One aspect of adoption law that is governed by federal law is interracial or cross-cultural adoption. To ensure fairness in the adoption process and equal opportunity, Congress enacted the Multiethnic Placement Act (MEPA) in 1994. Among other things, the law prohibits a federally assisted agency from categorically denying the opportunity for any person to become an adoptive or foster parent solely on the basis of the race, color, or national origin of the adoptive parent or the child. This act was amended in 1996 by the Interethnic Provision (IEP). This amendment, also known as Removal of Barriers to Interethnic Adoption, strengthened the mandate for fairness in the adoption process by penalizing states and adoption agencies who discriminate in the placement of children in foster care. In addition, it repealed Section 553 of the MEPA, which gave discretion to an agency or the state in considering the cultural, ethnic, and racial background of the child in their placement. The capacity of the adoptive parents to meet the child's needs based on the child's background is still a consideration and is typically examined within the framework of the best interests of the child. Partly in response to this law, a number of states (e.g., Arizona, California, Connecticut, Utah, and Washington) have enacted their own versions of the Multiethnic Placement Act.

RUSSIAN ADOPTIONS

Russian authorities require all of the following documents, and each must be translated, notarized, and witnessed.

1. Primary application to adopt

2. Financial statement

3. INS approval (I-171H)

4. Home study

5. Police clearance letters (both spouses)

6. Proof of home ownership

7. Marriage certificate (if single mother, just own birth certificate)

8. Power of attorney

9. Copies of passports (both spouses)

10. Medical examination letter (both spouses)

11. Agreement to do postplacement reports (from adoption or home study agency)

12. Two pages of family photos (no notary or witness needed)

A child declared an orphan (abandoned at birth or another time, parental rights revoked) by the court and registered with the Regional Department of Education in the Moscow Federal Data Bank for at least three months is eligible for adoption. Since Russian natives are favored over foreigners, during those three months, any approved Russian family may adopt the child. The child is removed from the Federal Data Bank when the Regional Department of Education receives notification that an adoptive family has expressed an interest in the child. Within ten days, the Federal Department of Education grants permission for the child to be adopted and issues an approval letter, which is submitted to the U.S. embassy in Moscow along with other documents to secure a visa for the child.

Local regional judges grant adoptions based on their review of the following: the portfolio of previously mentioned papers, a report from the local child-welfare department, a report from the orphanage director, and the judge's own impressions of the adoptive parents during the court hearing. Both parents are required to be at the court hearing, along with the orphanage director, state prosecutor, and the director of the child-welfare office. The judge issues a final decision the same day but its effect is delayed for ten calendar days. Once the decision takes effect, the adoptive parents gain absolute rights and full custody of the child.

The American embassy requires a medical exam along with a long list of documents, including the I-600. The documents, as well as photos of the child, are submitted to obtain a new birth certificate, visa, and passport.

The Russian government makes a diligent attempt at following up on their adopted children by requiring postplacement reports be submitted every six months for two years and then once a year for up to five years.

CHINESE ADOPTIONS

Abandonment in China is a side effect of strict population controls that allow only one child per family in cities and two in most rural areas if the first is a girl.

Adoptions from China have increased from 61 in 1991, when China passed its first adoption law, to 4,194 over the twelve months through September 1998. Well over half of Chinese babies adopted by foreigners go to Americans, and many of the others become children of Canadians and Europeans. In 1998, Americans adopted 13,621 foreign children, twice the total number of children adopted in the two previous decades. Second only to Russia, China is a very popular place for American adoptions overseas, followed by South Korea, Guatemala, and Romania. Several years ago, China's legislature expanded the eligibility field of potential foreign and Chinese adoptive parents for the nation's tens of thousands of abandoned baby girls. Amendments to the law revised the minimum parental age downward from thirty to twenty-five, and the law now allows people who already have children to adopt healthy abandoned babies. The law was passed over objections that it could become a way around the strict controls China places on births. These family size limits—plus a rural tradition favoring boys—result in a very large population of healthy abandoned baby girls waiting to be adopted. Many Americans and others are also attracted to China because it allows adoption by singles and people in their forties or older, who face eligibility hurdles elsewhere.

Linda J. Collier

See also: Children and Adolescent Immigrants, Family (Part II, Sec. 4); Illegal Immigration Reform and Immigrant Responsibility Act, 1996, Amerasian Children Act, 1997 (Part IV, Sec. 1).

BIBLIOGRAPHY

Bureau of Consular Affairs. *International Adoptions: Guidelines on Immediate Relative Petitions.* Washington, DC: Department of State, February 1997.

Horowitz, Robert A. *Summary of State Law Variations, ABA Center on Children and the Law.* Chicago, IL: American Bar Association. March 23, 1999.

Schoof, Renee. "More U.S. Couples Adopting Abroad," The Associated Press News Service. January 9, 1999: Guangzhou, China.

Taake, Angie. "Adoption." *National Adoption Information Clearinghouse,* (on-line publication at www.naic.com), February 23, 1999.

AMERICAN EMIGRATION ABROAD

"*H*uman wandering is as old as humankind, but the world has never seen so much of it. In crassly economic terms, migration involves the poor flowing to the rich," wrote B. Wysocki in the millennium edition of the *Wall Street Journal*. Nevertheless, American emigration abroad defies this generalization because it involves movement from a more developed part of the world to a somewhat less developed part. It is important to understand the extent of such emigration, the motivations for it, the dynamics of adjustment, and the factors involved in remaining or returning, as well as the consequences for American society.

EXTENT OF AMERICAN EMIGRATION ABROAD

While the United States has generally been regarded as a society based on immigration, there has been a substantial and surprising amount of emigration. According to sociologists R. Warren and E. P. Kraly, during the twentieth century the United States gained about 30 million immigrants and lost approximately 10 million people to emigration, a ratio of 3:1. Currently more than 195,000 people, mostly foreign-born persons, emigrate each year. Based on demographic analysis of completed U.S. censuses for the 1980s, the net emigration total was estimated at 1.6 million, of which 1.3 million were foreign-born residents. In general, it is easier to calculate the number of emigrants who were born abroad than to count those born in the United States. Indeed, estimating American emigration abroad remains a difficult challenge because such data are not collected regularly and systematically, as is the U.S. census, and what data there are come from several different federal government sources. Nevertheless, in comparing the average annual number of immigrants to the United States for the period 1995–98, 774,000, to the number of emigrants estimated by

Kraly, 195,000, it appears that the ratio of in-migrants to out-migrants is currently 4:1, in contrast to earlier in the twentieth century, as noted above, when it was 3:1.

Table 1 presents the average annual number of U.S. immigrants and emigrants and the net addition to the U.S. population for the period 1900–1979. Note that from the beginning of the twentieth century to the beginning of World War I, immigration was at its greatest level, but so was emigration. During World War I, emigration and immigration declined substantially, and during the Great Depression, emigration actually exceeded immigration.

After World War II, immigration increased and so did emigration. Thus there appears to be a relationship between the volume of emigration to that of immigration. But were not these emigrants from America simply disenchanted immigrants? Yes and no. For the years that data were available (1915–49), there was always a sizable portion of U.S. citizens among the pool of emigrants. Indeed, for emigrants, the ratio between non–U.S. citizens and U.S. citizens approached parity in the post–World War II years (see Table 1).

Table 2 presents data for nineteen countries that were among the leading recipients of emigrants from the United States. The seven leading destination countries, based on an average annual migration of Americans in the period 1960–76, in rank order were Mexico, Germany, the United Kingdom, Canada, Japan, Australia, and Israel. According to scholar Arnold Dashefsky and colleagues, these seven absorbed 88 percent of the average annual output of American migrants during this period. About one-half went to the U.S. neighbors, Mexico and Canada; about one-fourth went to European destinations, Germany and the United Kingdom; and most of the rest went to Japan, Australia, and Israel. Finally, Table 3 presents a picture with the cumulative total of American emigrants for twelve of the leading recipient nations.

In sum, emigration was a constant feature of

Table 1
Estimated Numbers in Thousands of U.S. Immigration, U.S. Emigration, and Net Additions to the U.S. Population, 1900–1979

Years	Immigrants	Emigration			Net Addition
		Total	Non-U.S. Citizen	U.S. Citizen	
1975–1979	2,411	629	629	NA	1,782
1970–1974	1,923	547	547	NA	1,376
1965–1969	1,795	510	510	NA	1,285
1960–1964	1,418	390	390	NA	1,028
1955–1959	1,401	211	211	NA	1,190
1950–1954	1,099	214	214	NA	885
1945–1949	653	185	94	91	468
1940–1944	205	96	57	39	109
1935–1939	272	206	153	53	66
1930–1934	427	443	336	107	-16
1925–1929	1,520	511	390	121	1,009
1920–1924	2,775	1,174	893	281	1,601
1915–1919	1,173	715	618	97	458
1910–1914	5,175	1,442	1,442	NA	3,733
1905–1909	4,947	1,793	1,793	NA	3,154
1900–1904	3,256	1,215	1,215	NA	2,041
All Periods	30,450	10,281	9,492	789	20,169

Source: U.S. Immigration and Naturalization Service and U.S. Bureau of Census.

twentieth-century American society. While rarely exceeding the volume of immigration, it did surpass it in several years. For the years for which data were available in the second half of the twentieth century, about half the emigration was to North America, and the other half was largely confined to the developed world.

SOURCES OF MOTIVATION

American emigration abroad belongs to that class of immigration called voluntary international immigration. In seeking to understand the sources and motivations for emigration, it is useful to compare the work of the classical European sociologist Emile Durkheim, who analyzed the social forces and facts affecting suicide. As Durkheim observed about the suicide rate, one might infer about the rate of emigration:

> The conclusion from all these facts is that the suicide [emigration] rate can be explained only sociologically. At any given moment the moral situation of society establishes the contingent of voluntary deaths [departures].

For Durkheim, the rate of suicide varied with the extent of integration within society; a like argument may be made for emigration.

While emigration is not the equivalent of suicide, voluntary international migration may be characterized similarly. Individuals with lower levels of integration in society are more likely to become emigrants. The general motivations can be divided into two categories: expressive and instrumental. The former concerns individuals seeking greater political or religious expression, rootless wanderers, persons seeking family unity, disciples of charismatic leaders, and adherents of religious and political groups. The latter motivates foreign students, migrant laborers, missionaries, and staffs of nongovernmental organizations.

DYNAMICS OF EMIGRATION

Having decided to emigrate, American migrants face another set of decisions and circumstances once they arrive in their new country of residence. These focus on problems of adjustment and the issue of remaining or returning to their country of origin. For many in-

Table 2
Average Annual Immigration to Selected Countries from the United States, 1960–1976

Country of destination	Total years reported	Average Annual Immigration from the United States*			
		1960 to 1974	1970 to 1974	1965 to 1969	1960 to 1964
All countries		180,200	281,000	151,700	66,100
Argentina	14	400	600	300	300
Australia	15	8,500	12,800	8,500	4,400
Belgium	16	3,100	4,300	3,200	1,700
Brazil	13	1,000	900	1,100	1,100
Canada	11	21,900	24,600	19,900	**
France	14	900	1,400	900	400
Germany	15	24,800	27,800	26,400	21,600
Hong Kong	12	2,900	3,400	2,000	**
Israel	17	3,898	5,449	4,550	2,154
Italy	17	2,700	5,400	1,400	300
Japan	17	1,720	23,400	15,100	12,100
Kenya	17	500	400	800	200
Mexico	13	64,600	142,000	40,600	17,300
Netherlands	13	3,400	3,800	3,100	**
New Zealand	15	1,400	2,300	1,300	1,000
Nigeria	13	1,400	1,700	1,100	1,300
Norway	17	2,900	3,200	2,800	2,600
Sweden	17	1,700	1,700	1,600	1,800
United Kingdom	12	20,900	21,300	21,500	**

*Averages are based on the number of years for which data are reported.
**Data are available for fewer than three years of the five-year period.
Source: Data derived from *United Nations Demographic Yearbook* as presented by Warren and Kraly 1985, p. 11, except for Israeli data, which were provided by the Israel Central Bureau of Statistics.

ternational emigrants, returning to their home country may not be an option for political, economic, social, or religious reasons. Nevertheless, for American emigrants, returning home is, in the great majority of cases, a realistic alternative. Therefore, such international migration should be viewed as cyclical. Emigrants may be drawn into a dynamic process of emigration, adjustment, and return migration, and in some cases may repeat that process.

Very little research has focused on emigrants from America in comparison to research on immigrants to the United States. A search of the *Sociological Abstracts* database of social science literature, covering the period 1963–99, yielded 253 articles on immigration and only 7 on emigration, yielding a ratio of 36:1 in comparison to a 3:1 ratio of actual immigration to emigration during much of the twentieth century. (This comparison presents only an approximation of the actual articles published, as some articles on migration may refer to either emigration or immigration or

both.) What little research that has been carried out and reported has largely examined American emigrants to Australia, Canada, and Israel. Based on a statistical model developed for the latter case, Dashefsky and colleagues proposed a more general model of the dynamics of American emigration:

1. This model suggests that absorption is affected by a set of demographic factors, for example, age . . . gender . . . and marital status. . . .

2. Staying (or leaving) is next affected by certain background factors prior to migration, such as knowledge of the language [of the host country] and organizational involvement [with those connected to the adopted country].

3. Experiences in the new society next affect absorption, such as contacts with veteran settlers and satisfactions with various basic areas of daily life including work, housing, and the like.

Table 3
Major Countries with Americans Living Abroad

Country	Number of Americans
Canada	626,585
Mexico	550,147
Britain	216,000
Israel	158,400
Italy	146,100
Germany	130,402
Philippines	118,000
France	86,037
Dominican Republic	85,900
Greece	82,500
Japan	73,301
Australia	63,800

Source: Richey 1997, p. 9.

4. Finally, all of the preceding experiences lead to the most important variable in explaining whether the emigrants stay, and that is "confidence of remaining."

IMPLICATIONS

Even as the United States receives immigrants, it will continue to produce emigrants, including those who previously immigrated as well as those who were native-born. Such Americans will emigrate seeking business opportunities, adventure, travel, and other forms of personal fulfillment. They will be drawn to countries that represent for them a greater compatibility of culture and technology as well as the opportunity to take advantage of economic and educational institutions. The degree of this adjustment will be rooted in the degree of differences between the United States and the new country. Finally, it is likely that only a minority of native-born American emigrants will remain abroad for their entire lives. For example, Dashefsky and colleagues reported that between the 1960s and 1980s only 25 percent of Americans who emigrated to Australia and 48 percent of those going to Israel remained in their adopted countries. Nevertheless, according to the director of statistics for the Immigration and Naturalization Service, American emigrants are a "big plus," as they represent an increasing involvement of the United States in the world.

Is American emigration good or bad for America? As it generally does not exceed immigration, emigration does not have serious consequences for the stability of the U.S. population. Indeed, as Kraly has noted, it is useful to consider emigration in regard to U.S. immigration policy. Despite the themes of alienation that have been attributed to such American migrants, it appears that many of them retain and espouse modern American values—efficiency in work, gender equality, and respect for civil rights and the environment—when they are abroad. Furthermore, they may in a sense serve as ambassadors of such values in the host countries and thereby narrow the cultural gap between the United States and these other nations. Finally, they are unlikely to surrender their American passports, an act that might confirm notions of alienation. As one American emigrant summed it up: "We've finally captured the American dream. It's just a shame that we had to come to New Zealand to do it."

Arnold Dashefsky

See also: Return Migration (Part II, Sec. 3); Renunciation of U.S. Citizenship, 1998 (Part IV, Sec. 2).

BIBLIOGRAPHY

Belsky, G. "Escape from America." *Money,* July 7, 1994, pp. 60–70.

Dashefsky, A., J. De Amicis, B. Lazerwitz, and E. Tabory. *Americans Abroad.* New York: Plenum, 1992.

Department of Justice, Immigration and Naturalization Service. "Legal Immigration, Fiscal Year 1998." In *Annual Report,* Washington, D.C., May 1999.

Durkheim, E. *Suicide.* Translated by J. A. Spaulding and G. Simpson. Glencoe, IL: Free Press, 1951 (originally published 1897).

Echikson, W. "Young Americans Go Abroad to Strike It Rich." *Fortune* 130:8 (October 17, 1994): 185–94.

Kraly, E. P. "Emigration: Implications for U.S. Immigration Policy Research." In *Migration Between Mexico and the United States: Binational Study.* Vol. 2, *Research Reports and Background Materials,* pp. 587–618. Mexico City: Mexican Ministry of Foreign Affairs; Washington, DC: U.S. Commission on Immigration Reform, 1998.

Richey, W. "Many Seek American Dream—Outside America." *The Christian Science Monitor,* March 19, 1997, pp. 9–12.

Warren, R., and E. P. Kraly. "The Elusive Exodus: Emigration from the United States." *Population Trends and Public Policy* 8 (1985): 1–17.

Woodrow-Lafield, K. A. "Viewing Emigration at Century's End." In *Migration Between Mexico and the United States: Binational Study.* Vol. 2, *Research Reports and Background Materials,* pp. 683–94. Mexico City: Mexican Ministry of Foreign Affairs; Washington, DC: U.S. Commission on Immigration Reform, 1998.

Wysocki, B. "On the Move." *Wall Street Journal,* January 1, 2000, p. R42.

COAST GUARD AND COASTLINES

For almost two hundred years the U.S. Coast Guard had only episodic involvement with maritime immigration enforcement, from antislavery laws enacted in 1794 to a ban on importing "coolie" laborers from China in 1862, to immigrant quotas in the 1920s, to the early arrival of Cubans in the 1960s. Today, the law enforcement effort to control illegal immigrants at sea, or "alien migrant interdiction operations" (AMIO) as it is now called, is an unusually complicated mission for the Coast Guard. The overwhelming majority of AMIO focuses on four source countries, as shown in Figure 1.

AMIO manifests an inherent tension. On one hand is national policy, incorporating international concerns and immigration policy. The Immigration and Naturalization Service (INS) heads overall immigration enforcement. Although the Coast Guard leads *maritime* immigration enforcement efforts, national policy is set by the National Security Council and involves other agencies, principally the INS and the State Department. On the other hand is the Coast Guard: AMIO inevitably overlaps with other missions, most obviously search-and-rescue (SAR) of mariners in distress, be they migrants or not. At the same time, the Coast Guard is carrying out other law enforcement duties, all the while allocating scarce resources among these and other missions. Thus the Coast Guard, despite leading the maritime enforcement effort, is actually struggling to carry out policy more than to make it.

COAST GUARD AUTHORITY

The Coast Guard is the nation's primary maritime law enforcement agency. This unusual component of the nation's armed forces enjoys extremely broad domestic law enforcement authority, principally under Title 14 U.S.C. Sections 2 and 89, which charge the Coast Guard with enforcing or assisting to enforce all federal laws on the high seas and on any other waters subject to U.S. jurisdiction.

International law, however, generally considers vessels on the high seas to be subject only to the jurisdiction of their flag states. Several exceptions in international law provide at least some basis for Coast Guard authority over foreign vessels. One is known as the "right of visit." This allows a warship to board any vessel that is not entitled to immunity (e.g., foreign warships have sovereign immunity) if there are reasonable grounds to suspect, among other things, that it is a stateless vessel, or is of the same nationality as the warship. This is a limited authority to confirm or refute such suspicions. If the suspicion is confirmed, the Coast Guard vessel may assert full jurisdiction.

Another basis for boarding foreign vessels, and perhaps the most versatile for AMIO, is consent. The Coast Guard routinely boards vessels with the consent of the vessel's master.

Another exception to the principle of exclusive flag state jurisdiction is the limited authority a coastal state, such as the United States, may claim over the Contiguous Zone, a belt of water lying adjacent to and immediately seaward of the Territorial Sea. In 1999 President Bill Clinton expanded the U.S. Contiguous Zone: it now covers the area from 12 to 24 miles offshore. Under accepted international law, a state may exercise the control necessary to prevent violations of its immigration laws, including boarding foreign vessels upon suspicion that they carry illegal immigrants.

However the Coast Guard comes to be on board, the vessel's registration is checked. If a vessel proves to be properly registered with a foreign nation, that nation may be asked to consent to the enforcement of U.S. laws aboard the foreign vessel—in other words, they may waive their exclusive jurisdiction in favor of the United States. This waiver, called "flag state consent," may be accomplished by any means, from a formal treaty in advance to a case-by-case agreement at the time of the boarding.

Figure 1
1998 Coast Guard Migrant Interdictions

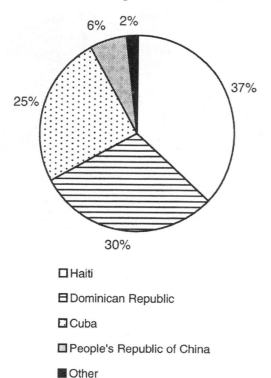

☐ Haiti

⊟ Dominican Republic

☐ Cuba

☒ People's Republic of China

■ Other

Source: Chart by author using official U.S. Goast Guard data published at www.uscg.mil/hg/g-o/mle/amiostatsl.htm (accessed April 3, 2000).

Thus, while the Coast Guard's broad domestic authority does not automatically extend to foreign vessels, the right of visit or the master's consent, when combined with flag state consent, allows the Coast Guard to stop vessels on the high seas, search for illegal immigrants, and enforce any relevant U.S. laws. Direct preventive enforcement is also possible in the Contiguous Zone.

The U.S. Immigration and Nationality Act (INA) of 1965 is one law that the Coast Guard enforces. Under the INA, it is unlawful for an alien to enter, or attempt to enter, the United States except under prescribed procedures. It is also a crime for anyone to knowingly bring, or attempt to bring, an alien into the United States at other than a designated port of entry.

"MIGRANT" VERSUS "REFUGEE"

An alien is someone who is not a citizen of the United States. Aliens seeking admission to the United States are often referred to as migrants (to avoid the confusion between emigrants and immigrants). "Refugee" is defined in Title 8 U.S.C. § 1101, and under international law, as one who is fleeing persecution or possesses a well-founded fear of persecution because of race, religion, nationality, membership in a particular social group, or political opinion. A refugee is entitled to special treatment because of U.S. obligations under international law.

The United States is a party to the United Nations Protocol Relating to the Status of Refugees. Although the protocol does not require that any country grant asylum, and does not prohibit resettling aliens in a third country, Article 33 of the protocol prohibits *refoulement*, that is, the return of a "refugee" to the source of the well-founded fear of persecution. However, under U.S. law the protocol has been held not to apply extraterritorially, which means that it does not apply to interdictions on the high seas. Furthermore, the attorney general's Office of Legal Counsel has opined that the protocol does not apply in the Territorial Sea either. This is the origin of the so-called wet feet–dry feet rule.

RECENT HISTORY

Current AMIO practice is a product of the last thirty-five years' experience, beginning in 1965 when Fidel Castro opened the port of Camarioca and allowed almost three thousand immigrants to come to Florida. Most came by private vessels, creating chaos and danger at sea to which the Coast Guard responded. Another major exodus from Cuba began in 1980, when the Castro government allowed 124,000 people to leave from the port of Mariel. Most came to the United States, once again, by private craft; and once again, the Coast Guard mixed life-saving and law enforcement missions as they sought to prevent mishaps in the stormy Florida Straits while enforcing immigration laws.

For Caribbean migrants, the United States is a natural target both because of proximity—Miami is only ninety miles from Cuba's northern coast—and because of family members already living in America.

Economic collapse under the Duvalier regime in Haiti in the late 1970s and early 1980s brought waves of Haitian migrants. Interdiction at sea became U.S. policy, in the form of Presidential Proclamation No. 4865 (which suspended the entry by sea of all undocumented aliens), issued by Ronald Reagan in 1981.

That proclamation was followed by Executive Order 12324 in 1981, under which the Coast Guard was

The U.S. Coast Guard is responsible for interdicting refugees found at sea, like these Haitians trying to reach Florida. *(United States Coast Guard)*

to stop certain "defined vessels" on the high seas upon suspicion of the "irregular carriage of persons," and to return them if possible to their country of origin. "Defined vessels" included vessels from nations that had authorized the United States to board them; at the time, the United States had such an agreement with Haiti, which provided also that Haiti would not prosecute those migrants who were returned to Haiti.

This measure was a practical step: mass migrations quickly overwhelmed the normal administrative channels for coping with illegal migrants, as well as overwhelming Coast Guard resources. Every nation has the inherent right to control its borders and determine who may enter; these presidential directives were essentially a policy decision that massed migrants, as a group, were not eligible for immigration. The novelty lay in that Executive Order 12324 had effect only beyond the Territorial Sea—that is, on the high seas. Because migrant vessels are often overloaded, unseaworthy, and ill-crewed, the U.S. policy of interdicting such vessels closer to Haiti saved many lives that would inevitably have been lost on a 600-

mile voyage to the United States. As an example, the Coast Guard has interdicted twenty-foot open vessels with more than seventy people on board in the Mona Passage between the Dominican Republic and Puerto Rico.

Of course, the U.S. government was also taking advantage of the fact that high-seas interdictions avoided any need for deportation hearings in that none of those interdicted had ever "entered" the United States. However, the Coast Guard vessels carried INS agents who interviewed all interdicted migrants to identify any with potential asylum claims—in other words, to separate possible refugees from other migrants, motivated mostly by economic concerns. The possible refugees were brought to the United States to investigate their asylum claims after the other migrants were repatriated to Haiti.

In 1991 a political coup in Haiti led to a huge increase in Haitian immigrants: from an annual average of 2,500 in the 1980s to an average of 17,000 between 1991 and 1994. Economic and political upheaval in other countries contributed to the burden: over one

Cubans fleeing the Castro regime have generally received a warmer welcome in the United States than refugees from noncommunist countries. Here Coast Guard guardsmen help Cuban refugees in Florida. *(United States Coast Guard)*

hundred twenty thousand migrants from twenty-three nations were interdicted by the Coast Guard between 1991 and 1995. Once again, Coast Guard resources were overwhelmed. In response, President Bush issued Executive Order 12807 in 1992, which directed the Coast Guard to interdict undocumented alien migrants at sea and return them whence they had come.

Executive Order 12807 replaced Executive Order 12324. The significant difference was that the new Executive Order 12807 no longer required any refugee screening whatever. Executive Order 12807 was upheld by the Supreme Court in 1993 and remains in effect today. Under its provisions the Coast Guard has been able to respond to further waves of Haitians, Cubans, and others. The strategy remains to interdict migrants as far at sea as possible, as this tactic saves lives, speeds repatriation, and avoids the burden of immigration processing ashore.

From 1993 to 1994, under Operation Able Manner, the Coast Guard concentrated on the Windward Passage between Haiti and Cuba to interdict Haitian migrants. Operation Able Vigil, in the Straits of Florida, responded to another surge of emigration from Cuba in 1994.

Yet another dedicated Coast Guard operation, Able Response, ran from 1995 to 1997, this time turning to migrants from the Dominican Republic. Some ninety-five hundred migrants, mostly in home-made open fishing vessels called *yolas*, were interdicted at sea or forced to return home. The operation succeeded in part because of the U.S. policy of interdicting migrants far at sea—in this case, in the Mona Passage between Puerto Rico and the Dominican Republic.

In 1995 the United States and Cuba agreed, through a joint communiqué, on steps to reduce the flow of Cuban migrants. The communiqué provided that Cuban migrants would be admitted only after applying for a visa, or for refugee status, at the U.S. Interests Section in Havana. In return, the United States agreed to allow up to 20,000 Cubans per year to enter the United States through this procedure. Thus illegal Cuban migrants interdicted at sea could be more readily repatriated to Cuba.

In 1996 the legal framework for AMIO changed. The INA had formerly distinguished between aliens who had "entered" the United States and those who had not. In general, those who had entered were entitled to deportation hearings and other proceedings, while other aliens were not and so could be summarily excluded. With the 1996 amendment to the INA came a significant change of terminology: the question became whether an alien had been "admitted" to the United States, and deportation was abandoned in favor of the broader term, "removal proceedings." As interpreted by the Justice Department, only aliens who were "applicants for admission," meaning those who had arrived on dry land, were entitled to removal proceedings.

The major effect of the 1996 amendments, from a maritime perspective, is that the Justice Department's interpretation of the amendments established a firmer basis for the "wet feet–dry feet" doctrine. Because procedural rights are now considered to accrue only when a migrant reaches land, there is no obligation of any kind for refugee screening or other procedures if a migrant is interdicted at sea, whether on the high seas or within U.S. territorial waters. Those with wet feet—those who are interdicted before reaching U.S. soil—are repatriated.

Since 1980, AMIO has been a matter of Haitian, Cuban, and Dominican migrants seeking to reach the Southeast United States via the Caribbean, and migrants from the People's Republic of China (PRC) who have sought entry on the coasts of the U.S. mainland as well as on Puerto Rico, the U.S. Virgin Islands, Hawaii, and, most recently, Guam and the Commonwealth of Northern Mariana Islands.

Migrants from the People's Republic of China were the immigration challenge of the 1990s. Several of the more notorious cases can be likened to slavery, with large numbers of migrants packed aboard freighters in miserable conditions, often under harsh discipline from "enforcers." Guam is a target because it is a U.S. territory but is 6,700 miles closer to China than the U.S. mainland. Every year, between fifteen and twenty thousand illegal Chinese migrants are thought to head for the west, most of them aimed at the United States. The migrants often pay $30,000 or more to be smuggled to the United States; a medium-sized vessel represents a $5 million human cargo to the organized criminals behind the scenes.

GOALS

The primary concern under U.S. policy, and as an international obligation, is to protect life at sea. Unsafe vessels crammed with weak people make deaths commonplace. After taking steps to save life, the Coast Guard's goal is to eliminate most illegal migrant flow. By policy, the Coast Guard also responds to refugee claims and asylum requests whenever they arise, whether during AMIO or other operations. Another task is to detain interdicted migrants on board Coast Guard cutters, outside the United States, until a decision is reached whether to repatriate them, transfer them to a third country, or in rare cases deliver them to Border Patrol or INS agents in the United States.

On the law enforcement front, the Coast Guard also seizes and arrests alien smugglers and gathers evidence against them. Fighting those who smuggle aliens is a nationwide effort and involves the INS, the Border Patrol, and the Customs Service. The goal is to raise both the costs and the likelihood of capture to deter criminals, a job made more difficult by the high financial return for smuggling.

Winning the resource tug-of-war is another goal. For example, if the Coast Guard decides to dispatch a cutter from the West Coast to Guam to buttress AMIO efforts there, it faces the cost in time and money for the 6,000-mile transit on top of the loss of that cutter from other duties such as enforcing fishing laws in U.S. offshore waters or deterring drug-runners. As a case in point, in 1995 the Coast Guard spent $11 million over 45 days and 6,000 miles, using three cutters and two aircraft, to interdict 147 illegal Chinese migrants aboard the motor vessel *Jung Sheng # 8.*

FUTURE TRENDS

The future of AMIO raises more concerns. Increases in migrant flow from all sources are attributed partly to professional smugglers. This shifts the U.S. concern from ordinary immigration control toward criminal law enforcement. The international community is awakening to the problem, as shown by a U.N. General Assembly resolution condemning alien smuggling and calling on nations to cooperate against alien smugglers. Unfortunately, international cooperation has been slower than the opportunism of criminal smugglers.

Even more disturbing, violence is on the rise in AMIO. AMIO is now the Coast Guard mission in which force is most likely to be needed: in Fiscal Year 2000 there were twice as many instances when force was required in AMIO cases as in drug cases. Desperate migrants and criminal smugglers have precipitated incidents such as boarding officers being attacked with machetes, migrants using children as fenders trying to keep Coast Guard boats away, migrants gashing themselves in hope of being evacuated to the United States for medical treatment, and even migrants dousing themselves with gasoline as a threat against apprehension and repatriation. Although none of these incidents ended in serious injury, any of them might easily have done so; if the trend continues, the likelihood is against a happy outcome.

National policy calls for action against suspected smuggling vessels all around the U.S. coasts and as far away as Guam. As the dangers to Coast Guard personnel rise and its operating budgets are drained, it is fair to ask how long the nation's present policies will serve.

Bruce P. Dalcher

The views expressed herein are solely those of the author and do not necessarily reflect those of the United States Coast Guard.

See also: The Immigration and Naturalization Service, Legal and Illegal Immigration: A Statistical Overview (Part II, Sec. 2); Cuba, Haiti and French-Speaking Caribbean (Part III, Sec. 2); China (Part III, Sec. 3); President Carter's Announcement on the *Marielitos*, 1980, President Bush and Courts on Return of Haitian Refugees, 1992, District Court on Admissions of Haitians, 1993 (Part IV, Sec. 1).

BIBLIOGRAPHY

Books and Government Publications

Coast Guard. *Commandant Instruction M 16247.1A Maritime Law Enforcement Manual.* Washington, DC: U.S. Coast Guard, January 1998.

Coast Guard. *Commandant Instruction M 16247.4 Maritime Counter Drug and Alien Migrant Interdiction Operations.* Washington, DC: U.S. Coast Guard, May 1999.

Convention on the High Seas of 1958. U.S. T.I.A.S. 5200; 13 U.S.T. 2312.

Executive Order 12807 of May 24, 1992. Interdiction of Illegal Aliens. 57 *Federal Register* 23133.

Executive Order 12324 of September 29, 1981. High Seas Interdiction of Illegal Aliens. 46 *Federal Register* 48109.

Johnson, Robert Erwin. *Guardians of the Sea: History of the United States Coast Guard, 1915 to the Present.* Washington, DC: Naval Institute Press, 1988.

Proclamation No. 4865 of September 29, 1981. High Seas Interdiction of Illegal Aliens. 46 *Federal Register* 48107.

Title 8, U.S. Code, Section 1101 *et seq. Immigration and Nationality Act,* as amended.

Title 14, U.S. Code, Sections 2, 89 (1999).

Title 46, U.S. Code, Section 2304 (1999). *Duty to Provide Assistance at Sea.*

United Nations Convention on the Law of the Sea. 10 December 1982. (Available online at <http://fletcher.tufts.edu/multi/texts/BH825.txt>.)

United Nations Protocol Relating to the Status of Refugees. U.S. T.I.A.S. 6577; 19 U.S.T. 6223.

Periodicals

Jones, Bob. "Haitian Migrant Interdiction Operations—*Chase* Report." *Commandant's Bulletin,* January 25, 1982, 8–14.

Kaplan, Herbert R. "Castro's 'Berlin Wall.' " *Sea Power* (November 1971): 14–20.

Nolan, Mary I. " 'What the Coast Guard Is All About [Operation Able Vigil].' "*Sea Power:* (November 1994), 41–43.

Palmer, Gary W. "Guarding the Coast: Alien Migrant Interdiction Operations at Sea." *Connecticut Law Review,* Summer 1997 (29 Conn. L. Rev. 1565).

Electronic Sources

Coast Guard, Office of Law Enforcement, <http://www.uscg.mil/hq/g-o/g-opl/mle/AMIO.htm>, April 2000.

Department of Justice, Immigration and Naturalization Service. <http://www.ins.usdoj.gov/text/index.htm>, April 2000.

Statement of Captain Anthony S. Tangeman on Coast Guard Migrant Interdiction Operations before the Subcommittee on Immigration and Claims, Committee on the Judiciary, United States House of Representatives, May 18, 1999 <http://www.uscg.mil/hq/g-o/g-opl/mle/testimony1.htm>, April 2000.

Unpublished Sources

Commandant, U.S. Coast Guard. Migrant Interdiction Policy. ALCOAST 016/00, message R122232Z, January 2000.

Department of Justice, Office of Legal Counsel, Opinion Memorandum of November 21, 1996 re: Rights of Aliens Found in U.S. Internal Waters.

CONNECTIONS TO HOMELAND

From the settlement of America by Europeans in the seventeenth century to the present-day mass influx of immigrants from Latin America, Asia, and Africa, each wave of newcomers maintained multifaceted links to their homeland through economic and social assistance, political involvement, and cultural exchange. Although immigrant connections with their home country have shared some common features over time, contemporary "transnational spaces," shaped by new developments in addition to enduring circumstances, are not exact replicas of those in the past. The two most distinctive features of homeland connections of present-day immigrants have been (1) the great increase in the frequency and intensity of transnational involvement that has made it an everyday immigrant experience and (2) emergence from the ethnic communities to which homeland involvements of past immigrants were largely confined by charges of civic-national disloyalty from the U.S. government and public opinion into the public spheres of mainstream American society.

New developments have intensified connections of present-day immigrants with their home country. The expansion of and the growing interconnectedness within the global system, accelerated by the transportation and communication revolution (called also the "compression of time and space") that makes frequent travel much easier than ever before and allows daily "virtual" (phone, the Internet) interactions between kin and friends in home and host countries. This has greatly increased human mobility and intensified the transnational communication networks.

Two other processes have combined to undermine the integration into American society of millions of mainly low-skill immigrants from underdeveloped parts of the world while strengthening their bonds with their homeland. Politicization—here, restrictive policing—of immigrant inflows by the U.S. government has created an army of marginalized, "illegal" (undocumented) immigrants, and the restructuring of

the American economy has produced a growing informal sector isolated from mainstream advancement/integration opportunities that employs large numbers of lower-skill new immigrants. At the other end of the political-economic spectrum, increased numbers of highly skilled immigrant professionals are very much in demand in the postindustrial American economy and, therefore, they are privileged by U.S. policies of immigrant admittance. The emergence of a transnational workforce servicing the global economy in both sending and receiving (here, U.S.) societies, have likewise—through positive reinforcements—contributed to the intensification of immigrant involvements with their homeland.

The developments prompting the legal-political and cultural legitimation in the United States of present-day immigrant involvement with the homeland have brought these connections, once closeted within ethnic communities, out into the public spaces of mainstream American life and have also contributed to their spread and fortification. Since the civil rights movement in the 1960s, the ideology of multiculturalism—often invoked throughout the nation's history as the founding principle of American society but never applied to all its citizens—has become the normative code in American public discourse, this time combined with practical implementation in the juridical system and public institutions. At the same time, civic-political movements and organizations of laws and declarations upholding universal human rights, civic entitlements of groups and individuals, social justice, and democratic representation and pluralism have proliferated across the globe and trickled down to the national level. As a result of these developments, whereas past immigrant involvement with the homeland was often seen as threatening American national integrity and interests and as such was openly discouraged, today, in the name of multiculturalism, immigrant social, cultural, and even civic-political connections with the home country

Psychological and cultural connections to homeland run strong in many immigrant communities, as evidenced by this flamboyant costume worn by a woman of Brooklyn's annual West Indian Day Parade, held every Labor Day weekend. *(Brian Palmer, Impact Visuals)*

have been recognized by U.S. institutions as legitimate and "natural" and by public opinion, which has generally become more tolerant and cosmopolitan regarding foreign things and people.

Present-day immigrants' transnational spaces differ from those in the past in yet another important way. They are much more variegated or plural in form and content because contemporary immigrants themselves are much more diverse than their predecessors in regional origins, racial identifications, home-country socioeconomic backgrounds and cultural orientations, and, in the host society, in their legal status, the sectors of the economy in which they are employed, and their modes of acculturation to the dominant society. Reflecting the diversity among immigrants and their circumstances, contemporary transnational connections vary greatly. They include intense economic, social, cultural, and civic-political involvements across two or more nation-states of people whose homes, work, incomes, friends, and entertainment actually (and symbolically) "happen" in between on two (or more) sides of state-national borders. These are increasingly common among the highly skilled professional globe-trotters whose identities and involvements reach vertically past (rather than horizontally across) territorial state/national-level memberships and commitments toward more encompassing, "postnational" ones such as universal humanity or panreligious solidarities.

Diversified in kind and more dense than those in the past, contemporary immigrants' transnational connections are not, however, uniformly intense. The level of homeland involvement depends on many factors, the most important of which are (1) geographic proximity of home and host countries; (2) close family members remaining in the home country; (3) economic dependence of home-country households on immigrant remittances; (4) immigrants' political status (legal versus undocumented, voluntary versus refugee) in the receiver society; (5) degree of similarity between home and host cultures (language, customs, values, and beliefs); (6) level of immigrants' residential concentration and segregation from mainstream American neighborhoods and workplaces; (7) inten-

Political issues in the homeland often continue to occupy the thoughts and actions of immigrants in their new land, as these anti-English, pro-Irish signs make clear. *(Hazel Hankin, Impact Visuals)*

sity of host-country nativism, racial prejudice, and rejection of immigrants (in public discourse, legal-institutional practices, and popular views and behavior); (8) foreign policy and international economic interests of sender- and receiver-country governments and their perception of relevant immigrant and ethnic groups as the facilitators of or obstacles to these interests; (9) intensity of immigrants' nationalistic (or other ideological) commitments to the home country; and (10) existence of diverse transnational institutional networks linking home and host countries. Immigrant transnational connections are sustained through different channels that can be classified as personal, hybrid personal-institutional, and institutional types.

PERSONAL CONNECTIONS

Today, as in the past, the immigration into and settlement in the United States of new immigrants have

been largely dependent on networks of information and assistance provided by family members and fellow nationals already in the country. Residents of the Dominican Republic and Mexico can rely on particularly extensive support networks: about 78 percent in the former group and 50 percent in the latter group have relatives or acquaintances in the United States. For Poles from the earlier wave of mass immigration, this proportion is more than 30 percent. This sustained assistance to kin and fellow nationals in making travel arrangements and then in finding places to live (the majority of immigrants concentrate in the regions, cities, and neighborhoods in which their families or fellow nationals reside) and work in America keeps established immigrants "connected" with their homeland through personal contacts and current information about affairs there and through a variety of the homemade items brought by the newcomers. These connections are further maintained through several other channels of transnational exchange: the Internet and fax machines (for those with sufficient education and income to have access to them); telephones; exchanges of videotapes; television (TV) programs and newspapers from the home country available in America; and immigrant return visits.

As long-distance phone calls have become affordable and convenient, immigrants make regular use of them to maintain ties with kin and friends in the home country. Some manage their household and business affairs at home through weekly or biweekly calls. On the phone they exchange news about day-to-day events in their lives and information and advice on family business matters and local community affairs. Regular exchanges of videotape recordings of weddings, religious celebrations, and other family occasions also allow immigrants to stay in close touch with their kin at home.

Facilitated by advances in transportation technology and the expansion of global tourism, immigrant visits to home countries are much more frequent today than they were during the mass immigration from Europe in the early 1900s. Large numbers of present-day immigrants originate from countries near the United States, such as Mexico and the Caribbean, which makes frequent visits even more convenient for immigrants with legal U.S. status and for *indocumentados* (undocumented residents) as well. Immigrants from more distant parts of the world such as Asia usually visit their home country every year or two and more often if they are involved in transnational business.

Home-country TV programs, widely available today via satellites and the Internet, along with national (published in sender countries) and ethnic (published in the United States) newspapers subscribed to by immigrants, constitute yet another connection with the homeland. Both the Internet and national/ethnic newspapers have also been used by immigrants to forge closer personal ties with their home country by seeking mates there through advertisements.

These frequent direct and virtual contacts with people and news from the home country sustain, in turn, immigrants' sense of identity with and commitment to their homeland. These personal attachments are outwardly expressed through the continued use in the home of native languages (reported by more than 50 percent to over 80 percent of immigrants depending on the group); the enduring preference for home-country cuisine; the maintenance of native customs; and, intrinsically, the preservation of the cultural values and beliefs of native regions or religions. Unless they remain in segregated socioeconomic niches and are rejected as unwelcome "others" by mainstream U.S. society and its legal-political system, over time immigrant native identities and customs "creolize" or blend with those of the United States.

They do retain, however, a transnational character and thus "symbolic connections" with the home country.

Regular remittances sent home by immigrants to support their families constitute an important material (financial) connection to their homelands. In 1990, remittances sent from the United States totaled an estimated $9 billion. The multimillion-dollar annual transfers from each immigrant group not only allow minimal survival or increased affluence of individual recipient households but in many underdeveloped sender countries also help balance national economies. In the Dominican Republic, for example, immigrant remittances have been the second most important source of foreign exchange.

PERSONAL-INSTITUTIONAL CONNECTIONS

These hybrid transnational connections have been maintained chiefly by highly skilled professional immigrants who make up between 25 and 30 percent of the contemporary foreign-born population in the United States, with Asian groups constituting a higher percentage and Latin American groups (except Cubans) a lower percentage. Such personal-institutional relations with the home country have primarily involved larger-scale (rather than family) business investments, which are often encouraged by sender-country governments interested in capturing immigrant capital for the development of national economies. Although the size of these transnational operations requires organized management, transportation, and communication, such enterprises commonly start and expand through immigrants' personal connections in business or political circles in their native country.

Asian-American transnational entrepreneurs have been called the "bridge builders" between the United States and the Pacific economies. In two-way business operations, Asian-American entrepreneurs serve as partners or mediators in the growing capital investments from the Far East in the United States, and they themselves engage in business activities overseas. Thus, encouraged by the Indian government, many Indian immigrants from New York invest in profit-making ventures in India such as urban real estate and the construction of factories and medical centers. Korean-owned retail businesses in America receive supplies from major department stores in large cities in Korea and deliver U.S.-made goods to immigrants' relatives in Korea. Of all Asian groups in America,

Chinese have been involved in transnational business most extensively. Because of language facility, familiarity with cultural customs, and local connections, Chinese-American entrepreneurs, in collaboration with Taiwanese and Hong Kong traders and financiers, have had a decided competitive advantage in accessing the vast markets of mainland China since it opened its doors to foreign investment in the 1980s. According to reports, in the 1990s, overseas Chinese accounted for 75 percent to 90 percent of the total foreign investment in a Chinese economy that grew more than 10 percent annually. At the same time, Chinese-American businesspeople have facilitated the influx of banking and real estate capital from Hong Kong and Taiwan into Chinatowns in American cities.

Among Hispanic immigrants, Cuban entrepreneurs have been the most active in business ventures in the Caribbean and South America (their own homeland has been closed to Western capital since the communist revolution in 1959). They have made Miami—the center of Cuban refugee diaspora in the United States—into a thriving global city with dense transnational networks of finance and trading operations and an intercontinental professional-managerial class. Other Hispanic immigrants build bilateral links between the U.S. cities in which they reside and their native countries or regions with smaller transnational business ventures. Taking advantage of the proximity of the two countries, Dominican entrepreneurs, for example, having established an investment base and business contacts in New York, travel back and forth, pursuing economic opportunities in both countries.

Immigrant involvement in transnational crime with their fellow nationals at home has been another form of personal connections between sender and receiver countries. Asian transnational organized crime groups are "into everything that is profitable," from hijacking cars in America for customers in China, Taiwan, or Hong Kong, trafficking in drugs and guns across the Pacific, and kidnapping people in China to extort money from their relatives in America, to smuggling undocumented Chinese immigrants into the United States for slave labor in Chinese-American sweatshops. Chinese immigrants have not been alone in transnational criminal ventures; similar activities have been reported among Mexicans, Cubans, Colombians, Nigerians, and other groups.

INSTITUTIONAL CONNECTIONS

Institutional connections of contemporary immigrants with their native homeland are maintained in two are-nas: inside and outside immigrant/ethnic communities. Inside, immigrant/ethnic associations engage in local and national affairs of their countries of origin, on the one hand, and in organized activities on behalf of their immigrant members' interests in preserving the languages and cultures of native countries/regions in the United States, on the other. Outside, in the mainstream public forum once largely inaccessible to "closet ethnics," that is, those who tried to hide their ethnic origins, organized immigrant/ethnic groups engage American public opinion, government institutions, and political lobbies in the causes of their home country.

In-group organized activities on behalf of immigrant homelands most commonly take the form of philanthropic projects to improve the welfare and standard of living of native communities. For example, the Miraflores Development Committee (MDC), composed of immigrants from a southern village in the Dominican Republic who now live in the Jamaica Plains section of Boston, has sponsored the construction of an aqueduct and the renovation of the village school. The New York Committee of Ticuanese immigrants from Mexico has financed the building of two schools, the reconstruction of public buildings after the 1987 earthquake, and, most important, a potable water project. Some immigrant-organized initiatives in home countries have a national scope. The association of Vietnamese physicians and health workers in America, for instance, has been regularly sending volunteer medical teams to work without charge in hospitals in Vietnam.

Through these and similar activities, immigrant organizations in America assist fellow nationals at home while assuming sender-state civic responsibilities toward its resident populations. Because in many poor communities the public welfare functions performed by immigrant organizations abroad are significant, sender-country governments actively seek and encourage these philanthropic transnational connections.

The engagement of organized immigrant groups in philanthropic projects on behalf of communities in the home country is a long-standing tradition in American ethnic history. More recently, as a result of the transnationalization of civic-political membership that accompanies globalization, immigrant/ethnic organized groups have become vocal public participants in the political affairs of their country of origin. Increased official recognition of dual citizenship by sender countries (e.g., Mexico, most of the Caribbean, Colombia, the Dominican Republic, Brazil) and its tacit toleration by the U.S. government have legitimized and encouraged such engagement.

The extension of voting rights to émigré citizens abroad has significantly empowered them politically, especially in countries (such as Mexico or the Dominican Republic) with very large and well-organized diasporas abroad. Public interventions by immigrant groups in the politics of the home country have become increasingly common. Thus, Palestinian Americans have criticized the radicals in the Palestine Liberation Organization (PLO) and lauded its moderate wing, and in the wake of the Tiananmen Square massacre, Chinese in America used the Internet and fax machines to spread antigovernment propaganda in China. In one of the most far-reaching expressions of transnational politics, in this case involving a sender-country government, the 1991 Colombian constitution provided for the political representation of émigrés abroad in the national congress.

Ethnic festivals and celebrations in immigrant communities have traditionally sustained cultural connections with home countries. Rapid advances in transportation and communication technologies and increased levels of education among present-day immigrants have made possible new forms of these connections, such as information sharing and planning shared activities on the Internet, organized "historical" and "cultural" tours of home countries, and cultural and educational exchange programs with home-country institutions. The most novel development of all, however, resulting from the legal-institutional implementation since the 1960s of the idea of multiculturalism as the organizing principle of U.S. society, has been the proliferation in the mainstream American public forum of the initiatives of organized immigrant/ethnic groups on behalf of or against political or military developments in their country of origin.

Political lobbying by immigrant groups on behalf of their fellow nationals in the home country has been practiced for a long time—for example, by American Jews in 1905 against the Kishinev pogrom in Russia, and by Poles, Czechs, and Slovaks during the Versailles Conference in 1918 for national independence of their homelands. Today, the lobbying is more open and self-assertive and is orchestrated on several public fronts at once. Besides political representatives who are often members of the lobbying group, these include the national media and U.S. civic associations and public opinion that can be reached by phone, fax, or the Internet to influence national and local public opinion.

Home-oriented politics of organized immigrant groups in the host country constitute a particularly strong connection to the native country in the case of political refugees. This connection is further rein-

forced and immigrant démarches become more effective in mobilizing American political establishment and public opinion if the cause coincides with U.S. foreign policy interests in the home country. The sustained anti-Castro activism of Cuban immigrants, ideologically and financially supported by the U.S. government, and the success of political pressures exerted between 1977 and 1981 by Cuban-American organizations for the admission of Cuban boat refugees, as compared with the largely ineffective actions of Haitian immigrant groups on behalf of their fellow nationals in the same situation, exemplifies very well this relationship.

Diverse organized activities conducted inside and outside immigrant groups that involve their home-country cultures and politics have sustained, as have personal and personal-institutional engagements with homelands, immigrants' continued identification with and sense of belonging to their native country. As immigrants put down roots over time in the host U.S. society and their involvement in its institutional structures multiplies through work, child education, social services, and civic-political participation, their multiple commitments extend across home- and host-country borders in a transnational "melting pot of identities" of the global world.

Ewa Morawska

See also: Return Migration (Part II, Sec. 3); Immigrant Politics III: The Home Country (Part II, Sec. 6); Impact on the Home Country Economy (Part II, Sec. 7).

BIBLIOGRAPHY

Basch, Linda, Nina Glick-Shiller, and Cristina Szanton Blanc. *Nations Unbound: Transnational Projects, Postcolonial Predicaments, and Deterritorialized Nation-States.* Zurich: Gordeon and Breach, 1994.

Bonilla, Frank, et al., eds. *Borderless Borders: U.S. Latinos, Latin Americans, and the Paradox of Interdependence.* Philadelphia: Temple University Press, 1998.

Cornelius, Wayne, Philip Martin, and James Hollifield. *Controlling Immigration: A Global Perspective.* Stanford: Stanford University Press, 1994.

Foner, Nancy. "What's New about Transnationalism? New York Immigrants Today and at the Turn of the Century." *Diaspora* 6:3 (1997).

Glazer, Nathan. *We Are All Multiculturalists Now.* Cambridge: Harvard University Press, 1997.

Guarnizo, Luis E. "On the Political Participation of Transnational Migrants: Old Practices and New Trends." In *Immigrants, Civic Culture, and Modes of Political Incorporation,* ed. Gary Gerstle and

John Mollenkopf, New York: Social Science Research Council, 2000.

Higham, John. *Send These to Me: Jews and Other Immigrants in Urban America*. New York: Atheneum, 1975.

Hu-DeHart, Evelyn, ed. *Across the Pacific: Asian Americans and Globalization*. Philadelphia: Temple University Press, 1999.

Joppke, Christian, ed. *Challenge to the Nation-State: Immigration in Western Europe and the United States*. Oxford: Oxford University Press, 1998.

Krauss, Clifford. "The Cali Cartel and the Globalization of Crime in New York City." In *The City and the World*, ed. Margaret Crahan and Alberto Vourvoulias-Bush. New York: Council on Foreign Relations, 1997.

Lessinger, Johanna. *From the Ganges to the Hudson*. Needham Heights, MA: Allyn and Bacon, 1995.

Levitt, Peggy. "Transnationalizing Community Development: The Case of Migration between Boston and the Dominican Republic." *Nonprofit and Voluntary Sector Quarterly*, 26:4 (1997).

Min, Pyong G. *Asian Americans: Contemporary Trends and Issues*. Thousand Oaks, CA: Sage, 1995.

Massey, Douglas, et al. *Worlds in Motion*. New York: Clarendon Press, 1998.

Morawska, Ewa, and Willfried Spohn. "Moving Europeans: Contemporary Migrations in a Historical Perspective." In *Global History and Migrations*, ed. Wang Gungwu. Boulder, CO: Westview Press, 1997.

Myrdal, Gunnar. *An American Dilemma*. New York: Harper and Row, 1962.

Pedraza, Sylvia, and Ruben Rumbaut, eds. *Origins and Destinies: Immigration, Race, and Ethnicity in America*. Belmont, CA: Wadsworth Publishing, 1996.

Portes, Alejandro, and Ruben Rumbaut. *Immigrant America*. Berkeley: University of California Press, 1990.

Sassen, Saskia. *Cities in a World Economy*. Thousand Oaks, CA: Pine Forge Press, 1994.

Sheffer, Gabriel. "Ethnic Diasporas: A Threat to Their Hosts?" In *International Migration and Security*, ed. Myron Weiner. Boulder, CO: Westview Press, 1993.

Smith, Michael, and Luis E. Guarnizo. *Transnationalism from Below*. New Brunswick, NJ: Transaction Publishers, 1998.

HUMAN SMUGGLING AND THE BUSINESS OF ILLEGAL IMMIGRATION

Wherever there have been state borders in human history that exclude some from entry into a country or city-state, professional smugglers have arisen to facilitate a clandestine crossing. The type of service provided by the smuggler varied from a simple river crossing on a boat to more sophisticated methods of deception and corruption of state agents. Likewise, the reasons that immigrants would use a professional or part-time smuggler are also varied; they may do so for economic, social, and political reasons, as in the case of avoiding religious or ethnic persecution. As states implemented more restrictive policies aimed at immigrants in the 1980s and 1990s, there was a corresponding increase in various types of immigration services offered to immigrants unwilling or unable to follow the legal immigration or asylum channels. A wide range of immigration merchants, including smugglers, profited from some aspect of the emigration process, including the financing, travel, or document services needed by a would-be immigrant. Thus, when considering the contemporary phenomenon of human smuggling, it is better to consider the broader business of illegal immigration, often linking several countries, than to think of human smuggling in the narrow sense of simply getting someone across a border.

While this is an area of immigration research in which few academic studies have been carried out, the International Organization for Migration, based in Geneva, estimates that the business of illegal immigration is now a $5 billion industry. The U.S. Immigration and Naturalization Service (INS) estimates a similar amount and asserts that profits are so great that large-scale drug smuggling operations are turning to the smuggling of immigrants as a lucrative but less risky alternative to drug smuggling. In fact, much of the current debate regarding the nature of human smuggling concerns the organization and operation of smuggling rings or networks; are they mostly coethnic "mom-and-pop" operations providing a limited service much like a legitimate enterprise, or has the seeming increase in human smuggling activities been driven by transnational criminal enterprises using the most sophisticated technology and enforcement techniques? The perception that various sorts of mafia are entering the illegal immigration business stems from the reasoning that greater profits attract bigger players who drive out the smaller operations. It also comes from empirical evidence that some immigrants are being lured into much more sinister smuggling rings that exploit an immigrant's illegality by turning them into slaves, especially women who are bought and sold among brothels. In 1998, one case of several Mexican teenage women forced into prostitution in the United States prompted a public press conference by U.S. Attorney General Janet Reno to announce the creation of a special antislavery and worker exploitation unit within the Department of Justice.

While it is true that large-scale, criminal enterprises have gotten into the immigration business and that the trafficking of women and children for sex has recently increased by all accounts on a global scale, some academic research suggests that professional criminals involved in other illicit trade do not necessarily drive out more locally organized immigration services. After all, with the demand for such services far outstripping supply in many regions of the world, an increase in smuggling operations does not necessarily entail putting existing operations out of business. Similarly, we must be careful to recognize the variety of smugglers and immigrants—ranging from return immigrants helping a cousin or neighbor to cross the border to transnational organized crime involved in trafficking women and children—if we are to understand the full impact of the business of illegal immigration apart from the human rights issues connected to the contemporary slave trade.

A problem with drawing conclusions from enforcement data and news reports, as is often the case, is that they reflect failed smuggling operations, not successful ones. This may lead to a systematic selection bias because the larger, more professional smuggling rings, including those which are part of ongoing criminal enterprises are actually easier to infiltrate and bust than small coethnic operations with a high degree of trust between immigrant and smuggler. Unfortunately, there is little alternative information and analysis to that of crime reports because it was not until the late 1990s that the first academic studies based on field research began to be published.

Drawing on this recent research, the remainder of this essay focuses on the social organization of illegal immigration as a business through an examination of three sending countries that typify the wide range of smuggling operations and their recent evolution into more sophisticated operations. Though related to human smuggling as an immigration service, the contemporary slave trade will not be considered. However, it is unavoidable to discuss human smuggling as a business without considering the more violent and coercive side of trafficking in human beings owing to the linkage in reality and in the rhetoric of state agents, lawmakers, and activists.

TRANSFORMATION OF THE ILLEGAL IMMIGRATION INDUSTRY: MEXICO AND ECUADOR

As the most important country of immigration to the United States for over a century and the country that shares its southern border, Mexico is a good starting point for understanding some of the social and political forces that led to an increase in the scale and scope of human smuggling operations in the late twentieth century. It is also an important case because it demonstrates the complexity of the social, economic, and political dimensions that shape human smuggling organizations and the policies meant to curb them.

According to Peter Andreas, professor of political science at Reed College, the flow of illegal immigrants across the United States–Mexico border has been transformed from a low-profile activity to a highly politicized one, highlighted by the massive buildup of border enforcement personnel and other physical barriers. The INS Border Patrol doubled in size between 1993 and 1998, with a budget that more than doubled in the same period. New high-tech equipment has been deployed alongside more traditional barriers such as high steel fences. The combined effect of this border buildup is to make a clandestine crossing much more than the almost casual affair it once was.

However, David Spener, professor of sociology at Trinity University, has conducted field research along the Texas-Mexico border and found that the increased difficulty in crossing illegally has raised smuggling fees, but not high enough to pose a deterrent to a clandestine entry. In addition, the claim by some INS officials that smugglers have turned to more ruthless methods and are linked to drug smuggling operations appears to be difficult to substantiate beyond a few cases. Several informants told Spener that many of the human smuggling operations remain apart from drug smuggling operations; it would, in fact, be a difficult task for a criminal syndicate to corner the mobile and diverse market of would-be immigrants seeking smuggling services. Similarly, illegal immigrants are often in danger of being robbed and violently attacked, but it is more often than not criminals along the clandestine routes who prey on illegal border crossers and not the smugglers themselves. In some instances, smugglers, forced now to take more risky routes through desert regions, have abandoned immigrants, resulting in their deaths. Once again, it is not always easy to interpret exactly what happened leading to the abandonment, though many immigration policymakers assert that these are cases of immigrant exploitation by smugglers. Yet it is also true that a current U.S. strategy is to force illegal border crossers into more desolate areas, which are inherently dangerous.

Unlike the long-standing case of Mexican immigration, Ecuadorian immigration exemplifies the evolution of human smuggling into transnational networks of immigration merchants engaged in the financing and facilitation of the surreptitious crossing of one or more national borders at great distances, thus allowing even cash-poor rural smallholders the opportunity for a household member to work abroad illicitly. The Ecuadorian province of Azuay is the site of a large-scale, clandestine emigration flow to New York City. Immigration from this region took off so rapidly that Ecuadorians went from obscurity to one of the largest immigrant communities in the New York metro area in a single generation. In Azuay, the business of immigration is often a part-time activity of return immigrants and nonimmigrants who—far from being full-time criminals using the latest technology—help distant relatives, neighbors, and coethnics out of Ecuador at prices below that of professional smugglers. The reason that small operators are able to smuggle people from rural Andean villages to Manhattan is that one mainly needs information of various sorts (who is corrupt, subcontractors en route,

Smuggling Asian immigrants into the United States is big business. Above, crewmen from the U.S. Coast Guard cutter *Jarvis* find seventy-five undocumented immigrants hidden in the hold of a ship docked in Midway, in the northern Hawaiian islands. *(United States Coast Guard)*

trusted "coyotes" or *polleros* at the border, and so on) and the ability to collect the smuggling fee, which is typically enforced through group norms or trust and reciprocity rather than violent coercion; the penalty for not repaying a smuggling debt is the inability to return to one's home community. Thus, the export of labor from Azuay is a profitable commodity for both immigrants and nonimmigrants alike, who are best viewed as "immigration merchants" rather than transnational gangsters.

IMMIGRANT MERCHANTS OR SLAVE TRADERS? THE CASE OF CHINA

Perhaps the case that has received the most media attention, including by Hollywood filmmakers, is that of illegal immigrants from China smuggled by individuals known as "snakeheads." While the overall number of illegal immigrants from China is still dwarfed by the case of Mexico, the novelty of the Chinese smugglers' multiple methods and the types of smuggling organizations they imply capture the public's attention.

Paul Smith, research fellow at the Asia-Pacific Center for Security Studies in Hawaii, argues that three developments have led to the outflux of Chinese in recent years. First, while economic growth in China has been impressive, it has also been highly uneven, with alarming rates of economic inequality. A significant consequence has been the growing internal, often illegal immigration from poor inland regions to more prosperous coastal cities within China. Second, as a result of this uneven development and domestic migration patterns, China is hard pressed to find employment for a workforce of over 700 million that is growing at a rate of 14 million every year. Thus, mass unemployment, a highly sensitive issue within China, is now over 150 million. Third, the burgeoning population growth rate itself is an enormous challenge to Chinese planners, who face increasing noncompliance with the unpopular birth control policy.

Peter Kwong, professor of Asian-American studies at Hunter College in New York, describes smuggled Chinese immigrants from Fujian Province as victims of a large-scale and sophisticated criminal network. He further tells of abuse of the immigrants by snakeheads upon arrival, such as threats of torture, rape, and kidnapping to pay off smuggling debts that can reach as high as $30,000. The high fees and abusive collection methods amount to what Kwong views as indentured servitude at the very least and often results in contemporary slavery, especially for women who are sometimes pressed into forced prostitution and sold from brothel to brothel.

Ko-Lin Chin, professor of criminology at Rutgers University, counters this uniformly negative view of Chinese smugglers or snakeheads with a description of a more diverse group of what people in Fujian referred to as "big snakeheads" and "little snakeheads": the former includes a range of business people and professional criminal organizations who act as the primary investors and masterminds of the smuggling operations, most of whom never see the "clients." Small snakeheads, in contrast, act as the recruiters and manage the actual smuggling operations. Similar to David Spener's findings along the Texas border, the claim that nearly all smugglers are part of larger criminal syndicates or gangs was not borne out in Chin's study.

THE GLOBAL MIGRATION INDUSTRY

Though social research on human smuggling remains inadequate and is often presented as preliminary and exploratory, a general theme of diversity emerges from the academic literature, which stands in contrast to more journalistic accounts based on claims by state officials, who nearly always portray smugglers as ruthless exploiters of immigrant victims. By examining three sending regions of clandestine immigrants to the United States, we find a diversity in types of sending regions and in the social organization of smuggling operations: smugglers and their organizations range from individuals who act like trusted businesspeople providing a service in high demand to some of the most depraved professional criminals who enslave immigrants as expendable commodities. James O. Finckenauer, director of the International Center of the National Institute of Justice, in examin-

ing human smuggling by Russian transnational organized crime, makes a useful distinction between crime that is organized and organized crime. While some human smuggling is conducted by sophisticated organized crime or mafia, most of it is organized by mom-and-pop operations that may be highly organized and break a narrow set of laws but are not part of ongoing professional criminal syndicates involved in such things as high-level government corruption and a multiplicity of areas of criminal activities.

Given these initial findings by researchers, it is best to conceive of illegal immigration as a business, much of which is carried out between two contracting parties with a high degree of trust; as with any type of industry, however, there are unscrupulous operators who are seeking only to con and exploit the client. Because of the clandestine and illegal nature of human smuggling, the risks of such abuse by those with more power is even greater. Professors John Salt and Jeremy Stein of the Migration Research Unit at the University College in London go one step further by conceptualizing immigration around the world as a type of industry that includes both legal and illegal immigration services offered by a range of individuals and institutions, including smugglers offering to traffic immigrants across borders for a fee.

David Kyle

See also: Coast Guard and Coastlines, The Immigration and Naturalization Service, Legal and Illegal Immigration: A Statistical Overview, Transit and Transportation of Recent Illegal Immigrants (Part II, Sec. 2); White Slave Traffic Act (Mann Act), 1910, California Proposition 187, 1994 (Part IV, Sec. 1).

BIBLIOGRAPHY

Andreas, Peter. "The Transformation of Migrant Smuggling across the U.S.-Mexico Border." In *Global Human Smuggling: Comparative Perspectives*, ed. David Kyle and Rey Koslowski. Baltimore: Johns Hopkins University Press, forthcoming.

Chin, Ko-Lin. *Smuggled Chinese: Clandestine Immigration to the United States*. Philadelphia: Temple University Press, 1999.

Finckenauer, James O. "Russian Transnational Organized Crime and Human Trafficking." In *Global Human Smuggling: Comparative Perspectives*, ed. David Kyle and Rey Koslowski. Baltimore: Johns Hopkins University Press, forthcoming.

International Organization for Migration. "Organized Crime Moves into Migrant Trafficking." *Trafficking in Migrants*, Quarterly Bulletin, no. 11 (June 1996).

Kyle, David. *Transnational Peasants: Migrations, Networks, and Ethnicity in Andean Ecuador*. Baltimore: Johns Hopkins University Press, 2000.

Kwong, Peter. *Forbidden Workers: Illegal Chinese Immigrants and American Labor*. New York: New Press, 1997.

Salt, John, and Jeremy Stein. "Migration as a Business: The Case of Trafficking." *International Migration Review* 35:4 (1997): 467–94.

Smith, Paul, ed. *Human Smuggling: Chinese Migrant Trafficking and the Challenge to America's Immigration Tradition*. Washington, DC: Center for Strategic and International Studies, 1997.

Spener, David. "Smuggling Mexican Migrants through South Texas: Challenges Posed by Operation Rio Grande." In *Global Human Smuggling: Comparative Perspectives*, ed. David Kyle and Rey Koslowski. Baltimore: Johns Hopkins University Press, forthcoming.

IMMIGRANT AID SOCIETIES AND ORGANIZATIONS

*T*hroughout its history, the United States has had a vibrant civil society with many immigrant community-based groups, organizations, voluntary associations, and aid societies. An immigrant aid society (or an immigrant organization) is an organization formed by individuals, who are members of a particular ethnic/national origin group, for the purpose of providing social services primarily to immigrants from their ethnic/national group. Immigrant aid societies deliver social services; provide programs aimed at assisting in the adaptation and incorporation of immigrants; give a sense of support and continuity to lives impacted by migration events; help immigrants reestablish their social contacts and networks; advocate on behalf of the group; and generally help immigrants navigate their new social environments. In New York City, for example, there are more than 300 community-based organizations that make up the immigrant service delivery system. These organizations are a vital part of the fabric of a diverse civil society. Some organizations, originally formed to provide services to particular groups, or to the general population, have evolved over time and tried to adapt, with varying success, to the needs of the new national origin groups that have come into the region. As new immigrant communities are established and grow, their families and children receive services from existing social service agencies. But, over time, as the ethnic/national group grows and develops a distinct sense of their social service needs, a social service professional base, connections to the metropolitan service delivery system, and organizational resources and capacity, immigrants form new organizations to provide a range of needed services for their particular communities. Immigrant organizations differ from other social service providers in that they explicitly incorporate cultural components, and a consciousness of ethnic/national origin identity, into their mission, practices, services, and programs.

HISTORY OF IMMIGRANT AID SOCIETIES

The large waves of immigrants that came to America between the 1820s and the 1880s were mostly of German, Irish, English, and Dutch descent. These groups developed a number of voluntary and philanthropic aid societies to provide services to their immigrant populations. Historian Robert Ernst states that "the mutual aid society provided sickness benefits to its members and paid the funeral expenses of those who died." According to Ernst, there was an inherent tension within some organizations between their functions as preservers of the cultural heritage and traditions from the countries of origin and their role as facilitators of cultural and socioeconomic adaptation and incorporation into North American society. Ernst adds that "genuine immigrants, planning to spend their entire lives in the United States, were more deeply concerned about their everyday existence, the welfare of their families, and the future of their children in the new world of opportunity. To satisfy their social and material needs, they founded a wide variety of institutions forming an intricate pattern of group activities which eased the adjustment of Europeans to American conditions."

In the late nineteenth and early part of the twentieth centuries, there were significant changes in the ethnic and national origin composition of the population in cities and, particularly, in what were then known as "slums." The "New Immigration" that began during the 1880s, and lasted until around 1915, involved a significant change in the sources of immigration from northern Europeans to Italians, Jews, and others from various parts of eastern and southern Europe. Much like many immigrants today, the "New Immigrants" of the early twentieth century were considered by many nativists to be of inferior sociocultural stock, more difficult to Americanize, and were

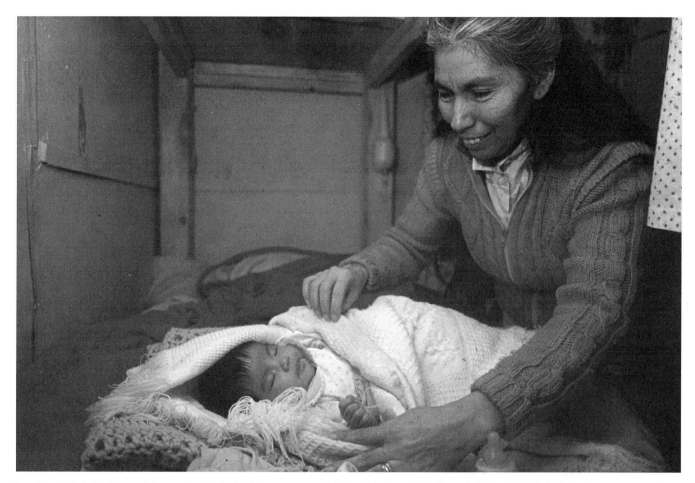

Fearing that Salvadoran refugees in the United States would be killed if forced back to their homeland during the war-torn 1980s, many Americans, like this San Antonio, Texas, woman, offered sanctuary. *(Wim Van Cappellen/Impact Visuals)*

perceived as a threat to the strength and unity of the nation. The importance of Americanization for immigrant socioeconomic incorporation has always been contested and immigrant aid societies have had to balance an awareness and respect of the particular cultural practices of their groups with the need for immigrants to adapt and incorporate into their new, often more complex, social environment. Historian Thomas Archdeacon, for example, states that "for the social activists who moved into immigrant neighborhoods and established settlement houses, the term [Americanization] meant giving the newcomers the wherewithal to survive in a modern industrial society. They tried to teach those who came to their settlement houses English, American social customs, and, when necessary, the rudiments of household management, health care, and sanitation. The best of those reformers, including the renowned Jane Addams of Chicago, performed their work without purposefully assaulting the immigrants' native cultures." Since the 1920s there have been two historical markers of American

immigration that have also been periods where a large number of immigrant organizations have been formed. The first period is during the late 1960s and early 1970s, following the civil rights movement and changes in the racial/ethnic/national origin composition of immigration flows to the United States more toward Asian, Latin American, and Caribbean populations. A second period of organizational growth occurred during the late 1980s following the Immigration Reform and Control Act (IRCA) of 1986.

TYPES OF IMMIGRANT ORGANIZATIONS

There are three broad types of immigrant aid societies. First, are immigrant groups, associations, and immigrant clubs. These groups are usually concerned with promoting social and economic ties, connections, and activities between immigrants from particular countries, or regions of countries. These groups often have close contact with the countries of origin but have a relatively small social service base. Second, are immigrant organizations that have been formally incorporated as nonprofit organizations, have a broad service portfolio, have a direct social service base with clients, have paid professional staff, and have offices open to the public with regular service hours. These organizations usually provide a variety of social services to immigrants from a particular country (or region) and are central to the social service delivery system for particular ethnic groups and in specific ethnic/immigrant neighborhoods. Third, are service providers with a large metropolitan-level social service base. These organizations provide social services to clients from a variety of countries, as well as services to a significant proportion of nonimmigrant clients (often from racial and ethnic minority groups).

Organizations can be categorized as immigrant, or ethnic, based on their mission and their history of providing services to particular ethnic groups. However, there are several other ways to categorize organizations: based on what they do, based on where they are, and based on who they serve. First, organizations vary based on the specific types of services or cluster of services that they provide. Some organizations concentrate on immigration services and legal help; others focus on services to the elderly; others specialize on youth services; others concentrate on health and related services; and others focus on general social services. The particular emphasis, main activities, and service portfolio are some of the defining features of an organization. Second, organizations differ in terms of their geographic area of work. Some agencies focus on specific communities, while others focus on a combination of neighborhoods, or the entire metropolitan area. Third, organizations differ in terms of the ethnicity of the clients that they serve. Some organizations serve clients from one country, but in many instances, because social service providers that receive public funding are barred from discriminating on the basis of national origin, organizations provide social services to clients from a cluster of countries within a region (Asia, Latin America, the Caribbean, Europe). Lastly, a fourth element that can be used to categorize immigrant organizations is the composition of the board of directors and the composition of the staff that works on the various programs offered by the organization. In addition to these elements and the number of years that the organization has been in operation, organizations vary in terms of other criteria such as number of clients served per year, size of the budget, and the sources of funding. Immigrant organizations vary in terms of size from large organizations serving thousands of clients from many parts of the world in a year to neighborhood-based organizations serving immigrants from a smaller cluster of countries. Organizations also vary in their operating funds from budgets below one hundred thousand dollars to several million dollars. Lastly, organizations vary in their sources of funding. The most common sources of funding for immigrant organizations are funds from the church; government contracts and subcontracts; corporate contributions; foundation grants; community fundraisers; individual donations; and, in rare instances, fees for services.

FUNCTIONS AND ROLES OF IMMIGRANT GROUPS AND ORGANIZATIONS

Immigrant aid societies serve several important social functions in their communities. The first is to assist families in the immigration process by providing advice and legal help for individuals who want to change their immigration status or sponsor relatives to come to the United States. Organizations also provide shelter and other forms of initial support and information to newly arrived immigrants. The second role of immigrant organizations is to provide services related to the adaptation and incorporation of immigrants into the new society. The third main function of immigrant organizations is to serve as an advocate and network for their ethnic groups, to articulate the needs of their community, to represent the needs and concerns of the group in metropolitan-level processes. A fourth main role of immigrant organizations is to serve as a liaison between immigrant communities and organizations in their countries of origin.

First, organizations help in the premigration and in the immigration process by providing advice and legal help for individuals who want to sponsor relatives to come to the United States. For those currently in the country, organizations provide a host of immigration/naturalization services related to the preparation of all of the legal paperwork involved in the immigration and naturalization process. Some of these services are legal advice and counsel; help with Immigration and Naturalization Service (INS) forms and procedures; certified fingerprinting; adjustment of status petitions; alien relative petitions; visa extensions and advanced parole; work authorization; affidavit of support (I-864 and I-134); diversity lottery visas; and replacement of green cards. Organizations also provide many forms of initial support to newly arrived immigrants and their families.

The second role of immigrant organizations is to provide services related to the adaptation and incorporation of immigrants into the new society. Most of these services are dispensed both to immigrant and nonimmigrant populations but there are specific challenges associated with providing social services to immigrant populations such as language differences, differences in knowledge about social services, cultural sensitivity, awareness of the most appropriate method to deliver services, and recognition of a group's particular needs. Many organizations provide Adult Basic Education (ABE), English as a Second Language (ESL), and General Equivalency Degree (GED) classes to their populations. Some organizations provide some kind of ABE or ESL program from beginners to intermediate to more advanced classes, native language literacy services, and GED classes coordinated with other community-based organizations (CBOs), or with nearby community colleges, with immigrants benefiting particularly from these kinds of services and programs. Many organizations also provide citizenship classes and support services that help immigrants with the naturalization exam. These services include civics classes and other services, programs, activities, and workshops that are explicitly designed to facilitate the adaptation and incorporation of immigrants into their new communities and into the country. In addition to social services, many organizations also prepare sociocultural activities and activities that link members of the origin group to each other and to the larger community.

The third main function of immigrant organizations is to serve as an advocate and network for their ethnic groups to articulate the needs of their community, and to mediate and facilitate in metropolitan-level processes. Many organizations are actively engaged in organizing immigrants in their communities as a way to influence service delivery and as a way to inform members of the group about social service needs in their communities. Organizations also provide social capital and are central to the reconstitution, formation, and management of immigrant social, political, and economic networks. Many organizations also represent the needs and concerns of their ethnic/national origin group (and the needs of similar social service organizations) in metropolitan-level policy discussions, commissions, conferences, and in media discussions on immigration, ethnicity, and social service provision to immigrant and other populations. Public education and information are central roles in many organizations as they seek to inform policy debates on matters related to the socioeconomic adap-

tation and incorporation of the group at the local and national level.

A fourth main role of immigrant organizations is to serve as a liaison and linkage between immigrant communities and their countries of origin. This is done in many ways, including facilitating the flow of news and information from and to the country of origin; facilitating and encouraging the flow of economic resources, remittances, and other investments; and the preparation of cultural, religious, patriotic, or other activities of importance to the country of origin. Many organizations have particular linkages to the main sending regions in the countries of origin and often sponsor delegations and visits to and from the countries of origin. Some immigrant organizational networks to the country of origin are central in providing linkages between elected officials, government bureaucrats, and political parties in the sending and receiving areas, and many organizations engage in activities designed to increase the level of information, public awareness, and political advocacy on U.S. policy toward the country of origin.

CHALLENGES TO IMMIGRANT GROUPS, ORGANIZATIONS, AND SERVICE PROVIDERS

Immigrant groups, organizations, and service providers face several challenges. The first set of challenges is related to recognizing social service needs in immigrant communities and providing an efficient delivery of services to their populations. In many organizations, there is a need for additional staff that is both trained and competent in their service area, and who are, at the same time, sensitive to the cultural particularities of the national origin groups that are being served by the organization. Another factor that impacts immigrant organizations is the low level of resources and funding for dedicated services given the large needs in many communities. A third factor that impacts immigrant organizations is changes in immigration and welfare policy.

Recent research suggests that changes in immigration and welfare laws are impacting individuals and families; groups, organizations, and service providers; and immigrant communities. Interviews conducted with immigrant organizations in New York City, revealed a shared sense among the various organizations that the living conditions of immigrants have deteriorated over the last four years and that many immigrant service providers are facing serious limitations in their capacity to react to policy changes and offer comprehensive services to immigrant families and children. At the *organization level*, our interviews indicate that changes in immigration and welfare laws have impacted the work of some organizations and their ability to respond to the evolving needs of clients, advocate for them, and, in many instances, fulfill their mission of providing support for everyone in the community in need of services regardless of legal status. During the initial phases of the implementation of immigration and welfare reform, many agencies felt that they did not have access to and were not provided with the information that they needed in order to help their clients and themselves adapt to the emerging policy environment and the new eligibility rules. Several agencies mentioned, however, that there were some positive efforts by organizations such as the New York Immigration Coalition and the Center for Immigrants Rights to keep them informed of changes and possible responses. Many organizations also felt that their ability to plan for and develop new programs was compromised by the energies that had to be spent adapting to the more restrictive policy climate. More specifically, organizations argued that they had experienced these impacts: (a) agencies were drawn away from direct service provision and more into advocacy; (b) more difficult program planning, a more unstable client base, and more difficult case management; and (c) problems with the elimination of basic immigration services and ESL/ABE training in many community centers.

Several agencies stated that since 1996 they have had to spend more time doing public education and advocacy on behalf of the organization, its services and programs, and their clients. For some agencies this was a positive development because it provided them with an opportunity to take stock of their organization, to examine their services and programs, and to try to be more aggressive and efficient at service delivery and in explaining to various constituencies inside and outside the community what their services are and who they serve. But for other agencies, the shift to more advocacy was negative in the sense that they felt it took time, organizational resources, and energy away from direct service provision, case management, and other work with clients. A federation of agencies in Manhattan suggested that it was providing assistance to startup programs that had an advocacy orientation and component, and that it was trying to work with its member agencies to develop the public education component of their work. Another agency in Queens indicated that it had increased its advocacy efforts to call attention to the backlog of citizenship applications and to the severe

application restrictions imposed on recent arrivals and their families. A large agency in Manhattan suggested that, like many other agencies serving immigrants and low-income populations, it has taken on more of an advocacy role on behalf of its clients and the services that they need. This organization has fought for the restoration of Social Security Insurance (SSI) benefits and filed several class actions, particularly on behalf of those ineligible for food stamps (mostly persons 18 to 59 years old without children). Another agency in Queens argued that it had played a larger advocacy role in trying to bring about the restoration of immigrant access to social services and programs. The organization participated in advocacy days at the state capital in Albany and in Washington, D.C., on these issues, and has been more aggressive about contacting policymakers and elected officials. The organization commented to us that while volunteer support and community needs have increased, their contracts and other funding for direct services has not. A midsized agency in Queens mentioned that its experience was similar to that of other immigrant service providers in that it has become increasingly involved in public education and advocacy efforts as a means to change certain aspects of the new laws, while a large Manhattan agency expressed the concerns of many when it stated that since immigration and welfare reform the organization has taken a more active role in advocating on behalf of its clients. The agency indicated that while the organization's goals have not changed, their dedication and level of commitment to defend their clients has increased, particularly for the growing number of victims of domestic violence and for those with pending deportation cases.

Second, many agencies suggested that changes in immigration and welfare laws, and the complex eligibility rules associated with them, had made program planning and management more difficult. Several organizations also argued that changes in immigration and welfare laws made their clients more unstable, which made providing adequate services, support, and case management more complicated and burdensome because clients moved around more and because eligibility rules have become more complicated. Agencies felt that they were operating in an unstable policy environment. This is exemplified by the comments made to us by a large agency in Brooklyn. Our interviewee mentioned that the agency's vocational programs were harder to manage due to new restrictions regarding the type of client it can serve and how long a client can seek services. They also pointed out that there has been a notable decline of immigrant clients on public assistance, many of whom are forced into job-readiness programs without regard to their basic educational needs. The agency described the practice of moving clients off the rolls as quickly as possible as "churning," or a cycle of dependency that does little to provide for the basic needs of immigrant workers, and thought that it was too early to assess the true impact of welfare reform but foresees a rise in homelessness and domestic violence.

Third, several agencies indicated that there was not enough funding available for Adult Basic Education (ABE), English as a Second Language (ESL), and General Equivalency Degree (GED) classes given the high demand for these services among the population. A large agency in Brooklyn stated that its ongoing programs such as ESL/ABE training had been replaced by shortsighted job clubs and résumé preparation programs. A federation of agencies in Manhattan suggested that cutbacks to ESL training due to a short-sighted focus on "welfare-to-work" were impacting the organization. Another federation of agencies mentioned that many of its member organizations were no longer receiving funds for ESL and ABE instruction. A large agency in Queens added that funding cutbacks and rule-bound restrictions to ESL and GED training were the result of a short-sighted focus on vocational development, and that the "welfare-to-work" program was having a negative effect on the organization and its clients. Another agency in Brooklyn echoed these sentiments and argued that the cutbacks to ABE/ESL discourages potential applicants for citizenship and sends a signal to immigrants that their educational development is not valued.

In response to these changes, many immigrant organizations are trying to foster working relations with some of the other community-based organizations and service providers in and around their service areas. Large metropolitan organizations have access to resources but often do not have sufficient outreach and need expertise in providing services to particular populations. Smaller, more neighborhood-based or national origin–based organizations often have expertise in their particular communities, but lack the organizational capacity to offer comprehensive services to individuals and families in need. Relations are sought and built based on complementariness between the work of each of the organizations. Collaborations are usually built around both particular programs and service areas and around expertise with particular populations. In some instances, another organization might have a more developed expertise in immigration services or adult education, and the particular group might try to partner with that organization to increase the available services to the community. In other areas, organizations might want to partner with another organization not so much to gain from the other organization's expertise in a particular service area, but to outreach and provide better services to particular national origin populations. There are three forms of partnership between organizations, and organizations develop each particular type of relationship depending on the particular service area, program needs, or populations served. The first form is cooperation that involves the exchange of information about activities and programs, some regular contact, and referral; the second form is coordination in which actual responsibilities for services and case management are decided and divided among the participating organizations. In the third form, there is collaboration in which funding, staff, management, and followup are shared between the member organizations. Each form of partnership requires a different level of sharing of responsibilities, intervention, and management, but the key is to use them to fit the needs of the organization.

We know very little, and we need to document more systematically, immigrant access to social services, the role of immigrant organizations in providing services to immigrants, and the impacts of changes in policy on families and children and on immigrant community-based organizations. However, we do know that by helping to foster contacts between immigrant communities and home countries; by providing social services and help in adaptation and incorporation; and by advocating for the service and other needs of immigrant communities, and, in some instances, representing communities in policy discussions, programs, committees, and policy task forces, these groups play a central role in both the preservation of the social and cultural heritage and fabric of immigrant communities and in the adaptation and incorporation of immigrants into the social, political, and economic structure of the United States.

Héctor R. Cordero-Guzmán

See also: Culture and Assimilation (Part I, Sec. 3); Chain Migration (Part II, Sec. 1); The Economic Debate over Immigration (Part II, Sec. 7); Social Services (Part II, Sec. 9); *LULAC et al. v. Wilson et al.,* 1995 (Part IV, Sec. 1).

BIBLIOGRAPHY

Archdeacon, Thomas. *Becoming American: An Ethnic History.* New York: Free Press, 1983.

Cardenas, Gilberto, and Antonio Ugalde, eds. *Health and Social Services Among International Labor Migrants.* Austin: University of Texas Press, 1998.

Cordero-Guzmán, Hector, and Jose G. Navarro. "Managing Cuts in the 'Safety Net': What Do Immigrant Groups, Organizations, and Service Providers Say About the Impacts of Recent Changes in Immigration and Welfare Laws?" *Migration World* 4 (April 2000).

Ernst, Robert. *Immigrant Life in New York City 1825–1863.* Syracuse, NY: Syracuse University Press, 1994.

Jenkins, Shirley, ed. *Ethnic Associations and the Welfare State: Services to Immigrants in Five Countries.* New York: Columbia University Press, 1988.

Lissak, Shpak Rivka. *Pluralism and Progressives: Hull House and the New Immigrants, 1890–1919.* Chicago: University of Chicago Press, 1989.

Ward, David. *Poverty, Ethnicity, and the American City, 1840–1925.* Cambridge, UK: Cambridge University Press, 1989.

THE IMMIGRATION AND NATURALIZATION SERVICE

The Immigration and Naturalization Service (INS) is the executive arm of United States government charged with regulating immigration into the country. As an agency of the Department of Justice, the INS is responsible for the administration and enforcement of laws relating to the immigration and naturalization of noncitizens. Performing the dual function of interior enforcement and border management, the INS is a much-criticized bureaucracy torn between the two opposing accusations of "not doing enough" to stop undocumented immigration and "doing too much," verging on being cruel and inhuman in its treatment of noncitizens.

INTERIOR ENFORCEMENT

Interior Enforcement consists of intelligence, investigations, and detention and deportation departments. The Intelligence Program of the INS is the chief source of immigration-related intelligence, providing factual and analytic information to all levels of INS staff. Such information helps the staff to make long-term, mid-term, and everyday decisions; acquire and allocate resources; and formulate future policies. The investigation branch is responsible for investigating infringement and violations of the provisions of the Immigration and Nationality Act (INA) and the United States Code. Broadly, this division identifies and removes foreigners charged with crime, counters foreign smuggling, and responds to immigration fraud and complaints regarding alien activity of a criminal nature.

The Detention and Deportation Branch is in charge of detaining, deporting, and supervising unauthorized foreigners. Although unwanted immigrants have always been held at INS detention centers, detaining large numbers of undocumented immigrants is a relatively recent development. For instance, in 1998, the INS spent more than $670 million nationwide to detain and deport 170,000 undocumented residents, including deportation by judicial order but excluding those who agreed to leave the United States. Top nationalities thus removed came from Mexico, Guatemala, El Salvador, Honduras, the Dominican Republic, and Colombia. Allegations of many injustices taking place in this increasingly repressive arena are common. There are also many detention centers near the border, controlled and run by the Border Patrol unit of the Immigration and Naturalization Service.

BORDER MANAGEMENT

The Border management units of the Immigration and Naturalization Service include the Border Patrol and Inspections. The Border Patrol is a mobile and uniformed branch of the INS. It is responsible for the detection and prevention of smuggling and the undocumented entry of people from neighboring nations, especially at ports of entry. There are approximately 250 ports of entry in the United States, including air, land, and sea locations. The agents of the Border Patrol preside over eight thousand miles of U.S. national borders by means as varied as aircraft, automobile, boat, motorcycle, snowmobile, horseback, bicycle, and foot. Inspections is the uniformed branch in charge of inspecting all persons seeking admission to or passing through the United States by air, land, or sea. The inspectors decide at various ports of entry whether the applicants qualify for entry and determine the status under which they can be admitted (for instance, permanent residence status or nonimmigrant status such as student, visitor, or employee). They carefully look for fraudulent documents and previous overstays. The inspectors are tasked with catching terrorists, narcotic smugglers, imposters, criminals, false citizenship documents, and undocumented foreigners

Under one name or another, the Immigration and Naturalization Service has been in operation since the 1890s. Here Border Patrol officers gather in front of their patrol cars outside Del Rio, Texas, in 1925. *(U.S. Department of Justice)*

seeking admission. Further, they not only preinspect foreigners overseas but also work with foreign governments and air, ground, and sea carriers to help them identify—prior to boarding—all unauthorized passengers.

In the 1980s and 1990s, amid heightened national concern with immigration, the INS intensified its efforts to police national borders, especially the Southwest's border, with additional floodlights, helicopters, and steel fences, which resulted in what scholars have called the "militarization" of the United States–Mexico border. Immigration and Naturalization Service efforts introduced computer and tracking technologies, including ground sensors, sophisticated infrared night-vision equipment, low-light-level television surveillance equipment, and an airborne infrared radar. Military technologies designed for Vietnam and Central America were borrowed from the Defense Department and applied to immigration control at the border. New modes of interagency collaboration were adopted that broadened, circulated, and extended federal police powers to state and local authorities. In the 1980s and 1990s, the Border Patrol grew exponentially in mission and staff. While the budgets of other fed-

eral agencies shrank in the same period, the INS—particularly its enforcement divisions—received additional resources to halt undocumented crossings of the United States–Mexico border. The measure almost doubled the number of Border Patrol agents and called for more detention space and a 14-mile fence along the Mexican border near San Diego. An unfortunate consequence of such militarization has been the reduction of the border to a kind of "constitution-free zone," where the INS, as noted by some scholars, is structurally less cautious in upholding basic civil liberties. Each year, the Border Patrol makes about 1.5 million arrests along the southwest border.

It is not wise, perhaps, to hold the INS bureaucracy solely responsible for all the related ills plaguing the United States and its immigrants, for the very structure of the nation-state constitutes many problems. In modern times, immigration in general emerges as a "problem" due chiefly to the rise of the nation-state, which treats its "borders" as absolute, inviolable, and definitive. Unlike loose, fuzzy territorial limits of earlier communities, such as dynastic realms and empires, whose borders faded indiscernibly into one another, the boundaries of nations not only rig-

The Immigration and Naturalization Service is responsible for deporting immigrants like these men at a detention center in Bayview, Texas, who lack proper documentation to be in the United States. *(Cindy Reiman/Impact Visuals)*

idly demarcate one cluster of regions and populations from another but also cut up the sky and the sea into exclusive national spaces. Such rigid, sharp, unyielding boundary maintenance both constructs categories of inclusion, such as the "citizen" or the "resident," and constitutes comparable categories of "exclusion"— the "alien," the "immigrant," the "refugee." In the beginning, before the United States became a nation, the people emigrating to America did not face the prospect of being termed "legal" or "illegal" aliens, because no fixed "national cast" existed with which to construct the category of outcasts. The creation of total national enclosures produced categories of people that spilled over the framework, such as aliens or refugees, who became objects of either derision or compassion depending on the situation. Prior to the advent of nations and their political-legal cast, humans migrated, like nonhumans from harsher climates to balmy regions, and the categories used to describe them included "settlers" or "nomads."

IMMIGRATION AND NATURALIZATION: CIVIL WAR TO WORLD WAR I

During the seventeenth and eighteenth centuries, when the United States was still in the process of becoming a nation, immigration was relatively unhindered. Americans did not question the policy of free and open immigration until the mid-nineteenth century, when large numbers of Irish, German, and Chinese immigrants began arriving. No national action was taken until the Civil War, when Congress created the office of commissioner of immigration. At this time, some states, such as California, had passed laws restricting immigration. These laws were thrown out by federal courts, and in 1875 the Supreme Court placed the responsibility of immigration regulation on federal shoulders. In the 1880s, the United States began to enact major immigration legislation, targeting and excluding at first immigrants who did not fit the

American self-conception of nationhood. The Chinese Exclusion Act of 1882 was an early sign of the imminent change in the previous philosophy of welcoming virtually all immigrants. The alien contract labor laws of 1885 and 1887 banned certain laborers—those who had signed labor contracts—from coming to the United States. The broader Immigration Act of 1882 levied a head tax of fifty cents on each immigrant and barred the entry of "idiots," convicts, "lunatics," and individuals likely to become a public charge. The economic viability of immigrant labor has always been an important aspect of U.S. immigration policy. In the 1880s, state boards or commissions enforced immigration law under the guidance of U.S. Treasury Department officials. At the federal level, U.S. Customs collectors at different ports of entry collected the head tax from immigrants, while "Chinese inspectors" enforced the Chinese Exclusion Act.

With deepening nationalistic concerns, the Immigration Act of 1891 assigned the federal government the task of inspecting, admitting, rejecting, and processing all immigrants seeking admission to the United States. Enforcing immigration law was a new federal function, and the 1890s witnessed the Immigration Service's first attempts to put into operation national immigration policy. Under the 1891 law, Congress expanded the categories of exclusion, and in the process made immigration regulation more complex, blocking the entry of polygamists, persons convicted of crimes of moral turpitude, and those suffering repugnant or communicable diseases. These national immigration laws produced the need for a federal agency that could enforce them. The Immigration Act of 1891 instituted the Office of the Superintendent of Immigration—a precursor to the INS. Placed within the Treasury Department, the superintendent supervised a new corps of U.S. immigrant inspectors stationed at U.S. principal national ports of entry.

Before the late nineteenth century, there were few federal immigration laws, and those in existence were mainly designed to address passengers arriving from Europe or Asia at seaports. It was not until 1891 that federal laws provided for the inspection of immigrants arriving at land border ports. As compared with tight surveillance of more than a hundred ports of entry today, during the early 1890s the service had opened only two immigration ports of entry along the border, one of which was perhaps at El Paso, Texas. Six years later, in 1899, there were only four U.S. immigrant inspectors functioning along the Mexican border, covering the ports of entry at Nogales, Arizona; El Paso and Laredo, Texas; and Piedras Negras, New Mexico. After 1900, the corps of inspectors swelled when the Chinese Service, which predated the

Immigration Service, came under control of the Bureau of Immigration. By 1901, there were inspectors stationed at Tucson, Arizona, and San Diego, California.

Even the Immigration Act of 1891 directed its attention primarily to the inspection of immigrants who arrived "by water" on a "steam or sailing vessel." A major new federal immigration station opened in New York Harbor on Ellis Island in early 1892 and became the largest and busiest station for the first half of the twentieth century. Ellis Island contained inspection facilities, hearing rooms, detention cells, hospitals, railroad ticket offices, administrative offices, and representatives of many immigrant aid societies. Out of the Immigration Service's entire staff of 180 in 1893, Ellis Island alone employed 119. Beginning in 1896, the majority of the immigrants arrived from southern and eastern Europe rather than from northern and western Europe, as in earlier years. As a result of growing national anxiety over the change in sources of immigration, the Immigration Service began to build additional immigrant checkpoints at other ports of entry through the early twentieth century, hiring more immigration inspectors in such places as New York, Boston, and Philadelphia. The national enterprise of inspecting immigrants for their fitness to join the new nation was initially financed by an "immigrant fund" established with collections from a head tax on immigrants paid by ship companies or ship captains. In 1909, Congress replaced the fund with an annual appropriation.

During the first few years at Ellis Island and other ports, the Immigration Service was still in the process of devising and formalizing basic immigration procedures. The new arrivals were questioned in detail, and their admission or rejection was noted on manifest records. Detention guards and matrons were in charge of the people detained pending decisions in their cases. If the decision was negative, they were deported at the expense of the transportation company that had brought the immigrants to the United States. There were also Boards of Special Inquiry for a closer review of each exclusion case. Often, the major reason for exclusion was an immigrant's impoverished status, especially if he or she had no friends or relatives nearby. The Board of Special Inquiry would admit a poor immigrant if someone could post bond or if an immigrant aid society would take responsibility for the person. The national control over immigration was further extended with the Immigration Act of 1895, which upgraded the Office of Immigration to the Bureau of Immigration, headed by the commissioner-general of immigration. By 1903, the economic and labor interests related to immigration, coupled with nationalist concerns, encouraged Congress to put both alien contract labor law and Chinese exclusion responsibilities under the control of the commissioner-general and transfer the Bureau of Immigration from the Treasury Department to the newly created Department of Commerce and Labor.

Immigration policy, however, was not limited to guarding the gates but also included naturalization. With the Basic Naturalization Act of 1906, Congress further consolidated the unified national hold over how the naturalization of future U.S. citizens would take place. It put an end to many discretionary powers of the nation's more than five thousand naturalization courts. Framing the rules for naturalization that are still in effect today, the act encouraged state and local courts to give up their naturalization jurisdiction to federal courts and expanded the Bureau of Immigration into the Bureau of Immigration and Naturalization. The need for the national consolidation of immigration and naturalization prompted the new bureau to collect copies of every naturalization record issued by every naturalization court. Tightening and extending the nation's control over every single immigration case, bureau officials checked immigration records to verify that each applicant for citizenship had been legally admitted into the United States. With the separation of the Department of Commerce and Labor into two cabinet departments in 1913, the Bureau of Immigration and Naturalization also divided into the Bureau of Immigration and the Bureau of Naturalization. The two bureaus existed separately within the Department of Labor until 1933.

BETWEEN THE WORLD WARS

Although immigration from Europe declined during World War I, the responsibilities of the agency expanded to include the internment of enemy aliens who were primarily seamen and worked on captured enemy ships. A 1918 presidential proclamation increased agency paperwork by adding passport requirements during inspection and deportation activities. Although the passport requirement disrupted routine traffic across U.S. land borders with Canada and Mexico, it strengthened the hold of the nation-state on each and every crossing of the national boundary. The Immigration Service consequently began to issue border crossing cards. As mass immigration resumed after the war, Congress devised a new immigration policy: the national origins quota system. The new system discriminated in favor of immigrants

from northern and western Europe, drastically reducing immigration from southern and eastern Europe as well as other parts of the world. The national origins quota system assigned each nationality a quota based on its representation in past U.S. census figures; thus Ireland, Germany, and Great Britain received more than 70 percent of the quota, which they rarely filled. The State Department distributed a limited number of visas each year through U.S. embassies abroad, and the Immigration Service admitted only immigrants who arrived with a valid visa.

One consequence of severely controlled immigration was the rise in illegal immigration. Congress's response to undocumented immigrant pressure, especially along the land borders, was the creation of the U.S. Border Patrol within the Immigration Service. By introducing an intensive vigil through the Border Patrol coupled with a new, strict immigration policy, the nation made the border more real and less crossable. Border Patrol success soon resulted in more agency staff and resources being moved to deportation activity. The establishment of a tighter and unyielding boundary management system also increased appeals enormously, which in turn required the enlargement of state structures to deal with such appeals. The new Immigration Board of Review was created within the Immigration Bureau in the mid-1920s.

While immigration is the crossing of the physical borders, naturalization—or Americanization—is a political act of border crossing. A popular Americanization movement prior to World War I prompted the Naturalization Bureau to publish the first *Federal Textbook on Citizenship* in 1918 to prepare naturalization applicants for rites of political and social passage. The Education for Citizenship Program circulated textbooks to public schools offering citizenship education classes and notified immigrants of available education opportunities. In 1933, the Bureau of Immigration and the Bureau of Naturalization merged again into one agency, the Immigration and Naturalization Service.

In the late 1930s, immigration became—amid the threat of war in Europe—more an issue of national security than of economic interests and significantly affected the INS. The president's Reorganization Plan of 1940 moved the INS from the Department of Labor to the Department of Justice. The entry of the United States into World War II led both to the shortage of experienced staff members, who were enlisted in the armed forces, and to the agency's rapid growth. During the war, the INS intensified its surveillance of noncitizens. It recorded and fingerprinted every foreign national in the United States through the Alien Registration Program, and organized and operated internment camps and detention facilities for foreigners belonging to the nations at war with the United States. The INS maintained constant guard of national borders, recorded checks related to security clearances for immigrant defense workers, and administered a program to import agricultural laborers to harvest the crops left untended by Americans who had gone to war. During the war, the INS also converted to a new record-keeping system, implemented the Nationality Act of 1940, and doubled its workforce from approximately four thousand to eight thousand employees.

World War II brought to light the American self-conception of nationhood and the associated complexity of immigration, ancestry, and nationalism, especially when many American citizens of Japanese ancestry on the West Coast were forcibly evacuated from their homes and moved to inland detention centers following the Japanese attack on Pearl Harbor on December 7, 1941. During the spring and summer of 1942, 110,000 Japanese Americans, including a number of Japanese immigrants, were placed in ten war relocation centers located in remote areas from the Sierra Nevada Mountains to the Mississippi River. Japanese Americans lived in these camps with few work opportunities for adults or little education for children. When the threat of a possible Japanese attack was over, 17,600 Nisei (second-generation Japanese in the United States) were accepted—after individual screening at the centers to prove their loyalty—for service in the U.S. armed forces. Ironically, many of the Nisei units were later cited for bravery. Following years of demands for redress for the harm and hurts suffered by the "evacuees" during the war, the U.S. government apologized in 1988 for the internments and provided partial monetary payments to the approximately sixty thousand surviving Japanese Americans who had been interned.

POST–WORLD WAR II PERIOD

After World War II, immigration stayed low as the 1920s national origins system, which favored immigration from Europe, remained in place. As a nation, however, the United States never lost sight of the economic benefits of immigrant labor. The flourishing American agriculture industry continued to import seasonal labor from Mexico, as it had during the war. A 1951 formal agreement between the United States and Mexico made permanent a program through which braceros, or Mexican laborers, were admitted to the United States for seasonal contract labor in agriculture.

The INS also addressed certain issues arising from conditions in postwar Europe. The War Brides Act of 1945 made easier admission of the spouses and families of returning American soldiers and the Displaced Persons Act of 1948 and the Refugee Relief Act of 1953 permitted admission of many refugees displaced by the war and unable to come to the United States under regular immigration procedures. In the postwar era, the nationalist concerns grew stronger, which made the INS reinforce border controls and begin targeted deportation programs, most notably Operation Wetback. Additional national worry over the possible existence of anti-American elements in the United States prompted INS investigations and deportation of persons who believed in communist doctrines, subversive ideas and activities, or engaged in organized crime.

Some major changes took place with the 1965 amendments to the 1952 immigration law. Having witnessed the consequences of systems of racial and national preference in Nazi Germany, Congress replaced the national origins system with a family preference system designed to reunite immigrant families and reduce the existing policy's predisposition to Europe. Additional changes were made to attract skilled immigrants to the United States. This transformation of national policy brought about fundamental changes in immigration patterns, as Asia and Central and South America, instead of Europe, became major sources of immigrants. However, the new system continued to limit the number of immigration visas available each year.

The arrival of large numbers of illegal immigrants in the 1980s led to the passage of the Immigration Reform and Control Act of 1986, which imposed sanctions against United States employers who hired undocumented immigrants, thus expanding the functional responsibilities of the Immigration and Naturalization Service. The INS now investigated, prosecuted, and levied fines against corporate and individual employers, as well as deporting those found to be working illegally. In fiscal year 1995, the INS made about twelve thousand employer arrests. The 1986 law also permitted certain undocumented immigrants to legalize their residence in the United States under INS administration.

Restrictions on both the number of people allowed to immigrate and their legal rights in American society have continued to climb through the 1990s. The United States passed the 1996 Immigration Reform and Immigrant Responsibility Act, which has increased the enforcement side of INS activities, giving rise to debates on the criminalization of immigration, racism, labor surpluses/shortages, and human rights.

In the 1990s, the INS was criticized for targeting specific minorities, especially people of color from Mexico and South America, in its raids related to worksite enforcement under the 1986 law, while ignoring immigrants from Europe and Canada. Another criticism about enforcement of the law is that it turns employers into INS agents by making them responsible for possible fake identification cards. Further, as part of Operation Vanguard, the INS goes through the personnel records of each workplace, checking Social Security numbers for duplications or for numbers that do not exist. Across the country, the Social Security Administration sends employers lists of workers whose numbers do not match its database. These "no-match letters" often lead to the firing of workers, as employers assume those listed are undocumented aliens.

Criticisms also center around the shabby treatment of immigrants at the detention centers. Esmor detention center in Elizabeth, New Jersey, was the scene of a riot in 1995 when tensions among three hundred immigrants erupted in the wake of long-standing complaints about crowding, substandard food, poor medical service, and abusive guards. After the riot, all immigrants were transferred to a county jail, where they were housed—though accused of no crime—with prisoners and brought into court for hearings dressed like felons in handcuffs and shackles. Human rights violations sometimes result from some of the arrests, especially when the deportation of an undocumented worker leaves the remaining spouse and children to fend for themselves and when children, having been born on U.S. soil, are citizens while parents are illegal aliens.

It must be noted, however, that the INS is only an instrument of the government, which possesses the power to define "aliens," "immigrants," and "citizens"; to differentiate among them; and to constitute them as a problem or an asset through legislation. Immigration and Naturalization Service officials have complained of "mission overload," which is a practical consequence of the rise in punitive legislative measures taken by Congress in the 1980s and 1990s. Interestingly, the move toward harsher treatment of immigrants is global. As a major agency controlling the flows of people across U.S. borders, the INS is caught between the two opposite pulls of globalization induced by mounting pressures of transnational capitalism—demanding a free flow of both capital and labor—on the one hand, and the nation-state's reaction against the increased possibility of the international penetration of its boundaries, on the other.

For instance, many corporate leaders have been pressing the United States government to relax the restriction on labor immigration because of what they perceive as a shortage of labor (especially in the information technology sector), upward wage pressure, and competitive advantage. Labor leaders and other groups fear that such immigration will take jobs, especially high-tech jobs, away from native-born Americans, as well as lower wages. The intensity of the debate is reflected in various bills that were introduced, defeated, revived, passed, and rewritten in House of Representatives, the Senate, and the White House in the 1990s. As a compromise, the final bill that was enacted allowed more visas (115,000) to be granted to foreign workers each year, but only for a limited period of time. The INS, as a federal agency, is not only caught between these opposing pressures that add to the complexity of the enterprise but also has benefited in terms of growth in funding and staff in times of campaigns for small government. The INS workforce, which numbered approximately eight thousand from World War II through the late 1970s, grew in the 1990s to more than thirty thousand employees in thirty-six INS districts at home and abroad. The original force of immigrant inspectors now carries out varied tasks relating to inspection, examination, adjudication, legalization, investigation, patrol, and refugee and asylum issues.

As the Immigration and Naturalization Service enters the twenty-first century, it continues to battle its reputation for being a poorly run federal agency. It is estimated that a third of all applicants abandon their quest for citizenship before any formal resolution of their cases. Possessing limited legal rights, immigrants have limited physical space for complaint or redress. Long lines of actual and potential immigrants start forming, in the rain and snow, as early as three in the morning outside various INS offices throughout the United States. Although INS officials now assert that they are gradually moving in the direction of treating immigrants as customers, most of the modernization efforts and enormous resources have been expended on adding and enhancing the efficiency of surveillance systems. Caught between "doing too much" and "not doing enough," the INS may undergo a major reorganization in the years to come. Congress is considering legislation that would eliminate the current INS structure and place immigration issues under the direction of an associate attorney general who would "supervise" and "oversee" two new major offices. One office would oversee naturalization, visa petitions, and refugee application services, and the other would enforce immigration law and oversee border patrols, deportation, and investigations. Because of the ongoing importance of immigration and its connection to global capitalism and national affairs, the Immigration and Naturalization Service—in whatever form—will likely continue to play a major role in the United States's economic and social development.

A. Aneesh

See also: Immigration Stations (Part I, Sec. 3); Legal and Illegal Immigration: A Statistical Overview (Part II, Sec. 2); Legislation I: Immigration (Part II, Sec. 5);

Immigration Reform and Control Act, 1986 (Part IV, Sec 1); Report by U.S. Commission on Immigration Reform, 1994 (Part IV, Sec. 2).

BIBLIOGRAPHY

Dunn, Timothy J. *The Militarization of the U.S.-Mexico Border, 1978–1992: Low-Intensity Conflict Doctrine Comes Home.* Austin: CMAS Books, University of Texas at Austin, 1996.

Jacobson, David. *The Immigration Reader.* Malden, MA: Blackwell, 1998.

Kurian, George T., ed. *A Historical Guide to the U.S. Government.* New York: Oxford University Press, 1998.

LEGAL AND ILLEGAL IMMIGRATION: A STATISTICAL OVERVIEW

During the mid-twentieth century, racist national origin quotas based on the 1890 census, which were mandated by the Quota Act of 1924, favored entry of northwestern Europeans and barred most potential immigrants from Asia, southeastern Europe, and developing countries throughout the world. This act was not revised until the passage of the Immigration and Nationality Act of 1952, also known as the McCarran-Walter Act, which allowed enlarged quotas for southeastern European immigrants. Relatively open, worldwide legal immigration, limited only by overall numbers, did not prevail until passage of the Immigration and Nationality Act of 1965 abolished the quota system based on race.

In 1965, family reunification became the major criterion for entrance, and this provision contributed to a change in immigration patterns which shifted immigration from developed European countries to underdeveloped countries. There was no limit on visas for immediate relatives of citizens, and a preference for relatives of resident aliens increased the admission of marital partners, children, and parents. As a result, in the 1980s, marriage became the principle method of gaining entry for new immigrants. Another consequence was that family-related migration greatly reduced the amount of return migration. As a partial result, the number of immigrants admitted in the 1980s and early 1990s reached an all-time high, and the origins of immigrants became very diverse.

Another criterion set by the Immigration and Nationality Act of 1965 was that the need for workers in particular occupations would be used to establish admission preferences. Thus, the immigration stream developed a pronounced professional and skilled component.

DEMOGRAPHIC COMPOSITION AND CAUSATION OF POST-1965 LEGAL IMMIGRATION

The Immigration and Nationality Act of 1965 greatly increased the number and degree of diversity of American immigrants. By the last decade of the twentieth century, the immigrant population numbered 25.8 million persons, or 9.7 percent of the United States population. Although this figure is considered high and is much remarked upon in the media, it does not represent a degree of immigration as extensive as early in the twentieth century. Between 1900 and 1920, the U.S. foreign-born population had increased in each decade. After 1930, the foreign-born population declined, but it began to grow rapidly again after 1970. Despite this trend, the current level of immigrant population is not at a peak, as 14.4 percent of the 1870 population, 14.8 percent of the 1890 population, and 14.7 percent of the 1910 population was foreign-born.

The major change in immigration which has occurred is that its contemporary geographic imbalance represents a complete reversal of early- to mid-twentieth-century trends. In 1900, 90 percent of American immigrants originated from Europe. This was reduced to 17 percent in the 1990s. The countries of origin of post-1965 immigrants are primarily located in the developing world. The vast majority of all immigrants originate from Latin America (approximately one-half) and Asia (over one-quarter). Latino sending societies in the southern half of the Americas include Mexico, El Salvador, Guatemala, Honduras, Peru, and Ecuador, and, from the Caribbean, the Dominican Republic, which has a Hispanicized, primarily African-origin national population. Former English

Every year hundreds of thousands of people attempt to enter the United States without proper documentation. Many, like these Haitian refugees being stopped by the U.S. Coast Guard, never make it. *(USCG/Photo by PA2 Robin Ressler)*

or French colonies in the Caribbean that are major sources of African-descent immigrants include Haiti and Jamaica. Mexico is the major sending society for both documented and undocumented immigration, but its relative proportion of all immigrants is decreasing due to vastly increased other Latino and Asian immigration. After 1980, almost half of all immigration originated from Asia, with a major undocumented component. Africa and Oceania are the source of almost 3 percent of immigrants.

Liberalization of legal immigration policy is one factor in the generation of the most geographically diverse group of migration streams in American history. Sociologist Rubén Rumbaut, however, contends that the degree to which the Immigration and Nationality Act of 1965 modified immigration is exaggerated because immigrants are both legal and eligible for citizenship and "illegal, without documents and disallowed such privilege." Macrostructural and historical forces have played an important role in the dramatic change away from the historical predominance of Eu-

ropean nations and Canada as sites of immigration. In 1980, Mexico became the most frequent country of origin for immigrants. At previous junctures of history, Ireland (1850–70), Germany (1880–1920), and Italy (1930–70) were the leading sending countries for immigrants.

Mexico demonstrates the importance of macrostructural factors and history in the new structure of immigration. Historically, Mexican labor has been encouraged to migrate to the United States when employers needed workers, and the Bracero Program, which lasted from 1942 to 1964, actually institutionalized this pattern for agricultural employers for a period of time. Despite its close proximity to the United States, Mexican immigration is most responsive to the degree of economic opportunity afforded by the American economy as its workers are a part of transnational movements in an emergent "global division of labor." Today, this linkage is even more complex as a stream of Mexican workers, documented and undocumented, enters the United States and a group of

Most Mexican immigrants—like these men and women lining up to cross the border from Las Palomas, Chihuahua, to Columbus, New Mexico—enter the United States legally. *(Jack Kurtz/Impact Visuals)*

American corporations establish manufacturing subsidiaries in Mexico.

Rumbaut believes that the U.S. involvement in world affairs and its post–World War II global hegemony has created the military, political, economic, and cultural linkages that encourage legal and unauthorized immigration. For example, as a result of U.S. involvement in the Persian Gulf War (1990–91), thousands of Iraqi soldiers and prisoners of war became refugees in America. Later, they will be able to apply for family reunification, and a new sending country relationship will become institutionalized. It is the repeated American involvement in the developing world through military and economic interventions that has created the seeds of the new movement. This massive population transfer, nevertheless, would probably not occur if global inequality in access to capital did not serve to attract both professional and unskilled workers to the United States.

Scholar Reed Ueda indicates that current sending countries reflect economic patterns in immigration which originated between 1924 and 1965. After 1924, increased numbers of professional workers, women, and children immigrated to the United States. After 1960, American women began to enter the economy in large numbers, and many immigrant women joined them. The growing number of service positions attracted women, while the decline in unskilled industrial labor provided less opportunities for male immigrants, although agriculture remains dependent on foreign-born workers. Women became a majority of immigrants, as they reunited with family members in the United States and/or came for employment.

The social formation of dynamic new sending country relationships since 1965 has contributed to intense immigration throughout the late twentieth century. Although legal admissions declined from 915,000 in 1996 to 798,378 in 1997, the demand factor is still present. The Immigration and Naturalization Service (INS) reduced the family preference limit

Figure 1
Foreign-Born Population and Percentage of Total Population for the United States: 1850 to 1997

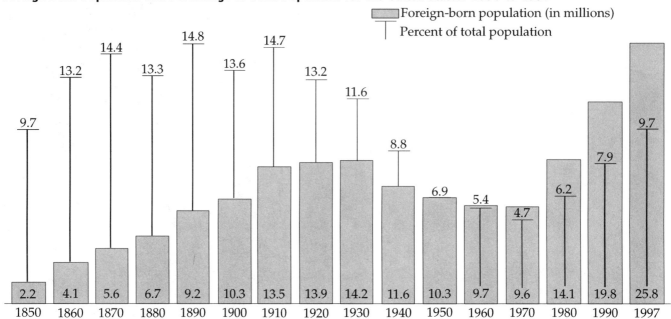

Source: Bureau of the Census, 1999a, Table 1, and 1999b, Table 1-1.
Note: For 1850–1990, resident population. For 1997, civilian noninstitutional population plus armed forces members living off-post or with their family on-post.

somewhat and had an increase in the number of applications pending status adjustment. Thus, a bureaucratic "paper" drop rather than reduced applications occurred. Again, legal immigration dropped to 660,477 in 1998, the lowest number of admissions since 1988 (643,025). Again, this is attributed to a paperwork backlog, as the number of applications that had not been decided increased.

The absolute number of legal immigrants "entering" the United States in a given year is sometimes cited as a cause for alarm by anti-immigration "nativists." The figure describing the level of immigration in any year is subject to fluctuation that may not be related to time of arrival. For example, it was widely publicized that 1,827,167 aliens were admitted as immigrants in 1991. This figure reflected 1,123,162 persons who were already present before 1991, some for many years or decades, and were given amnesty under the Immigration Reform and Control Act of 1986. In many years, individuals who were already present, such as those on temporary visas (e.g., student visas), are bureaucratically processed as "new arrivals." The INS paperwork backlog that developed in the late twentieth century will be responsible for distorting the statistics on new arrivals in the twenty-first century as well.

UNAUTHORIZED IMMIGRANT POPULATION

Many academic researchers have criticized INS apprehension statistics because they do not account for the possibility of multiple captures of individuals. Therefore, no reliable estimate can be made of the total apprehended and deported, only of the absolute number of times apprehensions and departures occurred. As Thomas Espenshade points out, the statistics do not identify repeat arrests and do not account for those who were successful on their first crossing. The statistics also fluctuate in relation to the intensity of Border Patrol enforcement at a particular historical juncture or location. The undocumented migrants face little legal repercussion if caught, because they are simply deported and can try again. It may be costly, however, if they have paid a smugglers fee and failed. Since the Border Patrol implemented Operation Hold the Line in Texas, Operation Gatekeeper in California, and Operation Safeguard in Arizona, certain areas of the border are much more tightly monitored. Evidence indicates, however, that more Mexicans are obtaining legal crossing cards or turning to other land routes. Finally, many undocumented immigrants enter the country legally, then

Table 1
Leading Countries of Birth of the Foreign-Born Population: Selected Years, 1850 to 1990

Subject	1850	1880	1900	1930	1960	1970	1980	1990
Number of 10 Leading Countries by Region								
Total	10	10	10	10	10	10	10	10
Europe	8	8	9	8	8	7	5	3
Northern America	1	1	1	1	1	1	1	1
Latin America	1	—	—	1	1	2	2	2
Asia	—	1	—	—	—	—	2	4
10 Leading Countries by Rank[1] (foreign-born population in thousands)								
1	Ireland 962	Germany 1,967	Germany 2,663	Italy 1,790	Italy 1,257	Italy 1,009	Mexico 2,199	Mexico 4,298
2	Germany 584	Ireland 1,855	Ireland 1,615	Germany 1,609	Germany 990	Germany 833	Germany 849	Philippines 913
3	Great Britain 379	Great Britain 918	Canada 1,180	United Kingdom 1,403	Canada 953	Canada 812	Canada 843	Canada 745
4	Canada 148	Canada 717	Great Britain 1,168	Canada 1,310	United Kingdom 833	Mexico 760	Italy 832	Cuba 737
5	France 54	Sweden 194	Sweden 582	Poland 1,269	Poland 748	United Kingdom 686	United Kingdom 669	Germany 712
6	Switzerland 13	Norway 182	Italy 484	Soviet Union 1,154	Soviet Union 691	Poland 548	Cuba 608	United Kingdom 640
7	Mexico 13	France 107	Russia 424	Ireland 745	Mexico 576	Soviet Union 463	Philippines 501	Italy 581
8	Norway 13	China 104	Poland 383	Mexico 641	Ireland 339	Cuba 439	Poland 418	Korea 568
9	Holland 10	Switzerland 89	Norway 336	Sweden 595	Austria 305	Ireland 251	Soviet Union 406	Vietnam 543
10	Italy 4	Bohemia 85	Austria 276	Czechoslovakia 492	Hungary 245	Austria 214	Korea 290	China 530

Source: Bureau of the Census, 1999a, Tables 3 and 4.

Note: — represents zero.

[1] In general, countries as reported at each census. Data are not totally comparable over time due to changes in boundaries for some countries. Great Britain excludes Ireland. United Kingdom includes Northern Ireland. China in 1990 excludes Hong Kong and Taiwan.

Table 2
U.S. Undocumented Immigrant Apprehensions:
1965–1995

Year	Apprehensions
1965	110,371
1967	161,608
1969	283,557
1971	420,126
1973	655,968
1975	766,600
1977	1,042,215
1979	1,076,418
1981	975,780
1983	1,251,357
1985	1,348,749
1987	1,190,488
1989	954,243
1991	1,197,875
1993	1,327,259
1995	1,536,520

Source: Immigration and Naturalization Service, *Statistical Yearbook.* Washington, DC: Immigration and Naturalization Service, 1966–1996.

overstay their visas, and thus are not accounted for in apprehension data to any great extent. Thus, it is difficult to obtain an accurate estimate of undocumented border crossing, although it may be possible to track visa violations.

The absolute number of INS apprehensions cited for 1997 was 1,536,520. Late in the twentieth century, the Border Patrol force was augmented by military technology and support, a phenomenon termed the "militarization of the border" by Timothy Dunn. Because of increased border enforcement, individual immigrants and human smugglers are choosing increasingly remote and dangerous overland routes for entry. As a result, death tolls rose during the 1990s, but the undocumented population is estimated as continuing to increase.

The INS estimates that from 4.6 to 5.4 million undocumented immigrants are residing in the United States. These statistics are criticized due to the impossibility of completely enumerating an underground population. The INS/Border Patrol has also been accused of inflating the arrest figures for purposes of attaining greater funding. Because of the problems involved in counting a fugitive population, these figures should be regarded with caution.

Mexico is estimated to be the source of over 50 percent of undocumented immigrants. Central American

nations affected by revolution and social turmoil (El Salvador, Guatemala, Honduras, and Nicaragua) are prominent source countries. Because all countries are subject to quotas, both Mexico and Canada are major sources of unauthorized immigrants, some of whom come for family reunification. Caribbean countries (Haiti, the Bahamas, the Dominican Republic, Trinidad and Tobago, and Jamaica) are near and send many clandestine immigrants. South American nations (Colombia, Ecuador, and Peru) are emerging as major sources of undocumented immigrants. South Asia (the Philippines, Pakistan, India, and Korea) is a region with many major source countries for the undocumented. California, the District of Columbia, and Texas are estimated to have the largest unauthorized populations.

Approximately 41 percent, or 2.1 million, of the unauthorized population are estimated to be "overstays," individuals who entered on a legal basis and did not depart. It is estimated that 16 percent of the Mexican undocumented population have overstayed,

Table 3
Estimated Unauthorized Immigrant Population for
Top Twenty Countries of Origin: October 1996

Country of Origin	Population
All Countries	4,990,000
1. Mexico	2,700,000
2. El Salvador	335,000
3. Guatemala	165,000
4. Canada	120,000
5. Haiti	105,000
6. Philippines	95,000
7. Honduras	90,000
8. Poland	70,000
9. Nicaragua	70,000
10. Bahamas	70,000
11. Colombia	65,000
12. Ecuador	55,000
13. Dominican Republic	50,000
14. Trinidad and Tobago	50,000
15. Jamaica	50,000
16. Pakistan	41,000
17. India	33,000
18. Dominica	32,000
19. Peru	30,000
20. Korea	30,000
Other	744,000

Source: Immigration and Naturalization Service. "Illegal Alien Resident Population." Washington, DC: Immigration and Naturalization Service, 1996.

26 percent of Central Americans, and 91 percent of unauthorized immigrants from other countries.

SOCIAL-CLASS BACKGROUND OF NEW IMMIGRANTS

Immigrants are divided into professional and working-class flows. Before the Great Depression, the vast majority of immigrants were working class. After the Immigration and Nationality Act of 1965 admissions criteria favoring professional workers whose skills were in demand facilitated the "brain drain," a flow of highly educated, talented individuals from developing countries. Immigrants brought extensive human capital, in the form of education and training, into the United States. These professional and skilled immigrants had the advantage of access to capital, entrepreneurial training, and family or ethnic support networks.

Early in the twenty-first century, roughly equivalent portions of the native-born and foreign-born populations over twenty-five years of age have attained four or more years of college. College education is associated with a high level of occupational attainment in the United States. Twenty-four percent of new immigrants work in managerial and professional occupations as compared with roughly 14.7 percent of the native-born. An additional 22 percent of the foreign-born worked in technical, sales, and administrative activities. A high percentage of certain groups are in managerial and professional positions: 38.7 percent of European-born workers are in managerial and professional positions, as are 36.7 percent of Asian-born workers. Twenty-three percent of workers from South America are managers and professionals, but only 6 percent from Mexico are. The chief countries of origin of the professional and managerial stratum are India, Taiwan, Iran, Hong Kong, the Philippines, Japan, Korea, and China. Additional countries with somewhat smaller numbers of individuals in this category are Nigeria, Egypt, Saudi Arabia, Kenya, Israel, Lebanon, Ghana, and Argentina. One significant result of this elite immigration is that over 20 percent of U.S. physicians are foreign-born and especially likely to be from India or the Philippines. Another consequence is that over one-half of all U.S. engineering degrees are held by the foreign-born immigrants, with 20 percent held by Taiwanese, Asian Indians, and South Koreans.

Almost half of arrivals have been working-class immigrants who are unskilled and relatively less educated. About 34 percent of new immigrants over the age of twenty-five did not complete high school in contrast to roughly 18.7 percent of the native-born population. This group is especially likely to have become laborers, service workers, and semiskilled operatives in a postindustrial economy with pockets of downgraded traditional manufacturing. In the final quarter of the twentieth century, the percentage of unskilled, less educated immigrants increased. Undocu-

Figure 2
Educational Attainment of the Foreign-Born Population

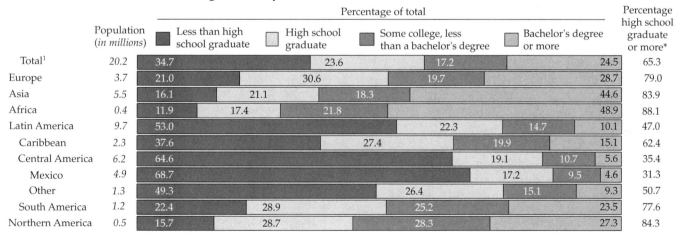

	Population (in millions)	Less than high school graduate	High school graduate	Some college, less than a bachelor's degree	Bachelor's degree or more	Percentage high school graduate or more*
Total[1]	20.2	34.7	23.6	17.2	24.5	65.3
Europe	3.7	21.0	30.6	19.7	28.7	79.0
Asia	5.5	16.1	21.1	18.3	44.6	83.9
Africa	0.4	11.9	17.4	21.8	48.9	88.1
Latin America	9.7	53.0	22.3	14.7	10.1	47.0
Caribbean	2.3	37.6	27.4	19.9	15.1	62.4
Central America	6.2	64.6	19.1	10.7	5.6	35.4
Mexico	4.9	68.7	17.2	9.5	4.6	31.3
Other	1.3	49.3	26.4	15.1	9.3	50.7
South America	1.2	22.4	28.9	25.2	23.5	77.6
Northern America	0.5	15.7	28.7	28.3	27.3	84.3

Source: Bureau of the Census, 1999, Table 13-10.
Note: Civilian noninstitutional population plus armed forces members living off-post or with their family on-post.
*Due to rounding off, figures in table do not necessarily correspond to figures in this column.
[1]Total includes Oceania and region not reported, not shown separately.

Figure 3
Major Occupation Group of Foreign-Born Workers 16 Years Old and Over by Region of Birth: 1997

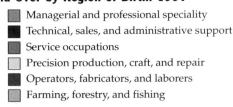

■ Managerial and professional speciality
■ Technical, sales, and administrative support
■ Service occupations
□ Precision production, craft, and repair
■ Operators, fabricators, and laborers
■ Farming, forestry, and fishing

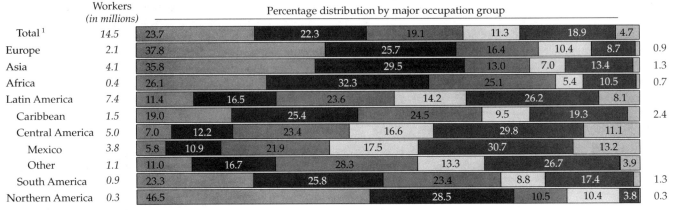

	Workers (in millions)	Managerial and professional speciality	Technical, sales, and administrative support	Service occupations	Precision production, craft, and repair	Operators, fabricators, and laborers	Farming, forestry, and fishing
Total[1]	14.5	23.7	22.3	19.1	11.3	18.9	4.7
Europe	2.1	37.8	25.7	16.4	10.4	8.7	0.9
Asia	4.1	35.8	29.5	13.0	7.0	13.4	1.3
Africa	0.4	26.1	32.3	25.1	5.4	10.5	0.7
Latin America	7.4	11.4	16.5	23.6	14.2	26.2	8.1
Caribbean	1.5	19.0	25.4	24.5	9.5	19.3	2.4
Central America	5.0	7.0	12.2	23.4	16.6	29.8	11.1
Mexico	3.8	5.8	10.9	21.9	17.5	30.7	13.2
Other	1.1	11.0	16.7	28.3	13.3	26.7	3.9
South America	0.9	23.3	25.8	23.4	8.8	17.4	1.3
Northern America	0.3	46.5	28.5	10.5	10.4	3.8	0.3

Source: Bureau of the Census, 1999, Table 15-10.
Note: Civilian noninstitutional population.
[1]Total includes Oceania and region not reported, not shown separately.

mented workers, who are often sojourners, take temporary, low-paid, unskilled work. Many are found in agriculture, where a majority of workers are foreign-born.

Both new documented and undocumented Latino, Asian, and Afro-Caribbean immigrants moved into the semiskilled and service labor market in U.S. metropolitan areas. Late in the twentieth century, noncitizen immigrants (8.4 percent) were twice as likely to be unemployed than naturalized immigrants (4.3 percent), while the native-born were intermediate (5.3 percent). In the process, tensions grew between unskilled African-American workers and new immigrants, but the contribution the new arrivals made during economic restructuring, the transition from a manufacturing to a service and information economy, accompanied an expansion of the urban economy in which many more-educated African Americans entered the public sector.

The social division between professional and working-class immigrants articulates with divergent countries of origin. Professional and skilled immigrants tend to originate from India, the Philippines, Korea, Taiwan, China, Great Britain, and Canada. In this group, there is a balanced sex ratio and a median age of thirty. Less skilled and less educated operatives, laborers, and service employees originate from

Mexico, Central America, Southeast Asia, and the Caribbean (Haiti, Dominican Republic, Cuba, Puerto Rico). Less well known sources of working-class immigrants include Italy and Portugal.

Mexican immigration is uncompassionately represented in the media as responsible for substantial "thirdworldization" of the United States because of immigrants' high concentration in unskilled, service, and farm employment. Frank Bean and Marta Tienda have estimated that Mexicans comprise 60 percent of all unauthorized immigrants. The vulnerability created by lack of documentation further precludes social mobility for many Mexicans. The Mexican contribution to both legal and undocumented immigration is the highest of any source country and reflects the shared border and binational history of U.S.-Mexico relations. It is useful to remember that the conflict over contemporary immigration expressed in the English Only movement and such laws as Proposition 187, which restricts the rights of undocumented immigrants in California, has been preceded by a nineteenth-century conflict in which the United States divested Mexico of approximately one-half of its national territory. The reemergence of Mexican immigration represents an extension over time of preexisting ties through migrant networks which some scholars have referred to as the *reconquista*, or reconquest, of the southwestern United States.

NEW ASIAN IMMIGRANTS

The Immigration and Nationality Act of 1965 permitted greatly increased Asian immigration after exclusionary laws passed in the late nineteenth and early twentieth centuries had greatly restricted it. The Chinese and Japanese were joined by diverse East and South Asian streams. The fastest growing Asian groups were South Koreans, Cambodians, Filipinos, Indians, Vietnamese, Thai, Indonesians, Burmese, Sri Lankans, Singaporeans, Malaysians, Pakistanis, and Bangladeshis. In addition, there are Asian immigrants from prior immigrant populations established in the West Indies and Latin American countries such as Peru. Twenty-seven percent of the new immigrant population has origins in Asia.

Professional and high-tech workers predominate among Asian immigrants. This group often entered on temporary visas as students at American universities before applying for permanent residency. Low-skill-education Asian immigrants went to New York, Boston, Chicago, and Los Angeles, taking jobs in manufacturing and service. Many Hong Kong immigrants entered garment sweatshops, hotels, and restaurants.

Northeast and Southeast Asia generated a series of refugee streams, including postcommunist Chinese refugees, Vietnamese, ethnic Chinese from Vietnam, Cambodians, and Laotians, including ethnic Hmong. Eight hundred thousand Southeast Asian refugees (approximately 50 percent of all displaced persons entering the United States) had settled in America by 1990. The Asian refugees have varied greatly. The urban Vietnamese were educated. Cambodian and Laotian refugees, on the other hand, were especially likely to receive U.S. welfare, which reflects their origins as a rural peasantry.

Contemporary Asian immigration has been familial rather than individual, as in the nineteenth century. Naturalization levels are high, and citizens have applied to bring their relatives. Chain migration involves heavy use of the "immediate relative" provision for expanding family presence. Family reunification is a major factor in the balanced sex ratio of current Asian immigration.

Asian immigrants had been geographically concentrated on the West Coast and in Hawaii. In addition to Chinese enclaves there are emergent Korean and Filipino communities.

NEW LATIN-AMERICAN IMMIGRANTS

After 1965 Latin American immigration increased markedly. The 13.1 million U.S. citizens born in Mexico, Central America, South America, and the Caribbean make up 51 percent of America's new immigrants. In 1997, there were 7 million Mexican immigrants in the United States, approximately 27 percent of the foreign-born population. Mexicans comprise the largest foreign-born population.

America's largest and medium-size central cities are developing sizable Latino populations as the Spanish-surnamed population is increasing at 1 million annually, ten times greater than the European-American population's rate of increase. This is due to increased immigration and higher levels of fertility.

Latin Americans comprise a diverse group in terms of racial origins. The use of country of origin to indicate nationality is misleading because descendants of European, Asian, and Jewish immigrants to Latin America have also moved to the United States. Regardless of the mestizo (Indian-Spanish) background of many Central and South American immigrants, a majority report themselves as white.

After 1965, Central American immigration originated from Costa Rica, El Salvador, Guatemala, Honduras, Nicaragua, and Panama. Later, civil wars resulted in increased immigration from El Salvador, Honduras, Nicaragua, and Guatemala. The sex ratio of Central American immigration is imbalanced, with women predominating. Many migrate individually to earn remittances to send back to their families. They often take jobs involving caregiving or cleaning in private homes, hospitals, and businesses.

Immigration from South America has been more steady. The sex ratio is balanced, and immigrants are likely to be older. South American immigrants are much more apt to be professionals than are Central Americans and less likely to be domestic servants. Both Central and South American immigrants were urban dwellers who sought upward mobility and were attracted to the major urban centers of North America.

Three emigrant segments from Cuban society arrived in different time periods. In the early 1960s, many members of the upper class—including industrialists, landowners, and government officials—abandoned communist Cuba. This group had a balanced sex ratio and tended to come as families. The second group of exiles, which arrived in the United States between 1965 and 1973, included many urban professionals, such as doctors, lawyers, engineers, and professors. In the early 1980s, the Mariel boat lift brought the third group of immigrants. This group was less educated than the first two groups. Over 500,000 Cubans were admitted as refugees during that time.

In the late twentieth century, a wave of immigration of people from the Dominican Republic eventually led them to surpass Puerto Ricans as the largest Hispanic population grouping in New York City. A majority were middle-class urbanites and laborers. They took work in New York's manufacturing and service sectors. Originally, Dominican males were likely to immigrate, but later they sent for wives, and women began to initiate migration for the purpose of taking industrial and service jobs.

DECREASED IMMIGRATION FROM EUROPE

Although the creators of the Immigration and Nationality Act of 1965 expected many Europeans to emigrate, this did not materialize. Earlier in the century, Europeans constituted more than one-half of all immigrants; but afterward, Europeans comprised less than 10 percent. The United Kingdom, Italy, Germany, and Portugal were the most frequent source nations. After the fall of communism in much of the region, eastern European and Russian immigration greatly increased.

In recent years many European immigrants have been professional and white collar. Some European immigrants are undocumented and work in the downgraded American manufacturing sector or personal services. Seventeen percent of the new immigrant population is from Europe. In 1900, 86 percent of the foreign-born population was from Europe, and this regional preponderance remained fairly stable at 83 percent in 1930 and 75 percent in 1960.

Another major social change in the European immigrant component of the U.S. population has been the increased entry of southern and eastern Europeans and the decline in northern and western European immigrants. Although northern and western European immigrants were a majority of all immigrants in 1850, southern and eastern European immigrants constitute the majority today.

REFUGEES

The United States refugee admittance policy has been discriminatory in that political considerations have often weighed more than the hard facts of human rights violations. For many years, most Cubans were admitted whereas most Haitians were not, despite the evidence of political turmoil and loss of life in Haiti. The desire of the U.S. government to embarrass communist states outweighed the evidence of threat to human life.

From 1949 to 1953, the United States admitted refugees under the Displaced Persons Act of 1948. In 1954–57, the Refugee Relief Act of 1953 allowed entrance. After the Soviet repression of the Hungarian anticommunist uprising, from 1956 to 1959, many Hungarians entered the United States. From 1966 through the establishment of the Refugee Act of 1980, many conditional entrants were allowed to immigrate. After the Cuban revolution in 1959, thousands of Cubans entered the United States, later followed by the Mariel boat lift in 1980. The darker skin of Haitians and lingering racism in the United States were also factors in the decision to return many to Haiti as economic migrants before U.S. military occupation occurred in 1991.

From 1978 to 1984, after the Vietnam War and in relation to civil conflicts in Southeast Asia, hundreds of thousands of Vietnamese, Cambodians, and Laotians entered under the conditions of the Indo-Chinese Refugee Resettlement Program. This is another group considered to have been fleeing communism. The number of refugee admissions peaked in the 1980s, with many South Asian "boat people" and Mariel Cubans entering the United States. The Refugee Act of 1980, which conforms to United Nations requirements, defines a refugee as "an alien outside the United States who is unable or unwilling to return to his or her country of nationality because of persecution or a well-founded fear of persecution." In any year, Congress reviews the refugee situation and the president establishes a numerical ceiling that is allocated primarily by region of origin.

ASYLEES

An "asylee" is legally defined as "an alien in the United States who is unable or unwilling to return to his or her country of nationality because of persecution or a well-founded fear of persecution." Refugees are outside the United States and people seeking asylum are present and allowed to apply for residency under provision of the Refugee Act of 1980. During the 1990s, asylee applications increased greatly. The criteria for designating refugees or asylees has been controversial. United States policy was to grant asylee status to Cubans on the grounds that imposition of the communist government represented political persecution.

Despite U.S. involvement in Central American conflict in Nicaragua, El Salvador, Honduras, and Guatemala, there was a political reluctance to assign the status of asylee to those who fled these countries. Although many arrived in the United States and applied for asylum, if detained, they were deported until the resolution of the case *American Baptist Church (ABC) v. Thornburg* in favor of exiled Central Americans in 1991. At present, many El Salvadorans and Guatemalans have pending filings. Other countries with large numbers of asylee applications include Mexico, Haiti, India, the People's Republic of China, and Iraq.

Haiti represents another case of failure to acknowledge political persecution. Although the United States intervened against a repressive military dictatorship by sending troops, there has been a reluctance to grant refugee or asylee status to Haitians.

Asylum may be granted to individuals fleeing "coercive population control procedures." China, which restricts couples to one child, is the primary source of individuals granted asylum under this criterion. One important asylum issue being considered is whether or not to allow girls and women fleeing the practice of genital mutilation to remain.

GEOGRAPHIC DESTINATIONS OF THE NEW IMMIGRANTS

New immigrants are primarily attracted to a limited number of American destinations. In 1997 six states had new immigrant populations of 1 million or more: California, 8.1 million; New York, 3.6 million; Florida, 2.4 million; Texas, 2.2 million; New Jersey, 1.2 million; and Illinois, 1.1 million. Five states had higher concentrations of new immigrants than the national average (9.7 percent): California, 25.7 percent; New York, 19.6 percent; Florida, 16.4 percent; New Jersey, 15.4 percent; and Texas, 11.3 percent.

As a result of immigrant concentration, the United States has two "majority-minority" states: California and the historically Spanish-American New Mexico. In California, the population of European-American descent is a statistical minority, although in terms of political efficacy, they often act as a dominant group. The term "Mexicanization of California" refers to the growing Latino population as symbolized by the de-

Figure 4

States with a Foreign-Born Population of 1 Million or More in 1997: 1990 and 1997

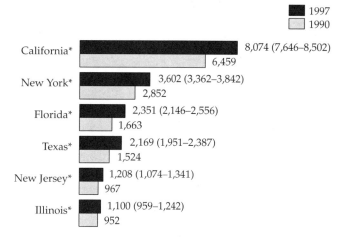

Source: Bureau of the Census, 1990 census of population, and 1999, Table 4-1A.

Note: Numbers in thousands. Ninety percent confidence intervals in parentheses for 1997 estimates. For 1990, resident population. For 1997, civilian noninstitutional population plus armed forces members living off-post or with their family on-post

*Change from 1990 to 1997 is statistically significant.

mographic majority in Los Angeles County and the city of Los Angeles. The label "browning of the Midwest" has been applied to the 50 percent increase in Latino growth in ten central region states. Even the New South has seen the development of sizable Latino population concentrations and urban neighborhoods.

IMMIGRANT URBAN CONCENTRATION

New immigrants are highly concentrated in a few major metropolitan areas. This represents a major urban transition, as the foreign-born population is present in greater numbers than the native-born in metropolitan and central city areas. As of 1990, five metropolitan areas have a million or more new immigrants: Los Angeles, 4.8 million; New York, 4.6 million; Miami, 1.4 million; San Francisco, 1.4 million; and Chicago, 1.1 million. Over one-quarter of the population in the nation's largest metro areas is of immigrant origin. As Table 5 shows, Los Angeles, with 30.5 percent of the population foreign-born, has the greatest proportion of new immigrants in metro areas of 4 million in population size or greater. Next come New York, with 22.8 percent, and San Francisco, with 20.8 percent.

Table 4
Foreign-Born Population in the 10 Largest Metropolitan Areas: 1997

Rank in total population	Metropolitan area	Percentage foreign-born
1	New York-Northern New Jersey-Long Island, NY-NJ-CT-PA	22.8
2	Los Angeles-Riverside-Orange County, CA	30.5
3	Chicago-Gary-Kenosha, IL-IN-WI	13.0
4	Washington-Baltimore, DC-MD-VA-WV	11.0
5	San Francisco-Oakland-San Jose, CA	20.8
6	Philadelphia-Wilmington-Atlantic City, PA-NJ-DE-MD	6.2
7	Boston-Worcester-Lawrence, MA-NH-ME-CT	8.1
8	Detroit-Ann Arbor-Flint, MI	6.7
9	Dallas-Ft. Worth, TX	9.6
10	Houston-Galveston-Brazoria, TX	15.0

Source: Bureau of the Census, 1999, Table 5-2A.
Note: Civilian noninstitutional population plus armed forces members living off-post or with their family on-post. Metropolitan areas as defined June 30, 1993.

THE LATINIZATION OF URBAN AMERICA

In the late twentieth and early twenty-first centuries, Latinos have come to or will surpass African Americans as the largest ethno-racial population in many major metropolitan cities. In 1996, the critical demographic juncture occurred in New York City. At present, Latinos outnumber African Americans in six of the ten largest U.S. cities: New York, Los Angeles, Houston, San Diego, Phoenix, and San Antonio. La-

tinos outnumber European Americans in Los Angeles, Houston, and San Antonio. The Dallas-Fort Worth metropolitan area is projected to attain a Latino majority by the year 2005.

Census statistics indicate that eighteen of the twenty-five largest metropolitan counties will have a Latino population larger than the African-American population by 2003. Despite the previous historical concentration of the Latino population in the Southwest, the entire United States is being influenced by demographic Latinization. In both New England and the Pacific Northwest, Spanish-surnamed individuals

Figure 5
Labor Force Participation Rates of the Population 16 Years Old and Over by Age and Gender for Selected Age Groups: 1997

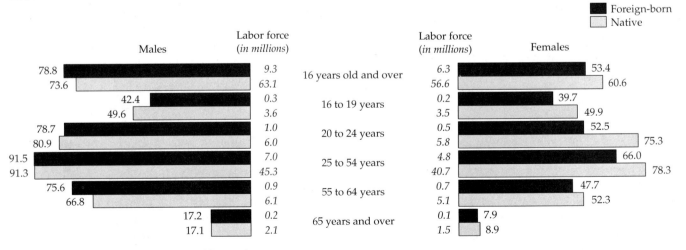

Source: Bureau of the Census, 1999, Table 14-1A.
Note: Percentage of the civilian noninstitutional population.

Figure 6
Income of Foreign-Born Households by Region of Birth of the Householder: 1996

	Households (in millions)	
Total[1]	10.4	$30,000
Europe	2.2	$31,300
Asia	2.7	$42,900
Africa	0.3	$31,300
Latin America	4.9	$24,100
Caribbean	1.2	$23,900
Central America	3.0	$23,000
Mexico	2.4	$22,400
Other	0.6	$25,400
South America	0.6	$31,800
Northern America	0.3	$35,000

Source: Bureau of the Census, 1999, Table 16-1D.
Note: Households as of March 1997. Civilian noninstitutional population plus armed forces members living off-post or with their family on-post.
[1]Total includes Oceania and region not reported, not shown separately.

now outnumber African Americans. It has long been projected that, in the twenty-first century, Latinos will come to be the largest U.S. ethnic group. Because of the urban concentration of the new immigration, this trend is happening more quickly in metropolitan regions. Although Latino immigration and settlement are concentrated in cities of varying size in the West and Midwest, they are exceptionally concentrated in America's twenty largest cities. New York has one-third of the nation's Spanish-surnamed population.

GENDER AND LABOR FORCE PARTICIPATION OF IMMIGRANTS

In 1997, 91.5 percent of foreign-born men age twenty-five to fifty-four work, as compared with 91.3 percent of native-born men. The rate of labor force participation was minimally affected by citizenship status or region of birth. Sixty-six percent of new immigrant women age twenty-five to fifty-four worked, as compared with 78 percent of native-born women. Among foreign-born women, 77 percent of naturalized citizens worked, as compared with 60 percent of noncitizens. Mexican women (52 percent) had the lowest rate of labor force participation of foreign-born women.

MEDIAN INCOME AND POVERTY

In 1996, the median income for households containing a foreign-born householder was $30,000, as compared with $38,100 for the native-born. The divergence between the managerial/professional and unskilled components of immigration contributes to this high degree of variation, as does region of origin. Asian householders had a median income of $42,900; European householders, $31,300; and Latin American householders, $24,100.

Male foreign-born workers earned a median income of $25,000 as compared with $20,800 for foreign-born female workers. Naturalized males had median incomes of $35,600 as compared with $20,500 for noncitizen males. Naturalized women earned a median income of $25,500 as compared with $17,500 for noncitizen females. The trend known as the "feminization of poverty," or the tendency for women heads of household with children to have much lower incomes, is found among both foreign- and native-born. Among foreign-born women heads of household with one or more children under eighteen years of age present, median income was $13,400 as compared with $16,800 for similarly situated native-born families.

Noncitizen new immigrants were significantly more likely to have below-poverty-level incomes (26.8 percent) than naturalized citizens (10.4 percent) and the native-born (12.9 percent). The Latin American poverty rate was 28 percent as compared with 12.7 percent for European immigrants and 14.7 percent for Asian immigrants.

NATURALIZATION

In 1997, approximately 9 million, or 35 percent, of the new immigrant population naturalized. The Census Bureau documented a decline in the rate of naturalization among the total immigrant population, with 64 percent in 1970, 51 percent in 1980, and 40 percent in 1990. Naturalization varied by region of birth. The rates in 1997 were: Europe, 53.3 percent; Asia, 44.3 percent; and Latin America, 24 percent. Mexican immigrants had the lowest rate of naturalization at 15 percent.

Naturalization is important because without it, immigrants lack political representation. The propensity to naturalize is greater among younger, upwardly mobile individuals with higher levels of education, occupational status, and human capital. Individuals whose spouses or children are citizens are also more

Figure 7
Median Earnings of Foreign-Born, Full-Time, Year-Round Workers by Gender and Region of Birth: 1996

Males ☐
Females ■

Males	Workers (in millions)		Workers (in millions)	Females	Female-to-male earnings ratio
$25,000	6.6	Total[1]	3.7	$20,800	.83
$40,500	0.9	Europe	0.6	$23,400	.58
$35,300	1.8	Asia	1.2	$24,600	.70
$18,600	3.5	Latin America	1.7	$16,700	.90
$23,900	0.6	Caribbean	0.5	$20,200	.85
$16,800	2.5	Central America	0.9	$14,200	.85
$16,800	2.0	Mexico	0.6	$13,700	.81
$16,700	0.5	Other	0.3	$16,400	.98
$25,200	0.4	South America	0.3	$21,100	.84

Source: Bureau of the Census, 1999, Table 17-10.
Note: Civilian noninstitutional population plus armed forces members living off-post or with their family on-post.
[1]Total includes Africa, Oceania, Northern America, and region not reported, not shown separately.

Figure 8
Poverty Rates for the Foreign-Born Population by Region of Birth: 1996

Population (in millions)

Region	Population (in millions)	Rate
Total[1]	25.8	21.0
Europe	4.3	12.7
Asia	6.8	14.7
Africa	0.6	17.1
Latin America	13.1	28.0
Caribbean	2.8	23.7
Central America	8.8	31.6
Mexico	7.0	33.9
Other	1.8	22.3
South America	1.5	15.1
Northern America	0.6	7.9

Source: Bureau of the Census, 1999, Table 18-1D.
Note: Population as of March 1997. Civilian noninstitutional population plus armed forces members living off-post or with their family on-post and excluding unrelated individuals under 15 years old.
[1]Total includes Oceania and region not reported, not shown separately.

Figure 9
Naturalized Citizens by Region of Birth: 1997

Foreign-born population (in millions)

Region	Foreign-born population (in millions)	Percentage
Total[1]	25.8	35.1
Europe	4.3	53.3
Asia	6.8	44.3
Africa	0.6	34.8
Latin America	13.1	23.6
Caribbean	2.8	41.3
Central America	8.8	16.6
Mexico	7.0	14.9
Other	1.8	23.7
South America	1.5	31.5
Northern America	0.6	43.8

Source: Bureau of the Census, 1999, Table 7-1.
Note: Percentage of foreign-born population. Civilian noninstitutional population plus armed forces members living off-post or with their family on-post.
[1]Total includes Oceania, and region not reported, not shown separately.

likely to naturalize. Restrictive legislation, such as Proposition 187 in California, and the 1996 Welfare Reform Act, which denied services for a period of time to resident aliens, may prompt immigrants to step up their rate of naturalization.

Judith Warner

See also: The Immigration and Naturalization Service, Transit and Transportation of Recent Illegal Immigrants (Part II, Sec. 2); Amnesty (Part II, Sec. 5); Immigration and Nationality Act, 1965, Immigration Reform and Control Act, 1986, Illegal Immigration Reform and Immigrant Responsibility Act, 1996, California Proposition 187, 1994 (Part IV, Sec. 1); Report by U.S. Commission on Immigration Reform, 1994 (Part IV, Sec. 2).

BIBLIOGRAPHY

Barkan, Elliot R. *Asian and Pacific Islander Migration to the United States: A Model of New Global Patterns.* Westport, CT: Greenwood Press, 1992.

Barringer, Herbert R., Robert W. Gardner, and Michael J. Levin. *Asians and Pacific Islanders in the United States.* New York: Russell Sage Foundation, 1993.

Bean, Frank D., and Marta Tienda. *The Hispanic Population of the United States.* New York: Russell Sage Foundation, 1987.

Brun, Michael, et al. "A Spatial Study of the Mobility of Hispanics in Illinois and the Implication for Educational Institutions." JSRI Research Paper no. 43, Julian Samora Research Institute, East Lansing, MI, 1998.

Bureau of the Census. *Estimates of Population of Metropolitan Areas.* Washington, DC: Government Printing Office, 1996.

———. *Profile of the Foreign-Born Population of the United States: 1997.* Current Population Reports Special Studies P23-195. Washington, DC: Government Printing Office, 1999.

Caplan, Nathan, John K. Whitmore, and Marcella H. Choy. *The Boat People and Achievement in America: A Study of Economic and Educational Success.* Ann Arbor: University of Michigan Press, 1989.

———. *Children of the Boat People: A Study of Educational Success.* Ann Arbor: University of Michigan Press, 1991.

Cornelius, Wayne. "The Structural Embeddedness of Demand for Mexican Immigrant Labor." In *Crossings: Mexican Immigration in Interdisciplinary Perspectives,* ed. Marcelo M. Suarez-Orozco, pp. 113–44. Cambridge: Harvard University Press, 1998.

Daniels, Roger. *Coming to America: A History of Immigration and Ethnicity in American Life.* New York: Harper Perenniel, 1991.

Davis, Mike. *Magical Urbanism: Latinos Reinvent the US City.* New York: Verso, 2000.

Department of Labor. *A Profile of U.S. Farm Workers.* Prepared by Richard Mines, Susan Gabbard, and Anne Stierman. Washington,

DC: Government Printing Office, 1997. www.dol.gov/dol/asp/public/programs/agworker/report/main.htm.

Dunn, Timothy J. *The Militarization of the U.S.-Mexico Border, 1878–1992: Low Intensity Doctrine Comes Home.* Austin, TX: Center for Mexican-American Studies, 1996.

Espenshade, Thomas. "Does the Threat of Border Apprehension Deter Undocumented U.S. Immigration?" *Population and Development Review* 20:4 (1994): 871–92.

Foner, Nancy. *New Immigrants in New York.* New York: Columbia University Press, 1987.

Frey, William, and Kao-Lee Liaw. "Immigrant Concentration and Domestic Migrant Dispersal: Is Movement to Nonmetropolitan Areas White Flight?" *Professional Geographer* 50:2 (1998): 217–18.

———. "Internal Migration of Foreign-Born Latinos and Asians: Are They Assimilating Geographically?" In *Migration and Restructuring in the United States,* ed. Kavita Pandit and Suzanne Withers. Latham, MD: University Press of America, 1999.

Hendricks, Glen. "Dominicans." In *Harvard Encyclopedia of American Ethnic Groups,* ed. Stephen Thernstrom. Cambridge: Harvard University Press, 1980.

Jasso, Guillermina, and Mark R. Rosenzweig. *The New Chosen People: Immigrants in the United States.* New York: Russell Sage Foundation, 1990.

Moss, Mitchell, Anthony Townsend, and Emmanuel Tobier. *Immigration Is Transforming New York City.* New York: Taub Urban Research Center, New York University, 1997.

National Center for Health Statistics. *Births of Hispanic Origin, 1989–1995.* Washington, DC: Government Printing Office, 1998.

Oboler, Susan. *Ethnic Labels, Ethnic Lives: Identity and the Politics of (Re)Presentation in the United States.* Minneapolis: University of Minnesota Press, 1995.

Orlov, Ann, and Reed Ueda. "Central and South Americans." In *Harvard Encyclopedia of American Ethnic Groups,* ed. Stephen Thernstrom. Cambridge: Harvard University Press, 1980.

Perez, Lisandro. "Cubans." In *Harvard Encyclopedia of American Ethnic Groups,* ed. Stephen Thernstrom. Cambridge: Harvard University Press, 1980.

Pessar, Patricia. "The Dominicans: Women in the Household and Garment Industry." In *New Immigrants in New York,* ed. Nancy Foner. New York: Columbia University Press, 1987.

Portes, Alejandro, and Rubén Rumbaut. *Immigrant America: A Portrait.* Berkeley: University of California Press, 1996.

Rumbaut, Rubén G. "Origins and Destinies: Immigration to the United States Since World War II." In *New American Destinies: A Reader in Contemporary Asian Immigration,* ed. Darrell Y. Hammamoto and Rodolfo E. Torres. New York: Routledge, 1997.

Sutter, Valerie O'Connor. *The Indochinese Refugee Dilemma.* Baton Rouge: Louisiana State University Press, 1991.

Ueda, Reed. *Postwar Immigrant America: A Social History.* New York: St. Martin's, 1994.

Waldinger, Roger. *Still the Promised City? African Americans and New Immigrants in Postindustrial New York.* Cambridge: Harvard University Press, 1996.

MARRIAGE MARKET

*G*enerally speaking, valid legal marriages of American citizens to foreign-born persons that occur abroad are equally valid and legal in the United States. Although federal regulations prohibit diplomatic and consular offices from performing marriages overseas, local civil or religious officials can and often do officiate over the ceremony.

While fighting raged in Europe during World War II, American men and women met and married foreigners in abundance, bringing numerous immigrants to the shores of America. In December 1945, Congress passed the War Brides Act, permitting the immigration of foreign women (and men) who had married or become engaged to U.S. military personnel while they were stationed overseas. Because of the favoritism afforded persons of British descent during this second wave of immigration, many British women became U.S. residents through this act. By 1964, a new movement to import foreign-born spouses had manifested itself. And by 1980, a surge in contract marriages, or mail-order brides, was in vogue.

The wife-import or mail-order bride business was not a new phenomenon, but had existed and been a part of American history since the early days of its settlement. As immigrants began to inhabit North America and establish their permanent homes, arranged marriages with local women in their own country were organized by relatives and often took place through proxy marriages. Even today, many cultures and religions still engage in the practice of contract and arranged marriages, but the popular view is that the use of such methods to find a partner has a negative implication.

PETITIONING FOR AN ALIEN FIANCÉE

A Petition for Alien Fiancée, or form I-129F, can be filed prior to a marriage and handled more expeditiously than the Petition for Alien Relative, form I-130. But only citizens of the United States by birth or naturalization who have the capacity to enter into a valid marriage can file the alien fiancée petition. The requirement of having the capacity to enter into a valid marriage can be proved by a showing that the U.S. citizen has never been married, was married and is now divorced, or is widowed. The inability to enter into a valid marriage nullifies a fiancée petition. According to the Immigration and Naturalization Service (INS) approximately eleven hundred more fiancées arrived per year in the 1970s and 1980s than attained permanent resident alien status. In the 1990s, the average yearly excess of arrivals has been approximately twenty-two hundred.

To satisfy the INS that the marriage is not a fraud or a fiction, there must be evidence that the petitioner and beneficiary have met in person within the last two years. The meeting is not required to be of any particular duration. It need not be purposeful or targeted, but it must take place. The requirement of a personal meeting can only be waived if it can be proved that the meeting would result in extreme hardship to the petitioner or that compliance would violate strict customs of the beneficiary's foreign land or culture.

Once a citizen files a fiancée petition with the INS service center with jurisdiction over his or her place of residence, the beneficiary receives an application for a K-1 visa. After the appropriate consulate approves the application, the beneficiary is permitted to enter the United States for the purpose of marriage. This admission is only valid for a period of ninety days and cannot be extended. The Petition for Alien Fiancée permits the principal beneficiary to include dependent children in the visa application. Such derivative dependents may be issued a K-2 visa, although their status is determined at the consulate abroad during the interview with the principal beneficiary.

The ninety-day period gives the parties an opportunity to get to know each other and determine if they will marry. If a valid marriage is going to occur, it must take place during that ninety-day period. If a valid marriage does occur, the alien fiancée then is

The expansion of the internet in recent years has made shopping for prospective brides more convenient and more subject to abuse. The web page advertises both potential Filipina spouses and sex tours of Southeast Asia. *(Maria Dumlao, Impact Visuals.)*

permitted to apply for an adjustment of status. If the couple decides not to marry, the beneficiary must leave the United States before the end of the ninety-day admission period. There are no extensions of time possible under this visa category, but compliance with the conditions of the K-1 visa authorizes both parties to use this type of petition in the future with other potential mates.

IMMIGRANT SPOUSES

From 1995 to 1998, more than 614,433 foreign-born spouses of American citizens were admitted to the United States. During this same period, 529,538 spouses and children of lawful permanent residents were granted visas. In fiscal year 1994, the last year for which detailed data were maintained, the INS reviewed 96,033 spousal applications for removal of conditional status and removed the conditions on 90,243, or 94 percent. This means that 94 percent of the cases were judged valid marriages. Only 717 of the 5,790 denied or closed cases (12 percent) were denied for cause. Of the cases denied for cause, 266 (37 percent) were foreign-born wives of U.S. citizens or lawful per-

manent residents. A study conducted by the INS based on a sample of these 266 women estimated that between 4 and 9 percent of their marriages were arranged through the international matchmaking industry.

INTERNATIONAL MATCHMAKING BUSINESS

Because of the absence of records regarding overseas marriages, the INS commissioned a study of the industry that estimated the number of mail-order marriages to be in the range of four thousand to six thousand yearly as of 1998. Another study commissioned by the INS uncovered the existence of two divergent opinions about the mail-order bride business. On the one hand, the report discovered some persons viewed it as an international personal ad service used by consenting adults and competent people. On the other hand, the study found that a small majority viewed the system as inequitable and believed that the transactions resulted in an international industry that involved the trafficking of women from developing countries to industrialized Western countries. Concluding that the mail-order bride transaction, unlike dating services or personal ads, is one where the consumer-husband holds all the cards, the INS found the industry uncompromisingly one-sided. The male customer has access to and chooses from a pool of women about whom personal details and information are provided, while the women are told virtually nothing about the male customer except what he chooses to reveal about himself. The woman's motivation may be something as simple as seeking a loving partner or something more specific, such as finding a partner who will facilitate her legal immigration to the United States. The male customer may be seeking a woman who is only eager to satisfy his expectations and meet his needs.

The popularity of the Internet in the 1990s has opened a Pandora's box of sorts. Anyone with a computer and Internet access can browse through the legions of international matchmaking organizations' catalogs and Web sites to find thousands of ready and willing women as dating candidates. Some of the Web sites are cosmopolitan mechanisms that provide photos and audio representations of the candidates. Other groups may include organized social gatherings and travel arrangements for a fee. "Crime and Servitude: An Exposé of the Traffic in Women for Prostitution from the Newly Independent States," the Global Survival Network (GSN), estimated that two hundred mail-order bride companies arrange between two thousand and five thousand marriages in the United States each year.

A recent documentary produced by GSN reveals how mail-order bride businesses are used as a facade to recruit and traffic Russian women to Germany, Japan, and the United States for the sex industry. Because of the particular ease with which fiancée visas are obtained, GSN reports that traffickers have become increasingly interested in sending women to the United States.

Many of the mail-order bride businesses are U.S.-based companies with Russia-based operators offering a wide range of services. Depending upon the amount of money the prospective spouse is willing to spend, he can have unlimited access to eligible women. The 1997 GSN report identified one marriage agency specializing in Russian women that charges customers a $1,850 membership fee, which entitles the client to buy the right to view photos and videos of 400 women. GSN discovered that at least eight U.S.-based mail-order bride companies operate in Moscow alone.

Abroad and stateside, the companies are part of an exploding multimillion-dollar industry that markets women from developing countries as potential brides to men in Western nations. Although the last two de-

cades have seen a significant influx of women from the Philippines or elsewhere in Asia, the Philippine government has pushed to cut the supply side of the equation, banning advertisement and recruitment in the islands. According to published reports, the Philippines, one of the poorest nations in Asia, annually exports more than twenty thousand mail-order brides worldwide.

In recent years, political changes and easy access to the Internet have sparked huge interest and enhanced business for companies seeking to introduce women from the former Soviet Union. A Phoenix-based company called A Foreign Affair, which features thousands of women from Russia, Eastern Europe, Asia, and Latin America on its Web site, estimates that it has had more than fifteen thousand male customers since it started in 1995, when there were a handful of competitors. Now, there are nearly two hundred and fifty introduction companies doing business in the United States. At least eighty focus exclusively on women from Russia and Eastern Europe; others expanded to include Russian women, who are portrayed as uncomplicated, traditional, family-oriented, and untainted by Western feminism. One organization stated, "Their views of relationships have not been ruined by unreasonable expectations." They cater to men who desire women who are white, but by virtue of their foreign origin, are exotic.

The usual format of an international marketing organization is that the company publishes a catalog listing hundreds of women of various ages (due to the lack of state, federal, or international regulation, minors are regularly included in the matchmaking portfolio), a physical description, and a brief statement of background. These are available through both printed material and the Internet. For an additional payment, customers may select video presentations of the women described in the catalog. The company may then organize a tour for customers to travel to Russia to meet a wide selection of women and girls. Consequently, as many as two thousand women may show up for a mixer party for a group of only a dozen men. For purposes of publicity, the company photographs the women for the catalog and videotapes the evening's activities for use on late-night cable infomercials.

FRAUDULENT OR ABUSIVE MARRIAGES

The volume of persons sponsored under the family preference provisions of the immigration law reflects the American ideal of family preservation and cohesiveness and therefore cannot be thought of as re-markable. In fiscal year 1997, 170,000 of the total 796,000 immigrants were the spouses of U.S. citizens, and 32,000 were the spouses of legal permanent residents—a total of more than one-quarter of all immigration. Among the spouses of U.S. citizens in 1997, 105,000 of the 170,000, or 61 percent, were women. A much higher proportion of the 32,000 spouses of legal permanent residents—28,000, or 87 percent—were women. In 1997, the total number of women directly immigrating through marriage was 132,000, or 66 percent of the spouses.

The INS has imposed two very specific rules to thwart attempts by individuals to involve themselves in fraudulent or fictitious marriages for the sake of immigration. One condition discussed earlier in this section is that the parties must meet within the two years before the fiancée petition. The other rule is that once an adjustment of status is conditionally approved, the parties who married must stay married for two years before the individual can be declared a permanent resident. An application to remove the threat of deportation is made six months prior to the expiration of the conditional green card.

The INS does, however, grant exceptions for women who can prove their new husbands are violent or abusive. The women may self-petition to remain in the United States. In fiscal year 1997, nearly twenty-five hundred self-petitions were filed with the INS, while more than thirty-three hundred self-petitions were filed by battered spouses or children in fiscal year 1998. The trend has been to accept and approve these petitions because there is an understanding and appreciation of the vulnerability and helplessness of the women involved. For two years, the American spouse holds the key to the successful immigration of the wife and the power to deport her. Most alien spouses who emigrate to the United States are from impoverished or disadvantaged backgrounds and stand on unequal footing with their American spouses. Many of these spouses latch on to a suitor who promises the world and delivers little. Advocates of the Violence Against Women Act (VAWA) of 1994 have closely monitored the situation of mail-order brides and their spouses. Recognizing the vulnerability of the women, these advocates have lobbied for the right of the women to self-petition for a status adjustment that would enable them to stay in the United States. As a result of the VAWA, the INS has been addressing some of the ways in which spousal abuse may be an immigration issue as much as it is a gender and a criminal justice issue. On March 26, 1996, the INS published interim regulations creating a self-petitioning process for battered spouses and children of U.S. citizens and legal permanent residents. The INS has been informing the public about the remedies that are available and informing INS workers about the extent and impact of domestic violence and its effect on victims. Although the number of battered spouses and children seeking relief through the self-petitioning process remains relatively low, it is clear from the dynamics of the mail-order bride industry that there is a strong possibility that the petitions will increase.

Linda J. Collier

See also: Human Smuggling and the Business of Illegal Immigration (Part II, Sec. 2); Ethnic Intermarriage, Family, Gender (Part II, Sec. 4).

BIBLIOGRAPHY

Basheda, Lori. "Wedded to Idea of U.S. Men." *The Orange County Register* (Santa Ana, CA), October 19, 1998: B1.

Bureau of Consular Affairs. *Visa Bulletin* 8:12 (1999). Washington, DC: Department of State.

Caldwell, Gillian. "Bought and Sold." Washington, DC: Global Survival Network, 1997.

Department of State. *Marriage of United States Citizens Abroad.* Travel Advisory. March 1998. Retrieved from Internet on January 5, 2000.

Glodava, Mila, and Richard Onizuka. *Mail-Order Brides: Women for Sale.* Fort Collins, CO: Alaken, Inc., 1994.

Immigration and Naturalization Service. *Annual Report: Legal Immigration, Fiscal Year 1998* 2 (May 1999). Washington, DC: Office of Policy and Planning, Statistics Branch.

———. *Report to Congress on "Mail-Order Bride" Businesses,* Congressional request under Section 652 of the Illegal Immigration Reform and Immigrant Responsibility Act of 1996 (IIRIRA), Washington, DC: Government Printing Office, 1999.

Meng, Eddy. "Mail Order Bride: Gilded Prostitution and the Legal Response." *University of Michigan Journal of Law Reform,* Fall (1994).

Mitchell, Charles. "For Love and Money, Russian Matchmakers Cater to American Men." Detroit Free Press/Knight-Ridder/Tribune News Service, October 6, 1994.

Scholes, Robert J. "AF ISO WM: How Many Mail-Order Brides?" *Immigration Review* 28, Spring (1997).

Sun, Lena H. "The Search for Miss Right Takes a Turn Toward Russia. 'Mail-Order Brides' of the '90s Are Met via Internet and on 'Romance Tours.'" *Washington Post,* March 8, 1998: A1.

Tizon, Alex, and Diedtra Henderson. "The World of the Mail-Order Matchmaker: Blackwells Met via Bellingham Bride Broker." *Seattle Times,* March 12, 1995: A1.

———. "Mail-Order Matchmaking Not Regulated." *Seattle Times,* March 12, 1995: A19.

SPONSORSHIP

Sponsorship is the act of recommending someone for entry (an alien beneficiary) into the United States and agreeing to maintain or support him or her by providing either financial subsidy or private employment. Employment-based immigration, or adjusting status through family-based preferences, is used to become a permanent resident or to acquire a green card.

To qualify as a sponsor, a person must be eighteen years of age or older, domiciled in the United States, and have an annual income of at least 125 percent of the federal poverty line. A sponsor who is on active duty in the Armed Forces and is petitioning for a spouse or child need only demonstrate an annual income of at least 100 percent of the federal poverty guidelines.

In the case of sponsorship, the Immigration and Naturalization Service (INS) places a numerical limitation on the number of alien beneficiaries seeking to immigrate to the United States who may qualify under this category. In 1999, the INS set the annual minimum family-sponsored preference limit at 226,000 persons, and the annual minimum employment-sponsored preference limit at 140,000. The law calculates the number of persons eligible to be admitted from each country by taking 7 percent of the total annual family-sponsored and employment-based preferences—25,620—and establishing the dependent area ceiling at 2 percent, or 7,320.

STATUS OF BENEFICIARIES

Family-sponsored preference visas accord the same status to both children and spouse and the same order of consideration is afforded the sponsor whom they are seeking to join. Each petition filed on behalf of a family member is handled in the order it is filed and received. Certain countries that are oversubscribed and have reached their per-country limit are subject to the allocation rules described by Section 202(e) of the Immigration and Naturalization Act.

THE SPONSOR'S PROMISE

A sponsor signs an affidavit ensuring the economic viability of his or her charge by swearing under oath that that he or she will support the alien beneficiary during times of hardship or financial difficulty. This promise serves as collateral to prevent the alien beneficiary from becoming a burden on the federal government or a public charge. As of December 19, 1997, all immediate relatives and family-based immigrants must have a sponsor fill out the Form I-864. Also, a sponsor is required for employment-based immigrants who are coming to work for a relative or for a company in which a relative owns 5 percent or more of the company.

To demonstrate current income at 125 percent of the poverty guideline and the ability to maintain the beneficiary at that level, petitioners must submit copies of their three most recent federal income tax returns or an explanation as to why returns have not been filed. If the petitioner is unable to submit the requisite copies of three filed tax returns, the INS will adjudicate the case based on the most recent tax return, current income and employment letters, and assets. Only assets that can readily be converted into cash within one year may be included. Evidence of assets may include bank statements covering the last year, evidence of ownership and value of stocks, bonds, and certificates of deposit, and evidence of ownership and value of other personal property or real estate. In order to be counted toward income requirements, the petitioner's assets, minus the petitioner's liabilities, must exceed five times the difference between the minimum poverty guideline requirements and the sponsor's household income.

The INS or consulate will look at the household size of the sponsor versus the amount of income shown. The numbers and exemptions will then be compared to a chart delineating the appropriate proportion of income to liabilities. If the number of all dependents and other aliens that may have been sponsored versus the income declared exceeds the minimal level, then the ability to sponsor is approved. If the income levels are below the required minimums, then the petition will be rejected unless the sponsor has enough additional assets, such as stocks, mutual funds, bank accounts, and the like, to prove to the INS that the sponsor has the ability to support the alien beneficiary. If the sponsor still cannot meet the required income or asset levels, the sponsor may find a joint sponsor to guarantee the support of the alien. The joint sponsor can be anyone who meets the criteria and is willing to provide an I-864 Affidavit of Support.

The immigration consequences of being labeled a "public charge" are very serious. A person likely to become a public charge in the United States is inadmissible and cannot become a legal permanent resident. Furthermore, anyone found to have become a public charge within five years of admission is subject to deportation.

The affidavit of support is enforced against the sponsor only if a sponsored individual receives any benefit under any means-tested public benefit program. The appropriate federal, state, or local agency may request reimbursement from the sponsor. If the sponsor fails to reimburse the agency or agree to a repayment plan, the agency may bring a court action against the sponsor based on the affidavit of support.

Sponsors must also notify the INS of changes of address within thirty days on Form 1-865. Failure to provide notice can result in fines of up to $2,000.

Although no single factor is determinative of whether a person has become a public charge, the INS looks at whether he or she is primarily dependent on the government for subsistence, receiving public cash assistance for income, or maintenance. Additional inquiries may consider whether the person has been institutionalized for long-term care at government expense, and their age, health, family status, assets, resources, financial status, education, and employment skills.

The Illegal Immigration Reform and Immigrant Responsibility Act of 1996 renders all support affidavits legally enforceable against the sponsor. This obligation continues until the immigrant becomes a citizen, or accrues forty qualifying quarters of work, whichever comes first.

FAMILY-SPONSORED PREFERENCES

Section 203 of the Immigration and Naturalization Act (INA) of 1965 describes four categories of family-sponsored preferences for American citizens and permanent residents seeking entry into the United States for their loved ones:

1. unmarried sons and daughters of citizens;
2. (A) spouses and children, and (B) unmarried sons and daughters of permanent residents;
3. married sons and daughters of citizens; and
4. brothers and sisters of adult citizens.

Also permitted without limitation are immediate family members of adult U.S. citizens such as parents and children born abroad to alien residents.

If visa allotments in any category remain undistributed, then they are added to the numbers in the succeeding categories. Seventy-seven percent of the overall limitation for the second family-based preference is reserved for the petitions for spouses and children. Twenty-three percent of the overall limitation is reserved for unmarried sons and daughters of permanent residents.

SPONSORING AN ALIEN SPOUSE

Although a petition may be filed under category 2A of Section 203 of the INA to sponsor a foreign spouse for entry into the United States, a foreign marriage does not necessarily guarantee the entry of an alien spouse. If a foreign marriage occurs, the American spouse must first file a Petition for Alien Relative. Once that is done, the petitioner may endure many months or even years of separation from his or her new spouse while the petition is approved and then finally processed at the foreign consulate abroad.

Another option available to an American spouse is the fiancé visa. American citizens can petition for a visa for alien fiancés to allow them admission to the United States for a ninety-day period to allow for them to prepare for their marriage and life together. The fiancé petition is generally completed in a much shorter time period than a spousal petition. Upon entry into the United States, the fiancé is permitted to remain for only ninety days, and the parties must marry within that ninety-day window or the alien fiancé must leave the United States. If marriage to the petitioner occurs, the married couple may then apply for adjustment of status to lawful permanent resident at the INS district office in their area. If the marriage does not occur and the fiancé returns to his or her home country within the ninety-day period, then the parties retain eligibility to pursue this option with other potential spouses in the future.

EMPLOYMENT-BASED PREFERENCES

There are five employment-based preference categories in which persons hoping to immigrate to the United States can have sponsors make application for them for permanent resident status. The first employment-based preference, under which about forty thousand visas are issued annually, is for priority workers. These workers include the following and do not require labor certification.

1. managers and executives subject to international transfer to the United States;

2. outstanding professors and researchers with universities or private employers with an established research department; and

3. aliens of extraordinary ability in the sciences, arts, education, business, and athletics.

The second employment-based preference, under which 40,000 visas are issued annually, plus those not used in the first preference, includes

1. aliens of exceptional ability in the sciences, arts, or business; and

2. professionals with advanced degrees.

These may come if they have acquired a labor certification and a job offer. This requirement may be eliminated if the immigrant qualifies for a "national interest" waiver. The approval of a national interest

waiver may allow an employment second-based preference worker to adjust status in the United States without having a job offer.

The third employment-based preference category, under which 40,000 visas are issued annually, plus those visas not used in the first and second preferences, may include:

1. professionals with bachelor's degrees not qualifying under the second preference;

2. skilled workers; and

3. unskilled workers with a labor certification and an offer of employment, but only 10,000 visas of the annual allotment may be assigned to unskilled workers.

The fourth employment-based preference concerns special immigrants, including religious workers, persons seeking reacquisition of citizenship, and returning residents.

The fifth employment-based preference includes at least three thousand visas issued annually to investors who can create jobs in targeted rural or high-unemployment areas.

Under the second and third categories, for which labor certification is required, employers must show that they attempted to find qualified American workers before the jobs they are seeking to fill can be offered to immigrants. This requires that the job be advertised for a period of time in either a newspaper or a professional journal. Once this search process is complete, documents verifying the quest are submitted to the Department of Labor, which investigates whether the employer has made a good-faith effort to find American workers who are willing, able, and qualified to do the job. Once the Department of Labor is satisfied that this has been done, it will approve the labor certification and permit the employer to fill the vacancy with an alien worker.

Linda J. Collier

See also: Family (Part II, Sec. 4); Professionals and the Brain Drain (Part II, Sec. 8); Science (Part II, Sec. 10); Immigration and Nationality Act, 1965, Illegal Immigration Reform and Immigrant Responsibility Act, 1996, Personal Responsibility and Work Opportunity Reconciliation Act, 1996, Amerasian Children Act, 1997 (Part IV, Sec. 1); Title IV: Restricting Welfare and Public Benefits for Aliens, 1996, Report on the Shortage of Technology Workers, 1997 (Part IV, Sec. 2).

BIBLIOGRAPHY

Bureau of Consular Affairs. *Visa Bulletin* VIII:12 (1999).

Department of State. "Immigrant Numbers for November 1999." *Visa Bulletin*. 3:12 (1999).

Fix, Michael, and Jeffrey S. Passel. *Immigration and Immigrants: Setting the Record Straight*, Washington, DC: Urban Institute, 1994. p. 25.

Siskind's Immigration Bulletin. "Border and Deportation News," June 1999.

U.S. Laws

8 CFR 1323

8 U.S.C. 551

8 U.S.C. 1185

TRANSIT AND TRANSPORTATION OF RECENT ILLEGAL IMMIGRANTS

The majority of people who emigrate to the United States initially arrive legally as visitors, students, or employees, by airplane, foot, ship, or vehicle, then overstay their visas and become illegal immigrants. Yet, in 1990, it was estimated that of the more than 3.3 million people believed to be illegally resident in this country, at least four of ten had migrated to the United States by subterfuge, deception, or concealment. These estimates include those being smuggled in on homemade boats, those brave enough to travel by inner tube or raft, and others who are smuggled into the United States in cargo holds by highly organized gangs on ships.

THE LAW AS IT RELATES TO THE TRANSPORT OF IMMIGRANTS

The Immigration and Nationality Act of 1965 makes it "unlawful for any person, including any transportation company, or the owner, master, commanding officer, agent, charterer, or consignee of any vessel or aircraft, to bring to the United States from any place outside thereof (other than from foreign contiguous territory) any alien who does not have a valid passport and an unexpired visa."

In addition, the act places an affirmative duty on all carriers—defined as "an individual or organization engaged in transporting passengers or goods for hire to the United States"—who transport passengers from foreign ports of embarkation to take reasonable steps to ensure that all passengers are documented and eligible to enter the United States. Failing to abide by this Immigration and Naturalization Service (INS) requirement, the carrier may be subject to certain fines and penalties.

It is the carrier's duty to screen each passenger and determine what, if any, documentation is required for his or her legal entry into the United States. If the passenger requires a visa, the carrier must determine if the holder, and any persons accompanying the holder, are the authorized users of the visa. And if the carrier suspects fraud, he must undertake a reasonable investigation to corroborate or dispel any inconsistencies.

Section 215 of the Immigration and Nationality Act states that "it shall be unlawful for any person to transport or attempt to transport from or into the United States another person with knowledge or reasonable cause to believe that the departure or entry of such other person is forbidden by this section." False statements, forged, counterfeit, mutilated, or altered documents supplied by another in an attempt to gain entry or permission to enter the United States are likewise punishable under immigration law. In some cases, when a conspiracy is alleged or implicated, violators have been tried and convicted under the applicable Racketeering Influenced Corrupt Organization statutes.

ENTRY BY BOAT

As early as 1607, with the arrival of English settlers in Jamestown, Virginia, people have been arriving by ship for purposes of emigrating to America. In 1980, the Mariel boatlift, a flotilla of a few hundred vessels and carriers, provided an illegal means of transportation for 124,000 undocumented Cubans to emigrate to the United States. The illegal contingent was interdicted by the Coast Guard and forced to turn back.

Undeterred by this history, in 1994, during a period of civil unrest, 63,000 Cubans and persons of Haitian descent took to the waters in a variety of vessels, only to be interdicted by the Coast Guard and sent back to their respective countries.

A combative Coast Guard attempted to interdict a raft carrying six Cubans in June 1999 by surrounding it and spraying it with a fire hose. Failing that, they attempted to use pepper spray on the immigrants. When the immigrants jumped from the boat and attempted to swim to shore, the Coast Guard attempted to block their passage. After all six were apprehended, they were detained for a short time and then permitted to stay in the United States.

In a desperate attempt to reach American shores in July 1999, one Cuban woman lost her life by drowning, when the boat in which she was traveling collided with a Coast Guard boat. Eleven other passengers traveling in the boat were also thrown into the water but survived.

On Thanksgiving Day in 1999, a five-year-old boy named Elian Gonzalez was rescued floating on an inner tube in the Atlantic Ocean after his mother and her brother drowned along with fourteen other persons making the perilous journey by raft from Cuba to Miami. Although the INS ordered the boy returned to his natural father in Havana, Cuba, relatives in Miami sparked furious protests in the United States and brought a custody petition to block his return to Cuba.

More than four hundred Haitians and Dominicans packed on a sixty-foot wooden boat were persuaded to abandon the boat once it ran aground in Biscayne Bay, Florida, on New Year's Day of 2000. The immigrants were transferred to smaller cutters, where they were to be detained until they could be returned to their countries of origin. It is believed that the Coast Guard turned back 363 Haitians and 406 Dominicans trying to reach the United States illegally by boat in 1999.

Regardless of safety, or futility, persons from the Dominican Republic are known to utilize a home-made fishing vessel known as a *yola* to traverse the body of water between the Dominican Republic and Puerto Rico called the Mona Passage. More than ninety-five hundred immigrants from the Dominican Republic were forced to return to their homeland in 1997 by the Coast Guard.

Smugglers take advantage of the desperation that often fuels migrants' desire to leave their country of origin. Paying between $20,000 and $40,000 per person, persons leaving the People's Republic of China often accept passage on overcrowded vessels with deplorable and unsanitary conditions. Some are commanded by Asian gang smugglers and others by shrewd businesspeople. Stowaways who make their way to the United States as cargo often spend the last leg of the journey in smaller boats for arrival at a U.S. port. Yet others are relegated to using their own feet or are transferred to a car to cross a land border into the United States.

Chinese stowaways have been discovered on ships docking at ports in California, Georgia, New York, New Jersey, Washington, and Michigan. The largest group of illegal Chinese immigrants was discovered in August 1999. The ship—the *Prince Nicholas*—has been deemed a modern-day slave ship because the 132 immigrants were found living in the bow of the ship, which had been outfitted with modern-day conveniences such as air conditioning, water, and electricity. The area housing the stowaways, known as the forepeak and generally used to store fresh water, or to hold a ballast tank that might hold sea water to keep the ship's nose level, was reconfigured into a maze of individual compartments to accommodate the stowaways. The space was divided into a number of 2-by-3-foot sections, and equipped with fans and electricity. Each compartment had a hole connecting each space, one to the next. Although the usable living space was more than 50 by 50 feet wide, the unusually large number of men made the space cramped and uncomfortable. Welded from the outside and bolted from the inside, it took the INS and Savannah (GA) firefighters equipped with the "Jaws of Life" several minutes to pry open the hatches and free the stowaways.

Prior to this voyage, only small numbers of Chinese immigrants are known to have been smuggled onto American soil. An undisclosed number of Chinese immigrants were left on the shores of New Jersey and the Bahamas in July 1998. Six Koreans and the ship's captain and mechanic were implicated and indicted in the smuggling plot. That incident was followed by the February 1999 arrival of eleven Chinese immigrants who were found in a cargo container in the bow of a ship at a port in Long Beach, California.

Twice in Seattle, Washington—once in June 1998 and again in April 1999—Chinese stowaways were discovered occupying a crate left on a ship docked at the Port of Tacoma. Although authorities were unsure how the nineteen stowaways had survived the harrowing, three-week journey from China to Seattle, it was clear that someone had specifically equipped the 40-by-8-foot crate for human cargo because it was outfitted with a fabric top, making it easier for the stowaways to breathe.

Not all stowaways receive such careful assistance when planning their journey abroad. On a cargo ship flying a Singapore flag, three stowaways were found dead in a sealed hold. A fourth man was found alive hidden elsewhere on the ship. It is believed that the aliens had concealed themselves on the ship during a stop in Abidjan, Nigeria, and were apparently overcome by fumes before its arrival in New York.

On Memorial Day weekend of 1999, the Coast Guard seized three boats off the coast of San Diego.

In one of the incidents, one passenger swam ashore seeking help for the seven other passengers in his boat, because the boat was sinking and none of the other passengers could swim. A lifeguard rescued the seven other men. While he was calling the sheriff's department to fill out a report on the incident, all eight of the men ran away.

A number of deadly excursions have been made through the All-American Canal in southern California. In 1999, the American Canal was the scene of more than seventeen fatalities. One fatality in June 1999 resulted when three migrants attempting to navigate the waters in a raft were interdicted by the Border Patrol. A Border Patrol officer fired a pellet gun at the raft and caused it to capsize. Although two of the rafters made it to shore unharmed, the third was never found, despite an intensive manhunt.

INS agents in Detroit, Michigan, boarded a Panamanian freighter bound for Chicago, where they discovered twenty-two stowaways from the Dominican Republic. Three aliens had already jumped ship in Trois-Rivières, Canada, complaining that they had not eaten for nine days and that some of the other aliens had turned violent. After the discovery, authorities found that the stowaways had been kept in an 18-by-20-foot room without windows, but they did have access to a bathroom. The ship owners were fined $10,000 per stowaway and assessed the costs for detention and return of the stowaways.

ENTRY BY VEHICLE

Illegal aliens are smuggled by vehicle across the U.S. border in places that border Mexico and Canada. In early 1999, police engaged in a harrowing two-hour chase in an attempt to stop a van carrying fifteen undocumented immigrants in San Diego County. And although the INS attempted to pull the van over on Interstate 10, it hastily sped away. Spike strips placed in the roadway to puncture the van's tires failed twice to stop the driver. After giving more chase, police were finally able to stop the van and apprehend the driver and all but one of his passengers.

In April 1999, the Arizona segment of the Border Patrol captured more than 47,000 undocumented immigrants crossing from Mexico, down from a total of more than 65,500 in March. Poor living conditions in Central America as a result of Hurricane Mitch in October 1998 are believed to be the reason for the 30 percent increase over the numbers in April 1998, when about 38,600 were apprehended.

Every so often a routine traffic stop leads to the discovery of illegal aliens. Such a stop in Missouri led to the discovery of fourteen undocumented Hispanics. Although the local sheriff's deputy who made the stop contacted the INS, it was unable to take custody of the men because it had no way to transport them or a safe location in which to house them.

Thirty-four illegal immigrants were discovered concealed in the rear of a U-haul truck as it made its way across the Mexican border into El Centro, California, in the spring of 1996. The truck sped away as the Border Patrol attempted to stop it. Chasing the truck at speeds of more than 75 miles per hour, the California Highway Patrol joined the Border Patrol in the chase, which took the agencies more than 200 miles through three counties. Once the immigrants were taken into custody by the INS, it was disclosed that they had paid $300 each for a ride in the truck.

A 1998 Ford pickup served as a mode of transportation for twenty-five illegal immigrants in Corpus Christi, Texas, in the spring of 1998. Together with the Border Patrol, the Brook's County Sheriff's Department gave chase for two hours in an attempt to stop the vehicle. Once the vehicle was interdicted, all passengers scattered. Within six minutes, ten of the twenty-five illegal immigrants had been corralled and captured. The remaining fifteen have still not been caught.

ENTRY BY RAIL

Although illegal immigrants have taken the liberty of hitching a ride with an unknowing commercial trucker on occasion, illegal aliens find more success in stowing away in a railway car. Peeling away open trailers or aluminum containers on rail cars often provides illegal immigrants with a way to gain safe passage across the U.S. border with minimal chance of detection. A Union Pacific spokesperson explained that sophisticated smugglers often use counterfeit or stolen seals on containers, to ensure that containers with human cargo are not opened. In some cases stowaways avoid detection by running out of a compartment as they feel the car slow at a checkpoint and reentering the railway car at another compartment as the train moves on again.

For swift and speedy transportation, there are numerous freight train carriers and countless passenger trains, which traverse more than a hundred thousand miles of rails that criss-cross the country. Railroad cars provide a prime opportunity for unsophisticated immigrants to make their way cross-country and cover many miles with little money and no discernible plan. Secreted in the boxcar of a freight train, immigrants can travel anonymously and freely. Far fewer immigrants travel by passenger train than by freight, because passenger trains are costly methods of travel.

Linda J. Collier

See also: Human Smuggling and the Business of Illegal Immigration (Part II, Sec. 2).

BIBLIOGRAPHY

Associated Press. "3 Stowaways Die in Cargo Hold on US-Bound Ship." *New Times National News,* March 19, 1996.

———. U-Haul Truck with Dozens of Illegal Immigrants Chased 200 Miles. March 6, 1996. 10 Illegal Immigrants Captured after Officials Chase Pickup for Two Hours. From the Internet at Corpus Christi News, March 2, 1998.

———. "Boat Packed with Haitians and Dominicans Runs Aground." *Burlington Free Press,* January 2, 2000, A1.

Coast Guard. "Alien Migrant Interdiction" http:www.uscg.mil/hq/g-o/g-opl/mle/AMIO.htm, October 23, 1999.

Department of State. "Immigrant Numbers for November 1999." *Visa Bulletin* 3:12 (1999).

Fix, Michael, and Jeffrey S. Passel. *Immigration and Immigrants: Setting the Record Straight,* 25. Washington, DC: Urban Institute, 1994.

Gold, Jeffrey. "Ship's Captain and Mechanic Convicted of Alien Smuggling." Associated Press, December 3, 1998.

Reed-Ward, Paula. "Chinese Aliens Found Hiding on Ship Docked in Savannah," *Savannah Morning News* on the Web, http://www.savannahmorningnews.com, August 13, 1999.

Siskind's Immigration Bulletin. "Border and Deportation News," June 1999.

———. *"Cuban Migrants Fight Coast Guard to Reach Florida,"* July/August 1999.

Trucker's Electronic Newspaper. "US Says Truck Stowaways Not Much of a Problem," http://www.ttnews/members/printEdition/0001158.html, October 29, 1999.

Wilson, Melinda. "22 Stowaways Found off Detroit." *Detroit News,* August 25, 1998.

U.S. LAWS

8 CFR 1323

8 U.S.C. 551

8 U.S.C. 1185

TRANSNATIONALISM: IMMIGRATION FROM A GLOBAL PERSPECTIVE

Since the late 1960s, United States immigration trends have become markedly different from those at the beginning of the century. Immigration waves of the late nineteenth and early twentieth centuries were largely comprised of European emigrants. The newly arrived Europeans were expected to become part of mainstream North American society by assimilating into the nation's society, culture, and politics. As a result of the enactment of the Immigration Act of 1965, immigration patterns shifted from European migrations toward those involving the emigration of people from Latin America, the Caribbean, and Asia. Today, rather than assimilating, the new immigrants, who are often bilingual, live their lives in the United States and in their home country, immersing themselves in two societies simultaneously. They often have homes, families, friends, and associates here and there; some have allegiance to two nations through dual citizenship. Because of the here-there quality of their lives, today's immigrants are often referred to by scholars as "transmigrants."

The new immigrants economically and emotionally support themselves and a plethora of others through a variety of employment, investment, communication, and social strategies. Global social, economic, and political changes, state-of-the-art technology, electronic mail and commerce, as well as affordable airfare enable today's immigrants to the United States to maintain social, economic, and political ties with their homeland. Businesses such as international phone centers, money transfer and shipping companies, courier services, and travel agencies have been established in and around immigrant enclaves to facilitate transnational ties and transactions. Immigrant entrepreneurs set up small businesses in the American cities and suburbs in which they settle, selling such ethnic commodities as groceries and newspapers and offering services that cater to the needs of the immigrant population. Through individual or collective efforts, entrepreneurial or state-sponsored enterprises, immigrants create transnational networks within which people, money, commodities, ideas, information and countless other resources flow. The media have reported on the gist of this, thus adding to the growing public awareness of the new immigration trends, but they have merely touched on the theoretical underpinning of this phenomenon, which in academic parlance is called "transnationalism." Since the late 1980s, transnationalism has been developing as a theory across social science disciplines in general and in international migration studies in particular.

Money plays a key role in transnationalism, linking people across national borders and creating webs of social obligations and dependencies. Money is also a catalyst for the political manipulation and maneuvering of emigrant subjects by the state; conversely, it is leverage used by those subjects to bargain with the state. In the global economy, the movement of people, labor, and money has resulted in a paradoxical situation, the fluidity of class and status relations, and the deepening social stratification. An economic perspective is merely one approach that discloses a myriad of social, cultural, and political interconnections inherent in transnational relations. Yet, because transnationalism has now become an intrinsic characteristic in the international labor system of the global economy, economic considerations are of prime importance.

TRANSNATIONALISM THEORY

In recent decades social sciences in general and anthropology in particular moved beyond bounded, temporally static, ahistoric studies toward research accentuating identity, power, and history in a global context. Much of this research cited, expanded, critiqued, or diverted from global theory. Global theory and its development often are traced to Immanuel Wallerstein's perspective on the origins of capitalism known as world-system economic theory. Wallerstein argued that capitalism is organized on a global, rather than national, basis. It is differentiated by spheres of influence in which economically and politically peripheral and semiperipheral countries are economically dependent on the hegemonic core. Globalization developed as a rubric subsuming disparate paradigms and modes of analyses for the movement of people, capital, knowledge, and culture. One such paradigm to emerge was that of transnationalism, which is nestled inside the multidimensional theory of globalization. Michael Kearney observed that transnationalism overlaps globalization but has a more limited purview and noted that global processes are decentered from specific nations. In transnational processes, the nation and the state are implicit; territorial, social, economic, political, and cultural aspects of a nation are shaped by the nation through its policies and institutions but transcend one or more nation-state. This notion is at the core of new migration studies that emphasize the movement and settlement of nationals across multiple national borders.

Contemporary migration studies have long abandoned former paradigms such as those that examined the success or failure of immigrants' adaptation to United States society. Concepts of the nation and the movement and settlement of people and borders have been reworked, yielding new models that link migration to global capitalism and nation building. With the advent of technological advances, time and space have been reconceptualized. A number of theorists began thinking about the transnational process in the late 1980s. Notable among those who have been instrumental in devising a new transnational framework in migration studies are Nina Glick-Schiller, Linda Basch, and Cristina Szanton-Blanc. In the late 1980s, they observed transnational practices in their respective anthropological fieldwork, began to speak and write about the phenomena, and set about to popularize the term "transnationalism" as part of their project to rethink international migration. They were organizers of a May 1990 conference aimed at analyzing transnational migration, formulating research questions, and developing a revised analytic framework. They also served as editors of *Towards a Transnational Perspective on Migration*, a compilation of the 1990 conference papers. In *Nations Unbound*, Basch, Glick-Schiller, and Szanton-Blanc defined transnationalism as "the process by which immigrants forge and sustain multi-stranded social relations that link together their societies of origin and settlement." They used the term transnationalism to signify the fluidity

with which ideas, objects, capital, and people move across boundaries and borders. The authors outlined a framework that situated migration within a global history and highlighted the agency of transmigrants. With their paradigm they examined migration within processes related to the changing conditions of global capitalism, the creation of social fields by transmigrants that cross national boundaries, the deconstruction of boundaries, and the nation-building processes of two or more nations.

In the ensuing years, researchers have augmented the early works of the pioneering researchers on transnationalism and utilized the newly developed transnationalism paradigms. Delmos Jones assessed the theoretical approaches, conceptualizations, and arguments made by the contributors to the May 1990 conference on transnationalism. He perceived the following conditions as inherent in transnationalism: First, migrants maintain ties to their country of origin and home society. Families, particularly extended families, remain functional across national boundaries; communications technology facilitates these processes. Second, transmigrants often do not establish permanent residency in the host society. Third, migrants seek upward mobility; migrants working in Western cities aim to improve their status in their home country. And, finally, migrants are important to their home country.

In 1999, Steven Vertovec made an assessment of the recent works on transnationalism. While noting that the disparate works presented a confusing array of perspectives, he uncovered some common ground in transnational studies and found that the meaning of transnationalism has been established on the following conceptual premises: First, the meaning of transnationalism involves structures or relationships spanning borders. Second, transnational migrations or diasporas create a "diaspora consciousness" that is marked by dual or multiple identities motivated by decentered attachments, a here-there or a multilocality awareness, or re-created identities. Third, transnationalism is associated with the production of hybrid cultural phenomena found in quotidian practices, social institutions, and styles. Transnational flows in the global media and electronic communications, such as satellite and cable networks, e-mail, and the Internet, facilitate this hybridity. Fourth, there exists a realm of global capitalism in which "big players" and "little players" engage in financial activities within global structures. The big players include the transnational corporations (TNC) and global elites comprised of TNC executives, state bureaucrats, and wealthy investors and consumers who operate on the global stage. The little players, through their remittances, transfer billions of dollars on which their kin and country depend. Fifth, transnationalism is a site for the articulation and implementation of transnational political activities. This incorporates transnational campaigning by political parties from home nations within a receiving country; resource distributors such as international nongovernmental organizations; and lobbying by transnational social movement organizations effecting global change in human rights, the environment, world peace, women's rights, and development. Finally, transnationalism has changed people's relation to space; some researchers have posited that social fields link actors, whereas others have argued that international migration has eroded social relationships.

Other scholars, in particular the anthropologist Nancy Foner, have challenged the very notion that transnationalism is a new phenomenon. Her research has shown that transnational activities, such as the maintenance of social ties through letters and monetary remittances, the financing of chain migration, return trips, and remigration, and political participation, were carried out by people of earlier immigration waves. The salient features that distinguish today's phenomenon from the past is that late-twentieth-century technology has compressed time and space, making the transfer and exchange of conversation, sentiments, knowledge, capital, and material goods minimal if not immediate.

Others have critiqued specific aspects of the transnational framework established to date. Alejandro Portes, Luis E. Guarnizo, and Patricia Landolt criticized transnational studies, writing that they are "highly fragmented," that the field "lacks both a well-defined theoretical framework and analytic rigor," and that the research narratives "often use disparate units of analysis." The authors redefined transnationalism by limiting the phenomenon to sustained social contacts and excluding such sporadic activities as occasional remittances, contacts, and trips. They give primacy to the individual and his or her support networks as the proper unit of analysis. Guarnizo and Michael Peter Smith suggest that the main concern for guiding transnational research should involve the study from above and below. As Sarah J. Mahler points out, "transnationalism from above" places emphasis on macrolevel structures and processes which are controlled by power elites and which transcend national boundaries, for example, transnational corporations, global media, and commodification. "Transnationalism from below" emphasizes the transnational activities of nonelites, that is, of "ordinary" transmigrants.

Transnationalism has encompassed an array of

perspectives. In general, any migration study with a here-there component is considered a transnational study, provided it contains the requisite citation of transnational theory as a starting point for its theoretical and contextual trajectory. As a result, the literature is disparate and might theoretically appear confusing or fragmented. But transnationalism itself is diverse and fragmented; by its very nature, it is simultaneously local and global, and it connects and disconnects. The process of international migration is highly heterogeneous due to the tremendous diversification of international migration, a process that is influenced by an enormous array of human, economic, political, social, spatial, and temporal factors. Introduce the concept of global capitalism into the study of migration, and the complexity increases exponentially.

TRANSNATIONALISM IN AN ECONOMIC CONTEXT

As most analysts of transnationalism point out, the relations between capital and labor and the changing conditions of global capitalism appear to be a common analytic premise in the field. This perspective follows the money and, by doing so, is certain to illuminate the agency of individuals; global structures, such as the state and worldwide institutions; and the causes and consequences of social, cultural, and political relationships. And this approach undoubtedly illustrates the economic inequities and social hierarchies inherent in capitalism and transmigrant activities. Yet even exploring the economic aspect of transnationalism is a complex task. It entails examining the structural aspects of global capitalism and the financial strategies—from survival to mega-investment—utilized by individuals within a range of economic classes who migrate from or to peripheral and semiperipheral countries to countries in the core.

The starting point for the discussion of economic transnationalism will begin with remittances. In migration studies, remittances can take several forms, ranging from noneconomic or sociocultural remittances to economic ones. In theorizing about social remittances, Peggy Levitt notes that they can include "ideas, behaviours, identities, and social capital that flow from receiving- to sending-country communities." Economic remittances involve the transmission of capital and are oriented toward global, regional, local, and family economic spheres. Social and economic remittances operate simultaneously in transnational affairs; both are significant at multiple levels.

For cash-poor countries, economic remittances may be the means by which a country keeps its economy afloat. Remittances supply foreign exchange and hard currency, provide liquidity for cash-deficient governments, assist in servicing debt, and have a favorable impact on the balance of payments. Money from remittances can enable a nation's economic agents to import basic consumer goods, raw materials for production, and food items. The importation of food items is often a consequence of farmers emigrating and leaving behind arable land that is no longer utilized, or it can be a result of changing consumption patterns influenced by transmigrants. For migrant households, remittances at the least provide income to purchase basic necessities for subsistence living and consequently improve the standard of living; remittances are often a substitute for state-funded welfare systems. Economic remittances create important linkages that involve a network of obligations between family members at home and abroad and provide the means for family networks to operate despite the spatial separation. Remittances often compensate family members who act as caretakers for a migrant's family and house back home. Immigrants also use remittances to invest in their economic future by building better or second houses in their country of origin, or they use the money to expand or start local businesses or to upgrade agricultural technology on their family farm. Some of this latter activity supports the local economy. Also, immigrants use remittances to invest in their own social status; they contribute to hometown associations, cooperatives, and such community projects as building schools, churches, and potable water systems, or they initiate capital ventures at home.

Charles B. Keely and Bao Nga Tran noted that the global phenomenon of labor migration has given rise to both a positive and a negative view of worker remittances and their consequences for economic development. A negative assessment posits that remittances increase the dependency of the sending country because it becomes reliant on a market that it does not control and can influence only minimally. Remittances contribute to economic and political instability because workforce demands are subject to swings; remittances will drop when labor power demands in receiving countries decline or when families join the worker in the receiving country. Also, remittances destroy the economic development of the sending country because they are spread over hundreds of thousands of households within which decisions are made about the money. It is assumed by the negativists that money is spent on newly desired imported luxury consumer goods; this increases local demand so that wages are pushed up and inflation increases. Conversely, a positive view suggests that remittances undeniably serve the interests of transmigrants and their families and the government. Studies in this camp show that remittances are spent not on wasteful consumption but on basic needs, health care, and education, all of which result in improved standards of living for migrant households and a higher standard in comparison with nonmigrant households. Governments realize gains in access to hard currency and public income and benefit from labor force absorption. In evaluating dependency, a positive perspective would view labor similar to other commodities in the market; while unequal exchange is inherent in the market, labor-exporting countries have some leverage in the market and must exercise skill in anticipating and adjusting to market forces.

Putting this in context, Nina Glick-Schiller and Georges E. Fouron have found that Haitians living and working in the United States continue to send remittances year after year and therefore sustain broad networks of people that include close kin and those they hardly know, as well as old friends and neighbors. Remittances are often a burden on those who remit. But as workers in an insecure labor market in the United States, Haitian immigrants send remittances and invest their earnings in property, businesses, and social relations back home as an economic strategy in which they hedge their bets about their economic future in the United States. The significant purchasing power of U.S. dollars in Haiti enables economic possibilities that are unmatched in the states. Also, Haitian immigrants view Haiti, a culture that respects the elderly, as a place to which they can return in old age or if they become disabled, where family and friends will care for them. After retirement, an immigrant returning with a steady and secure pension or Social Security income would be considered a person of substance. Remittances often elevate the status of Haitian immigrants who are marginalized because of race in the United States; when Haitians return for home visits, they are treated as visiting dignitaries.

While remittances are both a burden and an insurance policy for Haitian immigrants, they are essential to native Haitians and the government. Glick-Schiller and Fouron report that the average monthly remittance of $100 by 90 percent of the Haitian immigrants often makes the difference between life and death for residents of a country with a 45 percent unemployment rate and a 50 percent malnutrition rate. By 1980, remittances exceeded what Haiti garnered in foreign exchange, therefore making them crucial to the Haitian economy.

Steven Vertovec noted that the collective remittances of $75 billion sent by the "little players" to their countries of origin have made a huge impact on a global scale during the last thirty years. Citing 1995 World Bank figures, he explains that "in Algeria, the value of remittances climbed from $178 million in 1970 to $993 million in 1993; in India, from $80 million in 1970 to over $3 billion in 1993; and in Egypt, from $29 million in 1970 to nearly $5 billion in 1993." It is evident that national economies of many capital-poor countries rely heavily on remittances from nationals abroad. Conversely, regional economies in host countries have benefited from the surge in businesses that support social and monetary remittances sent by transmigrants. In a 1998 article on the new immigrants in the *New York Times*, Deborah Sontag and Celia W. Dugger investigated the money transfer activities in the region. They garnered statistics from the New York State Banking Department which indicated that since 1988 the number of companies licensed to send money increased by 40 percent; these companies had approximately two thousand storefronts and agents. While not successful in ascertaining the total estimate of immigrants' remittances in the New York area, reporters secured figures provided by local money transfer companies. The authors reported that "Body Express says it transfers about $1 million a year to Haiti; Habib Exchange sends about $6 million a year to India, Pakistan and Bangladesh; Pekao Trading wires about $320 million a year to Poland."

Economic remittances are intertwined with social and political forces and serve varying interests within a broad spectrum of constituencies from poor immigrants to international elites to nation-states. State involvement, influence, and manipulation are not unusual in transnational economic, political, and social spheres. Sarah Mahler provided an apt example of a state's manipulation to preserve the practice of remittances by emigrants. In 1994, 200,000 Salvadorans in the United States were at risk of deportation due to the expiration of their Temporary Protected Status. The El Salvador government claimed that returning immigrants would be prosecuted. Yet, it simultaneously provided legal aid and assistance to immigrants applying for political asylum in the United States in an attempt to prolong their stay abroad. This strategy was devised to ensure the continuation of remittances estimated at approximately $1 billion annually which was hundreds of millions of dollars more than the country's export earnings. Because El Salvador had recently emerged from a civil war and was not receiving much international aid to rebuild in the aftermath, loss of remittances could have destabilized the country.

Many countries rely on the collective remittances of hundreds of thousands of individual poor and middle-class immigrants, while other countries depend on middle-class and elite immigrants to boost their economic infrastructure and international image. Basch, Glick-Schiller, and Szanton-Blanc provided cases in which various governments have tried to convince immigrants, despite their limited capital, to invest in development plans in agricultural export crops, industry, and tourism. For example, former Haitian president Jean-Bertrand Aristide identified the Haitian transnational population as "the bank of the diaspora," which was grandiosely earmarked as a source for building an independent economic base. The Haitian government led by Aristide's successor advertised through immigrant organizations the sale of bonds in such development projects as a milk factory. And the Philippine government targeted its relatively wealthy constituency to invest in shrimp farming for international export. Immigrants often view home projects with skepticism, and some projects have proven financially unsound. Nevertheless, expatriates play the government courting strategy to their advantage. Filipino and Caribbean migrants have petitioned for greater incorporation into the political systems of their home country. For instance, Filipino migrants have requested dual citizenship, voting rights, the right to own land on a foreign passport, and the opportunity to run for elective office in the Philippines.

India provides the archetype for a government's courting of moneyed immigrants. Johanna Lessinger demonstrated how educated and professional Asian Indian expatriates who are now settled in the United States, Europe, Southeast Asia, and the Middle East are emerging as a new transnational business class. This is due largely to the restructuring of the global economy in the last decade. India has come under pressure from the international market to shift from protectionist to open market policies. As a result, India has liberalized its foreign investment laws; consequently, foreign investment has become attractive and advantageous to nonresident Indians (popularly called NRIs). The government sought investments from its 10 million immigrants, especially those living in the United States and Europe. Immigrants' education and management and technical expertise gave rise to employment and income opportunities abroad, enabling them to amass disposable income available for investment. Beginning in the 1980s and until 1991, NRIs were treated as a favored subcategory of the foreign investor; they were granted exemption from many of the tight investment restrictions imposed by India. They were given governmental assistance to set up new industries, become partners in existing firms, acquire raw materials, borrow start-up money, and find coinvestors and were encouraged to invest their savings in Indian banks. The total value of their investments in assorted industries from 1984 to 1988 was approximately $240 million. Economically, direct investment by NRIs has made an enormous impact on India's industrial growth; however, the jury is still out on its long-term success. Yet, these direct investments have yielded sustained employment opportunities, increased living standards, and enhanced the social status for investors' kin employed in NRI firms. And NRIs' savings deposits of $10 billion to $12 billion have assisted in maintaining India's precarious foreign currency reserves and helped to finance India's foreign imports. From a social standpoint, NRI investment has both positive and negative social consequences. Investment assuages the guilt immigrants might have about leaving India, and business ventures provide an incentive to return to India in the future. However, investments by elite expatriates further polarized existing class relations within India and initiated a growing hostility among the indigenous business elite. Also, it created a definite class stratification within the Indian immigrant community in the United States.

India's NRIs are merely one elite class being formed as a result of the restructuring of global capitalism. Aihwa Ong's study profiled the transpacific Chinese capitalist class. The educational, emigration, and investment strategies of capital-bearing, middle-class, upper-class, and mega-wealthy Hong Kong immigrants to California provided the foundations for self-made Chinese entrepreneurs. Since the mid-1970s, people from Hong Kong have invested in San Francisco's Bay Area real estate through a variety of schemes devised to minimize taxes and maximize profits. Middle-class investors operated on a comparatively modest scale and bought homes; others invested in shops and apartment and office buildings worth from $1 to $25 million. The extremely wealthy investors, which included Hong Kong's top sixty business families, whose capital holdings were estimated at over $400 million each, invested in such long-term ventures as Bay Area urban renewal projects and suburban developments. Companies and owners located primarily in Hong Kong made much of the latter investments through intermediaries. Overseas Chinese investments were estimated to range from $2 to $10 billion throughout California.

Yet it is not just the educated technical and professional elite who make transnational business deals. Patricia Landolt, Lillian Autler, and Sonia Baires mapped the commerce of tiny, small, and medium-size transnational enterprises that conduct business between El Salvador and Salvadoran settlements in Los Angeles and Washington, D.C. The researchers identified five types of enterprises that maintain important transnational links. They are circuit enterprises, cultural enterprises, ethnic enterprises, microenterprises (very low capitalization) by return immigrants, and transnational expansion enterprises. Microentrepreneurs are the most prolific and vulnerable group of capitalists from El Salvador. This group includes those who eke out a living as *viajeros* shuttling between El Salvador and the United States delivering money, letters, gifts, and consumer goods; distributors of ethnic newspapers and radio and TV programming; and small business owners operating groceries, restaurants, bakeries, beauty shops, and so on. And it includes those returning to El Salvador who utilize the savings they earned and skills they learned abroad to open small business ventures at home. The precarious nature of these latter businesses forces the returning migrant entrepreneurs to return regularly to wagework in the United States. In some of these ventures, significant investments are made in El Salvador and the United States, binding various settlements in the two countries through economic ties.

FLUIDITY OF CLASS AND STATUS IN THE TRANSNATIONAL TERRAIN

A close scrutiny of each of the aforementioned studies would reveal the agency of actors and the structural forces played out on a particular social, cultural, and political terrain. Yet an economic perspective is remiss without mention of the inequities and the fluidity of class and status in the transnational terrain. Blatant inequities among nations exist; I have shown how capital-poor countries are dependent on remittances earned in core countries. Also, Gerald Sider has argued that receiving countries benefit not only from the extraction of surplus value by productive workers but also do so without bearing educational costs. He wrote that working-class transnational migration "is specifically and necessarily a process of sucking value out of migrant's home countries and transferring that value to the host country." Noting that sending countries bear the cost of reproducing a human labor force until it reaches working age, they further incur the additional costs when immigrants return home sick, broken, or old to be cared for by their kin.

In transnational migration, class and status are

malleable and sometimes are transformed particularly for those whose occupational skills are mismatched in new labor situations. Immigrants experience shifts in social positions, either upward or downward, which consequently affect their social and occupational power and prestige. Unemployment, misemployment, and racial, ethnic, and sexual discrimination in the international labor market are factors that can induce alterations of social class and status. Rural farming immigrants with extremely low levels of education, English proficiency, and occupational skills now find themselves as service sector laborers among the urban working poor. Educated middle-class professionals are working double or triple shifts as domestics, garment workers, janitors, gardeners, construction workers, and a plethora of low-skilled and low-wage jobs in the host country. Yet, some returning immigrants who have worked these jobs and steadfastly invested in the social and economic infrastructures at home elevated their status in their home country. Others who have experienced downward occupational mobility due to lack of skills or discrimination in the host country carved out niches for themselves in the formal, informal, and ethnic labor markets, hence regaining their status and financial position as local or transnational entrepreneurs. For example, Pyong Gap Min observed that Korean male immigrants to New York who are generally highly educated but lack English proficiency are relegated to self-employment or blue-collar positions in the ethnic economy. He found that some Korean men who are dissatisfied with their downward mobility have returned to Korea for greater occupational and financial opportunities and begin a "commuter marriage," shuttling back and forth to their "transnational family" for business trips or personal visits. This arrangement is far from novel; circular immigrant labor is characteristic of capitalism. But the professional and technical class is increasingly adopting this practice, particularly as transnational corporations proliferate, setting up factories and offices to facilitate worldwide operations. This has given rise to a new class of business elites, technocrats, bureaucrats, and entrepreneurs.

Transnational entrepreneurship, which is wide ranging in character, is differentially constructed along economic and status lines. Yet successful participation in the market as an entrepreneur does not correlate with social acceptance. Landolt, Autler, and Baires have found that Salvadoran entrepreneur membership in Washington, D.C., business associations is largely absent, and it is negligible in the local Hispanic business associations, which are dominated by more affluent and established Hispanics such as Cubans and Venezuelans. Aihwa Ong wrote that wealthy Hong Kong immigrants face discrimination in their attempts to break into the highest social circles in California. She noted that in the transnational racial hierarchy, the California upper class perceives the Chinese as second-class world citizens despite their money and education.

An economic perspective is one entrée into the study of the multifaceted process of transnationalism, a highly diverse phenomenon in both theory and fact. Transnational theory and studies include social, economic, and political linkages; the movement and fluidity of tangible and intangible resources across national boundaries; the influence of the changing conditions of global capitalism on international migration, and the here-there aspect associated with migration and settlement.

Terese Lawinski

See also: Return Migration (Part II, Sec. 3); Segmented Assimilation (Part II, Sec. 4); Immigrant Politics III: The Home Country (Part II, Sec. 6).

BIBLIOGRAPHY

Basch, Linda, Nina Glick-Schiller, and Cristina Szanton-Blanc. *Nations Unbound: Transnational Projects, Postcolonial Predicaments, and Deterritorialized Nation-States.* Australia: Gordon and Breach Publishers, 1994.

Bohning, W. R. "Elements of a Theory of International Economic Migration to Industrial Nation States." In *Global Trends in Migration*, ed. Mary M. Kritz, Charles B. Keely, and Silvano M. Tomasi, pp. 28–43. New York: Center for Migration Studies of New York, 1981.

Foner, Nancy. "What's New about Transnationalism? New York Immigrants Today and at the Turn of the Century." *Diaspora* 6:3 (1997):355–75.

Glick-Schiller, Nina, and Georges E. Fouron. "Terrains of Blood and Nation: Haitian Transnational Social Fields." In *Ethnic and Racial Studies* 22:2 (1999): 340–66.

Glick-Schiller, Nina, Linda Basch, and Cristina Blanc-Szanton. "Towards a Definition of Transnationalism: Introductory Remarks and Research Questions." In *Towards a Transnational Perspective on Migration: Race, Class, Ethnicity, and Nationalism Reconsidered*, ed. Nina Glick-Schiller, Linda Basch, and Cristina Blanc-Szanton, ix–xiv. New York: Annals of the New York Academy of Sciences, 1992.

———. "Transnationalism: A New Analytic Framework for Understanding Migration." In *Towards a Transnational Perspective on Migration: Race, Class, Ethnicity, and Nationalism Reconsidered*, ed. Nina Glick-Schiller, Linda Basch, and Cristina Szanton-Blanc, 1–24. New York: Annals of the New York Academy of Sciences, 1992.

Guarnizo, Luis Eduardo, and Michael Peter Smith. "The Locations of Transnationalism." In *Transnationalism from Below*, ed. Michael

Peter Smith and Luis Eduardo Guarnizo, 6:1–31. New Brunswick, N.J.: Transaction Publishers, 1998.

Jones, Delmos. "Which Migrants? Temporary or Permanent." In *Towards a Transnational Perspective on Migration: Race, Class, Ethnicity, and Nationalism Reconsidered*, ed. Nina Glick-Schiller, Linda Basch, and Cristina Blanc-Szanton, pp. 217–24. New York: Annals of the New York Academy of Sciences, 1992.

Kearney, Michael. "The Local and the Global: The Anthropology of Globalization and Transnationalism." In *Annual Review of Anthropology* 24 (1995):547–65.

Keely, Charles B., and Bao Nga Tran. "Remittances from Labor Migration: Evaluations, Performance, and Implications. In *International Migration Review*. 23:3 (1989): 500–52.

Landolt, Patricia, Lillian Autler, and Sonia Baires. "From Hermano Lejano to Hermano Mayor: The Dialectics of Salvadoran Transnationalism. In *Ethnic and Racial Studies* 22:2 (1999): 290–315.

Lessinger, Johanna. "Investing or Going Home? A Transnational Strategy among Indian Immigrants in the United States." In *Towards a Transnational Perspective on Migration: Race, Class, Ethnicity, and Nationalism Reconsidered*, ed. Nina Glick-Schiller, Linda Basch, and Cristina Blanc-Szanton, pp. 53–80. New York: Annals of the New York Academy of Sciences, 1992.

Levitt, Peggy. "Social Remittances: Migration Driven Local-Level Forms of Cultural Diffusion." In *International Migration Review* 32: 4 (1998): 926–48.

Mahler, Sarah J. "Theoretical and Empirical Contributions toward a Research Agenda for Transnationalism." In *Transnationalism from Below*, ed. Michael Peter Smith and Luis Eduardo Guarnizo, 6: 64–100. New Brunswick, N.J.: Transaction Publishers, 1998.

Menjivar, Cecilia, Julie DaVanzo, Lisa Greenwell, and R. Burciaga Valdez. "Remittance Behavior among Salvadoran and Filipino Immigrants in Los Angeles." In *International Migration Review* 32: 1 (1998) 97–126.

Min, Pyong Gap. *Changes and Conflicts: Korean Immigrant Families in New York.* Needham Heights, MA: Allyn and Bacon, 1998.

Ong, Aihwa. "Limits to Cultural Accumulation: Chinese Capitalists on the American Pacific Rim." In *Towards a Transnational Perspective on Migration: Race, Class, Ethnicity, and Nationalism Reconsidered*, ed. Nina Glick-Schiller, Linda Basch, and Cristina Blanc-Szanton, pp. 125–43. New York: Annals of the New York Academy of Sciences, 1992.

Petras, Elizabeth McLean. "The Global Labor Market in the Modern World-Economy." In *Global Trends in Migration*, ed. Mary M. Kritz, Charles B. Keely, and Silvano M. Tomasi, pp. 44–63. New York: Center for Migration Studies of New York, 1981.

Portes, Alejandro, Luis E. Guarnizo, and Patricia Landolt. "Introduction: Pitfalls and Promise of an Emergent Research Field." In *Ethnic and Racial Studies* 22:2 (1999): 217–37.

Sider, Gerald. "The Contradictions of Transnational Migration: A Discussion." In *Towards a Transnational Perspective on Migration: Race, Class, Ethnicity, and Nationalism Reconsidered*, ed. Nina Glick-Schiller, Linda Basch, and Cristina Blanc-Szanton, pp. 231–40. New York: Annals of the New York Academy of Sciences, 1992.

Sontag, Deborah, and Celia W. Dugger. "The New Immigrant Tide: A Shuttle between Worlds." *New York Times*, July 19, 1998, A1, 27–30.

Vertovec, Steven. "Conceiving and Researching Transnationalism." In *Ethnic and Racial Studies* 22:2 (1999): 447–62.

Wallerstein, Immanuel. *The Modern World-System: Capitalist Agriculture and the Origins of the European World Economy in the Sixteenth Century.* New York: Academic Press, 1974.

GENERAL INDEX

442nd Regimental Combat Team, **1**:163–164
8, Code of Federal Regulations sec. 214.2(o), **2**:707
8, US Code sec. 1101(a)(15)(f), **2**:707
8, US Code sec. 1101(a)(15)(j), **2**:706
8, US Code sec. 1101(a)(15)(m), **2**:708–709
8, US Code sec. 1101(a)(15)(q), **2**:707
8, US Code sec. 1481(a), **4**:1459
8, US Code sec. 1481(b), **4**:1459
8, US Code sec. 1153(b)(1), **2**:705; **3**:837
8, US Code sec. 1153(b)(2), **2**:705–706; **3**:839
8, US Code sec. 1153(b)(3), **2**:706; **3**:840
8, US Code sec. 1153, **3**:837
20, Code of Federal Regulations sec. 656.21, **2**:706

A

Abbott, Grace, **4**:1488
Ability-motivation hypothesis, **2**:601
Academic institutions. *See* Education, higher
Academic Student. *See* F-1 Academic Student
Acadians, **1**:284; **4**:1265
Acculturation, **1**:94–96
  definition of, **4**:1505*g*
  factors aiding, **2**:717–719
  before leaving homeland, **3**:990
  stages in, **2**:721
  types of, **2**:424*t*
ACLU. *See* American Civil Liberties Union

Act Banning Naturalization of Anarchists (1903), **4**:1288
Act Conferring United States Citizenship on American Indians (1924), **4**:1297
Act of Union (Great Britain), **1**:54
Act to Establish a Uniform Rule of Naturalization, An (1790), **4**:1277
Activism. *See* Political activism
Adams, John, **1**:51, 71, 245; **2**:484
Adams, John Quincy, **1**:72
Addams, Jane, **1**:335; **2**:726, 730
Adolescence
  adjustment among, **2**:426–430
  community-based services, **2**:733
  crime, **2**:683–684
  demographics, **2**:422–424
  impact of immigration on, **2**:425
  See also Children
Adoption, **1**:307–310; **2**:506
Adventurer, **3**:858
Advocacy groups. *See* Interest groups
Affidavit of support, **4**:1443, 1449, 1505*g*
Affirmative action, **3**:972
Afghan immigrants, **4**:1210
AFL-CIO. *See* American Federation of Labor-Congress of Industrial Organizations
African Americans
  banned from AFL-affiliated unions, **1**:123
  employment, **2**:573–574, 593
  and Irish immigrant relations, **1**:61, 62
  racial/ethnic conflict, **1**:225
  response to South African immigrants, **3**:1068

African Americans *(continued)*
  San Francisco, **3**:970, 972
  in Union army, **1**:85
  Washington, D.C., **3**:974
African immigrants
  East, **3**:1056–1060
  and evangelicalism, **3**:879
  forced immigration (slave trade), **1**:28, 37–41, 53, 89; **3**:1065, 1072
  North, **3**:1027–1028, 1062–1064
  South, **3**:1065–1068
  Washington, D.C., **3**:981
  West, **1**:37–40; **3**:1070–1077
  women, **3**:1060, 1074
Aggravated felonies, **2**:514
Agribusiness. *See* Agriculture
Agricultural Act of 1949. *See* Bracero Program Act (1949)
Agricultural labor
  contemporary trends, **2**:627
  ethnic and racial shifts, **2**:621–622
  public awareness, **2**:622–623
  social movements, **2**:625–626
  temporary workers, **4**:1318, 1327
  unions. *See* Agricultural organizations
Agricultural laws
  Bracero Program Act. *See* Bracero Program Act (1949)
  California Farm Labor Act (1975), **4**:1305–1312
Agricultural organizations
  Agricultural Workers Organizing Committee (AWCO), **2**:539, 622–623, 626
  Farm Labor Organizing Committee (FLOC), **2**:596, 626

Numbers in bold indicate volume; g indicates glossary.

Americanization *(continued)*
  global, **1:**198–199, 248
  model housing, **2:**587
  in schools, **1:**151; **2:**725–726
  See also Assimilation
American-Mexican Victory Youth
    Club, **1:**171
AMIO. *See* Alien migrant
    interdiction operations
Amish, **1:**22; **3:**858–859; **4:**1505*g*
Amnesty, **1:**217; **2:**572–573
  AFL-CIO and, **2:**687
  applicants and implementation,
    2:475–479
  definition of, **4:**1505*g*
  policy, **2:**472–474
  public opinion on, **2:**564
  for undocumented workers. *See*
    Immigration Reform and
    Control Act
Amnesty International, **3:**1115–1116
Anarchists
  deportation of, **2:**504
  post–World War I, **1:**145
Anarchists, Act Banning
    Naturalization of (1903), **4:**1288
Ancient Order of Hiberians, **1:**62;
    2:490
Andean countries, **3:**1083–1088
Angel Island, **1:**109–110; **3:**968
Angell Treaty (1881), **4:**1282
Anglicanism, **1:**23
Anglo-Saxon
  definition of, **4:**1505*g*
  superiority, **3:**1003
Anschluss, **1:**157
Antebellum era, legislation,
    2:449–501
Antimiscegenation laws, **2:**436,
    442; **3:**968; **4:**1505*g*
  See also Miscegenation
Anti-Semitism
  1880s, **1:**286
  1920–1927, **1:**140; **4:**1245
  1930s, **1:**141, 156–157, 287–288
  1940s, **1:**158; **4:**1248
Appeals, **2:**511
Aquino, Corazon, **1:**274
Arab American Institute (AAI),
    3:1189
Arab American University
    Graduates, Inc. (AAUG), **3:**1189

Arab immigrants
  hate crimes toward, **1:**231
  literature, **2:**749–750
Archdale, John, **1:**23
Architecture
  American identity and, **2:**589
  See also Religious buildings
Argentinian immigrants, **3:**1083,
    1093
Aristide, Jean-Bertrand, **1:**380;
    3:934
Arizona, **1:**17
Arkansas, **1:**78
Armenian immigrants, **3:**1190–1191
  definition of, **4:**1505*g*
  literature, **2:**750
  refugees, **1:**286, 291–292
  theater, **2:**759–761
Arms embargo bill (1914) proposal,
    1:138, 151
Arranged marriages. *See* Marriage
Arrowheads, Clovis, **1:**11
Asian American Political Alliance
    (AAPA), **2:**540
Asian immigrants
  brain drain, **1:**200–202, 262, 269
  contemporary immigrants,
    1:357
  crime, **1:**326
  culture and cultural identity
    film, **3:**789–791
    pan-ethnic, **2:**540
    radio, **3:**798
    theater, **2:**761
  education/occupation level,
    1:206
  entrepreneurship, **1:**325–326
  family relations, elders,
    2:431–432, 433–434
  health, **2:**713–714
  immigration stations, **1:**109, 111,
    110
  marriage, **2:**440–441
  model minorities, **2:**541–542
  politics
    activism, **2:**536–537,
      540–543
    electoral, **2:**545, 549,
      550–551
    homeland, **2:**553
  racial/ethnic conflict, **1:**225,
    290–291

Asian immigrants *(continued)*
  settlement patterns, **2:**413–415
    Houston, **3:**906–908
    Los Angeles, **3:**915–916
    New York City, **3:**953
    rural America, **3:**957–958
    Washington, D.C., **3:**980
  violence against, **2:**542–543
  See also specific ethnic group
Asian immigration debate
    (Australia), **3:**1015
Asian Pacific American Legal
    Center (APALC), **2:**543
Asiatic Barred Zone, **3:**1002;
    4:1208
*Asociación Nacional México
    Americana*, **1:**172
Assimilation
  in Australia, **3:**1010
  classical theory of, **2:**609–610
  definition of, **4:**1505*g*
  downward mobility, **2:**463–464
  in Israel, **3:**1027
  language, **3:**810
  nativist resistance to, **2:**450
  post-1965, **2:**461–463
  segmented, **2:**460, 612; **3:**818;
    4:1514*g*
  social mobility, **2:**465
  See also Americanization
Assyrian immigrants, **3:**1191–1192;
    4:1505*g*
Astronauts, **4:**1231–1232
Asylum
  claimants by nationality
    (1992–1998), **1:**292*f*
  definition of, **4:**1506*g*
  policy, **4:**1427–1429
  policy changes, **1:**212, 297; **2:**507,
    575
  refugee status compared with,
    1:291, 358–359
  See also Refugees
Asylum for Women, New U.S.
    Rules on (1995), **4:**1437–1438
Atlanta Agreement, **4:**1352
Australia
  critics of policies, **3:**1015–1016
  diversity, **3:**1008–1010
  future of immigration, **3:**1016
  immigration selection policy,
    3:1009–1010

Central American immigrants
(*continued*)
  reasons for immigration, **3**:1099
  refugees, **1**:205, 300
  settlement patterns, **2**:416;
    3:1106–1107
    Houston, **3**:905–906
    Los Angeles, **3**:915
    Washington, D.C.,
      3:979–980
  See also specific ethnic group
Central American Refugees and U.S.
  High Schools, **2**:727
Central Pacific Railroad Company,
  1:77–78, 94; **3**:967
Chae Chan Ping v. United States,
  3:1002
Chain migration, **1**:249–255; **2**:440
  definition of, **4**:1507*g*
  impact on adolescents, **2**:425
Character loans, **2**:580
Chávez, César, **1**:172; **2**:539, 626;
  3:962; **4**:1305
Chavez-Saldo, Cabell v., **2**:512, 520
Chicago
  collective conflict, **1**:225–226
  culture and arts, **1**:129
  Hull House, **2**:730
  settlement patterns, **2**:411
  voting rights, **2**:519
Chicano Moratorium, **2**:540
Chicano movement, **2**:539–540;
  3:928
Child labor, **1**:124
Children
  adoption, **1**:307–310; **2**:506
  community-based services, **2**:733
  demographics, **2**:422–424
  education. *See* Education
  number of ever born, **2**:390–392
  parachute kids, **4**:1231–1232,
    1513*g*
  second-generation, **1**:127; **2**:422
    adjustment among,
      2:425–430
    bilingualism, **3**:811–813
    challenges for, **2**:425–426
  trafficking of, **1**:329
  See also Adolescence
Children's Health Insurance
  Program (CHIP), **2**:487;
    4:1447

Children's literature, for teaching
  ESL, **2**:783–784
Chilean immigrants, **1**:291; **3**:966,
  1083
Chin, Vincent, **2**:542
China
  adoption from, **1**:310
  Boxer Rebellion (1900), **2**:503
  discouragement of emigration,
    1:74
  human smuggling, **1**:331–332,
    373; **2**:667, 682
Chinese Exclusion Act (1882),
  1:81–82, 150; **2**:502, 621, 623;
  3:967, 1002
  definition of, **4**:1507*g*
  repeal of, **2**:505, 537; **3**:970; **4**:1298
  text, **4**:1283–1284
Chinese for Affirmative Action,
  3:972
Chinese immigrants
  acculturation, **1**:95
  at Angel Island, **1**:109, 110
  anti-Chinese legislation, **1**:80,
    150; **2**:502–503
    ban lifted on, **1**:153
    See also Chinese Exclusion Act
      (1882)
  coolie trade, **2**:501, 502; **3**:968
  crime, **2**:494–495, 681–682
  demographics, **3**:1157, 1158*t*,
    1160
  discrimination of, **1**:80–81, 123;
    2:623; **3**:967–968
  education, **1**:207; **3**:1162–1163
  entrepreneurship, **1**:207, 325–326,
    381; **2**:578, 582
  evangelicalism, **3**:877–878
  extraordinary, **3**:1165–1166
  family relations, **3**:1160–1161;
    4:1231–1232
    elders, **2**:431–432, 433–434
  family reunification, **1**:202
  health, **2**:714
  history of, **1**:74–82, 94
  from Hong Kong, **4**:1230–1231
  illegal immigrants, **1**:319, 320,
    373
  literature, **2**:750–751
  marriage, **3**:1161–1162
  number of, **1**:195
  occupation level, **1**:207

Chinese immigrants (*continued*)
  population by state (1870–1890),
    1:78*t*
  poverty, **1**:208
  religion, **3**:1164
  settlement patterns, **2**:413
    Chinatowns, **2**:543;
      3:1157–1160
    Hawaii, **3**:1160
    Houston, **3**:1160
    Los Angeles, **3**:915–916,
      1158–1159
    New York City, **3**:953, 1159
    rural America, **3**:957–958
    San Francisco, **3**:967–969,
      1159–1160
    Washington, D.C.,
      3:976–977, 980
  from Taiwan, **4**:1229–1230
  work, income and economic
    activity, **3**:1163–1164
Chinese Immigration Act (1885)
  (Canada), **3**:1020
Chinese Massacre of 1871, **3**:915
Chinese Six Companies, **1**:76–78;
  4:1507*g*
Christianity, evangelical. *See*
  Evangelicalism
CIC. *See* Citizenship and
  Immigration Canada (CIC)
Cinema. *See* Film
Circular migration, **2**:402
Citizen Wives' Organization
  (CWO), **2**:456
Citizens' Committee on Displaced
  Persons (CCDP), **1**:159–160
Citizenship
  classes, **2**:732
  dual, **2**:557, 558, 559
  and global economy, **3**:992–993
  renunciation, **2**:516; **4**:1459–1460
  status, **2**:509
  See also Naturalization
Citizenship and Immigration
  Canada (CIC), **3**:1018; **4**:1507*g*
Citizenship Day, **4**:1297
Civil and Political Rights, Cov-
  enant on, **3**:995, 996–997, 999
Civil Liberties Act (1988),
  1:165–166
Civil rights, **2**:484–488, 538–540
Civil Rights Act (1870), **2**:515

GENERAL INDEX

Europe, Western. *See* Western Europe

European Community law, **3:**997, 998, 999

European Convention on Human Rights, **3:**999

European Convention on Nationality (ECN), **3:**998–999

European Convention on the Legal Status of Migrant Workers, **3:**998

European Court of Human Rights, **3:**999

European Court of Justice, **3:**998

European immigrants
  colonial, **1:**30–36
  decline of, **1:**135, 195, 358
  Eastern, **4:**1238–1243
  film, **3:**787–788
  gender roles, **2:**457
  nineteenth century, **1:**51–53; **3:**988–989
  patterns of, **1:**100–105; **2:**739
  settlement patterns, **2:**417–418; **3:**957
  See also specific country

European Social Charter, **3:**998

European Treaty Series, **3:**998

European Union (EU), **3:**997, 998

Evangelicalism, **3:**874–880

Evian Conference, **1:**157

Exchange visitor, J-1. *See* J-1 exchange visitor

Excludable aliens, **2:**502, 503, 505, 710; **4:**1427

Exclusion, without hearing, **4:**1343–1344

Executive branch, policymaking, **3:**1002–1005

Executive Order 9066, **1:**142, 163; **2:**485, 538; **3:**970; **4:**1333, 1508g

Executive Order 9417, **1:**159

Executive Order 12324 (1981), **1:**316–317

Executive Order 12807 (1992), **1:**318

Exile, **4:**1508g

Expansionism, **1:**246–247
  cultural, **1:**198–199

Expansionists, **1:**229
  arguments used by, **2:**573–574

Expansionists *(continued)*
  compared with restrictionists, **2:**527–532
  definition of, **2:**526–527; **4:**1508g
  and globalism, **2:**533–534

Export-processing zones, **3:**991

Extraordinary Ability. *See* O-1 Extraordinary Ability

Extraordinary Alien. *See* O-1 Extraordinary Ability

F

F-1 Academic Student, **2:**707–708

F student visas, **2:**707–708; **3:**837

Factories. *See* Sweatshops and factories

Factories in the Fields, **2:**621, 622

Factory Act (1892), **2:**667

Factory farming, **2:**621

Factory-town homes, **2:**588

Failed migrants, **2:**402

Fainter, Bernal v., **2:**512

FAIR. *See* Federation for American Immigration Reform

Fair Housing Act (1968), **2:**589

Fair Labor Standards Act (1938), **2:**678

Fair Share Law. *See* Refugee Fair Share Law

FAIR v. Klutznick (1980), **2:**399

Family preferences. *See* Preference system

Family reunification, **1:**199–200, 202–203, 229, 346, 349
  chain migration and, **1:**254–255
  family-sponsored preferences, **1:**254–255
  international law and, **3:**998
  as a pull factor, **1:**262

Family unity, **4:**1321–1322

Farabundo Martí National Liberation Front (FMLN), **2:**556

Farm Labor Organizing Committee (FLOC), **2:**596, 626

Farming. *See* Agriculture

Farmworkers. *See* Agricultural labor

FCC, Campos v., **2:**515

February Revolution (1848), **1:**66

Federal Bureau of Investigation (FBI), **1:**146, 153

Federal government
  antebellum legislation, **2:**449–501
  employment restrictions, **2:**511–512
  regulation of alien admission, **2:**509–510, 518

Federal Public Benefit, **4:**1448

Federal Textbook on Citizenship, **1:**345

Federalist No. 2, **1:**45

Federalist No. 10, **1:**45

Federalists, **1:**71–72; **2:**484–485

Federation for American Immigration Reform (FAIR), **1:**229, 230; **2:**527, 575; **4:**1508g

FAIR v. Klutznick (1980), **2:**399

Federation of Hindu Associations (FHA), **3:**884, 885; **4:**1508g

Federation of Japanese Labor, **2:**536

Felonies, aggravated, **2:**514

Female genital mutilation (FGM), **1:**293; **2:**456–457; **4:**1327, 1508g

Feminization
  of poverty, **1:**361
  of the workforce, **2:**455

Fenian movement, **1:**63

Fertility
  data, **2:**390–392
  measures of, **2:**388–390
  theories of variation in, **2:**392–393

Feudal government, **1:**16–17

Fiancée Act (1947), **1:**288; **4:**1255

Fiancée petition, **1:**364–365

Fifteen Passenger Bill, **3:**1002

Fifth Amendment, **2:**515

Fifth columnists, **1:**137, 141, 142; **4:**1508g

Fifty-Sixers, **1:**301

Fijian immigrants, **4:**1194

Filipino immigrants
  agricultural labor, **2:**621; **4:**1200–1202
  ban lifted on, **1:**153; **2:**537
  contemporary immigration, **4:**1203–1204
  education, work, income and economic activity, **1:**207; **4:**1204–1205
  evangelicalism, **3:**878
  family reunification, **1:**202
  history of, **4:**1198–1200, 1198–1203

Numbers in bold indicate volume; g indicates glossary.

Haitian Refugee Immigration
Fairness Act (HRIFA), **1:**282;
4:1509*g*
Haitian refugees, **1:**204–205, 282,
289–290
Bush's order on return of,
4:1356–1366
interdiction at sea, **1:**316–319;
3:1006
refused asylum, **1:**289, 291; **3:**935,
1005–1006
See also Haitian immigrants
Haitians, District Court on
Admission of (1993),
4:1381–1386
Hamilton, Alexander, **1:**71
Harding, Warren G., **1:**152; **2:**504
Harrison, Benjamin, **2:**502
Hart, Philip, **1:**184; **2:**506
Hart-Cellar Act, **1:**167–168, 172,
184–185, 199–200; **3:**865
definition of, **4:**1509*g*
Harvard University, **2:**703
Hate Crime Statistics Act, **2:**497
Hate crimes, **1:**226; **2:**497–498;
4:1509*g*
Hawaii
Chinese immigrants, **1:**78; **3:**1160
Filipino immigrants, **4:**1200
Japanese immigrants, **1:**111, 162
Oceania immigrants, **4:**1193,
1195–1196
Hayakawa, Samuel Ichiye, **1:**230;
2:542
Hayes, Rutherford B., **1:**69, 81;
2:502; **3:**1002
Head tax. *See* Taxes
Health, **1:**116–117
of elderly immigrants,
2:433–434
food/nutrition services, **2:**732
general status of immigrant,
2:710–711
and passenger ship legislation,
2:500, 501, 502–503
and poverty, **2:**427–428
See also Disease; Health care;
Mental health; specific ethnic
group
Health care, **2:**486–487, 696–698
Health Professions Educational
Assistance Act (1976), **2:**644

Hebrew Immigrant Aid Society,
1:287; **4:**1245
Hegemony, **4:**1509*g*
Helms, Jesse A., **4:**1417–1418
Helms-Burton law, **2:**556
Hennessey, David, **2:**491–492
Hepatitis B, **2:**711
Herzegovina, **1:**301
Herzl, Theodore, **3:**1023–1024
Hesburgh, Theodore M., **1:**255
Hess, Moses, **3:**1023
Hindu temples, **2:**773–774
Hinduism, **3:**881–885
Hippies, **3:**803
Hirabayashi, Gordon, **1:**165
Hirabayashi v. United States (1943),
1:165; **4:**1369–1370
Hispanic immigrants. *See* Latin
American immigrants
History of the English Settlement
in Edwards County, Illinois
(1818), **4:**1466–1469
Hitler, Adolf, **1:**140, 156, 157, 158,
287
HIV. *See* AIDS/HIV
Hmong, **1:**191, 198, 291, 300;
4:1226, 1509*g*
Ho Ah Kow v. Matthew Noonan, **1:**80
Holocaust, **1:**158–159; **4:**1242, 1248
Home Teacher Act (1915), **1:**170
Homeland. *See* Country of origin
Homeownership, **2:**586–587
Homestead Act (1862), **1:**92;
2:619
Homestead strike, **1:**145
Homosexuals. *See* Gay and lesbians
Hong Kong immigrants,
4:1228–1229
Hoover, Herbert, **1:**69, 153, 156;
2:505
Hoover, J. Edgar, **1:**146
Horticulture. *See* Agriculture
Host polities, integration into,
3:998–999
Host societies, international law,
3:997–998
Hotel industry, New York, **2:**655–657
Hounds, **3:**966
House and Senate immigration
committees, **2:**527
Household services. *See* Domestic
services

Housing
architectural style, **2:**589
conditions, **1:**114–116; **2:**588–589,
590; **3:**960
effect of jobs on, **1:**119
homeownership, **2:**586–587
restrictive laws, **2:**589
social service programs, **2:**732
urban, **2:**586–587, 588–589
Houston
Asian immigrants, **3:**906–908
Central American immigrants,
3:905–906
Chinese immigrants, **3:**1160
contemporary immigration,
3:901–903
Indian immigrants, **3:**908
Japanese immigrants, **3:**907–908
Mexican immigrants, **3:**903–905
settlement patterns, **2:**411
How an Emigrant May Succeed in
the United States, **4:**1502–1503
Howitt, E., **4:**1472
Hsia, Maria, **2:**551
Huang, John, **2:**551
Hudson, Henry, **1:**21, 30
Huerta, Dolores, **2:**626; **3:**962
Huguenots, **1:**23, 35, 90; **4:**1265,
1509*g*
Hui. *See Kye*
Hull House, **1:**115; **2:**730, 117
Human capital, **2:**577, 581, 634
Human ingenuity, **2:**531–532
Human rights
integration, **3:**997–999
violations, **1:**347; **2:**497
Human Rights Committee, **3:**997
Human Rights Watch, **3:**1115–1116
Human smuggling. *See* Smuggling,
human
Hungarian immigrants,
4:1238–1243 *passim*
refugees, **1:**160, 191, 288,
300–301; **3:**1004

I

Idaho, **1:**77; **4:**1265
Identity
cultural. *See* Culture and cultural
identity
ethnic, **1:**126–127

McCarran, Patrick, **1:**154, 182; **2:**505
McCarran-Walter Act. *See* Immigration and Nationality Act (1952)
McCarran-Walter Immigration and Nationality Act. *See* Immigration and Nationality Act (1952)
McCarthy, Joseph, **1:**154
McDonald White Paper (1939), **3:**1025
McDonald's, **1:**248
McKinley, William, **1:**247
McWilliams, Carey, **2:**621, 622; **3:**911
Media industry, **3:**795–797
    alternative media, **3:**797–798
    portrayal of immigrants. *See* Stereotypes
Median income statistics, **1:**361, 362*t*
Medicaid, **2:**696–697; **4:**1447
Meissner, Doris, **4:**1437
Melanesian immigrants, **4:**1193–1197
Melting pot, **3:**997; **4:**1511*g*
Memorial of James Brown (1819), **4:**1470–1471
Mennonites, **1:**22, 94, 286; **4:**1511*g*
Mental health
    chain migration and, **1:**253
    children/adolescent immigrants, **2:**427–429
    counseling services, **2:**732
    depression, **2:**719–721
    elderly immigrants, **2:**434
    preventative measures, **2:**721–722
    self-help groups, **2:**719
    social networks and, **2:**717–718
Menzel, Gottfried, **4:**1480
Mex-America
    definition of, **4:**1511*g*
    demographics of, **3:**926
    economic restructuring of, **3:**926–927
    historical origins, **3:**922–926
    inequalities and identities in, **3:**927–928
    physical construction border, **3:**927

Mexican American Legal Defense Fund (MALDEF), **2:**541
Mexican American Political Association, **2:**538
Mexican American Youth Organization, **2:**539
Mexican Central Railroad, **2:**621
Mexican immigrants
    agricultural labor, **2:**621–627; **3:**1141
    Americanization of, **1:**170
    Bracero Program. *See* Bracero Program
    crime, **2:**495–496, 683
    demographics, **1:**195–196; **3:**1139–1140
    deportation, **1:**141, 154, 172; **2:**485
    Díaz era (1876–1911), **3:**1140–1141
    discrimination of, **1:**168, 170, 171
    education level, **1:**206; **2:**594, 595
    family relations, **2:**443–444
    fertility rate, **2:**595
    future of immigration, **3:**1143–1144
    gender roles, **2:**457–458
    Great Depression era, **3:**1141–1142
    health, **2:**712–713
    history of, **1:**170–172
    Immigration Reform and Control Act and, **3:**1142–1143
    literature, **2:**757
    occupation level, **1:**206
    politics
        activism, **1:**170–172; **2:**535–536, 538–541
        exclusion from electoral, **2:**545
        homeland, **2:**554
    and poverty, **1:**208
    public opinion on, **2:**562–565
    remittances, **2:**597, 598, 599, 607
    repatriation, **1:**153, 170; **2:**485, 545, 621, 623–625
    settlement patterns, **2:**415
        Houston, **3:**903–905
        Los Angeles, **3:**914–915
        rural America, **3:**958–959
    survival self-employment, **2:**582
    theater, **2:**765–766
    wages and income, **1:**171, 172

Mexican immigrants *(continued)*
    World War I, **3:**1141
    World War II, **1:**142, 153; **2:**538
Mexican Migration Project, **1:**252; **2:**405
Mexican Repatriation Program, **2:**485
Mexican Revolution, **2:**554; **3:**1140
Mexican-American War, **1:**17; **2:**620; **3:**909, 922, 1136
Mexico
    Bracero Program. *See* Bracero Program
    human smuggling, **1:**330
    Native Americans, **1:**12
    Spanish conquest of, **1:**14, 15, 17
Miami
    Cuban immigrants, **2:**416; **3:**931–933, 1112–1116
    demographics of, **3:**930–931
    future of immigration, **3:**935–936
    Haitian immigrants, **2:**674; **3:**933–934
    immigration policy and, **3:**934–935
    Los Angeles compared to, **3:**918
    settlement patterns, **1:**205, 289; **2:**411
    underground economy, **2:**673–675
Microenterprise, **4:**1511*g*
Micronesian immigrants, **4:**1193–1197
Middle Eastern immigrants, **3:**1186–1187, 1187–1192
Middle Immigration Series, **2:**393, 396; **4:**1511*g*
Middleman minority theory, **1:**226–227; **2:**578
    See also Ethnic enclaves
Migration, circular, **2:**402
Mining, **1:**94
    California Foreign Miners Tax (1849), **3:**923
    Foreign Miners License Law, **1:**80
    Foreign Miners Tax (1850), **3:**1138
Ministry of Immigrant Absorption (Israel), **3:**1026

Taxes *(continued)*
　head tax, **2:**502, 503; **3:**1020, 1141;
　　4:1509*g*
　obligation to pay, **2:**513
　paid by undocumented
　　immigrants, **2:**737
　poll, **2:**545, 546
　renunciation of citizenship and,
　　4:1460
　restrictionist/expansionist
　　views, **2:**574
T.B.-Orphan bill, **2:**506
Technology Workers, Report on the
　Shortage of (1997), **4:**1452–1456
Telephone Verification System/
　SAVE (TVS/SAVE), **4:**1435
Telephones, **1:**324–325
Television
　ethnic and foreign language,
　　3:798, 804, 816
　golden age, **3:**793–794
　history of, **3:**792
　narrowcasting, **3:**795–796
　portrayal of immigrants,
　　3:803–804, 824–825
　post-1960 programming, **3:**794
　for transnational
　　communication, **1:**325
Temporary Assistance to Needy
　Families (TANF), **2:**518; **4:**1439,
　1447
Temporary protected status, **2:**507;
　3:1101; **4:**1321–1322, 1515*g*
Temporary Relief Act (1847) (Great
　Britain), **1:**57
Temporary worker visa. *See* H-1B
　visa
Tenements, **2:**588; **4:**1515*g*
Tenth Amendment, **2:**519
Terrace v. Thompson (1923), **2:**515
Territorial Sea, **1:**315, 316, 317
Texas
　agricultural production, **2:**622
　Clovis-type arrowheads, **1:**11
　El Paso, **2:**621; **3:**923–925, 1139
　employment restrictions, **2:**520
　Galveston immigration station,
　　1:111
　Operation Hold the Line,
　　1:352; **3:**927, 1143; **4:**1404,
　　1512*g*
　restrictive legislation, **2:**521

Texas *(continued)*
　settlement patterns of (1990s),
　　1:205
　Spanish settlers, **1:**17
Thai immigrants, **4:**1218–1219
Thailand, export of workers,
　1:274
Theater, **1:**127–128; **2:**759–767,
　for organizing workers,
　　2:626
　portrayal of immigrants,
　　3:820–821
Third-world
　definition of, **4:**1515*g*
　number of immigrants,
　　1:197–199
　overpopulation, **1:**279–280
　reasons for immigration,
　　1:197–199
　and transnational corporations,
　　3:990, 991; **4:**1515*g*
Thirteenth Amendment, **1:**87
Thompson, Terrace v., **2:**515
Tie breaker rules, **2:**513
Tillam, Thomas, **1:**245
Title IV: Restricting Welfare and
　Public Benefits from Aliens
　(1996), **4:**1439–1451
Tobacco, **1:**32
Tocqueville, Alexis de, **1:**18; **3:**827
Tongan immigrants, **2:**597, 599; **4:**1194
Tour Through the United States
　(1819), **4:**1472
Trade Act, Freedom of Emigration
　Amendment, **4:**1248
Trading with the Enemy Act
　(1917), **3:**833
Trafficking, **1:**272, 273
　children, **1:**329
　drug, **2:**681, 682, 683
　of women, **1:**274–275, 329,
　　365–366; **2:**680
　See also Smuggling, human
Transfrontier loan employment,
　3:998
Translation services. *See*
　Interpretation services
Transmigrants, **1:**376
Transnational communication,
　1:322–327
Transnational communities, **1:**105;
　3:993

Transnational communities
　(continued)
　Dominican Republic,
　　3:1124–1125
　and poverty, **2:**611–612
Transnational corporations (TNCs),
　3:990, 991; **4:**1515*g*
Transnational crime, **1:**326
　See also Smuggling, human;
　　Trafficking
Transnationalism
　definition of, **4:**1515*g*
　economics and, **1:**378–381
　socioeconomic class and,
　　1:381–382
　theory of, **1:**376–378
Transportation, mechanisms of,
　1:372–375
Treaty of Ghent (1814), **4:**1253
Treaty of Guadalupe Hidalgo
　(1848), **1:**91; **2:**539, 620; **3:**909,
　922, 1049, 1136–1140
　definition of, **4:**1509*g*
　text, **4:**1280
Triangle Shirtwaist Company,
　1:124–125; **2:**665
Trinidadian immigrants, **2:**416–417;
　4:1210
Tripartite city, **2:**653
Triple minorities, **3:**1134–1115
Trotsky, Leon, **1:**145
Trudeau, Pierre, **3:**1020
Trujillo, Rafael, **1:**174
Truman, Harry, **1:**154, 159, 297;
　2:505; **3:**1003, 1004
　directive on European refugees,
　　4:1334–1335
Tuberculosis, **1:**117; **2:**506, 711;
　4:1457–1458
Turkish immigrants, **3:**1189–1190
Tuscarora War, **1:**34
TV Marti, **2:**556
Tweed, William M., **1:**63
Tydings-McDuffie Act (1934),
　4:1201

U

Ukrainian immigrants,
　4:1238–1243 *passim*
Underground economy
　contract slavery, **2:**680–681

GEOGRAPHICAL INDEX

LEGAL AND JUDICIAL INDEX

Numbers in bold indicate volume; g indicates glossary.